JOHN CATT'S GUIDE TO

International Schools 2014/15

Twelfth Edition
Editor: Jonathan Barnes

JOHN CATT
EDUCATIONAL
LIMITED

Published in 2014 by
John Catt Educational Ltd,
12 Deben Mill Business Centre,
Woodbridge, Suffolk IP12 1BL UK
Tel: 01394 389850 Fax: 01394 386893
Email: enquiries@johncatt.com
Website: www.johncatt.com
© 2013 John Catt Educational Ltd

Designed and typeset by John Catt Educational Limited
Printed and Bound in Great Britain by Cambrian Printers.

**A CIP catalogue record for this book is available from
the British Library.**

ISBN: 9781909717138

Contacts
Editor
Jonathan Barnes
Email: jonathanbarnes@johncatt.com

Advertising & School Profiles
Tel: +44 (0) 1394 389850
Email: sales@johncatt.com

Distribution/Book Sales
Tel: +44 (0) 1394 389863
Email: booksales@johncatt.com

We are grateful to the many individuals and associations who helped with the production of this guidebook

Contents

How to use this guide

John Catt's Guide to International Schools has been specifically designed with the reader in mind. Now in its twelfth year, this edition includes useful and informative information which is ideal for anyone looking for details of an international school, association, international curriculums, exams, tests and qualifications. There are clearly defined sections providing information for anyone looking at independent international education worldwide today.

Are you looking for help and advice? Take a look at our editorial section (see pages 7 to 55). Here you will find articles covering a wide variety of issues you are likely to come across when choosing a school for your child. Each year we try to find a differing range of topics to interest and inform you about the uniqueness of independent international education.

Perhaps you are looking for a school or college in a certain country? Then you need to look first in the directories (starting on page D187). Here you will find basic information about all the schools in each country (countries are featured in alphabetical order within their relevant continent), complete with contact details.

From this section you will be directed to more detailed information in the guide, where this is available. An example of a typical directory entry is given at the end of this article.

Some of you may already be looking for a specific school or college. In which case, if you know the name of the school or college but are unsure of its location, simply go to the index at the back of the guide where you will find all the schools listed alphabetically. Page numbers prefixed with the letter D denote the directory section; those without, a full profile.

This year we have also introduced a section to highlight schools that offer specialist facilities for students with special educational needs (see page 175).

In the appendix you will find up-to-date information about international curriculums and the examinations, tests and qualifications available (see page 353), editorial about international schools associations (see page 319), and contact details for Ministries of Education worldwide (see page 333).

Key to directory

Country	**Whereford**
Name of school or college	**College Academy**
Indicates that this school has a profile	*For further details see p.00*
Address and contact number	Which Street, Whosville, Wherefordshire AB12 3CD
	Tel: 01000 000000
Head's name	**Head Master:** Dr A Person
Age range	**Age range:** 11–18
Number of pupils. B = boys G = girls VIth = sixth form	**No. of pupils:** 660 B330 G330 VIth 200
Fees per annum. Day = fees for day pupils. WB = fees for weekly boarders. FB = fees for full boarders.	**Fees:** Day £11,000 WB £16,000 FB £20,000
Curriculum	**Curriculum:** National, IBDP, ALevs
Language of instruction	**Language instr:** English, French
Memberships/Accreditation	(AISA) (COB) (EAR)

Key to icons

Key to symbols:

- (†) Boys' school
- (♀) Girls' school
- (⚐) Boarding accommodation

Member of:

- (AISA) Association of International Schools in Africa
- (CEE) Central and Eastern European Schools Association
- (EAR) East Asia Regional Council of Overseas Schools
- (ECIS) European Council of International Schools
- (RS) Round Square

Accreditation:

- (CIS) Council of International Schools
- (COB) Council of British International Schools

International schools – markers of meaning

Kevin J. Ruth, Executive Director of ECIS, says that international schools are committed to being 'at the frontiers of what is possible in education'

International schools play an important role in creating a mission-driven community with intercultural intelligence – a community that helps young people to identify markers of meaning in our profoundly diverse and dynamic world. Just as German poet Günter Eich saw the value of poems 'as buoys that mark the course in an unknown area' (Trigonometrische Punkte, 1964), international schools provide value by connecting students with and across the world's cultures, helping them to establish markers that serve as buoys on their journey into the unknown that we call adulthood. The end result is that their international education will inform the relationships they create and nurture in their lives, irrespective of place, yet profoundly mindful of it.

We live in a time of relentless change, and perhaps the greatest test for any school is to help young people learn what it means to be human when their orientation is challenged by such change. There is no easy answer as to how to meet that test, yet, happily, international schools are poised to integrate new technologies into an existing core of wisdom that draws deeply on an orientation toward intercultural understanding and experiences. Drawing on that, let us examine three sets of orientation markers: first, those prominent markers along our present course; second, those markers that will define our next stage of development; and third, 'wicked markers', or those markers that require attention to mindset and behaviour to transform schools and societies in new and exciting ways. The third set will appear as questions designed to provoke thought.

Today: where international schools are engaging current energies

Learning
Schools obviously spend time on the act of learning. What is not so obvious, however, is how much change there has been in what we call 'learning'. When one thinks of school, one tends to think of formal learning – a classroom with desks, a teacher, a specific curriculum (including co-curriculars), and homework. What advances in technology have produced in the past five to seven years, though, is tremendous growth and opportunity in informal learning. According to a recent article in *Chief Learning Officer*, research shows that some 80% of learning that helps us to be successful occurs informally. Consider how much of that kind of learning

occurs via ever-expanding social networks, and it makes sense that international schools are determining how to integrate it with formal learning. Connectivism, the notion that learners are creating connections and developing a network that contributes to their development and knowledge, is impacting how 'school' occurs.

Curriculum
Given the aforementioned, schools are engaging in approaches to curriculum design that take into account those changes and developments. How pupils progress from Marker A to Marker B is of profound importance when we consider the increasing access to and impact of informal learning. International schools concern themselves with the practice of international mindedness, the role of culture and language, and the value of inquiry. Witness the many excellent curricular options being vetted and implemented in schools, whether the International Baccalaureate, Advanced Placement, Common Core, National Curriculum, Fieldwork Curriculum, Common Ground Curriculum, or others. One of the more salient questions at the moment, given the burgeoning interest

in opportunities for student creativity, is how curricula are oriented toward consumption and/or creation by students. Whatever the choice of curriculum, it influences daily practices and decision-making in schools. Therefore, schools tend to consider curriculum very carefully, as this choice contributes to the ethos of the school itself.

Innovation

Even the briefest perusal of conference programmes and blogs, social media, or recently-updated mission statements shows that innovation is on everyone's mind. Although it can be somewhat of a buzzword, international schools are making a link between innovation and strategy, to the benefit of students and families. Some schools provide pupils with access to online courses, others run their own online courses, still others are experimenting with blended learning models that incorporate face-to-face instructional time with asynchronous online instruction. Yet there are other non-technological innovations as well – new outdoor experiences, restructured travel-study programmes, clubs that empower underserved groups in communities. We have seen much innovation, and it shows no signs of decelerating as schools focus their strategies on enhancing the value proposition they offer families.

Tomorrow: where international schools will look to enhance the design of the educational experience

Contextualised Data

In a world that produces more data daily, including that produced by students themselves, international schools must become meaning-makers. Schools will move toward providing contextualisation around data points, from testing data (AP, SAT, IB, GCSE, A levels, and others) to learning data (LMS-generated, digital textbook-generated, adaptive learning platform-generated, *etc*). The goal will be to maintain and celebrate humanity in the midst of complex numbers, figures, and charts.

Professional Development

International schools recognise already that high-quality, impactful, and network-based professional development is central to their success. As schools develop according to the markers mentioned here, they will increase their scrutiny of quality programmes, looking for breadth, depth, affordability, and availability, so that all who work in international schools, from teaching assistants to heads, can grow as professionals and enhance the value proposition of schools. One example of how schools have begun to consider the design of professional development is the intense creation of professional learning communities, wherein faculty learners create connections and develop

a larger learning network, demonstrating that ongoing learning is a part of life in our schools.

Hiring

Schools will need to examine existing hiring practices and methods to determine whether they align with an enhanced design of the educational experience. Necessary changes to hiring will include new ways to identify and cultivate faculty and staff who are culturally flexible, agile learners: professionals who have been rapidly adaptive at something; who respond well to speed, volatility, and uncertainty; who collaborate as normal practice; who show the ability to teach and communicate intercultural understanding; and who take calculated risks.

Wicked markers: contemplating solutions that require attention to mindset and behaviour

Equity and Access

How might we increase access to education in ways that were not possible before, given advancements in technology coupled with a fusion of formal and informal learning, not only in our existing communities but in fragile and developing communities across the world?

Environmental Sustainability

How might we design experiential, entrepreneurial, place-based student learning experiences that provide direct engagement with real-world problems in the areas of food production, clean water, natural resource consumption, and renewable energy (among others)?

Longevity and Learning

How might we attune ourselves to those who have not benefitted from meaningful learning experiences in their younger years, so that, as they live longer and more active lives, they come to recognise and embrace the life-force of teaching and learning?

Transcultural Intelligence

How might we move from a perspective of learning about cultures to one of learning across cultures, as part of the formal and informal learning that occurs in international schools, whether in classrooms, professional learning communities, or elsewhere?

International schools are committed to orienting themselves to be at the frontiers, literally and figuratively, of what is possible in education, no matter the complexity of the aforementioned markers. Our dedication to intercultural understanding, complemented by a spirit of collaboration, ingenuity, and generosity, informs our pursuit of educational excellence, as we endeavour to serve and support families worldwide.

Avanti!

Kevin J. Ruth Ph.D is Executive Director of ECIS (www.ecis.org)

Innovative international school is 'training students for jobs that don't yet exist'

Continued campus development for a state-of-the-art international school in Singapore that continues to push educational boundaries

Since its inception, Stamford American International School has been a leader in education. Stamford provides a world-class experience for students from Nursery through High School featuring the International Baccalaureate (IB) programme integrated with the rigorous American Education Reaches Out (AERO) standards. Stamford was the first school in Singapore to offer a daily Mandarin and Spanish Foreign Language Program starting from age two. Stamford was also the first in Singapore to offer 1-to-1 iPad and MacBook Programs to integrate technology throughout the curriculum.

In fact, Stamford's $300 million campus has introduced some of the most state-of-the-art facilities for an international school in the world. Stamford continues

their advancement in bringing the best international school facilities to Singapore with the completion of the Phase II development.

The Phase II development includes additional classroom and specialist space to support the growth of Stamford's Secondary School. It includes enhanced sports facilities with an additional swimming pool, full gymnasium, fitness center, indoor climbing wall, Golf Academy and tennis courts. Additional specialist areas include a Performing Arts Center with 500 seats, additional Art rooms, an Art Gallery, additional Music facilities, additional technology rooms and another Learning Resource and Media Center complete with interactive iLEarn facilities.

Stamford American International School

Stamford's $300 million international school has introduced some of the most state-of-the-art facilities for an international school in the world

Phase II facilities also include a fully air-conditioned Student Cafeteria, a Senior School Study and the Stamford Courtyard, a green oasis for quiet contemplation or socializing. Sustainable operational features include sensor driven lights, air-conditioning which switches off when not in use and facilities for monitoring overall energy use at the school.

One of the most exciting additions of the Phase II campus development is the world-class Innovation Center which is unlike any facility or resource built in a Secondary School. The Innovation Center is more than just a physical facility; it is a place of partnership between Stamford's students and the corporate sector, bridging the gap between theory and real-world execution. Within the Innovation Center, project-based group activities where students discuss real-world issues will be a common activity.

By linking the education of Stamford's students with the realities of the commercial world, Stamford gives students the best possible start on their careers as entrepreneurs and business leaders. According to one of

Stamford's parents, Andrea West, "Stamford's curriculum trains students for jobs that don't yet exist. We are confident that Stamford will turn out global citizens with a competitive advantage. We are equally grateful that both the curriculum and the on-going community action encourages students to become responsible members of the community and the world."

Stamford's continued development includes many features that are not only new for Stamford but also groundbreaking educational additions to Singapore. Stamford ensures every new program and facility is firmly supported by proven educational principles and adds to the quality of student education. Stamford is a leader in education committed to improving the quality of education in Singapore.

Stamford parents, George and Lisa Horsington, add: "We like the fact that Stamford doesn't just have a vision for the future, it has clear plans for achieving the ambitious goals it has set. Stamford doesn't follow educational trends, it leads the way…and we look forward to being a part of the school for many years to come."

For more information about Stamford American International School, see pages 92-93

How a British education remains a firm anchor in a rapidly changing world

Sir Roger Fry, Chairman of King's Group, says that families benefit from the highest academic standards and principles at British international schools

Ironically, the one thing that is constant in our world is 'change' itself. Education, particularly British education, is sometimes thought of as being somewhat immune to change. Many people think of British education as being delivered by very traditional institutions with long histories and old-fashioned attitudes. Yet education is a form of communication and above all else technological change has revolutionised communications. These changes are also starting to make an impact on education.

Teachers transfer knowledge, understanding and culture to the next generation. This wisdom will help prepare children to be responsible, caring and successful adults. This puts teachers at the centre of the action and schools occupy a key position, not simply helping children to understand the way the world is changing, but also leading the change. On the one hand, teachers have to be expert at understanding the rapidly developing technology that is driving change in the classroom and on the other, they still have to focus on the basics, things that don't change so rapidly. There is little point in teaching children about a specific technology if it is going to be superseded in a few years' time. Many children at school today will be working in jobs that have yet to be invented.

What can British international schools offer in this context? What makes them stand out from other international schools? I think the answer lies in the very nature of the nation, whose educational tradition they are built upon; namely 'constant evolution'. Britain is one of just a handful of countries in the world without

a written constitution. British society has constantly evolved its traditions to meet changing circumstances. Its democratic roots run deep, and can be traced back to the Magna Carta, signed by King John in 1215. Its institutions are solid but they are able to adapt and adjust to new situations. The British educational system reflects the nation. For example, A levels have evolved from an examination system that was founded in 1857. Clearly the exams have been modified and updated over the last 157 years but their long history and expertise continue to add to their value and prestige.

The British exam system is well known as the 'gold standard' of exam systems. This is because the exams are impartial and unbiased, these are very British values. The British exam system is built upon the idea of 'fair-play', just as much as fair dealing is expected during a game of cricket. In addition to impartial exams, marked by unknown examiners, all good schools agree to be inspected on a regular basis by teams of impartial, more

> The British exam system is well known as the 'gold standard' of exam systems. This is because the exams are impartial and unbiased, these are very British values. The exam system is built upon the idea of 'fair-play', just as much as fair dealing is expected during a game of cricket.

Chemistry class at King's College, La Moraleja

or less anonymous experts. This all adds to the rigour and seriousness that makes British schools so widely admired.

Britain values its traditions, but at the same time, it is perhaps one of the countries that is most open to the world and receptive to other cultures. This is equally true of British schools. The Council of British International Schools (www.cobis.org.uk), of which I am proud to be Honorary President, has members in every continent, except Antarctica, and these schools teach students from virtually every country in the world. The Council supports its members in many ways and stands as a beacon for quality education.

British schools around the world depend on British teachers. What is it that these teachers do that is so different from other teachers? British education is based on simple, yet hugely effective and well-proven techniques. They seem to be common sense, but are often forgotten outside of the Anglo-Saxon tradition of education. Children learn best from first-hand experience, not books. Books can reinforce learning, but when a child is encouraged to experiment, test and sometimes even make a mess; real, meaningful and memorable learning takes place. Mixing paints in primary school is just as

much about science as it is about art. Building a machine to transport an egg across a school hall, is just as much about creativity in thought and problem solving, as it is about design and technology. Of course some parents are not particularly overjoyed when their child comes home with paint in their hair and stories about drawing creepy-crawlies, but these things are part and parcel of the British way of learning.

This very special way of teaching, delivered by well trained and qualified professional teachers, means that British schools, wherever they are located need a special kind of infrastructure. They need bright, open-plan classrooms for younger children, whilst older children need specialist laboratories and studios. These are not easy or cheap options. British schools have a very special attitude to education and this is reflected in the architecture and investment in buildings.

What are the results of this very British approach to education? Well you can see it in the numbers of UK universities that appear in the global rankings of top universities. Every year about 30 British universities are listed in the top 100. It is worth noting that these universities are open to students from all over the world. The tradition of excellence in education starts in pre-nursery and goes all the way up to university.

These universities produce great leaders. Not just in the world of Politics but in Art, Medicine, Chemistry, Mathematics, Astronomy, Physics, Computing, Dance, Music and Design. Since 2001, 18 'British' scientists and artists have won Nobel Prizes. Of these one third were not born in Britain, but all of them benefited from 'A British Education' at some level. This academic brilliance at the top helps convince parents of very young children, of the huge advantage that a British education will give their child.

As well as in academia, British educated people lead the way in business. Jon Ive who is head of design at Apple Inc. went to a very modest school in England and to a not very famous university, yet he has designed products that have changed the way that hundreds of millions of people communicate. Jon Ive remembers his primary school teacher as being his first source of inspiration. I am sure we all remember teachers from our past. Tim Berners-Lee, who invented the World Wide Web – which counts almost three billion users – remembers two teachers at his school in Putney who particularly inspired him. He also remembers building his first computer from cardboard boxes and an old clock. Taking a playful, creative and fun approach to learning, founded upon solid, rigorous, academic standards, nurtured by qualified teachers who pay special attention to the social and physical development of every child they teach, yields wonderful results.

British Education isn't perfect. The process of constant evolution is not painless. New ideas need testing, new initiatives and new subjects get added to the curriculum, while others get taken away. But the fundamentals, the central beliefs and ideals upon which British education

British schools outside the UK are often much more 'British' than schools in Britain. This is for one very simple reason: Parents value 'Britishness', they recognise the standards and principles that British education can bring to their children.

is built, remain relatively strong and consistent anchors in a rapidly changing world. British schools outside the UK are often much more 'British' than schools in Britain. This is for one very simple reason: Parents value 'Britishness', they recognise the standards and principles that British education can bring to their children. They know that 'the British way of seeing the world' will stay with their children through their lives and might well influence the way their grandchildren grow up. The big idea, the objective, is not simply to coach children to pass exams, but to allow them to become truly open-minded, creative and dynamic individuals.

Not that long ago products with the words 'Made in England' were held in high regard and exported in huge volumes all over the world. Today, Britain is not so dependent on manufacturing and the words 'Made in England' has been swapped for 'Educated at a British school'. These words are found on millions of curriculum vitaes all over the world. Long may British education continue to change and to innovate.

Sir Roger Fry is Chairman of King's Group and Honorary President of the Council of British International Schools (COBIS)

IB schools making the connection to online teaching and learning

Anne Keeling, of Pamoja Education, looks at the growth and influence of web-based teaching programmes

As online learning becomes an increasingly fundamental part of higher education and the workplace, schools are beginning to recognise its importance as part of the curriculum. The International Baccalaureate is leading the way with online learning globally. As a result, a growing number of international schools are embracing this new way of learning and teaching.

The benefits of online learning

Online learning benefits both the students and the schools themselves. It offers opportunities for students to develop valuable technology and self-management skills in preparation for independent learning at university and in the world of work.

For schools, online learning enables them to provide an expanded range of subject options for 16-18-year

-olds which, for many smaller or newer international schools, can be one of their most challenging issues. And, importantly, it moves the school towards providing a more blended approach to learning; combining traditional face-to-face classroom teaching with virtual learning and in so doing responding to the learning needs and preferences of today's digital-age students.

Online learning with the International Baccalaureate Diploma Programme

The International Baccalaureate has been offering an online option for its Diploma Programme (IBDP) subject courses for students for the past five years. During that time, an increasing range of online Diploma Programme subject courses have become available including Mathematics, Philosophy, Economics, Psychology,

Pamoja Education

Business Management, Information Technology in a Global Society, Spanish, Mandarin and Film.

All IBDP online subject courses have been created and are delivered by specialist online course provider UK-based Pamoja Education in collaboration with the International Baccalaureate, to ensure students are able to communicate effectively and fully engage in their IBDP learning through a range of innovative online educational tools.

In participating schools, students can choose to take one or more of their IB Diploma Programme subjects, for the entire two-year period of study, via the virtual classroom. They learn in groups of between 15 and 25 students, working alongside online classmates who are based in other schools around the world.

Their teacher – an experienced, qualified IB subject teacher who is also fully trained in online learning techniques – guides them throughout the course via a range of e-dialogue. This includes live online lessons which allow students synchronous time with their teacher and classmates, weekly assignments including online class discussions and blog entries, and learning activities that students work on either alone, with their classmates or with their teachers.

The students have structured yet flexible learning weeks, meaning that they have a weekly learning schedule to complete but which can be undertaken at a time and place that best suits each individual.

Growth and success

Interest in the IBDP online course options is growing significantly based on student and school success. In the May 2013 IBDP examinations, 83.5% of online students achieved a grade 4 or above, comparing very favourably with 78.5% for all IBDP students.

This academic year there are 1,400 students from over 300 schools participating in IBDP online subject courses. This includes seven schools that are members of the Council of British International Schools (COBIS). Colin Bell is the CEO of COBIS: "Regardless of school setting or location, continuity of quality education and access to engaging curriculum and effective learning resources, which include online learning platforms are of great importance to student achievement," he says. "Many students studying at British Schools Overseas are from highly mobile families who travel often. For these students

in particular, access to online learning platforms can provide essential continuity."

Tana Monk is one of this year's online students. She is a first year IBDP student studying two courses online; Business & Management and Economics through Yokohama International School in Japan. "I was expecting the IB [Diploma] to be really difficult, and that doing it online would make it even harder," she says. "But once I dove into the course and got familiar with the site, I found that it was really easy and organized. Pamoja Education's programme has a lot of tools that help you to communicate with your classmates and with your teacher. So whenever you need help or advice, you can contact them and they'll get back to you right away and help you as much as they can. I also like how the lessons are set up, because you can go at your own pace as long as you get everything done by the end of the week."

Tana says being in a genuinely global classroom has helped to give her a more international view of the subjects she is studying. "I get to see the world from many different cultural perspectives, meet different people and even make friends," she says.

In preparation for university

So how is the online learning experience helping IBDP students after completion of their course; once they reach university? Past international student, María Fernández-Martos Balson who studied IB Mathematics Higher Level online and is currently an Engineering student at the University of Cambridge in England reflects on her IBDP online learning: "The flexible pace of an online course suited me well," she says.

"I quite liked being able to skip or revisit topics, as necessary. Being able to submit questions in video format was also very useful. My teacher was extraordinary – very talented and extremely supportive. This is not something my school would have been able to provide otherwise. I am currently studying Engineering at the University of Cambridge. I do think that the Pamoja Education online course benefited my application: it shows that I can adapt to a new learning environment quickly, and that I am a proactive learner. The online Mathematics HL course has prepared me for university in ways that a traditional course cannot, both in terms of the quality of the teaching, and of the time management skills that I developed during the course."

More information about IBDP online learning and a range of informative YouTube videos from students, parents and teachers are available from Pamoja Education at www.pamojaeducation.com

The pioneering spirit of a school start-up

Corine van den Wildenberg, Vice Principal of GEMS World Academy – Etoy, shares her experiences of 'the blank canvas' of a new international school

GEMS World Academy – Etoy opened in September 2013

There are few opportunities in an educator's career to work with a blank canvas: to establish a new school, to be given the opportunity to create and build something that speeds past the slow process of change. I'm enjoying my second of such experiences having just moved from Montenegro, where I was Head of School, to Switzerland, where I am the Vice Principal, assisting the same process. Both situations were quite different, with diverse staff, resources, locations, and student communities. What I have learned from both school start-up projects is that they rely on key elements in order to achieve success.

Establish a clear vision
At the outset it is vital to articulate a clear vision, a reason for being, the school's purpose. The vision plays a key role in recruitment. There must be buy-in, a commitment to strive forward toward that illustrious goal. A shared understanding of the school's vision is important in order

to build commitment and to ensure everyone is working towards the same vision.

Curiosity, inquiry, creativity and passion are key outcomes that are highlighted in the vision for GEMS World Academy – Etoy. In addition, GEMS Education has established four core values that underpin the philosophy and vision of the school: global citizenship, growing by learning, pursuing excellence and leading through innovation. These four pillars provide a foundation from which a talented pool of educators can work to shape and build the school of our dreams. These are supported by the decision to implement the three International Baccalaureate programmes: the Primary Years, Middle Years and Diploma Programmes. If the start-up project is likened to a blank canvas, then the vision, core values and the curriculum become the colours on our palette through which all other aspects are mixed and illustrated.

There must be buy-in, a commitment to strive forward toward that illustrious goal. A shared understanding of the school's vision is important in order to build commitment and to ensure everyone is working towards the same vision.

Recruit staff with a pioneering spirit

Jim Collins, in his book *Good to Great: Why Some Companies Make the Leap ... And Others Don't* (2001), coined the phrase 'get the right people on the bus,' and while it may seem cliché, it continues to ring true. Though very exciting, thinking on your feet is also the reality of the day. New staff members will come with a variety of experiences and perspectives established from years of teaching and learning elsewhere. Their ideas, opinions and practice will influence the new 'How we do things around here'. What is required for whom and for what also places a stress on development during a start-up.

The established vision and core values are the lenses through which recruiting decisions are made. For some educators, a start-up school may be too demanding on time, energy and other resources. They may require

more stability and that much more be in place in order to function. Others will jump at the chance to redefine what learning experiences could and should be and are driven by the possibility of change. Engaging educators who are ready to review previously held practices or beliefs, and who want to venture into the unknown and who truly are flexible is vital. These are the educators who roll up their sleeves and dig in. They become the artists who, using the colours on their palette (vision, core values and curriculum), manage the resources and collaboratively create. They are 'doers', always ready to learn and innovate.

Safeguard learning

Time may be one of the most precious resources during a start-up project as there are many things happening at once. The leadership team should make a clear distinction of roles, allowing teachers the time and resources needed to provide the best learning experiences. All other matters are managed in order to allow learning to happen.

A school that embraces inquiry as a pedagogy also models and engages in it. Inquiries inevitably arise when decisions need to be made, or initiatives are taken, as there is a vast amount of literature, research and commentary on what is best practice in education. When reflecting on new issues or starting with new plans, the developing team does well to keep the best interests of students at heart. It is sometimes easier to respond to an issue or query with what is best for staff or parents. Nevertheless student learning is at the forefront of school success and therefore the response to all challenging questions is found by answering "What is best for students?"

Safeguarding student learning directly impacts word-of-mouth marketing. The founding families must also have trust in the pioneers and their ability to strive towards the vision and core values and to implement the curriculum holistically.

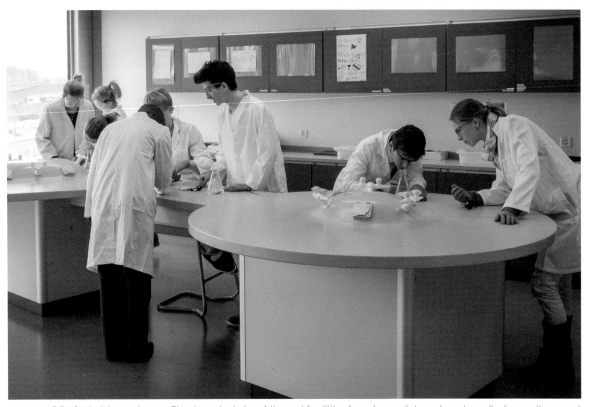

GEMS World Academy – Etoy boasts state-of-the-art facilities for science (above) and media (opposite page)

Balance the priorities

Experience will tell you that a myriad of policies and practices are in place in well-established schools. These aspects of formal schooling may also be anchors that prevent change. During a start-up there will be a drive to have much in place and to race to establish those factors that seem the norm and the necessity. However, it is more important to reflect on the implementation of such things carefully so that they truly embrace and emulate your vision and values. When in doubt, the issues that will help the school strive towards the vision might take precedence over other issues. Safety cannot be compromised, of course, yet perhaps there exist policies that require some fine tuning in order to better reflect a more current approach to good practice. A start-up allows you to do this.

We are partially through the 21st century and I've even heard people speak of 22nd century learning. Given the current tools at our disposal, the speed and ease of which we can access information, the numerous demands placed on education by various communities, it's beholden of the staff to take the time to reflect, review and revise aspects of their implementation in order to ensure that the school of their dreams truly comes to life.

Upon reflection, it is interesting to note how founding teams pass through the initial start up year much like a class of students passes through an authentic inquiry. Ours has been a learning journey of collaborative action and reflection. We have soared forward with collectivity with enthusiasm and now must step back to reflect and marvel at our work in progress. The process has required our founding "artists" to live up to the values of global citizenship, growing by learning, pursuing excellence and leading through innovation. A school start-up is an exciting venture that simultaneously provides both challenges and rewards and at the end of of the year, the canvas is no longer blank, rather, it is a colourful reflection of enthusiastic achievements on many levels.

Corine van den Wildenberg is Vice Principal/Early Childhood Coordinator at
GEMS World Academy – Etoy, Switzerland (for more information see page 119)

European University
Business School
www.euruni.edu

Muhammad Mahgoub
MBA in Leadership, 2014
Interned at Baker Hughes

Thomas Ruschke
BA in Business Administration, 2012
Interned at Mercedes-Benz do Brasil

YOU!

Fanny L. Fortier
BA in Business Administration, 2013
Interned at the Adidas Group

Roxana Flores
BA in International Marketing, 2012
Interned at Triumph International

At European University, a practical education comes with experiential learning!

Education and experience teach you skills useful in any business field: international experience, multiple languages and adaptability. European University meets the needs of students and helps recruiters identify talent. We actively engage in employer outreach, providing students with a wide variety of internship and career opportunities.

PEOPLE HAVE IDEAS.
ENTREPRENEURS MAKE THEM HAPPEN.

BARCELONA | GENEVA | MONTREUX | MUNICH | ONLINE

Internships offer great opportunities for enterprising students

Anna Wlodek, of European University, says that targeted work placements provide valuable real-world experience and boost career prospects

The way we work is changing. And as such, the recruitment process is evolving. Companies are becoming ever more demanding, and it has become about more than just what you've studied, where you've worked and what responsibilities you've had; now it's also about proving that you've taken that extra step and gone that extra mile.

Internships play a big part in modern education and a student's transition into today's business world. Not only do they show employers a willingness to work hard, they also enable personal development, facilitate growth and open doors to possibilities.

Theory learned in the classroom can simultaneously be applied to a real-life work scenario, and similarly, experience gained in a business setting can illustrate theory to support classroom learning. Because of the laws of supply and demand in the global job market; too many workers; and not enough work, it is becoming harder and harder for candidates to stand out among the current several hundred application average. It is up to students to find ways to demonstrate their work ethic and dedication to their careers; and it is up to their university to encourage, support and assist them.

A student undertaking an internship benefits from real-world experience that not only adds to their CV, but also gives them an edge in the job market, builds their confidence and allows them to learn first-hand about specific industries. Lessons learned in the classroom become real. Textbook theory on work processes, strategies, management systems and work methods is put into practice and better analysed and understood. Undertaking an internship while studying, either simultaneously or on breaks between terms, also enables students to take the experience from the business environment back to the classroom and use it to further excel in their learning.

On a personal level, internships enable students to identify their strengths and weaknesses, explore different career options and establish a network of business contacts. Experience in different sectors gives students the chance to branch out and try different areas of business, and find out what they enjoy and what they are good at. A short-term work placement is the ideal opportunity for gaining better insight into potential career paths. As Anna Wlodek, Career Advisor on the European University Barcelona campus, commented: "An internship is a great way of trying different departments; working in various areas of one company and discovering where your talents lie and what aspects of a business you enjoy most."

Stepping into the world of work connects students with current professionals who have a wealth of experience to share and opens doors to networking possibilities. Getting an early start on becoming part of such a community is an added bonus of undertaking an internship while still studying. A strong, varied network of contacts is an indispensable tool that can greatly contribute to success in the modern working world. An internship while studying

> Students can use an internship as an on-the-job, practical interview, work hard and excel, and in doing so show exactly what they could bring to the company as a full-time employee.

also allows students to procure full-time, permanent job offers immediately after graduating, allowing them to jump-start their careers rather than spend time on internships.

An internship demonstrates dedication to prospective employers. A commitment to working while studying highlights an eagerness to understand, a desire to gain experience, and a commitment to developing talents and improving skills. Instead of whiling away a summer or free time during term time, interns show that they are keen to work hard, use their time wisely and do everything they can to excel in their careers. While simultaneously studying and doing an internship is hard work, doing so adds unquestionable value to a CV.

The prospective employer in question may well be the company at which a student is interning. As Anna Wlodek says: "An internship gives you a golden opportunity to prove yourself, opening doors to potential job offers in the future."

Students can use an internship as an on-the-job, practical interview, work hard and excel, and in doing so show exactly what they could bring to the company as a full-time employee.

In order to keep pace with the current business environment, European University encourages students to engage in internships while studying. To further promote student opportunities, EU collaborates with companies that offer internships throughout the academic year and also during the summer. In doing so, they offer great opportunities to students. EU BBA graduate and current MBA student Emir Dagci recognizes the university's dedication to its students: "As a transfer student, I can easily say that European University is an extremely diverse, high-quality, dynamic and forward-thinking institution. It not only prepares students for business life in the best way but also offers students constant support and helps them find job and internship opportunities."

EU offers a variety of career services for students. There is a career counselor on all four main EU campuses: in Barcelona, Geneva, Munich and Montreux. They are available to students throughout the academic semester. They help them realize their career goals by coaching them and discussing their dreams and ambitions. This process is then used to highlight the students' key skills and help them map out a viable career path. Students are given advice on how to find internships and also matched to offers available through existing partnerships.

European University has collaborated and continues to collaborate with companies such as Vueling, Qatar Airways, KPMG and Credit Suisse, in order to offer internship positions for students who are interested in discovering the many varied values an internship can bring.

Anna Wlodek is Careers Advisor at European University

Thirty-five years of growth and prosperity

Rob Williams, Group Managing Director, explains how Braeburn Schools Ltd have developed an ethos that fosters confident, successful learners

Over its thirty-five year history, Braeburn has grown from a single primary school caring for the educational needs of approximately 70 children, to now looking after the well-being of over 3000 pupils between 2 and 19 years of age. Our responsibilities are not taken lightly. Despite the fact we run 15 schools in both Kenya and Tanzania, we pride ourselves that our brand values are consistently revealed in all our schools. An educational brand which reflects a desire to ensure children are happy and content in their learning. An educational brand where children really do come first. A brand where children of whatever creed or colour accept each other, don't notice apparent differences, but respect each other for what they believe in and what they are. Our children become confident individuals, responsible citizens and are learners enjoying success.

Our Headteachers all understand the ethos that prevails in our schools. They understand it, agree with it and develop it. Most have grown up professionally within it and now work as part of the group management team to ensure the ethos is maintained.

The curriculum we follow is the National Curriculum of England and Wales, which we supplement in the later stages of our students' education by offering IGCSE, AS level, A level, IB Diploma, National Diploma and Higher National Diploma programs (dependent on the educational institution attended). The curriculum is all about identifying and developing talents, whether academic, sporting, dramatic, or any of the other avenues which are presented for children to show what they are capable of. Indeed, the extra-curricular programs in all our schools are extensive and wide-ranging in what they offer. By supporting the academic aspects of school life with a plethora of cultural, social and interesting events and activities, we ensure our children and students are prepared for the experiences and challenges adult life brings.

At an academic level, in recent years we have consistently improved on previous records. Yet for a group of schools that is not extensively selective, our staff can take much pride in a student achieving at a much lower level than this, but achieving at their maximum. Historically we have had students enter our schools with specific learning difficulties, but have left achieving at A level with four maximum grades. Braeburn is providing an education to allow all children within its care to grow up happily, and at the same time to be equipped with the social, behavioural, intellectual, and life skills needed for them to be an asset to their families, communities and friends in adulthood, to be ambitious enough to succeed personally and professionally and to be ready to live a fulfilling life.

Our schools are well-resourced to ensure the chosen curriculum is covered and covered in an interesting way. Our biggest resource is our teachers, who are dedicated, well-qualified, enthusiastic and well-intentioned professionals.

Braeburn is about people – teaching and non-teaching staff who are committed to ensuring our children grow up in the right way. We are fortunate in that we have parents who have the desire to see their children grow up in the right way and finally, we have children who do grow up in the right way.

Our children are cared for and supported and, more importantly, they recognise that support. They experience success such that anxiety is reduced. They are provided with a whole range of opportunities to allow them to succeed, as success is the starting point from which all aspects of our practice and methodology begin. Most important of all, our children are happy, and a happy child is much more likely to succeed.

Our teachers are graduates, skillfully trained in their profession, but also carefully picked to fit into our ethos. They clearly care about our children and want them to succeed. Our group consistently provides refresher training programs for staff to enable them to meet the ever evolving changes and challenges of moving with the times in a dynamic educational world.

Our parents are actually involved in our schools. The mechanisms of communication between school and home are many, but we also actively promote the idea of parents spending time in the schools such that they know, understand and respect the education their children are receiving.

That triangle of children, teachers and parents is strengthened by open communication networks between the players. We actively encourage comment and suggestions by parents and students and have often acted on them. Our Headteachers operate an open door policy and we have social events and systems which mean parents are closely involved in our schools.

Our relative successes can be attributed to the teams in place within and between our schools. Loyal staff members, loyal parents and loyal students ensure that our ethos is maintained and developed. Our founding and current directors have placed and do place their own children in our schools. Their confidence is shared by many others.

Whichever Braeburn school, the atmosphere you will find is a warm and happy one, where children and students smile their way through their formative years, get actively involved in opportunities to learn and experience and prepare themselves to be successful, broad-minded, and capable adults. More to the point, they become 'nice' people.

Braeburn has a thirty-five year history, but its ambition lies not in the past but to a future where the great, great grandchildren of the present students would happily want their own children placed in the school where they were schooled, and where the ethos and values currently displayed would still be unchanged.

For more information about Braeburn Schools, please see pages 60-67

Putting theory into practice

An insight into how Ecole hôtelière de Lausanne students are trained and prepared for leading jobs in the hospitality industry

EHL student Estelle Murer, 20. Read about her internship at a hotel in Dubai on page 27

Ecole hôtelière de Lausanne students are trained to become top executives who possess solid managerial and teamwork skills and who are experts in the art of customer relationships.

EHL's academic teaching, combined with demanding hands-on experience, produces graduates who can adapt and evolve quickly in a competitive international environment.

Operational internships all over the world
Two semesters of internships are required, the first being an operational internship and the second an administrative internship. The first placement is an opportunity for students to immediately put the skills they have learned during their Preparatory Year into practice. Internships are a key part of the study programs and play a major role in the learning process. EHL therefore takes particular care to ensure that the internship runs smoothly so that both parties can benefit fully from the collaboration.

The Preparatory Year is a total immersion in the world of hospitality and allows students to acquire the necessary experience to carry out their future roles as managers. The study program reflects the school's unique teaching

philosophy, which combines the art and science of management. The first year of study aims to deepen students' understanding of the culture of hospitality through the teaching of academic subjects linked to the hotel industry, from social, political and human sciences to technology and economics.

EHL's values of excellence, 'savoir-faire' and 'savoir-être' are all passed on through teaching of culinary arts and other arts related to hospitality. Students develop their 'manual intelligence' by undertaking various operational roles, which enable them to acquire both practical knowledge and a good understanding of managerial responsibilities.

Their knowledge and practical experience allow them to be immediately operational and ready to face challenges in the companies where they undertake their internship.

The internship which takes place during the Preparatory Year is a complete introduction to the world of work. The placement is usually carried out in operational departments such as the kitchen, stewarding, restaurant service, room service, bakery, catering and all other activities linked to the restaurant industry.

Internships can also be undertaken in the accommodation sector, in areas such as housekeeping, laundry, reception and the concierge service.

The talent and professional skills demonstrated by EHL students during their internships are greatly appreciated: 87% of employers say that they would hire a student once they graduate.

Case study – Estelle Murer, EHL student, aged 20, from Switzerland Bachelor program (Year 2)

Attending a conference on hospitality management given by an EHL alumnus during a forum was a turning point for Estelle. This helped her to realise that she wanted to study hospitality, and since then her interest in hospitality has become stronger and stronger.

Since joining EHL, Estelle's passion for hospitality and its related fields has kept growing. Studying at EHL was the only option for her, nothing else would do.

A keen traveller, Estelle has already visited many different parts of the world including South East Asia. With the operational internship looming, it was time to choose a destination. Estelle could go anywhere in the world, and she had to choose one country: "Why not do my internship in a country that I do not know at all, so that I would face a real challenge?"

Her choice fell on Dubai and 5* hotels. Almost 25 applications and several interviews later, Estelle received the confirmation that she had been selected for a job on Reception at the Mövenpick Hotel Deira.

"After an integration week, during which I had the chance to spend one day in each department of the hotel, I worked on Reception. That was where I discovered teamwork during the day, during the evening and during the night. It is incredible to see everything that happens in a hotel in the middle of the night, and unless you have lived that unique experience it is almost impossible to imagine."

Two weeks after the start of her internship, Estelle was asked to manage one of the welcome desks while one of her colleagues was absent. From that moment, her

"I will never forget that six-month internship. It was a first step and a total immersion in the world of work which was extremely enriching. I learnt a huge amount in terms of hospitality and the hotel industry in general, but it also enabled me to develop and mature."

internship took on a new dimension and she undertook a fast-track training program. It was a learning process that required her to demonstrate responsibility, professionalism and rigor.

"I will never forget that six-month internship. It was a first step and a total immersion in the world of work which was extremely enriching. I learnt a huge amount in terms of hospitality and the hotel industry in general, but it also enabled me to develop and mature. The cultural differences and the long working hours gave me the opportunity to better understand the working of the hospitality industry in the Middle East. Working independently, taking on responsibilities, acting in a truly professional manner, developing a taste for adventure and finally surpassing oneself… such is the extraordinary context that my internship took place in".

'Crossing the divide' to deliver new international school

Alec Jiggins explains how Knightsbridge Schools International took on the challenge of setting up a school in Montenegro

Knightsbridge Schools International Montenegro belongs to a global network of international schools united through shared ethos and curriculum. Modelled on both the successful features of Knightsbridge School in London and the international standards expected of high quality schools across the globe, KSI Montenegro offers a unique and compelling approach to education in the beautiful Bay of Kotor.

The opening of the first international school in the KSI group was an exciting opportunity to 'cross the divide' and see the realisation of the KSI mission and ethos. KSI has developed further international schools in key strategic and emerging markets to ensure the provision of high-quality education to families in a variety of global locations.

Establishing our school in Montenegro has been a challenging, but also rewarding experience for all the members of KSI Community. Being the first international school in the country that implements the International Baccalaureate and aims to educate, not only foreign, but also Montenegrin citizens, required a lot of hard work. Our

staff members and constant cooperation between the school and the Government and local community and business to strive for our success, with the school currently working with the Montenegrin Ministry of Education to attain our secondary school license.

In addition, as a new educational concept in the country, it took time for people to understand its value and the benefit our programme has for students. The Montenegrin system of education is widely accepted and recognised by citizens and this has not changed, but with KSI, the door has opened to the IB and more and more Montenegrin nationals join our school each year.

After the hard work and excitement of these past four years on our journey, in Montenegro, we are well on the way to achieving many of our goals. We are the first authorised PYP IB World School in Montenegro; we have achieved candidacy for both the MYP and DP and are confident of achieving authorisation for both programmes; and we are the first international school to have obtained the Montenegrin Ministry of Education license. Most recently we have opened the very first

As a new educational concept in the country, it took time for people to understand it value and the benefit our programme has for students. The Montenegrin system of education is widely accepted and recognised by citizens and this has not changed, but with KSI, the door has opened to the IB and more and more Montenegrin nationals join our school each year.

British-ethos boarding school in Montenegro and the wider Balkans region. We are excited to begin teaching the IB Diploma Programme in September 2015.

Joining the KSI Montenegro family opens a world of opportunities to our students, as they are inspired and supported both in and out of school by their parents and teachers. Apart from the school's student-centered focus on learning, the driving force behind the school is perhaps better explained by the school's ethos of Keep Smiling, Keep Striving. Along with the "KSI Code", this shared ethos has been carefully shaped to support the unique learning environment of Montenegro and our location on the Adriatic Coast.

Within the school, we foster a strong sense of community and provide a supportive and warm environment within which, learners are encouraged to "work hard and play hard". As a result, our school in Montenegro has created its own KSI identity, which every child, parent and teacher can relate to and grows to appreciate more over time. That in itself is fundamental to the success of our holistic approach. Students are encouraged to use a range of different technologies in their learning, with the IB Learner Profile being kept at the heart of our learning experience. Students have access to Rosetta Stone for language development and teachers regularly use Khan Academy to facilitate independent learning in mathematics.

The motto of Knightsbridge Schools International, 'Be all you can be', remains central to each and every KSI School across the globe. By understanding and embracing this ethos, together, we have built a strong and caring KSI Community.

This culture permeates through every facet of the school's programme and recognises age appropriate strategies to discover and take ownership of the KSI ethos. Service learning is key to our programme, and students are encouraged to be involved with the local community through voluntary work, collaboration with other schools, and through learning the local language.

KSI Montenegro is located in a pristine coastal environment, where we are surrounded by the very mountains which gives this country its name, whilst also being only a few steps away from the clear blue waters of the Kotor Bay. Our students enjoy access to sports such as sailing, kayaking, hiking, tennis, and football. The clean air and healthy living makes it an ideal place to go to school. Our school chef prepares fresh, healthy meals every day for a variety of dietary requirements. Our boarding house is equipped to the highest standards, and our whole campus is wifi enabled. We offer After School Activities such as football, yoga, dancing, chess, Scrabble club, sewing club, and the International Award.

We are very proud of KSI Montenegro and our community. Please come and visit us, or contact us for more information on how our community is living our mission.

For more information about KSI Montenegro, see page 128

A passion for learning
is a passion for life

SEK International Schools
Est. 1892

Spain · France · Ireland · Qatar

+34 902 80 80 82 | www.sek.es

Tradition, innovation and leadership

Established in 1892, SEK International Schools combine innovation and pedagogical leadership with 120 years of tradition and history to offer educational programmes unlike any other.

An international learning community

Motivated by the IB mission, SEK International Schools offer a complete curriculum of academically rigorous international programmes in English and Spanish.

SEK schools are engaging and personalized learning communities, where students develop the intellectual, personal, emotional and social skills to become lifelong learners and shape their own future as global citizens.

SEK students enjoy state-of-the-art learning spaces and extensive sports facilities, as well as boarding facilities in Madrid, Dublin and SEK Campus Les Alpes (France).

IB pioneers, since 1977

SEK International Schools pioneered IB programmes in Spain more than 35 years ago.

Through Camilo José Cela University, the SEK Group is one of Europe's leading providers of IB professional development. UCJC offers a wide range of IB workshops as well as IB Certificates in Teaching and Learning.

CAMILO JOSÉ CELA
UNIVERSITY

More information at: www.ucjc.edu

International Schools
Est. 1892

+6,000 students
58 nationalities

SEK International School **El Castillo (Madrid, Spain)**
PYP, MYP and DP English, Spanish, Bilingual

SEK International School **Ciudalcampo (Madrid, Spain)**
PYP, MYP and DP English, Spanish, Bilingual

SEK International School **Santa Isabel (Madrid, Spain)**
PYP

SEK International School **Catalunya (Barcelona, Spain)**
PYP, MYP and DP Spanish and Bilingual

SEK International School **Alborán (Almería, Spain)**
PYP, MYP and DP Spanish and Bilingual

SEK International School **Atlántico (Pontevedra, Spain)**
PYP, MYP, DP Candidate School*

SEK International School **Dublin (Dublin, Ireland)**
MYP Candidate School*

SEK International School **Qatar (Doha, Qatar)**
PYP Candidate School*

SEK Campus **Les Alpes (Megève, France)**

Camilo José Cela University (Madrid, Spain)
Undergraduate, Postgraduate, Professional Degrees
On-campus and distance programmes

Supporting 'the complete learner's journey'

Sarah Lyons introduces new curriculum initiatives and the ongoing development of learning resources at Cambridge University Press

We at Cambridge University Press are driven by the simple imperative: to work alongside educators and learners to provide individuals with accessible, inspirational learning resources that lead them to a lifetime of achievement. Our bestselling resources offer the complete learning journey from Primary-age through to A level; they are endorsed by Cambridge International Examinations and provide comprehensive coverage of the Cambridge curriculum frameworks and syllabuses.

This year we introduced our Cambridge Primary series, the exciting new series for the Cambridge Primary curriculum frameworks, made up of Primary English (for First Language learners), Global English* (for English as a Second Language learners), Primary Mathematics and Primary Science. Cambridge Primary is an innovative set of resources designed to support teachers and help learners succeed in Primary Education. Designed to set

the foundations for future learning, Cambridge Primary focuses on academic achievement and is an ideal resource for any international or bilingual school.

Our comprehensive print, digital and online resources are designed to inspire young learners and support hardworking teachers. Our resources help learners to become independent, confident thinkers, who are able to express themselves clearly, with a focus on critical thinking, problem solving and creativity. Our resources encourage learners to take an investigatory approach and help learners to develop the skills and language to find answers, solve problems and apply their newly found knowledge through engaging activities and classroom discussion.

Hardworking teachers can expect the same level of thought which we give to our young learners, with a plethora of dedicated print, digital and online teacher

LEADING SWISS BUSINESS SCHOOL

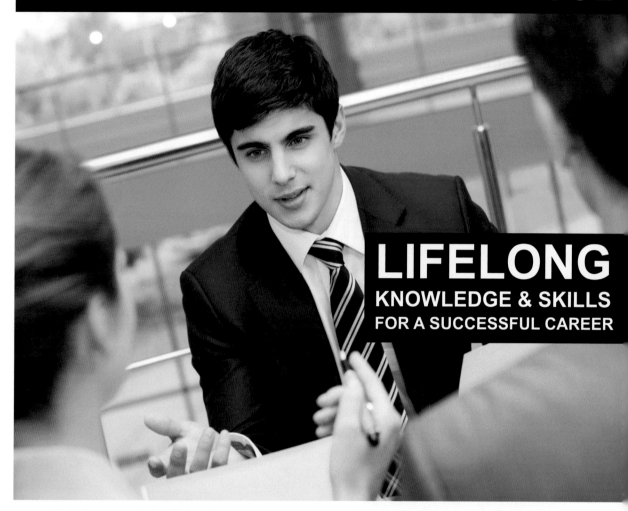

LIFELONG
KNOWLEDGE & SKILLS
FOR A SUCCESSFUL CAREER

MBA / MASTER
BACHELOR

International Business
Banking and Finance
Entrepreneurship
Family Business Management
Oil, Gas and Energy Management
Communication and Marketing
International Finance

OUR DISTINCTIONS

Study in a city top-ranked for quality of life
Central & urban campus in Geneva
Dynamic learning based on practice
Top faculty with real-world experience
Small classes & human-sized institution
Accredited programmes taught in English
International student body & environment
Career guidance & outstanding opportunities
3 intakes per year & online application system
Outstanding career opportunities

The educational environment is ever-changing and is one which is at the forefront of exciting new developments and innovations. We all know that it is important to grow and adapt with these exciting developments, however we also realise this is not without its challenges. For this reason we strive to work with students and teachers, to support and guide them throughout the learning journey and provide innovative and inspirational educational resources that lead to a lifetime of learning.

resources. Our teacher resources offer everything from defined learning objectives and lesson planning, to worksheets and advice on how to adapt lessons to different levels of ability.

We work with innovative and inspiring authors with extensive knowledge of the education market to create resources which are designed with the English as Second Language learner in mind. Our resources use accessible language and colourful illustrations throughout to best communicate concepts and aid visual learning.

As part of the complete learning journey we aim to support young learners at each stage of their journey; from the start of their journey at 5 years old when they are entering Primary School to 19 years old when they are completing their A level examinations. "But what about everything in between?" we hear you ask. We realise how important it is to support students from one level to the next, which is why we aim to ensure that all our resources from Primary to A level prepare students for a seamless progression onto the next stages of education. Starting at Cambridge Primary; our Cambridge Primary resources provide excellent foundations for Cambridge Checkpoint supporting the Secondary 1 Curriculum. Our Primary resources ensure students are ready for the next level in education and are equipped to make the change from Primary to Secondary school. This principle is replicated throughout our resources up to A-level, with our Cambridge Checkpoint resources in turn providing excellent foundations for Cambridge IGCSE and our Cambridge IGCSE resources providing important fundamentals for the International A level.

The educational environment is ever-changing and is one which is at the forefront of exciting new developments and innovations. We all know that it is important to grow and adapt with these exciting developments, however we also realise this is not without its challenges. For this reason we strive to work with students and teachers, to support and guide them throughout the learning journey and provide innovative and inspirational educational resources that lead to a lifetime of learning.

Cambridge Global English titles have not gone through the Cambridge Endorsement as they follow the curriculum frameworks developed by English Language Assessment

The importance of play – and what schools need to ensure

Ayca Mehlig, of ABC Team Playgrounds, looks at the issues surrounding the installation and maintenance of high-quality play equipment in schools

The UN Convention on the Rights of the Child sets out universally-accepted rights for children. According to Article 31 of the UN Convention, every child has the right to rest and leisure, to engage in play and recreational activities appropriate to the age of the child and to participate freely in cultural life and the arts. Play is actually in our nature. It is meaningful and it is freedom. Play is a child's main method of developing him or herself within their society.

Researchers have found evidence of privately-built play equipment within the yards of some noble families from 18th century Germany. The first built play area dates back to 1821, built in Massachusetts at the school yard of the Latin School. Improved designs followed in Germany and the first public playgrounds started to be built in 1837. These first playgrounds were very simple and mostly constructed from nature itself ie tree trunks and rocks. The advancement of play areas and play equipments has continued ever since. Playgrounds became widespread in the urbanization of the 20th century and this was supported by customization of individual sites and the introduction of equipment standards, to prevent against accidents. Today, playgrounds of various types are the theme of scientific research, from preventive medicine to pedagogy, in order to support the current developments.

Just as HSE England (2012) point out, play provides children with an understanding of their own abilities; helps them to learn and develop; and exposes them to the realities of the world in which they will live – this is a world not free from risk but rather one where risk is ever present. The opportunity for play develops a child's risk awareness and prepares them for their future lives.

Meeting the needs and demands of children of all ages at a playground requires an important balance between protecting children from serious risks and equally supplying high-quality play opportunities and activities. This, as adults, communities, schools, manufacturers and designers, is our responsibility to children.

But the safety of playgrounds doesn't depend solely upon the initial design of the play area or the play equipment. Proper management, routine professional inspections and maintenance are essential to support children's safe play. When handing over their projects, manufacturers submit the necessary inspection and maintenance requirements. The standards EN 1176 and/or CPSC and ASTM have to be clearly seen on every piece of equipment to ensure proper management of the play area and the equipment.

Safety inspection of a playground has to be run routinely, operationally and annually. For annual inspections it is recommended that a specialist carries out an inspection that looks at vandalism, minor and major wear, long-term structural problems, changes in standard compliance and design practice, risk assessment etc. Such inspections are offered by insurance companies, playground equipment manufacturers, commercial companies and safety organizations.

At this point it is important to mention the training of the managing team of a playground. It is highly recommended that staff responsible for ensuring the routine safety and upkeep of school playgrounds are given basic training for their inspections, to ensure that equipment is always conforming to the highest safety and quality standards and that any problems are flagged up as quickly as possible.

In summary, safety always has to be the first priority when providing play equipment for our children. And as playgrounds are developed to bring the greatest benefit to schools and their pupils, it's important to work with experienced companies with proven track records to ensure safety in design as well as sustainability, quality and proper management. This lays the foundations for children to play in an environment of safety, exploration and enjoyment.

ABC Team Playgrounds® and its qualified representatives work with a number of international schools across Europe. For more information contact infois@abc-team.de or visit www.abc-team.de

'We may not have it all together but together we have it all'

Rachael Westgarth explains the ethos behind Round Square schools and looks ahead to the group's forthcoming conference

The theme for the start of the Round Square 2014 International Conference, this year opening in India, is 'we may not have it all together but together we have it all'. It describes an idea of learning to live together in peace and harmony with mutual respect, compassion, social responsibility and tolerance of diversity amongst individuals; of interdependence, co-existence and collaboration.

Round Square (RS) is a not-for-profit network of more than 150 schools on five continents that collaborate on a holistic approach to learning that guides students into becoming well-rounded, informed, responsible, principled and confident Global Citizens. Together our schools build and benefit from a mutually supportive network that shares resources, ideas, methods, experience, opportunities, locally, regionally and internationally.

RS schools are characterised by a shared belief in an approach to education based on six pillars, our IDEALS, drawn from the theories of education philosopher Kurt Hahn. These are:

International understanding, empathy and tolerance for all cultures
Democratic governance and justice
Environmental stewardship
Adventure, motivating self-discovery and courage
Leadership, with courage and compassion
Service to others

The RS method recognises that learning is most effective when it is experiential, cross-cultural and collaborative, and when it is infused through a broad spectrum of inter, extra and intra-curricula activities.

Collaboration within the RS network takes many forms. Sometimes it is as simple as two schools working together. In late January, for example, a delegation from a RS college in Peru travelled to a fellow RS school in California to collaborate for ten days on a program that focussed on the topics of sustainable watersheds and intercultural understanding. They engaged with an integrated, experiential curriculum of environmental awareness, outdoor adventure, and community service focusing on stewardship and the critical role that healthy watersheds play as sources of clean, plentiful water supplies. During the programme, the students shared ideas about how each school is addressing issues such as community service, environmental awareness, intercultural understanding, and student government. The intensity of learning in these one-to-one exchanges can be profound.

On a larger scale, regional and international student-led Round Square Conferences encourage collaboration of thinking and learning across countries and continents. At a more intimate level, local, regional and international student and teacher visits and exchanges offer opportunities for students and teaching staff to experience each other's learning environments, countries and cultures.

Sometimes these begin with simple communication. In December Year 7 students from a RS school in England had a Skype interactive session with a RS school in Armenia. The group had discussions on how each country celebrates Christmas and New Year. As the students relaxed, they sang *Jingle Bells* together and then each school group sang their school hymn in their own language. The pupils discussed their daily schedule, what classes they enjoyed. The session ended with new friendships and pen pals established along with plans to skype again the following term.

More complex collaborative initiatives between clusters of RS schools include Service Projects that connect students directly with communities, both locally and around the world, where their hard work as volunteers can be of real practical benefit.

During a two-week term break a group of 19 participants from five RS schools within the Australasia and East Asia region came together for a Regional Project in Fiji. The group homestayed in the villages of Namuamua and Yanuya.

In both locations they ran daily classes in the village primary schools, with activities ranging from maths and science to music, dance, sport and art. In Namuamua the group also completed some much needed renovation work on two small boarding houses for children from other villages and planted trees in an area of damaged woodland. In Yanuya the project work had an environmental focus with students spending time

Students from five Round Square schools took part in a service project in Fiji , running classes for primary schools

removing rubbish from the beaches in a conservation area for turtles and iguanas.

The collaborative approach taken by RS schools extends to the community within the school. Themes of democracy and peace and working together for the greater good are borne out in everyday life, and RS students are encouraged to seek out and work together with communities that are less fortunate than themselves both now and in their adult life.

During December students from a number of African RS member schools collaborated on a service project in the small town of Philippolis in the Free State province of South Africa. During the week the group completed various projects including the setting up of two vegetable gardens, erecting a wire fence around the site and revamping the community church. Their main project was the completion of a soup kitchen so that the community could provide its most needy members with food.

A student reflects: "As the days passed we got to know the people in our groups better. We started off as individuals focused on finishing a specific job but as we neared the completion of the project it was clear that our mentality had changed - we didn't stop when the tenth bag of cement was mixed (manually), instead we worked

until the floor was covered and the walls were plastered. Even when the chance of rain gave the promise of an 'off day', there were people who volunteered to go back to the site to carry on working. The most amazing part was too see how the community members were eager and more than willing to work with us, side by side."

One of the most important lessons of a Round Square Service project comes from the collaborative nature of the work. Students learn through experience that working together can be more rewarding and more productive than working alone, and that working in collaboration with a community that is in need rather than for them extends the learning experience, bringing greater benefits to all parties.

The Round Square 2014 International Conference begins in India with the thought that together we might have it all. The conference will then travel this year to Jordan where the theme is a message of peace and the logo includes an olive tree with branches that reach out and intertwine. Very apt for a network whose schools, teachers and students collaborate on so many levels to reach out to, work and learn with, communities both at home and throughout the world.

For more information about Round Square, visit www.roundsquare.org

Political education in Italy – connecting past and present

Juliana DiBona says John Cabot University in Rome offers students the chance to 'extend their political education beyond their textbooks'

Italy has been a political and cultural Mecca for more than two millennia. From the great Roman Empire to its current prominent role on the world stage as a founding member of the G8, Italy's fascinating political history makes it an ideal location to study political science and international affairs.

As an American university located in Rome, Italy, John Cabot University provides its students with a unique political education and opportunities to study political science and international affairs in context. Students not only read Niccolo Machiavelli's political theories in textbooks, but also walk along the streets of the former Italian city-states he analysed. They learn about World War II by exploring Italian war sites and taking weekend trips to experience the remains of concentration camps firsthand. The University's location in Italy's capital provides students with a front row seat to both Italy's and the European Union's fascinating political and economic situations.

While intellectually challenging, studying international affairs in such a politically important and culturally diverse setting is truly a uniquely satisfying experience. Selina Strawley, an International Affairs major from the US, noted that: "International affairs at John Cabot has given me a broader view of the world. My classmates represent a variety of nationalities, and I have been able to learn from their perspectives in the classroom and by travelling with friends to their hometowns in Morocco and Italy, I have been able to experience their cultures firsthand."

John Cabot University provides students with a holistic foundation in international affairs, complemented by its location in such a politically prominent city. Students study national governments, international institutions and the processes by which international affairs are conducted, with particular focus on the forces which influence national and international policies. Professors incorporate real-life examples from Italian and European politics into class discussions, and the diverse nationalities represented in our classrooms result in conversations that force students to reexamine their preexisting biases and ethnocentric thought patterns so that they may view the world through a multilateral lens.

The faculty members at John Cabot University's department of political science and international affairs are undoubtedly the cornerstones of the program. Professor Sensi boasts a Ph.D. in Political Science from Rutgers University, a law degree from Harvard Law School, fluency in three languages, and a fascinating career that has allowed him to live in the United States, the Middle East and Europe. Students learn from his vast experience through John Cabot's small classes and through 'Pizza and Politics', a popular group he leads throughout each semester to discuss political events over lunch.

Professor Driessen earned his PhD in Political Science from the University of Notre Dame and was a resident post-doctoral fellow at Georgetown University's Center for International and Regional Studies in Doha, Qatar from 2011 to 2012. Professor Driessen teaches courses on religion and politics, comparative politics, Middle East studies and peace studies, and is currently organizing a conference on Rethinking Political Catholicism, which will be hosted at John Cabot University in May.

Outside of the classroom, the internships completed by John Cabot University students truly set them apart as they enter the job market. Leonardo Quattrucci, who is currently pursuing a Master of Public Policy at Oxford University, held internships with both the Italian parliament and the US Embassy as an undergraduate at JCU. He noted that his political science internships were "fundamental factors in my present and future development, both professionally and personally".

Fellow Oxford-bound graduate Tommaso Trillo completed several internships with international think tanks and organizations during his undergraduate career, and is currently working as a Research Assistant for the Budapest Centre for International Prevention of Genocide and Mass Atrocities. His internship experience was not only vital for his career, but has already been used by important policy makers; in April 2104 he was flown to Washington, DC, where his research on the role of development agencies in preventing mass atrocities was presented at a World Bank forum.

Students may also interact politically on campus by interning with the Guarini Institute of Public Affairs, which organizes lectures and seminars aimed at enhancing knowledge and understanding of challenges facing the world today. Anthony Vanicek, who is currently pursuing his law degree at the Catholic University of America, noted that his internship "not only gave me great work experience, but it forced me to re-evaluate my perspectives on critical issues facing Europe and the United States. Hearing the voices of men and women regarding prevalent concerns in the world, meeting and keeping correspondence with journalists, diplomats, ambassadors, scholars, and writers gave me an opportunity to learn in a unique way that a classroom is seldom able to offer'.

Due to the University's location in a major European capital, students have countless opportunities to gain practical experience in Rome's many international organizations, nonprofit foundations, and embassies. Each year, John Cabot University's students intern with organizations as prestigious as the World Food Program, the International Development Law Organization, and UNICEF.

Studying Political Science and International Affairs in Rome allows students to not only gain a solid academic foundation in political theory and history, but also to experience a front row seat in Italian, European and international politics. For students who wish to extend their political education beyond their textbooks, the undergraduate experience at John Cabot is truly a special experience.

For more information about John Cabot University, visit www.johncabot.edu

A future in hospitality – it's not what you think

Johan Stromsater, Vice-President Global Enrollment from Laureate Hospitality Education, says a hospitality degree program in Switzerland is the pathway to an elite career

Students at the Les Roches International School of Hospitality Management in Switzerland

Prepare to forget everything you thought about hospitality. Nowadays, it goes beyond hotels and restaurants to include sectors such as events, entertainment, financial services, travel, tourism and culinary arts. The industry offers exciting global career paths within top-tier brands: Louis Vuitton, Rolex and Bloomberg are as likely to recruit hospitality graduates for leadership and management roles, as much as the Four Seasons, InterContinental, Ritz-Carlton, or Kempinski hotels.

As the industry continues to expand worldwide, so does the need for hospitality management professionals who have the education and skills to grow with it. Few industries offer as much potential for a global business career as hospitality, because few industries in the world are growing as rapidly as hospitality. The World Tourism Organization estimates that the hospitality industry will grow 4.2% per year over the next 10 years. By 2024,

nearly 10% of all jobs in the world will be supported by the hospitality industry, representing a staggering 346,901,000 jobs.

A hospitality degree program in Switzerland is perhaps, par excellence, the degree pathway to some of the most elite-level career portfolios in the world.

What makes Swiss hospitality education unique for businesses?

Switzerland is the birthplace of classic hospitality education. Experiential learning is a perfected art amongst hospitality institutes in Switzerland, usually accompanied by a rigorous program of intellectual development.

Experiential learning demands that students manage real kitchens that create high-end cuisine, and master the art of bespoke service, thus developing

The Glion Institute of Higher Education

an intrinsic ability to deliver customer-oriented service with both impeccable aesthetics and precision. More than any other discipline perhaps, Swiss hospitality teaches students to recognise the psychological need of consumers to enjoy an experience, rather than conduct a transaction.

Experiential learning also implies professional internships and real-life projects within both Swiss-based and international companies. Through these internships, Swiss hospitality students develop a raft of soft-skills, such as leadership and inter-cultural fluency, which are transferable to any sector and give them a competitive edge over other graduates. By the time they graduate, Swiss-trained students already have an impressive professional resumé.

The reputation Swiss hospitality institutes enjoy is pertinently illustrated by the fact that top-tier companies will conduct regular recruitment sessions on the campuses of the highest-ranked Swiss hospitality institutes. At Les Roches International School of Hotel Management, for example, at least 50 companies visit each semester. It is not unusual for students to graduate with a dilemma: not, 'will I get a job?' but rather 'which job offer shall I take?'

These jobs can vary depending on the courses selected by the students. Some alumni take up Manager in Training positions in wealth management for private

banks or estate management. Some will choose to work in marketing or events for the Olympic Games or World Cup, and still others will opt for the travel and tourism sector and rise to executive-level positions within a global hotel chain, such as Rotana Hotels and Resorts or the Ritz-Carlton Hotel Company.

This highlights two important points: prospective students need to select a Swiss hospitality institute that offers a) business degrees; and b) course specializations, to tailor studies to professional objectives.

Course specialisations in Marketing, Innovation & Sustainability, Entrepreneurship, Event Management, Human Resources, Revenue Management and Culinary Business Management open a wider range of doors than a simple Swiss hospitality degree. They maximise the potential that the training and reputation of a Swiss hospitality education offers, by providing students with an extra level of specialist knowledge.

What makes Swiss hospitality education unique for students around the world?

A successful career in hospitality requires graduates to have a certain level of global exposure and experience. Both Glion and Les Roches foster this in abundance with students of around 90 nationalities and international campuses. The Glion London campus is located in

Roehampton, just outside of London's city center, while Les Roches has branch campuses Marbella, on the sunny Costa del Sol of Spain, and in Shanghai, China, as well as affiliate institutes in the USA and Jordan. Les Roches offers a Global Degree, a program which starts and ends in Switzerland, and includes one semester in Spain and China. Glion's Multicampus programs allow students to study for a year in London.

The Greek word for the hospitality concept is xenia. It means 'guest-friendship' and herein lies perhaps one of the most valuable outcomes of pursuing Swiss hospitality education. The international friendships made – because of the cultural diversity, because of the real-world professional assignments – last a lifetime.

And when you have a career that takes you around the world, a friendly face is always a bonus.

What the students say

Grisha Davidoff – Mexico
Glion Bachelor Degree in Hospitality Management - Semester 6
"I decided to study hospitality management at Glion because in contrast with other schools, we are a business school specialized in hospitality. This means that you get to know the foundation of hotel operations without losing the entrepreneurial, financial and general management courses that other business schools may offer to you and hence, you do not close your doors to other industries.

"With all aspects of Glion teaching methods, I feel highly prepared to enter the professional world and I already have entry-level offers in managerial positions."

Kristin Rieve – Germany
Les Roches Bachelor Degree in International Hotel Management - Semester 5
"Les Roches teaches us more than how to wear a suit, and prepare and give a presentation in front of an audience. Industry operations are taught from the outset, going through all levels of management to an intense concentration of leadership and management. Due to various kinds of projects that foster team work, students learn from each other, teach each other, and lead and guide each other, under the philosophy of 'learning by doing'.

"Les Roches inspires and supports us to be the best and innovate in what we're doing, and it trains us to be leaders."

'A structured and nurturing environment'

William Doherty, Executive Director of Chamberlain International School, looks at the increasing demand for therapeutic boarding schools

Across the globe there are scores of students who are impacted by learning differences and or emotional health issues. Whilst some of these students are able to manage through their education in a traditional setting, many are not so fortunate. Bright, capable, enthusiastic students facing learning or emotional challenges are often either not accepted at a traditional school or once there find that they require a higher level of support to meet with success and reach their full potential. Learning, emotional or neurological diagnoses are common in all regions of the world, affecting every community and age group across all income levels.

It has been estimated by the World Health Organization that 14% of the population faces mental health diagnosis and 10% of the world's population have learning disabilities. The UK mental health foundation has stated that estimates vary, but research suggests 20% of all children have a mental health problem in any given year and that rates of these problems increase as they reach adolescence. Specialized education and treatment allows these students the individualized attention they require and can lead the way to a very bright future whether that be in higher education or in obtaining the skills necessary to make a livelihood or both. Some of the recommended and proven strategies for success include, specialized academic programming, individual and group therapy, exercise, taking part in social activities, development of life skills, livelihood and financial literacy skills. A therapeutic boarding school offers such programming.

As the demands of a fast paced, technologically based world increase, so do the constant distractions and social pressures. Adolescence is inherently a challenging time in students' lives. When academic or emotional challenges are added to that equation it can be overwhelming. Therapeutic boarding schools offer a structured, supportive setting where students may discover and build upon their strengths while learning the techniques necessary to best navigate their challenges.

What is a therapeutic boarding school?

A therapeutic boarding school is a unique setting for students who may struggle emotionally or academically in a traditional school setting. A therapeutic boarding school provides intensive support both academically and clinically for students to reach their full potential and to experience success in school.

What does a therapeutic boarding school do?

A therapeutic boarding school looks at the areas of competency and strength which each student possesses and then develops a plan to build resiliency and achieve academic and social emotional goals. It offers a traditional college preparatory high school core curriculum with the flexibility to design individualized programs to ensure each student receives the courses needed to graduate with a high school diploma. Many therapeutic boarding schools also offer vocational and life skills curriculum and opportunities for those students who are more suited to move into the workforce post graduation. The small class size and trained special education teachers allow for meaningful accommodation of students' emotional, behavioral and academic needs. Close student-faculty relationships, small class size, and dormitory living provide a daily schedule, which is highly structured. The daily schedule helps students learn to manage their time, develop friendships and enhance their self confidence. While emphasizing the importance of achieving academically, a therapeutic boarding school also offers support through clinical, nursing and psychiatric departments.

What support services does a student receive?

When a student enters a therapeutic boarding school an individualized educational plan is developed. The plan addresses academic goals as well as social and emotional goals. When a student enters a therapeutic boarding school, he or she is assigned a clinician who meets with the student weekly and communicates with the parents regularly. If a student has a specific diagnosis or takes prescribed medication, the school psychiatrist will perform an assessment and monitor the student's medication throughout his or her stay. All the faculty and staff members are trained in a therapeutic management system, which includes crisis prevention to keep a student safe should that be necessary.

How does a student move on?

The therapeutic boarding school not only focuses on college or career preparation, but also on preparation

for successful adult living. This is accomplished by understanding one's unique challenges and needs, and how to advocate for help that may be needed. The dormitory experience provides guidance in developing self-discipline and contributing to a positive community environment. Students participate in daily scheduled extracurricular and recreational activities both on and off campus. Field trips and excursions allow the students to explore arts, culture and the environment.

Interdisciplinary team meetings are scheduled regularly to review the progress a student has made toward achieving individual goals. When the therapeutic staff, the family and other involved professionals determine a student is ready to move on, a transition plan is developed. The plan addresses all aspects of the student's future plans including college placement assistance.

What makes a therapeutic boarding school special?

The therapeutic school provides a unique setting for students who have experienced difficulty managing in the traditional school setting. Often such students and their families end up in a difficult situation of trying to find a school that will allow the student to continue on their educational path with the level of support they require to do so successfully. This can be an overwhelming process for all involved. That is the critical time for intervention and consideration of a therapeutic boarding school.

What to look for when choosing a therapeutic boarding school

It is highly recommended to personally visit the schools being considered. Some suggested questions to ask in advance should include finding out the licensure/ accreditation of the school; staff credentials; academic curriculum; credentials of the clinical director; availability of psychiatrist at the campus; does the school conduct background checks on all of their employees; criteria for admission; frequency and availability of contact between parent and their child and between the school and parents and what are the nursing and medical protocols in place should a student require such attention. Talk with students at the school and with parents of students currently enrolled. The overall environment should be structured and nurturing with a wide variety of opportunities socially and academically as well as plenty of physical exercise.

For more information about Chamberlain International School, see pages 150-151
This school features in our new section highlighting schools that offer support
for students with special educational needs, starting on page XX

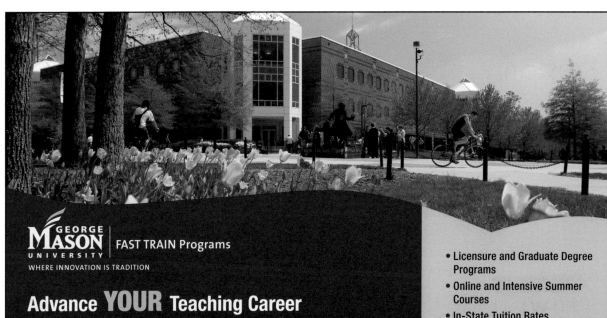

Preparing teachers for diverse classrooms

Ana Silva on how George Mason University is helping the educators of tomorrow meet the demands of international school teaching

The Division of Advanced Professional Teacher Development and International Education in the College of Education and Human Development at George Mason University is committed to the ongoing professional development of teachers, teacher leaders, and international educators around the world through the development of innovative programs, international partnerships, and authentic engagement in the world of teaching and learning. Our programs offer a variety of degree, certificate, and endorsement options for educators, including programs through FAST TRAIN and Transformative Teaching, designed to assist educators to meet the ever-changing demands of today's diverse classroom environments.

FAST TRAIN programs began in 1990 as a collaborative effort between the Virginia Department of Education, the U.S. State Department, and George Mason University. It has prepared over 1,400 graduates, currently teaching in over 40 different countries, in response to the demand for highly qualified teachers in international schools worldwide. Participants have the flexibility to live abroad and work in international schools while pursuing graduate study and teacher certification. FAST TRAIN offers initial teacher certification programs in Elementary Education and English as a Second Language, as well as professional development programs in Learning Support and International Baccalaureate® (IB) studies. FAST TRAIN Programs bring an international understanding

Through collaboration, leadership, and education research, educators will discover new ways to think, act, and have an impact on issues of teaching, learning, and social justice from the classroom outward.

into our teacher education programs by recruiting highly qualified faculty and globally-minded students. We have a stellar reputation among international educators and institutions of higher education that is parallel to none.

The FAST TRAIN Elementary Education Program is designed for prospective and current teachers who want to work with PK-6 students in international schools around the world. The program offers two scheduling options; the full-time summer program for students living abroad, and the part-time evening program for students living in the D.C. Metro area. The program is aligned with International Baccalaureate PYP standards; students have the option of completing additional requirements to be eligible for the IB Certificate in Advanced Teaching and Learning.

The FAST TRAIN English as a Second Language program offers flexible schedules to meet the needs of busy educators, including online study during the academic year and face-to-face courses on our Fairfax, Virginia Campus during a five-week summer intensive program. Our exceptional faculty and staff are globally minded and deliver curriculum specifically tailored to address the needs of culturally diverse language learners. Affordable on-campus housing is available for students participating in summer course work.

The Advanced International Baccalaureate® certificate or master's degree program is fully approved by the IB to provide graduate education for current and future IB teachers who wish to develop a superior understanding of the IB curriculum and student learner. Participants have the option to focus on the Primary Years, Middle Years, or Diploma programmes. They may choose to complete only the concentration comprising of fifteen credits to earn a graduate certificate and become eligible to apply to the IB for the IB Certificate in Teaching and Learning, or complete an additional twelve credits to earn a Master's Degree in Curriculum and Instruction and become eligible to apply for the IB Advanced Certificate in Teaching and Learning Research.

In service teachers and other educators interested in building foundational knowledge in learning support

and differentiated instruction may pursue the FAST TRAIN Learning Support graduate certificate program. Course work begins each spring and may be completed entirely online.

For more information about FAST TRAIN Programs including how to apply, please visit our website at http://fasttrain.gmu.edu/

Transformative Teaching, the newest program offered through the Division of Advanced Professional Teacher Development and International Education, is a unique, multi-faceted, online master's degree program that provides in practice classroom teachers with the opportunity to reflect on their teaching practices, create empowering learning environments, and become informed participants in the policy arena as well as transformative leaders in their schools. Through collaboration, leadership, and education research, educators will discover new ways to think, act, and have an impact on issues of teaching, learning, and social justice from the classroom outward. Participation in the Transformative Teaching master's degree program offers participants the opportunity to reinvigorate their commitment to teaching and learning as they advance their teaching career.

Courses in the Transformative Teaching program are taught online, allowing teachers from around the world to connect in deep collaboration while continuing to teach full time. The program is offered in a cohort model so participating teachers will work with a fixed group of students and faculty throughout the program; allowing the chance to build lasting relationships among peers. In addition to the online courses, the program includes two, week-long, intensive summer courses held on the George Mason University campus in Fairfax, Virginia. The first summer course is taken at the beginning of the program and the second summer course is taken midway through completion. On campus housing is available to students during participation in on-site course work.

For more information on the Transformative Teaching program, please visit our website at masononline.gmu.edu/programs/medtransformativeteaching/.

Education for a changing world

The British Institute of Technology looks at why a new sort of business course is required to meet the needs of a fast-paced business environment

The UK has always been good at doing business and, today, as the flow of inward investment shows, continues to gain the vote of confidence from global giants to high tech start-ups.

Even twenty years ago, nobody would have been able to foresee the impact innovation would have on every aspect of business. In a constantly changing environment the world of business requires dynamic individuals who can see and think beyond their role.

It's not surprising that business-related courses, too, have undergone a rapid period of expansion. They fulfil a vital function: blending theory and practice to ensure that new graduates enter the workplace with the skills and understanding to react quickly to the innovation and change that now characterises the business environment and maximise their potential.

Successful courses, such as those developed by the British Institute of Technology & E-commerce (BITE) BA in Business Management and MBA Strategic Management and Leadership won't just address the knowledge requirement but will also devote substantial time to ensuring students have an in depth understanding of how to apply that knowledge.

But there's more to it than that. Good business courses don't just stick to what is currently out there at the moment but ensure that students develop the flexibility of mind to adapt as new technology comes on stream.

In-depth analyses shared by business professionals allows student to be informed of cutting edge ideas and development at the same as developing the business know-how.

While BITE recognises the importance of in-depth subject knowledge, it is the application of this knowledge that is the key to individual and institutional success.

The aspirations of most graduates are to see their know-how put into action with the industry relation. So it's important to choose a course where first-class

Mirusha Adampulle receives a prize from Lord Erroll at the BITE Student Award Ceremony

relationships with business and industry enable them to progress into their chosen fields, through work placement and/or a fixed term of shadowing.

BITE is one of the leading institutes in the UK and is the 5th top private institute reported by the Times Higher Education. Its success lies in the partnership it has with the industry and how it nurtures this relationship by building career opportunities for students. Technology is driving the global economy, creating an ever increasing demand for trained and talented individuals. That is why BITE not only teaches skills needed for the future through its range of undergraduate and postgraduate degree programmes, it also champions the pioneering work of the best in the sector – the people who inspire others to follow their lead in creating the technologies that will transform the world. For more information, visit www.bite.ac.uk

Redesigned SAT exam aims to reward hard-working students

The College Board provide an update on significant developments designed to help young people succeed at university

The College Board, a global non-profit education membership organization, plans to move beyond delivering assessments to delivering opportunity — with initiatives to be used in concert with assessments to propel students around the world toward university success. Part of those initiatives includes changes to the SAT® exam.

The SAT was created in the late 1800s by a group of leading American universities that had concerns about not having a universal way to determine if students were prepared for college-level course work. They formed the College Entrance Examination Board, and working together they administered the first standardized exam in 1901. For the first time, students could take one entrance exam for several universities instead of taking a separate exam for each university to which they applied.

Today, the SAT is administered to over two million students in more than 7,000 test centers in 175 countries and territories.

The College Board's goal is to support university readiness and success for more students and to make sure that those who are prepared take full advantage of the opportunities they've earned through their hard work. The redesigned SAT will reward productive use of classroom time and a focus on rigorous course work.

Each change in the redesigned test draws upon evidence of the knowledge and skills that are most essential for university success, and the exam is also modeled on the work that students do in challenging high school courses.

"This is a clear message that good hard work is going to pay off and achievement is going to pay off," said William R. Fitzsimmons, Dean of Admissions at Harvard University.

"This is one of the most significant developments that I have seen in the 40-plus years that I've been working in admissions in higher education."

The redesigned exam will:

- have three sections: Evidence-Based Reading and Writing, Math, and the Essay.
- return to the 1600 scale. (The SAT is currently scored on a 2400 scale.) The essay will provide a separate score.
- be approximately three hours in length, with an additional 50 minutes for the essay. The precise time of the exam will be affirmed through research.

The first administration of the redesigned exam will take place in spring 2016. The College Board has already released the full specifications of the exam along with extensive sample items for each section on their website deliveringopportunity.org.

Major changes to the exam include:

1. Relevant words in context: "SAT words" will no longer be vocabulary students may not have heard before and are likely not to hear again. Instead, the SAT will focus on words that students will use consistently in college and beyond.
2. Evidence-based reading and writing. Students will be asked to support answers with evidence, including questions that require them to cite a specific part of a passage to support their answer choice.
3. Essay analyzing a source: The essay will measure students' ability to analyze evidence and explain how an author builds an argument

The College Board's goal is to support university readiness and success for more students and to make sure that those who are prepared take full advantage of the opportunities they've earned through their hard work. The redesigned SAT will reward productive use of classroom time and a focus on rigorous course work.

to persuade an audience. Responses will be evaluated based on the strength of the analysis as well as the coherence of the writing. The essay portion of the writing section will no longer be required.

4.   Math focused on three key areas: The math section will draw from fewer topics that evidence shows most contribute to student readiness for college and career training. The exam will focus on three essential areas: problem solving and data analysis; the heart of algebra; and passport to advanced math.

5.   Source documents originate from a wide range of academic disciplines, including science and social studies: The reading section will enable students to analyze a wide range of sources, including literature and literary non-fiction, science, history and social studies.

6.   Analyzing data and texts in real world context: Students will be asked to analyze both text and data in real world contexts, including identifying and correcting inconsistencies between the two. Students will show the work they do throughout their classes by reading science articles and historical and social studies sources.

7.   Founding Documents and Great Global Conversation: Each exam will include a passage drawn from the Founding Documents of America or the Great Global Conversation they inspire.

8.   Scoring does not deduct points for incorrect answers (rights-only scoring): The College Board will remove the penalty for wrong answers — and go to the simpler, more transparent model of giving students points for the questions they answer correctly.

Moving forward, the College Board will also support the practice of excellent work in classrooms by working with teachers and college faculty to design course frameworks and modules for use in grades 6–12.

"It's really exciting that students will be asked to read real documents and offer evidence to support their perception," said Pam Horne, Associate Vice Provost for Enrollment Management and Dean of Admissions at Purdue University. "And the math will now focus on areas that will be helpful for admissions officers and students as they go through high school."

In addition, the College Board is partnering with Khan Academy to provide the world with free test preparation materials for the redesigned SAT. Khan Academy is a non-profit with a mission of providing a free world-class education for anyone, anywhere and provides free online educational materials (e.g., practice exercises, instructional videos, teacher tools) that support personalized education for users of all ages in a scalable way.

"For too long, there's been a well-known imbalance between students who could afford test-prep courses and those who couldn't," said Sal Khan, founder and executive director of Khan Academy. "We're thrilled to collaborate closely with the College Board to level the playing field by making truly world-class test-prep materials freely available to all students."

College Board and Khan Academy will build SAT preparation material together for launch in spring 2015. This means for the first time ever, all students who want to take the SAT will be able to prepare for the exam with sophisticated, interactive software that gives students deep practice and helps them diagnose their gaps at absolutely no cost. In the meantime, students who will take the current SAT can now go to Khan Academy to work through hundreds of previously unreleased practice problems from actual SAT exams, accompanied by more than 200 videos that show how to solve the problems step-by-step.

The College Board will continue to present updated SAT information over the course of the two years leading up to the first administration of the redesigned exam. Updates will also be available on the organization's new microsite: deliveringopportunity.org.

The questions you should ask

However much a school may appeal on first sight, you still need sound information to form your judgement

Schools, particularly independent schools, attract pupils by their reputations, so most go to considerable lengths to ensure that parents are presented with an attractive image. Modern marketing techniques try to promote good points and play down (without totally obscuring) bad ones. But every Head knows that, however good the school website/prospectus is, it only serves to attract parents through the school gates. Thereafter the decision depends on what they see and hear.

When you choose a school for your son or daughter, the key factor is that it will suit them. Many children and their parents are instinctively attracted (or otherwise) to a school on first sight. But even if it passes this test, and 'conforms' to what you are looking for in terms of location and academic, pastoral and extracurricular aspects, you will need to satisfy yourself that the school does measure up to what your instincts tell you.

Choosing an international school can prompt additional questions for parents and students alike. The international school's intake is not restricted by geographical or educational authority boundaries. International schools have the added benefit of being able to embrace a sense of national pride while encouraging a respect of and interest in international thinking, standards and cultures.

Research we have carried out over the years suggests that in many cases the most important factor in choosing a school is the impression given by the Head. As well as finding out what goes on in a school, parents need to be reassured by the aura of confidence that they expect from a Head. How they discover the former may help them form their opinion of the latter.

So how a Head answers your questions is important. Based on our research, we have drawn up a list of varied points on which you may need to be satisfied. The order in which they appear below does not necessarily reflect their degree of importance to each parent, but how the Head answers them may help you draw your own conclusions:

- How accessible is the Head, whose personality is seen by most parents as setting the 'tone' of the school?
- Will the child fit in?
- What is the overall atmosphere?
- To which organisations does the school belong?
- How has it been accredited?
- What is the ratio of teachers to pupils?
- What are the qualifications of the teaching staff?
- How often does the school communicate with parents through reports, parent/teacher meetings or other visits?
- What are the school's exam results? What are the criteria for presenting them? Are they consistent over the years?
- How does the school cope with pupils' problems?
- What sort of academic advice is available?
- What is the school's attitude to discipline?
- Have there been problems with drugs or sex? How have they been dealt with?
- What positive steps are taken to encourage good manners, behaviour and sportsmanship?
- Is progress accelerated for the academically bright?

- How does the school cope with pupils who do not work?
- What is the attitude to religion?
- What is the attitude to physical fitness and games?
- What sports are offered and what are the facilities?
- What are the extracurricular activities?
- What cultural or other visits are arranged away from the school?
- What steps are taken to encourage specific talent in music, the arts or sport?
- What is the uniform?
- What steps are taken to ensure that pupils take pride in their personal appearance?
- What are the timetable and term dates?
- What are the boarding facilities like?
- Is there a dedicated person to look after new international students?
- Does the school have a recommended guardian service?
- Does the school have a dedicated and strong pastoral team?
- Is it possible to have the names and addresses of parents with children at the school to approach them for an opinion?
- Does the school have a dedicated teacher for Mother Tongue languages or ESL?

International school profiles

International schools in Africa

Schools ordered A–Z by Name

Braeburn Arusha School

Braeburn Schools
Summum Appeto

PO Box 14268, Arusha, Tanzania
Tel: +255 (0)250 5716
Email: secondary@braeburnschool.ac.tz
Website: www.arusha.braeburn.com
Head of School: Ms Alison Rogers
Head of Primary School: Ms Claire Baker

School type: Coeducational Day, Weekly and Full Boarding
Age range of pupils: 2–19
No. of pupils enrolled as at 01/09/2014: 450
Average class size: 20
Teacher/pupil ratio: 1:20

Renowned for its warm family feel, Braeburn School Arusha guarantees that students from all over the world soon feel valued and at home. Difference is celebrated and respected and individuals are set their own targets for improvement. This means that students are seen as individuals and not as a group. Our small class sizes, along with the care that each student receives from their form tutor, makes this approach possible.

We offer a wide range of subjects, both academic and vocational and we offer different approaches to qualifications, wherever possible including coursework as well as exam papers. Students can choose to study as many as 10 Cambridge IGCSEs or as few as 6 and some choose to take papers after one year instead of after two years. In the sixth form, students can opt for a vocational, coursework pathway to university (BTEC) or a more traditional exam based route (A levels), with both pathways guaranteed to lead onto success.

Our careers advice, work experience programme and post-16 mentoring interviews, combined with visits to higher education university fairs, means that all of our students are well informed about the various options available to them once they leave Braeburn. As a result, 100% our students over the past four years have found themselves accepted in universities across the world.

The Boarding facilities and care at Braeburn School Arusha were recently described as 'excellent' by a representative from the Council of International Schools. And the students in our care would agree. Unlike traditional boarding houses, our students from 10 different countries of the world, describe boarding as 'home away from home'. Dubbed as the best boarding home in East Africa, this million dollar investment boasts ensuite bedrooms, wireless internet, three lounges and two purpose built study areas. DSTV, wholesome home cooking and a wide array of books and games continue to make the place feel like home. Add to this a range of outings and activities at the weekend and teacher help with home learning during the week and you will understand why Braeburn Boarding is so popular.

Braeburn School Arusha takes great pride in the rich programme of activities that we offer all our students, whether it be sport, extra-curricular activities, community service or exciting trips. Not surprisingly, our students blossom and become the confident, polite and well adjusted young people that we are all so proud of.

Braeburn Garden Estate School

Braeburn Schools
Summum Appeto

PO Box 16944, 00620 Nairobi, Kenya

Tel: +254 20 501 8000
Fax: +254 20 8562450
Email: headmaster@braeburn.ac.ke
Website:
www.gardenestate.braeburn.com
Executive Head: John Herbert
Head of High School: Rob Jackson
Head of Primary School: Tim Richards

School type: Coeducational Day &
Weekly Boarding
Religious Denomination:
Non-denominational
Age range of pupils: 2–18
No. of pupils enrolled as at 01/09/2014: 605
Average class size: 12-20
Teacher/pupil ratio: 1:9

Braeburn Garden Estate School (BGES) would like to extend a very warm welcome to you as prospective students and parents. Our leafy 28 acre site boasts excellent facilities and its location, away from the city centre, offers the tranquillity and space to learn with pleasure.

BGES is an international, co-educational school educating students between 2 and 18 years old with the option of weekly boarding. We have full CIS accreditation status and we are an IB World School.

BGES students come from over 80 different countries and we teach them to respect each other and to show an interest in the opinions and beliefs of others. Opportunities are created for students to celebrate these differences in cultures and backgrounds as part of the curriculum and through school events.

Our holistic approach to education places an equal emphasis on academics, sport, music, drama and the arts. This rich and varied curriculum compliments and extends the students learning experiences and provides them with the skills they need to succeed in world beyond the school.

We adopt the British National Curriculum through Nursery to Year 11, whilst in Years 12 and 13 students study the International Baccalaureate Diploma Programme.

Small class sizes, high teacher-to-pupil ratios and differentiated teaching practices all work to ensure that each and every child is closely monitored and able to reach their full potential. We encourage our children to be open to new opportunities, to work hard and strive to excel, both within and beyond the classroom.

We aim to provide a stimulating, safe environment where students feel happy and excited about coming to school, where they can enjoy a wholesome, fulfilling education that prepares them for all walks of life.

It would be our pleasure to meet you and show you around our school.

Braeburn Imani International School

Braeburn Schools
Summum Appeto

PO Box 750, 00100 Thika, Kenya

Tel: +254 (0)20 2029322 / 44
Fax: +254 67 24130
Email: margaret.waithira@braeburn.ac.ke
Website: www.imani.braeburn.com
Head of Secondary School: Catherine Sat
Head of Primary School: Debbie Kasura

School type: Coeducational Day, Weekly and Full Boarding
Age range of pupils: 2–18
No. of pupils enrolled as at 01/09/2014: 175
Average class size: 11
Teacher/pupil ratio: 1:6

Braeburn Imani International School is the newest school in the Braeburn Group, situated on the outskirts of Thika town approximately 40km north of Nairobi. It offers quality education for children from playgroup (aged 2) to year 13 (A levels) in a peaceful twenty acre site that is conducive for study. The brand new purpose built school offers excellent facilities from a secure and attractive Early Years unit to specialist High School laboratories for science and ICT. All the classrooms are large, airy and well furnished.

The majority of students are day scholars, with an increasing number joining from the developing residential areas along the Thika super-highway which is served by the school transport system. The small personal boarding facility caters for up to 48 students and attracts pupils from further afield, either on a weekly or full boarding basis.

Like all schools in the group, the school follows the National Curriculum of England and Wales, with High School students preparing for IGCSE examinations offered by Cambridge International Examinations in year 11 and A levels in year 13. All staff are well qualified and enjoy the advantage of being part of a group which emphasises professional development.

Alongside academics, the school offers a wide range of extra-curricular activities to meet the interests of most children. Sport is always popular and a wide variety is available. The all round development of the student is actively encouraged and there are many opportunities to get involved in different competitions, activities and events.

The relatively small numbers in the school mean that each pupil receives personal attention in class and around the school. The atmosphere is very positive; the sense that the school has a very bright future is felt by the entire community, making it a very exciting school to be part of.

Braeburn Kisumu International School

Braeburn Schools
Summum Appeta

PO Box 1276, 4010 Kisumu, Kenya
Tel: +254 (057) 202 3471
Email: admin@kis.co.ke
Website: www.kisumu.braeburn.com
Head of School: Carmel O'Dolan

School type: Coeducational Day
Age range of pupils: 18 months–16 years
No. of pupils enrolled as at 01/09/2014: 104
Average class size: 7
Teacher/pupil ratio: 1:5

Braeburn Kisumu International School is nestled amidst colourful bougainvilleas in the leafy suburbs of Milimani in Kisumu City overlooking the serene ambience of Lake Victoria.

The school follows the National Curriculum of England and Wales from Pre-crèche (18 months) through to Year 11 (16 years) when the students take Cambridge International Examination Board IGCSE examinations. In addition to academic life, BKIS ensures that sports and co-curricular activities are an integral part of school life and so pupils are exposed to a wide range of sports as well as activities like Scouts, President's Award, Amnesty International, EAMUN and Tae Kwondo

helping to form the basis for a life long love of an activity. Music is also popular at BKIS with many pupils working towards ABRSM examinations, for which our school is an examination centre. Being a small school we are particularly proud of the fact that everyone in the school gets involved in school productions, helping to develop a passion for the stage.

As an international school we are eager to ensure that we do provide a true international education as we celebrate number of global initiatives such as World Book Day, World Francophone Day, to name just a couple, in addition to celebrating Diwali, Thanksgiving, Christmas and other cultural celebrations

as they fall within the school year.

Kisumu is a small community away from the big city life of Kenya's capital and BKIS is a focal point for families and friends as we have numerous whole family activities throughout the year including family picnics as well as dinner dances and murder mystery evenings organised by our very active parent teacher group.

This supportive community spirit, coupled with a highly qualified and experienced teaching team, ensures that BKIS pupils not only achieve highly academically but also have fun on their journey to success.

Braeburn Mombasa International School

Braeburn Schools
Summum Appeta

PO Box 83009, Mombasa, Kenya

Tel: +254 20 202 6156
Fax: +254 41 5485493
Email:
enquiries@braeburnmombasa.ac.ke
Website: www.mombasa.braeburn.com
Head of High School: Peter Barnard
Head of Primary School: Rebecca Barnett

School type: Coeducational Day &
Weekly Boarding
Age range of pupils: 2–18
No. of pupils enrolled as at 01/09/2014: 270
Average class size: 17
Teacher/pupil ratio: 1:12

Braeburn Mombasa International School (BMIS) is an EYFS, Primary and Secondary, National Curriculum of England and Wales School. There are 280 students of different cultures, religions and backgrounds, with 23 different nationalities in attendance at this fully accredited, Council of International Schools (CIS) and IAPS affiliated School. The language of learning is English.

BMIS is on its own spacious, purpose built site, close to the Indian Ocean on the Kenya coastline. The facilities fully cater for all students, aged 2 to 18 years, with a broad and balanced curriculum. Extra-curricular sport, drama, community programmes and music are available and are an important part of the whole school ethos.

The School is a Cambridge International Examination Centre (CIE) for IGCSE and

AS/A Levels. It will also soon offer BTEC Business in the post IGCSE sector.

Teaching staff are internationally trained and, working in conjunction with local staff, all teach in vibrant and inclusive teaching areas. This is a very friendly and welcoming school for all.

For more information visit: www.mombasa.braeburn.com or email: enquiries@braeburnmombasa.co.ke

Braeburn Nanyuki International School

Braeburn Schools
Summum Appeto

Cottage Hospital Road, PO Box 1537,
10400 Nanyuki, Kenya
Tel: +254 (0)20 211 3624
Email: nanyuki@braeburn.ac.ke
Website: www.nanyuki.braeburn.com
Head of School: Eva Kioko

School type: Coeducational Day
Age range of pupils: 2–11
No. of pupils enrolled as at 01/09/2014: 123
Average class size: 15
Teacher/pupil ratio: 1:10

Here at Braeburn Nanyuki International School, we believe all children can learn and we work hard to ensure all children can achieve and succeed.

Braeburn Nanyuki comprises of an Early Years Foundation Stage as well as a Primary School, offering National Curriculum of England and Wales to children of all nationalities and cultures in a calm, serene and secure learning environment, all our children are encouraged to be fully engaged in their learning in and out of the classroom. Situated at the foot of Mt Kenya, Braeburn Nanyuki is set in beautifully landscaped gardens with a panoramic view of the mountain. Our wood and stone classrooms ensure that our school fits neatly and unobtrusively into our environment. Our small class sizes ensure that all children are closely monitored to enable them to attain their full potential.

At Braeburn Nanyuki, the atmosphere is a happy one, a welcoming one and a truly caring one, as parents, guardians and staff all contribute each day, and in so many ways, to making learning a journey of discovery through first hand experience. As we aim to maintain the special community touch whose core values of respect, trust, honesty, integrity, support, cooperation and fraternity have a special place in our hearts, our firm commitment is to offer the merits of a well structured education that is as rigorous as it is broad, in an engaging and stimulating learning environment which is safe, orderly and nurturing.

We believe that with the continued, unwavering support of parents, guardians and the community that we have so far received, as well as the sustained spirit of teamwork, dedication and hard work of all the staff, the future can only be very bright indeed!

Braeburn School

Braeburn Schools
Summum Appeta

PO Box 45112, Gitanga Road, Lavington,

Nairobi GPO 00100, Kenya

Tel: +254 20 501 8000

Email: enquiries@braeburn.ac.ke

Website:
www.braeburnschool.braeburn.com

Executive Head: Scott Webber

Appointed: September 2008

Head of High School: Virginia Catlin

Head of Primary School: Charlotte Hilton

School type: Coeducational Day

Age range of pupils: 3–18

No. of pupils enrolled as at 01/09/2014: 993

Average class size: 22

Teacher/pupil ratio: 1:10

Founded in 1979, Braeburn School has undergone significant development and growth during its 35 years to date. Situated on a 14 acre site in the Lavington suburb of Nairobi, the school is conveniently located to serve many of the rapidly developing suburbs of the city. With over 80 nationalities represented within the student population, Braeburn is truly an international school which offers an excellent education to students from Early Years through to A level.

The school has recently undertaken and received accreditation with the Council of International Schools (CIS) and is enthusiastically ensuring its continued development and commitment to raising the high standards already established. The Primary section of the school is also a long established member of the Independent Association of Preparatory Schools (IAPS) therefore enjoying significant and particularly vibrant, extra-curricular involvement with other IAPS member schools in Kenya.

Braeburn School prides itself on having established a friendly and welcoming environment where everyone: students, parents and staff, are encouraged to be happy and feel valued. We actively promote an Open Admissions Policy in the Primary and therefore are privileged to enjoy a thriving student body which openly celebrates its diversity and achievement throughout the school. With over 80 teachers on site we also enjoy tremendous diversity and experience within our classrooms. We are fortunate to be able to recruit excellent teachers from Kenya, as well as from much further afield. All our teachers bring passion, energy and enthusiasm to their role and are incredibly committed to supporting the aspirations and achievements of our students both in and out of the classroom. It is worth noting that the High School's examination results have consistently improved year on year; a fitting tribute to the professionalism of our teachers and to the commitment of our students.

Please do take the time to further explore what Braeburn School has to offer.

Braeside Schools

Braeburn Schools
Summum Appeta

PO Box 25578, 1603 Nairobi, Kenya

Tel: +254 20 501 8000
Fax: +254 20 3870264
Email: headsec@braeside.ac.ke
Website: www.braeside.braeburn.com
Executive Head: Mr Andy Hill
Head of High School: Jennifer Kaumbulu

Head of Primary School: Gladys Wahinya
School type: Coeducational Day
Age range of pupils: 2–18
No. of pupils enrolled as at 01/09/2014: 900
Average class size: 18
Teacher/pupil ratio: 1:10

Braeside is a co-educational Council of International Schools (CIS) accredited day school offering academic programmes based on the British National Curriculum for 2 to 18 year-olds. Established in 1996, it is located on lush grounds off Muthangari Road in the quiet residential suburb of Lavington within Nairobi.

It has a warm, friendly and caring atmosphere with high standards of discipline, whilst providing an environment conducive to good learning. Braeside's aim is to allow all students to fulfil their academic potential, while at the same time developing social skills and graces to enable them to meet the challenges of society.

Braeside is the largest accredited University of Cambridge International Centre in Kenya and also has the prestigious status of being a Cambridge Fellowship Centre. The courses offered are numerous and cater for the needs of its students in an international environment. They lead to International Qualifications including the Qualifications and Curriculum Authority (QCA), Checkpoint, International General Certificate of Education (IGCSE), International Certificate of Education (ICE), General Certificate of Education (GCE 'O', AS/A2) and BTEC (Edexcel).

The school's Early Years Unit is housed in its own unique facility featuring a well-equipped playground and a sports field, the main focus being character building through play.

In the Primary Years the aim is to develop independent learners who feel that they belong in every facet of the school.

In the Secondary Years the focus is on equipping learners with life skills that will enable them to be ready for adult life.

Whilst the importance of academic achievement is recognised, it also offers a wide range of extra-curricular opportunities for its students. Individual timetables for activities are prepared for pupils to pursue their interests at lunch times, after school and at weekends. Regular school excursions are also an integral part of the school's programme.

Confident Individuals, Responsible Citizens and Learners Enjoying Success

British International School, Victoria Island

(Founded 2001)

PO Box 75133, 1 Landbridge Avenue,
Oniru Private Estate, Victoria Island,
Lagos, Nigeria
Tel: +234 1 774 8066
Email: registrar@bisnigeria.org
Website: www.bisnigeria.org
Principal: Mr Peter Yates M.B.E
School type: Coeducational Day & Boarding

Age range of pupils: 11–18
No. of pupils enrolled as at 01/04/2013: 330
Boys: 180 **Girls:** 150
No. of boarders: 90
Fees per annum as at 01/05/2014:
Day: $17,300
Full Boarding: $30,400
Teacher/pupil ratio: 1:9

Founded in 2001, based on a secure and spacious 30-hectare purpose-built campus close to the centre of Lagos, BIS provides students with an oasis of tranquility one of Africa's most vibrant cities.

Serving the needs of local and expatriate children aged 11-18 this co-educational day and boarding school has consistently produced outstanding results in Cambridge International Examinations. Our latest results show a 92% pass rate A*-C in English and Maths at IGCSE, comparable with top UK and international schools around the world. Our continued success at IGCSE has enabled BIS to develop a reputation as a centre of academic excellence. In the

coming year BIS will introduce MIDYIS testing that will enable the school to track student progress and further respond to their learning needs.

The school's curriculum follows the national curriculum of England adapted to meet Nigerian needs. A blend of Nigerian and expatriate teachers ensure that BIS can offer a broad based education based on a traditional subject spread. Class size is limited to 20 students by school policy. In these small classes students and teachers are able to build strong working relationships.

BIS students are encouraged to take an active role in school life by participating in co-curricular, inter house and inter school

competitions. With an increasingly varied extracurricular programme, based around sporting, dance and cultural activities students have the opportunity to excel outside the classroom as well as within. The Student Council plays a vital role within the school; meeting regularly with senior staff to represent the views of the students and actively organizing school events.

BIS Students regularly participate in the school's annual dramatic production, science projects, maths competitions, educational trips in Nigeria and overseas, and the Duke of Edinburgh's International Award programme.

BIS is proud to be a member of Council of British International Schools.

Brookhouse School

(Founded 1981)
PO Box 24987, Nairobi, 00502 Kenya
Tel: +254 02 243 9261

Fax: +254 02 243 0269
Email: info@brookhouse.ac.ke
Website: www.brookhouse.ac.ke
Director: John O'Connor
Appointed: September 2004
School type: Coeducational Day & Boarding
Religious Denomination:
Non-denominational

Age range of pupils: 2–19
No. of pupils enrolled as at 01/01/2014: 750
Boys: 375 **Girls:** 375
Fees per annum as at 01/01/2014:
Day: US$17,500
Boarding: US$30,000
Average class size: 16
Teacher/pupil ratio: 1:10

Situated in a leafy suburb of Nairobi ten minutes from the city centre, Brookhouse is a Round Square member school offering coeducational pre-school, preparatory, secondary and pre-university foundation levels. The school delivers an adapted form of the British National Curriculum leading to IGCSE and A levels, and caters for the professional, business and diplomatic communities of the East African region.

Brookhouse balances traditional values with an innovative approach, with small classes and a wide range of subject choices. Graduates proceed to leading UK universities, with an increasing number choosing the USA, Canada, Australia and South Africa.

With more than 45 nationalities represented, the school prides itself on fostering international understanding, and promotes a diverse programme of extra-curricular activities to ensure the development of the whole child, including the President's Award Scheme, Model United Nations, and commitment to Round Square service projects.

Teachers are recruited from the UK and East Africa.

Situated on a 13 acre campus adjacent to Nairobi National Park, the school has secure on-site co-educational boarding accommodation for 200 students and a dozen or more staff, helping to create a strong sense of community.

Academic facilities include computer and science laboratories, libraries, Art and Music studios, Careers Centre and a world-class performance auditorium; many classrooms have interactive smart boards.

The Arts receive major emphasis at Brookhouse: the Fine Art department mounts an annual public exhibition; there are regular drama productions; and the Music department includes choirs, orchestral and instrumental groups. Individual instrumental lessons are also offered.

The Learning Support Unit caters for Special Educational Needs and for ESL backgrounds, as well as providing an Academic Extension Programme. Sporting facilities include a state-of-the-art gym and aerobics studio, indoor sports centre for tennis and basketball, squash courts, swimming pool and irrigated playing fields for a range of team and individual sports.

Écoles Al Madina

Écoles Al Madina

تربية، قيم و انفتاح
Éducation, Valeurs et Ouverture

(Founded 1993)

Site Californie, Lotissement Bellevue 2, Rue 3 Californie, Casablanca, Morocco

Site Ain Sebaa, Km 9, route de Rabat, Hay Chabab, Ain sébàa, Casablanca, 20250, Morocco
Site Polo, 52 Bd Nador, Casablanca, 20420, Morocco
Tel: +212 522 5050 97
Fax: +21222 50 49 60
Email: almadina@madina.ma
Website: www.almadina.ma

Head of School: Mme Hayat Cherrouk
Appointed: 1996
School type: Coeducational Day
Age range of pupils: 2–18
No. of pupils enrolled as at 01/09/2014: 3686
Boys: 1899 **Girls:** 1787
Fees per annum as at 01/09/2014:
MAD14,000 – MAD28,000

Un groupe scolaire de renom à l'échelon national marocain, fondé en 1993, il compte aujourd'hui 4 sites répartis sur différents quartiers de Casablanca : Californie, Ain Sebâa, Polo et Ghandi. Cette extension des Ecoles Al Madina est le résultat d'une demande croissante de répondre au besoin de faire bénéficier la communauté scolaire d'un enseignement de qualité visant la réussite académique ainsi que l'épanouissement des élèves et leur développement personnel.

Les quatre sites sont bâtis sur de grandes superficies, faites de verdures et d'air pur alliant la pratique de l'acte pédagogique au plaisir de récréation constructive.

Le projet pédagogique des Ecoles Al Madina s'appuie sur un programme intégré de la maternelle au Baccalauréat. De surcroît, dans sa quête de répondre aux besoins du secteur de l'éducation, le groupe a la première université privée au Maroc « Mundiapolis ».

Notre mission aux écoles Al Madina est de former un citoyen ouvert d'esprit, porteur des valeurs universelles et contributeur à l'édification d'un avenir meilleur. Notre ambition est la participation au développement du système éducatif aux échelons national et mondial, par l'adoption de programmes internationaux et d'approches pédagogiques innovantes, assurés par une équipe attachée aux qualités du profil professionnel et social de l'acteur éducatif.

Les Ecoles Al Madina, « Ecoles du Monde », un label accrédité aux Ecoles Al Madina par l'organisation du BI (Baccalauréat International) pour leur mission distinguée, leur quête de la qualité et leur souci d'ouverture à l'international dans un esprit de respect et d'attachement aux valeurs et à l'identité nationale.

Les Ecoles Al Madina sont agréées depuis l'an 2000 à dispenser le programme du Premier Cycle secondaire de l'organisation du BI (Baccalauréat International) un programme qui couvre les tranches d'âge de 12 à 16 ans et qui est sanctionné par un certificat de reconnaissance internationale.

Les études secondaires (lycée) sont couronnées aux Ecoles Al Madina par l'obtention du Diplôme du Baccalauréat International. Ce programme, de par la formation riche et enrichissante qu'il offre, permet aux élèves aussi d'accéder aux universités les plus prestigieuses du monde.

L'accès à l'éducation **internationale**

FAMAKS International Schools

Plot 8 Fajuyi Adekunle Crescent, Off Ajayi
Crowther Street, Asokoro, Abuja, Nigeria
Tel: +234 (0)8109884780
Email: info@famakschools.com
Website: www.famakschools.com

Head Teacher: Mr Franklin Adjetey
School type: Coeducational Day &
Boarding
Age range of pupils: 2–10

Established in January 2009 and situated in the secure and prosperous district of Asokoro, the Federal Capital Territory of Abuja and serving both local and expatriate families, FAMAKS International Schools is home to over 200 pupils from a range of religious and national backgrounds. The Kaduna Campus was opened in January 2010.

Our vision is focused on achieving excellence in a secure and stimulating learning environment offering high quality education from Early Years to Key Stage 2. We achieve this by providing a well-structured, well planned curricular – the English National Curriculum and the International Primary School Curriculum

(IPC) – and employ British trained teachers from the UK. We also engage a British educational consultant who visits regularly from the UK and spends time in the school advising, training, ensuring high quality lessons are delivered and monitors pupil progress and achievement.

FAMAKS prides itself on providing a school fit for purpose in the 21st Century. In addition to an excellent adult pupil ratio, we are also an inclusive school that provides individual educational plans, as well as health care plans for children with special educational needs. Provision is made for all children to receive high quality and nutritious meals which include breakfast, lunch and afternoon snack.

All classrooms are air-conditioned coupled with interactive white boards. There are state of the art facilities including a music room, a dance studio, a science laboratory, an ICT suite, two libraries and several play areas including a basketball and football pitch. The school also operates a flexible boarding house facility.

A leader in the provision of world class learning facilities and environments, FAMAKS draws upon the practices of leading international schools in the world. We are a member of the Council of British International Schools (COBIS) and the Association of International Schools in Africa (AISA).

Rainbow International School Uganda

(Founded 1991)
P.O. Box 7632, Kampala, Uganda

Tel: +256 312 266696/7
Fax: +256 312 266999
Email: info@risu.sc.ug
Website: www.risu.sc.ug
Head of Primary: Mrs Audrey Dralega
Head of Secondary: Mr Jason Lewis
Admissions: Mr Allen Onzima
School type: Coeducational Day & Boarding

Age range of pupils: 2–18
No. of pupils enrolled: 850 (approx.)
Fees per annum as at 01/09/2014:
Primary: US$4,560 – US$7,900
Secondary: US$9,500 – US$13,200
Average class size: 24-26
Teacher/pupil ratio: 1:12

Curriculum

All teaching is in English and follows the guidelines of the British National Curriculum with a philosophy of learning by means of investigation, experimentation and practical involvement. Children are encouraged to interact in order to facilitate the learning process and to develop their social skills.

In Primary School, emphasis is on Mathematics, English and Science together with Information Communication Technology (ICT) and the foundation subjects of Geography, History, Design Technology, Physical Education (PE), Art, Music and Swimming. French is also offered from Year 2.

The Primary Curriculum content is delivered through three main vehicles: International Primary Curriculum (IPC), Cambridge International Primary Programme (CIPP) and the Early Years Foundation Stage Curriculum (EYFS).

In Secondary School, at Key Stage 3 (Years 7, 8 and 9), emphasis is on English, Mathematics and Science. English is taught mainly as a first language, with a focus on use of language through speaking, listening and the study of both fictional and non-fictional texts.

Science at Key Stage 3 is taught as a single subject, integrating components of Biology, Chemistry and Physics and following the Spotlight Science course. In Mathematics, the course focuses very much on developing skills in numeracy, with the emphasis being on applying mathematical principles to solve problems. These three core subjects are assessed formally at the end of Year 9 in preparation for IGCSE.

All Key Stage 3 students take either French or German, whilst ICT is compulsory up to Year 11. They also take History, Geography and four essentially practical subjects – Drama, Music, Art and Physical Education. Personal Social and Health Education (PSHE) and Citizenship, which deal with aspects of personal development, not necessarily covered in the formal curriculum.

The curriculum at Key Stages 4 and 5 is very much determined by the Cambridge International Examinations (CIE) Board with International General Certificate of Secondary Education (IGCSE) examinations and Advanced Level examinations in Years 12 and 13. At IGCSE all students must take English, Mathematics, ICT and either Co-ordinated Science or the three separate sciences. They can also choose three or four additional subjects from Accounts, Art and Design, Business Studies, Drama, Economics, French, Geography, German, History, Music, Physical Education (taken as an examination subject) and Sociology.

To qualify for the 6th form, students need 5 subjects at IGCSE at C grade or above, including Mathematics and English, although this is a minimum requirement.

Accreditation

RISU is registered with the DfES (Department for Education & Skills) in the United Kingdom and is a member of the Council of British International Schools (COBIS).

Studying at RISU

Rainbow has three purpose built science laboratories, three high-tech computer rooms with internet connection, a music room, two multi-purpose halls, a drama room and two new art rooms. There are also extensive playing areas with a tennis court, two football pitches, a basketball court, a volleyball court and a 25 metre-long swimming pool.

Careers service

The Careers Department is led by two highly qualified and experienced teachers that offer advice and guidance to parents and students from Year 9 upwards on choice of options for IGCSE. In addition, A Level students receive guidance on subject combinations and international university admissions as well as counselling on further education.

International schools in Asia

Schools ordered A–Z by Name

Ascend International School

5 'F' Block, Opp. Govt. Colony,
Bandra Kurla Complex (Bandra E),
Mumbai 400051 India
Tel: +91 022 7122 2000
Email: admin@ascendinternational.org
Website: www.ascendinternational.org

Head of School: Aditya Patil
School type: Coeducational Day
Age range of pupils: 3–12
Average class size: 18
Teacher/pupil ratio: 1:8

Inspiring Curious Minds
AIS Mission Statement
Ascend International School delivers a rigorous and collaborative 21st century education where students discover a lifelong love of learning. Our innovative programme is grounded in contemporary educational research. Through individualized education, we foster academic excellence and cultivate self-confident, creative, reflective, and analytical thinkers. AIS students are motivated to act in the selfless tradition of the Indian heart, actively contributing to their expanding global community.

Educational Partnership
Ascend International School was established in 2012 and is an initiative of the Kasegaon Education Society. Founded in 1945, KES began as a small initiative, established to bring educational opportunities to the rural sector of Maharashtra.

As India braced itself for the changing needs of students, the KES Governing Council began to consider how to incorporate the values and traditions of Indian society within the framework of a dynamic education model. Their goal was to create a school that offered families

living in Mumbai the type of innovative education that is required to prepare students for the changing landscape of 21st century. Council members sought an existing school to work beside that highlighted some specific traits: problem solving, collaboration, big ideas, tenacity, generosity, high expectations and above all, a school where everyone had an enthusiasm for learning. After touring University Child Development School, established in 1911 in Seattle, USA, the AIS founders discovered a true partner for their visionary project. This partnership provides Ascend with a platform for learning new

ideas, systems and cultures that we can infuse into our classroom communities at AIS and the continuity of a shared, far reaching vision.

Curriculum

Ascend International School is a Candidate School* for the International Baccalaureate Primary Years Programme (PYP). We are pursuing authorization to become an IB World School. IB schools share a common philosophy – a commitment to high quality, challenging, international education that AIS believes is important for our students.

Only schools authorized by the IB Organization can offer any of its academic programmes: the Primary Years Programme (PYP), the Middle Years Programme (MYP), or the Diploma Programme (and in addition the IB Career-related Certificate). Candidate status gives no guarantee that authorization will be granted.

Inquiry

At AIS, learning is meaningful because students study skills and apply concepts in real-world contexts. The curriculum at AIS is structured to generate questions and inspire curious minds. Inquiry-based thinking, planning, implementation and reflection are a part of every lesson. Ascend students learn how to investigate topics thoroughly and gain a comprehensive understanding of each subject area. Rigorous academic skills are embedded in the context of this inquiry-based work. AIS offers specialist instruction in science, art, music, technology, language, yoga and physical education. As students work on projects, gain experience in academic realms and expand their knowledge base, they begin to see themselves as artists, mathematicians, scientists, writers and community members.

Collaboration

The abilities to work with others, innovate and expand upon ideas are necessary tools for the 21st century. Collaboration provides the vehicle to build, practice and enhance these skills. AIS gives its students the opportunity to work as both leaders and learners in multi-age classrooms. Student projects are designed to promote flexible thinking and active community participation. We think it is vital for students to learn to explain their own thinking, consider alternative perspectives, build on someone else's ideas, and reconsider their own thinking based on feedback from others. Within these settings, students have the opportunity to carry out their investigations with a wide variety of peers and experience different roles, while receiving individualized instruction to develop their academic fluency.

International Mindedness

Modern education demands that students not only understand and appreciate their role in Indian culture but in the broader global community as well. AIS students are supported to consider multiple viewpoints and perspectives. Students from AIS pursue opportunities to enhance the lives of others and to support the health and well-being of our planet. We teach our students to listen carefully to others, to participate in group discussions and hone their individual skills. We believe that developing understanding and compassion for different perspectives and empathy for the needs of others is essential to the moral development of a child.

Campus

AIS is located in the heart of Mumbai in the Bandra Kurla Complex on a 2.5 acre campus. Our educational spaces are open and purposeful, designed to emphasize collaboration and reflect the open layout of modern architecture. Classrooms are designed to promote experiential learning and function more as studio workshops with worktables, informal gathering places and private study nooks. Each floor of the school is organized around a 'central design studio' for technology integration and investigations. Sports facilities include turf playfields, a 2800-sq ft multi-purpose hall, and a 25-meter rooftop pool. Athletic choice, commitment, competition, and teamwork are the core values that drive the athletic programme.

Australian International School, Singapore

Australian International School

1 Lorong Chuan, 556818 Singapore

Tel: +65 6883 5155

Fax: +65 6285 5255

Email: enquiries@ais.com.sg

Website: www.ais.com.sg

Principal: Dr Nick Miller

School type: Coeducational Day

Age range of pupils: 3–18

No. of pupils enrolled as at 01/09/2014: 2600

Fees per annum as at 01/09/2014:
S$16,276 – S$40,034

AIS – We're not looking for the ordinary.

"There could not be a better time to join the Australian International School ('AIS') in Singapore. Australia has an integral part to play in Asia's course on the brink of their destiny. AIS seeks to prepare and equip young Australian leaders to play their part in making a difference for good in what is posed to be the most influential part of the world. The Asian Century White Paper sets out a clear call to young people to prepare themselves in terms of Asian literacy, integrated relationships and skill in Asian languages.

"AIS strategically could not be better located to deliver this agenda. We have a wonderful school. It is a vibrant and caring community and lives its values of respect, achievement and opportunity. We are committed to the notion of a rounded education, individualised learning and the notion that each child is special and each child is successful."

Dr Nick Miller, Principal

The AIS Curriculum and teaching philosophy

AIS is the only southern-hemisphere school in Singapore that offers an Australian curriculum-based global education for students from the age of three to 18 years. This truly international education begins in with the International Baccalaureate Primary Years Programme from Preschool to Year 5, a recently developed school-specific curriculum framework for Years 6 to 8, Cambridge IGCSE in Years 9 and 10, and the NSW Higher School Certificate or International Baccalaureate Diploma Programme for Years 11 and 12. The Australian Curriculum (AC) underpins the entire curriculum at AIS from Prep through to Year 8.

AIS is committed to differentiation to ensure our students realise their full potential through a range of resources, including the Lower Elementary School Inquiry Centre, the collection and use of meaningful data and the creation of individualised learning plans.

Unsurprisingly, AIS students are academically in the high-ability range and experience superior average growth compared to the best performing Australian state or territory – the ACT. This combined with daily Mandarin lessons from Prep to Year 5, a 1:1 Apple iPad/MacBook program from Prep to Year 12 and a dedicated professional learning centre to develop teachers of the highest calibre, ensures AIS students are in the best environment to exceed our expectations, and their own.

The Arts

Music, Drama and Visual Arts are integral to the curriculum at AIS. Students are exposed to the Arts from Preschool and continue their studies as part of the core curriculum until Year 8, at which time they may continue in the discipline(s) of their choosing. Through the expertise of passionate and experienced specialist teachers in dedicated rooms and open air venues in the Elementary and Secondary Schools, students are encouraged to hone their craft and pursue a deeper understanding and appreciation of the Arts.

Sports

The AIS Sports Program aims to develop well rounded athletes and individuals who understand the benefits of lifelong engagement in physical activity. Our programs introduce sport at a young age to encourage the development of friendships, healthy habits and physical skills from which to build on. Our representative sports program, AIS Sharks, covers 13 sports in a range of local, regional and international competitions.

Community Service

Community service is an integral part of the School's globally focused philosophy. The goal of community service at the AIS is to foster a sense of responsibility as members of the community. As responsible citizens, students develop character and integrity through voluntary actions to help the community around them. They will establish a clear connection to their school, local community and abroad.

The AIS Community

The AIS community extends well beyond the classroom, the partnership between the school, the parents and the students is key to our collective success. AIS parents are extremely active within our community be it as members of AISPA (the AIS Parents' Association), coaching sporting teams, reading in class or sharing their expertise. Our collective mission is to develop young people who instinctively strive to make a difference for good. Our school-wide pastoral care program is based on restorative practices, which ensure the cultivation of positive relationships between students and the teaching faculty and breeds respect at all levels.

American School of Bombay

(Founded 1981)

Elementary School: Commercial 2, Tower 4,Kohinoor City, Kirol Road, Off LBS Marg Kurla (W), Mumbai 400 070
Tel: +91 22 6131 3600
Secondary School: SF 2, G-Block, Bandra Kurla Complex Road, Bandra East, Mumbai, 400 098 India
Tel: +91 22 6772 7272

Email: asb@asbindia.org
Website: www.asbindia.org
Head of School: Craig Johnson
School type: Coeducational Day
Age range of pupils: 3–18
No. of pupils enrolled as at 01/09/2014: 750
Fees per annum as at 01/09/2013:
US$15,250 – US$32,400
Teacher/pupil ratio: 1:5

The American School of Bombay is a 30-year-old school deeply rooted in a 2000-year-old city. A kaleidoscope of traditions, cultures, and values, every major world religion and dozens of languages are represented in our community and spoken on our campus. We are a village of people from over 50 countries, with one educator for every five students. This world of plurality is held together by our community's drive to fulfill our mission.

We know who we are, we know what we have committed to, and we authentically and enthusiastically endeavour to pursue our mission: to inspire continuous inquiry; to empower students to be courageous, optimistic, and full of integrity; to pursue dreams; and to enhance the lives of others.

An independent, coeducational day school, ASB serves 750 students from the international and expatriate community of Mumbai – early childhood through Grade 12. We are an IB World School offering the Primary Years and Diploma Programmes. Graduates are awarded an American high school diploma and/or the IB Diploma.

Students focus on communication skills, being digitally literate and inventive thinkers through effective teaming, collaboration and interpersonal skills. We believe that mutual trust and respect are essential for healthy, enduring relationships and that practice and perseverance are essential to a culture of excellence.

ASB graduates are accepted at the world's finest colleges and universities including MIT, Stanford, University of Pennsylvania, Columbia, Cornell, Brown, Johns Hopkins, Emory, Duke, McGill, University College London, Harvard University, University of Sydney and the University of Paris and contribute personally and professionally across a diversity of fields.

It is said: '...if there is one place on the face of Earth where all the dreams of living men have found a home... it is India.' We agree, and believe the same about ASB. After all, what better place for dreams to find a home than in a school?

British International School, Ho Chi Minh City

BRITISH INTERNATIONAL SCHOOL
HO CHI MINH CITY

(Founded 1997)

An Phu Secondary Campus, District 2
An Phu Primary Campus, District 2
Tu Xuong Primary Campus, District 3
Tel: +84 83 744 2335 (Ext:230)
Fax: +84 83 744 2334
Email: info@bisvietnam.com
Website: www.bisvietnam.com
CEO & Principal: Shaun Williams
School type: Coeducational Day

Age range of pupils: 2–18
No. of pupils enrolled as at 01/09/2014: 1859
Boys: 909 **Girls:** 950 **Sixth Form:** 137
Fees per annum as at 01/09/2014:
US$9,300 – US$25,000
Average class size: 20
Teacher/pupil ratio: 1:10
Secondary: 1:21

The BIS Group of Schools in Vietnam has been operating the hugely successful British International School (BIS) in Ho Chi Minh City since 1997. From very modest beginnings the school has grown to become the largest international school in Vietnam and is one of the leading international schools in the South East Asia region. Further expansion of the BIS Group of Schools will take place in August 2014 with the opening of the first British International School in Hanoi.

BIS is a selective, independent and co-educational day school providing a British style curriculum for an international student body. Both Primary campuses cater for students from the Foundation Stage (Pre-school) through to Year 6 and the Secondary campus caters for students from Year 7 to Year 13.

All three of the campuses have been designed fully in line with international

standards and host large libraries, music suites, computer suites, indoor 25 metre swimming pools, large sports halls and grass playing fields. The Secondary campus has excellent specialist facilities including a gymnasium, auditorium, mini theatre, science laboratories, music technology suite, drama studio, dance studio, art and design technology rooms as well as ICT suites. Foundation aged children have their own mini swimming pools, sand pits, dedicated playgrounds and climbing apparatus.

The school provides a broad, balanced and differentiated curriculum to meet the wide ranging needs of the students. Staffed by British qualified and trained teachers with relevant British curriculum experience, the education on offer is amongst the best available anywhere in the world. BIS operates within the framework of the National Curriculum for

England and students are prepared for both the International General Certificate of Secondary Education (IGCSE) and the International Baccalaureate Diploma Programme (IBDP). BIS students then progress to top universities around the world.

The school is fully accredited by the prestigious Council of International Schools (CIS) and is a registered centre for the UK examination boards Cambridge International Examinations (CIE). It is also designated as an IB World School and is registered with the UK Government DfE as an overseas school. It is a full member of the Federation of British International Schools in Asia (FOBISIA).

BIS has been inspected, approved and rated as 'Outstanding' by the British Government as detailed in a British Schools Overseas (BSO) Inspection Report, March 2013.

British International School, Phuket

(Founded 1996)

59 Moo 2, Thepkrasattri Road, Koh Kaew,
Muang, Phuket 83000 Thailand
Tel: +66 (076) 335555
Fax: +66 (076) 238750
Email: info@bisphuket.ac.th
Website: www.bisphuket.ac.th
Head of School: Mr Neil M Richards MBE

School type: Coeducational Day & Boarding
Age range of pupils: 18 months–18 years
No. of pupils enrolled as at 01/09/2014: 840
Fees per annum as at 01/09/2014:
Day: THB245,000–THB600,600
Weekly Boarding: THB251,200–THB294,800
Full Boarding: THB300,300–THB327,600

The British International School Phuket (BISP) in Thailand is an English medium, co-educational, day and boarding school (est. 1996). Its purpose-built 39-acre campus includes high quality boarding accommodation and provides world-class facilities that enable students to excel in sports, the expressive arts, and in their studies. The student population consists of 840 day and boarding students with over 50 different nationalities represented.

BIS Phuket provides a Pre-school, Primary and Secondary school education of the highest international standard. External examinations are offered in the IB Diploma, IGCSE, and Cambridge ESOL. In addition, an externally assessed programme for spoken English is provided

through the London Academy of Music and Dramatic Arts (LAMDA), and the music department offers 'Rock School' and ABRSM qualifications.

In the Early Years, Primary and Key Stage Three sections of the school the UK National Curriculum has been enriched and adapted to meet the needs of our international student body. The school has a wide choice of IGCSE and IB courses. Language instruction is given by mother-tongue teachers in English, Thai, Russian, Mandarin, French and Spanish. An International Learning Centre (ILC) has been established at the school as a part of its commitment to the creation of a 'learning community'.

The sports facilities are exceptional, with

two swimming pools and 10 x 7-a-side and two x 11-a-side football pitches. Within the recently introduced high performance Sports Academies structure, our swim, football, golf and tennis teams are professionally coached. Loughborough University graduates support the sporting life of the school through a GAP programme.

The school is accredited by the Council of International Schools (CIS) and the New England Association of Schools and Colleges (NEASC), and is a member of the International School's Association of Thailand (ISAT), the Federation of British International Schools in South and East Asia (FOBISSEA) and the Boarding Schools Association of the United Kingdom (BSA).

Dwight School Seoul

DWIGHT SCHOOL SEOUL
Igniting the spark of genius in every child
PERSONALIZED LEARNING · COMMUNITY · GLOBAL VISION

(Founded 2012)

21 World Cup Buk-ro 62-gil, Mapo-gu,

Seoul, 121-835 Republic of Korea

Tel: +82 2 6920 8600

Fax: +82 2 6920 8700

Email: admissions@dwight.or.kr

Website: www.dwight.or.kr

Head: Kevin Skeoch

Appointed: January 2011

School type:

Coeducational International Day

Age range of pupils: 3–18

No. of pupils enrolled as at 02/10/2013:

Boys: 186 **Girls:** 145

Established in 2012, Dwight School Seoul is an independent international school dedicated to igniting the spark of genius in every child.

Dwight School Seoul is a member of The Dwight Schools, with campuses and programs in New York, USA; London, UK; Vancouver Island, Canada; and Beijing, China. Following the tradition of its sister campuses, Dwight School Seoul is an authorized International Baccalaureate World School, providing all three International Baccalaureate programmes: Primary Years Programme (Pre-K-grade 5), Middle Years Programme (grades 6-10) and the Diploma Programme (grades 11-12). Widely known as the most challenging and respected pre-university course of study worldwide, the IB is the only universal curriculum that evaluates students according to international benchmarks. Dwight is unique to Seoul as it is the only school in the city offering all three IB programmes. Through blending the best of a traditional curriculum with the innovative IB, Dwight School Seoul students have opportunities to learn and develop as well-balanced individuals.

Dwight School Seoul is located in Seoul's Digital Media City, the silicon valley of South Korea. Its 200,000 square foot campus was designed by the award-winning D&B Architecture Group in accordance with sustainable design

principals. The campus includes two indoor gymnasiums, an outdoor soccer field, a large climbing wall, two large media rooms, a library, two purpose-built acoustic music classrooms with eight individual rehearsal rooms, a 400+ seat performing arts center, gallery space, and a rooftop garden with an open-air stage.

At Dwight School Seoul, our educational model is built with innovation and leadership in mind. Supporting our mission and philosophy are our three pillars:

personalized learning, community and global vision. Our teachers are committed to recognizing and developing each child's individual 'spark of genius' and our focus is on individual progress and growth. Through an extensive language and theater arts programmes, a wide-ranging sports programme, state-of-the-art technology instruction, community service projects, trips and excursions, Dwight students are well-prepared for university entrance and to become empowered global citizens.

Hokkaido International School

(Founded 1958)

1-55 5-jo, 19-chome, Hiragishi, Toyohira-ku, Sapporo 062-0935, Japan

Tel: +81 11 816 5000

Fax: +81 11 816 2500

Email: his@his.ac.jp

Website: www.his.ac.jp

Head of School: Mr Barry Ratzliff

School type: Coeducational Day & Boarding

Age range of pupils: 3–20

No. of pupils enrolled as at 01/09/2014: 190

Boys: 95 **Girls:** 95

No. of boarders: 14

Fees per annum as at 01/09/2014:

Day: US$9,500

Boarding: US$15,000

Average class size: 15

Teacher/pupil ratio: 1:10

Curricular Program: Hokkaido International School is located in the beautiful northern city of Sapporo, capital of Japan's northernmost island and prefecture, Hokkaido. HIS is a close community of approximately 200, day and resident (dormitory) students. The elementary school program is centered around the theme- based and integrated International Primary Curriculum (IPC). The Language Arts program is driven by the Common Core aligned Reading and Writing Workshop approach while the math program is Singapore Math (US version). At the secondary level, the integrated International Middle Years Curriculum defines the Middle School (grades 6-8) while the high school program

(9-2) ladders up to the flexible university preparatory, Advanced Placement (AP) program.

Areas of Emphasis: Beyond its curricular core, HIS has two curricular areas of emphasis, music and outdoor education. The school believes strongly in taking advantage of the island's beautiful natural environment and incorporates outdoor educational experience throughout its physical education program and through two dedicated high school courses, the Outdoor Pursuits and Outdoor Leadership courses, which together develop leadership skills, environmental understandings and appreciation for the world we live in. The Adventure Hokkaido Club, AdHoc, compliments Outdoor

Education by providing weekend and after-school opportunities to ski, snowboard, kayak, ice- fish, camp, hike and travel on the beautiful island of Hokkaido.

After HIS: In its 55-year history, the school has met the educational needs of expatriate and bicultural families as well as Japanese nationals who have returned from living abroad. Our students fully prepare themselves for entrance into universities around the world with the most popular English speaking destinations being the United States, Canada, the UK and Australia. Other options include the growing number of English and bilingual programs being offered at Japanese universities.

We invite you to visit us at www.his.ac.jp.

Ibn Khuldoon National School

(Founded 1983)
Building 161, Road 4111, Area 841, Isa
Town, Kingdom of Bahrain
Tel: +973 177 80661
Fax: +973 177 689028
Email: hr@ikns.edu.bh

Website: www.ikns.edu.bh
President: Dr Kamal Abdel-Nour
School type: Coeducational Day
Age range of pupils: 4–18
No. of pupils enrolled as at 01/09/2014: 1500
Average class size: 18-22

IBN Khuldoon National School (IKNS) is a non-profit, self-supporting, coeducational institution that is dedicated to providing high quality education for local and expatriate students. The school is licensed by the Ministry of Education to offer a bilingual programme of study for students from Kindergarten to Grade 12. A diverse faculty, whether teaching in Arabic or English, provides a rich and supportive learning environment for students. The faculty is supported by a dedicated team of administrative, IT and support staff.

IKNS has been affiliated with the International Baccalaureate (IB) since 1990, as an IB Diploma Programme provider. The first group of students sat for the IB diploma examinations in 1992. Since then, the results of the students have been a great source of pride to IKNS.

In addition to the IB Diploma, IKNS offers an American high school diploma. Both are tertiary education preparatory programmes, and are considered to be equivalent to the Bahraini "Tawjihi".

The school received its full accreditation from the Middle States Association of Colleges and Schools (MSA) in 1994, and it continues to be in good standing with the association. The accredited status of the school affirms that it provides the level of quality in its educational programmes, services, activities and resources expected by its stakeholders.

The National Authority of Qualifications and Quality Assurance for Education and Training awarded the school an 'Outstanding' rating in September 2013.

The school facilities include two libraries, six science laboratories, six computer laboratories, seven art rooms, three indoor sports halls, around a hundred classrooms, in addition to outdoor playgrounds and sports fields.

The new IKNS Sports Complex has an indoor multipurpose facility and an outdoor football field. The indoor section has a total area of 2,314 square meters. It houses a swimming pool, two basketball courts (that are also used for volleyball and badminton), a well-equipped fitness hall, a multipurpose hall, a class/meeting room and a first aid room.

International Community School

PO Box 2002, Amman 11181, Jordan

Tel: +962 6 4790666

Fax: +962 6 5725416

Email: office@ics.edu.jo

Website: www.ics-amman.edu.jo

Principal: John Bastable

Appointed: July 2010

School type: Coeducational Day

Age range of pupils: 3–18

No. of pupils enrolled as at 01/09/2014: 614

Boys: 334 **Girls:** 280

Fees per annum as at 01/09/2014:

US$5,873 – US$18,610

The International Community School (ICS) is a well established international school where students matter and where children come first. It is a non-profit making organization; all money goes back into the school, which provides very good standards of education to over 50 different nationalities.

In September 2009 the school moved to brand new purpose-built premises, which are set in beautiful countryside on the outskirts of Amman. These new premises offer high quality facilities in many specialist areas such as music, drama, science and ICT as well as purpose-built facilities for nursery and reception aged children and a sixth form suite. The school offers an inclusive British style education to children from the age of 3 to 18 delivered by a highly motivated and largely British trained and qualified staff. The school follows the UK three term year, which runs from August to July. The curriculum is taught in line with the British National Curriculum leading to IGCSEs and GCSEs in Year 10 and 11 through to AS and A levels in Year 13. This is supported by a Gifted & Talented programme and BTEC courses.

Learning a foreign language is seen as important and a choice of additional English, Arabic or French is introduced as part of the curriculum from Year 1 onwards. Wherever possible, good use is made of the local environment though field trips and outings. Each term a broad range of extracurricular activities is offered to help the students develop a wide range of interests and a healthy zest for life. Parental involvement in the school is encouraged, with a range of activities being arranged for families and staff. The International Community School's mission is to provide the highest quality British-style education to the national and international community in Jordan, striving for excellence and achievement in all fields in caring, diverse and inclusive environment.

International School of London (ISL) Qatar

International School of London Qatar

(Founded 2008)

PO Box 18511, North Duhail, Doha, Qatar
Tel: +974 4433 8600
Fax: +974 4499 5208
Email: mail@islqatar.org
Website: www.islqatar.org
Head of School: Chris Charleson

School type: Coeducational Day
Age range of pupils: 3–18
No. of pupils enrolled as at 01/04/2013: 900
Fees per annum as at 01/09/2014:
QR31,250 – QR66,950

Founded in 2008 as part of the Qatari Supreme Education Council's Outstanding Schools Initiative, the International School of London (ISL) Qatar enrols over 900 students, ages 3-18 from over 68 countries, seeking an outstanding 21st Century education. ISL Qatar is an International Baccalaureate (IB) World School, authorised to offer the Primary Years, Middle Years and Diploma Programmes. The IB curriculum fulfils the School's vision of combining intellectual rigour and high academic standards with a strong emphasis on the ideals of international mindedness, global engagement and responsible citizenship.

ISL Qatar is a culturally diverse community which fosters a passion and enthusiasm for learning, through outstanding educational practices. Students' cultural and linguistic identities are valued and nurtured through the international curriculum and Mother Tongue programme. ISL Qatar develops the attitudes, skills and understanding needed for active and responsible contributions to both local and global communities. The team of experienced and qualified teachers and administrators provides every student with the opportunity to grow and learn in an environment that respects diversity and promotes identity, understanding, and a passion for learning.

The school's approach to personalized learning enables students to find their unique talents, encourages them to think critically and find solutions, and enables them to make informed moral judgments based on sound principles. Through the ISL Qatar values, students develop key attributes, such as courage, integrity, resilience, and perseverance, by exposure to challenges in their experience of an ever-changing world.

Through the pastoral and social programmes, students receive advice and guidance to help them through the sometimes confusing path to maturity and adulthood. The goal is to foster the leaders of tomorrow committed to the ideals of peace, integrity, fairness, and compassion. ISL Qatar students are given a solid reference point based on deeply embedded principles that are learned through experiences and interactions with a diverse range of people from across the globe, gaining key skills and attributes such as creativity, adaptability, valuing and embracing diversity, working collaboratively with others, and tolerating ambiguity – all necessary for future success.

ISL Qatar is part of the International School of London Group which celebrated its 40th anniversary in 2012. The other ISL schools are in London and Surrey, England. The International School of London is one of the oldest IB Diploma schools in the world with a proud history of international college and university placement.

1 community
60 nationalities

Jerudong International School

(Founded 1997)

Jalan Universiti, Kampong Tungku, Bandar Seri Begawan, BE2119 Brunei Darussalam

Tel: +673 2 411000

Fax: +673 2 411010

Email: office@jis.edu.bn

Website: www.jis.edu.bn

Principal: Andrew Fowler-Watt MA(Cantab)

Appointed: August 2011

School type: Coeducational Day & Boarding

Age range of pupils: 2–18

No. of pupils enrolled as at 01/09/2014: 1650

Sixth Form: 360

No. of boarders: 260

Fees per annum as at 01/09/2014:

Day (non corporate, non Bruneian):

B$15,912 – B$17,496

Weekly Boarding

(non corporate, non Bruneian): B$17,688

Full Boarding

(non corporate, non Bruneian): B$23,688

Average class size: 23

Jerudong International School (JIS) founded in 1997 is in the small, beautiful country of Brunei Darussalam, on the island of Borneo. It is a large, thriving school with over 1650 students offering a broad, liberal education in the best traditions of western independent schools. It is one of the leading British international schools in South East Asia preparing students for I/GCSEs, A levels and the IB Diploma. JIS has almost 200 highly qualified teachers primarily from the UK but also from Australia, New Zealand, France and Brunei. We pride ourselves on providing an education that is not only academically challenging but also seeks to develop the whole student.

The facilities at JIS are exceptional. The purpose-built, ICT networked school occupies over 300 acres on a single campus in Jerudong, near the coast – a short drive from the capital city. Students are able to use the Arts Centre (containing a 725 seat auditorium, dance studios, smaller theatres and rehearsal rooms), Senior Academic and Administration Centre, 26 science laboratories, extensive music faculty (including recording studio), art, design and technology and textile studios, libraries and traditional classrooms as well as the swimming pool, gymnasium, netball/basketball courts, tennis courts and soccer/rugby pitches. The Boarding facilities for students age 11

years + are purpose designed and built for the community of 270 students. Boarders are also able to use the school facilities.

All students and teachers in the School are members of a House which provides a key role in providing opportunities for internal sports competition and other House Events (eg Debating, Dance and Music). The Houses play a vital role in establishing the spirit of the School. A strong extracurricular programme exists with over 200 activities on offer each term including a wide range of sports and arts activities, the International Award, Model United Nations, environmental groups and "Make A Difference" community programme.

Kellett School

KELLETT
啓歷學校
The British International School
in Hong Kong

(Founded 1976)

Pok Fu Lam Prep Campus: 2 Wah Lok Path, Wah Fu, Pok Fu Lam, Hong Kong, SAR,

Hong Kong, China
Kowloon Bay Prep and Senior Campus: 7 Lam Hing St., Kowloon Bay, Hong Kong
Tel: +852 3120 0700
Fax: +852 2875 0262
Email: kellett@kellettschool.com
Website: www.kellettschool.com
Principal: Ms Ann McDonald
School type: Coeducational Day

Age range of pupils: 4–18
No. of pupils enrolled as at 01/04/2012: 670
Boys: 335 **Girls:** 335
Fees per annum as at 01/09/2014:
Preparatory: HK$130,300
Senior: HK$169,600
Sixth Form: HK$178,100
Average class size: 23
Teacher/pupil ratio: Approx 1:13

Kellett School, The British International School in Hong Kong was founded in 1976 as a not-for-profit Association by like-minded parents providing a high quality British style education to English speakers in Hong Kong. The School's aim is to engender 'a love of learning and confidence for life' in each of its students. This aim is accomplished by ensuring the students achieve personal academic excellence, are confident, articulate and gain a wide range of transferable skills.

Kellett is a through train school with two campuses, the Pok Fu Lam campus and the Kowloon Bay campus. The Pok Fu Lam campus is a Preparatory school and is located in Hong Kong's Southern district

of Wah Fu at the foot of Mount Kellett and overlooking Kellett Bay. Kowloon Bay campus offers Preparatory and Senior places. The Senior school is four form entry, guaranteeing all Kellett preparatory students a senior school place and at capacity offering up to 600 places. Kellett School follows the Early Years Foundation Stage (EYFS) and English National Curriculum, which begins in Reception and runs through to the end of Year 13 and includes GCSE, IGCSE and A levels.

Kellett has grown to earn an enviable reputation as one of Hong Kong's leading independent International Schools where students learn with growing independence, in a challenging and

stimulating environment. High academic achievement is realised within a broad curriculum embracing 21st Century learning, creativity, the arts and sport, whilst taking into account their unique position in South East Asia at the gateway to China.

Kellett School looks to develop students both inside and outside the classroom. The school offers a rich and varied programme of extracurricular activities that contribute to the development of the whole student. These include local and overseas educational visits, a rich repertoire of performing arts opportunities and sport and activities of general interest.

KIS International School

Knowledge Inspiration Spirit

(Founded 1998)

999/124 Pracha Utit Road, Samsennok,

Huay Kwang, Bangkok, 10320 Thailand

Tel: +66 (0)2 2743444

Fax: +66 (0)2 2743452

Email: admissions@kis.ac.th

Website: www.kis.ac.th

Head of School: Sally Holloway

School type: Coeducational Day

Age range of pupils: 2–18

No. of pupils enrolled as at 01/09/2014: 550

Fees per annum as at 01/09/2014:

Baht281,000 – Baht591,000

KIS International School is a full IB World School in Bangkok, Thailand. The school was founded in 1998 and offers an international curriculum of high academic standards which challenges students to become responsible and effective world citizens.

The green, spacious campus is situated in the centre of town in the gated and guarded Kesinee Ville housing estate, providing a fine learning environment away from the noise and pollution while being easily accessible from both central Bangkok and the suburbs. The school facilities are excellent, with laboratories, libraries, an arts centre, a 500-seat auditorium, tennis courts, games pitches and a rooftop swimming pool.

KIS offers the well-respected International Baccalaureate programmes exclusively, starting with the Primary Years Programme for ages 3-11, the Middle Years Programme for ages 11-16 and the pre-university IB Diploma Programme for ages 16-18. The programmes are well-balanced and instil students with a positive attitude to learning, while engaging them with a world perspective in the humanities, languages, mathematics, the arts, technology and the sciences. The wide range of extra-curricular activities further allows students to develop their interests outside of the classroom. Teachers at KIS are a group of vibrant, highly qualified, IB trained, supportive and, above all, exceptional educators.

KIS graduates have gone on to study at excellent universities, frequently with scholarships, in the UK, the US, Canada, Europe, Thailand and elsewhere.

The atmosphere at KIS is one of the school's great strengths. Students and parents quickly feel at home and develop a sense of pride in their school. KIS's smaller size means there is individual attention for each student and openness to creative and progressive ideas.

We invite you to visit KIS and experience our blend of Knowledge, Inspiration and Spirit first hand.

Naseem International School
'STUDENTS FIRST'

Naseem International School
"STUDENTS FIRST"

(Founded 1982)

PO Box 28503, Riffa, Kingdom of Bahrain

Tel: +973 17 782 000

Fax: +973 17 687 166

Email: naseem@batelco.com.bh

Website: www.nisbah.com

President/Director: Sameera Al Kooheji

School type: Coeducational Day

Age range of pupils: 3–18

No. of pupils enrolled as at 01/09/2013: 985

Boys: 592 **Girls:** 393

Naseem International School provides a balanced education, which enables its students to fulfill their potential in all areas of growth, and empowers them to become critical thinkers who compassionately care for others and who play an active, responsible role in shaping our society and saving our world.

Naseem International School offers a rigorous academic dual language programme (Arabic and English) beginning at the pre-school level through to Grade 12. The teacher-student ratio average is around 1:9. Its dedicated leadership and faculty prepare students for both the IB and the High School Diploma programmes. The school was awarded IB Diploma authorization in 1996, MYP authorization in 2012, and PYP authorization in 2008; making Naseem International School the first fully authorized IB World School in Bahrain.

A variety of extra-curricular activities, including sports, drama, art and music are offered to address the creative and physical needs of our students.

Naseem International School emphasizes the importance of co-operation between the school and home, and promotes ongoing communication involving parents, students and teachers, in order to facilitate this co-operation. Naseem International School has a proud history of being founded in 1982 by Mrs. Sameera Abdul Jabar Al Kooheji in response to a demand for a national school that would provide a high-quality education within a traditional Arabic environment. Its mission is to offer a holistic education which adequately prepares our students for the challenges they are to face in the future.

NIST International School

NIST INTERNATIONAL SCHOOL

(Founded 1992)

36 Soi 15 Sukhumvit Road, Wattana, Bangkok, 10110 Thailand
Tel: +66 2 651 2065
Fax: +66 2 253 3800
Email: admissions@nist.ac.th
Website: www.nist.ac.th
Headmaster: Mr James MacDonald

Appointed: July 2013
School type: Coeducational Day
Age range of pupils: 3–18
No. of pupils enrolled as at 01/09/2014: 1538
Fees per annum as at 01/09/2014:
US$12,000 – US$22,000
Average class size: 23

The first and only full, not-for-profit IB World School in Thailand, NIST International School was established in 1992 with the guidance and support of the United Nations. The school now welcomes over 1,500 students of over 50 nationalities and provides all three International Baccalaureate programmes: the Primary Years Programme (PYP), Middle Years Programme (MYP) and Diploma Programme (DP). NIST is governed by the Foundation for International Education and is accredited through the Council of International Schools (CIS) and New England Association of Schools and Colleges (NEASC).

Recognized worldwide for its progressive approach, the IB programmes provide students with critical 21st century skills. The academic structure emphasizes exploration, risk-taking and trans-disciplinary learning. All students are required to take part in community service activities that encourage participants to empathize with others and take an active role in solving issues. As of 2014, NIST has also partnered with other top international schools to offer the Global Citizen Diploma, a supplementary component that assesses graduates' leadership, service and community engagement.

In addition to its rigorous academics, NIST provides students with an expansive World Languages Programme and more than 300 extra-curricular activity options. As one of the founding members of the Southeast Asia Student Activity Conference (SEASAC), the NIST Falcons compete against their peers from other top schools in Southeast Asia. NIST has also committed itself to IT excellence and innovation. The school offers students the use of MacBook Air computers, iPads, a completely wireless campus, SMART Boards, FrontRow classroom amplification system, and LCD-equipped classrooms.

NIST represents the future of education through its stellar academic achievements; engaged, community-driven culture; forward-looking philosophy; and expansive resources. With its graduates attending the best universities in the world and going on to become community leaders, NIST International School has become recognized as one of the world's leading learning institutions.

Shrewsbury International School

SHREWSBURY INTERNATIONAL SCHOOL

BANGKOK

1922 Charoen Krung Road, Wat Phrayakrai, Bang Kholame, Bangkok 10120, Thailand
Tel: +66 2 675 1888
Fax: +66 2 675 3606
Email: admissions@shrewsbury.ac.th

Website: www.shrewsbury.ac.th
Principal: Stephen Holroyd
School type: Coeducational Day
Age range of pupils: 3–18
No. of pupils enrolled as at 01/09/2014: 1600

Since opening its doors in 2003, Shrewsbury International School has built a reputation for academic success as well as excellence in sport, music and the creative and performing arts. The school's exam results speak for themselves. In 2013, 65% of IGCSE passes were at A*-A grade and 77% of A level passes were at A*-B grade. Shrewsbury's graduating students in 2014 will take up places at the world's leading universities including Oxford, Cambridge, UCL and LSE in the UK as well as UCLA, UPenn and Carnegie Mellon in the US.

Shrewsbury International School offers an inspirational English language education for carefully selected students, caring for them in an organization committed to continuous improvement, and providing outstanding opportunities both in and out of the classroom.

The school, which caters for children age 3-18 from 35 nationalities, enjoys a stunning location on the banks of the Chaophraya River in Central Bangkok with many of Shrewsbury's 1,600 pupils travelling to school by boat. The spacious, purpose-built campus – staffed by hand-picked teachers mostly from the UK – provides excellent facilities and resources.

Pupils are stretched to meet their potential through the varied and challenging British curriculum and small class sizes ensure that each student receives the individual support they require in their all-round development as people. Field trips out of school, concerts, productions, sports competitions and a vast range of extracurricular activities add breadth and interest as our pupils move up through the school.

The school enjoys genuine and close links with Shrewsbury School in the UK. The Board of Governors includes Sir David Lees, Chairman to the Court of the Bank of England, and two members who act as governors to both schools. Stephen Holroyd worked at Shrewsbury UK for 20 years before taking over as Principal at the Bangkok School.

Stamford American International School

1 Woodleigh Lane (off Upper Serangoon Road), 357684 Singapore

Tel: +65 6602 7247
Fax: +65 6602 7259
Email: admissions@sais.edu.sg
Website: www.sais.edu.sg

Superintendent: Mr Malcolm Kay
School type: Coeducational Day
Age range of pupils: 2–18
No. of pupils enrolled as at 01/09/2013: 1650

School Profile

Centrally located in Singapore, Stamford's state-of-the art campus welcomes children from Nursery (age 2) through Secondary School. Easily accessible, Stamford is centrally located next to the Woodleigh MRT and is a short drive from all the major expatriate residential areas. Stamford is truly a diverse community with students representing over 60 different nationalities.

Best of American and International Learning

Stamford offers two rigorous programs of learning – the International Baccalaureate (IB) Programme integrated with the American Education Reaches Out (AERO) standards. The program builds on children's natural curiosity through formal content mixed with a broad range of associated 'real-world' experiences. This creates a solid platform for information and concepts which students will build on

while at Stamford and for the rest of their lives.

Stamford believes that students can achieve more than they think they can and challenges students according to their individual ability level by differentiating course instruction. Stamford focuses on the whole child, offering instruction in Art, Music, Dance, Drama, Physical Education and Library. The curriculum is concept-based, building on children's natural curiosity through formal content mixed with a broad range of associated 'real-world' experiences.

Stamford is fully accredited by the Western Association of Schools and Colleges (WASC) and is an IB World School authorized for the Primary Years Programme (PYP), Middle Years Programme (MYP) and Diploma Programme (DP). Additionally, Stamford is a proud member of the Council of International Schools (CIS) as well as

Edutrust and Council of Private Education (CPE) certified.

Daily Foreign Language – Mandarin & Spanish

At Stamford, daily foreign language is part of the core curriculum for all students from Nursery (age 2) through Secondary School. Speaking, reading, writing and intercultural awareness is taught in order to create international-mindedness and global citizenship for all students. Classes are divided to ensure that each child is challenged at an appropriate level.

Stamford takes pride in engaging highly-qualified, native-speaking teachers who are able to use their experience and traditions as a platform for integrating the core curriculum into the language program. In addition to celebrations and engaging learning opportunities, technology is also woven into the framework of the language program.

Integrated Technology – 1:1 iPads & MacBooks

Stamford believes that the implementation of Information and Communications Technology (ICT) prepares students for university and the workplace, where technology is an integral part of academia and business. Stamford integrates ICT into the curriculum as a tool; there are interactive Promethean boards in every learning space, a 1-to-1 iPad Program for students from Kindergarten 2 through Grade 5 and a 1-to-1 MacBook Program for Secondary School students.

The 1-to-1 dedicated technology program allows students to challenge themselves in applying practical and creative thinking skills to solve problems and communicate their ideas to a wider audience. Students are progressively challenged as they advance through the program. Stamford teachers are also linked into an extensive Apple network of sharing and collaborating to bring the best ICT practices into the classroom.

World-Class Facilities

Stamford's campus has introduced some of the most state-of-the-art facilities for an international school in the world. Stamford will continue their advancement in bringing the best school facilities to Singapore with the completion of the Phase II development, opening in August 2014.

The Phase II development will include additional classroom and specialist space to support the growth of Stamford's Secondary School. It will include enhanced sports facilities with an additional swimming pool, another full gymnasium, fitness center, indoor climbing wall, Golf Academy and tennis courts. Additional specialist areas will include a Performing Arts Center with 500 seats, additional Art rooms, an Art Gallery, additional Music facilities, additional technology rooms and another Learning Resource and Media Center complete with interactive iLEarn facilities.

There will also be another fully air-conditioned Student Cafeteria, a Senior School Study and the Stamford Courtyard, a green oasis for quiet contemplation or studying. Sustainable operational features will include sensor driven lights, air conditioning which switches off when not in use and facilities for monitoring overall energy use at the school.

Stamford's campus also includes a world-class Innovation Center unlike any facility or resource built in a Secondary School. The Innovation Center will be more than just a physical facility; it will be a place of partnership between Stamford's students and the corporate sector, bridging the gap between theory and real-world execution. Within the Innovation Center, project-based group activities where students discuss real-world issues will be a common activity. By linking the education of Stamford's students with the realities of the commercial world, Stamford will give students the best possible start on their careers as entrepreneurs and business leaders.

Stamford's continued development includes many features that are not only new for Stamford but also groundbreaking educational additions to Singapore. Stamford ensures every new program and facility is firmly supported by proven educational principles and adds to the quality of student education. Stamford is an education leader committed to improving the quality of education in Singapore.

Tanglin Trust School, Singapore

92 Portsdown Road, 139299 Singapore
Tel: +65 67780771
Fax: +65 67775862
Email: admissions@tts.edu.sg
Website: www.tts.edu.sg
Head of School: Peter Derby-Crook

School type: Coeducational Day
Age range of pupils: 3–18
No. of pupils enrolled as at 01/09/2014: 2730
Fees per annum as at 01/09/2014:
Day: S$23,754–S$39,467
Average class size: 24

Established in 1925, Tanglin has almost 90 years' experience of providing British based education to the international community in Singapore. Tanglin is a non-profit company limited by guarantee and is registered as an educational charity. It is dependent on school-fee income and all revenue is devoted to the provision of education.

Tanglin is a vibrant co-educational school of over 2,700 students aged from 3 to 18 years, representing over 50 different nationalities. The school is split into the Infant School (3-7 years), Junior School (7-11 years) and Senior School (11-18 years), which includes Sixth Form.

Learning is based on the English National Curriculum, which is enriched to reflect the school's location in Asia. Tanglin is unique amongst international schools in Singapore in offering both A Levels and the International Baccalaureate in Sixth Form, both of which yield consistently outstanding academic results to complement the school's excellent results at I/GCSE.

In addition to its outstanding academic performance, Tanglin offers an extensive range of sporting, musical, creative and recreational co-curricular activities. Tanglin students are also encouraged to contribute actively to the local community, support service projects and participate in a wide variety of extra curricular pursuits. Pastoral care is a key strength of the school and, along with high standards and achievement; this has been consistently recognised in recent school inspections.

Tanglin is inspected every year within the British Schools Overseas (BSO) framework, recognised by Ofsted. All three schools have been awarded 'Outstanding', the highest possible grade, in their latest inspections (2012, 2013 and 2014).

Tanglin is a place where children can thrive, inspired by passionate teachers and supported by excellent pastoral care. Underpinning life at Tanglin are a set of ten attributes, closely aligned with the IB's Learner Profile which the school strives to develop in its students; balanced, caring, risk-takers, knowledgeable, resilient inquirers, communicators, principled, open-minded, thinkers and reflective.

The British School of Bahrain

PO Box 30733 – Budaiya, Building
1080, Road 1425, Block 1014, Hamala,
Kingdom of Bahrain
Tel: +973 1 761 0920
Fax: +973 1761 0371
Email: admissions@thebsbh.com

Website: www.britishschoolbahrain.com
Head: Charles Wall
School type: Coeducational Day
Age range of pupils: 3–18
No. of pupils enrolled as at 01/04/2013:
Boys: 821 *Girls:* 762

The British School of Bahrain (BSB) is a high-performing, international school with a reputation and vision for excellence and innovation. Based on the English National Curriculum, the school has an international outlook and fosters in its students a global perspective of respect, open-mindedness and acceptance of diversity. The BSB is very fortunate to have all three schools on one campus, which provides a wonderful opportunity for sharing across schools and year groups to build a strong sense of community. 'The BSB Spirit' is what really makes the British School special. It flourishes because our dedicated, caring staff, talented and enthusiastic students, and extremely supportive parent community work together as one team in pursuit of learning', reports Charles Wall, Head of School. Last year BSB's A level results continued their upward trend with a 100% pass rate; 32% of students were awarded an A or A* grade, while the number of students who were awarded A* to C grades rose to 84%. This year we have four students have gained interviews for Oxbridge and one has been offered a place to read law. We intend to offer the IB Diploma alongside A levels within the next couple of years.

In April 2012, the BSB received 'outstanding' in all six categories from the QAAET (Quality Assurance Authority for Education and Training) and the recommendation to share their excellent practice with others in Bahrain. Already, the BSB Academies offer professional coaching in sports and the performing and creative arts to all students throughout Bahrain. *West Side Story* last year was an amazing performance featuring talented students from five different schools trained at the BSB Academies and this year *Peter Pan* was totally awesome with flying special effects. The BSB is committed to promoting professional learning by bringing specialists to Bahrain and sharing the training opportunities with other Bahrain schools. The school has been instrumental in hosting Bahrain's first TEACHMEET.

The Gulf English School

PO Box 2440, Doha, Qatar
Tel: +974 4457 8777
Email: info@gulfenglishschool.com
Website: www.gulfenglishschool.com
Managing Director's Advisor & Business
Manager: Ms Mona El Helbawi
Head of Secondary: Mr David Frame

Head of Primary: Mrs Ina Gerrard
School type: Coeducational Day
Age range of pupils: 3–18
No. of pupils enrolled as at 01/09/2014: 1535
Fees per annum as at 01/09/2014:
Available on request

The Gulf English School opened in 1993 to meet the need for an educational facility which would provide a broad and balanced curriculum based on the English National Curriculum and also offer an Arabic Language and Islamic Studies programme as authorised by the Supreme Education Council. The school is housed in modern purpose built facilities of a coeducational programme up until Year Five and a segregated programme from Year Six onwards.

From a small beginning in two villas, the school has rapidly developed and now occupies two large modern purpose-built premises with all facilities available to educate students to a high standard.

The Gulf English School only employs fully qualified teachers of the highest calibre from all over the world. All teachers are fluent and competent English speakers who are experts in their particular field of knowledge and skills.

Teachers bring a wide breadth of experience and pedagogical practice and many hold masters degrees or equivalent.

The present campus was opened in 2003 and has been expanding since to meet the constantly ever growing numbers of students. In The Gulf English School we have a range of facilities in the purpose built buildings.

The Infant School is housed in a two storey purpose built building, which provides a very pleasant environment for both staff and children. The infant building consists of 19 classrooms, each classroom is equipped with a networked computers, an outside playground, facilities for music practice, library and computer lab.

The Primary School is housed in a larger two storey building including classrooms with interactive whiteboards, Junior Library, multi-purpose hall, swimming pool, ICT lab, art studio, music room and cafeteria.

The Secondary building is the E shape building which includes classrooms, a library, four science labs, three ICT labs, large multi-purpose hall, large swimming pool, two art studios, climate controlled swimming pools and an all weather pitch playground.

The International School Of Penang (Uplands)

(Founded 1955)

Jalan Sungai Satu, Batu Feringgi, 11100 Penang, Malaysia

Tel: +604 8819 777
Fax: +604 8819 778
Email: info@uplands.org
Website: www.uplands.org
Principal: Ian Williams
Appointed: August 2012
School type: Coeducational Day & Boarding
Age range of pupils: 4–19
No. of pupils enrolled as at 01/09/2014: 633

Boys: 331 **Girls:** 302 **Sixth Form:** 104
No. of boarders: 42
Fees per annum as at 01/09/2014:
Day: RM9,667–RM14,500 per term
Full Boarding: RM12,100–RM12,677 per term
Average class size: 24
Teacher/pupil ratio: 1:8

Our motto: Respect for self. Respect for others.

We are a coeducational, secular, non-profit day and boarding educational institution offering quality international education to children aged 5-19. Our students' examination results have consistently been above global averages for the IB Diploma Programme and the IGCSE examinations.

The school was originally founded in 1955 by the Incorporated Society of Planters (ISP) to provide expatriate planters a place to school their children. Over 50 years later we continue to provide a nurturing environment for expatriate and Malaysian children alike, offering for our boarders a 'home away from home'.

Uplands' roots are firmly in Penang, an island itself rich in the history of dynamic international and inter-ethnic exchange. We educate young people of over 40 nationalities and are fully committed to the concept of Universal Values and International Ideals, and believe that the hope for peace in the future lies in an interdependent international community where 'Respect for self. Respect for others' is paramount.

The Campus

A purpose-built four-acre campus is conveniently situated in the resort township of Batu Feringgi, Penang Island. The school features 36 classrooms, five science laboratories, a multipurpose hall with gymnasium, a new artificial-turf sports field and a 25-metre swimming pool. The modern classroom buildings encircle a beautiful garden courtyard creating a peaceful environment conducive for play and learning.

Extracurricular activities

There are many opportunities for all students to excel in and enjoy ECAs. Our annual performing arts events and visual exhibitions, successes on the sports field at state and international levels are testament to our successes in educating a person as a whole.

Learning support

The Learning Support Department aims to support those who are struggling to meet the demands of mainstream curriculum. It tailors individual programmes called Individualised Education Programmes (IEPs) for students who need help.

Vientiane International School

(Founded 1991)

PO Box 3180, Ban Saphanthong Tai,
Vientiane, Laos
Tel: +856 21 486001
Fax: +856 21 486009
Email: contact@vislao.com
admissions@vislao.com
Website: www.vislao.com

Director: Greg Smith
School type: Coeducational Day
Age range of pupils: 3–18
No. of pupils enrolled as at 01/06/2014: 447
Fees per annum as at 01/08/2014:
US$6,650 – US$17,720
Average class size: 18-20

Vientiane International School (VIS) is an independent, non-profit, fully authorized IB World School offering the International Baccalaureate Primary Years (PYP), Middle Years (MYP) and Diploma (DP) Programmes from Early Years through Grade 12. The school received initial accreditation in 2001 from both the Western Association of Schools and Colleges (WASC) and the Council of International Schools (CIS) and was re-accredited in December 2011. Vientiane International School is the only school in Lao PDR to receive accreditation from international accreditation agencies.

Our mission is to **challenge, inspire and prepare learners for life**. We provide a safe, respectful, collaborative and sustainable learning environment. We offer a high quality, holistic education that empowers learners to be internationally minded global citizens and also offer enriching learning experiences through interaction with the Lao community and our international communities.

The school has a strong ethos of **Community, Action and Service** and has made many connections in the Lao community that have developed the cultural understanding and global awareness of our students and the school community as a whole. Strong connections have been made through the relationships and partnerships that students have developed through supporting our Lao sister school and

through Secondary Action Learning Service Adventure (SALSA) trips.

VIS students come from diverse backgrounds with over 40 different nationalities represented within the student body. A large percentage of the parents are professionals from embassies, NGOs and international companies. Our student body has a transient rate of approximately 20% each year and our curriculum ensures students successfully transition to their next international school or English-medium school in their home

country. Our Diploma students are likewise well prepared for acceptance into a college or university with the majority of students attending a quality university upon graduation.

VIS also offers an extensive co-curricular programme where students can engage in a wide variety of activities after school and at the weekends. The school is part of the regional association, MRISA, which enables our students and those from neighbouring countries to regularly take part in sporting and cultural exchanges.

International schools in Australasia

Schools ordered A–Z by Name

The Hutchins School

HUTCHINS

(Founded 1846)
71 Nelson Road, Sandy Bay, Tasmania,
7005 Australia
Tel: +61 3 6221 4200
Fax: +61 3 6225 4018

Email: hutchins@hutchins.tas.edu.au
Website: www.hutchins.tas.edu.au
Headmaster: Mr Warwick Dean
School type: Boys' Day & Boarding

An internationally minded community of learners

In the tradition of its education international mindedness The Hutchins School respects and welcomes all faiths and cultures. The Hutchins School was founded in 1846 and is an Anglican day and boarding school for boys currently enrolling over 1000 boys from Kindergarten to Year 12. Our school is sited in spacious beautiful grounds beside the University of Tasmania. The school also has magnificent views overlooking the nearby Derwent River which runs through Hobart, the capital of the State of Tasmania, Australia. Tasmania is an energetic, exciting city with numerous cultural, sporting, artistic and heritage events and activities. Food and cultural activities from many areas around the world are celebrated throughout the year in the city's temperate climate; an environment which is clean, safe and friendly.

The Hutchins School has three campuses in Early Learning and Junior School, Middle School and Senior School all of which exist on one extensive site and are coordinated, coherent and connected, operating from a community with a shared vision, mission and established core values.

The School has a culture rich in academic achievement. As an Early Learning to Year 12 school The Hutchins School has a clear scope and sequence curriculum that provides many pathways for success for our students.

Our most successful students are offered places in international and Australian universities. With a consistent record of academic high achievement Hutchins students often win scholarships to study at well-known universities. The Hutchins School has an excellent reputation for its annual Year 12 results and capacity to facilitate a wide range of further studies through its national and international connections, exchange programs and its academic pathway planning and Careers Counselling Centre.

An example of diversity in curriculum is the existence of our Marine Studies Centre, a High Achievement Program attached to the University of Tasmania, Bridging Programs in Years 7 and 8 and a very special program for students in Year 9 – 'The Power of 9' – as a bridge from the Middle Years to studies in the Senior Years. Our professionally developing staff is well known for their expertise and commitment to assisting boys achieve their goals.

Students enrolling from overseas experience a boarding environment in a first class facility which provides an 'at home' feeling supported by Director of Boarding with international experience, a nurse and medical support, house cleaning staff and a full time chef and catering staff. Teachers specialising in Chinese, French and Intensive English tuition are employed at the school to assist overseas enrolments and enhance the academic performance of boarding students at Burbury House.

Students enrolling from overseas who take up residence at Burbury House in The Hutchins School are on acceptance of their enrolment also offered a future place at the University of Tasmania.

Because we specialise in boys' education our purpose is to maintain a tradition of challenging boys to participate in today's world and prepare them for their future. In doing so we aim to develop young men who are: balanced in intellectual, spiritual, emotional, social and physical skills; in possession of relevant knowledge, skills and attributes; who possess a love of learning and who are willing to unselfishly serve their contemporaries and the wider local, national and international community.

Our vision is to provide an inspirational education where each student develops his personal best. As such, we hold these values as the foundation of our endeavours: relationships based on integrity and mutual respect, a safe and secure environment for all, education of each student, compassion and pastoral care, the pursuit of excellence appropriately celebrated, accepting best practice and academic challenge, active local, national and international citizenship, community connectedness and, building resilience through purposeful effort. In carrying out our vision and mission. The Hutchins School provides a large and diverse range of educational opportunities for students so that each is enabled to discover that in his school which he enjoys and in which he is encouraged to excel.

An extensive range of sports and co-curricular activities is provided throughout the School. Summer sports such as; Rowing, Cricket, Athletics, Swimming, Tennis, Badminton, Basketball, Cycling, Sailing, Surfing, and Water polo are complemented by Winter sports such

as; Australian Rules Football, Soccer, Cross Country running, Hockey, Rugby, and Sports Shooting. Co-curricular activities such as; Debating, Chess, Student Council, Community Service, International Exchanges, Musical bands, orchestra and ensembles encourage

students to participate in teams as well as develop a commitment to community service based on the belief that, 'What you do matters'.

The Hutchins School is a member of the Council of International Schools
www.hutchins.tas.edu.au

The Scots College

The Scots College
Sydney Australia

Locked Bag 5001, Bellevue Hill, Sydney, NSW 2023 Australia
Tel: +61 2 9391 7600
Fax: +61 2 9327 6947
Email: reception@tsc.nsw.edu.au

Website: www.tsc.nsw.edu.au
Principal: Dr Ian PM Lambert BA, Grad DipT, MA, PhD, MACE
School type: Boys' Day & Boarding

Located in leafy Bellevue Hill in Sydney's Eastern suburbs, The Scots College is one of the oldest and most prestigious private boys' schools in Australia, drawing students from around the world. Scots is a non-selective Presbyterian GPS day and boarding school for boys from the age of three in the Early Years Centre, right through to Year 12.

The Scots College is located in close proximity to some of Sydney's iconic attractions; a short bus trip in any direction will take the boys to Bondi Beach, the Sydney Opera House, and the Harbour Bridge. Sydney's Botanical Gardens and Centennial Park are also in close proximity of the College, boasting flora and wildlife such as wild pelicans, black swans and freshwater turtles.

Boarding has been central to the life and culture of the College since it was established in 1893. When asked about his boarding experience, Will Carruthers a Year 7 boarder from Young in NSW, stated, "My first week in boarding … 'wow'! … taking in the city culture and all the buzzing of the traffic! It is a big move for a 13-year-old coming from a small country town of only 12,000 people." Loic Cameron from Singapore, also a Year 7 boarder said, "Boarding – it was a huge step and now I'm here having the time of my life with my best friends and I am really enjoying both sports and academics."

"The Scots College is proud of its cultural diversity. International students are a welcome and valued part of our community as they provide a deeper

cross-cultural understanding and consequently, a broader worldview," said Dr Ian PM Lambert, Principal, The Scots College.

Hamish Dunbar graduated in 2013 after having started his journey at Scots in 2010 as a boarder in Fairfax House, one of the College's five boarding houses. "What I enjoyed most about Scots was the friendships. Living with your mates from all over the world and forging lifelong friendships. Maybe one little thing I missed was my mum's homemade cooking!" Hamish admitted.

The College's desire for each boy to strive to be a confident, well-grounded young man of integrity with a strong sense of identity, values, and character is encapsulated in the unique Brave Hearts

At Scots, teachers serve as classroom coaches to bring out a student's best performance and help him achieve his academic goals. The Thinking Sportsman academic coaching model is centred around learning in teams and inspires boys to be responsible for their own learning. Teachers encourage a spirit of willingness and focus on building a culture of empowerment in the classroom in which boys can thrive.

A myriad of sports is on offer at Scots encouraging boys to discover personal strength born of competition and camaraderie. Additionally a wide range of co-curricular activities can be passionately pursued at every stage of a Scots boy's brave hearts bold minds journey along with outdoor and community-based learning initiatives. These programs inspire the boys to become principled, compassionate and engaged citizens of their College, community and world.

Bold Minds education philosophy. "This College has a big picture. We can see the forest and not just the trees. We aim to equip all different types of boys with brave hearts and bold minds that will provide them with a chest full of confidence," said Dr Ian PM Lambert.

When boys begin their journey to brave hearts and bold minds, an innovative curriculum, a rigorous academic program and state-of-the-art learning facilities awaits them. These elements combine to create an atmosphere of excellence where boys can become creative, confident and accomplished learners.

The principles of the Reggio Emilia philosophy form the basis of learning in the Preparatory School, encouraging boys to discover and develop their interests. In the early years, educational specialists introduce boys to learning experiences in the Creative Arts with classes in Dance, Music, Drama and Visual Arts. As these little boys become fine Scots boys, they work with their classmates to develop thinking skills.

In the Senior Preparatory School, boys are challenged with leadership training and an expanded Honours Program extends the academic interests of eligible students. A notebook computer program empowers the boys to become contemporary learners as they progress into the Senior School.

In the Senior School, adventure is core to a boy's experiences. In Year 9, boys undertake the Glengarry Outdoor Education Program – a two-term residential experience in Kangaroo Valley, two hours south west of Sydney. Glengarry has the highest level of ORIC Accreditation with extensive safety and risk management procedures and is renowned at Scots as a rite of passage into manhood.

The overall aim of the College is to develop confident, well-grounded men, who are motivated and equipped to pursue rich and rewarding lives. The College is very proud of its fine young men who embody the Scots vision of integrity and support each other in their quest for excellence.

To discover how your son can embark on his own Scots brave hearts bold minds journey, please visit www.tsc.nsw.edu.au.

Mentone Girls' Grammar School

(Founded 1899)

11 Mentone Parade, Mentone,
VIC 3194 Australia
Tel: +61 3 9581 1200
Fax: +61 3 9581 1291
Email: info@mentonegirls.vic.edu.au
Website: www.mentonegirls.vic.edu.au

Head of School: Fran Reddan
School type: Girls' Day
Age range of girls: 3–18
No. of pupils enrolled as at 01/09/2014: 730
Fees per annum as at 01/09/2014:
AUS$10,903 – AUS$24,565

Mentone Girls' Grammar is one of the finest schools for girls in Melbourne, Australia, consistently ranked among the best schools in the State of Victoria. We have been providing a premium education for girls from Kindergarten to Year 12 since 1899; accepting students of all talents and abilities, faiths and cultures.

We understand how girls think, learn and interact. Our curriculum is specifically designed to engage girls at each age and stage, to support the best possible learning outcomes. Our beautiful beachfront location has inspired our **WAVES** priorities – key principles that guide the way we meet the particular learning needs of girls by contributing to their **W**ellbeing, **A**chievement, positive **V**alues, **E**nterprising

nature and **S**uccess as women in society. These priorities contribute to the unique culture and success of our School, as well as our personalised approach to learning.

As a member of the prestigious Council of International Schools (CIS) and an International Baccalaureate (IB) World School (primary), we are often benchmarked against some of the best schools in the world. Our curriculum challenges and inspires our students to learn, lead and live with an international focus. The curriculum includes both Asian and European languages and senior students can participate in a range of international experiences. Our aim is to develop compassionate, connected, articulate young women who have fun in

learning and the confidence to succeed no matter where their journey takes them.

As you would expect, we offer all the advantages of a quality independent school, from excellent teaching and small classes in purpose built, technology-rich learning centres, to a wide range of subject choices and co-curricular opportunities. In addition, strong community alliances provide many opportunities, from water skills with Mentone Life Saving Club, to quality competition through Girls Sport Victoria.

Mentone Girls' Grammar is filled with staff and students who have passion, dedication and perseverance. We have high expectations and take great pride and joy in exceeding them.

International schools in Europe

Schools ordered A–Z by Name

Anglo-American School of Sofia

**ANGLO-AMERICAN
SCHOOL OF SOFIA**

(Founded 1967)

16 Kozyak St, Sofia 1407, Bulgaria
Tel: +359 2 923 8810
Fax: +359 2 923 8859
Email: ipapazova@aas-sofia.org
Website: www.aas-sofia.org

Director: Jim Urquhart
Appointed: July 2011
School type: Coeducational Day
Age range of pupils: 4–18
No. of pupils enrolled as at 01/09/2014: 438

The Anglo-American School of Sofia is an independent, non-profit school, offering an educational program from Pre-Kindergarten through Grade 12 for students of all nationalities.

We engage, support and prepare each student for today and tomorrow. We

- Foster a love of learning, healthy living and international community
- Develop the knowledge, skills and values to communicate, find solutions and innovate
- Enhance critical thinking, resourcefulness and creativity
- Cultivate leadership, compassion and responsible citizenship in both attitudes and actions
- Nurture the abilities to interact effectively with others and to act independently with confidence

Our core values are commitment, respect and excellence.

Founded in 1967, AAS has a rich history of providing a high-quality education to the children of the international community residing in Sofia, the capital city of Bulgaria. Currently we have more than 430 students, aged 4 to 18, from more than 45 countries.

The Anglo-American School of Sofia is accredited by the Council of International Schools (CIS) and the New England Association of Schools and Colleges (NEASC). AAS is an authorized International Baccalaureate World School.

AAS is a member of the Central and Eastern European Schools Association (CEESA), as well as the Council of British International Schools (COBIS). Students and staff have opportunities to participate in a variety of activities, athletics and professional development in the region.

The Program

Education at the Anglo-American School of Sofia is viewed as more than acquisition of knowledge. Our curriculum is based on the best practices of international education. The language of instruction is English. The foreign languages taught at AAS include Bulgarian, French, and Spanish.

AAS offers a rich selection of co-curricular activities (more than 50) for students at all grade levels. The processes of inquiry, discovery, application and creativity are considered essential to the quality education we provide our students.

AAS recognizes each child's unique needs and potential through diverse educational experiences and methods, with teachers, students and parents as partners in the learning process.

Elementary School (Pre-K – Grade 5)

AAS provides its youngest students with a stimulating and supportive introduction to school life. During these classes, children take their first steps towards acquiring the physical, intellectual and social skills necessary for a successful and happy life at school. The Elementary School atmosphere is one of warmth, friendliness and caring. Regular communication with parents is valued and each individual's growth is nurtured and supported in the AAS Elementary School.

Middle School (Grades 6 – 8)

Middle School is an important stage in the path to maturity and independence both academically and socially. It is a time of physical, emotional and intellectual change and development. The atmosphere in the Middle School encourages and supports the development of a well-rounded young adolescent. Students work with small advisor groups, denoted as Wolf-Pack Time, to further foster community.

High School (Grades 9 – 12)

A balanced international curriculum is designed to encourage high academic standards and social development. The High School years at AAS promote inspires high academic standards, international understanding and responsible citizenship, and critical thinking and lifelong learning. Studies include English, the Sciences, Social Studies, Mathematics, Languages, Physical and Health Education and the Arts. A variety of elective choices offer students further

opportunities in Technology, Robotics, Theatre, Multimedia, Yearbook, Art and Music. Students work with small advisor groups, denoted as Wolf-Pack Time, to further foster community.

We look to help each student match themselves with the best post-secondary opportunities in accordance with their strengths and passions. Our graduates are accepted to top-tier universities around the world, including Cambridge, Harvard and other highly selective schools in our graduates' respective home countries.

The Faculty

The AAS faculty is comprised of teachers from a variety of countries, including the USA, UK, Canada, New Zealand, Australia, Poland, France, Mexico and Bulgaria. All faculty members have extensive experience and most hold advanced degrees.

The Community

AAS has a very active parent-teacher organization that supports student development by providing enhancement grants and organizing numerous community-building events throughout the year. We believe one of the keys to our success in education is the close cooperation and partnership with our parents.

AAS Facility

Our state-of-the-art campus is located at the foot of Vitosha Mountain, in the Pancharevo region of Sofia. AAS boasts seven hectares of land.

The AAS award winning building (Building of the Year 2006) LEED Gold EBOM Award 2012 (Leading in Energy and Environmental Design) has a unique layout, which successfully combines exceptional design and functionality with energy efficiency. Our building boasts a green roof, many open multi-purpose areas for flexible learning environments, solar panels for heating water, photo-voltaic roofed covered parking to collect energy, and a self-supporting water system that allows us to reuse grey-water for our toilets and irrigate our green spaces with biologically cleaned grey-water.

Our students enjoy a rich variety of indoor and outdoor sports facilities including two outdoor sports fields, outdoor basketball courts, two tennis courts, two large gymnasiums, a fitness room, and a student designed playground that includes a zip-line and a toboggan hill. All classes have access to modern and well maintained ICT labs, four fully equipped Art and Music rooms, modern Science labs, a performance stage and a Black Box Theatre in addition to spacious, well-equipped classrooms. Our Library is over 800 m² with more than 18,000 volumes.

In the Words of our Students

"AAS is my home away from home."

"I am happy and inspired."

"I love AAS; I cannot wait to get to school every day."

Aiglon College

(Founded 1949)
Avenue Centrale 61, 1885 Chesières-
Villars, Switzerland

Tel: +41 (0)24 496 6161
Fax: +41 (0)24 496 6162
Email: admissions@aiglon.ch
Website: www.aiglon.ch
Head Master: Mr Richard McDonald
Appointed: August 2009
School type: Coeducational Day & Boarding
Age range of pupils: 9–18
No. of pupils enrolled as at 01/01/2014: 341

Boys: 180 **Girls:** 161 **Sixth Form:** 113
Prep: Boys: 39 **Girls:** 32
Upper Sixth: 50
No. of boarders: 306
Fees per annum as at 01/01/2014:
Day: CHF31,150–CHF70,180
Full Boarding: CHF63,000–CHF97,280
Average class size: 10-12
Teacher/pupil ratio: 1:5

Founded in 1949 by John Corlette, Aiglon is a not-for-profit independent school occupying a spectacular position on a sheltered plateau high in the Swiss Alps, in the French-speaking village of Chesières-Villars. Classes are taught in English.

The school day begins with meditation to promote a habit of reflection. There is strong pastoral care and boarding houses provide a caring and supportive environment. A large staff permits a staff:student ratio of 1:5. The students are from many different international backgrounds, representing 58 nationalities. They study for IGCSEs and the IB Diploma as well as IELTS and SAT. Academic results are strong and the great majority of leavers go on to universities around the world, including leading institutions on both sides of the Atlantic. Music, drama and art are strong and there

is a wide range of extracurricular activities. Sports are an important part of the curriculum. There is a large sports centre, a variety of sporting surfaces, a fitness room and access to swimming pools, a skating rink, and extensive ski slopes. The school operates a unique outdoor expeditions programme featuring ski-mountaineering, rock climbing, kayaking and camping. Cultural excursions are arranged annually to major European cities. Many students participate in the Duke of Edinburgh's Award Scheme and the whole school is committed to community service – within the school, the local community and with international service projects around the world.

Aiglon is a founding member of Round Square, a worldwide association of schools sharing a commitment, beyond academic excellence, to personal

development and responsibility. Thirty subjects are offered to IB level. All sixth formers take six subjects, including three subjects at higher level, three at standard level and theory of knowledge. Learning development specialists provide diagnosis and support for students with additional learning needs; intensive ESL support is available. In addition to English, Aiglon offers eight foreign languages. Eight single sex houses accommodate up to 45 students each. There are resident qualified nurses and doctors in the village. There are termly parent-teacher meetings and weekend exeats authorised by houseparents. Visits to the village are allowed at fixed times according to age.

The Aiglon College Eagle Alumni Association is well-established and provides a strong global network for alumni.

Bordeaux International School

bis

(Founded 1988)

252 Rue Judaïque, 33000 Bordeaux, France

Tel: +33 5 57870211
Fax: +33 5 56790047
Email: bis@bordeaux-school.com
Website: www.bordeaux-school.com
Principal: Mrs Cussac
Appointed: September 1999
School type: Coeducational Day & Boarding
Religious Denomination: NIA

Age range of pupils: 3–19
No. of pupils enrolled as at 01/09/2014: 130
Boys: 64 **Girls:** 66
No. of boarders: 4
Fees per annum as at 01/09/2014:
Day: €3,180–€13,980
Full Boarding: €6,110–€9,100
Average class size: 10
Teacher/pupil ratio: 1:7

Bordeaux International School (BIS) is situated in the heart of the city. For children aged three to fourteen, the school offers a bilingual English/French education, and for older students, an English programme with a strong international dimension, leading to IGCSE and Advanced level examinations. A maximum class size of 12 students ensures a great deal of personal attention, and with students from over 20 different nationalities, the school offers the opportunity to flourish in a truly international environment.

BIS is an accredited member of the Council of International Schools (CIS), recognised by the French Ministry of Education, and a registered examination centre with The University of Cambridge.

The school offers a boarding system either living with a French host family or in residential apartments. There are also regular visits to theatres, art galleries and museums in Bordeaux, a sports programme within the school, which is integrated with sports clubs in Bordeaux, plus participation in the International Award Scheme.

At **IGCSE** level the students follow a programme of subjects with extra features: support and extended lessons either to help those students who are having difficulties or those who wish to extend their understanding and take exams a year early; conversational French lessons to give students extra confidence in using the language; access to an e-learning portal, where homework is set and help is available directly from teachers using a dedicated website.

At **Advanced level**, reflecting their age, students are encouraged to involve themselves in the life of Bordeaux and to use the research and library facilities. Students also have the options of a work placement, extended excursions within France and abroad. With the dual aims of intense academic study and of discovering French culture, the Sixth Form offers students an opportunity to complete their education in an international environment before progressing to university either in Britain, France or worldwide.

British Council School

(Founded 1940)
Calle Solano, 5 – 7, Pozuelo de Alarcon,
Madrid, 28223 Spain
Tel: +34 91 337 3612
Fax: +34 91 337 3634

Email: school@britishcouncil.es
Website: www.britishcouncilschool.es
Head of School: Gillian Flaxman
Appointed: August 2010
School type: Coeducational Day

Age range of pupils: 3–18
No. of pupils enrolled as at 01/09/2014: 1950
Boys: 987 **Girls:** 963 **Sixth Form:** 233
Average class size: 22
Teacher/pupil ratio: 1:11

British Council School

The British Council School is the only school managed by the British Council in Spain, and one of the most renowned bilingual schools in the country. We follow the British educational system intertwined with Spanish culture. Our students are future citizens of the world, prepared to approach any challenge with a positive attitude.

Academic Excellence

We were the first British school established in Spain, now with over 70 years' experience. Our continuing fine reputation and prestige are founded on our spirit of innovation, our highly qualified teaching staff and on standards of excellence in the British and Spanish education we offer.

Our academic approach, as well as our school environment, are designed and developed to respond to the times we live in. We are clearly focused on the future, as evidenced by our unique BiBac® system, which complemented by our excellent results in IGCSEs, helps our students to access the best universities in the world (Imperial College, Yale, ICADE...).

Student life

Life in British Council School is inspired by London dynamism. Music, expressive arts, science, literature, sports and public speaking events fill the school calendar.

We know that every child is unique, and it's our mission to offer an integrated value-based education, exploring all types of opportunities to achieve the child's full potential. We focus on strengthening self-esteem, creativity and talent, and encouraging students to explore their freedom responsibly along with a very strong community service programme.

With our *Family System*, each student forms part of a 'Family', which encourages a sense of belonging and helps to develop strong social and interpersonal skills.

Student profile

More than 90% of our students are Spaniards but our student body is diverse, including over 30 nationalities. Usually our students start school at three years old and finish their school career at eighteen.

Our School is therefore the ideal option for families looking to take advantage of the British educational system and at the same time willing to integrate fully into Spanish society.

Brussels International Catholic School

Chaussée de Wavre, 457, Brussels,
1040 Belgium
Tel: +32 264 035 36
Email: info@bicschool.be

Website: www.bicschool.be
School type: Coeducational Day
Fees per annum as at 01/09/2014:
Day: €7,500–€8,500

The Brussels International Catholic School is an independent school located in central Brussels very close to the European institutions. It offers a bilingual education (English-French) to over 400 students coming from over 40 different nationalities. The school follows the curriculum of the Cambridge Examinations of which it is a recognised test centre (IGCSE). The school is also fully accredited, and is a full member of the European Council of International Schools (ECIS).

The school believes that 'Happy children achieve more' and places the individual child at the centre of its attention. Working as a committed and dedicated community, and inspired by Christian values, the school seeks to achieve academic excellence in a caring environment where the individual needs of every child are fully catered for.

The school accepts children aged from two and a half to sixteen (at the time of going to press the school hopes to open the Sixth Form offering A levels). Specialist language support teachers ensure that children can integrate the school at all levels, regardless of their level of English and French.

The school attempts to maintain the school fees as low as possible: for 2014-15 fees are €7,500-€8,500 per annum.

The school believes that education is a collective endeavor, in partnership with parents and children alike. Seeking to incorporate new technology with tried and trusted methods, the school combines modernity with classical methods of education, especially in those critical years where children are learning to read and write, and acquire those life skills which will prepare them for leadership in the future.

Believing that the creative arts are an invaluable means of personal development, the school offers the opportunity to excel in music and drama, producing two plays every year.

In addition the school offers a wide range of extra-curricular activities ranging from Golf, Tennis and Rugby to Opera and Science clubs.

Collège Champittet

COLLEGE
CHAMPITTET
FONDÉ EN 1903

(Founded 1903)

Ch. de Champittet, PO Box 622, Pully-Lausanne, 1009 Switzerland
Tel: +41 21 721 0505
Fax: +41 21 721 0506
Email: info@champittet.ch
Website: www.champittet.ch
Director General: Dr Steffen Sommer

School type: Coeducational Day & Boarding
Age range of pupils: 3–18
No. of pupils enrolled as at 01/09/2014: 800
Fees per annum as at 01/09/2014:
Day: CHF18,100–CHF31,550
Full Boarding: CHF70,500–CHF77,750

Collège Champittet is an educational community, for boarders and day students, whose philosophy embraces the challenges of high academic achievement, responsibility and leadership, spiritual awareness and participation in a wide variety of activities.

Academic excellence across our three curricula – Swiss Maturité, French Baccalaureate and IB – draws on the finest tradition of Swiss, French, and British international education, enhanced by a truly bilingual setting. It is encouraged and enabled by a highly motivated and deeply caring body of staff who within the spirit of our Christian values, understand

and provide for the specific needs of every student.

Our Pully campus is both a day school (for students aged 4 to 18) and a boarding school (for students aged 12 to 18). Spread out over 40,000 m, the campus offers a unique setting and exceptional conditions, in which students learn and thrive.

Located on the picturesque banks of Lake Geneva, the campus is close to the centre of Lausanne and our students can easily enjoy the rich cultural life of the city.

Academic performance is of course our top priority, but we are also fully aware that our students need to find fulfillment in a variety of activities. Our

magnificent campus offers a wide array of opportunities for sport, including tennis, handball, basketball, football or volleyball as well as aquatic sports and skiing owing to our close proximity of Lake Geneva and the Alps.

As a forward-looking, well-resourced school, we are steeped into the mindset of 21st century education. Modern technology in the form of individual tablet computers allows our students to engage in active, teacher-led independent learning, problem solving and research activities that enhance creativity, promote higher order thinking and develop transferrable skills.

Collège du Léman International School

COLLÈGE DU LÉMAN
Geneva — Switzerland

(Founded 1960)

74, route de Sauverny, 1290 Versoix,

Geneva, Switzerland

Tel: +41 22 775 55 55

Fax: +41 22 775 55 59

Email: admissions@cdl.ch

Website: www.cdl.ch

Director General: Mr Yves Thézé

Appointed: August 2011

School type: Coeducational Day & Boarding

Age range of pupils: 2–18

No. of pupils enrolled as at 01/04/2014: 2002

No. of boarders: 252

Fees per annum as at 01/04/2014:

Day: CHF19,900 – CHF32,900

Boarding: CHF83,000

Average class size: 18

Teacher/pupil ratio: 1:9

Collège du Léman is an international college preparatory school located in Geneva, Switzerland. Our boarding and day school programmes offer individual growth, academic excellence and life-long learning to students from Pre-K through Grade 12. We are part of the Meritas Family of Schools, a worldwide family of elite college preparatory schools that offer students the highest standards in education and unique, international learning opportunities.

Collège du Léman is an 8-hectare landscaped campus, nestled between the Jura Mountains and Lac Léman on the outskirts of Geneva. It offers attractive residential facilities and recreational areas, providing our students with a wide range of sport and leisure activities.

Collège du Léman is committed not only to excellence in education but also to stimulating enthusiasm for lifelong learning and intellectual growth.

We open our doors to students who benefit from our multicultural learning environment. We nurture a sense of social responsibility and respect for others so that our students are well-prepared to become respected world citizens. In this spirit, we endeavor to add value to our teaching through its diversity. The knowledge students gain must be applicable across cultures and be supported by qualifications recognized worldwide. We value each student's individuality as well as his or her integration into society.

Our academic programme prepares our students for the demands of the 21st century. These programmes integrates both bilingualism and multilingualism and leads to:

• English-language diplomas: American High School with or without

Advanced Placement (AP), IGCSE, International Baccalaureate (IB)
• Bilingual diplomas: Swiss Maturité, International Baccalaureate (IB)
• French-language diplomas: French Baccalaureate, Swiss Maturité

ESL Programme: There is a credit bearing academy on campus for students whose first language is not English and who require additional language support. These students will work to raise their proficiency by attending a variety of English courses through the semester.

Bilingual Programme: From the age of 5, students have the opportunity to follow a bilingual (English and French) programme. Bilingualism leads to more open-mindedness and tolerance and helps children easily learn new languages, creating numerous opportunities for the future.

College and Career Guidance

Our team of college advisors at Collège du Léman are dedicated to guiding students through the college preparation and selection process, helping them

access the most prestigious universities world-wide. Parents are also involved in the process and invited to information evenings. In addition, College fairs are organized throughout the academic year, allowing our students to meet representatives from top universities.

Student Life

Athletics offered: Badminton, Basketball, Cricket, Dance, Football/Soccer, Floor Hockey, Golf, Horse riding, Rugby, Sailing, Skiing,Swimming, Track & Field, Tennis, Volleyball, Yoga and many more!

Fine arts: Music, painting, theatre, dance, choir, orchestra, piano improvisations and many more!

Clubs: School magazine, Student government, Model United Nations (MUN).

Charities: MADS (Make A Difference Society), ZOA (Zambian Orphans Appeal). Students can enjoy our swimming pool, gym, weight and exercise rooms, track, library, computer labs, art studios, music and dance studios, basketball courts, and much more on the school's campus.

Dwight School London

(Founded 1885)
6 Friern Barnet Lane, London, N11 3LX UK

Tel: +44 (0)20 8920 0600
Fax: +44 (0)20 8211 4605
Email: admissions@dwightlondon.org
Website: www.dwightlondon.org
Head: Mr David Rose MA(Ed), BA, CertEd, FRSA
School type: Coeducational Day

Age range of pupils: 2–18+
No. of pupils enrolled as at 01/05/2014:
Lower School: 170
Upper School: 200
Fees per annum as at 01/09/2014:
May vary upon application
Average class size: max 20

Dwight School London is an independent international school established in 1972 dedicated to igniting the spark of genius in every child.

Dwight London is one of the first schools in the UK to offer the full International Baccalaureate programme. Widely known as one of the most challenging and respected pre-university courses of study in the world, the IB is the only universal curriculum where students are graded according to international benchmarks.

At Dwight School London education is built on three pillars: personalised learning, community and global vision. We are committed to helping our students achieve more by providing a caring, stimulating and positive environment. Through blending the innovative IB with Dwight's unique pillars, students are able to attain their goals and be prepared for life as responsible, confident, compassionate, and capable citizens.

Our teachers are committed to recognizing and developing each child's spark of genius, and our focus is on individual progress and growth. Through extensive language and theatre arts programmes, a wide-ranging sports programme, state-of-the-art technology instruction, public service activities and international trips, Dwight London students are well-prepared for university entrance and global citizenship.

Dwight School London is a member of The Dwight Schools, which is a global network of campuses and programs in New York, Canada, Seoul, and Beijing.

Ecole Active Bilingue Jeannine Manuel

(Founded 1954)

70 rue du Théâtre, Paris, 75015 France

Tel: +33 1 44 37 00 80

Fax: +33 1 45 79 06 66

Email: admissions@eabjm.net

Website: www.eabjm.org

Principal: Elisabeth Zéboulon

School type: Coeducational Day

Age range of pupils: 4–18

No. of pupils enrolled as at 01/04/2014: 2390

Boys: 1148 **Girls:** 1242

Fees per annum as at 01/04/2014:

Day: €5,118–€5,414

IB Classes: €16,920

Average class size: 27

EABJM is a non-profit pre-K-12 coeducational school founded in 1954 with the mission to develop international understanding through bilingual (French/English) education. An associated UNESCO school, EABJM has become the largest non-denominational independent school in France, with more than 2300 pupils representing over 70 nationalities and every major cultural tradition. The school's academic excellence matches its diversity: EABJM is regularly ranked among the top five of all 121 Paris high schools (state and independent) for its overall academic performance.

Each year, EABJM welcomes more than 100 new non-French speaking pupils who enrol in 'adaptation' classes where they follow a French immersion programme. A senior advisor follows them closely and, the following year, they join the mainstream where they continue to be supported with a special French programme, which involves three weekly hours of special French classes over and above the standard French curriculum.

THE LOWER AND MIDDLE SCHOOL follow the National Curriculum with several exceptions: English is taught every day and, in middle school, sciences, history and geography are taught in English. The curriculum is enriched at all levels, not only with a more advanced English language and literature curriculum, but also, for example, with Chinese language instruction (compulsory in grades 3-4-5), an integrated science programme in lower school, and independent research projects in middle school.

IN UPPER SCHOOL, tenth graders follow the National Curriculum. In 11th grade, pupils choose between the standard French Baccalaureate, the French OIB (International Option within the French

Baccalaureate) and the International Baccalaureate. Out of a graduating class of 192 students in 2013, 50 took the IB, 131 opted for the French OIB, and the balance chose the standard French Baccalaureate. (As the IB is not subsidized, its tuition is more than three times the French curriculum tuition.)

Over the past three years, approximately 22% of our students have gone to US colleges or universities, 28% chose the UK, 12% chose Canada, 36% entered the French higher education system, and the balance pursued their education all over the world.

Admission

Although admission is competitive and applications typically exceed available spaces by a ratio of 5:1, every effort is made to reserve space for international applicants, including children of families who expect to remain in France for a limited period of time and wish to combine a cultural immersion in French education with the ability to re-enter their own school systems and excel.

EF Academy Oxford

EF Academy
International Boarding Schools

Pullens Lane, Headington, Oxfordshire
OX3 0DT UK

Tel: Admissions: +41 41 41 74 525
Email: admissionsia@ef.com
Website: www.ef.com/academy
Head of School: Ms Ted McGrath
School type: Coeducational Boarding

Age range of pupils: 16–19
No. of pupils enrolled as at 01/04/2014: 180
Fees per annum as at 01/04/2014:
Full Boarding: £25,000

EF Academy International Boarding Schools prepare students from 75 countries for a global future with a superior secondary school education in the US or UK. At EF Academy, we believe in every student's ability to succeed. We empower them to do so through our renowned curricula, as well as quality one-on-one relationships with teachers and mentors alike.

Built into every course is an emphasis on multi-lingualism, International travel, and intercultural exchange which helps distinguish our student's academic credentials to both university admissions officers and future employers.

The School

Our school is situated in the illustrious city of Oxford, renowned for its scholastic tradition and rich cultural and architectural heritage. EF Academy students join Oxford's vibrant academic community, which attracts leading scholars from around the world.

Ten minutes from Oxford's center, the newly renovated campus has multimedia classrooms, a fully-equipped gym, state-of-the-art science and computer labs, wireless internet access, a library, cafeteria and lounge. The school has a truly international atmosphere, with students from over 75 different countries living and studying alongside each other.

Academics

We offer proven academic programs that cater to a range of learning goals. Students who plan to attend university in the USA or UK can prepare for the IB Diploma. Those interested pursuing their studies in the UK benefit from EF Academy's A level preparation program.

We have a track record of academic excellence with 45% of students receiving A/A* grades at A level, compared with the national average of 27%.

University Placements

Not only have many of our students been accepted into Top 10 universities including Oxford, Cambridge, LSE, Warwick and Bath, they have also been admitted to courses that are deemed to be the best in the country for their subject, such as accounting at the University of Warwick, law at University College London, and chemical engineering at the University of Birmingham.

Pastoral Care

At EF Academy teachers are passionate about preparing students for a multicultural world. Each student is assigned a personal tutor whose role is to monitor the student's academic progress and general welfare.

Students are encouraged to nurture their talents and develop new skills and confidence. In addition, dedicated university counselors work 1-on-1 with each student to ensure the highest possible university placement.

Residential Life

Accommodation is offered in on-campus dormitories or with host families, where students can benefit from full immersion into British culture and language; both options provide a safe, supportive and comfortable home away from home.

EF Academy Torbay

International Boarding Schools

EF House, Castle Road, Torquay, Devon
TQ1 3BG UK

Tel: Admissions: +41 41 41 74 525
Email: admissionsia@ef.com
Website: www.ef.com/academy
Head of School: Mr Trevor Spence
School type: Coeducational Boarding

Age range of pupils: 14–19
No. of pupils enrolled as at 01/04/2014: 280
Fees per annum as at 01/04/2014:
Full Boarding: £22,650
IGCSE Grades 9 & 10: £22,050

EF Academy International Boarding Schools prepare students from 75 countries for a global future with a superior secondary school education in the US or UK. At EF Academy, we believe in every student's ability to succeed. We empower them to do so through our renowned curricula, as well as quality one-on-one relationships with teachers and mentors alike.

Built into every course is an emphasis on multi-lingualism, International travel, and intercultural exchange which helps distinguish our student's academic credentials to both university admissions officers and future employers.

The School

The EF Academy campus is situated in a modern-day castle on a hill overlooking the city of Torbay, a popular tourist destination on England's scenic south-west coast. The school recently underwent a multi-million dollar renovation which included a new state-of-the-art building with spacious multimedia classrooms, technology center, interactive science laboratories, art studios, student lounge and study areas.

Academics

Education at EF Academy is highly personal and a range of internationally renowned programs are offered to meet the individual needs of each student. Our academic staff prepares students who are interested in continuing on with university studies in the United Kingdom, for the IGCSE, A level and IB Diploma exams.

EF Academy has a track record of academic excellence with 45% of students receiving A/A* grades at A level, compared with the national average of 27%.

University Placements

The EF Academy class of 2014 is on course for another year of success. Our students have been accepted into some of the best universities in the United Kingdom, including Top 10 schools like Cambridge, UCL, Durham, Exeter, Imperial, Warwick and Bath. 36% of our students have been admitted into one of the Top 10 UK universities for their chosen subject.

Pastoral Care

Personal tutors provide one-to-one individualized support and guidance. Each student is assigned a personal tutor whose role is to monitor the student's academic progress and general welfare. Students are encouraged to nurture their talents and develop new skills and confidence. In addition, dedicated university counselors work 1-on-1 with each student to ensure the highest possible university placement.

Residential Life

Most students at EF Academy Torbay live with local host families, which helps to immerse them in British culture and lifestyle. An off-campus dormitory is also available for students that prefer a residential environment.

GAU The American College

AMERICAN COLLEGE
NICOSIA · KYRENIA

Karmi Campus, Karaoglanoglu, Girne, via Mersin 10, Turkey
Tel: +90 392 650 2220
Fax: +90 392 650 2232
Email:
gaucollege@gau-americancollege.k12.tr

Website: www.gau-americancollege.k12.tr
Founder & Chairman of the Board:
Serhat Akpinar
College Principal: Aysu Balkanlar
College Vice Principals: Koray Emirhoca/
Sermin Mayin
International Prep School Principal:
Paula Branch
Elementary School Principal:
Nagihan Diner
Nursery Principal: Binnur Saymaz

Summer School Director: Celal Sakka
Summer School Email: summerschool@
gau.edu.tr
School type: Coeducational Day
Age range of pupils: 2–18
No. of pupils enrolled as at 01/09/2014: 858
Boys: 407 *Girls:* 447
Fees per annum as at 01/09/2014:
Annual Fees: €3,655 – €5,365
Registration Fee: €100
Transportation Fee: €655

GAU The American College is an independent school offering education to students between the ages of 2 and 18. It aims to provide a high quality, internationally based education to students of different nationalities.

GAU The American College follows a British-based curriculum with Turkish taught throughout the grades. In the elementary sections of the College our students are prepared for the Cambridge Young Learners exams (Starters, Movers and Flyers). In the College our students are offered KET, PET, IELTS, IGCSE as well as AS/A. All staff are fully qualified and hold degrees and teaching credentials. The teaching staff has been recruited internationally with eight different nationalities represented.

The school is located at the base of the Besparmak Mountains, overlooking the Mediterranean. The facilities have fully functional multimedia, internet connected computer labs, science labs, music hall, art studio, dance studios, basketball and tennis courts, indoor sports salon and swimming facilities in addition to the classrooms.

The program offered by the school includes a variety of non-curricular activities for all pupils to ensure that the education offers creative, artistic and expressive areas to complement the academic areas. Participation in the local and regional tournaments such as basketball, track and field, football, swimming, fencing as well as art, mathematics, science and language continue throughout the year.

The school academic year begins in September and finishes in June. Summer programmes are available. An English examination is required for those students wishing to enter second, third, fourth, fifth and sixth grade. Provision is made for ESL students.

GEMS World Academy – Etoy International School

GEMS World Academy
ETOY

La Tuilière 18, Etoy, 1163 Switzerland

Tel: +41 (0)21 964 18 18
Fax: +41 (0)21 964 12 79
Email: registrar_gwe@gemsedu.com
Website:
www.gemsworldacademy-etoy.com

Founding Principal: Ms Audrey Peverelli
School type: Coeducational Day, Weekly and Full Boarding
Age range of pupils: 2–16

Preparation for success

GEMS World Academy-Etoy International School prepares young people for success, ensuring they fulfil their potential.

Every teacher brings a wealth of first-class teaching expertise and a genuine passion to actively engage students in the learning process.

Technology-rich learning environments, dedicated parent engagement programmes, and a unique focus on individual development ensure our students acquire the vital skills and versatility they need for the future.

We offer tuition in English for children aged 3-16, Pre-Kindergarten to Grade 10. We also provide extensive language availability in French, German and Spanish and our World Language Learning Centre provides even further opportunities for linguistic competence.

The Little GEMS Nursery's unique approach to learning is carefully planned to provide an outstanding early years education for children aged 2-3.

Scholarships are offered across all disciplines including the arts, music, academic subjects and sports.

The school also offers after-school programmes led by school staff and qualified sport coaches.

GEMS Education is a pioneering education company. Through our schools, consulting practice and our charitable foundation we are advancing education for all. Every day in our schools around the world, we prepare thousands of children of all ages for real world success.

We are a catalyst and delivery partner. We work with governments, donor agencies and private clients to improve education systems, and provide vital training for young people in an increasingly competitive world.

Through the Varkey GEMS Foundation we campaign for, and support initiatives that change lives through education.

International College Spain

International College Spain

A NORD ANGLIA EDUCATION SCHOOL

(Founded 1980)

C/Vereda Norte, 3, La Moraleja, 28109

Alcobendas, (Madrid) Spain

Tel: +34 91 650 2398

Fax: +34 91 650 1035

Email: icsinfo@wclschools.org

Website: www.icsmadrid.org

Director: Jeremy Singer

School type: Coeducational Day

Age range of pupils: 3–18

No. of pupils enrolled as at 19/05/2014: 705

Fees per annum as at 01/09/2014:

Day: €8,700 – €16,530

Teacher/pupil ratio: 1:8

International College Spain, founded in 1980 by the late Manouchehr Farhangi, is the leading international school in Madrid. ICS is a day school offering primary and secondary education to boys and girls of more than 56 nationalities from 3 to 18 years old. The school is the only one in Madrid to offer a full international curriculum throughout the whole age range (kindergarten 3 to grade 12) in English, by means of the three prestigious International Baccalaureate Programmes. The IB diploma gives access to the top universities worldwide.

The school campus is situated on three hectares of land in La Moraleja, ten kilometers north of the centre of Madrid. School bus routes serve much of the city and there is excellent public transport. The facilities include separate buildings for primary and secondary schools, five science laboratories, a large art department, music rooms, computer labs, two libraries, an interactive learning centre, extensive rooms for independent study, an auditorium, a gymnasium and a cafeteria. The teaching staff is multinational, experienced and fully-qualified. The school year, from September to June with winter and spring breaks, is divided into three academic terms.

ICS has acquired a reputation for encouraging high academic achievement within a caring and stimulating environment. Central to the educational philosophy of International College Spain is the desire to promote international understanding whilst preparing its students for the challenges of life in a multicultural global society.

ICS is part of the renowned Nord Anglia Education Group that enhances learning in 28 and growing schools across the globe, bringing the best of the world's educational practice to the student. The school is accredited by the International Baccalaureate Organisation, The New England Association of Schools and Colleges and The Council of International Schools. ICS is approved by the Spanish Ministry of Education as a foreign school for the education of both Spanish and foreign students.

International Community School

International Community School

(Founded 1979)

4 York Terrace East, Regents Park, London, NW1 4PT UK

Primary Tel: +44 20 7935 1206

Secondary tel: +44 20 7402 0416

Email: admissions@ics.uk.net

Website: www.icschool.co.uk

Head of Secondary School: Ms Rose Threlfall

Head of Primary School: Mr Stuart Pollard

School type: Coeducational Day

Age range of pupils: 3–18

No. of pupils enrolled as at 01/09/2013: 250

Fees per annum as at 01/09/2014:

Day: £22,100

Average class size: 16

The International Community School is an independent, International Baccalaureate World School, located in central London. The School is accredited by the IB, the British Council and is also a member of the European Council of International Schools.

We have a Primary campus for students aged 3-11 years on the edge of Regents Park and a Secondary School campus for 11-18-year-olds close to Hyde Park. ICS offers the IB Primary Years, Middle Years and Diploma programmes. Our class sizes are small, and there is a strong focus on personalised learning. We have also developed our own specialised programmes for those seeking English language development or support with Special Educational Needs.

Our School community of approximately 260 students represent 45 different nationalities and around 15% of our students are British. The teaching faculty is also representative of our student body, originating from all parts of the world and this adds to the richness of our curriculum and extra-curricular programmes.

At ICS, we strive to ensure that each of our students has a fully integrated and supported, dynamic personalised learning programme that meets their specific educational requirements. We use Information Communication Technology in a variety of innovative ways to engage and encourage our students to become lifelong learners. In addition we ensure curriculum enrichment through the 'Outdoor Classroom'. This entails frequent educational visits within London, spending time at our Outdoor Education Centre at Bawdsey Manor in Suffolk and our unique 'Travel and Learn' opportunities.

The extensive Travel and Learn programme operates throughout the year for all students with expeditions to places such as, the Galapagos Islands, South Africa, Iceland, Ghana and China. We also offer lunchtime and after school clubs and activities for students ranging from football and basketball to rock climbing, capoeira and cooking clubs. Each year we also have a large drama production at the Secondary school and concerts and exhibitions at the Primary school.

The School also provides a door-to-door minibus service that serves most of central London.

For more information please contact the Admissions Office – admissions@ icschool.co.uk

Germany

International School of Bremen

(Founded 1998)
Badgasteiner Str 11, D-28359 Bremen,
Germany

Tel: +49 421 5157790
Fax: +49 421 51577955
Email: office@isbremen.de
Website: www.isbremen.de
Director: Malcolm Davis
Appointed: 2005
Head of Secondary School: Kim Walton
Head of Elementary School:
Susanna Bergmann

School type: Coeducational Day
Age range of pupils: 3–18
No. of pupils enrolled as of 01/09/2014: 400
Fees per annum as of 01/09/2014:
€9,950 – €15,150
Average class size: 9-18
Teacher/pupil ratio: 1:10

The Mission
In partnership with family and community, The International School of Bremen (ISB) seeks a high educational excellence through establishing a varied and dynamic learning environment. It provides an academic, social and physical education in English that promotes the development of responsible, global citizens who are prepared for our ever-changing world.

The City
Bremen is located in the north of Germany. Its city centre reflects a rich medieval trading background, while its modern industrial base draws high tech business that supports the image of Germany's 'Space City'. A public and private university creates a strong academic tradition of which the ISB is part.

The School
ISB is a private, coeducational, college-preparatory, English-speaking school. It was established in 1998 to serve students of the international community of Bremen providing an educational alternative to the German State system. Presently our students and staff represent 42 countries from across the world. Class sizes are generally small with an average of 18 students per grade. The school occupies a purpose-built facility in the Technology Park adjacent to the University Bremen. ISB is a non-selective school, however SEN support is limited.

Faculty
The dedicated and experienced teachers at ISB come from a number of countries (Australia, Germany, India, The Netherlands, Canada, Spain, United Kingdom, South Africa, Burma and USA). The members of our teaching staff are

certified according to the standards of their home countries. Many of our teachers hold Master Degrees or Doctorates.

Membership & Accreditation

The School is a member of CfBT, ECIS, CIS and IBO and is accredited by the State of Bremen, Germany.

The Curriculum

Students range in age from 3-19 years. The school offers an international curriculum drawing upon best practices from the UK, USA, Australia and the host country with all instruction in English except for foreign language classes. Specialist teachers provide instruction in music, physical education, art, drama and languages. An ESAC (English Support across the curriculum) is offered for those students who need assistance with English.

Elementary (Early Learning 1-3 through Grade 5) Within the ISB Elementary Section the International Primary Curriculum (IPC) is offered. This is a widely recognized course of study that has clear academic benchmarks that set standards for basic skills on which to build an upper level education.

IMYC (Grades 6 through 8) All students pursue a broad based academic programme guided by the International Middle Years Curriculum. Additionally, three foreign languages are offered: Spanish, French and German. Students

bringing other mother languages can often be accommodated within the tradition of an international school. We have been able to support Farsi, Chinese and Russian. Those students with weak English are supported in additional classes.

IGCSE (Grades 9 and 10) The students participate in the IGCSE programme with a culminating examination in May of Grade 10. Completion and success is not a prerequisite to enter into the IB but is used as an indicator of achievement and future success.

International Baccalaureate (IB) Diploma Programme (Grades 11 and 12) The IB is a two year pre-university course designed to facilitate the mobility of students and promote international understanding. The comprehensive course of study for the IB Diploma is designed to provide students with a balanced education. All students are assessed externally by the IB and if successful are awarded International Baccalaureate Diplomas.

International School of Düsseldorf e.V.

Learning to Be a World Citizen

INTERNATIONAL SCHOOL OF DÜSSELDORF E.V.

(Founded 1968)
Niederrheinstrasse 336, Düsseldorf,

40489 Germany
Tel: +49 211 (0) 9406 712
Fax: +49 211 (0) 9406 804
Email: info@isdedu.de
Website: www.isdedu.de
Head: Simon Head
Appointed: 2014

School type: Coeducational Day
Age range of pupils: 4–19
No. of pupils enrolled as at 01/09/2014:
Boys: 540 *Girls:* 542
Average class size: 16-18
Teacher/pupil ratio: 1:8

ISD, a school with a tradition

Founded more than 46 years ago, the International School of Düsseldorf is serving the needs of more than 1,080 students from around 50 countries. ISD is first and foremost a community of learners gathered together on a bright and inviting

campus situated a short walk from the Rhine in the beautiful, historic suburb of Kaiserswerth; a safe place where inquiry precedes the construction of knowledge and where teamwork precedes success. Here, dedication, continuous evaluation and review as well as mentoring and

parental involvement encourage local and international students to develop holistically.

The early childhood centre houses four year olds and provides a full-day programme. A careful mix of structure and play encourages children to explore and find success in a broad range of classroom activities. Elementary school is where children from preparatory to grade 5 enjoy an educational programme in a caring environment designed to foster the love of learning at a very early age. The Senior School academic programme covering grades 6-12 is broadly based throughout as well as rigorous, challenging and stimulating.

School buildings are spacious, modern and well-equipped. A 400 seat theatre supports an extensive visual and performing arts programme. Two gymnasiums and three football fields serve a comprehensive physical education and competitive sports programme. School teams regularly compete in local and international competitions.

An emphasis on teaching and learning for understanding is underpinned by an extensive professional development programme. Small classes are led by a creative, enthusiastic and committed faculty.

The rigorous academic programme is complemented by an extensive counseling and pastoral care programme, as well as EAL and learning support. Over 98% of graduating students gain admission to universities.

ISD carries full accreditation through CIS and NEASC.

It is the aim of the International School of Düsseldorf to help all its students to become responsible world citizens and leaders in tomorrow's world.

International School of London (ISL) Surrey

(Founded 1991)
Old Woking Road, Woking, Surrey
GU22 8HY UK

Tel: +44 (0)1483 750409
Fax: +44 (0)1483 730962
Email: admissions@islsurrey.org
Website: www.islsurrey.org
Head of School: Dr James A Doran
Appointed: Feb 2011
School type: Coeducational Day

Age range of pupils: 2–14
No. of pupils enrolled as at 01/09/2014:
Boys: 95 **Girls:** 95
Fees per annum as at 01/09/2014:
Day: £9,000–£17,550
Average class size: 14
Teacher/pupil ratio: 1:7

The International School of London (ISL) Surrey is a coeducational day school currently accepting students from age 2 through 15 (rising 16), nursery through grade 10, expanding one grade level per year, reaching 12th grade in the academic year 2016-17. The school has consistently achieved outstanding Office for Standards in Education (Ofsted) reports and is one of only nine schools of over 1600 worldwide accredited at the International Primary Curriculum Mastering Level.

The vibrant Middle Years Programme provides students with learning attitudes appropriate for adolescents in a global society. Attributes of the programme include an iPad Technology Programme and the Open World Experience, a regular cycle of planning, experience and reflecting on student-directed activities.

ISL Surrey is a candidate school for both the International Baccalaureate (IB) Middle Years and Diploma Programmes.

ISL Surrey provides a student-centred and inquiry-based academic programme which values both independent and collaborative work. The school's low teacher-student ratio permits a high degree of individualisation, ensuring that each student is both supported and challenged. Although the language of instruction is English, mother tongue literacy is supported from an early age. Beginning with the three-year-olds, up to five class periods of mother tongue lessons are provided each week within the class day. Students whose first language is English begin foreign language study at age three. EAL is provided as necessary.

The school is situated on a 10.3-acre campus. Its purpose built facilities include an early childhood centre and a primary building with classrooms, gymnasium and stage, music room, library, IT centre, an art room and state-of-the-art science laboratory for Middle Years students. With the active participation of students, parents and staff, the school is currently engaged in a building project which will more than double the size of the current school and include a new gymnasium, theatre, library, science laboratories, dining room, offices and specialised classrooms.

ISL Surrey is part of the International School of London Group which celebrated its 40th anniversary in 2012. The other ISL schools are situated in London, UK and Doha, Qatar.

King's College, The British School of Madrid

King's College
The British School of Madrid

(Founded 1969)

Paseo de los Andes 35, 28761 Soto de Viñuelas, Madrid, Spain
Tel: +34 918 034 800
Fax: +34 918 036 557
Email: info@kingscollege.es
Website: www.kingscollege.es
Head: Andrew Rattue MA (Oxon) MA (London) PGCE (London)

Appointed: September 2014
School type: Coeducational Day & Boarding
Age range of pupils: 2–18
No. of pupils enrolled as at 01/09/2014: 1405
No. of boarders: 44

King's College Madrid is a coeducational day and boarding school which provides British education for children from the age of 2 to 18 years (Pre-Nursery to Year 13). It is located on an attractive 12-acre site in a leafy suburb, just 20 minutes' drive from Madrid and the main airport.

King's College is one of the most successful British schools in Europe. After IGCSEs and A levels, students go on to study at top universities in the UK, Spain and the USA.

The school has over 1400 pupils which allows a wide range of subjects to be offered at IGCSE and at A level.

Since it was founded in 1969, King's College has gained a reputation for high academic standards. An experienced careers and university entrance advisory department is available to all pupils and the Oxbridge preparatory group prepares students applying to Oxford and Cambridge universities. Just recently pupils have gone on to study at Oxford, Cambridge, Berkeley, Yale, LSE, Imperial College London, UCL, Stanford and many other top universities in the UK, Spain and the USA.

Our boarding house opened in September 2011 and offers some of the best boarding accommodation in Europe. Tenbury House is home to over 44 pupils from all over the world. The new facilities offer a 'home from home' environment with shared and individual bedrooms all with en-suite bathrooms, underfloor heating and wireless internet. In addition there is a dining room, a common room, a TV room, a study room, a kitchen that pupils can use to make light meals and a laundry. During the evenings and weekends, the students in Tenbury House have full use of these facilities and can also take advantage of many of the school's sports facilities.

King's College is the only school in Madrid currently inspected by the Independent Schools Inspectorate.

King's Saint Michael's College

King's *Saint Michael's* College

(Founded 1856)

Oldwood Road, Tenbury Wells,
Worcestershire WR15 8PH UK
Tel: 01584 811300
Fax: 01584 811221
Email: info@st-michaels.uk.com
Website: www.st-michaels.uk.com
Principal: Stuart Higgins BA, MEd, FRSA
Appointed: September 1996

School type: Coeducational Boarding
Age range of pupils: 14–18
No. of pupils enrolled as at 01/09/2014: 108
No. of boarders: 108
Fees per annum as at 01/09/2014:
Full Boarding: £24,995–£26,895
Average class size: av 9-10
Teacher/pupil ratio: 1:7

Saint Michael's College, part of King's Group, is a small, friendly, international secondary boarding school offering GCSE and A levels, university foundation and summer courses to students from all over the world.

Specialist English language provision is provided and plays a major role in the curriculum with almost all students going on to study at universities in Britain.

The college, which has been listed by English Heritage for its architectural interest, is an impressive Victorian building set in 10 hectares of its own grounds. Great Britain has a reputation for the quality of its education. Saint Michael's continues in this tradition by offering intensive tuition by well-qualified teachers in small classes. The great variety of nationalities who study at the school provides a stimulating intellectual atmosphere for all.

The school is coeducational and offers the choice of residential or host family accommodation in carefully selected local families. A varied and exciting sports and social programme, including excursions, sports teams and cultural activities, is also provided. Two new halls of residence have recently been constructed and opened in September 2013, they provide an extremely high quality accommodation for students, offering a 'home from home' environment with shared and individual bedrooms,

common rooms and fully-equipped kitchens. During the evenings and weekends, the students have full use of these facilities and can also take advantage of many of the school's sports facilities.

The students are closely supervised by friendly, approachable staff who are

on hand 24 hours a day to offer close personal attention. On arrival students are allocated a member of the teaching staff as their personal tutor. It is the role of the tutor to ensure that each student settles into school, is happy, feels looked after and is given any help required on academic and non-academic matters.

KSI Montenegro

KNIGHTSBRIDGE
SCHOOLS INTERNATIONAL

Seljanovo bb, Porto Montenegro, Tivat,
Montenegro
Tel: +382 32 672 655

Fax: +382 32 672 368
Email: info@KSI-Montenegro.com
Website: www.KSI-Montenegro.com
Head of School: Linda Winch
Head of Boarding: Rachael Murfet
School type: Coeducational Day & Boarding

Age range of pupils: 3–16
Fees per annum as at 01/04/2014:
Day: €11,850–€13,500
Full Boarding: €11,500
Average class size: 6-12

KSI Montenegro was founded in 2010 on the principles of global citizenship, as a member of an international network of schools. KSI has a proud history and heritage of academic excellence in all aspects of international education.

Located in the tranquil surroundings of the Boka Bay, in one of the most beautiful fjords in the world, KSI offers students a challenging and rewarding educational experience. Students benefit from our stimulating surroundings which promote our healthy body, healthy mind philosophy.

KSI Montenegro is authorised by the International Baccalaureate to offer the Primary Years Programme, and is has achieved candidacy for the MYP and DP. In due course, the school intends to offer the IBDP in September 2015. It is also a school licensed by the Montenegrin Ministry of Education.

Boarding at KSI is new to our community, opened in September 2013 and offering a British model of pastoral support with an international ethos. KSI Montenegro strives to create an environment of comfort, safety and fun for boarders, offering a homely, yet challenging education experience.

The main language of instruction is English, with the school is committed to the implementation of the International Baccalaureate Programmes as our curriculum.

KSI Montenegro provides a holistic, balanced and varied curriculum that addresses the needs of all learners and supports the development of learning strategies that prepare them for each stage of their education. All students are encouraged to take initiative and develop personal responsibility, and are expected to actively participate in developing a friendly, welcoming and culturally understanding environment. This adds to the holistic experience of boarding and allows students to develop as a community of empowered and engaged global citizens.

KSI Montenegro aims to develop the knowledge, skills and values of learners through active inquiry, participation and reflection, so that they may become collaborative and compassionate global citizens who are committed to making a positive difference.

The school is developing multilingualism through its language programmes by currently offering the host country language, as well as French, Spanish, Russian and German lessons. In addition, all learners have access to over 25 other languages, through the approach which integrates both technology and language learning, Rosetta Stone.

KSI has developed an inspirational learning environment that supports the multiple and interconnected learning needs of each child through the use of technology, various sports and the arts.

Marymount International School London

(Founded 1955)
George Road, Kingston upon Thames,
Surrey KT2 7PE UK

Tel: +44 (0)20 8949 0571
Fax: +44 (0)20 8336 2485
Email:
admissions@marymountlondon.com
Website: www.marymountlondon.com
Headmistress: Ms Sarah Gallagher MA,
HDip in Ed
School type: Girls' Day & Boarding
Age range of girls: 11–18

No. of pupils enrolled as at 01/09/2014: 252
Sixth Form: 115
No. of boarders: 90
Fees per annum as at 01/09/2014:
Day: £18,090–£20,670
Weekly Boarding: £30,840–£33,420
Full Boarding: £32,325–£34,905
Average class size: 12
Teacher/pupil ratio: 1:6

Marymount International School is an independent Catholic day and boarding school – welcoming girls of all faiths, aged 11-18.

A small school with only 250 pupils, Marymount offers a supportive, nurturing environment which prepares the students for life in a global setting. Part of an international network of schools, Marymount has an inclusive ethos which achieves a common purpose for young women from over 40 nationalities.

In 1979 Marymount was the first girls' school in the UK to adopt the IB Diploma programme in the belief that it provides the most challenging and stimulating educational offering to the Sixth Former. The IB programme sets out to develop inquiring, critical minds, enabling pupils to become independent thinkers and 'active, lifelong learners'. In concert with Marymount's Catholic values the IB also sets out 'to develop caring young people who help to create a better and more peaceful world through intercultural understanding and respect'. Graduates attest that they feel they have been stretched academically, spiritually and socially: they are fully prepared for university and for life.

The School has a proud history of excellent academic results, consistently ranking within the top 5% of IB schools globally. Typically 20% of our graduates achieve more than 40 points (achieved by only 4% worldwide) and up to 40% graduate with a Bilingual Diploma. Although the largest single national group is British, additional languages taught include Spanish, German, French, Japanese, Korean and Mandarin for native speakers. In preparation for the IB, the school offers the Middle Years Programme: stretching students without the need for incessant testing.

Set in a leafy campus close to the London South West postcodes, school buses cover routes from amongst others Sloane Square, South Kensington and Fulham.

The School has a rolling admissions programme and students go on to top universities worldwide.

MEF International School

INTERNATIONAL SCHOOLS

(Founded 1998)

Ulus Mah. Öztopuz Cad., Leylak Sok.

34340, Ulus/Besiktas, Istanbul, Turkey

Tel: +90 (212) 287 6900 ext 1340

Fax: +90 (212) 287 3870/4681

Email: contact@mef.k12.tr

Website:

www.mefinternationalschools.com

Head of School: Figen Sönmez

Primary Principal: Dr. Michael Keppler

Secondary Principal: Jeffrey Woolley

School type: Co-educational Day

Religious Denomination: Non-denominational

Age range of pupils: 3–18

No. of pupils enrolled as at 01/09/2014: 425

Fees per annum as at 01/09/2014:

US$10,066 – US$25,817

Our Motto

"Building Bridges between Countries and Cultures"

Our School

MEF International School (MEF IS) is accredited by the Council of International Schools (CIS) and New England Association of Schools and Colleges (NEASC). MEF IS, with its fully authorized International Baccalaureate Primary Years Programme (IBPYP) in the primary school to its IB Diploma Programme

(IBDP) in the secondary school, provides quality education. It is a fully authorized Cambridge International Examinations Centre (CIE), offering Cambridge Secondary 1 with Checkpoint exams, Cambridge Secondary 2 with IGCSEs, and AS/A levels in the secondary school. Additionally, MEF IS is the sole ACT Examination Center in Istanbul. In order to meet the needs of diverse learners, support is provided through English Language Learning (ELL), learning

support, enrichment/extension, guidance counseling and university counseling.

MEF IS high school students have the opportunity to join Model European Parliament (MEP) and Model United Nations (MUN) sessions. Students participate in international MEP conferences to represent Turkey. MUN students attend both local and international conferences and represent the school by serving on the delegations of various countries.

Our Students

MEF IS has a diverse student body with students from over 48 different countries. All enrolled students hold a passport other than Turkish. However, the IBDP accommodates both international and Turkish national students who meet entry requirements.

Academic Success

MEF IS middle school students scored well above average in maths, science, and English on the Cambridge Checkpoint examinations in 2013. At IGCSE, 74% of our students scored A*-C in June 2013 exams. Since IB Diploma Programme authorization in September 1998, over 90% of our students have successfully obtained their IB Diploma.

Our Faculty

There are 74 full-time fully certified staff members, representing over 15 different nationalities. All teachers hold a university degree and a teaching certificate in their field of instruction. The whole school student to teacher ratio is 6:1.

Our Location

The school is situated in the heart of Istanbul on a four acre campus nestled in the hills above Ortaköy, only minutes away from the Bosphorus Strait in the midst of residential neighborhoods.

Mougins School

MOUGINS
SCHOOL

(Founded 1964)

615 Avenue Dr Maurice Donat, CS 12180,
06252 MOUGINS Cedex, France

Tel: +33 (0)4 93 90 15 47
Fax: +33 (0)4 93 75 31 40
Email: information@mougins-school.com
Website: www.mougins-school.com
Headmaster: Mr Brian G Hickmore
Appointed: September 1995
Deputy Head: Ms Jane Hart
Secondary Head: Mrs Joanna Povall
Primary Head: Mrs Christine Bearman

School type: Coeducational International Day
Age range of pupils: 3–18
No. of pupils enrolled as at 01/09/2014: 518
Boys: 275 **Girls:** 243 **Sixth Form:** 79
Fees per annum as at 01/09/2014:
€5,600 – €15,520
Average class size: 22
Teacher/pupil ratio: 1:14

Prepare for tomorrow's world with an education worthy of today

Unique on the Côte d'Azur, Mougins School follows the British curriculum and offers an advanced international programme to students of 3-18 years of age, of over 40 nationalities. On completion of their (I)GCSE, AS and A level examinations, students gain worldwide entry into further education in prestigious universities.

Situated in Mougins and within the high technology park of Sophia Antipolis, the purpose-built campus comprises six state-of-the-art buildings as well as sports areas, recreational areas and areas of quiet contemplation. The campus houses not only well equipped classrooms, but four science laboratories, two computer suites, two art studios, two music studios, a superb gymnasium, an examinations room, a dedicated performing arts building, a library containing over 10,000 volumes, as well as computers for research, overseen by a librarian. A dining room provides freshly cooked food on a daily basis. These facilities ensure that, together with a high academic standard, the students' physical and cultural development is also encouraged. The school produces two annual concerts and two musicals, together with more intimate theatre and musical performances throughout the year.

The student body regularly participates in fund-raising challenges. In the past the School has purchased a Guide Dog for the Blind. Associated with Comic Relief, the School has supported Red Nose Day for fourteen years. Financial aid, food and clothes were recently given to the Visayas Association in support of the Philippines and action will be taken this year to raise money for education in Cambodia.

Pastoral care is readily available for new families in assisting with the hurdles of relocation. An active Parent Teacher Association organises social events for parents on a regular basis and assists students and staff with activities. Despite its growth; Mougins School retains its caring family atmosphere which complements the high quality of teaching reflected in a 100% pass rate at A level for the past four years.

Oeiras International School

oeiras
international
school

(Founded 2010)
Quinta Nossa Senhora da Conceicao,
Rua Antero de Quental no 7, Barcarena,

2730-013 Portugal
Tel: +351 211935330
Email:
info@oeirasinternationalschool.com
Website:
www.oeirasinternationalschool.com
Principal/IBCC Coordinator: Chari Empis
Head of Curriculum: Francisco Vargas
Head of Pastoral Care: Steven Bruce-Lomba

School type: Coeducational Day
Age range of pupils: 10–18
No. of pupils enrolled as at 01/09/2014:
Boys: 128 *Girls:* 94
Fees per annum as at 01/09/2014:
€10,700 – €17,900
Average class size: 16
Teacher/pupil ratio: 0.1

OIS – Oeiras International School, offers the International Baccalaureate (IB) programmes for Years 6 to 13 (ages 10-18), where students with a range of abilities find success.

Why OIS?

- We invest in our students. OIS is a not-for-profit school: all generated earnings are re-invested in the school for the benefit of the children.
- We have individual care and attention to *each* child – class sizes do not exceed 16 students, so as to facilitate multi-level teaching and to focus on individual learning styles.

- We have created a supportive, caring environment in which students take responsibility for their own learning process.
- Its beautiful campus (3.5 acres) and facilities with separate computer labs, library, science labs, art rooms and versatile sports fields.
- OIS only hires experienced IB teachers with degrees and teaching credentials from their home countries.

This non-for-profit school was founded by a group of parents and teachers deeply committed to academic excellence and intellectual rigour. The sense of community

and freedom amongst the students and teachers is maintained under the IB learner profile umbrella.

For students this means that the school has an innovative and creative character, provides an environment of openness and mutual respect, and develops the individual talents of each and every student. Extracurricular and co-curricular (on Wednesday afternoons) activities focus on creativity and community service. A huge variety of sports activities are also provided.

At OIS happy students are taught by committed and contented teachers.

Queen Ethelburga's Collegiate Foundation

(Founded 1912)
Thorpe Underwood Hall, Ouseburn, York,
North Yorkshire YO26 9SS UK

Tel: 01423 33 33 30
Fax: 01423 33 37 54
Email: info@qe.org
Website: www.qe.org
Principal: Steven Jandrell BA
Appointed: September 2006
School type: Coeducational Day & Boarding
Religious Denomination: Multi-Denominational

Age range of pupils: 3–19
No. of pupils enrolled as at 01/09/2014: 1278
Boys: 684 **Girls:** 594 **Sixth Form:** 557
No. of boarders: 868
Fees per annum as at 01/09/2014:
Day: £7,185–£12,960
Average class size: 20
Teacher/pupil ratio: 1:10

Founded in 1912, Queen Ethelburga's Collegiate is a day and boarding school with 1150 pupils aged from 5 years to 18 years and from over 40 different countries. Set in 220 acres of beautiful North Yorkshire countryside, the campus has some of the most impressive study, boarding and leisure facilities in the independent school sector.

Last year, QE celebrated its best ever A-Level results. Queen Ethelburga's College was ranked the top day and boarding school in the North of England, according to the Daily Telegraph 2013 League Table for percentage A*/A A-Levels and equivalent qualifications. It scored 80% which ranked it top in the North and the fourth UK day and boarding school overall.

Younger pupils study from the age of three years in Chapter House Preparatory School, starting with the Early Year Foundation Stage and child-led and adult-led activities to foster their skills in reading, language and number work.

King's Magna Middle School takes pupils from age 10 years to 14 years. Here the transition is made from class-based teaching to specialist teaching, so that by Years 8 and 9, all subjects will be taught by specialist teachers. The curriculum is based on the National Curriculum, but extends beyond this with a comprehensive programme of sports and creative activities.

By Year 11 students will choose to attend the College, which offers a more traditional academic route of learning with GCSEs and A-Levels, or the Faculty, which offers GCSEs and A-Levels but also more vocational BTEC subjects such as performing arts, fashion or sports science.

For many students though, Queen Ethelburga's is more than a school, it is their home too, and the boarding facilities are simply exemplary. Student bedrooms and apartments are all air-conditioned and have their own en-suite facilities and for the older students, their own kitchen area. Each room has a direct dial telephone, satellite plasma television with timed gaming port and DVD player. House parents are on hand 24 hours a day to help with prep, heat up hot chocolate or to listen to career ideas.

When the school day is over, there are hundreds of activities including regional coaching in sports such as archery and fencing; various arts and music based clubs which regularly perform in QE's King's Theatre, debating societies, science forums and a very active Duke of Edinburgh Scheme and Combined Cadet Force.

New to September 2014 are two sporting academies – the Rugby Academy, supported by Leeds Rugby Academy and Foundation at Leeds Carnegie and the Netball Academy run by Yorkshire Jets. There will be further development of existing programmes in football, swimming, cricket, hockey and basketball.

Queen Ethelburga's motto is about ambition and excellence – "to be the best that I can with the gifts that I have" – it is a school rich in talent and opportunities and well deserves such a maxim.

Rydal Penrhos School

(Founded 1880)
Pwllycrochan Avenue, Colwyn Bay,
Clwyd LL29 7BT UK

Tel: +44 (0)1492 530155
Fax: +44 (0)1492 531872
Email: info@rydalpenrhos.com
Website: www.rydalpenrhos.com
Headmaster: Mr P A Lee-Browne MA
Appointed: April 2008
School type: Coeducational Day &
Boarding
Religious Denomination: Methodist

Age range of pupils: 2–18
No. of pupils enrolled as at 01/09/2014: 537
Boys: 308 **Girls:** 229
No. of boarders: 132
Fees per annum as at 01/09/2014:
Day: £6,360–£14,625
Weekly Boarding: £21,285–£26,250
Full Boarding: £23,655–£29,145
Teacher/pupil ratio: 1:8

Rydal Penrhos offers the kind of education that any parent would wish for their child, in a stunning location. It's a school that allows pupils of all ability to fulfil their academic potential and expects them to develop at least one abiding non-academic passion. It is also a community where everyone benefits from the outstanding pastoral care that is as strong for our day pupils as it is for our boarders. All our pupils aspire to the best while retaining the distinctive Rydal Penrhos respect and consideration for other people. This ethos exists from the start of the Prep school, aged 2½, right through to the Upper Sixth.

The school is a meeting point for international cultures. It nurtures mutual understanding and develops sensitivity to people from all walks of life. It is, above all, a school to which parents can send their children confident in their physical and emotional safety, knowing that the school provides the opportunities and resources for them to flourish and move on fully prepared for the next stage of their lives.

- Top 75 Independent Co-ed boarding schools in the UK, 2013
- Top 40 UK IB Schools, 2013
- GCSE, IGCSE, pre-Sixth (1-year GCSE), A Level and International Baccalaureate all offered
- Pupil to teacher ratio of 1:8, with an average of one form tutor to every 12 pupils

- Small class sizes (max 20 at GCSE, 18 in Sixth form)
- 'Gifted and Talented' programme and Learning Support
- Day and Boarding, full, weekly and flexible
- All major boys' and girls' sports, and weekly sports fixtures against other schools
- RYA accredited sailing school, WRU Rugby Academy
- 45 clubs and societies every week including kayaking, chess, climbing, jewellery design, Model United Nations and Duke of Edinburgh to Gold Level
- Annual educational trips eg 2013-2014 to Thailand, Uganda, France and USA
- Upgraded drama studio, choirs, orchestra and ensembles

"Boarding has taught me to be more social and how to be organised. Rydal Penrhos is awesome and now I have a whole family of new friends." (Gabby, Year 7)

"I love that I can balance my studies with sport, music, drama and community service – and it is thanks to the support of my teachers at RP that I am able to do this. I am grateful to them for always having time for me." (Laura, Upper VI)

"From our point of view the school provides, and has provided, all that we could wish for. We have invested well for our child's future." (Current senior school parent)

Seaford College

(Founded 1884)
Lavington Park, Petworth, West Sussex
GU28 0NB UK

Tel: 01798 867392
Fax: 01798 867606
Email: jmackay@seaford.org
Website: www.seaford.org
Headmaster: J P Green MA BA
School type: Coeducational Boarding & Day
Age range of pupils: 7–18
No. of pupils enrolled as at 01/09/2014: 621

Boys: 436 **Girls:** 185 **Sixth Form:** 143
No. of boarders: 137
Fees per annum as at 01/09/2014:
Day: £8,505–£17,850
Weekly Boarding: £17,625–£23,850
Full Boarding: £27,900
Average class size: 15-20
Teacher/pupil ratio: 1:9

Seaford is a small, friendly co-educational College, situated in an unrivalled position near Petworth, West Sussex. With its own Prep School, Senior School and Sixth Form, the College is located away from the distractions of city life, yet is still within easy reach of cultural and commercial centres. The College accepts day pupils and also offers both full and flexi-boarding for pupils aged 7-18. Seaford College is non-selective school and we are proud to offer an inclusive environment where each individual is known and valued; is given attention and respect. Our aim is to educate the whole person; to find the strengths of each boy and girl and to enable them to succeed. We are a warm, friendly school with excellent teaching and learning across all departments. In addition to this very strong academic core we offer outstanding pastoral care and an impressive programme of extra-curricular activities. With its purpose-built music school and state-of-the-art classrooms for maths and science, plus all-new boys' boarding houses. A typical Seafordian will be an articulate, confident and well-rounded young person. Seaford College offers an inspirational environment where personal bests are achieved both in and outside the classroom. Seaford College is a hidden gem, tucked away at the foot of the picturesque South Downs. Seaford College is easily accessible from London and the M25 and is only 45 minutes by car from Gatwick.

Sherborne International

(Founded 1977)

Newell Grange, Newell, Sherborne, Dorset
DT9 4EZ UK

Tel: 01935 814743

Fax: 01935 816863

Email:
reception@sherborne-international.org

Website: www.sherborne-international.org

Principal: Mrs Mary Arnal BA, MSc, PGCE, FRSA

Appointed: September 2013

School type: Coeducational Boarding

Age range of pupils: 11–16

No. of pupils enrolled as at 01/09/2014: 157

Boys: 100 **Girls:** 57

No. of boarders: 157

Fees per annum as at 01/09/2014:

Full Boarding: £37,500

Average class size: 7

Teacher/pupil ratio: 1:4

Sherborne International (formerly International College) was founded in 1977 by the prestigious Sherborne School and is located close to the centre of the beautiful and historical town of Sherborne. Its own purpose-built campus accommodates up to 165 boys and girls aged 11-16. Sherborne International has an unrivalled reputation for providing the very best start to British independent education for children from non-English speaking, non-British educational backgrounds.

Many students enrol on the one-year I/GCSE programme, although there is also a popular two-year option for those whose English skills are not quite as strong. The junior programmes, for students aged 11-14, provide solid foundations on which students can build their future learning.

Classes are small – usually a maximum of 8 students – and the full British curriculum is provided. Teachers are exceptional and all are trained, and most qualified, in teaching English as an Additional Language, as well as in their own specialist subject. Each student is prepared for any appropriate public examinations, for example GCSEs, IGCSEs, or Cambridge English language examinations. Each year the school records far above average examination results.

Sherborne International aims to equip each student to take his or her place successfully at a traditional British independent boarding school – and a dedicated Future Schooling Adviser offers students expert advice on the best school for them.

In the five boarding houses experienced house parents, supported by teams of residential house tutors, provide excellent pastoral care to ensure the happiness, health and welfare of all students.

Sherborne International offers a long-established, intensive residential summer school programme with a full English curriculum for boys and girls aged 8-17, covering all levels of English from beginner to advanced.

Sherborne International is accredited by both the Independent Schools Inspectorate and by the British Council. It is a member of COBIS, ECIS, ISA, BSA and English UK.

St Andrew's College

(Founded 1894)
Booterstown Avenue, Blackrock,

County Dublin, Ireland
Tel: +353 1 288 2785
Fax: +353 1 283 1627
Email: information@st-andrews.ie
Website: www.st-andrews.ie
Headmaster: Mr Peter Fraser
Appointed: January 2014
School type: Coeducational Day

Religious Denomination: Presbyterian
Age range of pupils: 4–18
No. of pupils enrolled as at 01/09/2014: 1264
Boys: 634 *Girls:* 630 *Sixth Form:* 176
Fees per annum as at 01/09/2014:
Day: €6,400 – €8,450
Average class size: Av 16
Teacher/pupil ratio: 1:12

St Andrew's College was founded in 1894 by members of the Presbyterian community in Dublin. The school was originally located in the centre of the city but, in order to acquire the additional space needed to cope with continuous expansion, a new site in Booterstown, a residential suburb on the south side of the city, was acquired in 1971, inaugurating a period of unprecedented development.

The College is now an international, co-educational, inter-denominational school which caters for approximately 1,250 students whose ages range from 4 to 18.

The campus has been greatly enhanced following the construction of a new building which now houses the English, mathematics and art faculties. A new fitness studio and additional changing rooms were also constructed. We have recently upgraded our computer networking and students can access our VLE from all parts of the campus.

Operating within the Irish education system, St Andrew's is recognized by the Department of Education and Skills. It is also fully accredited by CIS and NEASC and is also an IB World School.

The school aims to provide a balanced, liberal education which, while encouraging high academic achievement, ensures a supportive environment for pupils with a wide range of abilities and aspirations. The academic programme culminates in the Leaving Certificate and International Baccalaureate Diploma exams, in which students regularly achieve results which

surpass the national average. Over 98% of students are offered places in universities and other third level colleges in Ireland and abroad.

A professionally-staffed counselling and career guidance service is provided, and students who wish to take them are prepared for College Board Tests (PSATs and SATs).

Languages taught include Irish, French, German, Spanish, Italian, Korean and Japanese. Many other languages are taught within the context of the European School, set up in 2001 to cater for the needs of children of EU Commission personnel based in Ireland.

There is an EAL department to assist students whose first language is not English. The sports programme includes rugby, hockey, basketball, soccer, swimming and tennis, and this is complemented by numerous co-curricular activities such as Model United Nations, choir, orchestra, drama and MEP. Educational, sporting and cultural trips to locations of interest in Ireland and abroad are organised throughout the year. Pupils are admitted to the College on the basis of a published set of criteria and, where practicable, personal interview.

St Andrew's College Dublin Limited is a registered charity. (No. CHY 4055.)

St Columba's College

(Founded 1843)

Kilmashogue Lane, Whitechurch, Dublin 16, Ireland

Tel: +353 1 4906791

Fax: +353 1 4936655

Email: admin@stcolumbas.ie

Website: www.stcolumbas.ie

Warden: L J Haslett BA, DPhil, PGCE

Appointed: 2001

School type: Coeducational Day & Boarding

Religious Denomination: Church of Ireland (Anglican)

Age range of pupils: 11–18

No. of pupils enrolled as at 01/09/2014: 295

Boys: 159 **Girls:** 136 **Sixth Form:** 137

No. of boarders: 240

Fees per annum as at 01/09/2014:

Day: €3,452–€4,944

Full Boarding: €6,207–€7,450

Average class size: 15 (junior); 10 (senior)

Teacher/pupil ratio: 1:8

St Columba's College is an HMC, Church of Ireland (Anglican) boarding and day school for boys and girls aged 11-18. Situated on the slopes of the Dublin mountains, overlooking Dublin Bay, the College enjoys the benefits of easy access to the Irish capital with the charms of a rural setting.

Ours is a deliberately small school of just 295 pupils. This size is a fundamental part of our ethos because we believe in a strong sense of togetherness in an atmosphere that is caring and supportive of all. We value the quality of the relationships we enjoy between teachers and pupils who live side-by-side and work together productively on a daily basis.

We have high academic standards – among the very best in Ireland – and almost all of our pupils go on to universities in Ireland and the UK. We encourage every individual pupil to get involved in the broader life of the college, whether it be in music, sport, drama, debating or public speaking. We aim to develop well-rounded and happy boys and girls with the self-confidence to mix freely and easily with others, whatever their background or age.

Occupying 150 acres, St Columba's has buildings dating from its establishment in 1843, through the last century and into the new millennium. In the past five years, the college has invested around €15million to ensure that it continues to offer its pupils the best facilities in terms of classrooms, sports facilities and accommodation. Recent additions have been new, purpose-built and refurbished boarding houses, state-of-the art music rooms, a second Astroturf hockey pitch and an additional dining room, as well as classrooms and common rooms. In addition, the College boasts a library and study rooms that are second to none in terms of facilities and resources, and a sports hall that provides facilities for indoor sport as well as a health and fitness suite and a dance studio.

The College offers seven-day boarding, which includes Saturday morning classes, six afternoons of sport for all, and a comprehensive range of weekend activities for its pupils. Our emphasis is on participation and involvement. Please visit our website (www.stcolumbas.ie) or phone for a prospectus. We welcome prospective parents and their children, and we look forward to a visit from you in the future.

St George's International School Luxembourg A.S.B.L.

St George's
International School, Luxembourg
A.S.B.L.

(Founded 1990)

11 Rue des Peupliers, L-2328 Luxembourg,
Tel: +352 423224
Fax: +352 423234
Email: reception@st-georges.lu
Website: www.st-georges.lu
Principal: Dr Christian Barkei
Appointed: September 2013
School type: Coeducational Day

Age range of pupils: 3–18+
No. of pupils enrolled as at 01/09/2014: 674
Boys: 332 **Girls:** 342
Fees per annum as at 01/09/2014:
Day: €5,625 – €13,715
Average class size: 20
Teacher/pupil ratio: 1:7

St George's International School, Luxembourg A.S.B.L. is an independent, not-for-profit school whose curriculum is based on the National Curriculum of England and Wales and the International Primary Curriculum. We believe that learning should be accessible to everyone, with every student able to find the tools and opportunities they need to achieve their full potential within an environment that is challenging and supportive. This philosophy is at the heart of our school's motto *"Achieving potential through challenge and care"*.

With over 50 nationalities represented, the rich diversity of our student community provides a unique and exciting learning environment for every child. Considerable care is taken to ensure that learning is personalised according to individual needs.

We believe that students thrive when there is a strong partnership between school and home, and pride ourselves on offering a warm welcome and providing ongoing support for all families.

Located in the beautiful and historic city of Luxembourg, the school is situated within easy reach of the city centre in modern, purpose-built accommodations. The school offers a wide range of I/GCSE and AS/A level subjects in preparation for

university entrance, and the vast majority of our leavers will go on to universities around the world. The school offers a variety of extra-curricular activities, after-school support and care, private music lessons and the opportunity to participate in international projects such as World Challenge, the Comenius project, and various COBIS competitions throughout the academic year.

St George's is an accredited executive member of the Council of British International Schools (COBIS) and is inspected by the International Schools Inspectorate (ISI). It is also an accredited Cambridge and Edexcel examination centre as well as being a member of the European Council of International Schools (ECIS), the Society of Heads and the Council of International Schools (CIS).

St. George's School in Switzerland

(Founded 1927)

Chemin de St Georges 19, CH 1815
Clarens/Montreux, Switzerland
Tel: +41 21 964 3411
Fax: +41 21 964 4932
Email: admissions@stgeorges.ch
Website: www.stgeorges.ch
Head of School: Mr Ian Tysoe

School type: Coeducational Day &
Boarding School
Age range of pupils: 3–18
No. of pupils enrolled as at 01/09/2014: 400
Fees per annum as at 01/09/2014:
Please enquire
Teacher/pupil ratio: 1:5

Almost 100 years of academic excellence
Reflecting back on 87 years of exciting activity at St. George's School, we can proudly say that we have successfully provided our students with the best international education in Switzerland while retaining many of the excellent values of a British school.

Under an hour's drive from Geneva, our 12-acre campus is located in the residential suburb of Clarens, near Montreux, overlooking the Lac Leman and the Alps.

The high quality of our staff and the outstanding on-campus sport facilities ensure that students receive a holistic approach to their education.

Academia – *Levavi Oculos*
Our mission is to provide a global sense of excellence in education, reaching the perfect balance between intellectual stimulation, physical activity and the development of social skills. Our academic programmes give access to the world renowned IGCSE exam and IB Diploma. They guarantee a solid learning base including science, humanities, the arts and foreign languages preparing your children for a bright and strong academic future.

We aim to provide our students with a sense of initiative and the self confidence needed to help them become worldly, reliable, caring and responsible adults.

Boarders
St. George's has proved to be a 'home away from home' for thousands of young women and men giving them the chance to experience a unique way of life. Everything at the school is designed to help students adapt easily and quickly to their second home.

By enrolling your children at St. George's School in Switzerland, you are giving them the chance to appreciate different cultures, instill in them the need for daily discipline, the values of respect, and monitor their development into mature caring achievers.

Summer Camp
Since the 1980s, St. George's School in Switzerland Summer Camps have been a continued success, welcoming boys and girls aged 10 to 17 from over 20 countries throughout July and August. We provide our summer campers with a safe, happy, stimulating atmosphere in a beautiful environment. Campers are given the opportunity to improve their language skills while making friends from around the world. Excursions, sports and outdoor entertainment remain a major part of the program to guarantee exciting lifelong memories.

St. Stephen's School

(Founded 1964)

Via Aventina 3, Rome, 00153 Italy
Tel: +39 06 575 0605
Fax: +39 06 574 1941
Email: ststephens@ststephens-rome.com
Website: www.sssrome.it
Head of School: Mr Eric Mayer
School type: Coeducational Day & Boarding

Age range of pupils: 14–19
No. of pupils enrolled as at 01/09/2014: 270
Fees per annum as at 01/09/2014:
Day: €21,900
Full Boarding: €34,500
Average class size: 13
Teacher/pupil ratio: 1:7

St. Stephen's is a coeducational, non-denominational, boarding and day school, enrolling students from age 14-19 in grades 9-12 and for a postgraduate year. Founded in 1964, St. Stephen's provides a demanding classical liberal arts education taking full advantage of its location in the historic centre of Rome. Primary objectives are academic excellence, fellowship and cooperation among students and faculty, and the development of students as independent, responsible, and involved members of the larger world community. The curriculum prepares students for the American high school diploma, including a variety of Advanced Placements subjects, and the International Baccalaureate (IB), which helps students to enter universities worldwide.

The campus of St. Stephen's occupies two and one-half acres in the centre of Rome. Constructed around a central courtyard, the traditional Roman-style building contains 13 classrooms, two art studios, a music room, four science laboratories, a 13,500 volume automated library (including a collection of DVDs, videos, periodicals, and wireless internet access), two desktop computer rooms, a mobile laptop computer lab, a writing centre, a multimedia centre, photography laboratory, dining room, snack bar and student's lounge, laundry room, theatre/auditorium, dormitory rooms, resident faculty apartments, tennis, basketball and volleyball courts.

The only international school in Rome to offer a boarding programme,

St. Stephen's can accommodate approximately 40 students living in single, double or triple rooms, all with internet and network access. Boarders are housed in the school building, where resident faculty supervisors provide social and academic support around the clock. Meals are served family-style in the dining hall, and boarders have access to a snack bar and lounge equipped with audio-video devices. Rome and its surroundings provide many opportunities for weekend boarding activities such as visits to historical and cultural sites, day trips to nearby beaches and ski areas, and overnight stays in scenic Tuscan or Umbrian hill towns.

TASIS The American School in England

The American School in England

(Founded 1976)
Coldharbour Lane, Thorpe, Surrey
TW20 8TE UK

Tel: +44 (0)1932 582316
Fax: +44 (0)1932 564644
Email: ukadmissions@tasisengland.org
Website: www.tasisengland.org
Head: Mr Michael V McBrien
Appointed: July 2010
School type: Coeducational Boarding & Day

Religious Denomination: Non-denominational
Age range of pupils: 3–18
No. of pupils enrolled as at 01/09/2014: 750
Fees per annum as at 01/09/2014:
Day: £6,670–£21,630
Full Boarding: £36,870
Average class size: 15
Teacher/pupil ratio: 1:7

TASIS The American School in England offers a challenging American university-preparatory curriculum, as well as the International Baccalaureate (IB) Diploma Programme. Located in a quiet village 18 miles southwest of London and eight miles from Heathrow Airport, the school's spacious campus combines Georgian mansions and 17th century cottages with new, purpose-built facilities.

The TASIS experience prepares young people from fifty nations to meet the challenges of a demanding world. This cultural diversity, along with small classes and a dedicated, experienced faculty, provides an outstanding environment for learning.

Individualised college counseling assists students in every step of the university selection and application process. Success in Advanced Placement (AP) courses (similar to A levels) and the IB Diploma has resulted in acceptances to prestigious universities in the US, the UK, Canada, and worldwide.

TASIS England includes three divisions: Lower (ages three to nine), Middle (ages 10-13), and Upper (ages 14-18). Committed to providing the very best educational experience, the school combines excellent facilities for science, theatre, visual arts, music, sports, fitness, and technology with a strong traditional academic programme. All students regularly benefit from working closely with visiting artists, actors, musicians, and sports professionals.

While academics are emphasised,

students participate in the extensive extracurricular activities, sports, arts, and community service opportunities that are essential to TASIS England's mission of ensuring a balanced education.

Taking full advantage of the opportunities that England and Europe offer as extensions to classroom learning, TASIS students enjoy numerous field trips, weekend activities, and travel abroad.

Accredited by the Council of International Schools (CIS) and the New England Association of Schools and Colleges (NEASC), TASIS England is an IB World School and was inspected by Ofsted in 2012. The school is a member of The Association of Boarding Schools (TABS) and the National Association of Independent Schools (NAIS).

The American School in London

The American School in London

(Founded 1951)

One Waverley Place, London NW8 0NP UK
Tel: 020 7449 1221
Fax: 020 7449 1350
Email: admissions@asl.org
Website: www.asl.org
Head: Mrs Coreen Hester

School type: Coeducational Day
Age range of pupils: 4–18
No. of pupils enrolled as at 01/09/2014: 1350
Boys: 696 **Girls:** 654
Fees per annum as at 01/09/2014:
Day: £21,950–£25,650

The American School in London is a non-profit, independent, Kindergarten through Grade 12 school, founded in 1951, which offers a singular opportunity to students – an American curriculum delivered by a first-rate faculty in one of the great cultural centers in the world. Our student body of 1,350 represents more than 45 nationalities with 30-plus languages spoken at home in addition to English.

The School's mission is to develop the intellect and character of each student by providing an outstanding American education with a global perspective.

London thrives, and our students take full advantage of this wonderful city as a classroom, participating actively in its vibrant historical, artistic, and cultural venues. At the threshold of continental Europe, we introduce our students to the background and experiences that will create the international citizens of tomorrow.

Our curriculum offers the challenge of high expectations, the excitement of engaging learning experiences, and the support of a caring community.

Samuel Johnson once ventured about London that "there is more learning and

science within the circumference of 10 miles from where we now sit than in all the rest of the kingdom." From studying architecture at a nearby Tudor castle to competing at the English-Speaking Union to exploring nature at the School's outdoor education garden, our students come to see the truth of Johnson's assertion. They learn to apply their newfound knowledge both inside and outside of the classroom, and they come to appreciate the importance of leadership and the value of service to a wider world. Best of all, they are happy to be here, and the smiles are wide.

The British School of Brussels

THE BRITISH SCHOOL OF BRUSSELS

(Founded 1969)
Leuvensesteenweg 19, 3080 Tervuren,

Belgium
Tel: +32 (0)2 766 04 30
Fax: +32 (0)2 767 80 70
Email: admissions@britishschool.be
Website: www.britishschool.be
Principal: Mrs Sue Woodroofe BA(Hons) NPQH
School type: Coeducational Day

Age range of pupils: 1–18
No. of pupils enrolled as at 01/03/2014: 1300
Sixth Form: 200
Fees per annum as at 01/03/2014:
€23,950 – €30,650
Average class size: 16-25
Teacher/pupil ratio: 1:10

The school was founded in 1969 and officially opened in 1970. It has a beautiful site of ten hectares, surrounded by woodlands and lakes near the Royal Museum of Central Africa in Tervuren, and is 20 minutes drive from central Brussels. The school is a coeducational non-selective day school for students aged 1-18, with over 1300 currently on roll. There is an Early Learning & Development Centre (Kindercrib) for children aged 1-3. Currently 39% of the students are British and there are 70 other nationalities represented in the school.

A British-based curriculum is offered within an international context with courses leading to GCSE and IGCSE examinations at 16 years old and GCE A levels, as well as Vocational Courses (BTEC in Business, Hospitality and Sports). The International Baccalaureate (IB) Diploma Programme is offered (bilingual French & Dutch options also) in addition to A levels. French is compulsory from the age of 4. To compliment the existing English-medium teaching, the school has established a French/English programme for ages 4-14 years.

As an international school operating in the heart of one of the world's most multilingual countries, the school offers Dutch from age 7-11 (mother tongue and beginners) as well as the choices of German and Spanish from age 11 as an additional language. There is an English Language Immersion programme for non-native English speakers and an Additional Educational Needs Department.

The school has excellent facilities including a state-of-the-art design & technology workshop, Food & Nutrition Workshops, networked IT suites, dance and drama studios as well as eight science laboratories, four art studios and comprehensive modern languages and humanities suites plus a self-service cafeteria.

The arts play a major role in the life of the school; music, drama and dance thrive and a wide range of performances are held regularly in the 240-seat theatre. The music department has a music technology suite, full-scale recording studio and a rehearsal studio.

A wide range of sports is offered, including rugby, football, hockey, tennis, swimming, gymnastics, athletics and basketball and the school participates successfully in GISGA as well as ISST. Similarly there is a wide range of extracurricular activities in sport, music and drama with frequent opportunities for overseas travel and school journeys. BSB will be the only international school in Belgium to have its own swimming pool by 2016.

Advice on higher and further education and on a choice of career is available to all students. Throughout the year multinational careers counsellors run events and host guest speakers to guide students in making their post-graduate plans.

Our academic results are impressive. In 2013, we achieved the best IB results in Belgium in many categories, and almost three times higher than the international average. (Over 16% of students passed with the highest marks of 40 or over, compared to last year's global average of 6.6%.) To be so far above the worldwide average is a measure of how well students do at BSB. This is all the more remarkable because BSB is a non-selective school, taking students from all abilities and all national education systems. In 2013, 29.5% of students sitting A level examinations scored A or A*. Over half the GCSE examinations taken in 2013 were passed at Grades A* and A – an increase of 2% on 2012. In 2013 in Primary School, 100% of children in Year 6 achieved Level 4 and above in Mathematics. 70% of the children achieved Level 5 in Reading, indicating attainment levels above the national average.

From Harvard to Cambridge from medicine to architecture, our students head for top universities worldwide. There is a long list of famous BSB alumna including authors, TV series producers, actresses and Olympic medallists.

The International School of the Algarve

(Founded 1972)

Apartado 80, 8401-901 Lagoa, Algarve, Portugal

Tel: +351 282 342547

Fax: +351 282 353787

Email: geral@eialgarve.com

Website: www.eialgarve.com

Head: Graciete de Sá e Cid

Appointed: September 1982

School type: Coeducational Day & Boarding

Age range of pupils: 3–18

No. of pupils enrolled as at 01/09/2014:

Boys: 373 *Girls:* 365 *Sixth Form:* 110

Fees per annum as at 01/09/2014:

€3,624 – €13,400

Average class size: 16

Teacher/pupil ratio: 1:10

The International School of the Algarve has been providing a quality education, through the medium of English, to the international community of the Algarve for 42 years. It is fully licensed and accredited by the Ministry of Education.

Senior students prepare for IGCSE and AS/A2 LEVEL qualifications from the UK examinations boards.

The teaching staff are qualified and experienced.

At present Students are from 30 different nationalities. There is support from EAL and SEN departments as well as a school psychologist.

The school is fully integrated with other international Schools in Portugal in terms of sporting events, careers and staff training.

The school occupies a nine-hectare site in the central Algarve, approximately 35 minutes from Faro International Airport. The school bus service serves a wide area, from Burgau in the west to Faro in the east.

There are extensive sports fields, a rollerblading rink, modern science laboratories and ICT suites as well as the biggest School library in Southern Portugal.

We are proud to announce that since the summer of 2012 we are part of the Nobel Education Network, having now created a local school group with Primary sites in Espiche and Almancil.

Boarding facilities are available for students from the age of 12: full-time, term time and on a temporary basis.

Summer School with intensive teaching of the English Language and a wide range of activities available in July and August.

UWC Atlantic College

 ATLANTIC COLLEGE

(Founded 1962)
St Donat's Castle, St Donat's, Llantwit Major, Vale of Glamorgan CF61 1WF UK

Tel: +44 (0)1446 799000
Fax: +44 (0)1446 799277
Email: principal@atlanticcollege.org
Website: www.atlanticcollege.org
Principal: John Walmsley
Appointed: January 2012

School type: Coeducational Boarding
Age range of pupils: 16–19
No. of pupils enrolled as at 01/09/2014: 350
Fees per annum as at 01/09/2014:
Full Boarding: £27,025
Average class size: 15
Teacher/pupil ratio: 1:9.5

Our Mission: *"UWC Atlantic College makes education a force to unite people, nations and cultures for peace and a sustainable future."*

Located in the 12th Century St Donat's Castle in the United Kingdom, UWC Atlantic College is the founding college of a global education movement and international residential school.

Each year, 350 students aged 16-19 from over 90 different countries benefit from a world-class International Baccalaureate (IB) educational experience. It offers one of the most comprehensive scholarship programme at pre university level.

Transformational Education

The two-year Atlantic Diploma has two linked parts: the IB 16-19 academic curriculum and an equally important extra-curricular programme focusing on global, social justice, environmental and physical challenge activities.

The college has an excellent academic record (average grade 37) and is highly valued by many of the world's leading universities, including Oxford and Cambridge in the United Kingdom and Deans of Admission from Ivy League universities such as Harvard, Princeton, Yale and Brown visit annually to interview students.

Campus and Facilities

St Donat's Castle houses classrooms, a performance hall, dining hall and a library collection of more than 25,000 volumes in a variety of languages. Also on campus are student boarding houses, well-equipped science laboratories, computer facilities, music practice rooms, a theatre, a student social centre and an independent arts centre.

Graduates emerge committed, motivated, socially responsible and internationally aware, with the potential to make a real and lasting difference in the world.

For more Information please contact us quoting reference IS14.

International schools in North America

Schools ordered A–Z by Name

Alcuin School

A MONTESSORI AND INTERNATIONAL
BACCALAUREATE EDUCATION

(Founded 1964)

6144 Churchill Way, Dallas, TX 75230 USA

Tel: +1 972 239 1745

Fax: +1 972 239 3650

Email: annie.villalobos@alcuinschool.org

Website: www.alcuinschool.org

Head of School: Walter Sorensen

Appointed: July 2009

School type: Independent

Coeducational Day

Religious Denomination: Non-sectarian

Age range of pupils: 18 months–18 years

No. of pupils enrolled as at 01/09/2014: 500

Fees per annum as at 01/09/2014:

US$13,000 – US$22,600

Average class size: 24

Teacher/pupil ratio: 1:13

A vibrant, nurturing, coeducational academic community serving students from toddler to 12 grade, Alcuin School uses the Montessori and International Baccalaureate program methods to foster critical thinking and a lifelong passion for learning. With faculty support, students at Alcuin School are eager to embrace change, question the status quo, and prepare for their future as leaders in a global society.

Nestled in the heart of north Dallas on 12 acres with lovely gardens and a small winding creek, the Alcuin School has provided a lovely learning environment for its students for 50 years. In 1964 Albert A. Taliaferro, an Episcopal priest, created the vision for a school of excellence through implementation of a world class educational program. As a result, Alcuin School has achieved the authorization to

provide the International Baccalaureate Middle Years Programme in grades 6 through 8 as well as the Montessori program in Toddlers through grade 5. Beginning in August 2014, an Upper School will be added and the school is currently a candidate school for the Diploma Programme. Through its rich history, the school has developed a culture of respect and peace with a foundation of genuine kindness.

Parents select the Alcuin School for a progressive education which focuses on the 21st Century skills of communication, collaboration, critical thinking and creativity. An inquiry-based curriculum, classroom interactions, and individualization inspire students to grow and flourish. Honing these skills comes through unique Alcuin educational experiences including a wide range of

outdoor learning opportunities and travel programs. Providing instruction in Spanish and Mandarin Chinese demonstrates Alcuin's commitment to language development of both the mother tongue and other languages. Through their studies, students make daily connections between academics and the outside world.

A current parent expresses the spirit of the Alcuin community with these thoughts, "Our most sacred obligation to our students is to open their hearts, inform their minds and encourage their dreams that they may be ready when life calls them to greatness." This spirit has led the community to generously support the School's capital campaigns. As a result, students study in state of the art classrooms and also benefit from other excellent facilities including libraries, the Wyly Performing Arts Center, a completely modern gymnasium, athletic fields, art studios and dedicated science laboratories. Beginning in August 2014, students will have access to a 21st Century Innovation Studio enabling them to explore beyond the classroom. An Innovation Speakers Series bringing outstanding scientists, artists, humanitarians and entrepreneurs will bring an additional unique dimension to the school.

Alcuin presents an opportunity for families to choose a school which provides a world-class Montessori and IB education that inspires the spirit of whole student to become an "Innovative Thinker and Passionate Learner."

For more information, please visit www. alcuinschool.org.

Baton Rouge International School

Baton Rouge International School

5015 Auto Plex Drive, Baton Rouge,
LA 70809 USA
Tel: +1 225 293 4338
Fax: +1 225 293 4307
Email: info@brisla.com
Website: www.brintl.com

Head of School: Nathalie Guyon
School type: Coeducational Day &
Residential
Age range of pupils: 6 weeks–18
Average class size: 14-16
Teacher/pupil ratio: 1:7

The Baton Rouge International School (BRIS) is an independent, non-profit school offering a rigorous college preparatory curriculum in a multilingual environment (English, French, Spanish, Portuguese and Chinese) from preschool through 12th grade. By engaging our students in this unique program of foreign language immersion, technology education, language arts, math and science, music, physical education and the visual and performing arts, they are equipped with the tools and resources needed to succeed in College and beyond. Our highly-qualified and diverse faculty includes certified native teachers. They are a daily example, bringing to light harmony in a world of differences. The Baton Rouge International School is currently authorized to offer the International Baccalaureate Middle Years Programme (MYP) for grades 6-10 and the IB Diploma Programme for grades 11-12. At the end of their studies, BRIS graduates receive an American High School Diploma with Advanced Placement (AP) and the International Baccalaureate Diploma (IB).

Accreditation

The Baton Rouge International School is an IB World School authorized to offer both the MYP and the DP. BRIS is also approved by the BESE and the Louisiana Department of Education/US Department of Education. In addition, BRIS is a full member of many professional/educational organizations in the United States and abroad.

Campus Facilities

The BRIS campus is located in Baton Rouge, Louisiana, USA. The modern facilities have been built on an 18-acre property in the heart of Baton Rouge. Its peaceful, green environment includes a lake visited by geese and falcons and plenty of space for playgrounds, fields for soccer and other sporting activities. The wooded site offers the tranquility needed for young minds to stay focused while enjoying campus life. BRIS recently completed a comprehensive campus Master Plan to design and build larger buildings to serve as administrative, educational and recreational facilities for the future. The design and planning reflects the innovative education that BRIS provides through contemporary and environmentally sustainable architecture.

Live Locally, Think Wisely, Communicate Globally!

Chamberlain International School

Chamberlain
International School

(Founded 1976)
1 Pleasant Street, PO Box 778, Middleboro,
MA 02346 USA

Tel: +1 508 946 9348
Fax: +1 508 947 1593
Email: admissions@flcis.com
Website: www.chamberlainschool.org
Head of School: William Doherty
School type: Co-educational Therapeutic
Boarding & Day

Age range of pupils: 11–22
No. of pupils enrolled as at 01/09/2014: 115
No. of boarders: 98
Fees per annum as at 01/09/2014:
Contact admissions@flcis.com for details
Average class size: 12
Teacher/pupil ratio: 12:1:1

Chamberlain School is a therapeutic co-educational boarding and day school for students aged 11-22 years. Students come to us from across the United States and throughout the world. We see the brightness and uniqueness in all of our students and focus on developing those positive qualities and abilities. Chamberlain is SEVIS approved by US Department of Homeland security to accept international students and issue an I-20.

Campus and facilities:
Students feel a sense of home on a peaceful and picturesque campus of historic buildings complimented by modern facilities all surrounding a traditional New England village green.

We have excellent road and rail links to Boston, Massachusetts and Providence, Rhode Island both of which have international airports that are within one hour's drive. The beautiful campus includes 9 New England style dormitories as well classroom buildings, therapists and psychiatrist's offices, nurse's station, swimming pool, automotive technology facility, art studio and gym.

Our students
Chamberlain students are between the ages of 11 and 22. They share similar challenges in their lives. Our students work hard, with the support of our faculty and staff, to balance both their gifts and their challenges. Some of our students' challenges may include emotional

dysregulation as a result of medical conditions such as bipolar disorder, depression, attentional issues, autism spectrum disorder, anxiety, obsessive-compulsive disorder and or specific learning disabilities. Our students benefit from a higher level of supervision and therapeutic support than a traditional school environment.

Hidden disabilities may prevent some students from achieving their potential. The frustrations related to unidentified strengths and disabilities can result in behavioral and social/emotional issues. School can become a frustrating experience for students who face these multiple challenges. The literature regarding best practices in teaching these

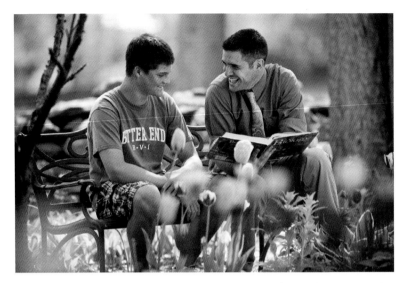

students consistently supports strength-based teaching strategies while at the same time working toward developing accommodations and compensation strategies that empower the students. Chamberlain has a wealth of experience in utilizing all of these strategies for the past 38 years.

Academic curriculum and enrichment courses

Chamberlain International School is a diploma granting institution. We offer college preparatory and general education courses to both middle and high school students. A strong focus of our academic program is on the core academic subjects: Literature, Writing, Mathematics, Social Studies, and Science. Our students benefit from additional studies in Foreign Language, Visual Arts, Automotive Technology, Physical Education, Health, and Study Skills.

The academic program at Chamberlain International School works within a larger interdisciplinary team of professionals to ensure that students successfully meet their academic potential. Teachers and Educational Supervisors work collaboratively with Speech Language Pathologists, Occupational Therapists, Clinicians and medical professionals to ensure that all strategies are being used to meet the students' goals. This team approach, coupled with the low student to teacher ratio, allows our educators to tailor and individualize content and instruction to optimize success.

Our core curriculum is further enhanced by Chamberlain's SAT/ACT Preparation Program, Vocational Training Programs, and Enrichment Course Program.

Therapeutic and clinical Support

Chamberlain students receive a high level of therapeutic support. This benefit enhances their overall experience at school which in turn leads to a higher level of success academically and socially. Having both individual and group therapy with masters level clinicians, students learn strategies to cope with stress; how to manage emotions and valuable education about the varying challenges they are facing that at times interfere with everyday life.

Each students individual therapist works closely with our two on site Psychiatrists as well as the nursing department for any medication or medically related needs our students may have.

Student life

Chamberlain International School has created a home like environment in each of its nine dormitories. The atmosphere is designed to be relaxed and calming, so that students may focus on their individualized goals. Chamberlain students learn the value of good nutrition and are taught how to budget for and prepare healthy meals. Students are encouraged to participate in a physically active schedule, through unparalleled access to activities that challenge body, heart and mind. Students have daily access to the community, enabling them to develop the necessary skills they will need to navigate the modern world. On- and off-campus student life activities include:

- Hiking
- Rock climbing
- Horseback riding
- Soccer
- Basketball
- Swimming
- Crew
- Golf
- Ski trips
- Europe, Bemuda and China trips
- Athletic club and gym
- Aviation
- The Automotive Tech program
- Movies and theater
- Professional sports games
- Student dances
- Community Service opportunities

Canada

CCI – The Renaissance School

59 Macamo Court, Maple, Ontario L6A-1G1, Canada
Tel: +1 905 508 7108
Website: www.canadiancollegeitaly.com
Head of School: Marisa DiCarlo D'Alessandro

School type: Coeducational Day & Boarding
Age range of pupils: 15–19
No. of pupils enrolled as at 01/09/2014: 70
Boys: 30 **Girls:** 40

Canadian College Italy is Canada's first high school in Italy. CCI is a co-educational boarding school that offers an academically rigorous curriculum in a semester format. Founded in 1995, we have provided a unique high quality English-language based educational experience that prepares students for success in their university studies. Our professional teaching staff dedicates itself to ensure extensive individual attention is available for every student. CCI prides itself on its excellent student achievement and graduates have accepted offers and received scholarships from a variety of universities throughout Canada, the USA, the UK, Australia and Europe.

The essence of CCI is that challenging learning takes place in the country of the Renaissance where archaeological, historical and art treasures are visited as a formally instructed integral part of the CCI educational experience. Classroom and book learning, upon which the School places the highest value, is dramatically enhanced when students are learning in the very places where the events being studied occurred. All students visit the major art cities within Italy and optional trips are also organized throughout Europe.

The Town of Lanciano, where CCI is located, is an ancient-yet-modern, safe, and well serviced small city of 45,000 in the eastern Abruzzo Region. It is a 15 minute drive from the sand and stone beaches of the Adriatic Sea and less than three hours by bus from Rome. An important part of the student experience is to live in an Italian town and be immersed in its culture, and Lanciano has warmly embraced CCI and our students.

Students attend CCI from – Canada, Europe, the United States, the United Kingdom, Mexico, South America and Italy to name a few. This assemblage of students and concentration of experience promotes strong friendships with classmates from all over the world.

Canadian College Italy's mission: To provide a unique environment in which students experience a renaissance academically, socially and culturally.

Dwight School

DWIGHT SCHOOL
Igniting the spark of genius in every child
PERSONALIZED LEARNING · COMMUNITY · GLOBAL VISION

(Founded 1872)
291 Central Park West,
New York, NY 10024 USA

Tel: +1 212 724 7524
Fax: +1 212 874 4232
Email: admissions@dwight.edu
Website: www.dwight.edu
Chancellor: Stephen H. Spahn
Head of School: Dianne Drew

School type: Coeducational Day
Age range of pupils: 2–18
No. of pupils enrolled as at 01/09/2014: 806
Fees per annum as at 01/09/2014:
US$40,000

Founded in 1872, Dwight School is an independent school located on Manhattan's Upper West Side dedicated to igniting the 'spark of genius' in every child. The School's world-class education is built on three pillars: personalized learning, community, and global vision.

Dwight has been an accredited International Baccalaureate (IB) World School since 1980 and was the first school in the US to offer the comprehensive programme for students from preschool through twelfth grade. Dwight is one of six IB schools originally selected from over 3,700 worldwide to be an IB Open World School to pilot IB Diploma Programme courses online.

Widely known as one of the most challenging and respected pre-university courses of study anywhere in the world, the IB is the only universal curriculum where students are graded according to international benchmarks. The IB focuses on the development of critical thinking. Students often lead classroom discussions; are challenged to be open-minded inquirers and risk-takers; reflect on their learning; and relate it to the real world.

Dwight School is committed to developing every student's passion – or unique 'spark of genius' – through personalized learning, allowing students to immerse themselves in a comprehensive range of subjects across all three IB programmes: Primary Years Programme (preschool-grade 5), Middle Years Programme (grades 6-10), and the Diploma Programme (grades 11-12).

Master teachers from all corners of the globe provide an enriched and innovative learning experience, guiding students through extensive language programmes, state-of-the-art technology instruction, rich visual and performing arts productions, and on a wide range of championship-winning athletic teams and international trips. Each of these components encourage students to pursue excellence in all endeavors.

Dwight students are internationally-minded leaders who are accepted by a number of the world's top colleges and universities, including Harvard, Yale, Princeton, MIT, Stanford, Dartmouth, Cornell, Columbia, McGill, Oxford, and The University of Edinburgh.

Dwight School is the flagship campus of The Dwight Schools, which is a global network of programmes and campuses in London, Beijing, Shanghai, Seoul, and on Vancouver Island.

Dwight School Canada

PERSONALIZED LEARNING · COMMUNITY · GLOBAL VISION

(Founded 2009)

2371 East Shawnigan Lake Road,
Shawnigan Lake BC, V0R 2W5 Canada
Tel: +1 250 929 0506
Fax: +1 250 743 3664
Email: admissions@dwightcanada.org

Website: www.dwightcanada.org
Head: Jerry Salvador
School type: Coeducational Day & Boarding
Age range of pupils: 11–18

Dwight School Canada is an independent international day and boarding school dedicated to igniting the spark of genius in every child. Our 24-acre campus, situated on Shawnigan Lake, provides the perfect backdrop for community and environmental engagement.

Dwight Canada is an International Baccalaureate (IB) World School, and it is the only school in North America to provide three diplomas: IB, American High School, and British Columbia High School. Through blending the best of a traditional curriculum with the innovative IB, which grades students according to international benchmarks, all Dwight Canada students have opportunities to learn in depth and develop as well-balanced individuals.

Dwight's teachers are committed to recognizing and developing each child's unique spark of genius, and our focus is on individual progress and growth. In addition to academics, Dwight Canada has strong athletics and arts programming, offering students a wide range of extracurricular activities, from violin instruction to ice hockey.

Dwight School Canada is a member of The Dwight Schools, a global network of schools with campuses and programs in New York, London, Seoul, and Beijing. All Dwight Schools share a commitment to three pillars: personalized learning, community and global vision. Dwight Canada also serves as home to the Dwight Global Leaders Academy, a summer program designed to teach young people the principals of leadership and social entrepreneurship.

EF Academy New York

Tel: Admissions: +1 914 597 7241
Email: admissionsia@ef.com
Website: www.ef.com/academy
Head of School: Brian Mahoney
School type: Coeducational Boarding

100 Marymount Avenue, Tarrytown,
NY 10591-3796 USA

Age range of pupils: 14–19
No. of pupils enrolled as at 01/04/2014: 590
Fees per annum as at 01/04/2014:
IB: $44,700
IGCSE Grades 9 & 10: $39,900

EF Academy International Boarding Schools prepare students from 75 countries for a global future with a superior secondary school education in the US or UK. At EF Academy, we believe in every student's ability to succeed. We empower them to do so through our renowned curricula, as well as quality one-on-one relationships with teachers and mentors alike.

Built into every course is an emphasis on multi-lingualism, International travel, and intercultural exchange which helps distinguish our student's academic credentials to both university admissions officers and future employers.

The School
Study at an idyllic campus located in Upper New York State. A mere 40-minute train ride from Manhattan, EF Academy's secure campus offers 100 acres of landscaped grounds, running trails, and playing fields in the village of Thornwood.

Our educational facilities feature updated multimedia classrooms, a premier science center, performance theater, and studios for art, dance, and music. There's an on-site cafeteria, multiple student lounges, a gymnasium, as well as basketball and tennis courts.

Academics
Education at EF Academy is highly personal. A guidance counselor meets with students regularly, either one-on-one or in a group setting to monitor their academic progress. A range of internationally renowned programs are offered to meet the individual needs of each student; including the IB Diploma, North American High School Grades 9-12, as well as the International GCSE program.

University Placements
The EF Academy class of 2014 is on course for another year of success. Not only have the majority of our students been accepted into top ranked universities such as NYU, UC Berkeley, UCLA and Williams, they have also been admitted to premier business schools such as the University of Virginia, engineering schools such as Georgia Tech and arts schools such as Pratt Institute.

Pastoral Care
In contrast to the formal teacher–student relationship of most traditional educational systems, EF Academy's instructional philosophy is highly interactive and participatory. We keep classes small (the maximum student-teacher ratio is 15:1).

Students are encouraged to nurture their talents and develop new skills and confidence. In addition, dedicated university counselors work 1-on-1 with each student to ensure the highest possible university placement.

Residential Life
Students live in comfortable, on-campus dormitory accommodation. House parents and teachers provide support and mentorship around the clock, and ensure a safe home away from home for all students.

Lycée International de Los Angeles (LILA)

(Founded 1978)

1105 W. Riverside Drive,
Burbank, CA 91506 USA
Tel: +1 626 695 5159
Fax: +1 818 994 2816
Email: admissions@lilaschool.com
Website: www.lilaschool.com
Interim CEO: Mr John Fleck

Head of School (beginning October 2014): Mr Michael Maniska
School type: Coeducational Day
Age range of pupils: 2–18
No. of pupils enrolled as at 01/09/2014: 1003
Fees per annum as at 01/09/2014:
$13,900 – $16,700

The Lycée International de Los Angeles (LILA) is an international, preschool through 12th-grade school with approximately 1,000 students on five campuses in the greater Los Angeles area: Los Feliz (PreK-5th), Pasadena (Preschool-5th), West Valley (Preschool-5th), Orange County (Preschool-5th), and Burbank (6th-12th). It is the only school in Los Angeles to teach a bilingual (French and English) program culminating in the French Baccalauréat or the International Baccalaureate Diploma. Students are taught to read, write, and speak both languages by the end of their elementary education. Satisfying both the Common Core State Standards and the French Ministry of Education's requirements

necessitates a rigorous schedule; the percentage of instruction in each language varies at each grade level.

LILA is committed to academic excellence in a nurturing and intimate environment that encourages personal initiative, creativity and curiosity. The school's goal is to develop confident, caring, and open-minded critical thinkers who will thrive in a diverse competitive world. LILA aims to offer more than mere knowledge of at least two languages; the ultimate goal is to form fully multi-literate students capable of functioning in two or more linguistic worlds. To achieve this goal, LILA specifically avoids dividing students based upon their dominant

language. At LILA, ways of thinking and expression are adopted that reflect an appreciation for cultural differences and multiple world views. Diverse groups learn more from each other when exchanging different points of view, introducing new pieces of information, and confronting alternative ideas. LILA's small and nurturing classes facilitate the sharing of different viewpoints. LILA teachers, staff and students come from all over the world, and the students study and live in a world community every day. Since its inception in 1978, LILA has earned an esteemed reputation with the placement of graduates in top international and American universities.

Meadowridge School

(Founded 1985)

12224 240th Street, Maple Ridge BC,
V4R 1N1 Canada
Tel: +1 604 467 4444
Fax: +1 604 467 4989
Email: info@meadowridge.bc.ca
Website: www.meadowridge.bc.ca
Head of School: Mr Hugh Burke

School type: Coeducational Day
Age range of pupils: 4–18
No. of pupils enrolled as at 01/09/2014: 530
Fees per annum as at 01/09/2014:
Domestic Fees:: C$17,800
International Fees:: C$24,300

Situated in the shadow of the Golden Ears Mountains on a 27 acre campus in beautiful Maple Ridge, British Columbia, Canada, Meadowridge is an International Baccalaureate, coeducational, university preparatory day school serving students from junior kindergarten (age four) to grade 12.

With an emphasis on the development of well-rounded individuals, our students learn to live well, with others and for others, in a just community. The foundation of that learning is the safe and supportive environment of the school. Through outstanding teaching, programmes and facilities, Meadowridge develops in students the confidence not only to meet the future, but also to create it.

Meadowridge is one of only 12 IB World Continuum Schools in Canada and one of only five in British Columbia accredited to offer three IB programmes, PYP, MYP and DP. As an IB Continuum World School in British Columbia, we adhere to the principles of accreditation outlined by the Canadian Accredited Independent Schools (CA+IS), Canada's only internationally recognized school accreditation agency.

We are also a member of the Council of International Schools and are committed to providing our students the highest quality of education and the knowledge to become engaged participants in the global community. Only two schools in Canada have this dual accreditation as both IB Continuum and CIS.

Our 103,000 square foot facility hosts state-of-the-art science labs; a theatre; two athletic fields, one which serves as an international sized soccer pitch; a greenhouse; the largest school library collection in the province with close to 43,000 resources; and two gyms, one containing an eight foot bouldering wall. We recently purchased 13.6 acres of surrounding, forested land to further enhance our academic programmes at all levels.

Mulgrave School

(Founded 1993)

2330 Cypress Bowl Lane, West Vancouver
BC, V7S 3H9 Canada

Tel: +1 604 922 3223

Fax: +1 604 922 3328

Email: admissions@mulgrave.com

Website: www.mulgrave.com

Head of School: John Wray

School type: Coeducational Day

Age range of pupils: 3–18

No. of pupils enrolled as at 01/09/2014: 800

Average class size: 19

Mulgrave School is a non-denominational, coeducational IB World School (pre-kindergarten to grade 12) authorized to offer all three IB programmes. By inspiring excellence – the continuous pursuit of personal best – in education and life, Mulgrave strives to equip lifelong learners to thrive in a culturally diverse and interdependent world and to embrace, with passion and confidence, their responsibility always to do their best to support others and to make a difference by serving their communities, both locally and in the world at large.

Developing growing independence in learning, service and leadership are inherent to the school's ethos, as is a strong culture of caring and support. Nestled in the forested slopes of Vancouver's North Shore with a spectacular view overlooking Burrard Inlet and the Pacific Ocean, Mulgrave School is highly valued for its positive community spirit and vibrant atmosphere. Experienced teachers from around the world provide a comprehensive and challenging IB curriculum to an equally diverse student body.

Mulgrave has a key focus on 21st century learning skills and personalized learning. Wireless technology is utilized throughout the school. Starting with an iPad program in grade 2, students switch to laptops and tablets in grades 6 to 12, where they are encouraged to use technology to explore global perspectives and expand the boundaries of learning. Personalized learning is a cornerstone for the Middle School, where students have the option to select a wide range of electives to pursue personal passions and interests, in conjunction with core MYP courses.

Mulgrave graduating students go on to top colleges and universities worldwide.

In the past three years, Mulgrave students have attended Princeton, Harvard, Oxford, Stanford, McGill, University of British Columbia, Cornell and University College of London.

The school's commitment to athletics, service, outdoor education, arts, leadership and co-curricular activities provides ample opportunity for students to find and develop their unique passions. We foster the development of young leaders who demonstrate international understanding and meaningful action as responsible citizens of the global community.

The school is a member of ISABC and CIS and is accredited by IBO as an IB Continuum school.

For more information, please contact our admissions office at admissions@mulgrave.com.

St. Timothy's School

(Founded 1832)

8400 Greenspring Ave, Stevenson, MD 21153 USA

Tel: +1 410 486 7400

Fax: +1 410 753 8504

Email: admis@stt.org

Website: www.stt.org

Head of School: Randy Stevens

School type: Girls' Day & Boarding

No. of pupils enrolled: 180

Fees per annum as at 01/09/2014:
$50,330

St. Timothy's School provides an exceptional college-preparatory education and unparalleled opportunities for young women in grades 9-12. Situated on a beautiful 145-acre campus in Baltimore County, St. Timothy's offers a full boarding and day program for highly motivated students wishing to pursue the International Baccalaureate Diploma Programme. St. Timothy's is an easy commute to Washington, DC, Annapolis, Philadelphia and New York, and the school is located just twenty minutes from Baltimore's Inner Harbor.

Since its founding in 1832, St. Timothy's has prepared students for matriculation to the most select colleges and universities in the United States and abroad; and it has educated young women to live confidently in the world, to lead with courage and conviction, and to act responsibly and ethically in all areas of their lives.

St. Timothy's School provides a unique and dynamic combination of classroom and real-world learning through its award-winning Global Immersion Program, the Winterim experience, and travel abroad opportunities. The school's curriculum has an international focus, and students and teachers from around the world bring a unique and rich blend of cultures, languages, and experiences.

St. Timothy's School offers unparalleled leadership opportunities for young women and a highly individualized academic program with small classes. The school has a new, state-of-the-art academic facility featuring the latest teaching technologies; a new outdoor athletic complex; and a full equestrian center including indoor and outdoor rings.

St. Timothy's welcomes students of all faiths and draws strength from a diversity of beliefs and experiences.

St. Timothy's School welcomes students who are committed to pursuing challenging academics within a supportive environment and who would benefit from and contribute to the overall life of the school community.

For more information about St. Timothy's School or to begin the application process, please contact the Admissions Office at +1 410 486 7401 or admis@stt. org. The Admissions Office can help you schedule a campus tour and your personal interview, and the staff can arrange additional meetings with faculty, coaches, and administrators.

Stoneleigh-Burnham School
International Baccalaureate World School

(Founded 1869)
574 Bernardston Road, Greenfield,
MA 01301 USA
Tel: +1 413 774 2711
Fax: +1 413 772 2602
Website: www.sbschool.org

Head of School: Sally Mixsell
School type: Girls' Boarding & Day
Age range of girls: 11–20
No. of pupils enrolled as at 01/09/2014: 155
No. of boarders: 112

Stoneleigh-Burnham School, founded in 1869, is a girls' boarding and day school nestled in the beautiful Pioneer Valley of western Massachusetts. Educating girls grades 7-12 and post-graduate on its 100-acre campus, the School inspires its students to value intellectual curiosity, to embrace diversity, and to act with integrity. Stoneleigh-Burnham is the only girls' school in New England to offer the International Baccalaureate Diploma Programme.

Stoneleigh-Burnham is proud to be a girls' school – years of research confirm that the all-girl environment creates a culture of achievement. Girls in single-sex schools develop stronger self-esteem, are exposed to broader leadership opportunities, and graduate from high school with higher aspirations and greater self-confidence. Based on research that shows connectedness, competence, and confidence are the core elements of self-esteem in girls, our progressive curriculum cultivates in each girl an appreciation for all aspects of a liberal arts education and stretches her to understand the multi-sensory, collaborative process by which she learns about herself and her world. From seventh grade through senior year, our teachers focus on interactive learning that encourages collaboration and self-expression while promoting healthy competition.

Stoneleigh-Burnham offers an array of challenging academic courses that launch students into focused study and leadership to prepare them for college and beyond. With small class sizes and a research-based curriculum, Stoneleigh-Burnham School provides its students with a safe and inclusive environment that encourages self-discovery, adventurousness, and strong academic pursuit. Passionately committed to its multi-cultural environment, Stoneleigh-Burnham School is proud of its rich diversity of students hailing from over sixteen countries around the world.

The International Baccalaureate (IB) Diploma Programme is an internationally-acclaimed, comprehensive, academically rigorous course of study that encourages highly motivated juniors

The school's Equestrian Center is right on campus and that means girls can walk from their classes and dorm rooms directly to the barn. Every rider, from the complete novice to the advanced jumper, receives personalized instruction that reflects her interests, goals, and abilities. Licensed coaches provide instruction tailored to all levels with training in equitation, hunters, jumpers, eventing, dressage, and equine studies. Our four-time National Champion IEA (Interscholastic Equestrian Association) team competes at both the Middle School and High School levels within the largest zone in the country. Stoneleigh-Burnham is now the only secondary school in the United States to offer British Horse Society International Certification.

Girls develop best when they are in a community that knows them and where they feel connected. With its history of fostering the development of strong female identities, its safe and inclusive multi-cultural environment, and its dedication to understanding how girls best learn and grow, Stoneleigh-Burnham School guides emerging women to become active agents of their own destiny. To learn more, please visit our website www.sbschool.org or call our Admissions Office at 413-774-2711.

and seniors to draw connections across disciplines, to approach subject areas from multiple perspectives, and to be active participants in their own intellectual pursuit. Students who choose to enroll in the optional IB Diploma Programme will spend their junior and senior years studying advanced material in six subject areas. As part of the curriculum, students will also complete an extended essay, take an integrative Theory of Knowledge course, and work to achieve personal goals focused on creativity, athletic pursuit, and community service. All Stoneleigh-Burnham juniors are invited to enroll in the optional two-year IB Diploma Programme because unlike the AP (Advanced Placement), student access to the IB Programme is based on motivation to work, not grades.

Stoneleigh-Burnham offers dynamic opportunities outside the classroom for a well-rounded educational experience that challenges each student to develop confidence and to discover her best self. These include athletics, numerous clubs and after-school activities as well as nationally recognized equestrian, debate, and performing arts programs.

Stoneleigh-Burnham girls are known for their ability to speak with confidence and clarity. Our world-class debate and public speaking program regularly sends qualifiers to the World Individual Debate and Public Speaking Championships as part of the United States team. Our program boasts fourteen students who have ranked as world competitors. The Debate and Public Speaking Society is open to any girl interested and students will participate in public speaking tournaments, in Lincoln-Douglas, cross-examination, extemporaneous, and parliamentary-style debate.

The Newman School

(Founded 1945)

247 Marlborough Street, Boston,
MA 02116 USA
Tel: +1 617 267 4530
Fax: +1 617 267 7070
Email: hlynch@newmanboston.org
Website: www.newmanboston.org
Head of School: J Harry Lynch
Appointed: 1985

School type: Coeducational Day
Age range of pupils: 13–18
No. of pupils enrolled as at 01/04/2013: 240
Fees per annum as at 01/09/2014:
US$32,000
Average class size: Av 14
Teacher/pupil ratio: 1:10

The Newman School, founded in 1945 in the heart of Boston, the educational capital of America, provides a diverse student body, a college preparatory, liberal arts education, based on intellectual rigor and trust, and guided by the philosophy of Cardinal John Henry Newman.

Situated in Boston's Back Bay, The Newman School is within short walking distance of the Boston Public Library, Symphony Hall, the Boston Ballet, the Museum of Fine Arts, and the many colleges and universities – including Harvard, Boston University, Northeastern and MIT - for which Boston is world-renowned. International students comprise 35% of the student body,

representing 14 countries including China, Korea, Vietnam, Russia, Kazakhstan, Spain, Nigeria, Italy, Germany, Saudi Arabia, Ghana, Greece, Thailand and Brazil. Homestays are arranged through an established network of experienced families. Newman is approved to issue the paperwork needed in order to apply for the F-1 student visa required for study in the US, is accredited by the New England Association of Schools and Colleges, and is approved to offer the International Baccalaureate Diploma Programme.

International student transfers are welcome, generally joining the school in the second half of the 10th or the beginning of the 11th grade. An intensive

English as a second language program is offered to students needing English study prior to entering the high school program. Senior transfers are considered. All students completing the school's course of study are eligible to receive the Newman diploma. The IB Diploma, an additional credential, is awarded based upon success on external examinations.

Newman students participate in sports and extracurricular programs including: boys and girls crew, sailing, soccer, cross country, boys and girls basketball, tennis, and baseball, as well as literary journal, SAT prep, recycling, Model United Nations, chess instruction, mock trial and a range of service opportunities.

United World College – USA

(Founded 1982)
PO Box 248, Route 65, Montezuma,
NM 87731 USA

Tel: +1 505 426 3394
Fax: +1 505 454 4275
Email: admission@uwc-usa.org
Website: www.uwc-usa.org
President: Dr. Mukul Kumar

School type: Coeducational International Boarding
Age range of pupils: 16–19
No. of pupils enrolled as at 01/09/2014: 200
Boys: 100 **Girls:** 100

UWC-USA: Turning Dreams into Action

UWC-USA students share a common trait: they are passionate change-agents who strongly identify with the school's mission of using education as a force to unite people and cultures for a peaceful, sustainable world.

While UWC-USA students embrace the same mission, you couldn't imagine a more diverse group of young people. The 200 students who fill the campus hail from 75 to 80 different countries and represent a broad range of ethnicities, religions, and socio-economic backgrounds. In this rich milieu, students learn about the world in a deeply personal way. As a result, they develop a profound sense of empathy and an international outlook that impacts them and those around them throughout their lives.

UWC-USA is part of a 14-school consortium that includes campuses on five continents. Located in northeastern New Mexico, the 200-acre boarding school is surrounded by a majestic pine forest, springs, and the rich cultural environment of the American Southwest. All students are enrolled in the International Baccalaureate Diploma Programme, the US equivalent of 11th and 12th grade, and the faculty-to-student ratio is 9:1. In addition to their academic studies, students learn advanced outdoor skills and leadership through UWC-USA's flagship wilderness programme. They study conflict resolution to become mediators, and they engage with the local community by volunteering for organizations that provide services to some of the area's neediest residents.

When they graduate, UWC-USA students matriculate at many of the world's most highly regarded colleges and universities. From there, they go on to become community leaders, entrepreneurs, doctors, attorneys, and more. UWC-USA was founded in 1982 and has 3,000 proud and accomplished alumni; more than 90 percent of them say UWC-USA was the most transformative educational experience of their lives.

To learn more about UWC-USA, visit the school website at www.uwc-usa.org.

International schools in South America

Schools ordered A–Z by Name

Craighouse School

(Founded 1959)
Casilla 20 007, Correo 20, Santiago, Chile
Tel: +56 2 756 0218
Fax: +56 2 216 9139
Email: headmaster@craighouse.cl

Website: www.craighouse.cl
Headmaster: Peter Lacey
School type: Coeducational Day
Age range of pupils: 3–18
No. of pupils enrolled as at 01/09/2014: 1720

Have you thought about the kind of education you want for your children? We have.

Craighouse School seeks to understand your child's learning needs so that they can progress to his or her maximum potential.

Our aim is to prepare our pupils with the skills, knowledge and caring attitude required to make a significant contribution to the world. Our community works towards this aim, both from inside and outside the classroom, through our excellent curriculum and the many extracurricular activities and events we participate in, organize and host. Our recently inaugurated 24-hectare campus was built for the purpose of delivering our educational project and to provide state of the art spaces in which to develop the knowledge, skills, talents and interests of all our pupils.

We believe that continuity and consistency in education is essential to student achievement. The implementation of the three IB programmes puts our pupils at the centre of inquiry-based learning from playgroup to Year 12. In age-appropriate ways, we work to achieve and applaud the qualities identified in our student profile. We want Craighouse pupils to be mindful of being: inquirers, thinkers, communicators, risk-takers, knowledgeable, principled, open-minded, caring, balanced, reflective, and resilient. Achieving this profile is a fantastic goal for all of us!

Implemented in every year level, our personal and social development programme is another way we attain coherence and consistency in our school. This programme teaches children, from their early years, to talk about matters including identity, school culture, sex education, alcohol and drug abuse.

Craighouse is a Chilean school with British roots and an international approach and outlook. Pupils from playgroup to Year 6 are taught through the medium of English, within a context of total immersion. From Year 7 to Year 12, pupils have upwards of five hours a week of English language and literature classes, often with native English language teachers. All trips within and outside Chile are organized around cultural themes and sports venues. These occasions not only enrich the curriculum but also give our pupils opportunities for fine-tuning their language and communication skills.

Finally, our school is a place where your children can grow and achieve their dreams. We invite you to contact us for further information.

Gimnasio Británico

Calle 21 No 9A-58, Chia, Cundinamarca, Colombia
Tel: +571 8615084
Fax: +571 8615081
Email: gb@gimnasio-britanico.edu.co

Website: www.gimnasio-britanico.edu.co
Head of School: Jorge Piraquive Arévalo
School type: Coeducational Day
Age range of pupils: 2–16
No. of pupils enrolled as at 01/09/2014: 1500

Gimnasio Británico is located near the town of Chía, known for its warm-hearted citizenry and exceptional climate. We are a day school of approximately 1500 students between the ages of 2 and 16. Our students are nurtured in mind and body in accordance with the highest educational standards. Towards this goal, we have created a living/learning environment that remains unsurpassed in the field of private education. Beside intellectual growth, our goal is to instill essential values such as love, compassion, respect, and integrity in each student.

The Gimnasio Británico is the first officially recognized trilingual school in Colombia and this has led us to offer academically rigorous programs for preschool, elementary, junior high and high school that are coordinated to provide integrated curricula in a trilingual education in Spanish, English, and French. Comfortable classrooms meet the needs of our small groups of students and create an effective ambience for both teaching and learning. Science and language laboratories are modern (high-tech) and well-equipped, ensuring that students can progress comfortably and proficiently at their own pace. Also onsite is a complete research library with literary and didactic materials.

The Gimnasio Británico has fostered relationships with national and international public libraries, universities and institutes such as Rosario University, Indiana University, REF (Réseau d'Excellence en français des lycées, Alliance Française Bogota) and many others that could make the foundation for a lifelong learning. These relationships facilitated the learning process and creativity with independent thought; one of the hallmarks of the school. Students excel academically and position themselves for acceptance to the finest colleges or universities of their choice, both nationally and internationally where English or French is spoken, due to high scores on national and international exams. Once they enter undergraduate studies, they are equipped to succeed in the classroom, manage their time efficiently and fit in socially and academically. They arrive with critical thinking, communication and written skills, as well as research skills due to the technology tools offered by the school.

Students are encouraged to be inquisitive and open to growth, thus discovering and exploring new ideas and issues.

International School of Curaçao

International
School of
Curaçao

(Founded 1968)

PO Box 3090, Koninginnelaan z/n,
Emmastad, Curaçao
Tel: +599 9 737 3633
Fax: +599 9 737 3142
Email: info@isc.cw
Website: www.isc.cw
Director: Ms Margie Elhage-Cancio PhD
School type: Coeducational Day

Age range of pupils: 2–19
No. of pupils enrolled as at 01/09/2013: 454
Boys: 239 **Girls:** 216
Fees per annum as at 01/09/2013:
Contact Mrs Loraine van Rosberg at:
vanrosbergl@isc.cw
Average class size: 15
Teacher/pupil ratio: 1:7

Our School
The International School of Curaçao is an accredited, non-profit, private, co-educational, day school (K-12) that provides instruction in English.

Vision
An international education today for the global citizens of tomorrow.

Mission
The International School of Curaçao (ISC) educates students from diverse cultures to have the skills to think creatively, communicate effectively, reason critically, and act compassionately. ISC has pledged to achieve this by providing a high quality English medium education using United States and internationally recognized standards.

Elementary School
ISC offers the First Steps Program, a nursery program for 2 year-olds. The Elementary School begins with kindergarten for 3 years old and extends to Grade 5. In addition to Language, Mathematics, Science and Social Studies, students receive formal instruction in Art, Music, Library, Physical Education, Computer, Spanish and Dutch. We expect children to become skilled thinkers, problem solvers, readers, authors and mathematicians, to be able to succeed in later grades.

Middle School
Our Middle School offers a program tailored to the unique social and learning needs of adolescent students in grades 6, 7 and 8. We strive to enable students to think, create, solve problems, organize themselves, research essential questions, and most importantly to celebrate the differences within themselves and those around them.

High School
Our high school offers a vigorous liberal arts education for every student and fosters international understanding. Advanced Placement (AP) courses are offered in Spanish and Spanish Literature. Students can take a full IB Diploma in the 11th and 12th grade or opt to pursue individual certificates in the different subject areas.

Special Programs
English as a Second Language, Learning Resource, Highly Able Program, Guidance Counseling and College Placement.

Memberships
Association of American Schools in South America (AASSA), College Board National Association for College Admission Counseling.

Accreditation
Southern Association of Colleges and Schools (SACS), Council of International Schools (CIS).

King's College, The British School of Panama

King's College
The British School of Panama

Edificio 518, Calle al Hospital, Clayton, Panama
Tel: +507 282 3300
Email: kcp.admissions@kingsgroup.org
Website: www.kingscollege.com.pa

Headteacher: Vanessa Whay BEd (Hons), Cantab, NPQH
School type: Coeducational Day
Age range of pupils: 3–18
No. of pupils enrolled as at 01/09/2014: 176

King's College, The British School of Panama is part of King's Group. With over 45 years of experience, our schools create an environment that inspires pupils, giving them the confidence and enthusiasm to achieve the highest possible academic results.

The British School of Panama, located in the residential suburb of Clayton, is just 20 minutes' drive from the centre of Panama City.

At present the school educates children from Nursery (age 3) through to Year 8 (age 13).

The school is the newest addition to King's Group and will continue to grow, to eventually educate pupils from age 3 to 18 years old, where they shall complete their IGCSEs and A levels, to help them secure entrance to top universities around the globe, as our sister school currently does in Madrid.

Much more than buildings and grounds, establishing a new school requires experience, understanding and leadership. The best schools are, without exception, filled with happy children who love going to school. These are the children who will achieve the highest grades and go on to do great things. Happy children are busy children. The best teachers make sure that their pupils discover new things, explore new ways of seeing and learn to love the process of learning itself.

All of the teaching staff have British teaching qualifications and recent experience of delivering the English national curriculum.

King's College understands how to work with local governments and communities, ensuring that our schools comply with local as well as British standards.

We believe that child-centered, exploratory learning teaches young people how to think, question and explore new ideas. All learning is based upon these core skills; not simply a list of memorised facts, but knowledge and understanding. We give your son or daughter the best possible chance to reach their full potential, as an independent thinking and conscientious young person.

Northlands School

(Founded 1920)

Olivos Site: Roma 1248, Olivos,
Provincia de Buenos Aires, Argentina
Tel: +54 11 4711 8400
Fax: +54 11 4711 8401
Email: admissionsolivos@northlands.edu.ar

Nordelta Site:
Av de los Colegios 680 Nordelta, Provincia
de Buenos Aires, Argentina
Tel: +54 11 4871-2668/9
Email:
admissionsnordelta@northlands.edu.ar

Website: www.northlands.edu.ar
Acting Principal: Marisa Perazzo
School type: Coeducational Day
Age range of pupils: 2–18

Northlands is all-embracing, bilingual education from multiple perspectives.
It is all embracing because of our conception of a person as a whole, made up of a mind, a body and a soul.

It is bilingual because of our British roots and because English is the language of

instruction for at least fifty percent of our curriculum content. In this way, our students acquire a command of the language that allows them to sit for international exams at First Language level.

Our students' education is approached from multiple perspectives because we

offer them the opportunity to look at reality from different vantage points, with different and broad outlooks, always showing respect and appreciation of different cultures, beliefs and values.

We make our proposal come to life through:

- The **Development of the Areas of Knowledge**, which fundamentally refers to developing thinking skills and a capacity for meta-cognition, focusing on learning and reflecting upon how we learn.
- **Personal and Social Development**, which is founded on the great universal values, has integrity as a core human value. To put them into practice, we have designed a Personal and Social Education (PSE) Programme on the basis of those values and the attributes of the IB community profile, which we have incorporated as it coincides with our educational principles.
- **Physical Development**, which encourages widespread participation and competitive at health improvement, awareness of the importance of taking care of our body, life quality and contact with nature.

These three great areas are intertwined with one another and they overlap continuously because, as human beings, we are ONE.

Kindergarten Education

Northlands offers an all-embracing curriculum that works on physical, social, emotional, intellectual, ethic and aesthetic aspects through teaching and learning strategies focused on encouraging curiosity and the desire to know in children. Our young students strengthen their self-esteem, develop their understanding of their immediate surroundings and acquire the necessary

An International programme that develops essential educational skills including recall of knowledge, oral skills, problem solving, initiative, team work and investigative skills. It is recognized as the equivalent to the last two years of compulsory education in Great Britain.

IBO Diploma Programme

A challenging and stimulating curriculum that is widely recognized by the world's leading universities. It develops in students the ability to learn how to learn, a strong sense of their own identity and culture, and the ability to communicate with and understand people from other countries and cultures.

*Compulsory for all NORTHLANDS students.

Physical Education

We believe the practice of physical and sports activities to be an essential part of our students' education. We take part in national and international interschool events that promote team spirit and healthy competition.

Arts

Students are guided so that they may find in the arts an outlet for their self-expression. At an early stage, learning is based on games as a way of discovering and experimenting with the possibilities of each discipline. As students mature, they are offered a wide range of techniques, instruments and cultures to explore through the formal study of the dramatic arts, music and the visual arts.

skills to do work and express their ideas in both English and Spanish.

Primary Education

Northlands offers an all-embracing curriculum based on inquiry and research as the ideal vehicles for learning. We provide a caring and stimulating environment where children enjoy doing their work and develop positive academic and inter-personal attitudes, self-confidence and self-discipline. Students take the lead by making the learning process their own: they are encouraged to make choices, take decisions and ask questions, thus broadening their range of interests and knowledge.

Secondary Education

Northlands offers high quality secondary education, awakening in students an interest in and curiosity for the academic world, raising an international awareness and cultivating the appreciation of culture. During this phase students develop critical thinking skills, creativity and autonomy. Individual talents and personal interests are nurtured so that students can make satisfactory career choices at the end of their school life.

International Accreditation

Northlands, as a leading educational institution, is internationally accredited by the International Baccalaureate Organization (IB), the English Speaking Scholastic Association of the River Plate (ESSARP), the Latin American Heads Conference (LAHC) and the Council of International Schools (CIS).

International Programmes (*)

IBO Primary Years Programme (PYP)

An international education programme in which teachers and students explore in a transdisciplinary way the road to knowledge. Having a central axis based on the development of the child as a whole, this programme proposes an educational framework that is interesting, stimulating, relevant and committed to a structured inquiry that encourages students to act according to new perspectives and knowledge.

Cambridge International General Certificate of Secondary Education (IGCSE)

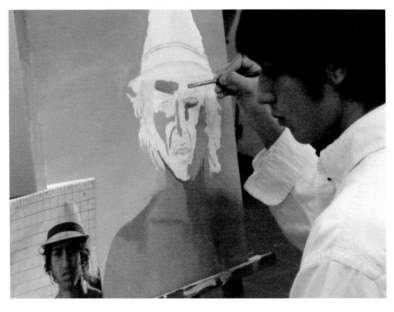

Santiago College

(Founded 1880)
Av. Camino Los Trapenses 4007,
Lo Barnechea, Santiago, Chile
Tel: +56 2 27338800
Email: master@scollege.cl
Website: www.scollege.cl

Director: Lorna Prado Scott
Academic Coordinator: Claudia Rose
School type: Coeducational Day
Age range of pupils: 4–18
No. of pupils enrolled as at 01/09/2014: 1846
Sixth Form: 253

Santiago College is a bilingual, independent, co-educational day school, founded as a non-sectarian institution in 1880 with support from the US Methodist Church.

The educational programme at Santiago College meets the requirements of the Chilean Ministry of Education and the International Baccalaureate Organization and the school is a member of CIS and NEASC.

Students normally enter Santiago College at PK level and stay until they graduate from 12th Grade. The students are mainly Chilean, but a considerable number of students come from other countries and priority admission is given to overseas applicants. Approximately 90% of the graduating class enters Chilean universities and the remainder pursues studies in the USA or Europe. The school operates a 180-day minimum calendar starting in early March and ending in mid-December. PK and kindergarten children have a half-day schedule. All other grades have a full school day beginning at 7:55am and ending at 3:35pm. The school campus of 11 hectares is located in Lo Barnechea, 20 minutes drive from the city centre. Facilities include a library of 40,000 volumes, 98 classrooms, AV rooms, an auditorium, gymnasium, playing fields, science labs and computing labs, music and art studios and one cafeteria. Students applying for admission to PK must be four years old by December 31st of the year prior to school entry. Santiago College accepts students without regard to gender, colour, creed, or ethnic, nationality or social origin. The selection process includes an interview with prospective students and their parents.

The British School Caracas

PO Box 668708, c/o Jet International 489,
Miami, Fl 33166, USA
Tel: +58 212 267 9443
Fax: +58 212 264 2141
Email: headmaster@tbscaracas.com
Website: www.tbscaracas.com
Head of School: John Plommer

Deputy Head of School & Head of
Primary: Keith Bailey
Secondary Heads: Steve Bolton & Yasir
Patel
School type: Coeducational Day
Age range of pupils: 3–18
No. of pupils enrolled as at 01/09/2014: 350
Boys: 184 **Girls:** 166

Primary Years: 220
Secondary Years: 130
Fees per annum as at 01/09/2014:
US$8,050 – US$19,923
Enrolment Fee: Early Years & Primary:
US$8,050
Enrolment Fee: Secondary Years:
US$4,025

The British School Caracas was established in 1950 and is located in a purpose-built facility in Altamira, a pleasant suburb of Caracas. The school has developed considerably over the years and offers an English language programme based upon the English National Curriculum for students aged 3 to 18 years of age. The rich English medium primary curriculum also includes first and second language Spanish and Venezuelan culture.

The secondary programme has a full range of elective courses in the IGCSE and IB Diploma years. The majority of staff is British trained. The school has well-established learning support and P.S.H.E programmes The ESL programme uses individual tuition and in class support for those students who require it. School facilities include a computer laboratory and each classroom has at least two computers, all connected to the intranet and Internet. There are well-equipped facilities for science, music, media studies, design technology, theatre and physical education. The school operates a northern hemisphere school year based upon three terms from September to July with a three-week break at Christmas and two-week break at Easter. The school day runs from 07:30 to 14:45 Monday to Friday. The school's extracurricular programme is varied, open to all ages, and includes sports such as hockey, judo, karate, basketball and football as well as music, drama, arts and craft, storytelling, ballet, computing and science clubs. Residential trips are a part of the curriculum for students from Year 5 to Year 13. They include hiking, white water rafting, camping and bird watching in the cloud forest and trips to Los Llanos and coastal national parks. In Secondary there are MUN and CAS trips. Admission is via personal interview and assessment.

The British School, Rio de Janeiro

The British School
Rio de Janeiro
KNOWLEDGE AND FRIENDSHIP

A caring community, striving for excellence,
where every individual matters.

(Founded 1924)

Rua Real Grandeza 99, Botafogo, Rio de

Janeiro, 22281-030 Brazil

Tel: +55 21 2539 2717

Fax: +55 21 2539 2717 (ext 151)

Email: edu@britishschool.g12.br

Website: www.britishschool.g12.br

Directors: John Nixon MBE & Therezinha Pientznauer

School type: Coeducational Day

Age range of pupils: 2–18

No. of pupils enrolled as at 01/09/2014: 2166

Boys: 1052 **Girls:** 1108

Fees per annum as at 01/09/2014:

R$50,000 approx

Average class size: 12-24

Teacher/pupil ratio: 1:9.4

Founded in 1924, we are a non-profit, independent and coeducational day school offering a complete and coherent curriculum for pupils of all nationalities from ages 2-18.

The school is an IB World School accredited by the Council of International Schools (CIS). One of the directors is a member of the Latin American Heads Conference (LAHC). The school has approximately 2160 pupils located on three sites. Botafogo houses a primary school and the first year of secondary school. The secondary school is based at Urca, close to the Sugar Loaf. The Barra site opened in February 2006. It is a major project to establish a 2-18 school in the Barra suburb by 2014. From 2014 onwards, the intake of pupils at Barra is from age 2 (Pre-Nursery) to age 18 (Class 11 – Year 13).

We aim to cultivate well-informed, open-minded, confident, caring and enquiring young people who strive to do their best. The emphasis on academic achievement is balanced by our concern to meet our pupils' physical, emotional and social needs and to ensure that they are prepared for active and well

balanced citizenship.

English is the language of teaching and learning. From Pre-Nursery to Class 9 the programme broadly follows the IPC and the British National Curriculum. Secondary students are prepared for the International General Certificate of Secondary Education (IGCSE) examinations and the International Baccalaureate (IB) Diploma Programme. The school has a history of creditable results in both IGCSE and the IB Diploma Programme and evident success in university entrance worldwide.

Classes are generally small and the school environment is pleasant, well-resourced and stimulating, with a strong focus on health, safety and security. Performing arts, sports, Model United Nations, Duke of Edinburgh's Award Scheme and work experience provide a wide range of co-curricular opportunities. Experiences beyond the school include numerous local day visits and national or international residential trips for most year groups from primary Class 3 upwards.

Our teachers are well-qualified (some 30% being recruited from overseas) and supported by a robust and effective

programme of continuing professional development. Foundation stage, primary and secondary education (IPC, UK National Curriculum, IGCSE; and Brazilian curriculum) and secondary – pre-university education (IB and Brazilian curriculum).

Extracurricular Activities

The extracurricular activities offered include football, capoeira, volleyball, basketball, ballet, artistic gymnastics, judo, choir, music (instruments and singing), cooking, drama and arts. Depending on the age and interest of the students, hiking and climbing, rowing and sailing lessons are offered.

Facilities

Air-conditioned classrooms, interactive Whiteboards in all classrooms and computers connected to the internet, eight science laboratories and nine computer laboratories, five libraries, gymnasium and open space for sports and games, playgrounds with a variety of toys, four auditoriums for drama classes, drama presentations and art exhibitions, five sickbays (first-aid – nurses), and five dining halls.

International schools with provision for students with special educational needs

This section features schools with specific provision for students with special educational needs

Schools ordered A–Z by Name

Baton Rouge International School

5015 Auto Plex Drive, Baton Rouge,
LA 70809 USA
Tel: +1 225 293 4338
Fax: +1 225 293 4307
Email: info@brisla.com
Website: www.brintl.com

Head of School: Nathalie Guyon
School type: Coeducational Day &
Residential
Age range of pupils: 6 weeks–18
Average class size: 14-16
Teacher/pupil ratio: 1:7

The Baton Rouge International School (BRIS) is an independent, non-profit school offering a rigorous college preparatory curriculum in a multilingual environment (English, French, Spanish, Portuguese and Chinese) from preschool through 12th grade. By engaging our students in this unique program of foreign language immersion, technology education, language arts, math and science, music, physical education and the visual and performing arts, they are equipped with the tools and resources needed to succeed in College and beyond. Our highly-qualified and diverse faculty includes certified native teachers. They are a daily example, bringing to light harmony in a world of differences. The Baton Rouge International School is currently authorized to offer the International Baccalaureate Middle Years Programme (MYP) for grades 6-10 and the IB Diploma Programme for grades 11-12. At the end of their studies, BRIS graduates receive an American High School Diploma with Advanced Placement (AP) and the International Baccalaureate Diploma (IB).

Accreditation

The Baton Rouge International School is an IB World School authorized to offer both the MYP and the DP. BRIS is also approved by the BESE and the Louisiana Department of Education/US Department of Education. In addition, BRIS is a full member of many professional/educational organizations in the United States and abroad.

Campus Facilities

The BRIS campus is located in Baton Rouge, Louisiana, USA. The modern facilities have been built on an 18-acre property in the heart of Baton Rouge. Its peaceful, green environment includes a lake visited by geese and falcons and plenty of space for playgrounds, fields for soccer and other sporting activities. The wooded site offers the tranquility needed for young minds to stay focused while enjoying campus life. BRIS recently completed a comprehensive campus Master Plan to design and build larger buildings to serve as administrative, educational and recreational facilities for the future. The design and planning reflects the innovative education that BRIS provides through contemporary and environmentally sustainable architecture. **Live Locally, Think Wisely, Communicate Globally!**

British International School, Ho Chi Minh City

BRITISH INTERNATIONAL SCHOOL
HO CHI MINH CITY

(Founded 1997)

An Phu Secondary Campus, District 2
An Phu Primary Campus, District 2
Tu Xuong Primary Campus, District 3
Tel: +84 83 744 2335 (Ext:230)
Fax: +84 83 744 2334
Email: info@bisvietnam.com
Website: www.bisvietnam.com
CEO & Principal: Shaun Williams
School type: Coeducational Day

Age range of pupils: 2–18
No. of pupils enrolled as at 01/09/2014: 1859
Boys: 909 **Girls:** 950 **Sixth Form:** 137
Fees per annum as at 01/09/2014:
US$9,300 – US$25,000
Average class size: 20
Teacher/pupil ratio: 1:10
Secondary: 1:21

The BIS Group of Schools in Vietnam has been operating the hugely successful British International School (BIS) in Ho Chi Minh City since 1997. From very modest beginnings the school has grown to become the largest international school in Vietnam and is one of the leading international schools in the South East Asia region. Further expansion of the BIS Group of Schools will take place in August 2014 with the opening of the first British International School in Hanoi.

BIS is a selective, independent and co-educational day school providing a British style curriculum for an international student body. Both Primary campuses cater for students from the Foundation Stage (Pre-school) through to Year 6 and the Secondary campus caters for students from Year 7 to Year 13.

All three of the campuses have been designed fully in line with international standards and host large libraries, music suites, computer suites, indoor 25 metre swimming pools, large sports halls and grass playing fields. The Secondary campus has excellent specialist facilities including a gymnasium, auditorium, mini theatre, science laboratories, music technology suite, drama studio, dance studio, art and design technology rooms as well as ICT suites. Foundation aged children have their own mini swimming pools, sand pits, dedicated playgrounds and climbing apparatus.

The school provides a broad, balanced and differentiated curriculum to meet the wide ranging needs of the students. Staffed by British qualified and trained teachers with relevant British curriculum experience, the education on offer is amongst the best available anywhere in the world. BIS operates within the framework of the National Curriculum for England and students are prepared for both the International General Certificate of Secondary Education (IGCSE) and the International Baccalaureate Diploma Programme (IBDP). BIS students then progress to top universities around the world.

The school is fully accredited by the prestigious Council of International Schools (CIS) and is a registered centre for the UK examination boards Cambridge International Examinations (CIE). It is also designated as an IB World School and is registered with the UK Government DfE as an overseas school. It is a full member of the Federation of British International Schools in Asia (FOBISIA).

BIS has been inspected, approved and rated as 'Outstanding' by the British Government as detailed in a British Schools Overseas (BSO) Inspection Report, March 2013.

Chamberlain International School

Chamberlain
International School

(Founded 1976)

1 Pleasant Street, PO Box 778, Middleboro, MA 02346 USA

Tel: +1 508 946 9348

Fax: +1 508 947 1593

Email: admissions@flcis.com

Website: www.chamberlainschool.org

Head of School: William Doherty

School type: Co-educational Therapeutic Boarding & Day

Age range of pupils: 11–22

No. of pupils enrolled as at 01/09/2014: 115

No. of boarders: 98

Fees per annum as at 01/09/2014:

Contact admissions@flcis.com for details

Average class size: 12

Teacher/pupil ratio: 12:1:1

Chamberlain School is a therapeutic co-educational boarding and day school for students aged 11-22 years. Students come to us from across the United States and throughout the world. We see the brightness and uniqueness in all of our students and focus on developing those positive qualities and abilities. Chamberlain is SEVIS approved by US Department of Homeland security to accept international students and issue an I-20.

Campus and facilities:

Students feel a sense of home on a peaceful and picturesque campus of historic buildings complimented by modern facilities all surrounding a traditional New England village green.

We have excellent road and rail links to Boston, Massachusetts and Providence, Rhode Island both of which have international airports that are within one hour's drive. The beautiful campus includes 9 New England style dormitories as well classroom buildings, therapists and psychiatrist's offices, nurse's station, swimming pool, automotive technology facility, art studio and gym.

Our students

Chamberlain students are between the ages of 11 and 22. They share similar challenges in their lives. Our students work hard, with the support of our faculty and staff, to balance both their gifts and their challenges. Some of our students' challenges may include emotional

dysregulation as a result of medical conditions such as bipolar disorder, depression, attentional issues, autism spectrum disorder, anxiety, obsessive-compulsive disorder and or specific learning disabilities. Our students benefit from a higher level of supervision and therapeutic support than a traditional school environment.

Hidden disabilities may prevent some students from achieving their potential. The frustrations related to unidentified strengths and disabilities can result in behavioral and social/emotional issues. School can become a frustrating experience for students who face these multiple challenges. The literature regarding best practices in teaching these

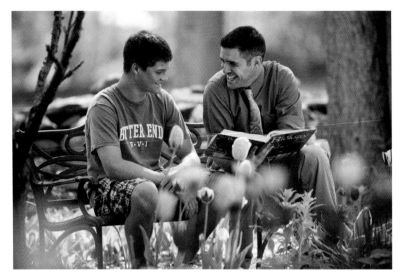

students consistently supports strength-based teaching strategies while at the same time working toward developing accommodations and compensation strategies that empower the students. Chamberlain has a wealth of experience in utilizing all of these strategies for the past 38 years.

Academic curriculum and enrichment courses

Chamberlain International School is a diploma granting institution. We offer college preparatory and general education courses to both middle and high school students. A strong focus of our academic program is on the core academic subjects: Literature, Writing, Mathematics, Social Studies, and Science. Our students benefit from additional studies in Foreign Language, Visual Arts, Automotive Technology, Physical Education, Health, and Study Skills.

The academic program at Chamberlain International School works within a larger interdisciplinary team of professionals to ensure that students successfully meet their academic potential. Teachers and Educational Supervisors work collaboratively with Speech Language Pathologists, Occupational Therapists, Clinicians and medical professionals to ensure that all strategies are being used to meet the students' goals. This team approach, coupled with the low student to teacher ratio, allows our educators to tailor and individualize content and instruction to optimize success.

Our core curriculum is further enhanced by Chamberlain's SAT/ACT Preparation Program, Vocational Training Programs, and Enrichment Course Program.

Therapeutic and clinical Support

Chamberlain students receive a high level of therapeutic support. This benefit enhances their overall experience at school which in turn leads to a higher level of success academically and socially. Having both individual and group therapy with masters level clinicians, students learn strategies to cope with stress; how to manage emotions and valuable education about the varying challenges they are facing that at times interfere with everyday life.

Each students individual therapist works closely with our two on site Psychiatrists as well as the nursing department for any medication or medically related needs our students may have.

Student life

Chamberlain International School has created a home like environment in each of its nine dormitories. The atmosphere is designed to be relaxed and calming, so that students may focus on their individualized goals. Chamberlain students learn the value of good nutrition and are taught how to budget for and prepare healthy meals. Students are encouraged to participate in a physically active schedule, through unparalleled access to activities that challenge body, heart and mind. Students have daily access to the community, enabling them to develop the necessary skills they will need to navigate the modern world. On- and off-campus student life activities include:

- Hiking
- Rock climbing
- Horseback riding
- Soccer
- Basketball
- Swimming
- Crew
- Golf
- Ski trips
- Europe, Bemuda and China trips
- Athletic club and gym
- Aviation
- The Automotive Tech program
- Movies and theater
- Professional sports games
- Student dances
- Community Service opportunities

Collège du Léman International School

COLLÈGE DU LÉMAN
Geneva — Switzerland

(Founded 1960)
74, route de Sauverny, 1290 Versoix,

Geneva, Switzerland
Tel: +41 22 775 55 55
Fax: +41 22 775 55 59
Email: admissions@cdl.ch
Website: www.cdl.ch
Director General: Mr Yves Thézé
Appointed: August 2011
School type: Coeducational Day & Boarding

Age range of pupils: 2–18
No. of pupils enrolled as at 01/04/2014: 2002
No. of boarders: 252
Fees per annum as at 01/04/2014:
Day: CHF19,900 – CHF32,900
Boarding: CHF83,000
Average class size: 18
Teacher/pupil ratio: 1:9

Collège du Léman is an international college preparatory school located in Geneva, Switzerland. Our boarding and day school programmes offer individual growth, academic excellence and life-long learning to students from Pre-K through Grade 12. We are part of the Meritas Family of Schools, a worldwide family of elite college preparatory schools that offer students the highest standards in education and unique, international learning opportunities.

Collège du Léman is an 8-hectare landscaped campus, nestled between the Jura Mountains and Lac Léman on the outskirts of Geneva. It offers attractive residential facilities and recreational areas, providing our students with a wide range of sport and leisure activities.

Collège du Léman is committed not only to excellence in education but also to stimulating enthusiasm for lifelong learning and intellectual growth.

We open our doors to students who benefit from our multicultural learning environment. We nurture a sense of social responsibility and respect for others so that our students are well-prepared to become respected world citizens. In this spirit, we endeavor to add value to our teaching through its diversity. The knowledge students gain must be applicable across cultures and be supported by qualifications recognized worldwide. We value each student's individuality as well as his or her integration into society.

Our academic programme prepares our students for the demands of the 21st century. These programmes integrates both bilingualism and multilingualism and leads to:

- English-language diplomas: American High School with or without Advanced Placement (AP), IGCSE, International Baccalaureate (IB)
- Bilingual diplomas: Swiss Maturité, International Baccalaureate (IB)
- French-language diplomas: French Baccalaureate, Swiss Maturité

ESL Programme: There is a credit bearing academy on campus for students whose first language is not English and who require additional language support. These students will work to raise their proficiency by attending a variety of English courses through the semester.

Bilingual Programme: From the age of 5, students have the opportunity to follow a bilingual (English and French) programme. Bilingualism leads to more open-mindedness and tolerance and helps children easily learn new languages, creating numerous opportunities for the future.

College and Career Guidance

Our team of college advisors at Collège du Léman are dedicated to guiding students through the college preparation and selection process, helping them access the most prestigious universities world-wide. Parents are also involved in the process and invited to information evenings. In addition, College fairs are organized throughout the academic year, allowing our students to meet representatives from top universities.

Student Life

Athletics offered: Badminton, Basketball, Cricket, Dance, Football/Soccer, Floor Hockey, Golf, Horse riding, Rugby, Sailing, Skiing,Swimming, Track & Field, Tennis, Volleyball, Yoga and many more!

Fine arts: Music, painting, theatre, dance, choir, orchestra, piano improvisations and many more!

Clubs: School magazine, Student government, Model United Nations (MUN).

Charities: MADS (Make A Difference Society), ZOA (Zambian Orphans Appeal). Students can enjoy our swimming pool, gym, weight and exercise rooms, track, library, computer labs, art studios, music and dance studios, basketball courts, and much more on the school's campus.

FAMAKS International Schools

Plot 8 Fajuyi Adekunle Crescent, Off Ajayi
Crowther Street, Asokoro, Abuja, Nigeria
Tel: +234 (0)8109884780
Email: info@famakschools.com
Website: www.famakschools.com

Head Teacher: Mr Franklin Adjetey
School type: Coeducational Day &
Boarding
Age range of pupils: 2–10

Established in January 2009 and situated in the secure and prosperous district of Asokoro, the Federal Capital Territory of Abuja and serving both local and expatriate families, FAMAKS International Schools is home to over 200 pupils from a range of religious and national backgrounds. The Kaduna Campus was opened in January 2010.

Our vision is focused on achieving excellence in a secure and stimulating learning environment offering high quality education from Early Years to Key Stage 2. We achieve this by providing a well-structured, well planned curricular – the English National Curriculum and the International Primary School Curriculum

(IPC) – and employ British trained teachers from the UK. We also engage a British educational consultant who visits regularly from the UK and spends time in the school advising, training, ensuring high quality lessons are delivered and monitors pupil progress and achievement.

FAMAKS prides itself on providing a school fit for purpose in the 21st Century. In addition to an excellent adult pupil ratio, we are also an inclusive school that provides individual educational plans, as well as health care plans for children with special educational needs. Provision is made for all children to receive high quality and nutritious meals which include breakfast, lunch and afternoon snack.

All classrooms are air-conditioned coupled with interactive white boards. There are state of the art facilities including a music room, a dance studio, a science laboratory, an ICT suite, two libraries and several play areas including a basketball and football pitch. The school also operates a flexible boarding house facility.

A leader in the provision of world class learning facilities and environments, FAMAKS draws upon the practices of leading international schools in the world. We are a member of the Council of British International Schools (COBIS) and the Association of International Schools in Africa (AISA).

International School of Curaçao

International
School of
Curaçao

(Founded 1968)

PO Box 3090, Koninginnelaan z/n,
Emmastad, Curaçao
Tel: +599 9 737 3633
Fax: +599 9 737 3142
Email: info@isc.cw
Website: www.isc.cw
Director: Ms Margie Elhage-Cancio PhD
School type: Coeducational Day

Age range of pupils: 2–19
No. of pupils enrolled as at 01/09/2013: 454
Boys: 239 **Girls:** 216
Fees per annum as at 01/09/2013:
Contact Mrs Loraine van Rosberg at:
vanrosbergl@isc.cw
Average class size: 15
Teacher/pupil ratio: 1:7

Our School
The International School of Curaçao is an accredited, non-profit, private, co-educational, day school (K-12) that provides instruction in English.

Vision
An international education today for the global citizens of tomorrow.

Mission
The International School of Curaçao (ISC) educates students from diverse cultures to have the skills to think creatively, communicate effectively, reason critically, and act compassionately. ISC has pledged to achieve this by providing a high quality English medium education using United States and internationally recognized standards.

Elementary School
ISC offers the First Steps Program, a nursery program for 2 year-olds. The Elementary School begins with kindergarten for 3 years old and extends to Grade 5. In addition to Language, Mathematics, Science and Social Studies, students receive formal instruction in Art, Music, Library, Physical Education, Computer, Spanish and Dutch. We expect children to become skilled thinkers, problem solvers, readers, authors and mathematicians, to be able to succeed in later grades.

Middle School
Our Middle School offers a program tailored to the unique social and learning needs of adolescent students in grades 6, 7 and 8. We strive to enable students to think, create, solve problems, organize themselves, research essential questions, and most importantly to celebrate the differences within themselves and those around them.

High School
Our high school offers a vigorous liberal arts education for every student and fosters international understanding. Advanced Placement (AP) courses are offered in Spanish and Spanish Literature. Students can take a full IB Diploma in the 11th and 12th grade or opt to pursue individual certificates in the different subject areas.

Special Programs
English as a Second Language, Learning Resource, Highly Able Program, Guidance Counseling and College Placement.

Memberships
Association of American Schools in South America (AASSA), College Board National Association for College Admission Counseling.

Accreditation
Southern Association of Colleges and Schools (SACS), Council of International Schools (CIS).

NIST International School

NIST INTERNATIONAL SCHOOL

(Founded 1992)

36 Soi 15 Sukhumvit Road, Wattana,
Bangkok, 10110 Thailand
Tel: +66 2 651 2065
Fax: +66 2 253 3800
Email: admissions@nist.ac.th
Website: www.nist.ac.th
Headmaster: Mr James MacDonald

Appointed: July 2013
School type: Coeducational Day
Age range of pupils: 3–18
No. of pupils enrolled as at 01/09/2014: 1538
Fees per annum as at 01/09/2014:
US$12,000 – US$22,000
Average class size: 23

The first and only full, not-for-profit IB World School in Thailand, NIST International School was established in 1992 with the guidance and support of the United Nations. The school now welcomes over 1,500 students of over 50 nationalities and provides all three International Baccalaureate programmes: the Primary Years Programme (PYP), Middle Years Programme (MYP) and Diploma Programme (DP). NIST is governed by the Foundation for International Education and is accredited through the Council of International Schools (CIS) and New England Association of Schools and Colleges (NEASC).

Recognized worldwide for its progressive approach, the IB programmes provide students with critical 21st century skills. The academic structure emphasizes exploration, risk-taking and trans-disciplinary learning. All students are required to take part in community service activities that encourage participants to empathize with others and take an active role in solving issues. As of 2014, NIST has also partnered with other top international schools to offer the Global Citizen Diploma, a supplementary component that assesses graduates' leadership, service and community engagement.

In addition to its rigorous academics, NIST provides students with an expansive World Languages Programme and more than 300 extra-curricular activity options. As one of the founding members of the Southeast Asia Student Activity Conference (SEASAC), the NIST Falcons compete against their peers from other top schools in Southeast Asia. NIST has also committed itself to IT excellence and innovation. The school offers students the use of MacBook Air computers, iPads, a completely wireless campus, SMART Boards, FrontRow classroom amplification system, and LCD-equipped classrooms.

NIST represents the future of education through its stellar academic achievements; engaged, community-driven culture; forward-looking philosophy; and expansive resources. With its graduates attending the best universities in the world and going on to become community leaders, NIST International School has become recognized as one of the world's leading learning institutions.

Shrewsbury International School

**SHREWSBURY
INTERNATIONAL
SCHOOL**
BANGKOK

1922 Charoen Krung Road, Wat
Phrayakrai, Bang Kholame, Bangkok
10120, Thailand
Tel: +66 2 675 1888
Fax: +66 2 675 3606
Email: admissions@shrewsbury.ac.th

Website: www.shrewsbury.ac.th
Principal: Stephen Holroyd
School type: Coeducational Day
Age range of pupils: 3–18
No. of pupils enrolled as at 01/09/2014: 1600

Since opening its doors in 2003, Shrewsbury International School has built a reputation for academic success as well as excellence in sport, music and the creative and performing arts. The school's exam results speak for themselves. In 2013, 65% of IGCSE passes were at A*-A grade and 77% of A level passes were at A*-B grade. Shrewsbury's graduating students in 2014 will take up places at the world's leading universities including Oxford, Cambridge, UCL and LSE in the UK as well as UCLA, UPenn and Carnegie Mellon in the US.

Shrewsbury International School offers an inspirational English language education for carefully selected students,

caring for them in an organization committed to continuous improvement, and providing outstanding opportunities both in and out of the classroom.

The school, which caters for children age 3-18 from 35 nationalities, enjoys a stunning location on the banks of the Chaophraya River in Central Bangkok with many of Shrewsbury's 1,600 pupils travelling to school by boat. The spacious, purpose-built campus – staffed by hand-picked teachers mostly from the UK – provides excellent facilities and resources.

Pupils are stretched to meet their potential through the varied and challenging British curriculum and small

class sizes ensure that each student receives the individual support they require in their all-round development as people. Field trips out of school, concerts, productions, sports competitions and a vast range of extracurricular activities add breadth and interest as our pupils move up through the school.

The school enjoys genuine and close links with Shrewsbury School in the UK. The Board of Governors includes Sir David Lees, Chairman to the Court of the Bank of England, and two members who act as governors to both schools. Stephen Holroyd worked at Shrewsbury UK for 20 years before taking over as Principal at the Bangkok School.

St Columba's College

(Founded 1843)

Kilmashogue Lane, Whitechurch, Dublin 16, Ireland

Tel: +353 1 4906791

Fax: +353 1 4936655

Email: admin@stcolumbas.ie

Website: www.stcolumbas.ie

Warden: L J Haslett BA, DPhil, PGCE

Appointed: 2001

School type: Coeducational Day & Boarding

Religious Denomination: Church of Ireland (Anglican)

Age range of pupils: 11–18

No. of pupils enrolled as at 01/09/2014: 295

Boys: 159 **Girls:** 136 **Sixth Form:** 137

No. of boarders: 240

Fees per annum as at 01/09/2014:

Day: €3,452–€4,944

Full Boarding: €6,207–€7,450

Average class size: 15 (junior); 10 (senior)

Teacher/pupil ratio: 1:8

St Columba's College is an HMC, Church of Ireland (Anglican) boarding and day school for boys and girls aged 11-18. Situated on the slopes of the Dublin mountains, overlooking Dublin Bay, the College enjoys the benefits of easy access to the Irish capital with the charms of a rural setting.

Ours is a deliberately small school of just 295 pupils. This size is a fundamental part of our ethos because we believe in a strong sense of togetherness in an atmosphere that is caring and supportive of all. We value the quality of the relationships we enjoy between teachers and pupils who live side-by-side and work together productively on a daily basis.

We have high academic standards – among the very best in Ireland – and almost all of our pupils go on to universities in Ireland and the UK. We encourage every individual pupil to get involved in the broader life of the college, whether it be in music, sport, drama, debating or public speaking. We aim to develop well-rounded and happy boys and girls with the self-confidence to mix freely and easily with others, whatever their background or age.

Occupying 150 acres, St Columba's has buildings dating from its establishment in 1843, through the last century and into the new millennium. In the past five years, the college has invested around €15million to ensure that it continues to offer its pupils the best facilities in terms of classrooms, sports facilities and accommodation. Recent additions have been new, purpose-built and refurbished boarding houses, state-of-the-art music rooms, a second Astroturf hockey pitch and an additional dining room, as well as classrooms and common rooms. In addition, the College boasts a library and study rooms that are second to none in terms of facilities and resources, and a sports hall that provides facilities for indoor sport as well as a health and fitness suite and a dance studio.

The College offers seven-day boarding, which includes Saturday morning classes, six afternoons of sport for all, and a comprehensive range of weekend activities for its pupils. Our emphasis is on participation and involvement. Please visit our website (www.stcolumbas.ie) or phone for a prospectus. We welcome prospective parents and their children, and we look forward to a visit from you in the future.

Directory of
international schools

International schools in Africa

Schools ordered A–Z by Country

Key to directory

Country

Name of school or college

Indicates that this school
has a profile

Address and contact number

Head's name

Age range

Number of pupils.
B = boys G = girls VIth = sixth form

Fees per annum.
Day = fees for day pupils.
WB = fees for weekly boarders.
FB = fees for full boarders.

Curriculum

Language of instruction

Memberships/Accreditation

Whereford

College Academy

For further details see p.00

Which Street, Whosville,
Wherefordshire AB12 3CD

Tel: 01000 000000

Head Master: Dr A Person

Age range: 11–18

No. of pupils:
660 B330 G330 VIth 200

Fees: Day £11,000
WB £16,000 FB £20,000

Curriculum:
National, IBDP, ALevs

Language instr:
English, French

(AISA) (COB) (EAR)

Key to icons

Key to symbols:

(♦) Boys' school

(♦) Girls' school

(♦) Boarding accommodation

Member of:

(AISA) Association of International
Schools in Africa

(CEE) Central and Eastern European
Schools Association

(EAR) East Asia Regional Council of
Overseas Schools

(ECIS) European Council of
International Schools

(RS) Round Square

Accreditation:

(CIS) Council of International Schools

(COB) Council of British International
Schools

Please note: Schools are coeducational day schools unless otherwise indicated

Angola

English School Community of Luanda
Rua de Cambambe, No 21-23, Bairro Patrice Lumumba, Luanda, Angola
Tel: +244 222 443 416
Head: Trevor Munroe
Age range: 4–13
(ECIS)

Luanda International School
Rua de Talatona, Caixa Postal 1566, Luanda, Angola
Tel: +244 222 460752
Director: Anthony Baron
Age range: 3–18
No. of pupils: 389 B199 G190
Curriculum: IBDP, IBMYP, IBPYP
Language instr: English
(CIS)

Benin

American International School of Cotonou
Fifatin, Akpakpa, Cotonou, Benin
Tel: +229 21 048 999
Head of School: Richard Houmbie
Language instr: English
(AISA)

English International School
Haie Vive, Cotonou, Benin
Tel: +229 21 30 32 65
Head of School: Rebecca Khelseau-Carsky
Language instr: English
(AISA)

International Christian School of Benin
PO Box 62457, Cotonou, Benin
Tel: +229 339 431
Head of School: Edna Tounou
Language instr: English
(✝) (AISA)

Botswana

Broadhurst Primary School
Private Bag Br 114, Broadhurst, Gaborone, Botswana
Tel: +267 3971221
Head Teacher: Rehana Khan
Age range: 5–13
No. of pupils: 405 B196 G209

Kopano Primary School
PO Box 206, Selebi Phikwe, Botswana
Tel: +267 2610552
Headmaster: Nasim Miller
Age range: 3–13
No. of pupils: 439 B210 G229
Language instr: English

Legae Academy
PO Box 750, Mogoditshane, Botswana
Tel: +267 3924 313
Principal: Easo Oommen
Age range: 11–21
No. of pupils: 677
Fees: P33,600
Curriculum: UK, IGCSE, ALevs
Language instr: English

Maru A Pula School
Private Bag 0045, Gaborone, Botswana
Tel: +267 391 2953
Principal: Andrew Taylor
Age range: 12–20
No. of pupils: 618 B320 G298
Curriculum: ALevs
(🏛)

Northside Primary School
Plot 2786, Tshekedi Crescent, Gaborone, 0000 Botswana
Tel: +267 3926210
Head of School: Mark McCarthy
Age range: 5–13
No. of pupils: 497 B254 G243
Curriculum: IBPYP
Language instr: English

Northside School
PO Box 897, Gaborone, Botswana
Tel: +267 3952440
Head: Mark McCarthy
Age range: 5–13
No. of pupils: 462 B236 G226
Curriculum: National, UK
(CIS)

Westwood International School
Plot 22978, Mmankgwedi Road, P.O. Box 2448, Gaborone, Botswana
Tel: +267 3906 736
Head of School: Helge Gallinger
Age range: 5–19
No. of pupils: 435
Fees: $6,318.18–$10,954
Curriculum: IBDP, IBMYP, IBPYP, IGCSE
Language instr: English
(AISA) (CIS)

Burkina Faso

International School of Ouagadougou
s/c Ambassade des Etats Unis, 01 BP 35, Ouagadougou, Burkina Faso
Tel: +226 50 36 21 43
Director: Sean Goudie
Age range: 3–16
No. of pupils: 106
Curriculum: SAT
(AISA)

Cameroon

American School of Douala
BP 1909, Douala, Cameroon
Tel: +237 3342 1437
Director: Beverly Sortland
Age range: 3–16
No. of pupils: 110 B50 G60
Fees: US$6,300–US$13,560
Curriculum: USA
(AISA)

American School of Yaounde
BP 7475, Yaounde, Cameroon
Tel: +237 2223 0421/2222 9465
Director: Sheena Nabholz
Age range: 3–18
No. of pupils: 170 B85 G85 VIth20
Fees: US$5,000–US$15,000
Language instr: English
(🏛) (AISA) (CIS)

Rain Forest International School
S I L BP 1299, Yaounde, Cameroon
Tel: +237 7793 7162
Director: Lois Anderson
Age range: 12–19
No. of pupils: 105
Curriculum: ACT, AP, SAT, TOEFL, USA
Language instr: English
(🏛) (AISA)

Yondo International High School
PO Box 14387, Yaoundé, Cameroon
Tel: +237 97 83 65 79
Head of School: Georges Fouda
(AISA)

Democratic Republic of the Congo

Cartesian School (Gs le Cartesien)
Kinshasa, Democratic Republic of the Congo
Tel: +243 999942280
Director: Steve Mbikayi
Language instr: French, English, Spanish
(ISA)

English-Speaking School of Lubumbashi
1 Route Kipopo (Quartier Golf), Lubumbashi, Democratic Republic of the Congo
Tel: +243 81 19 87 013
Head of School: Ellen Hoover
Language instr: English

International School Pointe Noire
Lotissement Tchikobo, Pointe-Noire, Democratic Republic of the Congo
Tel: +234 748 7700
Head of School: Garry Gibbons
Language instr: English
(AISA)

Jewels International School of Kinshasa
O.U.A., Commune of Ngaliema, Kinshasa, Democratic Republic of the Congo
Tel: +243 99 99 09 163
Principal: Najma Munshi
Language instr: English
(AISA)

The American School of Kinshasa
Rue de Matadi, Kinshasha, Democratic Republic of the Congo
Tel: +243 81 70 05 567
Head: Ronald Brown
No. of pupils: 163
Curriculum: AP, SAT
(AISA)

Egypt

Alexandria International Academy
Villa 7, Road 61, off Kamal El-Din Salah Street, Alexandria, Egypt
Tel: +20 12 224 8228
Casado: Nesreen El Sabban
Curriculum: IBPYP

British School of Alexandria
Mahmoud Aboul Ela Street, Kafr Abdou, Roushd, Alexandria, Egypt
Tel: +2 03 544 5426
Head Teacher: Terry Garbett
Age range: 3–18
(COB)

Cairo American College
PO Box 39, Maadi, Cairo, 11431 Egypt
Tel: +20 2 2755 5555
Head of School: Wayne Rutherford
Age range: 4–18
No. of pupils: 1400 B497 G440
Fees: US$20,000–US$20,700
Curriculum: AP, IBDP, SAT, USA
Language instr: English
(ECIS)

Cairo British School
39 El Kods El Sharif Street, Lebanon Square, Mohandeseen, Cairo, 12411 Egypt
Tel: +20 23 346 0109
Principal: R W W Swan
Age range: 2–11
No. of pupils: 99 B50 G49
Fees: Day £1,910–£2,727
Curriculum: SAT, UK
Language instr: English

Cairo English School
PO Box 8090, Masaken Nasr
City, New Cairo Egypt
Tel: +20 2 2448 3433
Head of School: Craif Monaghan
Age range: 3–15
No. of pupils: 457 B297 G160
Fees: Day £2,250–£4,100
Curriculum: IBDP, UK
Language instr: English
(CIS) (ECIS)

**Deutsche Schule
Beverly Hills Kairo**
Beverly Hills Compound,
Sheikh Zayed, 2 Egypt
Tel: +20 238 570 510 +11
Curriculum: IBDP
Language instr: English

Ecole Oasis Internationale
Zahraa El Maadi, Quarter no 3
and no 7 Part A & B, Cairo, Egypt
Tel: +202 16949-16979
Principal: Esmat Lamei
Age range: 3–18
No. of pupils: 1181 B535 G646
Curriculum: IBDP, IBMYP, IBPYP
Language instr: French
(CIS)

**Egypt British
International School**
5th Urban District, El Banafseg Zone,
Area 1, New Cairo City, Egypt
Tel: +20 2 2920 0101
Principal: Lyn Howard-Mitchell
Age range: 3–18
No. of pupils: 1000
Curriculum: UK
(COB)

**El Alsson British
& American
International School**
PO Box 13, Embaba,
Cairo, 12411 Egypt
Tel: +20 2 3388 8510
Age range: 3–18
No. of pupils: B799 G785
Curriculum: AP, SAT, UK,
USA, IGCSE, ALevs
Language instr: English

**El Gouna International
School**
El Gouna, Nr Hurghada,
Red Sea, Egypt
Tel: +20 265 580080
Age range: 4–16
No. of pupils: 285 B145 G140
Curriculum: National, UK

**Green Land – Pré
Vert International
Schools – GPIS-Egypt**
405 Gezirat Mohamed
Street, Giza, Egypt
Tel: +20 (010) 2226052
Founding Chairman: Amr
Ahmed Mokhtar
Age range: 1 –18
Curriculum: IBDP, IBMYP, IBPYP
Language instr: French,
English, Arabic

**Hayah International
Academy**
South of Police Academy, 5th
District, New Cairo, Egypt
Tel: +202 29299582-4
Head of School: Abeya Fathy
Age range: 3–18
No. of pupils: 1100
Fees: $9,200
Curriculum: IBDP
Language instr: English

**Integrated Thebes
American College in Cairo**
Box 3021 Madinat
Alsalam, Cairo, Egypt
Tel: +20 22 4772317
Age range: 3–18
No. of pupils: 500
Curriculum: USA

**International Arab
Egyptian School**
Kilo 4.5, Ezz El Din, Ismailia, Egypt
Tel: +20 264 3312327
Principal: Mohamed
Fouad Rasheed
Age range: 3–18
No. of pupils: 145 B40 G105
Curriculum: National
(symbol)

**International School
of Choueifat**
PO Box 2760, Al Horreya,
Heliopolis, Cairo, Egypt
(ECIS)

**International School
of Choueifat – City
of 6 October**
PO Box 31, PCode 12582,
Dreamland, City of 6
October, Al Giza, Egypt
Tel: +202 3855 3210
Acting Director: Robert Kleynhans
Age range: 3–15
No. of pupils: 102 B58 G44
(ECIS)

**International Schools
of Egypt – Alexandria**
PO Box 402, Sidi Gaber,
Alexandria, Egypt
Tel: +20 3 54 4498
Headmaster: Frank Znideric
Age range: 3–18
No. of pupils: 210 B120 G90
Fees: US$2,620–US$6,200
Curriculum: National, UK, IGCSE
(ECIS)

**Maadi British
International School**
4th District next to Wadi Degla
Club, Zahraa El Maadi, Egypt
Tel: +20 22 7058671/2/3/4/5
Head Teacher: Richard White
Age range: 3–11
No. of pupils: 370 B180 G190
Fees: Day £6,420
Curriculum: SAT, UK
Language instr: English
(COB) (ECIS)

**Modern English
School Cairo**
South of Police Adademy, PO Box 5
New Cairo, New Cairo, 11835 Egypt
Tel: +202 2618 9600
Principal: Matthew Kirby
Age range: 3.5–18
No. of pupils: 2097
Fees: Day £3,050–£6,800
Curriculum: ACT, AP, IBDP,
SAT, UK, USA, IGCSE, ALevs
Language instr: English
(ECIS)

Narmer American College
20 El-Narguis Service Area, New
Cairo City, Cairo, 11477 Egypt
Tel: +202 29201200
Head: Youssef Salah El Din
Curriculum: USA

**New Cairo British
International School**
Road 17, 1st Zone, 3rd
Settlement, 5th District, New
Cairo City, Cairo, Egypt
Tel: +20 (0)2 2758 2881
Principal: Raymond Williams
Age range: 3–18
No. of pupils: 720
Fees: Day £4,406–£9,526
Curriculum: IBDP, IBPYP,
National, UK, IGCSE
Language instr: English
(CIS) (COB) (ECIS)

**New Horizon Junior
& High School**
PO Box 1079, Zahraa Al Maadi City,
Sector #3, Maadi, Cairo, Egypt
Tel: +20 22 516 2685
Director: Aicha Wassef
Age range: 4–17
No. of pupils: 539 B277 G262
(ECIS)

**New Vision International
Schools**
S1-14 Beverly Hills, Sheikh
Zayed, Giza, 12588 Egypt
Tel: +202 3857 1220
Head of School: Geoffrey Darlison
Curriculum: IBPYP
Language instr: Arabic, English

Schutz American School
Post Box 1000, Alexandria, Egypt
Tel: +20 3 576 2205
Head of School: Joyce Martinez
Age range: 3–18
No. of pupils: 219
Curriculum: AP, SAT
(CIS)

**Smart International
School in Egypt**
K22 Cairo-Alexandria Desert
Road, adj Hazem Hassan
(KPMG), Giza, Egypt
Tel: +202 353 62004/6
Principal: W El Salmi
Age range: 2–16
Curriculum: UK
Language instr: English

**The American
International School in
Egypt, Main Campus**
PO Box 8090, Masaken, Nasr
City, Cairo, 11371 Egypt
Tel: +20 2 2618 8400
Director: Bill Delbrugge
Age range: 4–18
No. of pupils: 1408 B829 G579
Fees: $5,900–$10,300
Curriculum: AP, IBDP, SAT, USA
Language instr: English
(CIS) (ECIS)

**The American
International School in
Egypt, West Campus**
Sheikh Zayed City, Entrance
2, Greens Compound,
Cairo, 12588 Egypt
Tel: +20 2 3851 0616
Head of School: Walther Hetzer
Curriculum: IBDP
(ECIS)

**The British International
School of Cairo**
PO Box 137, Gezira, Cairo, Egypt
Tel: +202 3827 0444
Principal: Simon O'Grady
Age range: 3–18
No. of pupils: 580
Fees: E£8,881
Curriculum: IBDP, UK
Language instr: English
(COB) (ECIS)

The British School Al Rehab
Al Rehab City, Suez Road,
New Cairo, Egypt
Tel: +202 2 607 0292
Principal: Ian Harrison
Age range: 3–18
No. of pupils: 780 B390 G390
Fees: LE20,000–LE45,000
Curriculum: SAT, UK, IGCSE
Language instr: English
(COB)

The British School in Cairo
D3 Ring Road Maadi, Cairo, Egypt
Tel: +20 100 250 67 08
Age range: 3–18
No. of pupils: 400
Curriculum: National, UK

Eritrea

**Asmara International
Community School**
PO Box 4941, 117-19 Street,
#6, Asmara, Eritrea
Tel: +291 1 161705
Director: Paul Neary
Age range: 4–19
No. of pupils: 155 B99 G56
Curriculum: ACT, IPC,
SAT, TOEFL, USA
Language instr: English
(AISA)

Ethiopia

Andinet International School
PO Box 1289, Addis Ababa, Ethiopia
Tel: +251 011 618 6541
Principal: Nefertiti Makeda
Age range: 4–16
(AISA)

British International School, Addis Ababa
Ring Road, Bole, Addis Ababa, Ethiopia
Tel: +251 11 663 07 07
Head of School: Neil Page
Curriculum: UK
Language instr: English
(AISA)

German Embassy School Addis Ababa
PO Box 1372, Addis Abeba, Ethiopia
Tel: +251 11 553 4465
Head of School: Monika Biegel
Age range: 3–18
No. of pupils: 143 B77 G66
Fees: €8,625
Curriculum: IBDP
Language instr: English, German

International Community School of Addis Ababa
PO Box 70282, Addis Ababa, Ethiopia
Tel: +251 113 711544
Head of School: James Laney Jr
Age range: 3–18
No. of pupils: B405 G394
Fees: US$7,100–US$23,200
Curriculum: ACT, IBDP, SAT, USA
Language instr: English
(AISA)

Sandford International School
PO Box 30056 MA, Addis Ababa, Ethiopia
Tel: +251 111 552 275
Head of School: Kumlachew Aberra
Age range: 3–18
No. of pupils: 673 B372 G301
Curriculum: IBDP
Language instr: English

Gabon

American International School Libreville
BP 4000, Quartier Glass, Libreville, Gabon
Tel: +241 0174 3332
Head of School: Robert Bennett
Language instr: English
(AISA)

Ghana

Galaxy International School
3rd Osu Badu Link Airport, West Residential Area, Accra, Ghana
Tel: +233 302 911 646
Head of School: Yusuf Coskun
Language instr: English
(AISA)

Ghana International School
PO Box 2856, Accra, Ghana
Tel: +233 21 777163/773299/775143
Principal: Diana Nyatepe-Coo
Age range: 3–18
No. of pupils: 1174 B624 G550
Curriculum: UK, USA, ALevs
Language instr: English
(AISA) (CIS)

International Community School
Pakyi No. 2, Kumasi, Ghana
Tel: +233 32 209 1443
Language instr: English
(RS)

International School of Ahafo
C825/26 Lagos Ave., Accra, Ghana
Tel: +233 244 311 493
Head of School: Peter Single-Liertz
(AISA)

Lincoln Community School
N126/21 Dedeibaa St, Abelenkpe, Accra, Ghana
Tel: +233 30 277 4018
Head of School: Dennis Larkin
Age range: 3–18
No. of pupils: 580 B290 G290
Fees: US$5,985–US$14,150
Curriculum: IBDP, IBMYP, IBPYP, SAT
Language instr: English
(AISA) (CIS)

SOS-Hermann Gmeiner International College
Private Mail Bag, Community 6, Tema, Ghana
Tel: +233 303 202907
Principal: I T Ofei
Age range: 14–18
No. of pupils: 319 B157 G162
Fees: US$1,000
Curriculum: IBDP, ALevs
Language instr: English
(AISA) (ISA)

Takoradi International School
PO Box 453, Takoradi, Ghana
Tel: +233 31 20 25 681
Head of School: Naana Wereko
(AISA)

Tema International School
PO Box CO 864, Tema, Ghana
Tel: +233 303 305134, +233 303 308737
Head of School: Uzoamaka Agyare-Kumi
Age range: 12–18
No. of pupils: 330 B168 G163
Fees: US$7,800
Curriculum: IBDP, GCSE
Language instr: English
(ISA)

The Roman Ridge School
PO Box GP 21057, 8 Onyasia Crescent, Roman Ridge, Accra, Ghana
Tel: +233 302 780456 / 7
Principal: V Mainoo
Age range: 4–18
No. of pupils: 434 B226 G208 VIth30
Fees: US$1,450–US$1,850
Curriculum: National, ALevs
Language instr: English

Guinea

American International School of Conakry
US Department of State, 2110 Conakry Place, Washington, DC 20521-2110, USA Guinea
Tel: +224 622 66 15 35
Director: Timothy Casey
Age range: 2–18
Fees: US$2,700–US$15,000
Curriculum: USA
Language instr: English
(AISA)

Ivory Coast

International Community School of Abidjan
Po Box 06 BP 544, Abidjan, Ivory Coast
Tel: +225 22 471152
Principal: Daphne Neal
Age range: 5–19
No. of pupils: 110 B60 G50
Fees: US$8,000–US$13,900
Curriculum: AP, SAT, USA
(AISA) (CIS)

Kenya

Aga Khan Academy, Mombasa
PO Box 90066 – 80100, Mombasa, Kenya
Tel: +254 41 223 0413
Head of Academy: Rob Burrough
Age range: 2–18
No. of pupils: 780 B410 G370
Curriculum: IBDP, IBMYP, IBPYP
Language instr: English
(AISA)

Banda School
PO Box 24722, Nairobi 00502, Kenya
Tel: +254 020 8891220/260/8890337/3547828
Head: Alison Francombe
Age range: 1–13
No. of pupils: 400 B185 G215
Fees: Ksh60,500–Ksh437,500
Curriculum: UK
Language instr: English

BRAEBURN GARDEN ESTATE SCHOOL
For further details see p. 61
PO Box 16944, 00620 Nairobi, Kenya
Tel: +254 20 501 8000
Email: headmaster@braeburn.ac.ke
Website: www.gardenestate.braeburn.com
Executive Head: John Herbert
Age range: 2–18
No. of pupils: 605
Curriculum: IBDP, UK, IGCSE, ALevs
Language instr: English
(CIS)

BRAEBURN IMANI INTERNATIONAL SCHOOL
For further details see p. 62
PO Box 750. 00100 Thika, Kenya
Tel: +254 (0)20 2029322 / 44
Email: margaret.waithira @braeburn.ac.ke
Website: www.imani.braeburn.com
Head of Secondary School: Catherine Sat
Age range: 2–18
No. of pupils: 175
Curriculum: UK, IGCSE, ALevs
Language instr: English

BRAEBURN KISUMU INTERNATIONAL SCHOOL
For further details see p. 63
PO Box 1276, 4010 Kisumu, Kenya
Tel: +254 (057) 202 3471
Email: admin@kis.co.ke
Website: www.kisumu.braeburn.com
Head of School: Carmel O'Dolan
Age range: 18 months–16 years
No. of pupils: 104
Curriculum: UK

BRAEBURN MOMBASA INTERNATIONAL SCHOOL
For further details see p. 64
PO Box 83009, Mombasa, Kenya
Tel: +254 20 202 6156
Email: enquiries@
braeburnmombasa.ac.ke
Website:
www.mombasa.braeburn.com
Head of High School: Peter
Barnard
Age range: 2–18
No. of pupils: 270
Curriculum: UK, ALevs

BRAEBURN NANYUKI INTERNATIONAL SCHOOL
For further details see p. 65
Cottage Hospital Road, PO Box
1537, 10400 Nanyuki, Kenya
Tel: +254 (0)20 211 3624
Email: nanyuki@braeburn.ac.ke
Website:
www.nanyuki.braeburn.com
Head of School: Eva Kioko
Age range: 2–11
No. of pupils: 123

BRAEBURN SCHOOL
For further details see p. 66
PO Box 45112, Gitanga
Road, Lavington, Nairobi
GPO 00100, Kenya
Tel: +254 20 501 8000
Email: enquiries@braeburn.ac.ke
Website: www.braeburnschool.
braeburn.com
Executive Head: Scott Webber
Age range: 3–18
No. of pupils: 993
Curriculum: IGCSE, ALevs
Language instr: English

BRAESIDE SCHOOLS
For further details see p. 67
PO Box 25578, 1603
Nairobi, Kenya
Tel: +254 20 501 8000
Email: headsec@braeside.ac.ke
Website:
www.braeside.braeburn.com
Executive Head: Andy Hill
Age range: 2–18
No. of pupils: 900
Curriculum: UK

BROOKHOUSE SCHOOL
For further details see p. 69
PO Box 24987, Nairobi,
00502 Kenya
Tel: +254 02 243 9261
Email: info@brookhouse.ac.ke
Website:
www.brookhouse.ac.ke
Director: John O'Connor
Age range: 2–19
No. of pupils: 750 B375 G375
Fees: US$17,500
Curriculum: IGCSE, ALevs
Language instr: English

Cavina School
PO Box 43090, Nairobi, Kenya
Tel: +254 2 3866011/3877079
Headmaster: R A Massie-Blomfield
Age range: 3–13
No. of pupils: 200 B100 G100
Curriculum: UK
Language instr: English

Greensteds International School
Private Bag, Nakuru, Kenya
Tel: +254 50 50770
Headmaster: M P Bentley
Age range: 6–18
No. of pupils: 280
Fees: Ksh138,000–Ksh776,250
Curriculum: UK

Hillcrest International Schools
PO Box 24819, Karen
00502, Nairobi, Kenya
Tel: +(254 20) 806 7783/4
Principal: Chris Wheeler
Age range: 18 months–18 years
No. of pupils: 750
Curriculum: UK, IGCSE, ALevs
Language instr: English

International School of Kenya
End of Peponi Road/Kirawa Road,
PO Box 14103, Nairobi, 00800 Kenya
Tel: +254 20 209 1308/9
Director: John S Roberts
Age range: 4–18 B4–18 G4–18
No. of pupils: 874
Fees: US$10,450–US$20,895
Curriculum: IBDP, SAT, USA
Language instr: English

Kenton College Preparatory School
PO Box 30017, Nairobi, 00100 Kenya
Tel: +254 20 4347000
Headmistress: M Cussans
Age range: 6–13+
No. of pupils: 294 B135 G140
Fees: Ksh430,000
Curriculum: UK
Language instr: English

Mombasa Academy
PO Box 86487, Mombasa, Kenya
Tel: +254 41 471629
Head: P R Uppal
Age range: 3–18
Curriculum: UK, IGCSE, ALevs

Nairobi Academy Secondary School
PO Box 24817-00502, Nairobi, Kenya
Tel: +254 20 891156
Head Teacher: Nina Rebeiro
Age range: 12–18
Fees: Ksh465,000–Ksh855,000
Curriculum: UK, IGCSE, ALevs
Language instr: English

Oshwal Academy Nairobi
PO Box 1130 00606, Sarit
Centre, Nairobi, Kenya
Tel: +254 20 3748334
Principal: Chimnoy Banerjee
Language instr: English

Pembroke House School
PO Box 31, 20116 Gilgil, Kenya
Tel: +254 (0)20 231 2323
Headmistress: Deborah Boyd-Moss
Age range: 6–13
No. of pupils: 190 B101 G89
Curriculum: UK

Peponi House Preparatory School
PO Box 23203, Lower Kabete,
Nairobi 00604, Kenya
Tel: +254 (0)20 2585710
Headmaster: Robert Blake
Age range: 6–13
No. of pupils: 387 B193 G194
Language instr: English

Peponi School
Box 236, Ruiru, Kenya
Tel: +254 020 3546456
Principal: David J Marshall
Age range: 12–19
No. of pupils: 92 B64 G58
Fees: Day £4,646–£4,980
FB £5,650–£5,770
Curriculum: UK, ALevs

Rosslyn Academy
PO Box 14146, Nairobi, 00800 Kenya
Tel: +254 20 263 5294
Superintendent: Phil Dow
Age range: 4–18
No. of pupils: 650
Curriculum: ACT, SAT, USA
Language instr: English

Sandpiper's Preparatory School
PO Box 1188, Malindi, Kenya
Tel: +254 42 30432
Headmaster: Ivan Gannaway
Age range: 2–10
No. of pupils: 60 B30 G30
Curriculum: UK
Language instr: English

St Andrew's Prep School
Private Bag, Molo, 20106 Kenya
Tel: +254 20 2025 709/8
Headmaster: Paddy Moss
Age range: 5–13

St Andrew's Senior School
Private Bag, Molo, 20106 Kenya
Tel: +254 735 337736
Headmaster: Adrian Palmer
Language instr: English

St Mary's School
PO Box 40580, Rhapta Road,
Nairobi, 00100 Kenya
Tel: +254 20 4444 569
Head of School: Francis Mburu
No. of pupils: 814
Fees: Kshs320,000
Curriculum: IBDP
Language instr: English

The Aga Khan Academy, Nairobi
1st Avenue Parklands, PO Box
44424-00100, Nairobi, Kenya
Tel: Junior: +254 20 374 0733,
Senior: +254 20 374 9495
Head of Senior School: Jerri-
Lynn Hainstock
Age range: 3–19
No. of pupils: 900
Curriculum: IBDP, IBMYP, IBPYP
Language instr: English

The Aga Khan Nursery School, Nairobi
PO Box 14998, Nairobi, 00800 Kenya
Tel: +254 020 374 2114
Head of School: Dorena Maina
Curriculum: IBPYP

Tigoni Academy
Box Box 999, Limuru, Kenya
Tel: +254 66 40961/50145
Headmaster: Duncan Kelly
Age range: G10–16
No. of pupils: 30 B5 G25

Lesotho

American International School of Lesotho
14 United Nations Road,
Maseru, Lesotho
Tel: +266 223 229 87
Head of School: Dwight Mott
Language instr: English

**Machabeng College,
International School
of Lesotho**
PO Box 1570, Maseru, 100 Lesotho
Tel: +266 2231 3224
Head of School: Bruce Gilbert
Age range: 11–23
No. of pupils: 565 B295 G270
Curriculum: IBDP,
National, SAT, ALevs
Language instr: English
(AISA) (CIS)

**Maseru English Medium
Preparatory School**
PO Box 34, Maseru 100, Lesotho
Tel: +266 22 312276
Acting Principal: Muhali
Age range: 3–12
No. of pupils: 300 B150 G150
Curriculum: IBPYP, UK

Liberia

**American International
School of Monrovia**
Old Road, Congo Town,
Monrovia, Liberia
Tel: +231 777 818 775
General Director: Jeff Trudeau
Age range: 4–12
Curriculum: USA
(AISA)

Libya

**International School
of Benghazi**
Alhawarree Road, Benghazi, Libya
Tel: +218 91 445 9504
Principal: Peter Hodge
Curriculum: UK
Language instr: English
(COB)

Madagascar

**The American School
of Antananarivo**
Lot II J 161 A, Ambodivoanjo,
Ivandry, Antanarivo, Madagascar
Tel: +261 20 22 420 39
Principal: Amy Parish
Age range: 2–18
Fees: $4,240–$15,325
Curriculum: IBPYP, USA
Language instr: English
(AISA)

Malawi

**Bishop Mackenzie
International Schools**
PO Box 102, Lilongwe, Malawi
Tel: +265 1 756 631
Director: Nikolas Bishop
Age range: 5–18
No. of pupils: 660 B330 G330 VIth60
Curriculum: IBDP, IBMYP, IBPYP, UK
Language instr: English
(AISA) (CIS)

**Hillview International
Primary School**
PO Box 5809, Limbe, Malawi
Tel: +265 1 843540
Head: Chris Maultby
Age range: 4–11
No. of pupils: 175
Curriculum: National, SAT, UK

Kamuzu Academy
Private Bag 1, Mtunthama, Malawi
Tel: +265 1 259 288
Headmaster: Francis J Cooke
Age range: 10–18
No. of pupils: 521 B266 G255 VIth92
Fees: US$8,700–US$9,100
Curriculum: UK, IGCSE, ALevs
Language instr: English
(学)

**St Andrew's International
High School**
Private Bag 211, Brereton Drive,
Blantyre, 0000 Malawi
Tel: +265 823688/822585
Headteacher: Gordon Benbow
Age range: 11–18
No. of pupils: B327 G283
Fees: US$7,500
Curriculum: IGCSE, ALevs
Language instr: English
(学) (COB)

**St Andrew's International
Primary School**
PO Box 593, Blantyre, Malawi
Tel: +265 1833 4281
Head Teacher: P B Sloan
Age range: 4–11
No. of pupils: 402 B210 G192
Fees: US$3,300
(学) (AISA) (COB)

Mali

**American International
School of Bamako**
Bougouba, Rue 90, Bamako, Mali
Tel: +223 2022 4738
Director: Caroline Jacoby
Age range: 3–18
No. of pupils: 160 B80 G80
Fees: $4,328–$19,523
Curriculum: ACT, AP, SAT, USA
Language instr: English
(AISA)

Mauritania

**American international
School of Nouakchott**
PO Box 3107, Nouakchott,
Mauritania
Tel: +222 45252967
Director: Frank Walsh
Age range: 3–20
Fees: Day US$5,925–US$15,955
Curriculum: USA
Language instr: English
(AISA)

Mauritius

Alexandra House School
King George V Avenue,
Floreal, Mauritius
Tel: +230 69 64108
Headmistress: Bridget Langlois
Age range: 4–11
No. of pupils: 100 B50 G50 VIth14
Fees: Day £3,300
Curriculum: UK
Language instr: English
(COB)

**Clavis International
Primary School**
Montagne Ory, Moka, Mauritius
Tel: +230 433 4439/4337708
Head of School: Nicholas Hamer
Age range: 3–11
No. of pupils: 490 B239 G251
Fees: Rs195,800
Curriculum: IBPYP
Language instr: English, French

**International
Preparatory School**
Labourdonnais, Mapou, Mauritius
Tel: +230 266 1973
Head of School: Anne Pönisch
Age range: 3–12
No. of pupils: 384 B200 G184
Fees: MRU66,000–MRU110,000
Language instr: English
(AISA) (CIS)

**Le Bocage
International School**
Montagne Ory, Moka, Mauritius
Tel: +230 433 9900
Head of School: Andrew R Scott
Age range: 11–19
No. of pupils: 568 B315 G253
Fees: MUR340,300–MUR371,400
Curriculum: IBDP, IGCSE
Language instr: English
(CIS)

**Northfields International
High School**
Labourdonnais Village,
Mapou, Mauritius
Tel: +230 266 9448/9
Headmaster: Barnes
Curriculum: IBDP
Language instr: English
(COB)

Mauritania

**American international
School of Nouakchott**
(see above)

Morocco

**Al Akhawayn School
of Ifrane (ASI)**
Al Akhawayn University, BP
104, Ifrane, 53000 Morocco
Tel: +212 535 86 21 99
Director: Stephen Trevathan
Curriculum: USA
Language instr: English

**American School
of Marrakesh**
Route de Ouarzazate, BP
6195, Marrakech, Morocco
Tel: +212 (0)24 32 98 60/61
Age range: 4–18
Curriculum: USA

**American School
of Tangier**
Rue Christophe Colomb,
Tangier, Morocco
Tel: +212 39 939827/8
Headmaster: Joseph A McPhillips
Age range: 2–19
No. of pupils: 340 B178 G162
Curriculum: SAT, TOEFL, USA
Language instr: English,
French, Arabic

**Casablanca
American School**
Route de la Mecque, Lotissement
Ougoug, Quartier Californie,
Casablanca, 20150 Morocco
Tel: +212 522 21 4115
Director: Stephane Ruz
Age range: 3–18
No. of pupils: 537
Curriculum: AP, IBDP, SAT
Language instr: English
(ECIS)

**Écoles Al Madina,
Site Ain Sebaa**
Km 9, route de Rabat,
Hay Chabab, Ain sébàa,
Casablanca, 20250 Morocco
Tel: +212 0522 75 69 69
Head of School: Touriya El Otmani
Curriculum: IBMYP
Language instr: French, Arabic

**ÉCOLES AL MADINA,
SITE CALIFORNIE**
For further details see p. 70
Lotissement Bellevue
2, Rue 3 Californie,
Casablanca, Morocco
Tel: +212 522 5050 97
Email: almadina@madina.ma
Website: www.almadina.ma
Head of School: Hayat Cherrouk
Age range: 2–18
No. of pupils: 3686 B1899 G1787
Fees: MAD14,000–MAD28,000
Curriculum: IBDP,
IBMYP, National
Language instr: French, Arabic

Écoles Al Madina, Site Polo
52 Bd Nador, Casablanca,
20420 Morocco
Tel: +21 20 22 210 505
Head of School: Rajâa Boukhriss
Curriculum: IBMYP
Language instr: French, Arabic

George Washington Academy
Km 5.6 Rte d'Azemour, Dar
Bouazza, Casablanca,
20220 Morocco
Tel: +212 522 953 000
Head of School: David Welling
Curriculum: USA
Language instr: English, French, Arabic

Groupe scolaire Alkaraouiyine
350 Boulevard Sebta,
Lotisement Anfa, Mohammedia,
28000 Morocco
Tel: +212 23 30 13 57
Head of School: Elham Hamdi
Age range: 11–16
Curriculum: IBMYP, National
Language instr: Arabic, French

Groupe Scolaire La Résidence
87-89 Avenue 2 mars,
Casablanca, Morocco
Tel: +212 22809050/51
Age range: 3–20
No. of pupils: 3000
Curriculum: IBMYP
Language instr: French

International School of Morocco
3 Impasse Jules Gros, Quartier
Oasis, Casablanca, 20150 Morocco
Tel: +212 0 552 993 987
Pedagogical
Director: Meredith Achlim
Language instr: English
(COB) (ECIS)

Rabat American School
c/o US Embassy, BP 120
Rabat, Morocco
Tel: +212 (0) 53 671 476
Head of School: Paul W Johnson
Age range: 4–18
No. of pupils: 422 B230 G192
Fees: $9,720–$19,975
Curriculum: IBDP, SAT, USA
Language instr: English
(ECIS)

Mozambique

American International School of Mozambique
PO Box 2026, Maputo, Mozambique
Tel: +258 2 1491 994
Head of School: Mary Jo Heatherington
Curriculum: IBDP, IBMYP, IBPYP
Language instr: English
(AISA)

Maputo International School
C.P. 4152 Maputo, 389
Rua da Nachingwea,
Maputo, Mozambique
Tel: +258 21 492131/195
Director: Elia Bila
Age range: 3–18
No. of pupils: 436 B220 G216
Fees: MTn133,200–MTn332,400
Curriculum: National, UK, IGCSE
(AISA)

Namibia

St George's Diocesan School
PO Box 68, Windhoek, Namibia
Tel: +264 61234133
Language instr: English
(RS)

St Paul's College
PO Box 11736, Windhoek
9000, Namibia
Tel: +264 61 227783
Headmaster: R J Church
Age range: 6–18
No. of pupils: 574 B274 G300
Fees: N$23,110–N$36,840
Curriculum: National
Language instr: English

Windhoek International School
P/Bag 16007, Scheppmann Street,
Pioneerspark, Windhoek, Namibia
Tel: +264 61 241 783
Principal: Anthony Millward
Age range: 2–18
No. of pupils: 425 B214 G211
Curriculum: IBDP, IBPYP, IGCSE
Language instr: English
(AISA) (CIS)

Niger

American International School of Niamey
BP 11201, Niamey, Niger
Tel: +227 20 72 39 42
Director: Heidi Cavanagh
Age range: 3–18
No. of pupils: 84
Fees: US$4,435–US$19,959
Curriculum: USA
(AISA)

Nigeria

American Christian Academy
PO Box 19629, 2,4,6 Shell Close,
Onireke, Ibadan, Nigeria
Tel: +234 22 41 3240
Head of School: Karen Nwulu
Age range: 3–18
(AISA)

American International School of Abuja
Plot 346, Cadastral Zone B
02, Durumi District, Abuja,
P.M.B. 5080 Wuse Nigeria
Tel: +234 9 672 2224
Principal: Amy Uzoewulu
Age range: 2–14
No. of pupils: 185 B90 G95
(AISA)

American International School of Lagos
Behind 1004 Federal
Estates, Lagos, Nigeria
Tel: +234 11 77 64 535
Head of School: Timothy Travers
Age range: 4–15
No. of pupils: 476 B256 G220
Curriculum: IBDP, SAT
Language instr: English
(AISA) (CIS)

Avi-Cenna International School
6 Harold Shodipo Crescent,
GRA Ikeja, Lagos, Nigeria
Tel: +234 1 3426273
Head of School: David Ogburn
Curriculum: UK
Language instr: English
(AISA)

BRITISH INTERNATIONAL SCHOOL, VICTORIA ISLAND
For further details see p. 68
PO Box 75133, 1 Landbridge
Avenue, Oniru Private Estate,
Victoria Island, Lagos, Nigeria
Tel: +234 1 774 8066
Email: registrar@bisnigeria.org
Website: www.bisnigeria.org
Principal: Peter Yates
Age range: 11–18
No. of pupils: 330 B180 G150
Fees: *Day* $17,300 FB $30,400
Curriculum: UK, ALevs
Language instr: English
(AISA) (COB)

Brookstone School
Off Sani Abacha Road, GRA Phase
3, Port Harcourt, Rivers State Nigeria
Tel: +234 084 789584
Director: Ken Baines
Age range: 3–17
No. of pupils: 525
Fees: £640–£1,040
Curriculum: National, UK
Language instr: English
(ECIS)

Cedar Court British International School
10 Imgbi Road, Amarata,
Yenagoa, Bayelsa State Nigeria
Age range: 2–10
Curriculum: National, UK
(ECIS)

Children's International School
Italian School Site, Off Admiralty
Way, Lekki Phase 1, Lagos, Nigeria
Tel: +234 17 918 030
Head of School: Folushade Omokorede
Language instr: English
(AISA)

Chrisland Educational Organisation
26 Opebi Road, Ikeja, Lagos,
PMB 21612 Nigeria
Tel: +234 14 964 529
Head of School: Ibironke Adeyemi
(AISA)

Cradle to Crayon/ Springhall British School
37 Lake Chad Crescent,
Maitama, Abuja, Nigeria
Tel: +234 703 595 4101
Head Teacher: Kimberley Jones
Language instr: English
(COB)

D-Ivy College
32 Allen Avenue, Ikeja,
Lagos, Nigeria
Tel: +234 1 7914447/8
Head of School: Oyinlola Ilo
No. of pupils: 80
Curriculum: IBDP
Language instr: English

Day Waterman College
18B Thompson Avenue,
Ikoyi, Lagos, Nigeria
Tel: +234 (1) 279 3836
Principal: Jeni Sayer
Age range: 11–13
No. of pupils: 38
Curriculum: UK

Dowen College
18 Adebayo Dohery Road,
Lekki Phase 1, Lagos, Nigeria
Tel: +234 12 706 010
Head of School: Olawumi Togonu-Bickersteth
Language instr: English
(AISA)

Emerald Schools
c/o 8/10 Olawale Daodu Street,
Ifako Gbagada, Lagos, Nigeria
Tel: +234 18 54 57 78
Executive Director: Edna Obaze
Language instr: English
(AISA)

FAMAKS INTERNATIONAL SCHOOLS
For further details see p. 71
Plot 8 Fajuyi Adekunle Crescent,
Off Ajayi Crowther Street,
Asokoro, Abuja, Nigeria
Tel: +234 (0)8109884780
Email: info@famakschools.com
Website:
www.famakschools.com
Head Teacher: Franklin Adjetey
Age range: 2–10
Curriculum: IPC
Language instr: English
(AISA) (COB)

Grange School
6 Harold Shodipo Crescent, PO
Box 22, Ikeja, Lagos, Nigeria
Tel: +234 1 497 4351
Principal: Graham J Stothard
Age range: 4–16
No. of pupils: 720
Curriculum: UK
Language instr: English
(AISA) (COB) (ECIS)

Greenoak International School, Nigeria
99 Tombia Street Extension, Gra
Phase 3, Port Harcourt, Nigeria
Tel: +234 80 86 73 74 01
Principal: Anetta Papadopoulou
Curriculum: IPC
Language instr: English
(AISA)

Greensprings School, Lagos
32 Olatunde Ayoola Avenue,
Anthony, Lagos, Nigeria
Tel: +234 8776874
**Head of School/Director of
Education:** Harry McFaul
Curriculum: IBDP
Language instr: English
(⚖)

Hillcrest School (Jos)
13 Old Bukuru Road, Jos, Nigeria
Tel: +234 803 7190351
Head of School: Mike Stonecypher
Language instr: English
(⚖) (AISA)

Ibadan International School
24 Jibowu Crescent, Iyaganku,
Ibadan, L1 4HL, UK Nigeria
Tel: +234 2 231 0742
Head of School: C M Ige
Curriculum: IBPYP
Language instr: English
(AISA)

Inspire Academy
Plot 7, Abdulhahab Folawiyo
Ave, Forner First Ave, Gwarinpa
Housing Estate, Abuja, Nigeria
Tel: +234 802 5068312
Director: Maryam Mohammed
Curriculum: UK
Language instr: English
(COB)

International Community School, Abuja
PO Box 3972, Abuja, Nigeria
Tel: +234 9 523 3520
Superintendent: Jan Okpanachi
Age range: 2–18
No. of pupils: 500 B220 G280
Fees: US$3,520–US$10,680
Curriculum: ACT, AP,
SAT, USA, IGCSE
Language instr: English
(AISA) (CIS)

International School of Iita
c/o Lambourn & Co, Carolyn
House, 26 Dingwall Road, Croydon,
Surrey, CR9 3EE, UK Nigeria
Tel: +234 22 41 2626
Head: Carole Inniss-Palmer
Age range: 3–12
No. of pupils: 58 B27 G31
Curriculum: UK, USA
Language instr: English
(⚖) (AISA)

James Hope College
Obi Ikechukwu Road (Formerly
Old Lagos-Asaba Road),
Agbor Obi, Agbor, Nigeria
Tel: +234 704 597 7883
Principal: Malcolm Phillips
Curriculum: UK
Language instr: English
(COB)

Kaduna International School
PO Box 2947, 1 Wurno
Road, Kaduna, Nigeria
Tel: +234 62 31 11 21
Principal: Veronica Bernas Snoxell
Age range: 3–12
No. of pupils: 154 B79 G75
Fees: Day £1,200–£1,650
Curriculum: National, UK
(COB)

Lagos Preparatory School
36-40 Glover Road, Ikoyi,
Lagos, Nigeria
Tel: +234 1 7408325
Headteacher: John Samuel
Age range: 3–11
Curriculum: UK
(AISA) (COB)

Lekki British International Schools
Victoria Arobieke Street, Off
Admiralty Way, Lekki Peninsular
Phase 1, Lagos, Nigeria
Tel: +234 12 708 300
Head of School: Clement Adedeji
Curriculum: UK
Language instr: English
(⚖) (AISA) (COB)

Lifeforte International School
Lifeforte Boulevard, Awotan
Gra, Ibadan, Nigeria
Tel: +234 28 103 832
Head of School: Sarah Johnson
Language instr: English
(AISA)

Nigeria LNG School
Nigeria LNG Residential Area,
Bonny Island, Nigeria
Tel: +234 80390 52602
Head of School: Dirk Schuiling
Language instr: English
(AISA)

Noble Hall Leadership Academy for Girls
Plot 273, Institutes and Research
District, Abuja, Nigeria
Tel: +234 8032 032291
Head: Stewart Cowden
Language instr: English
(♣) (⚖)

Norwegian International School
GPA Phase 111, Port
Harcourt, Nigeria
Tel: +234 70662029
Head of School: Linda Onwuteaka
Language instr: English
(AISA)

Olashore International School
Prince Oladele Olashore Way,
Iloko-Ijesa, PMB 5059, Ijebu-Ijesa,
Oriade IGA 237-101, Ilesa, Nigeria
Tel: +234 813 609 7630
Principal: S A Valentine
Language instr: English
(⚖) (AISA)

Oxbridge Tutorial College
49 Sobo Arobiodu Street,
GRA, Ikeja, Nigeria
Tel: +234 1740 7577
Principal: Carol Scott-Mchale
Language instr: English
(COB)

Pampers Private School
Lagos, Nigeria
Tel: +234 15 835 703
Head of School: A Laoye
Language instr: English
(AISA)

Redeemers International Secondary School
350 Ikoredu Road, Maryland,
Lagos, Nigeria
Tel: +234 17 74 38 88
Principal: Olatundun Adetoye
Language instr: English
(AISA) (COB)

Regent Secondary School
Plot 858 Mabushi District,
FCT, Abuja, Nigeria
Tel: +234 80784 87966
Head of School: Ian McCutcheon
(AISA)

Sacred Heart Primary School
Independence Way, PO Box
620, Kaduna, Nigeria
Tel: +234 62 21 2929
Headmaster: Thomas Avadu
Age range: 5–12
No. of pupils: 296 B159 G137

St Saviour's School
54 Alexander Avenue,
Ikoyi, Lagos, Nigeria
Tel: +234 1 8990153
Head Teacher: A Tempest
Age range: 4–11
No. of pupils: 320
Curriculum: UK
(COB)

Surefoot American International School
Plot 5 Murtala Mohammad
Hyway, Opposite Zone 6 Police
Station, Calabar, Nigeria
Tel: +234 808 072 7168
Head of School: Michael Church
(AISA)

Temple Preparatory and Secondary School
Temple drive off Olusoji Idowu
Street, Ilupeju, Lagos, Nigeria
Tel: +234 18 940 981
Head of School: Shirley Okharedia
Language instr: English
(AISA)

Temple School
1 Temple Drive, Off Olusoji Idowu
Street, Ilupeju, Lagos, Nigeria
Tel: +234 18940981
Head: Okharedia
Age range: 1–16
Curriculum: UK, IGCSE
Language instr: English
(AISA) (COB)

The Regent School
1 Euphrates Street, Federal
Capital Territory, Abuja, Nigeria
Tel: +234 703 779 3322
Headteacher: Mike Dickson
Age range: 2–11
No. of pupils: 249 B142 G107
Fees: US$10,405
Curriculum: National, UK
Language instr: English
(AISA) (COB)

Vivian Fowler Memorial College for Girls
Plot 5 Balogun Street, Chief T
A Doherty Layout, Oregun,
Ikeja, Lagos, Nigeria
Tel: +234 1 793 8424
Head of School: Francis Fasuyi
(♣) (⚖) (AISA) (COB)

Rwanda

Green Hills Academy
PO Box 6419, Nyarutarama,
Kigali, Rwanda
Tel: +250 252 580 746
Head of School: Ron Wallace
Age range: 3–19
No. of pupils: 1450
Curriculum: IBDP
Language instr: English
(RS)

International School Kigali
PO Box 6217, Kigali, Rwanda
Tel: +250 78 83 02 899
Director: Brian Roach
Age range: 3–18
Curriculum: USA
(AISA) (CIS)

Senegal

Dakar Academy
BP 3189, Dakar, Senegal
Tel: +221 33 832 0682
Age range: 5–20
No. of pupils: 236 B117 G119
Fees: $12,600
Curriculum: ACT, AP, SAT, USA
Language instr: English
(⚓)

International
School of Dakar
BP 5136 Fann, Dakar, Senegal
Tel: +221 33 860 2332
Interim Director: Paul Olson
Age range: 3–18
No. of pupils: 393 B204 G189
Fees: US$14,400
Curriculum: IBDP, USA
Language instr: English
(AISA) (CIS) (ECIS)

West African College
of the Atlantic
BP 24340, Ouakam, Dakar, Senegal
Tel: +221 33 820 4929
Head of School: Jacqueline Ferreira
Curriculum: IBDP
Language instr: French, English

Seychelles

International School,
Seychelles
PO Box 315, Mont Fleuri,
Victoria, Mahe Seychelles
Tel: +248 610444
Head Teacher: Jane Lincoln
Age range: 3–18
No. of pupils: 520 B290 G230 VIth35
Fees: SR27,000–SR35,000
Curriculum: SAT, UK, IGCSE, ALevs
Language instr: English

Sierra Leone

American International
School of Freetown
(Sierra Leone)
c/o American Embassy, Freetown,
Department of State, 2160
Freetown Place, Washington, DC
20521-2160, USA Sierra Leone
Tel: +232 22 232 480 /
+232 76 622 453
Director: Jim Gerhard
Age range: 3–14
No. of pupils: 10 B4 G6
(AISA)

Somalia

Imran Binu Hussein
Near Unicef Office, Bulo-
Hubey, Wadajir District,
Mogadishu, Somalia
Tel: +252 185 6699
Director: Kaise Maio Abulhussein
Language instr: English

South Africa

American International
School of Cape Town
42 Soetvlei Avenue, Constantia
7806, Cape Town, South Africa
Tel: 27 21 713 2220
Head of School: Kevin Coordt
Age range: 4–18
No. of pupils: 302
Fees: R30,650–R81,378
Curriculum: AP, SAT, USA
Language instr: English
(AISA)

American International
School of Johannesburg
Private Bag X4, Bryanston,
2021 South Africa
Tel: +27 11 464 1505
Director: Andy Page-Smith
Age range: 4–19
No. of pupils: 894 B489 G405
Curriculum: AP, IBDP,
SAT, TOEFL, USA
Language instr: English
(AISA)

Bishops Diocesan College
Camp Ground Road, Rondebosch,
Cape Town, 7700 South Africa
Tel: +27 21 659 1000
Principal: Grant R B Nupen
Age range: B5–18
No. of pupils: 1350
Fees: R64,000
Curriculum: National
Language instr: English
(⚓)

Bridge House School
PO Box 444, Franschhoek,
7690 South Africa
Tel: +27 021 874 8100
Head of School: Mike Russell
Language instr: English
(RS)

Cornwall Hill College
PO Box 621, Nellmapius Drive,
Irene, 0062 South Africa
Tel: +27 12 667 1360
Executive Principal: Leon Kunneke
Language instr: English
(⚓) (RS)

Dainfern College
Broadacres Drive, Dainfern,
Johannesburg, South Africa
Tel: +27 011 469 0635
Principal: Matthew Davies
(⚓) (RS)

Hilton College
Private Bag 6001, Hilton 3245,
Kwazulu Natal South Africa
Tel: +27 33 383 0100
Headmaster: Dave Lovatt
Age range: B11–18
Fees: R129,000
(♂) (⚓)

International School
of Cape Town
Woodland Heights, Edinburgh
Close, Wynberg, 7800 Cape
Town, South Africa
Tel: +27 21 761 6202
Principal: David Hunter
Age range: 3–18
No. of pupils: 346 B171 G175
Fees: R26,505–R67,070
Curriculum: National, SAT, UK, ALevs
Language instr: English

International School
of Helderberg
Postnet Suite 214, Private Bag
X29, Somerset West, Cape
Town, 7310 South Africa
Tel: +27 21 851 6290
Head of School: Annette Austin
(ISA)

International School
of Hout Bay
Suite 164, Private Bag X14, Hout
Bay, Cape Town 7872 South Africa
Tel: +27 21 790 6285
Head of School: Andy Wood
Curriculum: IBDP, IBPYP
Language instr: English

International School
of South Africa
Private Bag, X2233, Mafikeng
South 2791, South Africa
Tel: +27 18 3811102
Headmaster: James Haupt
Age range: 11–19
No. of pupils: 440 B215 G225 VIth53
Fees: R36,280–R46,940
Curriculum: SAT, UK, IGCSE, ALevs
Language instr: English
(⚓) (ECIS)

Michaelhouse
Balgowan 3275, Kwazulu-
Natal, South Africa
Tel: +27 33 234 1000
Rector: Guy N Pearson
Age range: B13–17
No. of pupils: B555
Fees: ZAR158,000
Language instr: English
(♂) (⚓)

North American
International School
PO Box 14582, Hatfield,
Pretoria, South Africa
Tel: +27 124 601 154
Principal: Craig Van Zyl
Language instr: English
(AISA)

Penryn College
PO Box 2835, Nelspruit,
1200 South Africa
Tel: +27 013 758 9000
Principal: Chris Erasmus
Language instr: English
(RS)

Roedean School
Princess of Wales Terrace,
Parktown, 2193 South Africa
Tel: +27 11 647 3200
Executive Headmistress: Mary
Williams
Language instr: English
(♂) (RS)

St Andrew's College
PO Box 182, Grahamstown,
6140 South Africa
Tel: +27 (0) 46 603 2300
Headmaster: Paul Edey
Age range: B13–18
No. of pupils: 470
Fees: R69,000
Language instr: English
(♂) (⚓)

St Cyprian's School
Gorge Road, Oranjezicht,
8001 South Africa
Tel: +27 021 461 1090
Head of School: Sue Redelinghuys
Language instr: English
(♀) (⚓) (RS)

St Stithian's College
Private Bag 2, Randburg 2125,
Gauteng, South Africa
Tel: +27 11 577 6000
Rector: Stephen Lowry
Age range: 4–18
Fees: R31,795–R58,149

Stanford Lake College
PO Box 271, Haenertsburg,
Magoebaskloof, 0730 South Africa
Tel: +27 015 276 6103
Headmaster: Craig Carolan
Language instr: English
(♣) (RS)

The Oprah Winfrey Leadership Academy For Girls
P.O. Box 1485, 534 Wargrave Ave,
Henley on Klip, 1961 South Africa
Tel: +27 016 366 9000
Head of School: Anne Van Zyl
Curriculum: IBMYP
(♣)

Tiger Kloof Educational Institution
Portion 5, Waterloo Farm,
Kimberley Road (N18),
Vryburg, 8601 South Africa
Tel: +27 053 928 7000
Director: Mark Boobbyer
Language instr: English
(RS)

Vela School
Thronhillfarm, Mtahtha, South Africa
Tel: +27 200 601 167
(RS)

Sudan

Khartoum American School
c/o US Embassy, P.O. Box
699, Khartoum, Sudan
Tel: +249 15 577 0105 /
+249 15 577 0107
Superintendent: Steve Alexander
Age range: 3–18
No. of pupils: 222 B132 G90
Fees: US$5,500–US$16,600
Curriculum: SAT, USA
(AISA) (CIS)

Khartoum International Community School
PO Box 1840, Khartoum, Sudan
Tel: +249 183 215 000
Head of School: Nigel J Winnard
Age range: 3–18
No. of pupils: 400 B222 G178
Fees: US$6,240–US$21,276
Curriculum: ACT, IBDP, IBPYP
Language instr: English
(AISA) (CIS) (ECIS)

Swaziland

Sifundzani School
PO Box A286, Swazi Plaza,
Mbabane, Swaziland
Tel: +268 404 2465
Principal: Ella Magongo
Age range: 5–17
No. of pupils: 623 B279 G344
(AISA)

United World College of Southern Africa/ Waterford Kamhlaba
PO Box 52, Mbabane, Swaziland
Tel: +268 242 20866/7/8
Principal: Laurence Nodder
Age range: 11–19
No. of pupils: 602 B279 G323 VIth120
Curriculum: IBDP, IGCSE
Language instr: English
(♣)

Usutu Forests Primary School
PO Box 264, Mhlambanyats
H115, Swaziland
Tel: +268 4674134/412
Head of School: B Frost
Age range: 5–13
No. of pupils: 351 B180 G171
Curriculum: National, UK
Language instr: English

Tanzania

Academic International School
PO Box 63333, Dar es
Salaam, Tanzania
Tel: +255 222 780 444
Head of School: Yusuf Kalindaga
Language instr: English

Aga Khan School, Dar-es-Salaam
PO Box 125, Dar es
Salaam, Tanzania
Tel: +255 22 215 0700/215 0406
Head of School: Annie Thomson
Age range: 11–18
No. of pupils: 445 B241 G205
Fees: US$1,000–US$5,800
Curriculum: IBDP, IBPYP,
National, ALevs
Language instr: English

Al Muntazir School
PO Box 21735, Dar es
Salaam, Tanzania
Tel: +255 22 215 0161
Principal: Naserah Karim
Age range: 3–18
No. of pupils: 3173 B1501 G1672
Fees: TSh520,000–TSh800,000
Curriculum: National, UK

BRAEBURN ARUSHA SCHOOL
For further details see p. 60
PO Box 14268, Arusha, Tanzania
Tel: +255 (0)250 5716
Email: secondary@
braeburnschool.ac.tz
Website:
www.arusha.braeburn.com
Head of School: Alison Rogers
Age range: 2–19
No. of pupils: 450
Curriculum: UK
(♣) (ECIS)

Canon Andrea Mwaka School
PO Box 228, Dodoma, Tanzania
Tel: +255 26 2323220
Principal: Vicki Squibbs
Age range: 3–15
No. of pupils: 280 B130 G150
Curriculum: UK, IGCSE
Language instr: English

Dar es Salaam International Academy
PO Box 23282, Dar es
Salaam, Tanzania
Tel: +255 22 2600 202
Head of School: Shaista Juma
Age range: 5–16
No. of pupils: 134 B70 G64
Curriculum: IBMYP
Language instr: English
(AISA)

Geita Gold International School
Mchauru Village, Geita Gold
Mine, Geita Town, Tanzania
Tel: +255 282 520 500
Headmaster: Ryan Krause
Language instr: English
(AISA)

Genesis Schools
1408 Itagi Street, Dar es
Salaam, Tanzania
Tel: +255 222 666 147
Head of School: Josephine
Mutahangarwa
(AISA)

Haven of Peace Academy
PO Box 70020, Dar es
Salaam, Tanzania
Tel: +255 22 2650604
Director: Ben Snyder
Age range: 5–18
No. of pupils: 300 B145 G155
Fees: US$4,150–US$5,700
Curriculum: UK
(AISA)

International School Moshi, Arusha Campus
PO Box 2691, Arusha, Tanzania
Tel: +255 27 250 5029
Head of Campus: Éanna O'Boyle
Age range: 3–19
No. of pupils: 200 B100 G100
Curriculum: IBMYP, IBPYP
Language instr: English
(AISA) (CIS)

International School Moshi, Moshi Campus
PO Box 733, Lema Road,
Moshi, Kilimanjaro Tanzania
Tel: +255 767 534766
Head of Campus: Keiron White
Age range: 3–19
No. of pupils: B160 G150 VIth89
Fees: Day US$5,800–US$14,600
WB US$14,150–US$21,700
FB US$14,150–US$21,700
Curriculum: ACT, IBDP,
IBMYP, IBPYP, SAT, TOEFL
Language instr: English
(♣) (AISA) (CIS)

International School of Tanganyika Ltd
United Nations Road, PO Box
2651, Dar es Salaam, Tanzania
Tel: +255 22 2151700
Head of School: Martin Hall
Age range: 4–19
No. of pupils: 1020 B515 G505
Fees: US$10,300–US$20,000
Curriculum: IBDP, IBMYP,
IBPYP, SAT, TOEFL
Language instr: English
(AISA) (CIS) (ECIS)

International School of Zanzibar
PO Box 1787, Zanzibar, Tanzania
Tel: +255 777 477 053
Head Teacher: Terry Binns
Age range: 3–18
Curriculum: UK, IGCSE, ALevs
Language instr: English
(AISA)

Iringa International School
PO Box 912, Lumumba Street,
Gangilonga, Iringa, Tanzania
Tel: +255 26 2702018
Head of School: Kristeen
Chachage
Age range: 3–17
No. of pupils: 123 B60 G63 VIth2
Fees: US$2,670–US$7,680
Curriculum: IBPYP, IGCSE, ALevs
Language instr: English
(♣) (AISA)

Isamilo International School
PO Box 42, Mwanza, Tanzania
Tel: +255 282 550 0497
Headmaster: Joe Davies
Curriculum: UK, IGCSE, ALevs
Language instr: English
(AISA)

Kwanza International School
Bagamoyo Road, Dar es Salaam, Tanzania
Tel: +225 222 771 961
Head of School: Josephat Kaimenyi
(AISA)

Morogoro International School
PO Box 1015, Morogoro, 1015 Tanzania
Tel: +255 23260 4864
Headteacher: Jason Lewis
Age range: 3–16
No. of pupils: 158 B91 G67
Fees: TSh1,164,000–TSh2,056,800
Curriculum: IGCSE
Language instr: English
(icon) (AISA)

Savannah Plains International School
PO Box 56, Shinyanga, Tanzania
Tel: +255 282 764 016
Principal: Edward Mwanza
Language instr: English
(AISA)

St. Constantine's International School
PO Box 221, Arusha, Tanzania
Tel: +27 250 0104
Head of School: Francois Taljaard
Language instr: English
(icon) (AISA)

Tanga International School
PO Box 1178, Ocean Drive, Raskazone, Tanga, Tanzania
Tel: +255 27 264 2979
Head of School: Leanne Cook
Age range: 3–12
No. of pupils: 36 B20 G16
Fees: Day £1,800–£3,000
Language instr: English
(AISA)

The Gambia

Banjul American Embassy School
P.O. Box 2596, Serrekunda, The Gambia
Tel: +220 4495920
Director: Raymond Lemoine
Age range: 3–12
Curriculum: USA
Language instr: English
(AISA)

Marina International School
P.O.Box 717, Banjul, The Gambia
Tel: +220 449 7178 / +220 449 4387
Language instr: English
(AISA)

Shiloh Bilingual Education Centre International School
Bijilo, Serreku, The Gambia
Tel: +220 996 1756
Curriculum: UK
Language instr: English, French
(AISA)

Togo

American International School of Lome
35 Kayigan Lawson, Lome, Togo
Tel: +228 22 61 1896
Director: Clover J Afokpa
Age range: 3–18
No. of pupils: 73
Curriculum: USA
(AISA)

British School of Lomé
Hellman House, Lakeside Industrial Estate, Colnbrook, Slough, SL3 0EL, UK Togo
Tel: +228 226 46 06
Head of School: Helen Brocklesby
Age range: 3–18
No. of pupils: 241 B135 G103
Curriculum: IBDP, SAT, UK, IGCSE
Language instr: English
(icon)

École Internationale Arc-en-Ciel
BP 2985, Lomé, Togo
Tel: +228 222 0329
Director: Firouz Rahimi
Age range: 3–18
No. of pupils: 450
Curriculum: IBDP, IBMYP
Language instr: French
(ECIS)

International Christian School of Lomé
PO Box 582, Lomé, Togo
Tel: +228 222 1404
Head of School: Rigobert Tounou
Language instr: English
(AISA)

Tunisia

American Cooperative School of Tunis
ACST BP150, Cite Taieb M' Hiri, 2045 Laouina, Tunisia
Tel: +216 71 760 905
Head of School: Allan Bredy
Age range: 4–18
No. of pupils: 600 B300 G300
Fees: US$21,580
Curriculum: AP, IBDP, SAT, TOEFL
Language instr: English
(CIS) (ECIS)

British International School of Tunis
49 Rue du Parc, La Soukra, Tunis, 2036 Tunisia
Tel: +216 71 865 682
Principal: David Wilson
Age range: 3–11
Curriculum: UK
Language instr: English
(COB)

Uganda

Aga Khan High School, Kampala
PO Box 6837, Kampala, Uganda
Tel: +256 413 47 246
Headmaster: John Pragnell
No. of pupils: 1680
Fees: USH620,000
Curriculum: IBDP, IGCSE
Language instr: English

Ambrosoli International School
PO Box 10546, Kampala, Uganda
Tel: +256 414 220416
Head of School: Rachel Rice
Age range: 3–12
Curriculum: IPC, UK
Language instr: English
(AISA)

International School of Uganda
PO Box 4200, Kampala, Uganda
Tel: +256 414 200 374/8/9
Head of School: Chris Maggio
Age range: 2–19
No. of pupils: 485 B247 G238
Curriculum: IBDP, IBMYP, IBPYP
Language instr: English
(AISA) (CIS)

Kampala International School Uganda (KISU)
Plot No. 447, Block 213, Old Kira Road, Bukoto, PO. Box 34249, Kampala, Uganda
Tel: +256 414 453005
School Director: Neil Wrightson
Age range: 2–18
No. of pupils: 600
Curriculum: IBDP, IGCSE
Language instr: English
(CIS)

RAINBOW INTERNATIONAL SCHOOL UGANDA
For further details see p. 72
P.O. Box 7632, Kampala, Uganda
Tel: +256 312 266696/7
Email: info@risu.sc.ug
Website: www.risu.sc.ug
Head of Primary: Audrey Dralega
Age range: 2–18
No. of pupils: 850
Fees: US$4,560–US$7,900
Curriculum: UK, IGCSE, ALevs
Language instr: English
(icon) (COB) (EAR)

Zambia

American International School of Lusaka
PO Box 31617, Lusaka, Zambia
Tel: +260 211 260509
Director: Thomas Pado
Age range: 2–18
No. of pupils: 580 B301 G279
Curriculum: IBDP, IBMYP, IBPYP
Language instr: English
(AISA) (CIS)

International School of Lusaka
PO Box 50121, Ridgeway, Lusaka, Zambia
Tel: +260 211 252291
Head of School: Martin Gough
Age range: 2–18
No. of pupils: 676 B348 G328 VIth56
Fees: Day US$5,000–US$20,000
Curriculum: IBDP, IBPYP, IGCSE
Language instr: English
(AISA) (CIS)

Lechwe School
PO Box 20830, Kitwe, Zambia
Tel: +260 21 2 222530/227040
Principal: Brian Bentley
Age range: 2–18
No. of pupils: 390
Fees: $2,000–$7,500
Curriculum: SAT, UK, IGCSE, ALevs
Language instr: English
(icon)

Lusaka International Community School
PO Box 30528, Lusaka, Zambia
Tel: +260 211 290 626
Headmaster: Martin van der Linde
Age range: 2–17
No. of pupils: 242
Curriculum: UK
(CIS)

Zimbabwe

Falcon College
PO Esigodini, Esigodini, Zimbabwe
Tel: +263 288 331/674
Headmaster: R W Querl
Age range: B13–18
No. of pupils: 370
Fees: US$8,325
Curriculum: UK, ALevs
Language instr: English
(icon) (icon)

Harare International School
66 Pendennis Rd, Mount Pleasant, Harare, Zimbabwe
Tel: +263 4 870514
Head of School: Kathryn Carter-Golden
Age range: 3–18
No. of pupils: 395 B195 G200
Fees: US$5,500–US$17,300
Curriculum: AP, IBDP, IBPYP, USA
Language instr: English
(AISA) (CIS)

Peterhouse Boys
Private Bag 3741,
Marondera, Zimbabwe
Tel: +263 (0)279-24951/3,
+263-(0)279-22200/4
Rector: J B Calderwood
Age range: 12–18
No. of pupils: 915 B515 G400
Fees: US$12,000–US$13,000
Curriculum: UK, IGCSE, ALevs
Language instr: English

Peterhouse Girls' School
Private Bag 3774,
Marondera, Zimbabwe
Tel: +263 79 23599
Principal: S M Davidson
Age range: G12–18
No. of pupils: 310
Curriculum: UK, ALevs
Language instr: English

St George's College
Private Bag 7727, Causeway,
Harare, Zimbabwe
Tel: +263 4 704064
Headmaster: Brendan Tiernan
Age range: B13–18
No. of pupils: 750
Fees: US$6,840
Curriculum: UK, IGCSE, ALevs
Language instr: English

St John's Preparatory School for Boys
PO Box BW300, Fisher Avenue,
Borrowdale, Harare, Zimbabwe
Tel: +263 4885128/121
Headmaster: Michael
Noel Mackenzie
Age range: B6–12
No. of pupils: B545
Fees: US$5,550
Curriculum: National, UK
Language instr: English

St Johns College
Po Box BW 600, Borrowdale,
Harare, Zimbabwe
Tel: +264-4-885102
Head of School: Ross Fuller
Age range: 12–18
No. of pupils: 562 B538 G24
Curriculum: IBDP
Language instr: English

International schools in Asia

Schools ordered A–Z by Country

Key to directory

Country

Name of school or college

Indicates that this school has a profile

Address and contact number

Head's name

Age range

Number of pupils.
B = boys G = girls VIth = sixth form

Fees per annum.
Day = fees for day pupils.
WB = fees for weekly boarders.
FB = fees for full boarders.

Curriculum

Language of instruction

Memberships/Accreditation

Whereford

College Academy

For further details see p.00

Which Street, Whosville,
Wherefordshire AB12 3CD

Tel: 01000 000000

Head Master: Dr A Person

Age range: 11–18

No. of pupils:
660 B330 G330 VIth 200

Fees: Day £11,000
WB £16,000 FB £20,000

Curriculum:
National, IBDP, ALevs

Language instr:
English, French

(AISA) (COB) (EAR)

Key to icons

Key to symbols:

(†) Boys' school

(♀) Girls' school

(⚓) Boarding accommodation

Member of:

(AISA) Association of International Schools in Africa

(CEE) Central and Eastern European Schools Association

(EAR) East Asia Regional Council of Overseas Schools

(ECIS) European Council of International Schools

(RS) Round Square

Accreditation:

(CIS) Council of International Schools

(COB) Council of British International Schools

Please note: Schools are coeducational day schools unless otherwise indicated

Bahrain

Abdul Rahman Kanoo International School
PO Box 2512, Salmabad, Bahrain
Tel: +973 17875055
Principal: Aisha Janahi
Age range: 3–18
No. of pupils: 2090 B1109 G981
Curriculum: IBDP, IPC, National, IGCSE, ALevs
Language instr: English
(CIS)

Al Hekma International School
Building No 1962, Road 4363, Sanad 743, PO Box 26489, Adliya Bahrain
Tel: +973 17 620 820/17 623 999
President: Mona Rashid Abdul Rahman Al Zayani
Age range: 3–18

Arabian Pearl Gulf School
PO Box 26299, Manama, Bahrain
Tel: +973 1740 3666
School Principal: Ebtisam Al-Zeera
Age range: 3–18
No. of pupils: 1327
Curriculum: IBDP, IGCSE
Language instr: English, French, Arabic

Bahrain Bayan School
Road No 4112, Isa Town, 32411 Bahrain
Tel: +973 7712 2244
Director General: Peter Nanos
No. of pupils: 1082
Curriculum: IBDP, National, USA
Language instr: English

Bahrain School
PO Box 934, Manama, Bahrain
Tel: +973 17719822
Head of School: Douglas McEnery
Age range: 5–19
No. of pupils: 450
Fees: US$21,000
Curriculum: IBDP
Language instr: English
(🏛)

IBN KHULDOON NATIONAL SCHOOL
For further details see p. 83
Building 161, Road 4111, Area 841, Isa Town, Bahrain
Tel: +973 177 80661
Email: hr@ikns.edu.bh
Website: www.ikns.edu.bh
President: Kamal Abdel-Nour
Age range: 4–18
No. of pupils: 1500
Curriculum: IBDP, National, SAT, TOEFL, USA
Language instr: English, Arabic

Modern Knowledge Schools
PO Box 15826, Manama, Bahrain
Tel: +973 17 727724
Head of School: David Bailey
Fees: Day £0
Curriculum: IBDP
Language instr: English

Nadeen School
PO Box 26367, Adliya, Bahrain
Tel: +973 1772 8886
Principal: Pauline Puri
Age range: 2–12
No. of pupils: 370
Fees: BD1,740–BD2,580
Curriculum: UK
Language instr: English

NASEEM INTERNATIONAL SCHOOL
For further details see p. 89
PO Box 28503, Riffa, Bahrain
Tel: +973 17 782 000
Email: naseem@batelco.com.bh
Website: www.nisbah.com
President/Director: Sameera Al Kooheji
Age range: 3–18
No. of pupils: 985 B592 G393
Curriculum: IBDP, IBMYP, IBPYP, National, SAT, IGCSE
Language instr: English / Arabic
(ECIS)

Riffa Views International School
PO Box 3050, Manama, 934 Bahrain
Tel: +973 1656 5000
Director: Bernadette P Carmody
Age range: 4–12
Fees: BD5,600–BD7,000
Curriculum: IBDP, USA
Language instr: English
(CIS)

Shaikha Hessa Girls' School
PO Box 37799, Riffa, Bahrain
Tel: +973 17 756 111
Head of School: Samia Alkooheji
Fees: BD3,080
Curriculum: IBDP
Language instr: English
(🏛)(CIS)

St Christopher's School
PO Box 32052, Isa Town, Bahrain
Tel: +973 1759 8496
Principal: Ed Goodwin
Age range: 3–18
No. of pupils: 286 B1041 G1045
Curriculum: IBDP, SAT, UK, GCSE, IGCSE, ALevs
Language instr: English

THE BRITISH SCHOOL OF BAHRAIN
For further details see p. 95
PO Box 30733 – Budaiya, Building 1080, Road 1425, Block 1014, Hamala, Bahrain
Tel: +973 1 761 0920
Email: admissions@thebsbh.com
Website: www.britishschoolbahrain.com
Head: Charles Wall
Age range: 3–18
No. of pupils: B821 G762
Curriculum: UK
(AISA)

Bangladesh

American International School, Dhaka
PO Box 6106, Gulshan, Dhaka 1212, Bangladesh
Tel: +880 2 882 2452
Head of School: Richard Boerner
Age range: 3–18
No. of pupils: 730
Fees: US$5,140–US$20,030
Curriculum: ACT, AP, IBDP, IBPYP, SAT, USA
Language instr: English

Chittagong Grammar School
321/11 Sarson Road, Chittagong, Bangladesh
Tel: +88 031 622 472
Head of Upper School: Mahine Khan
(RS)

International School, Dhaka
Dhaka Bag, Knightsbridge Schools International, 124/128 Barlby Road, Unit 43, London, W10 6BL, UK Bangladesh
Tel: +880 2 840 1101/7
Chief Executive Officer: Craig Salmon
Age range: 2–17+
No. of pupils: 700
Fees: US$4,300–US$17,500
Curriculum: IBDP, IBMYP, IBPYP
Language instr: English
(CIS)

The Aga Khan School, Dhaka
House 37#, Road# 6, Sector #4, Uttara, Dhaka, 1230 Bangladesh
Tel: +88 02 8914042, +88 02 8950029, +88 02 8920481/82
Head of School: Nicola Sum
No. of pupils: 1216
Fees: US$828–US$1,032
Curriculum: IBPYP

Brunei Darussalam

International School, Brunei
Jalan Dato Haji Ahmad, Bandar Seri Begawan, BB 1114 Brunei Darussalam
Tel: +673 2330608
Executive Principal: Steven P Geraghty
Age range: 2–18
No. of pupils: 948 B504 G444
Fees: B$7,000–B$13,000
Curriculum: IBDP, National, SAT, UK, IGCSE
Language instr: English
(🏛)(CIS)(EAR)

JERUDONG INTERNATIONAL SCHOOL
For further details see p. 86
Jalan Universiti, Kampong Tungku, Bandar Seri Begawan, BE2119 Brunei Darussalam
Tel: +673 2 411000
Email: office@jis.edu.bn
Website: www.jis.edu.bn
Principal: Andrew Fowler-Watt
Age range: 2–18
No. of pupils: 1650 VIth360
Fees: B$15,912–B$17,496
Curriculum: IBDP, UK, ALevs
Language instr: English
(🏛)(COB)

Cambodia

Hope International School
PO Box 2521, Phnom Penh, 12000 Cambodia
Tel: +855 23217565
Head of School: Brent Willsmore
Age range: 3–18
Curriculum: IBDP, ALevs
Language instr: English

International School of Phnom Penh
PO Box 138, Phnom Penh, Cambodia
Tel: +855 23 213 103
Director: Barry Sutherland
Age range: 2–18
No. of pupils: 340
Curriculum: IBDP, IBPYP
Language instr: English
(CIS)(EAR)(ECIS)

Jay Pritzker Academy
PO Box 93298, Siem Reap, Cambodia
Tel: +855 (0)92 655 322
Director: Mark Fox
Age range: 4–12

Northbridge International School
PO Box 2042, Phnom
Penh 3, Cambodia
Tel: +855 23 886000/006
School Head: Roy Crawford
Age range: 3–18
No. of pupils: 300 B139 G161
Fees: US$4,500–US$12,400
Curriculum: AP, IBDP,
IBMYP, IBPYP, SAT, USA
Language instr: English
(EAR)

Zaman International School
PO Box 2508, Phnom
Penh, Cambodia
Tel: +855 23 214040
Age range: 5–19
No. of pupils: 765 B401 G364
Fees: US$2,000
Curriculum: National, SAT, UK
Language instr: English

China

Access International Academy Ningbo
No1 Ai Xue Road, Beilun District,
Ningbo, Zhejiang, 315800 China
Tel: +86 574 8686 9999
Head of School: Jeff Walker
Age range: 4–18
Curriculum: USA
Language instr: English
(EAR)

Alcanta International College
No 1130 Baiyun Dadao Nan, Baiyun
District, Guangzhou, 510420 China
Tel: +86 20 8618 3999/3666
Head of School: David Cao
Age range: 14–19
Fees: Day RMB160,000
WB 6,800–8,600 FB 6,800–8,600
Curriculum: IBDP
Language instr: English, Mandarin
(血)

American International School of Guangzhou
No 3 Yan Yu Street South, Er
Sha Island, Yuexiu District,
Guangzhou, 510105 China
Tel: +86 20 8735 3392/3393
Director: Joe Stucker
Age range: 3–18
No. of pupils: 975
Fees: US$11,600–US$25,000
Curriculum: IBDP, IBPYP
Language instr: English
(EAR)

Beanstalk International Bilingual School
No.6 North Road of East Fourth
Ring Road, Chaoyang District,
Beijing, 100016 China
Tel: +86 10 8456 6019
Curriculum: IBDP
Language instr: English

Beijing BISS International School
No 17, Area 4, An Zhen
Xi Li, Chaoyang District,
Beijing, 100029 China
Tel: +86 10 64 433151
Head of School: Gwyn Underwood
Age range: 4–19
No. of pupils: 380
Fees: RMB96,000–RMB172,000
Curriculum: IBDP, IBMYP, IBPYP, SAT
Language instr: English
(EAR)

Beijing City International School
77 Baiziwan Nan Er Road,
Chaoyang District, Beijing,
100022 China
Tel: +86 10 8771 7171
Head of School: Bill O'Hearn
Age range: 3–18
No. of pupils: 652 B321 G331
Fees: RMB123,900–RMB194,900
Curriculum: IBDP, IBMYP, IBPYP
Language instr: English
(CIS)

Beijing Concord College of Sino-Canada
Conglin, Zhuangyuan, Tongzhou
District, Beijing, 101118 China
Tel: +86 108 959 1234
Principal: Wang Bengzhong
Language instr: English

Beijing Huijia Private School
157 Changhuai Road, Changping
District, Beijing, 102200 China
Tel: +86 (10) 697 44794
Head of School: Wang, Zhize
Age range: 3–18
No. of pupils: 2200
Fees: RMB100,100–RMB171,200
Curriculum: IBDP, IBPYP
Language instr: Chinese, English
(血)

Beijing Huijia Wanquan Kindergarten
No. 35 Bagou South Road, Haidian
District, Beijing, 100089 China
Tel: +86 10 82551751
Head of School: Aidong Luo
Curriculum: IBPYP

Beijing International Bilingual Academy
Monet Garden, No 5 Yumin
Road, Houshayu, Shunyi,
Beijing, 101300 China
Tel: +86 10 80410390
Head of School: Vivian Gao

Beijing Shuren-Ribet Private School
Beijing Tongzhou District,
Songzhuang Xiaopu South
1, Beijing 101118, China
Tel: +86 (10) 80856318
Principal: Jaimie Skinner
Age range: 4–18
Curriculum: ACT, SAT, USA
(血)

Beijing World Youth Academy
18 Hua Jia Di Bei Li, Chao Yang
District, Beijing 100102, China
Tel: +86 10 6461 7787
Head of School: Wang Hong
Age range: 9–18
No. of pupils: 520
Fees: RMB80,000–RMB140,000
Curriculum: IBDP, IBMYP
Language instr: English
(血)

Canadian International School of Beijing
38 Liangmaqiao Lu, Chaoyang
District, Beijing, 100125 China
Tel: +86 10 64657788
Head of School: Douglas Prescott
Age range: 1 –18
Curriculum: IBDP, IBMYP, IBPYP, SAT
Language instr: English
(血)

Changchun American International School
2899 Dong Nan Hu Road,
Changchun, Jilin Province
130033 China
Tel: +86 431 8458 1234
Head of School: Bryan Manditsch
Age range: 3–18
No. of pupils: B54 G51
Curriculum: IBDP, IBMYP, IBPYP
Language instr: English

Changsha WES Academy
8 Dongyi Road, Xingsha,
Changsha National Economic
& Technical Development Zone,
Changsha, Hunan 410100 China
Tel: +86 731 82758900
Head of School: David Priest
Curriculum: IBPYP
Language instr: English

Chengdu International School
68 Tong Gui Road, Jin Jiang
District, Chengdu, 61066 China
Tel: +86 28 8608 1162
Head of School: Debbie-Sue Blanks

Chengdu Meishi International School
#1340 Middle Section of Tianfu
Avenue, Chengdu, 610042 China
Tel: +86 28 8533 0653
Principal: Thomas Liu
Age range: 11–19
Curriculum: IBDP
Language instr: English
(血)

Chongqing Yew Chung International School
M 38 Orchard Manor,
Renhe Town, Yubei District,
Chongqing, 401121 China
Tel: +86 23 6763 8482
Age range: 2–15
No. of pupils: 20 B11 G9

Concordia International School Shanghai
999 Ming Yue Road, JinQiao,
Pudong, Shanghai, 201206 China
Tel: +862 1 5899 0380
Head of School: Gregg Pinick
Age range: 3–18
No. of pupils: 1180 B587 G593
Fees: RMB146,000–RMB195,000
Curriculum: ACT, AP, SAT, USA
Language instr: English
(EAR)

Dalian American International School
No 2 Dianchi Road, Golden
Pebble Beach National
Resort, Dalian Development
Area, PC 116650 China
Tel: +86 411 8757 2000
Director: Kurt Nordness
Age range: 4–18
No. of pupils: 262
Fees: RMB105,460–RMB126,570
Curriculum: AP, USA
Language instr: English
(CIS) (EAR)

Dulwich College Beijing
89 Capital Airport Road,
Shunyi District, Beijing
101300, 101300 China
Tel: +86 10 6454 9000
Head of School: David Mansfield
Age range: 1–18
No. of pupils: B720 G710
Fees: RMB27,200–RMB191,100
Curriculum: IBDP, IGCSE
Language instr: English
(ECIS)

Dulwich College Shanghai
222 Lan An Road, Shanghai,
201206 China
Tel: +8621 5899 9910
Headmaster: Paul Friend
Age range: 2–18
No. of pupils: 1400
Fees: RMB27,500–RMB220,600
Curriculum: IBDP, IGCSE
Language instr: English, Chinese
(CIS)

Dulwich College Suzhou
360 Gang Tian Road,
Suzhou Industrial Park,
Suzhou, 215021 China
Tel: +86 (512) 6295 9500
Headmaster: John Todd
Age range: 2–18
Fees: Day RMB86,500–
RMB190,000 WB RMB263,000–
RMB283,000 26,700–287,000
Curriculum: IBDP, UK, IGCSE
Language instr: English
(血) (CIS)

ELCHK Lutheran Academy
25 Lam Hau Tsuen Road, Yuen Long,
New Territories, Hong Kong, China
Tel: +852 8208 2092
Head of School: Andy
Wa-chau Fung
Curriculum: IBDP
Language instr: English
(血)

EtonHouse International School – Wuxi

Regent International Garden, Junction of Taishan Road & Xixing Road, New District, Wuxi, Jiangsu Province 214028 China
Tel: +86 510 8522 5333
Executive Principal: Rob Stewart
No. of pupils: 180
Curriculum: IBMYP, IBPYP
Language instr: English, Mandarin, Japanese, Korean, Dutch

EtonHouse International School, Suzhou

102 Kefa Road, Suzhou Science & Technology Town, 215011 China
Tel: +86 0512 6825 5666
Head of School: Scott Taprell
Age range: 18 months–14
No. of pupils: 85
Curriculum: IBMYP, IBPYP
Language instr: English

Guangdong Country Garden School

ShundeCountry Gardens, Beijiao Town, Shunde District, Foshan City, Guangdong Province 528312 China
Tel: +86 757 26677 888
Head of School: Chunlei Li
Curriculum: IBDP, IBMYP, IBPYP
Language instr: English

Guangzhou Nanhu International School

No 55 Huayang Street, Tiyu Dong Lu, Tianhe District, Guangzhou 510620, China
Tel: +86 20 3886 6952
Principal: Jenny Roosmalen
Age range: 2–17
Fees: RMB58,500–RMB121,550
Curriculum: IBDP, UK, IGCSE, ALevs

Hangzhou International School

78 Dongxin Street, Bin Jiang District, Hangzhou, 310053 China
Tel: +86 571 8669 0045
Head of School: Robert van der Eyken
Age range: 2–18
No. of pupils: 350
Fees: RMB95,000–RMB155,000
Curriculum: IBDP
Language instr: English

Harrow International School Beijing

No.287 Hegezhuang Village, Cuigezhuang County, Chaoyang District, Beijing 100102, China
Tel: +86 10 6444 8900 6900
Head Mistress: Lynne Oldfield
Age range: 9 weeks–18 years
Curriculum: UK

Hua Mao Multicultural Education Academy

No 2 Yinxian dadao (Middle), Ningbo, Zhejiang Province 31519 China
Tel: +86 574 8821 1160
Head of School: Ivan Moore
Curriculum: IBDP, IBPYP

International Academy Beijing

Lido Office Tower 3, Lido Place, Jichang Road, Chaoyang District, Beijing, 100004 China
Tel: +86 10 6430 1600
Headmaster: Tim McDonald
Age range: 45–18
Fees: RMB105,000–RMB181,000
Curriculum: ACT, AP, SAT, USA
Language instr: English, Chinese

International Montessori School of Beijing

Building 8, 2A, Xiang Jiang Bei Lu, Chao Yang District, Beijing 100103, China
Tel: +86 (10) 6432 8228
Academic Principal: Marie Hoffman
Age range: Co-ed 18 months–12 years
Fees: RMB95,000–RMB140,000
Language instr: English, Chinese

International School of Beijing-Shunyi

No 10 An Hua Street, Shunyi District, Beijing, 101318 China
Tel: +86 10 8149 2345 ext 1001
Head of School: Tarek Razik
Age range: 4–19
No. of pupils: 1850
Curriculum: ACT, AP, IBDP, SAT
Language instr: English

International School of Sino-Canada

166 Nanguang Road, Nanshan District, Shenzhen, China
Tel: +86 755 266 1000
Principle: Donna Trafford
Age range: 4–18
Fees: US$19,950–US$22,500
Language instr: English

International School of Tianjin

Weishan Road, Shuanggang, Jinnan District, Tianjin, 300350 China
Tel: +86 22 2859 2001
Director: Steve Moody
Age range: 3–18
No. of pupils: 450
Fees: RMB63,000–RMB197,000
Curriculum: ACT, IBDP, IBMYP, IBPYP, SAT
Language instr: English

Ivy Academy

East Lake Villas, No 35 Dongzhimenwai Street, Suite D-102, Beijing, 100027 China
Tel: +86 10 8451 1380
Chief Education Officer: Londi Carbajal
Age range: 2–6
Language instr: English, Chinese

Kunming International Academy

Yan Jia Di Xiao Qu, Kunming, Yunnan 650034 China
Tel: +86 871 412 6887
Age range: 4–16
No. of pupils: 200
Curriculum: USA
Language instr: English

Manila Xiamen International School

No 735 Long Hu Shan Lu, Zeng Cuo An, Si Ming District, Xiamen, 361005 China
Tel: +86 592 2516373/5
Head of School: Mildred A Go
Curriculum: IBDP
Language instr: English

Nanjing EtonHouse Kindergarten

No 6 West Songhuajiang Street, Jianye District, PRC, Nanjing, 210019 China
Tel: +86 25 866 96 788
Curriculum: IBPYP

Nanjing International School

Xian Lin College and, University Town, Qi Xia District, Nanjing, 210046 China
Tel: +86 25 85899111
Head of School: Laurie McLellan
Age range: 3–19
No. of pupils: 710 B361 G349
Fees: RMB193,200
Curriculum: IBDP, IBMYP, IBPYP
Language instr: English

Ningbo Zhicheng School

No 377 Jiangbei Road, Jiangbei District, Zhejiang Province, Ningbo, 315033 China
Tel: +86 0574 87564017
Head of School: Nancy Sanderson Swartz
Curriculum: IBDP

Oriental English College, Shenzhen

No 10 Xuezi Road, Bao An Education Town, Baoan, Shenzhen, Guangdong 518128 China
Tel: +86 755 27516124
Head of School: Bamidele Akinbo
No. of pupils: 2600
Curriculum: IBDP
Language instr: English

Qingdao Amerasia International School

68 Shandongtou Lu, Qingdao, 266061 China
Tel: +86 532 8388 9900
Head of School: Chris Vicari
Curriculum: IBDP
Language instr: English

Qingdao MTI International School

Baishan Campus, Shazikou, Dongjiang, Lacshan District, Qingdao, 266102 China
Tel: +86 532 8881 5668
Principal: David Pattison
Age range: 5–18
Curriculum: National, USA
Language instr: English

Qingdao No.1 International School of Shangdong Province (QISS)

232 Songling Road, Shandong Province, Quingdao, 266061 China
Tel: +86 532 6889 8888
Director: Jay Teston
Age range: 3–17
Curriculum: UK
Language instr: English

QSI International School of Chengdu

#188 Nan 3 Duan, 3rd Ring Road, American Garden, Chengdu, 610041 China
Tel: +86 28 8511 3853
Director: Timothy Kruger
Age range: 3–18
No. of pupils: 100 B48 G52
Fees: US$6,300–US$17,300
Curriculum: ACT, AP, SAT, USA
Language instr: English

QSI International School of Chongqing

Chongqing University West Road, University Town, Shapingba, Chongqing, 401331 China
Tel: +86 23 6562 0115
Director: Roy Douthitt
Age range: 3–17
No. of pupils: 19
Curriculum: USA
Language instr: English

QSI International School of Dongguan

2nd Floor, Block A2, Dong Cheng Center, Dongguan City, Guangdong 523000 China
Tel: +86 769 2230 0131
Director: Karen Hall
Age range: 2–17
No. of pupils: 117
Curriculum: USA
Language instr: English

QSI International School of Shekou
5th Floor, Bitao Building, 8 Taizi Road, Shekou, Shenzhen, Guangdong, 518069 China
Tel: +86 755 2667 6031
Head of School: Scott D'Alterio
Age range: 2–13
No. of pupils: 813 B402 G411
Fees: US$12,300
Curriculum: AP, IBDP, SAT, USA
Language instr: English
(EAR)

QSI International School of Shenzhen
8063 Hongli West Road, Futian District, Shenzhen, Guangdong China
Tel: +86 755 8371 3122
Director: Matt Lake
Age range: 2–13
No. of pupils: 62
Curriculum: USA
Language instr: English

QSI International School of Suzhou
Yangcheng Lake East Road 98, Xiang Cheng District, Suzhou City, China
Tel: +86 512 6618 1009
Director: Daniel Waterman
Age range: 3–13
No. of pupils: 7
Curriculum: USA
Language instr: English

QSI International School of Zhuhai
No. 168 Anning Road, Xianzhou District, Guangdong, Zhuhai 519000 China
Tel: +86 756 815 6134
Director: Matthew Farwell
Age range: 2–18
No. of pupils: 39 B21 G18
Fees: $6,000–$16,100
Curriculum: USA
Language instr: English

Rainbow Bridge International School
2381 Hong Qiao Road, Shanghai, 200335 China
Tel: +86 21 6268 2074
Principal: Rebecca Zipprich
No. of pupils: 347
Curriculum: IBPYP

School of the Nations
Rua de Minho, Taipa, Macau (SAR), China
Tel: +853 2870 1759
Head of School: Vivek Nair
Age range: 3–18
Fees: MOP23,850–MOP39,250
Curriculum: IBDP, ALevs
Language instr: English

Shanghai American School (Pudong Campus)
Shanghai Links Executive Community, 1600 Lingbai Road, Sanjiagang, Pudong, Shanghai 201201 China
Tel: +86 21 6221 1445 Ext 3000
Superintendent: Richard Mueller
Age range: 4–18
No. of pupils: 3400
Curriculum: AP, IBDP, SAT
Language instr: English
(EAR) (ECIS)

Shanghai American School (Puxi Campus)
258 Jinfeng Road, Huacao Town, Minhang Dist., Shanghai 201107 China
Tel: +86 21 6221 1445
Superintendent: Richard Mueller
Age range: 4–18
No. of pupils: 3400
Curriculum: AP, IBDP, SAT
Language instr: English
(EAR) (ECIS)

Shanghai Changning International School
No 79, Lane 261, Jiangsu Lu, Shanghai, 200050 China
Tel: +86 21 6252 3688
Age range: 3–15
No. of pupils: 510 B260 G250

Shanghai Community International School – Hongqiao
1161 Hongqiao Road, Shanghai, 200051 China
Tel: +86 21 6261 4668
Superintendent of Schools: Jeffry R Stubbs
Age range: 2–18
No. of pupils: 1450
Curriculum: AP, IBDP, USA
Language instr: English
(EAR)

Shanghai Community International School – Pudong Campus
800 Xiuyan Road, Kangqiao, Pudong, Shanghai, 201315 China
Tel: +86 21 5812 9888
Head of School: Daniel Jubert
Age range: 2–18
No. of pupils: 650
Curriculum: IBDP
Language instr: English
(EAR)

Shanghai Pinghe School
261 Huang Yang Road, Pudong, Shanghai, China
Tel: +86 21 5031 1866
Head of School: Ren GuoFang
Age range: 5–18
No. of pupils: 1550
Curriculum: IBDP
Language instr: English, Chinese
(symbol)

Shanghai Rego International School
189 Dong Zha Lu, Xinzhuang Town, Minhang District, Shanghai, 201100 China
Tel: +86 21 5488 3431
Principal: Richard Naylor
Age range: 2–18
No. of pupils: 400 B190 G210
Fees: RMB140,000–RMB180,000
Curriculum: UK, IGCSE
Language instr: English

Shanghai Shangde Experimental School
No 1688 Xiu Yan Road, Pudong New District, Shanghai, 201315 China
Tel: +86 21 6818 0001 or +86 21 6818 0191
Head of School: Jiang Xiaoyong
Curriculum: IBDP
Language instr: English
(symbol)

Shanghai Singapore International School
301 Zhu Jian Road, Hua Cao Town, Shanghai, Minhang District 201106 China
Tel: +86 21 6221 6488
Headmaster: Low Eng Kee
Curriculum: IBDP
Language instr: English
(CIS)

Shanghai United International School
248 Hong Song Road (E), Minhang District, Shanghai, 201103 China
Tel: +8621 51753030
Head of School: Martin Donnellan
No. of pupils: 1200
Curriculum: IBDP, IBPYP
Language instr: English, Mandarin

Shanghai Victoria Kindergarten (Huating)
No 1, Lane 71 Huating Road, Shanghai, 200031 China
Tel: +86 21 5403 6803
Head of School: Maggie Koong
Curriculum: IBPYP
Language instr: Chinese

Shanghai Victoria Kindergarten (Minhang)
300 Gumei Road, Shanghai, 201102 China
Tel: +86 21 6401 1084
Head of School: Maggie Koong
Curriculum: IBPYP
Language instr: English

Shanghai Victoria Kindergarten (Pudong)
No.38, Lane 39, Yin Xiao Road, Pudong, Shanghai, 201204 China
Tel: +86 21 5045 9084
Head of School: Maggie Koong
Curriculum: IBPYP

Shanghai Victoria Kindergarten (Xin Zhuang)
#15-155 BaoCheng Rd, MinHang District, Shanghai, 201100 China
Tel: +86 (021) 5415 2228
Head of School: Joanne Lu
Curriculum: IBPYP
Language instr: Chinese, English

Shanghai World Foreign Language Middle School
380 Pu Bei Road, Xu Hui District, Shanghai, 200233 China
Tel: +8621 6436 3556
Head of School: Jian Xu
Curriculum: IBDP, IBMYP
Language instr: Chinese
(symbol)

Shanghai World Foreign Language Primary School
No 380 Pubei Road, Xu Hui District, Shanghai, 200233 China
Tel: +86 21 5419 2245
Head of School: Wang Xiao Ping
Curriculum: IBPYP
Language instr: English, Chinese

Shekou International School
Jing Shan Villas, Nan Hai Road, Shekou, Shenzhen, Guangdong Province 518067 China
Tel: +86 755 2669 3669
Director: Robert Evans
Age range: 2–18
No. of pupils: 650 B340 G310
Curriculum: IBDP, SAT
Language instr: English
(EAR)

Shenyang International School
55 Zusheng Road, Heping District, Minzu Economic Development Zone, Dongling District, Shenyang, 110117 China
Tel: +86 24 89 12 1177
Head Principal: Andy Lasiewicz
Age range: 4–18
No. of pupils: 161 B85 G76
Curriculum: USA
Language instr: English
(EAR)

Shenzhen College of International Education
1st Huanggang Park Street, Futian District, Shenzhen 518048, GuangDong China
Tel: +86 755 89804333
Principal: Joe Greenwood
Age range: 14–19
Curriculum: UK, IGCSE, ALevs

Shenzhen Concord College of Sino-Canada
166 Nanguang Road, Nanshan District, Shenzhen, China
Tel: +86 755 2656 8886
Language instr: Chinese
(RS)

Shenzhen Futian Funful Bilingual School
Goldfield Seaview Gardens, South Xinzhou Road, Futian District, Shenzhen, Guangdong, China
Tel: +86 755 2381 0830
Head of School: Delia Pei
Age range: 3–12
Language instr: English, Putonghua

Suzhou Singapore International School
208 Zhong Nan Street, Suzhou Industrial Park, Jiangsu, 215021 China
Tel: +86 512 6258 0388
Head of School: Nicholas Little
Age range: 2–18
No. of pupils: 1340
Curriculum: ACT, AP, IBDP, IBMYP, IBPYP, SAT
Language instr: English
(CIS) (EAR)

Taihu International School
Jin Shi Road, Bin Hu District, Jiangsu Province, Wuxi, 214121 China
Tel: +86 510 850 70333
Head of School: Simon Mark Saunders
Age range: 2–18
No. of pupils: 133 B65 G68
Fees: RMB160,000
Curriculum: IBDP, IBMYP, IBPYP
Language instr: English
(CIS)

Teda International School
72 Third Avenue, Teda, Tianjin, 300457 China
Tel: +86 22 6622 6158
Headmaster: Joseph Azmeh
Age range: 3–18
No. of pupils: 326 B166 G160
Fees: RMB109,500
Curriculum: AP, SAT, USA
Language instr: English
(CIS) (EAR)

The British International School of Shanghai (Puxi Campus)
111 Jinguang Road, Huacao Town, Minhang District, Puxi, Shanghai 201107 China
Tel: +86-21-5226-3211
Head of School: Kevin Foyle
Curriculum: IBDP, UK
Language instr: English
(COB)

The British International School Shanghai – Pudong Campus
600 Cambridge Forest New Town, 2729 Hunan Road, Pudong, Shanghai 201315 China
Tel: +86 21 5812 7455
Principal: Patrick Horne
Age range: 1–18
No. of pupils: 1150
Fees: RMB96,210–RMB271,530
Curriculum: IBDP, National, SAT, UK, IGCSE
Language instr: English
(COB)

The British International School, Nanxiang Shanghai
151 Baoxiang Road, Nanxiang Town, Jiading District, Shanghai 201802 China
Tel: +86 21 5912 5755
Principal: Mark Angus
Age range: 2–16
No. of pupils: 100 B50 G50
Fees: RMB224,862
Curriculum: UK, IGCSE
Language instr: English
(COB)

The British School of Beijing
5 Xiliujie, Sanlitun Road, Chaoyang District, Beijing 100027, China
Tel: +8610 8532 3088
Executive Principal: Mike Embley
Age range: 2–18
(COB)

The British School of Guangzhou
828 Tonghe Road, Nanhu, Guangzhou, Guangdong Province China
Tel: +86 20 8709 4788
Headmaster: Mark Thomas
Age range: 2–14
No. of pupils: 249
Fees: RMB75,300–RMB134,700
Curriculum: UK
Language instr: English
(COB)

The British School of Nanjing
Building 2, Jinling Resort, Jiahu Dong Lu, Nanjing 211100, China
Tel: +86 25 5210 8987
Head Teacher: Matthew Shephard
Age range: 3–13
No. of pupils: B45 G56
Fees: RMB102,600–RMB160,200
Curriculum: UK
(COB)

The International School of Macao
Macau University of Science and Technology (Block K), Avenida Wai Long, Taipa, China
Tel: +853 2853 3700
Head of Schools: Howard Stribbell
Age range: 3–17
No. of pupils: 840 B420 G420
Fees: MOP35,000–MOP75,000
Language instr: English
(🏛)

Tianjin Experimental High School
No 1 Pingshan Road, Hexi District, Tianjin, 300074 China
Tel: +86 22 2335 8689
Principal: Zhang Hong
Fees: RMB40,000
Curriculum: IBDP, IBMYP
Language instr: Chinese/English
(🏛)

Tianjin International School
1 Meiyuan Road, Huayuan Industrial Garden, Nankai District, Tianjin, 300384 China
Tel: +86 22 8371 0900
Head Principal: Scott Finnamore
Curriculum: USA
Language instr: English
(EAR)

Tianjin Rego International School
38 Huan Dao Dong Road, Mei Jiang Nan Residence Zone, Tianjin 300221, China
Tel: +86 22 8816 1180
Acting Principal: Michael Owens
Age range: 3–19
Curriculum: UK, IGCSE, ALevs

Utahloy International School Guangzhou
800 Sha Tai Bei Road, Bai Yun District, Guangzhou, Guangdong 510515 China
Tel: +8620 87202019
Head of School: Elaine Whelen
Age range: 2–18
No. of pupils: 940 B495 G425 VIth140
Fees: US$15,952–US$25,476
Curriculum: IBDP, IBMYP, IBPYP, TOEFL
Language instr: English
(CIS) (EAR)

Utahloy International School Zengcheng
San Jiang Town, Zeng Cheng City, Guangdong 511325 China
Tel: +86 20 8291 3201
Head of School: Michael Wylie
Age range: 2–18
No. of pupils: 168
Curriculum: IBDP, IBPYP
Language instr: English
(🏛) (CIS)

Wellington College International Tianjin
No 1 Yide Dao, Hong Qiao District, Tianjin 300120, China
Tel: +86 22 8758 7199
Master: David Cook
Age range: 2–18
Fees: RMB123,000–RMB399,900
Curriculum: IBDP, UK

Western Academy Of Beijing
PO Box 8547, 10 Lai Guang Ying Dong Lu, Chao Yang District, Beijing, 100102 China
Tel: +86 10 5986 5588
Director: J. Courtney Lowe
Age range: 3–18
Fees: Day RMB94,000–RMB243,000
Curriculum: IBDP, IBMYP, IBPYP
Language instr: English
(CIS) (EAR)

Western International School of Shanghai
555 Lian Min Road, Xujing Town, Qing Pu District, Shanghai, 201702 China
Tel: +86 21 6976 6388
Head of School: Tom Kline
Curriculum: IBDP, IBMYP, IBPYP
Language instr: English

WHBC of Wuhan Foreign Languages School
7th Floor Administration Building, 48 Wan Song Yuan Road, Wuhan, Hubei Province, 430022 China
Tel: +86 027 8555 7389
Curriculum: IBDP
Language instr: English
(🏛)

Wuhan Yangtze Internation School
San Jiao Hu Xiao, XueWuhan Economic & Technology Development Zone, Wuhan, 430056 China
Tel: +86 27842 38713
Head Principal: Jeff Kingma
Curriculum: USA
Language instr: English
(EAR)

Xiamen International School
262 Xing Bei San Lu, Xinglin, Jimei District, Xiamen, 361022 China
Tel: +86 592 625 6581
Headmaster: John M Godwin
Age range: 2–18
No. of pupils: 350 B190 G160
Fees: US$10,500–US$16,700
Curriculum: ACT, IBDP, IBMYP, IBPYP, SAT
Language instr: English
(EAR)

Yew Chung International School of Beijing
Honglingjin Park, 5 Houbalizhuang, Chaoyang District, Beijing, 100025 China
Tel: +86 10 8583 3731
Co-principal: Wayne Richardson
Age range: 3–18
No. of pupils: B407 G373
Curriculum: IBDP, IGCSE
Language instr: English, Chinese
(CIS)

Yew Chung International School of Chongqing
No 2, Huxia Street, Yuan Yang Town, New Northern Zone, Chongqing, 401122 China
Tel: +86 23 6763 8482
Age range: 3–18
No. of pupils: 93 B48 G45
Fees: RMB145,410–RMB147,870
Curriculum: National, UK
Language instr: English

Yew Chung International School of Qingdao
Bld. 7, 36 Laoshan Lu,
Laoshan District, Qingdao,
Shandong 266100 China
Tel: +86 532 8880 0003
Age range: 2–18
Curriculum: IGCSE
Language instr: English, Chinese
(EAR)

Yew Chung International School of Shanghai – Century Park Campus
1433 Dong Xui Road, Pudong,
Shanghai 200127 China
Tel: +86 21 5045 6475
Age range: 9–18
Curriculum: IBDP
Language instr: English
(CIS)

Yew Chung International School of Shanghai – Hongqiao Campus
11 Shui Cheng Road, Puxi,
Shanghai 200336 China
Tel: +86 21 6242 3243
Age range: 1–8
No. of pupils: 755
Curriculum: IBDP
Language instr: English
(CIS)

Zhuhai International School
Qi ' Ao Island, Tang Jia Wan,
Zhuhai, Guangdong, 519080 China
Tel: +86 756 331 5580
Head of School: Hadyn Adams
Curriculum: IBDP, IBMYP, IBPYP
Language instr: Chinese

East Timor

Dili International School
14 Rue Avenue de Portugal,
Pantai Kelapa, Dili, East Timor
Tel: +670 77316065
Head of School: Curtis Beaverford
Curriculum: IBMYP, IBPYP

QSI International School of Dili
Marconi, Aldea 4, Fatuhada,
Dili, Timor Leste East Timor
Tel: +670 3322389
Director: Jason Moore
Age range: 5–13
No. of pupils: 31
Curriculum: USA
Language instr: English

Hong Kong, China

American International School Hong Kong
125 Waterloo Road, Kowloon
Tong, Kowloon, Hong Kong, SAR
Tel: +852 2336 3812
Age range: 3–17
No. of pupils: B430 G390
Fees: HK$61,320–HK$113,440
Curriculum: AP, USA
Language instr: English
(EAR)

Australian International School Hong Kong
3A Norfolk Road, Kowloon
Tong, Hong Kong, SAR
Tel: +852 2304 6078
Age range: 4–18
No. of pupils: 1125 B564 G561
Fees: HK$76,300–HK$164,200
Curriculum: IBDP
Language instr: English

Beacon Hill School
23 Ede Road, Kowloon
Tong, Hong Kong, SAR
Tel: +852 2336 5221
Head of School: John Brewster
Age range: 5–11
No. of pupils: 540
Fees: HK$70,000
Curriculum: IBPYP, UK
Language instr: English
(CIS)

Bradbury School
43C Stubbs Road, Hong Kong, SAR
Tel: +852 2574 8249
Head of School: Sandra Webster
Age range: 5–11
No. of pupils: 720
Fees: HK$70,000
Curriculum: IBPYP
Language instr: English
(CIS)

Canadian International School of Hong Kong
36 Nam Long Shan Road,
Aberdeen, Hong Kong, SAR
Tel: +852 2525 7088
Head of School: Dave McMaster
Age range: 3–18
No. of pupils: 1835
Fees: HK$79,500–HK$134,800
Curriculum: IBDP, IBMYP, IBPYP
Language instr: English
(EAR)

Carmel School Association Elsa High School
460 Shau Kei Wan Road, Shau
Kei Wan, Hong Kong, SAR
Tel: +852 3665 5388
Head of School: Rachel Friedmann
Age range: 11–18
Fees: HK$123,900–HK$145,500
Curriculum: IBDP, IBMYP
Language instr: English

Causeway Bay Victoria & International Kindergarten
32-36 Hing Fat Street, G/Floor
– 2 Floor & Rooftop, Causeway
Bay, Hong Kong, SAR
Tel: +852 2578 9998
Head of School: Sabrina Lee
Curriculum: IBPYP

Chinese International School
1 Hau Yuen Path, Braemar
Hill, Hong Kong, SAR
Tel: +852 2 510 7288
Head of School: Theodore S Faunce
Age range: 4–18
No. of pupils: 1471 B691 G780
Fees: HK$114,800–HK$182,000
Curriculum: ACT, IBDP, IBMYP, SAT
Language instr: English
(CIS) (EAR) (ECIS)

Clearwater Bay School
DD229, Lot 235, Clearwater
Bay Road, New Territories,
Hong Kong, SAR
Tel: +852 2358 3221
Head of School: Chris Hamilton
Age range: 5–11
No. of pupils: 720
Fees: HK$70,000
Curriculum: IBPYP, UK
Language instr: English
(CIS)

Creative Primary School
2A Oxford Street, Kowloon Tong,
Kowloon, Hong Kong, SAR
Tel: +852 2336 0266
Head of School: Clio Chan So Ming
Curriculum: IBPYP

Diocesan Boys' School
131 Argyle Street, Mong Kok,
Kowloon, Hong Kong, SAR
Tel: +852 2768 5609
Headmaster: R K Y Cheng
Age range: B12–18
No. of pupils: 1420
Fees: HK$37,700
Curriculum: IBDP
Language instr: English

Discovery College
38 Siena Avenue, Discovery Bay,
Lantau Island, Hong Kong, SAR
Tel: +852 3969 1000
Principal: Mark Beach
Age range: 5–18
No. of pupils: 1500
Fees: HK$89,500
Curriculum: IBDP, IBMYP, IBPYP
Language instr: English
(CIS)

ESF Abacus International Kindergarten
Mang Kung Uk Village, Clearwater
Bay Road, Hong Kong, SAR
Tel: +852 27195712
Head of School: Frances Hurley
Age range: 2–5
No. of pupils: 176
Fees: HK$57,900
Curriculum: IBPYP
Language instr: English, Mandarin

ESF International Kindergarten (Hillside)
43B Stubbs Road, Hong Kong, SAR
Tel: +852 2540 0066
Head of School: Christopher Duncan
Curriculum: IBPYP
Language instr: English

ESF International Kindergarten (Tsing Yi)
Maritime Square, 33 Tsing
King Road, Tsing Yi, New
Territories, Hong Kong, SAR
Tel: +852 2436 3355
Head of School: Victoria Bewsey
Age range: 3–5
No. of pupils: 352
Fees: HK$5,820
Curriculum: IBPYP
Language instr: English

ESF International Kindergarten (Wu Kai Sha)
599 Sai Sha Road, Ma On Shan,
Sha Tin, Hong Kong, SAR, China
Tel: +852 2435 5291
Age range: 3–5
No. of pupils: 325
Fees: HK$61,400
Curriculum: IBPYP
Language instr: English

French International School
165 Blue Pool Road, Happy
Valley, Hong Kong, SAR
Tel: +852 2 577 6217
Head of School: Christian Soulard
Age range: 3–18
No. of pupils: 3707 B1210 G2497
Fees: HK$90,688–HK$146,094
Curriculum: IBDP,
FrenchBacc, IGCSE
Language instr: English, French

Funful Sear Rogers International School
1 Cumberland Road, Kowloon
Tong, Hong Kong, China
Tel: +852 2408 6683
Principal: Delia Pei
Age range: 5–11
Language instr: English

**German Swiss
International School**
11 Guildford Road, The
Peak, Hong Kong, SAR
Tel: +852 2849 6216
Principal: Annette
Brandt-Dammann
Age range: 3–18
No. of pupils: B634 G661
Fees: HK$85,500–HK$154,150
Curriculum: Abitur, IBDP,
National, UK, ALevs
Language instr: English, German

Glenealy School
7 Hornsey Road, Mid Levels,
Hong Kong, SAR
Tel: +852 2522 1919
Head of School: Brenda Cook
Age range: 5–11
No. of pupils: 360
Fees: HK$70,000
Curriculum: IBPYP
Language instr: English
(CIS)

**HKMA David Li Kwok
Po College**
8 Hoi Wang Road, Mongkok West,
Kowloon, Hong Kong, China
Tel: +852 2626 9100
Principal: Nicholas Puin
Age range: 12–20
No. of pupils: 921 B493 G428
Curriculum: National
Language instr: English,
Cantonese and Putonghua

Hong Kong Academy
12 Ka Wai Man Road, Kennedy
Town, Sai Wan, Hong Kong, SAR
Tel: +852 2655 1111
Head of School: Stephen Dare
Age range: 3–18
No. of pupils: 500
Fees: HK$100,800
Curriculum: ACT, IBDP,
IBMYP, IBPYP, SAT
Language instr: English
(CIS) (EAR) (ECIS)

**Hong Kong
International School**
1 Red Hill Road, Tai Tam,
Hong Kong, SAR, China
Tel: +852 3149 7000
Head of School: Kevin Dunning
Age range: 4–18
No. of pupils: 2600
Curriculum: AP, USA
Language instr: English
(EAR)

**Hong Lok Yuen
International School**
20th Street, Hong Lok Yuen, Tai Po,
New Territories, Hong Kong, SAR
Tel: +852 26586935
Principal: Ruth Woodward
Age range: 3–11
No. of pupils: 427 B229 G198
Fees: HK$88,160
Curriculum: IBPYP
Language instr: English
(CIS)

**International
Christian School**
1 On Muk Lane, Shek Mun,
Sha Tin, Hong Kong, SAR
Tel: +852 3920 0000
Headmaster: John Nelson
Fees: HK$52,200
Language instr: English
(EAR)

**International College
Hong Kong**
60 Sha Tau Kok Road, Shek
Chung Au, Sha Tau Kok, New
Territories, Hong Kong, SAR
Tel: +852 2655 9018
Head of School: Roy White
Age range: 11–18
No. of pupils: 170 B85 G85
Fees: HK$116,000–HK$121,000
Curriculum: IBDP, UK, IGCSE
Language instr: English

Island School
20 Borrett Road, Hong Kong, SAR
Tel: +852 2524 7135
Head of School: Christopher Binge
Age range: 11–18
No. of pupils: 1200
Fees: HK$101,400
Curriculum: IBDP, UK, IGCSE
Language instr: English
(CIS)

**Japanese International
School**
4663 Tai Po Road, Tai Po, New
Territories, Hong Kong, SAR
Tel: +852 2834 3531
Principal: Simon Walton
Age range: 4–11
No. of pupils: B85 G84
Fees: HK$81,500
Curriculum: IBPYP
Language instr: English

**Jockey Club Sarah
Roe School**
2B Tin Kwong Road, Homantin,
Kowloon, Hong Kong, SAR
Tel: +852 2761 9893
Principal: Alan Howells
Age range: 5–19
Curriculum: UK
Language instr: English

KELLETT SCHOOL
For further details see p. 87
2 Wah Lok Path, Wah Fu, Pok
Fu Lam, Hong Kong, SAR
Tel: +852 3120 0700
Email: kellett@kellettschool.com
Website: www.kellettschool.com
Principal: Ann McDonald
Age range: 4–18
No. of pupils: 670 B335 G335
Fees: HK$130,300
Curriculum: UK, IGCSE, ALevs
Language instr: English

Kennedy School
19 Sha Wan Drive, Pokfulam,
Hong Kong, SAR
Tel: +852 2855 0711
Head of School: Paul Hay
Age range: 5–11
No. of pupils: 900
Fees: HK$70,000
Curriculum: IBPYP, UK
Language instr: English
(CIS)

**Kiangsu-Chekiang
College, International
Section**
20 Braemar Hill Road, North
Point, Hong Kong, SAR
Tel: +852 2570 1281
Head of School: Jane Daniel
Age range: 3–18
No. of pupils: 960
Fees: HK$51,000
Curriculum: IBDP, UK, IGCSE
Language instr: English, Mandarin

King George V School
2 Tin Kwong Road, Homantin,
Kowloon, Hong Kong, SAR
Tel: +852 2711 3029
Principal: Ed Wickins
Age range: 11–18
No. of pupils: 1760
Fees: HK$101,400
Curriculum: IBDP, UK, IGCSE
Language instr: English
(CIS)

**Kingston International
Kindergarten**
12-14 Cumberland Road,
Kowloon Tong, Hong Kong, SAR
Tel: +852 2337 9049
Head Principal: Eliza Wong
Curriculum: IBPYP

**Kingston International
School**
113 Waterloo Road, Kowloon
Tong, Hong Kong, SAR
Tel: +852 2337 9031
Head of School: Emily Ngan
Age range: 1–12
No. of pupils: 298 B155 G143
Curriculum: IBPYP

**Kowloon Junior School,
Hung Hom Campus**
20 Perth Street, Homantin,
Kowloon, Hong Kong, SAR
Tel: +852 3765 8700
Principal: Mark Cripps
Age range: 5–11
No. of pupils: 900
Fees: HK$66,100
Curriculum: IBPYP, UK
Language instr: English

**Kowloon Junior School,
Rose Street Campus**
4 Rose Street, Yau Yat Chuen,
Kowloon, Hong Kong, SAR
Tel: +852 2394 0687
Head of School: Mark Cripps
Language instr: English

**Li Po Chun United World
College of Hong Kong**
10 Lok Wo Sha Lane, off
Sai Sha Road, Ma On
Shan, Hong Kong, SAR
Tel: +852 2640 0424
Head of School: Arnett Edwards
Age range: 16–19
No. of pupils: 256 B117 G139
Fees: HK$200,000
Curriculum: IBDP
Language instr: English
(🏛)

**Parkview International
Pre-school**
Tower 18 Parkview, 88 Tai Tam
Reservoir Road, Hong Kong, SAR
Tel: +852 2812 6023
Head of School: Mary Scarborough
Age range: 1–5
Fees: HK$77,800
Curriculum: IBPYP
Language instr: English, Putonghua

Peak School
20 Plunkett's Road, The
Peak, Hong Kong, SAR
Tel: +852 2849 7211
Head of School: William
(Bill) Garnett
Age range: 4–11
No. of pupils: 360
Fees: HK$70,000
Curriculum: IBPYP
Language instr: English
(CIS)

**Po Leung Kuk Choi
Kai Yau School**
6 Caldecott Road, Piper's Hill,
Kowloon, Hong Kong, China
Tel: +852 2148 2052
Head of School: Siu Ling Lau
Curriculum: IBDP
(🏛)

Quarry Bay School
6 Hau Yuen Path, Braemar Hill,
North Point, Hong Kong, SAR
Tel: +852 2566 4242
Head of School: Mina Dunstan
Age range: 4–11
No. of pupils: 716 B396 G320
Fees: HK$70,000
Curriculum: IBPYP, UK
Language instr: English
(CIS)

Renaissance College
5 Hang Ming Street, Ma On Shan,
New Territories, Hong Kong, SAR
Tel: +852 3556 3556
Head of School: Harry Brown
Age range: 5–18
No. of pupils: 2050
Fees: HK$86,800–HK$117,400
Curriculum: IBDP, IBMYP, IBPYP
Language instr: English
(CIS)

Sha Tin College
3 Lai Wo Lane, Fo Tan, Sha Tin,
New Territories, Hong Kong, SAR
Tel: +852 2699 1811
Head of School: Marc Morris
Age range: 11–18
No. of pupils: 1200
Fees: HK$98,000
Curriculum: IBDP, ALevs
Language instr: English
(CIS)

Sha Tin Junior School
3A Lai Wo Lane, Fo Tan, Sha Tin,
New Territories, Hong Kong, SAR
Tel: +852 2692 2721
Head of School: Perry Tunesi
Age range: 5–11
No. of pupils: 900
Fees: HK70,000
Curriculum: IBPYP, UK
Language instr: English
(CIS)

Singapore International School (Hong Kong)
2 Police School Road,
Aberdeen, Hong Kong, SAR
Tel: +852 2919 6916
Head of School: Wee Haur Pek
Age range: 4–17
Curriculum: IBDP, IGCSE
Language instr: English/Chinese

South Island School
50 Nam Fung Road, Aberdeen,
Hong Kong, SAR
Tel: +852 2555 9313
Principal: Graham Silverthorne
Age range: 11–18 AGE1 e–e
No. of pupils: 1400
Fees: HK$101,400
Curriculum: IBDP, IGCSE
Language instr: English
(CIS)

St. Paul's Co-educational College
33 MacDonnell Road,
Central, Hong Kong, SAR
Tel: +852 2523 1187
Principal: Anissa Chan
Age range: 11–18
No. of pupils: 1300
Fees: HK$78,000
Curriculum: IBDP
(符)

The Harbour School
Kennedy Town Centre Office Block,
23 Belchers St, Hong Kong, SAR
Tel: +85 228 165 222
Language instr: English
(EAR)

The Hong Kong Chinese Christian Churches Union Logos Academy
1 Kan Hok Lane, Tseung
Kwan O, Hong Kong, SAR
Tel: +852 2337 2123
Head of School: Paul Cho
Age range: 6–18
No. of pupils: 2085 B1074
G1011 VIth105
Fees: US$9,230
Curriculum: IBDP
Language instr: English

The Independent Schools Foundation Academy
1 Kong Sin Wan Road,
Pokfulam, Hong Kong, SAR
Tel: +852 2202 2000
Head of School: Malcolm Pritchard
Age range: 5–18
No. of pupils: B671 G646
Fees: HK$140,000–HK$190,000
Curriculum: ACT, IBDP, IBMYP, SAT
Language instr: English, Chinese
(CIS)

Think International School
117 Boundary Street, Kowloon
Tong, Hong Kong, SAR
Tel: +832 2338 3949
Curriculum: IBPYP

Victoria (Homantin) International Nursery
Carmel-on-the-Hill, 9 Carmel
Village Street, Ho Man Tin,
Kowloon, Hong Kong, SAR
Tel: +852 2762 9130
Head of School: Maggie Koong
Curriculum: IBPYP
Language instr: English

Victoria Belcher Kindergarten
Portion of Level 3 (Kindergarten
Area), The Westwood, 8 Belchers
Street, Hong Kong, SAR
Tel: +852 2542 7001
Head of School: Maggie Koong
Age range: 2–6
Fees: HK$30,804–HK$75,625
Curriculum: IBPYP
Language instr: English, Chinese

Victoria Shanghai Academy (VSA)
19 Shum Wan Road, Aberdeen,
Hong Kong, China
Tel: +852 3402 1000
Head of Academy: Christine Shain
Age range: 6–18
No. of pupils: 1657 B919 G738
Fees: HK$95,000–HK$137,250
Curriculum: IBDP, IBMYP, IBPYP
Language instr: English, Putonghua
(CIS)

West Island School
250 Victoria Road, Pokfulam,
Hong Kong, SAR
Tel: +852 2819 1962
School Principal: Jane Foxcroft
Age range: 11–18
No. of pupils: 1225
Fees: HK$101,400
Curriculum: IBDP, UK, IGCSE
Language instr: English
(CIS)

Yew Chung International School – Hong Kong
3 To Fuk Road, Kowloon,
Hong Kong, SAR
Tel: +852 2338 7106
Head of School: Iyad Matuk
Age range: 11–18
No. of pupils: 2000
Curriculum: IBDP, ALevs
Language instr: English, Chinese

India

Aditya Birla World Academy
Vastushilp Annexe, Gamadia
Colony, J D Road, Tardeo,
Mumbai, 400034 India
Tel: +91 22 2352 8400/1/2/3
Head of School: Radhika Sinha
Curriculum: IBDP
Language instr: English

Ahmedabad International School
Opp Rajpath Row Houses,
Behind Kiran Motors, Judges
Bungalow Road, Bodakdev,
Ahmedabad 380015 India
Tel: +91 79 2687 2459
Head of School: Tarulata Hirani
Age range: 3–17
No. of pupils: 1200
Curriculum: IBDP, IBPYP,
IGCSE, ALevs
Language instr: English

Ajmera Global School
Yogi Nagar, Eksar Road, Borivali
West, Mumbai, 400092 India
Tel: +91 22 32401053
Head of School: Hima Doshi
Curriculum: IBPYP
Language instr: English

Akal Academy Baru Sahib
Via Rajgarh, Teh. Pachhad,
Distt. Sirmore, Himachal
Pradesh, 173101 India
Tel: +91 9816400538
Head of School: Neelam Kaur
Curriculum: IBPYP
Language instr: English
(符)

All Saints' College
Nainital, Uttarakhand, 263002 India
Tel: +91 5942 235121
Principal: K E Jeremiah
Age range: G5–18
No. of pupils: 800
Curriculum: National
(符) (RS)

American Embassy School
Chandragupta Marg,
Chanakyapuri, New
Delhi, 110021 India
Tel: +91 11 2 688 8854
Head of School: Bob Hetzel
No. of pupils: 1332
Fees: US$6,350–US$17,350
Curriculum: IBDP
Language instr: English

American International School – Chennai
100 Feet Road, Taramani,
Chennai, 600113 India
Tel: +91 44 2254 9000
Head of School: Andrew Hoover
Age range: 3–18
No. of pupils: 226 B116 G110
Curriculum: IBDP
Language instr: English
(CIS) (ECIS)

AMERICAN SCHOOL OF BOMBAY
For further details see p. 78
SF 2, G-Block, Bandra Kurla
Complex Road, Bandra East,
Mumbai, 400 098 India
Tel: ESC: +91 22 6131 3600,
SSC: +91 22 6772 7272
Email: asb@asbindia.org
Website: www.asbindia.org
Head of School: Craig Johnson
Age range: 3–18
No. of pupils: 750
Fees: US$15,250–US$32,400
Curriculum: AP, IBDP,
IBPYP, SAT, USA
Language instr: English
(ASIA)

Amity Global School
Sector 46, Gurgaon,
Harayana, 122002 India
Tel: +91 8447525557
Head of School: Lon McDaniel
No. of pupils: 60
Curriculum: IBDP
Language instr: English

Amity International School Saket
M Block, Saket, New
Delhi 110017, India
Tel: +91 11 29561606
Principal: Bharati Sharma
Age range: 4–12

ASCEND INTERNATIONAL SCHOOL
For further details see p. 74
5 'F' Block, Opp. Govt. Colony, Bandra Kurla Complex (Bandra E), Mumbai 400051 India
Tel: +91 022 7122 2000
Email: admin@ascend international.org
Website: www.ascend international.org
Head of School: Aditya Patil
Age range: 3–12

Bangalore International School
Geddalahalli, Hennur Bagalur Road, Kothanur Post, Bangalore, 560077 India
Tel: +91 80 2846 5060/2844 5852
Head of School: Anuradha Monga
Age range: 3–18
No. of pupils: 282 B153 G129
Curriculum: AP, IBDP, UK, USA, IGCSE, ALevs
Language instr: English

BD Somani International School
625 GD Somani Marg, Cuffe Parade, Mumbai, 400 005 India
Tel: +91 22 2216 1355
Head of School: Don Gardner
Age range: 13–17
No. of pupils: 190
Curriculum: IBDP, IGCSE
Language instr: English

Bishop Cotton School
Shimla 171002, Himachal Prabesh, India
Tel: +91 177 2620880
Headmaster: Roy Christopher Robinson
Age range: B7–18
Fees: Rs145,000–Rs150,000

Bluebells School International
Kailash (Opp) Lady Shriram College, New Delhi – 110048, India
Tel: +91 011 29232963
Principal: Suman Kumar
Age range: 4–18
No. of pupils: B976 G893
Curriculum: National
Language instr: English

Bombay International School
Gilbert Building, 2nd Cross Lane, Babulnath, Maharashtra, Mumbai 400 007, India
Tel: +91 (22)2364-8206
Head of School: Mona Seervai
Curriculum: IBDP

Calcutta International School
724 Anandapur, E M Bypass, Kolkata 700107, India
Tel: +91 33 2443 2054
Director: Anuradha Das
Age range: 3–18
No. of pupils: 642 B360 G282
Fees: INR60,000–INR81,600
Curriculum: IBDP, UK, IGCSE, ALevs
Language instr: English

Cambridge International School
Chhoti Baradari, Opposite Medical College, Jalandhar, Punjab, 144003 India
Tel: +91 181 4623954
Head of School: Deepa Dogra
Curriculum: IBDP

Canadian International School
Survey No 4 & 20, Manchenahalli, Yelahanka, Bangalore, 560 064 India
Tel: +91 80 4249 4444
Head of School: Shane Kells
Age range: 3–19+
No. of pupils: 420 B220 G200
Fees: US$12,830
Curriculum: IBDP, SAT
Language instr: English

Candor International School
Begur-Koppa Road, Hulahali, Bangalore, Karnataka 560105 India
Tel: +91 80 2572 9999
Head of School: Pradip Das Kumar
Curriculum: IBDP

Chennai Public School
TH Road, SH 50, Thirumazhisai, Chennai, Tamil Nandu 600124 India
Tel: +91 44 2654 4477
Head of School: Suman Babu Yarlagadda
Curriculum: IBDP

Chinmaya International Residential School
Nallur Vayal Post, Siruvani Road, Coimbatore, Tamil Nadu 641 114 India
Tel: +91 422 261 3300/3303
Principal: Shanti Krishnamurthy
Age range: 10–19
No. of pupils: 500 B320 G180
Curriculum: IBDP, National
Language instr: English

CHIREC Public School
1-22 Kondapur, Botanical Garden Road, Hyderabad, Andhra Pradesh 500084 India
Tel: 91 40 44760999
Head of School: Ratna Reddy
Curriculum: IBDP

Choithram International
5 Manik Bagh Road, Choithram Hospital Campus, Indore, MP 452014 India
Tel: +91 0731 2360345/46
Head of School: Dilip Vasu
Curriculum: IBDP, IBMYP, IBPYP
Language instr: English

Christ PU College – Residential
Mysore Road, Kanmanike, Kumbalgodu, Bangalore, Karnataka 560060 India
Tel: +91 80 65338855
Head of School: Thomas Mangara
Curriculum: IBDP
Language instr: English

D Y Patil International School
Opp MIG Colony Adarsh Nagar, Worli, Mumbai, 400 030 India
Tel: +91 22 24305555
Head of School: Meera Mahadevan
Curriculum: IBDP, IBPYP
Language instr: English

D Y Patil International School, Nagpur
MIHAN Project Area, Village Khapri (Railway), Nagpur, Maharashtra State 441 108 India
Tel: +91 22 3928 5999
Head of School: Chalapathi Rao Gali
Curriculum: IBDP
Language instr: English

D Y Patil International School, Nerul
Dr D Y Patil Vidhyanagar, Sector 7, Nerul, Navi Mumbai, 400706 India
Tel: +91 22 47700840
Head of School: Nivedita Sinha
Curriculum: IBDP

Dhirubhai Ambani International School
Bandra-Kurla Complex, Bandra (East), Mumbai, 400098 India
Tel: +91 22 40617000
Head of International Curriculum: Dermot Keegan
Age range: 4–18
No. of pupils: 1026
Curriculum: IBDP, National
Language instr: English

DPS International, Saket
P-37 MB Road, Sector VI, Pusph Vihar, Saket, India
Tel: +91 11 2956 1187
Head of School: Aruna Ummat
Age range: 11–18
Curriculum: National, IGCSE, ALevs
Language instr: English

Dr Pillai Global Academy
Plot No 1, RSC 48, Gorai – II, Borivali (W), Mumbai, 400092 India
Tel: +91 22 2868 4467/87
Head of School: Maurice Coutinho
Age range: 3–18
Curriculum: IBDP, IGCSE, ALevs
Language instr: English

Dr Pillai Global Academy, New Panvel
Sector 7, New Panvel (W), Navi Mumbai, Dist Raigad, Mumbai, 410 206 India
Tel: +91 22 2522 4856
Head of School: Derek Hamilton
Curriculum: IBDP
Language instr: English

DRS International School
Survey No 523, Opposite Appeal Park Gundla, Pochampally, Kampally, RR District, Andhra Pradesh 0000 India
Tel: +91 40 237 92123/4/5
Head of School: Janajit Ray
Curriculum: IBDP, IBPYP
Language instr: English

DSB International School
76 Bhulabhai Desai Road, Mumbai, 400 026 India
Tel: +91 (22) 2362 0110
International Principal: Edward Bantry-White
Age range: 3–16
Curriculum: IBDP, UK, IGCSE
Language instr: German, English

DY Patil International School
Charoli Bd., Lohagaon, Pune, Maharashtra 411-012 India
Tel: +91 020 30612 714
Head of School: Brian Parker
Curriculum: IBPYP

Eastern Public School
Ward 1, Abbas Nagar, Bhopal, Madhya Pradesh, 462036 India
Tel: +91 755 2805695
Head of School: Mansoor Durrani
Curriculum: IBDP, IBMYP, IBPYP

Ecole Mondiale World School
9th Cross Rd, Tilak Udyan, Gulmohar, Vile Parle West, Mumbai, JPVD Scheme 400049 India
Tel: +91 22 2623 7265
Principal: Finbarr O'Regan
Age range: 2–18
Fees: Rs690,000–Rs890,000
Curriculum: IBDP, IBMYP, IBPYP
Language instr: English

Edubridge International School
Wadilal A. Patel Marg,
Grant Road (East), Mumbai,
Maharashtra 400 007 India
Tel: +91 22 61325555
Head of School: Michael Purcell
Curriculum: IBDP
Language instr: English

Fazlani L'Académie Globale
Shiv das Chapsi Marg, Opp.
Wallace Flour Mills, Mazagaon,
Mumbai, 400009 India
Tel: +91 022 32642730
Head of School: Linda Shaw
Curriculum: IBDP, IBPYP
Language instr: English

Fountainhead School
Opp Ambetha Water Tank,
Kunkni, Rander – Dandi Road,
Surat, Gujarat 395005 India
Tel: +91 261 3103441
Head of School: Vardan Kabra
Curriculum: IBDP, IBPYP

G D Goenka World School
Gurgaon-Sohna Road,
Haryana, Sohna, 122103 India
Tel: +91 12 4236 2895-6
Head of School: Neeta Bali
No. of pupils: 576
Fees: INR114,480
Curriculum: IBDP, IBPYP
Language instr: English

Garodia International Centre for Learning
153 Garodia Nagar, Ghatkopar
(E), Mumbai, 400077 India
Tel: +91 22 3263 9297
Head of School: Nishant Garodia
Curriculum: IBDP
Language instr: English

Genesis Global School
A-12, Sector 132, Noida,
201301 India
Tel: +91 9711 000626
Director cum
Principal: Pramod Sharma
Curriculum: IBDP, IBPYP
Language instr: English

Goldcrest International
Sector 29, Plot No: 59, Near Rajiv
Gandhi Park, Navi Mumbai,
Vashi, 400 703 India
Tel: +91 22 2789 2261
Curriculum: IBDP

Good Shepherd International School
Good Shepherd Knowledge
Village, M Palada PO,
Ootacamund 643 004, The
Nilgiris, Tamil Nadu 643004 India
Tel: +91 423 2550371
Principal: P C Thomas
Age range: 8–17
No. of pupils: 880 B609 G271
Curriculum: AICE, IBDP,
National, SAT, TOEFL, IGCSE
Language instr: English

Greenwood High
No.8-14, Chickkawadayara
Pura, Near Heggondahalli,
Gunjur Post, Varthur via,
Bangalore, 560087 India
Tel: +91 80 27822888
Head of School: Aloysius D'Mello
Age range: 3–19
Curriculum: IBDP

Hebron School
Lushington Hall, Ootacamund
643001, Nilgiris, Tamil Nadu India
Tel: +91 423 2442372/2442587
Principal: John Barclay
Age range: 5–19
No. of pupils: 373 B194 G179
Fees: Rs138,000–Rs276,000
Curriculum: UK, IGCSE, ALevs
Language instr: English

HFS International
Hiranandani Complex, Powai,
Mumbai, 400076 India
Tel: +91 22 2570 0045
Head of School: Kalyani Patnaik
Curriculum: IBDP
Language instr: English

Hillside Academy
Road No -46, Jubilee Hills,
Hyderabad, 500033 India
Tel: +91 40 2354 6113
Head of School: Pratima Sinha
Curriculum: IBPYP

HVB Global Academy
79 Marine Drive, Mumbai
400 020, India
Tel: +91 22 6143 6000/71
Head of School: Chandrakanta
Pathak
Curriculum: IBDP

India International School
Kshipra Path, Opp VT
Road, Mansarovar, Jaipur,
Rajasthan 302020 India
Tel: +91 141 2786401
Principal & Director: Ashok Gupta
Age range: 6–18
No. of pupils: 2182 B1330 G852
Curriculum: IBDP,
National, UK, ALevs

India International School
26/1, Sarjapur Road,
Chikkabellandur, Bangalore,
Karnataka 560035 India
Tel: +91 080 2843 9001
Curriculum: IBDP

Indus International School
Billapura Cross, Sarjapur,
Bangalore, 562125 India
Tel: +91 80 2289 5900
Principal: Sarojini Rao
Age range: 8–18
No. of pupils: 600
Curriculum: IBDP, IBPYP
Language instr: English

Indus International School, Hyderabad
Survey No 424 & 425,
Kondakal Village, Near
Mokila (M), Shankarpally,
Hyderabad 501203 India
Tel: +91 8417 302100
Head of School: Arvind
Kumar Chalasani
No. of pupils: 300
Fees: US$5,000–US$9,500
Curriculum: IBDP, IBPYP
Language instr: English

Indus International School, Pune
576 Bhukum, Near Manas
Resort, Tal Mulshi, Maharashtra,
Pune, 411042 India
Tel: +91 80 2289 5900
Head of School: Shouquot Hussain
Curriculum: IBDP, IBPYP

International School Aamby
Aamby Valley City,
Ambavene, District-Pune,
Maharashtra, 410401 India
Tel: +91 20 3910 2500
Principal: Jason Kirwin
Age range: 8–18
No. of pupils: 100
Fees: US$10,000
Curriculum: IBDP, IPC, IGCSE
Language instr: English

International School Kashmir (ISK)
Baghat Chowk, Srinagar, India
Tel: +91 9419038733
Language instr: English

International School of Hyderabad
ICRISAT-Patancheru, Hyderabad,
Andhra Pradesh 502324 India
Tel: +91 40 30713869
Principal: Oli Tooher-Hancock
Age range: 3–18
No. of pupils: 266 B142 G124
Curriculum: IBDP, UK, USA, IGCSE
Language instr: English

Jain International Residential School
Jakkasandra Post, Kanakpura
Road, Ramanagara District,
Bangalore, Karnataka 562112 India
Tel: +91 80 2757 7750
Principal: W R David
Age range: 9–18
No. of pupils: B500 G250
Curriculum: IBDP, National,
SAT, TOEFL, IGCSE, ALevs
Language instr: English

Jamnabai Narsee School
Narsee Monjee Bhavan,
NS Road #7, JVPD Scheme,
Vile Parle (W), Mumbai,
Maharashtra 400 049 India
Tel: +91 22 2614 7575
**Head – International
School:** Jasmine Madhani
Age range: 16–19
Curriculum: ACT, AP, IBDP,
National, SAT, TOEFL, IGCSE
Language instr: English

JG International School
JG Campus of Excellence, Opp.
Gulab Tower, Off Sola Road,
Ahmedabad, 380061 India
Tel: +91 79 27492315
Head of School: Kavita Sharma
Curriculum: IBDP
Language instr: English

Johnson Grammar School ICSE&IBDP
Street No 3, Kakatiya Nagar,
Habsiguda, Hyderabad-07,
Andhra Pradesh 500007 India
Tel: +91 40 27150555
Principal: Gita Iyengar
No. of pupils: 5500
Curriculum: IBDP
Language instr: English

KiiT International School
KiiT Campus 9, Patia, Bhubaneswar,
Orissa, 751024 India
Tel: +91 99 3706 4660
Head of School: Achyuta Samanta
Age range: 5–17
No. of pupils: 456 B460 G248
Fees: US$4,000–US$10,000
Curriculum: IBDP, National, IGCSE
Language instr: English

Kodaikanal International School
PO Box 25, Kodaikanal, Tamil
Nadu, 624 101 India
Tel: +91 4542 247 500
Head of School: Corey Stixrud
Age range: 4–17
No. of pupils: 565 B305 G260
Fees: US$7,360
Curriculum: ACT, IBDP,
IBMYP, IBPYP, SAT, USA
Language instr: English

Lakshmipat Singhania Academy
12B Alipore Road, Kolkata
700 027, India
Tel: +91 33 2479 3600
Head Mistress: Anjali Chopra

Lancers International School
DLF Phase V, Sector 53, Gurgaon,
Haryana, 122001 India
Tel: +91 124 4171900
Head of School: Y K Sindhwani
Curriculum: IBDP, IBPYP

Learning Panorama School
Plot no 25c,Old MHB Colony,
OPP Vaidya Kumar Gdn, Nr Don
Bosco School, Gorai Link Road,
Borivali(W) – MUMBAI, 400092 India
Tel: +91 22 6553 9224
Head of School: Shubha Sagar
Curriculum: IBDP

M Ct M Chidambaram Chettyar International School
179 Luz Church Road, Mylapore,
Chennai, 600004 India
Tel: +91 44 2499 2962/4210 8215
Head of School: Anandam Das
Age range: 11–19
No. of pupils: 39 B21 G18
Curriculum: IBDP, IGCSE
Language instr: English

Mahatma Gandhi International School
Sheth Hirabhai Motilal Bhavan,
Mithakali, Ahmedabad,
Gujarat, India
Tel: +91 79 646 3888
Head of School: Pascal Chazot
No. of pupils: 180
Curriculum: IBDP, IBMYP
Language instr: English

Mahindra United World College of India
PO Paud, Taluka Mulshi,
District Pune, 412108 India
Tel: +91 97644 42751/2/3/4
Head of College: Pelham
Lindfield Roberts
No. of pupils: 240
Curriculum: IBDP
Language instr: English

Mainadevi Bajaj International School
Plot No: 23-A, 24-28 Swami
Vivekanand Road, Malad
(West), Maharashtra,
Mumbai, 400064 India
Tel: +91 22 28733807
Head of School: Shagufta Parkar
Curriculum: IBDP

Mallya Aditi International School
PO Box 6427, Yelahanka,
Bangalore, 560 064 India
Tel: +91 80 846 2506/7/8
Principal: Sathish Jayarajan
Age range: 5–18
No. of pupils: 464
Curriculum: National

Mayo College
Srinagar Road, Ajmer,
PIN 305008 India
Tel: +91 145 266 1154
Principal: Kanwar Vijay
Singh Lalotra
(RS)

Mayo College Girls' School
Mayo Link Road, Ajmer, India
Tel: +91 145 266 1286
Principal: Kanchan Khandke
Language instr: English
(RS)

Mercedes Benz International School
Plot No P-26, Rajeev Ganhi Infotech
Park, Hinjewadi, Pune, 411057 India
Tel: +91 20 229 344 01
Head of School: Michael Thompson
Age range: 3–19
No. of pupils: 296 B160 G136
Fees: US$4,080–US$23,220
Curriculum: IBDP, IBMYP, IBPYP
Language instr: English
(🏛)(CIS)

MGD Girls' School
Tonk Rd, Ashok Nagar,
Jaipur, 302001 India
Tel: +91 1412 364478
Principal: Suniti Sharma
Language instr: English
(🏛)(RS)

Mody School (A Div. of Mody Institute of Education & Reseach)
Mody Institute of Education &
Research, NH-11, Lakshmangarh,
Rajasthan, 332311 India
Tel: +91 1573 225001 12
Curriculum: IBDP
Language instr: English
(🏃)(🏛)

Motilal Nehru School of Sports
Grand Trunk Rd, Rajiv Gandhi
Education City, Rai, 131029 India
Tel: +91 1302 366201
Language instr: English
(🏛)(RS)

Navrachana International School
Vasna Bhayali Road, Bhayali,
Vadodara, Gujarat, 391410 India
Tel: +91 265 225 3851/2/3/4
Principal: Theophane D'Souza
Curriculum: IBDP, IBMYP, IBPYP
Language instr: English
(🏛)

Neerja Modi School
Shipra Path, Near Building
Technology Park, Mansarovar,
Jaipur, Rajasthan 302020 India
Tel: +91 141 2785 484
Head of School: Indu Bubey
Curriculum: IBDP

NES International School Mumbai
Malabar Hill Road, Vasant Garden,
Mulund(W), Mumbai, 400082 India
Tel: +91 22 25911478
Head of School: R Varadarajan
Curriculum: IBDP, IBPYP
Language instr: English

Niraj International School
132, 133, Kandlakoya, 5 km from
Dhola-ri-Dhani, Hyderabad, India
Tel: +91 08418-200476, 96524 49666
Principal: H G Pant
Curriculum: IBPYP, IGCSE
Language instr: English

NSS Hill Spring International School
C Wing, NSS Educational
Complex, MP Mill Compound,
Tardeo, Mumbai, 400 034 India
Tel: +91 22 2352 6297 / 2354 0106
Principal: Nalini Pinto
No. of pupils: 320
Curriculum: IBDP, IBPYP
Language instr: English

Oakridge International School
Khajaguda, Nanakramguda
Road, Cyberabad,
Hyderabad, 500008 India
Tel: +91 40 20042460
Head of School: Rohit Bajaj
Age range: 2–18
Curriculum: IBDP, IBPYP
Language instr: English

Oakridge International School
Survey No 166/6, Bowrampet
Village, Near Bachupally,
Hyderabad, Andhra
Pradesh 500043 India
Tel: +91 040 6464 8111
Head of School: Adilakshmi
Chinnatalapathi
Curriculum: IBPYP

Oaktree International School
Diamond Harbour Road,
Bhasa, PO Bishnupur, District/
South 24 Parganas, Kolkata,
West Bengal 743503 India
Tel: +91 9830016555
Head of School: Paul Regan
Curriculum: IBDP
(🏛)

Oberoi International School
Oberoi Garden City, Off Western
Express Highway, Goregaon
(E), Mumbai, 400 063 India
Tel: +91 22 4236 3131
Head of School: Vladimir Kuskovski
Curriculum: IBDP, IBPYP
Language instr: English
(CIS)(EAR)

Olive Green International School
Besides Moha Dental College, Nr
Arjun Farm, Ranchodpura-Bhadaj
Road, Ahmedabad, India
Tel: 91 079 32516832
Head of School: Dilip Mehta
Curriculum: IBPYP

Pathways School (Gurgaon NCR South)
Baliawas, Off Gurgaon Faridabad
Road, Gurgaon, 122003 India
Tel: +91 9560121222
Head of School: Paramjit Narang
Curriculum: IBDP, IBPYP
Language instr: English

Pathways School Noida
Sector 100, Noida NCR East
(Delhi), New Delhi, 110062 India
Tel: +91 (11)2955 1090
Head of School: Shalini Advani
Curriculum: IBDP, IBPYP
Language instr: English

Pathways World School
Aravali Retreat, Off, Gurgaon
Sohna Road, Gurgaon,
Haryana 122004 India
Tel: +91 124 2318881
Head of School: Rima Singh
Age range: 2–19
No. of pupils: 748 B483 G265
Fees: US$10,500–US$15,500
Curriculum: IBDP, IBPYP
Language instr: English
(CIS)

Podar International School
Above Ramniranjan Podar Hall,
Saraswati Road, Santacruz (West),
Mumbai, Maharashtra 400054 India
Tel: +91 22 6711 1111
Director: Vandana Lulla
Age range: 3–18
No. of pupils: 1013 B500 G513
Fees: INR97,000–INR575,000
Curriculum: IBDP, IBPYP
Language instr: English
(CIS)

Pranjali International School
155-157 A.K. Marg, Next to St. Stephen Church, Kemps Corner, Mumbai, 400036 India
Tel: +91-22-2363-9166
Head of School: Smita Pandya
Curriculum: IBDP
Language instr: English

Punjab Public School
Nabha, Punjab, 147201 India
Tel: +91 9316 780250
Headmaster: Jagpreet Singh
RS

Rasbihari Internationals School
Vrindavan, Nashik-Ozar Road, Nashik 422003, India
Tel: +91 253 230 4622
Head of School: Suchitra Sarda
Curriculum: IBPYP
Language instr: English

RBK International Academy
Opp. Indian Oil Nagar, Ghatkopar-Mankhurd Link Road, Chembur, Mumbai, 400 088 India
Tel: +91 22 65218124/5/6
Head of School: James Paul
No. of pupils: 125
Curriculum: IBDP, IBMYP, IBPYP
Language instr: English

Ryan Global School
Yamuna Nagar, Lokhandwala, Andheri (west), Mumbai, 400058 India
Tel: +91 22 2632 0203/05
Head of School: Snehal Pinto
Curriculum: IBPYP, IGCSE

Sangam School of Excellence
N.H. 79, Atun, Bhilwara By Pass, Chittorgarh Highway, Bhilwara, Rajasthan 311001 India
Tel: +91 1482 312 251, +91 9784 599 077
Principal: Madhu Nagpal
No. of pupils: 1200
Curriculum: IBDP
Language instr: English

Sarala Birla Academy
Bannerghatta PO, Jigni Road, Bangalore, 560083 India
Tel: +91 80 41348200/03
Head of School: Santanu Das
Curriculum: IBDP
Language instr: English

Scindia Kanya Vidyalya
Moti Mahal Road, Gwalior, 474009 MP India
Tel: +91 7512 334080
Principal: Nishi Mishra

Scottish High International School
G-Block, Sector 57, Sushant Lok-II, Haryana, Gurgaon, 122011 India
Tel: +91 124 4112781-90
Head of School: Sudha Goyal
Age range: 3–17
No. of pupils: B767 G927
Curriculum: IBDP, IBPYP, National, IGCSE
Language instr: English

SelaQui International School
PO Sela Kui, Chakrata Road, Dehradun, 248197 India
Tel: +91 992 7000 585
Head: Rohit Pathak
Language instr: English

Sharad Pawar International School, Pune
Charoli Budruk, Taluka Haveli, District Pune, India
Tel: +91 20 30612700/752
Head of School: Gopalraj Rangaswamy
Age range: 3–17
Curriculum: IBDP, IGCSE
Language instr: English

Silver Oaks – The School of Hyderabad
Miyapur-Dindigal Road, Bachupally, Hyderabad, 500090 India
Tel: +91 40 23047777
Head of School: Sita Murthy
Curriculum: IBPYP

Singapore International School
On National Highway No. 8, Post Mira, Dahisar, Mumbai, 401104 India
Tel: +91 222 828 5200
Head of School: Sharonee Mullick
No. of pupils: 400 B240 G160
Curriculum: IBDP, UK
Language instr: English

Sreenidhi International School
8-2-579/ A, House No. 76, Road # 8, Banjara Hills, Hyderabad, 500034 India
Tel: +91 40 2355 2362
Head of School: V Srinivasan
Curriculum: IBDP, IBPYP
Language instr: English

SS Mody Cambridge International School
Behind BDK Hospital, Road No 2, Jhunjhunu 333001, Rajasthan India
Tel: +91 9967045342
Trustee & Executive Co-ordinator: Adittya Mody
Age range: 4–16
No. of pupils: 712
Fees: INR55,000–INR85,000
Curriculum: UK, IGCSE

Step by Step High School
3 Chitrakoot Square, Adjoining Stadium, Ajmer Road, Jaipur, India
Tel: +91 141 4132222

Step by Step International School
Mahapura, SEZ Road, Ajmer Road, Jaipur, Rajasthan, 302026 India
Tel: +91 97827 44444/44445
Head of School: Jayshree Periwal
Age range: 12–18
No. of pupils: 800 B500 G300
Curriculum: IBDP, IBPYP
Language instr: English

Step by Step School
Plot A 10, Sector 132 Taj Expressway, Noida, Uttar Pradesh 201303 India
Tel: +91 120 2472300
Head of School: Richa Agnihotri
Curriculum: IBDP
Language instr: English

Stonehill International School
1st Floor Embassy Point, 150 Infantry Road, Bangalore, 560001 India
Tel: +91 80 4341 8300
Director: Peter Mackenzie
Age range: 3–17
Curriculum: IBDP, IBMYP, IBPYP
Language instr: English

Sunflower English School
Sunflower House, 80 Feet Road, Near Bhaktinagar Circle, Rajkot, 360002 India
Tel: +91 2825294467
Principal: Rajesh Sharma
Language instr: English

SVKM International School
Dadabhai Road, Off. S.V. Road, Vile Parle West, Mumbai, 400056 India
Tel: +91 22 4233 3030/1
Head of School: Swaminathan Gurumurthy
Curriculum: IBDP

Symbiosis International School
Survey #231, HISSA 3A & 4, Symbiosis Viman Nagar Campus, Viman Nagar, Pune 411014 India
Tel: +91-20-2663-4550
Head of School: Narendra Kumar Ojha
Curriculum: IBDP, IBPYP
Language instr: English

The Aga Khan Academy, Hyderabad
Survey No 1/1 Hardware Park, Maheshwaram Mandal RR District, Hyderabad, Andhra Pradesh 500005 India
Tel: +91 40 66291313
Head of Academy: Ian Kerr
Curriculum: IBDP, IBPYP

The Assam Valley School
Sessa T.E. No.3, Assam, 784105 India
RS

The British School
Dr Jose P Rizal Marg, Chanakyapuri, New Delhi, 110021 India
Tel: +91 11 2467 8524
Head of School: Graham Ranger
Age range: 4–18
No. of pupils: 512 B260 G252 VIth84
Curriculum: IBDP, IGCSE
Language instr: English
CIS RS

The Calorx School
Nandoli, Thaltej-Shilaj Road, Ahmedabad, Gujarat 380058 India
Tel: +91 79 6544 4362
Head of School: Jayachree Kad
Curriculum: IBDP, IBMYP, IBPYP
Language instr: English

The Cathedral & John Connon School
6 Purshottamdas Thakurdas Marg, Fort, Mumbai, 400001 India
Tel: +91 22 2200 1282
Principal: Meera Isaacs
Age range: 5–18
No. of pupils: 1980 B1009 G971
Fees: IRup60,000
Curriculum: National, UK, USA, IGCSE
Language instr: English

The Cathedral Vidya School, Lonavala
Village Shilatne, Taluk Maval, Post Office Karla, Pune, Maharashtra 410405 India
Tel: +91 2114 282 693
Head of School: Meera Sain
Curriculum: IBDP
Language instr: English

The Daly College
Residency Area, Indore, 452001 India
Tel: +91 7312 719000
Principal: Sumar Bahadur Singh
Language instr: English

The Doon School
Mall Road, Dehradun, Uttarakhand, 248001 India
Tel: +91-135 2526 400
Head of School: Peter McLaughlin
Age range: B12–18
No. of pupils: 540 B532 G8
Curriculum: IBDP, National
Language instr: English

The Galaxy School
c/o Bhalodia Farm, Rajkot
Jamnagar Highway, Opp Gold
Coin Ceramic Fac, Targhadi, Distr
Rajkot, Gujarat 360110 India
Tel: +91 2820 282 501
Head of School: Kiran Bhalodia
Curriculum: IBDP

The Heritage School
994 Maduraha, Chowbaga
Road, Anandpur, PO East
Kolkata Township, Kolkata,
West Bengal 700107 India
Tel: +91 33 2443 0448
Head of School: Seema Sapru
Curriculum: IBDP

The Indian Public School
Fr. Abel Nagar, Edachira,
Kakkanad, Kochin,
Kerala, 682030 India
Tel: +91 4324 6456666
Head of School: Sonali Geed
Curriculum: IBDP
Language instr: English

The Indian Public School-Coimbatore
93 Sathy Road, S.S.Kulam P.O.,
Coimbatore, 641107 India
Tel: +91 422 6456666
Head of School: Sonali Geed
Curriculum: IBDP, IBPYP

The International School Bangalore
Whitefield-Sarjapur Road, Near
Dommasandra Circle, Bangalore,
Karnataka 562125 India
Tel: +91 80 22634900
Principal: Peter Joseph Armstrong
Age range: 3–18
No. of pupils: 1000
Fees: US$13,800
Curriculum: IBDP, IGCSE
Language instr: English

The Lawrence School
Sanawar, MDR 10, Distt. Himachal
Pradesh, Solan, 173202 India
Tel: +91 1792 261208
Headmaster: Praveen Vashisht
Language instr: English

The Modern School
Sector E, Aliganj, Lucknow,
Uttar Pradesh 226024 India
Tel: +91 522 402 1406
Head of School: Rakesh Kapoor
Curriculum: IBPYP

The Rajkumar College
Dr Radha Krishnan Road,
Gavliwad, Rajkot, 360001 India
Tel: +91 281 246 6064
Principal: Shankar Singh Adhikari
Language instr: English

The Sanskaar Valley School
The Sanskaar Valley
School, Chandanpura,
Bhopal, 462016 India
Tel: +91 755 325 5346
Director: Jyoti Agarwal
Language instr: English

The Scindia School
The Fort, Gwalior, 474008 India
Tel: +91 751 2480750
Principal: Samik Ghosh
Language instr: English

The Shri Ram School
Moulsari Avenue DLF Phase-3,
Gurgaon, Haryana 122002 India
Head of School: Komal Sood
No. of pupils: 227
Fees: Rs320,000
Curriculum: IBDP
Language instr: English

Trivandrum International School
Edackcode, PO Korani,
Trivandrum, Kerala 695104 India
Tel: +91 471 2619051
Principal: Rupa Sen
Curriculum: IBDP, IBPYP

Victorious Kidss Educares
Survey No. 53, 54 & 58, Hissa No.
2/1A, Off. Shreeram Society, Nagar
Road, Kharadi, Pune, 411014 India
Tel: +91 20 66355566/93
Founder President: Robbin Ghosh
Age range: 6 weeks–18 years
No. of pupils: 1050
Fees: US$2,751
Curriculum: IBDP, IBMYP, IBPYP
Language instr: English

Vidya Devi Jindal School
Delhi Road, Hisar, 125044 India
Tel: +91 1662 281000
Principal: Nandita Sahu
Language instr: English

Vidya Global School
Vidya Knowledge Park, Baghpat
Road, Meerut, 250002 India
Tel: 91 121 2439188/89/92
Head of School: Saurabh Jain
Age range: 4–16
Curriculum: IBPYP, National, IGCSE

Vishwashanti Gurukul
Rajbaug, off Pune-Solapur
Highway, Loni, Pune,
Maharashtra 412201 India
Tel: +91 20 39210000
Head of School: Anand Deodhar
Age range: 5–18
No. of pupils: 350 B200 G150
Curriculum: IBDP, IBPYP, UK, IGCSE
Language instr: English

Vivek High School
Vidya Path, Sector 38-B,
Chandigarh, 160036 India
Tel: +91 172 269 8988
Principal: P K Singh
Language instr: English

Welham Boys' School
5 Circular Rd, Dalanwala,
Dehradun, 248001 India
Tel: +91 135 265 7120

Woodstock School
Mussoorie, Uttrakhand, 248179 India
Tel: +91 135 661 5000
Principal: Jonathan Long
Age range: 4–18
No. of pupils: 508 B274 G234
Fees: Rs880,000–Rs1,060,000
Curriculum: ACT, AP, SAT, UK, USA
Language instr: English

Yadavindra Public School
New Lal Bagh, Patiala, India
Tel: +91 1752 215634
Principal: Stanley Vinod Kumar
Language instr: English

Indonesia

ACG International School – Jakarta
Jl Warung Jati Barat, Taman
Margasatwa, No 19 Ragunan,
South Jakarta, 12510 Indonesia
Tel: +62 21 780 5636
Head of School: Christine Rawlins
Curriculum: IBPYP
Language instr: English

Al Jabr Islamic School
Jl Bango II No 38, Pondok Labu,
Jakarta, 12450 Indonesia
Tel: +62 21 75913675
Head of School: Roestriana Riza
Curriculum: IBPYP
Language instr: English

Bali International School
PO Box 3259, Denpasar,
Bali, Indonesia
Tel: +62 361 288 770
Head of School: Brian Kissman
Age range: 3–18
No. of pupils: 290 B141 G149
Fees: US$7,000–US$13,500
Curriculum: IBDP, IBMYP, IBPYP
Language instr: English

Bandung Alliance International School
Jalan Bujanggamanik Kav
2, Kota Baru Parahyangan,
Bandung 40553, Indonesia
Tel: +62 22 8681 3949
Director: Pete Simano
Age range: 4–18
No. of pupils: 200
Curriculum: AP, USA

Bandung International School
Jl. Surya Sumantri No. 61, Bandung,
West Java 40164 Indonesia
Tel: +62 22 201 4995
Head of School: David Tigchelaar
Age range: 3–18
No. of pupils: B107 G119
Fees: US$4,870–US$16,710
Curriculum: ACT, AP,
IBDP, IBPYP, SAT, USA
Language instr: English

Batu Hijau International School
PT Newmont Nusa Tenggara,
Jl. Sriwijaya 258, Mataram
NTB, 83127 Indonesia
Tel: +62 372 635318 ext. 48424
Principal: Dave Forbes
Age range: 4–14
No. of pupils: 281 B159 G122
Fees: $18,000
Language instr: English

Binus International School Simprug
Jl Sultan Iskandar, Muda
Kav G-8, Simprug, Jakarta
Selatan, 12220 Indonesia
Tel: +62-21-724-3663
Head of School: Peter
Matthew Saidi
No. of pupils: 1300
Curriculum: IBDP, IBMYP, IBPYP
Language instr: English

British International School, Jakarta
Bintaro Jaya Sector IX, Jl. Raya
Jombang, Ciledug, Tangerang
15227, Jakarta Indonesia
Tel: +62 21 745 1670
Principal: Simon Dennis
Age range: 3–18
No. of pupils: 1370
Fees: US$8,625–US$22,950
Curriculum: IBDP, IGCSE
Language instr: English

Canggu Community School
Jalan Subak Sari, Banjar Tegal
Gundul, Canggu – Badung,
Bali 80361 Indonesia
Tel: +62 361 8446391
Head of School: Jeanie Forde
Age range: 4–16
Fees: US$4,410–US$9,240
Curriculum: IBDP, UK, IGCSE

Cita Hati Christian Senior School – East Campus
JL, Kejawan Putih Barat 28-30, Pakuwon City, Surabaya 60112 Indonesia
Tel: +62 31 591 5774
Head of School: Erlangga Pramudya
No. of pupils: 228
Curriculum: IBDP
Language instr: English

Cita Hati Christian Senior School – West Campus
Jalan Bukit Bali, B3 No. 6, Citraland, Surabaya, East Java 60211 Indonesia
Tel: +62 31 7404959
Head of School: Magdadena Nugroho
Curriculum: IBDP
Language instr: English

Gandhi Memorial International School
Jalan Landas Pacu Timur, Kota Baru Bandar, Kemayoran, Jakarta Utara, Asia Pacific 14410 Indonesia
Tel: +62 21 658 656 85
Head of School: A P Singh
No. of pupils: 697
Curriculum: IBDP, IBMYP, IBPYP
Language instr: English

Gandhi Memorial International School, Bali
Jl Tukad Yeh Penet No 8A Renon, Bali, Denpasar, 80235 Indonesia
Tel: +62 361 239744
Principal: Jaba Biswas
Age range: 3–18
No. of pupils: 550
Curriculum: IBDP, TOEFL, IGCSE
Language instr: English

Global Jaya International School
Emerald Boulevard, Bintaro Jaya Sektor IX, Pondok Aren, Tangerang, 15224 Indonesia
Tel: +62 21 745 7562
Head of School: Chris Chambers
Age range: 4–18
No. of pupils: 934
Fees: US$2,530–US$10,110
Curriculum: IBDP, IBMYP, IBPYP
Language instr: English, Indonesian

Green School
Jalan Raya Sibang Kaja, Banjar Saren, Abiansemal, Badung, Bali 80352 Indonesia
Tel: +62 361 469 875
Principal: John Stewart
Age range: 3–17
Curriculum: UK, IGCSE, ALevs

Hillcrest International School
PO Box 249, Sentani 99352, Irian Jaya, Papua Indonesia
Tel: +62 967 591460
Director: Paige A Adams
Age range: 5–18
No. of pupils: 160 B77 G83
Curriculum: ACT, AP, SAT, USA
Language instr: English

Jakarta International Multicultural School
Jl Pisangan Raya No.99, Cirendeu, Ciputat Timur, 15419 Indonesia
Tel: +62 21 744 4864
Principal: Karen Rudian
Curriculum: IBPYP

Jakarta International School
Administration, PO Box 1078 JKS, Jakarta, 12010 Indonesia
Tel: +62 21 769 2555
Head of School: Tim Carr
Age range: 3–21
No. of pupils: B1325 G1275
Fees: US$14,400–US$22,900
Curriculum: ACT, AP, IBDP, SAT, TOEFL
Language instr: English

Makassar International School
Jalan Botolempangan No.19, PO Box 1327, Sulawesi Selatan 9013, Indonesia
Tel: +62 411 315 889
Principal: Richard Gordon Hall
Age range: 5–13
No. of pupils: 26
Curriculum: UK

Medan International School
PO Box 1190, Jl Letjend Jamin Ginting Km10 / Jl Tali Air No 5, Medan, North Sumatra 20111 Indonesia
Tel: +62 61 836 1816
Principal: Matthew Gaetano
Age range: 3–16
No. of pupils: 70 B35 G35
Fees: US$5,300–US$10,500
Curriculum: IBMYP, IBPYP
Language instr: English

Mentari International School Bintaro
Jalan Perigi Baru No.6-7A Pondok Aren Bintaro, Tangerang, Jakarta, Indonesia
Tel: +62 21 745 8418
Curriculum: IBDP
Language instr: English

Mentari International School Jakarta
Jalan Haji Jian No 6-A, Cipete Utara, Jakarta Sealatan, Jakarta, 12150 Indonesia
Tel: +62 21 727 95288
Head of School: Clarissa Subagyo
Age range: 5–17
Curriculum: IBMYP, National, UK
Language instr: English

Mountainview International Christian School
Jl. Nakula Sadewa Raya No 55, Salatiga 50711, Jateng, Indonesia
Tel: +62 298 311673
Superintendent: Don McGavran
Age range: 5–19
No. of pupils: 180
Curriculum: ACT, SAT, USA
Language instr: English

Mutiara Harapan
Jl. Pondok Kacang Raya No 2, Pondok Aren, Bintaro, Tangerang, 28300 Indonesia
Tel: +62 21 7486 7788

Mutiara Nusantara International School
Kompleks Graha Puspa, Jl. Sersan Bajuri – Setiabudhi, Bandung, West Java, 40559 Indonesia
Tel: +62 22 278 8558
Head of School: Wade Johnson
Curriculum: IBDP
Language instr: English

North Jakarta International School
Jalan Raya Kelapa Nias, PO Box 6759/JKUKP, Kelapa Gading Permai, Jakarta 14250 Indonesia
Tel: +62 21 4500683
Head of School: Gary Lloyd Lafoy
Age range: 4–16
No. of pupils: 295 B149 G146
Curriculum: SAT

Penabur International School
Jl Bahureksa No 26, Bandung, West Java 40115 Indonesia
Tel: +62 22 9110 2255
Head of School: Lovanka Hambali Adam
Curriculum: IBPYP
Language instr: English

Sekolah Bina Tunas Bangsa, Pluit Campus
Jl Pluit Timur, Blok MM, Jakarta, 15224 Indonesia
Tel: +62 21 3003 1300
Head of School: Yudo Prima Cahyadi
Curriculum: IBDP
Language instr: English

Sekolah Bogor Raya
Perumahan Danau Bogor Raya, Bogor, 16143 Indonesia
Tel: +62 251 837 8873
School Director: Gerald Donovan
No. of pupils: 500
Curriculum: IBPYP
Language instr: English

Sekolah Buin Batu
Jl. Kayu Besi 400 Townsite PTNNT, Buin Batu, West Sumbawa, NTB, Indonesia
Tel: +62372-635318 Ext. 48443
Head of School: Ari Ardianto
Curriculum: IBPYP

Sekolah Cikal
Jl TB Simatupang Kav 18, Cilandak, Jakarta, 12430 Indonesia
Tel: +62 21 75902570
Head of School: Najelaa Shihab
Age range: 3–12
No. of pupils: 363 B191 G172
Fees: IDR27,500,000
Curriculum: IBMYP, IBPYP
Language instr: English, Indonesian

Sekolah Ciputra, Surabaya
Kawasan Puri Widya CitraRaya, Kota Mandiri. Kec Lakarsantri, Surabaya, 60213 Indonesia
Tel: +62-31-741-5018
Head of School: Erik Hoekstra
Curriculum: IBDP, IBMYP, IBPYP
Language instr: English

Sekolah Global Indo-Asia
Jalan Raya Batam Centre Kav SGIA, Batam Centre, Batam Island, Indonesia
Tel: +62 778 467333
Head of School: Dewi Diana Lukitasari
Curriculum: IBPYP
Language instr: English

Sekolah Mutiara Harapan
Complex PT RAPP Town Site I, PKL, Kerinci, Riau, 28300 Indonesia
Tel: +62 761 955550
Head of School: Lei Suang
Curriculum: IBPYP
Language instr: English

Sekolah Pelita Harapan (Sentul Campus)
Academic, Jl Babakan Madang, Bukit Sentul, Bogor, Jawa Barat 16810 Indonesia
Tel: +62 21 879 60135
Head of School: Peter Wells
Age range: 4–20
No. of pupils: 380 B190 G190
Fees: US$4,150–US$7,500
Curriculum: IBDP, IBMYP, IBPYP, National
Language instr: English

Sekolah Pelita Harapan International
#2500 Bulevar Palem Raya, Lippo Village, Tangerang, Banten, 15811 Indonesia
Tel: +62 21 5460233-4
Head of School: Brian Cox
Age range: 3–18
No. of pupils: 1074 B501 G573
Curriculum: IBDP, IBMYP, IBPYP, SAT
Language instr: English

Sekolah Pelita Harapan International Kemang Village
Jl Pangeran Antasari 36, Kemang Village, Jakarta Selatan, 12150 Indonesia
Tel: +62 21 290 56789
Head of School: David Michel
Curriculum: IBDP

Sekolah Pilar Indonesia
Jl Dewa 9, Ciangsana, Kawasan Cibubur, Bogor, 16968 Indonesia
Tel: +62 21 84936222
Head of School: Natasha Sijatauw
Age range: 3–17
No. of pupils: 320
Curriculum: IBPYP

Sekolah Tunas Bangsa
Jalan Arteri Supadio, (Achmad Yani II) Km 2, Pontianak, West Kalimantan 78391 Indonesia
Tel: +62 561 725555
Head of School: Liong Fui Na
No. of pupils: 377
Curriculum: IBPYP
Language instr: English

Sekolah Victory Plus
Jl Kemang Pratama Raya, AN 2-3 Kemang Pratama, Bekasi, 17116 Indonesia
Tel: +62 21 8240 3878
Head of School: Yustina Ries Sunarti
Fees: IDR24,000,000
Curriculum: IBMYP, IBPYP, National, UK
Language instr: English

Semarang International School
Jl. Jangli 37, Candisari, Semarang, 50254 Indonesia
Tel: +62 24 8311424
Principal: Diana Hoskin
Age range: 1–11
No. of pupils: 72 B32 G40
Language instr: English

Sinarmas World Academy
Jl TM Pahlawan Seribu, CBD Lot XV, BSD City, Tangerang, 15322 Indonesia
Tel: +62 21 5316 1400
Head of School: Wayne Richardson
Age range: 3–18
No. of pupils: B261 G239
Curriculum: IBDP, IBMYP, IBPYP
Language instr: English, Chinese
(CIS) (EAR)

Singapore International School – Indonesia (Bona Vista Campus)
Jalan Bona Vista Raya, Lebak Bulus, Selatan, Jakarta, 12440 Indonesia
Tel: +62 21 759 14414
Head of School: Joël Carré
Curriculum: IBDP
(🏛)

Singapore School, Kelapa Gading
Jl. Pegangsaan Dua No.83, Kelapa Gading, Jakarta Utara, Jakarta, 14250 Indonesia
Tel: +62 21 460 8888
Head of School: Andrew Paterson
Curriculum: IBDP
Language instr: English

SPH International Lippo Cikarang
Jl Dago Pemrai No 1, Komplek Dago Villas, Lippo Cikarang, Bekasi, 17550 Indonesia
Tel: +62 21 897 2786
Head of School: Amy Jungemann Hidajat
Age range: 3–18
Curriculum: IBDP, IBPYP
Language instr: English

STB-ACS (International) Jakarta
Jl Bantar Jati, Kelurahan Setu, Jakarta Timur, 13880 Indonesia
Tel: +62 21 8459 7175
Executive Principal: Ng Eng Chin
Age range: 3–18
No. of pupils: 633 B341 G292 VIth38
Fees: US$5,000–US$12,000
Curriculum: IBDP, ALevs
Language instr: English
(🏛)

Stella Maris School
Sektor 8A, Vatican Cluster, Gading Serpong, Tangerang, 15310 Indonesia
Tel: +62 21 54 212 999
Head of School: Anna Indarwati
Curriculum: IBDP
Language instr: English

The International School of Bogor
Jalan Papandayan No 7, Bogor, 16151 Indonesia
Tel: +62 251 8324 360
Head of School: Riki Teteina
Age range: 2–13
No. of pupils: 104 B54 G50
Fees: US$2,500–US$11,800
Curriculum: IBPYP
Language instr: English
(EAR)

The New Zealand International School
Jl. Kemang Selatan I No. 1 A, Kemang, Jakarta 12730 Indonesia
Tel: +62 21 7183222
Principal: Maree Butler
Curriculum: IGCSE, ALevs
Language instr: English

Tunas Muda International School Kedoya
Jl Angsana Raya D8/2, Taman Kedoya Baru, Jakarta Barat, 11520 Indonesia
Tel: +62 21 581 8766
Principal: Rachel Groves
No. of pupils: 274
Curriculum: IBPYP
Language instr: English, Indonesian

Tunas Muda International School Meruya
Jl Meruya Utara Raya, No 71 Kembangan, Jakarta Barat, 11620 Indonesia
Tel: +62 21 587 0329
Principal: Frances Hazle
Age range: 3–18
No. of pupils: 433
Curriculum: IBDP, IBMYP, IBPYP
Language instr: English, Indonesian

Wesley International School
Kotak Pos 275, Malang 65101, Malang, Indonesia
Tel: +62 341 586410
Director: Jonathan Heath
Age range: 5–18
No. of pupils: 110 B55 G55
Curriculum: AP, SAT, USA
Language instr: English

Yayasan Surabaya International School
Lakarsantri, Tromol Pos 2/SBDK, Surabaya, 60225 Indonesia
Tel: +62 31 741 4300
Superintendent: James A Mains
Age range: 3–18
No. of pupils: 480
Curriculum: ACT, IBPYP, SAT
(EAR)

Yogyakarta International School
PO Box 1175, Yogyakarta, 55011 Indonesia
Tel: +62 274 625965
Head of School: Orin A Stephney
Age range: 3–16
No. of pupils: 97 B56 G41
Fees: US$8,000
Curriculum: IPC, IGCSE, ALevs
Language instr: English
(EAR)

Iran

Shahid Mahdavi Educational Complex
West Kouh-Daman, Mina, Zanbagh, E'jazi, Zafaranieh, Tehran, 1988875361 Iran
Tel: +98 21 22435550
Head of School: Sedigheh Mahdavi
Curriculum: IBPYP
Language instr: English, Persian
(🏛)

Iraq

Ihsan Dogramaci Bilkent Erbil College
General Post office, PO box 43/0383, Erbil, Iraq
Tel: +964 75033 60382
Head of School: George Piacentini
Curriculum: IBPYP
Language instr: Arabic, English, Kurdish,Turkish

Israel

Anglican International School
PO Box 191, 82 Rechov Haneviim, Jerusalem, 91001 Israel
Tel: +972 2 567 7200
Director of School: Owen Hoskin
Age range: 3–18
No. of pupils: 230
Curriculum: IBDP, IBMYP, SAT
Language instr: English

Walworth Barbour American International School
P.O. Box 484, 65 Hashomron Street, Netanya, Even Yehuda 40500 Israel
Tel: +972 9 890 1000
Superintendent: John E Gates
Age range: 5–19
No. of pupils: 432 B222 G210

Japan

AICJ Junior & Senior High School
2-33-16 Gion, Asaminami-ku, Hiroshima, 731 0138 Japan
Tel: +81 82 832 5037
Principal: David Cooper
Curriculum: IBDP
Language instr: English
(🏛)

Aoba-Japan International School
7-5-1 Hikarigaoka, Nerima-ku, Tokyo, 179-0072 Japan
Tel: +81 3 6904 3189
Principal: Regina Doi
Age range: 4–16
No. of pupils: 300
(CIS) (EAR) (ECIS)

Canadian Academy
4-1 Koyo-Cho Naka, Higashinada-ku, Kobe 658-0032 Japan
Tel: +81 78 857 0100
Headmaster: David J Condon
Age range: 3–18
No. of pupils: 678 B348 G330
Curriculum: ACT, AP, IBDP, IBMYP, IBPYP, SAT, USA
Language instr: English
(🏛) (CIS) (EAR)

Canadian International School Tokyo
5-8-20 Kitashinagawa, Shinagawa-ku, Tokyo, 1410001 Japan
Tel: +81 03 5793 1392
Head of School: Ian Robertson
Curriculum: IBPYP
Language instr: English
(EAR)

Christian Academy in Japan
1-2-14 Shinkawacho, Higashikurume, Tokyo, 203-0013 Japan
Tel: +81 424 710 022
Language instr: Japanese
(EAR)

Doshisha International School, Kyoto
7-31-1 Kizugawa-dai, Kizugawa City, Kyoto, 619-0225 Japan
Tel: +81 774 71 0810
Head of School: Yoshitaka Nishizawa
Curriculum: IBDP, IBPYP
(⚐)

European School Kobe
3-2-8 Koyochonaka, Higashinada-ku, Kobe City, 658-0032 Japan
Tel: +81 (0) 78 857 9777
Principal: Ursula Shioji
Age range: 2–12
Curriculum: IBPYP
Language instr: English

Fukuoka International School
Momochi 3 – chome 18-50, Sawara-ku, Fukuoka-shi 814, Japan
Tel: +81 92 841 7601
Head of School: Diane Lewthwaite
Age range: 3–18
No. of pupils: B106 G110 VIth12
Fees: ¥1,245,000–¥1,484,000
Curriculum: IBDP, IBPYP, SAT
Language instr: English
(⚐) (EAR)

Gunma Kokusai Academy
1361-4 Uchigashima-cho, Ota-shi, Gunma-Ken, 373-0813 Japan
Tel: +81-276-47-7711
Head of School: Keizo Ogasawara
Curriculum: IBDP

Hiroshima International School
3-49-1 Kurakake, Asakita-Ku, Hiroshima, 739-1743 Japan
Tel: +81 82 843 4111
Head of School: Mark Exton
Age range: 3–18
No. of pupils: 120 B60 G60
Curriculum: IBDP, IBPYP, IGCSE
Language instr: English
(CIS)

HOKKAIDO INTERNATIONAL SCHOOL
For further details see p. 82
1-55 5-jo, 19-chome, Hiragishi, Toyohira-ku, Sapporo 062-0935, Japan
Tel: +81 11 816 5000
Email: his@his.ac.jp
Website: www.his.ac.jp
Head of School: Barry Ratzliff
Age range: 3–20
No. of pupils: 190 B95 G95
Fees: US$9,500
Curriculum: AP, IPC, SAT
(⚐) (EAR)

Horizon Japan International School
1-38-27 Higashi Terai, Tsurumi-ku, Yokohama, 230-0077 Japan
Tel: +81 45 584 1945
Principal: Mustafa Kara
Age range: 3–14
No. of pupils: 95 B52 G43
Fees: ¥1,500,000
Curriculum: IBDP, UK
(ECIS)

India International School in Japan
1-20-20, Ojima, Koto-Ku -135-0004, Tokyo, 136-0072 Japan
Tel: +81 03 3635 7850
Curriculum: IBDP
Language instr: English

International School Kitakyushu
Yahata Higashi-ku, Takami 2-chome, Shinnittetsu, Shijo Kaikan, Kitakyushu 7805, Japan
Tel: +81 (0)93 882 0020
Principal: Ann Ratnayake
Age range: 3–19

International School of the Sacred Heart
4-3-1 Hiroo, Shibuya-ku, Tokyo 150-0012, Japan
Tel: +81 3 3400 3951
Headmistress: Yvonne Hayes
Age range: B3–5 G3–18
No. of pupils: 594 B12 G582
Fees: ¥1,890,000
Curriculum: AP, SAT
Language instr: English
(♟) (CIS) (EAR)

K. International School Tokyo
1-5-15 Shirakawa, Koto-ku, Tokyo, 135-0021 Japan
Tel: +81 3 3642 9993
Head of School: Yoshishige Komaki
Age range: 3–18
No. of pupils: B300 G300
Fees: Day ¥1,480,000–¥1,780,000
Curriculum: IBDP, IBMYP, IBPYP
Language instr: English
(CIS)

Katoh Gakuen Gyoshu Junior & Senior High School
1361-1 Nakamiyo Okanomiya, Shizuoka, 4100011 Japan
Tel: +81 55 924 3322
Head of School: Michael Bostwick
Age range: 3–18
No. of pupils: 590 B280 G310
Curriculum: IBDP, IBMYP
Language instr: English, Japanese

Kyoto International School
252 Shinhigashidoin-cho, Sakyo-ku, Kyoto, 606-8355 Japan
Tel: +81 75 761 8600
Head of School: Kimberly Conlin
Age range: 3–14
No. of pupils: 75
Fees: ¥823,000–¥1,658,000
Curriculum: IBPYP
Language instr: English
(EAR)

Linden Hall High School
3-10-1 Futsukaichi-kita, Chikushino, Fukuoka, 818-0056 Japan
Tel: +81 (0)92 929 4558
Head of School: Hirokazu Osako
Curriculum: IBDP
(⚐)

Marist Brothers International School
1-2-1 Chimori-Cho, Suma-Ku, Kobe, 654-0072 Japan
Tel: +81 78 732 6266
Head of School: Marijana Munro
Age range: 3–19
No. of pupils: 296 B152 G144
Fees: ¥1,375,000
Curriculum: AP, USA
Language instr: English
(EAR)

Nagoya International School
2686 Minamihara, Nakashidami, Moriyama-ku, Nagoya, 463-0002 Japan
Tel: +81 52 736 2025
Head of School: Matthew Parr
Age range: 3–18
No. of pupils: B147 G171
Fees: ¥1,595,000–¥1,780,000
Curriculum: IBDP, IBPYP
(CIS) (EAR)

New International School of Japan
3-18-32 Minami-Ikebukuro, Toshima-ku, Tokyo 171-0022, Japan
Tel: +81 3 3980 1057
Head of School: Steven Parr
Age range: 3–15
Fees: ¥1,350,000–¥1,700,000

Nishimachi International School
2-14-7 Moto-Azabu, Tokyo 106, Japan
Tel: +81 3 3451 5520
Headmaster: Terence Christian
Age range: 5–15
No. of pupils: 423
(CIS) (EAR) (ECIS)

Okinawa International School
2-34-22 Sobe, Naha City, Okinawa, 9000023 Japan
Tel: +81 098 835 1851
Head of School: Masato Chinen
Curriculum: IBPYP

Osaka International School
4-4-16 Onohara Nishi, Mino-shi, Osaka, 562-0032 Japan
Tel: +81 72 727 5050
Head of School: Bill Kralovec
Age range: 4–18
No. of pupils: 261 B120 G141
Curriculum: ACT, AP, IBDP, IBMYP, IBPYP, TOEFL
Language instr: English
(CIS) (EAR)

Osaka YMCA International School
6-7-34 Nakatsu, Kita-ku, Osaka, 531-0071 Japan
Tel: +81 6 6345 1661
Head of School: John Murphy
Age range: 3–13
Curriculum: IBPYP
(EAR)

OYIS – Osaka YMCA International School
1-2-2-800 Benten, Minato-Ku, Osaka, 552-0007 Japan
Tel: +81 6 4395 1002
Principal: John Murphy
Age range: 3–12
No. of pupils: 95 B46 G49
Fees: ¥1,092,000–¥1,370,000
Language instr: English
(EAR)

Ritsumeikan Uji Junior and Senior High School
33-1 Hachikenyadani, Hirono-cho, Uji-shi, Kyoto 611-0031, Japan
Tel: +81 774 41 3000
Head of School: Charles Fox
Age range: 12–18
No. of pupils: 1630
Fees: ¥1,600,000
Curriculum: IBDP
Language instr: English, Japanese
(⚐)

Saint Maur International School
83 Yamate-cho, Naka-ku, Yokohama, 231-8654 Japan
Tel: +81 45 641 5751
Head of School: Catherine Osias Endo
Age range: 2–18
No. of pupils: B194 G243
Fees: ¥1,208,000–¥2,145,000
Curriculum: AP, IBDP, IPC, SAT, UK, USA, IGCSE
Language instr: English
(CIS) (EAR)

Seisen International School
1-12-15 Yoga, Setagaya-ku,
Tokyo, 158-0097 Japan
Tel: +81 3 3704 2661
Head of School: Margaret D Scott
Age range: B3–5 G3–18
No. of pupils: 630
Curriculum: IBDP, IBPYP,
SAT, USA, IGCSE
Language instr: English
(CIS) (EAR)

Seta International School
27-12, Seta 1-chome, Setagaya-
ku, Tokyo, 158-0095 Japan
Tel: +81 3 5717 6769

St Mary's International School
1-6-19 Seta, Setagaya Ku,
Tokyo, 158-8668 Japan
Tel: +81 3 3709 3411
Head of School: Michel Jutras
Age range: B5–18
No. of pupils: 920
Curriculum: IBDP, SAT
Language instr: English
(CIS) (EAR)

St Michael's International School
3-17-2 Nakayamate-Dori, Chuo-
ku, Kobe, 650-0004 Japan
Tel: +81 78 231 8885
Head of School: Gill Tyrer
Age range: 3–11
No. of pupils: 172 B85 G87
Fees: ¥1,000,000
Curriculum: SAT, UK
Language instr: English
(CIS) (COB) (EAR)

Tamagawa Academy K-12 & University
6-1-1 Tamagawa Gakuen,
Machida, Tokyo, 194-8610 Japan
Tel: +81 42 739 8601
President: Yoshiaki Obara
Age range: 12–19
No. of pupils: 3000
Fees: ¥13,000–$18,000
Curriculum: IBDP, IBMYP
Language instr: English, Japanese

The American School in Japan
1-1-1 Nomizu, Chofu-shi,
Tokyo 182-0031, Japan
Tel: +81 422 34 5300
Head: Edwin V Ladd
Age range: 3–19
No. of pupils: 1540
Curriculum: ACT, AP,
SAT, TOEFL, USA
(EAR)

The British School in Tokyo
1-21-18 Shibuya, Shibuya-
ku, Tokyo 150, Japan
Tel: +81 3 5467 4321
Head Teacher: Michael G Farley
Age range: 3–16
No. of pupils: 630 B328 G302
Fees: ¥2,050,000
Curriculum: UK
Language instr: English
(COB)

Tohoku International School
7-101-1 Yakata, Izumi-ku,
Sendai, 981-3214 Japan
Tel: +81 22 348 2468
Headmaster: James Steward
Age range: 4–18
No. of pupils: 92 B45 G47
Curriculum: AP, SAT
(EAR)

Tokyo International School
3-4-22 Mita, Minato-Ku,
Tokyo, 108-0073 Japan
Tel: +81 3 5484 1160
Head of School: Des Hurst
Age range: 3–12
No. of pupils: 340
Fees: ¥1,850,000
Curriculum: IBMYP, IBPYP
Language instr: English
(CIS) (EAR)

Tsukuba International School
Kamigo 7821-1, Tsukuba,
Ibaraki, 3002645 Japan
Tel: (81) 29 886 5447
Head of School: Shaney Crawford
Age range: 3–16
Curriculum: IBPYP
Language instr: English

Yokohama International School
258 Yamate-cho, Naka-ku,
Yokohama, 231-0862 Japan
Tel: +81 45 622 0084
Head of School: Craig Coutts
Age range: 3–18
No. of pupils: 630
Curriculum: IBDP, IBMYP, IBPYP, SAT
Language instr: English
(CIS) (EAR) (ECIS)

Yoyogi International School
1-15-12 Tomigaya, Shibuya-
ku, Tokyo 151-0063, Japan
Tel: +81 3 5478 6714
Director: Yuko Muir
Age range: 2–6
No. of pupils: 110
Curriculum: IBPYP, UK, USA
Language instr: English

Jordan

Abdul Hamid Sharaf School
PO Box 6008, Amman, 11118 Jordan
Tel: +962 6 592 4188
Director: Sue Dahdah
Age range: 3–18
No. of pupils: 525 B275 G250
Fees: $1,500–$5,000
Curriculum: National,
SAT, USA, ALevs
Language instr: English, Arabic

American Community School Amman
PO BOX 310, Amman 11831, Jordan
Tel: +962 6 581 3944
Superintendent: Larry McIlvain
Age range: 3–18
Fees: $3,410–$13,590
Curriculum: USA
Language instr: English

Amman Academy
PO Box 840, Khalda, 11821 Jordan
Tel: +962 6 535 4118
Head of School: Faten Muqattash
Curriculum: IBDP, IBMYP
Language instr: English

Amman Baccalaureate School
Al Hijaz Street, Dabouq,
PO Box 441 Sweileh 11910,
Amman, 441-11910 Jordan
Tel: +962 6 5411191
Principal: Stuart Bryan
Age range: 4–18
No. of pupils: 1163
Curriculum: IBDP, IBMYP
Language instr: English, Arabic
(CIS) (ECIS) (RS)

Amman National School
PO Box 140565, Amman,
11814 Jordan
Tel: +962 654 11067/8
Head of School: Dara Taher
Curriculum: IBDP
Language instr: English

Aqaba International School
PO Box 529, 77110 Aqaba, Jordan
Tel: +962 3 203 9933
Principal: Danny Harrison
Age range: 4–16
Curriculum: National, UK

Cambridge High School
Al Rabia, Abdel Kareem Al
Dabbas Street, PO Box 851771,
Amman, 11185 Jordan
Tel: +962 6 5512556
Head of School: Diana Afranji
Age range: 4–18
No. of pupils: 1056 B559 G497 VIth82
Fees: Day JD6,600
Curriculum: IBDP
Language instr: English

IBN Rushd National Academy
PO Box 940397, Amman,
11118 Jordan
Tel: +962 6 568 3490
Head of School: Fouad Majdalawi
Curriculum: IBPYP
Language instr: English

International Academy – Amman
PO Box 144255, King Hussein
Parks, King Abdullah II Street,
Amman 11814, Jordan
Tel: +962 6550 2055
Director: Hana Kanan
Age range: 4–18
No. of pupils: 1050 B525 G525 VIth75
Curriculum: IBDP, IBMYP, IPC
Language instr: English
(CIS) (ECIS)

INTERNATIONAL COMMUNITY SCHOOL
For further details see p. 84
PO Box 2002, Amman
11181, Jordan
Tel: +962 6 4790666
Email: office@ics.edu.jo
Website:
www.ics-amman.edu.jo
Principal: John Bastable
Age range: 3–18
No. of pupils: 614 B334 G280
Fees: US$5,873–US$18,610
Curriculum: UK, IGCSE, ALevs
Language instr: English
(ECIS)

International School of Choueifat – Amman
PO Box 316, Amman 11810, Jordan
Tel: +962 6 4291133
Age range: 3–18
No. of pupils: 1274 B742 G532
Fees: JD2,300–JD6,500
Curriculum: AP, SAT
Language instr: English

Islamic Educational College
Al Kulliyah Al Elmiyah, Al Eslamiyah
St A23, Amman, 11118 Jordan
Tel: +962 6464 1331
Director General: Jumana
Abu-hiljeh
(ECIS)

King's Academy
PO Box 9, Madaba,
Manja 16188 Jordan
Tel: +962 6 4300230
Headmaster: John Austin
Age range: 13–18
No. of pupils: 130 B62 G68
Fees: US$19,000
Curriculum: USA
Language instr: English
(CIS) (RS)

Mashrek International School
PO Box 1412, Amman, 11118 Jordan
Tel: +962 79 9577771
School Principal: Hana Al-Nasser Malhas
Age range: 3–18
No. of pupils: 1199
Fees: US$2,470–US$7,670
Curriculum: IBDP, IBMYP, IBPYP, National
Language instr: Arabic, English
(ECIS)

Modern American School
PO Box 950553-Sweifieh, Amman 11195, Jordan
Tel: +962 6 5862779
Director: Omaya Zamel
Age range: 3–18
No. of pupils: 940 B570 G370
Fees: US$3,964–US$10,000
Curriculum: National, UK, USA

Modern Montessori School
PO Box 1941, Khilda, Amman, 11821 Jordan
Tel: +9626 5535190
Principal: Randa Hasan
Age range: 3–18
No. of pupils: 1568
Curriculum: IBDP
Language instr: English
(ECIS)

New English School
PO Box 154, Khalda, Amman 11821, Jordan
Tel: +962 (0)6 5517111
Principal: Irene Beatrix Hofayz
Age range: 4–19
No. of pupils: 2050
Curriculum: National, SAT, UK, ALevs
(ECIS)

The Ahliyyah School for Girls
PO Box 2035, Jabal Amman, Amman, 11181 Jordan
Tel: +962 6 4649861
Superintendent: Haifa Najjar
Age range: G6–18
No. of pupils: 1000
Curriculum: IBDP, IBPYP, National, ALevs
Language instr: English

The Bishop's School for Boys
PO Box 2001, Amman, 11181 Jordan
Tel: +962 6 4653668
Head of School: Haifa Najjar
Curriculum: IBDP

The Little Academy
PO Box 143771, Amman, 11844 Jordan
Tel: +962 65858282
Head of School: Maha Al Alami
Curriculum: IBPYP
Language instr: English

Kazakhstan

Almaty International School
185 Auezov Str. Auezov District, Kalkaman Village, Almaty, 050006 Kazakhstan
Tel: +7 727 381 87 10/11
Director: Bruce A Kleven
Age range: 3–18
No. of pupils: 508 B252 G256
Curriculum: AP, USA
Language instr: English

Haileybury Almaty
Al-Farabi 112, Almaty 050040, Kazakhstan
Tel: +7 727 355 0100
Headmaster: John Price
Age range: 5–18
No. of pupils: 600
Curriculum: IBDP, UK
(COB)

Haileybury Astana
Tauelsyzdyk Avenue, Astana, Kazakhstan
Tel: +7 717 255 9855
Headmaster: Andrew Auster
Age range: 3–10
(COB)

International College of Continuous Education Astana
2 Molodezhny Microdistrict, Astana 0100000, 473000 Kazakhstan
Tel: +7 7172 224590
Head of School: Ludmila Shelukhina
Age range: 3–17
No. of pupils: 140 B70 G70
Curriculum: IBMYP, IBPYP
Language instr: English, Russian

International College of Continuous Education, Almaty
69A Zheltoksan Street, Almaty, 480004 Kazakhstan
Tel: +7 3272 399736
Head of School: Ludmila Shelukhina
Age range: 3–18
No. of pupils: 324 B175 G149
Curriculum: IBMYP, IBPYP
Language instr: English

International School of Almaty
40b Satpayev Street, Almaty, 050057 Kazakhstan
Tel: +7 727 2744808 / +7 727 2748189
Head of School: Zhibek Akasheva
Age range: 7–18
No. of pupils: 350
Curriculum: IBMYP, IBPYP
Language instr: Russian, English

Kazakhstan International School
102a Utegen Batyra, 050062 Almaty, Kazakhstan
Tel: +7 727 395 33 54
Principal: Elena Maksymova
Age range: 2–11
Curriculum: IBPYP
Language instr: English, Kazakh, Russian

Miras International School, Almaty
190 Al-Farabi Avenue, Almaty, Kazakhstan
Tel: +7 7272 55 1025
Head of School: Irina R Vlassyants
Age range: 3–18
No. of pupils: 600
Fees: US$9,870–US$21,680
Curriculum: IBDP, IBMYP, IBPYP
Language instr: English
(CIS)(ECIS)

Miras International School, Astana
30 Ablai Khan Avenue, Astana, 010009 Kazakhstan
Tel: +7 7172 369867
Head of School: Yelena Khamitova
Age range: 5–18
No. of pupils: 300 B142 G158
Fees: US$13,800
Curriculum: IBDP, IBMYP, IBPYP, National
Language instr: English, Russian, Kazakh
(CIS)(ECIS)

QSI International School of Aktau
Micro District #2, Building 74, Aktau, Kazakhstan
Tel: +7 7292 502398
Director: Sam Thomas
Age range: 3–13
Language instr: English

QSI International School of Astana
21 Akyn Sara Street, Komsomolsky Village, Astana, 010000 Kazakhstan
Tel: +7 7172 472 990/88
Director: Sandra Smith
Age range: 3–14
No. of pupils: 33
Curriculum: USA
Language instr: English

QSI International School of Atyrau
163 Mamekuly Street, Atyrau, 060002 Kazakhstan
Tel: +7 712 232 1751
Director: Eben Plese
Age range: 3–17
Language instr: English

Tien Shan Educational Center
10a Basenova Street, Almaty, 0500600 Kazakhstan
Tel: +7 727 932602
Director: Craig Johnston
Age range: 5–18
No. of pupils: 203 B106 G97
Fees: US$2,000–US$14,000
Curriculum: AP, USA
Language instr: English

Kuwait

Al Ghanim Bilingual School
PO Box 3014, Safat – 31013, Kuwait
Tel: +965 2564 4953
Director: Afaf El-Gemayel
Age range: 4–15
No. of pupils: 1000
Curriculum: National, USA
(ECIS)

Al Ru'ya Bilingual School
PO Box 44230, Hawalli 32057, Kuwait
Tel: +965 1804818
Director: Summayah Al-Mutawah
Age range: 2–18
No. of pupils: 1547 B920 G627
(CIS)(ECIS)

Al-Bayan Bilingual School
PO Box 24472, Safat 13105, Kuwait
Tel: +965 222 75 000
Director: Thomas Quinn
Age range: 3–18
No. of pupils: 1850 B995 G855
Curriculum: AP, National, SAT, TOEFL, USA
(CIS)

American Arab Bilingual Academy
PO Box 237, Safat 13098, Kuwait City, Kuwait
Tel: +965 2263 9681
Principal: Ahlam Khattab
Age range: 3–18
No. of pupils: 644 B447 G197
Curriculum: National, USA

American Creativity Academy
PO Box 1740, Hawalli, 32018 Kuwait
Tel: +965 2267 3333
Superintendent: Gertrude Gomez
Age range: 3–18
No. of pupils: B1551 G1652
Curriculum: IBDP, USA
Language instr: English
(CIS)(ECIS)

American International School of Kuwait
PO Box 3267, Salmiya, 22033 Kuwait
Tel: +965 1 843 247
Director: Samera Al Rayes
Age range: 4–18
No. of pupils: 1840
Fees: KD1,720
Curriculum: AP, IBDP, IBMYP, IBPYP, SAT, USA
Language instr: English
(ECIS)

Dasman Model School
PO Box 3366, Salmiya, 22034 Kuwait
Tel: +965 2243 0704/6
Superintendent: Roberto Santos
Age range: 3–19
No. of pupils: 1488 B925 G563
Curriculum: National, SAT, TOEFL, USA
(CIS)

Fahaheel Al Watanieh Indian Private School
49, South St., P.O.Box: 9951, Ahmadi 61010, Kuwait
Tel: +965 23983595
Principal: Anju Dheman

Gulf English School
PO Box 33106, 25562 Ruhaithiya, Kuwait
Tel: +965 575 7022
Director: Gillian Raper
Age range: 3–18
No. of pupils: 1700 B1000 G700
Fees: KD1,200–KD2,300
Curriculum: UK, ALevs
Language instr: English

Ideal Education School, Kuwait
PO Box 27557, Safat 13136, Kuwait
Tel: +965 240 3668
Principal: Sania Khattab
Age range: 3–21
No. of pupils: 186 B110 G76
(CIS)

International British School, Kuwait
PO Box 47401, Kuwait City, Kuwait
Tel: +965 2392 2430
Headmaster: William Deacon
Curriculum: UK
Language instr: English
(COB)

Khalifa School
PO Box 58, Safat 13001, Kuwait
Tel: +965 2574 4105
Principal: Humra Khan
Age range: 3–21+
No. of pupils: 197 B125 G72
Fees: KD5,656
Curriculum: UK, USA
Language instr: English, Arabic
(CIS)

Kuwait American School
PO Box 5150, Salmiya – 22062, Kuwait
Tel: +965 2572 0920
Principal: Peter Williams
Age range: 2–16
Fees: KD1,300–KD3,098
Curriculum: USA

Kuwait Bilingual School
PO Box 2107, Al Jahra City, 1023 Kuwait
Tel: +965 2458 1118
Curriculum: IBPYP

Kuwait English School
PO Box 8640, Salmiya 22057, Kuwait City, Kuwait
Tel: +965 565 5216/218
Principal: Rhoda Elizabeth Muhmood
Age range: 3–18
No. of pupils: 2008
Curriculum: ALevs
(ECIS)

Kuwait International English School
PO Box 93, Dasman 15451, Kuwait
Tel: +965 2262 8447; +965 22642047
Principal: John P Brewer
Age range: 3–18
No. of pupils: 327
Curriculum: IGCSE

Kuwait National English School
PO Box 44273, Hawally, Kuwait City 32057, Kuwait
Tel: +965 265 6904/5/6 & 265 2457/8
Director: Chantal Al-Gharabally
Age range: 3–16
No. of pupils: 600
Curriculum: UK
(CIS) (ECIS)

Manarat School
PO Box 27557, Safat, 13136 Kuwait
Tel: +965 257 22 083
Principal: Elizabeth Naert
Language instr: English
(CIS)

New English School
PO Box 6156, 32036 Hawelli, Kuwait
Tel: +965 25318060
Director: Ziad S Rajab
Age range: 3–18
No. of pupils: 1850 VIth70
Curriculum: ALevs
(ECIS)

New Pakistan International School
Block-9, Surraqa Bin Malik Street, (Near Doctor's Complex), Hawally, Kuwait
Tel: +965 22639720
Director: Anita Bukharey
No. of pupils: 2345
Curriculum: IGCSE, ALevs

The American Academy for Girls
PO Box 22156, Safat, Kuwait City 13082, Kuwait
Tel: +965 2563 9612
Superintendent: Jane Blazek
Age range: 3–18
No. of pupils: 830
Fees: KD700–KD2,100
Curriculum: USA

The American School of Kuwait
Hawalli-Al-Muthanna st, Block 7, Bldg 90017, PO Box 6735 Hawalli, Kuwait 32042 Kuwait
Tel: +965 2 266 4341
Superintendent: Rebecca Ness
Age range: 3–18
No. of pupils: 1325
Curriculum: AP, SAT, TOEFL

The British School of Kuwait
Safat 13130, Kuwait 26922, Kuwait
Tel: +965 2562 1701
Principal: Paul Shropshire
Age range: 3–19
No. of pupils: 1700 B925 G775 VIth85
Fees: KD1,425–KD3,520
Curriculum: National, UK, GCSE, IGCSE, ALevs
Language instr: English

The English Acadamy
PO Box 1081, Surra 45701, Kuwait
Tel: +965 2534 0427/8
Principal: Horace Vernall
Age range: 3–18
No. of pupils: 1000 B700 G300
Curriculum: UK, ALevs
Language instr: English, Arabic

The English School Fahaheel
PO Box 7209, Fahaheel, Kuwait City, 64003 Kuwait
Tel: +965 2371 1070/7263
Principal: Russell Dunlop
Age range: 3–18
No. of pupils: 1050 VIth37
Curriculum: UK, IGCSE, ALevs
Language instr: English

The English School, Kuwait
PO Box 379, Safat 13004, Kuwait
Tel: +965 2563 7206
Headmaster: John Allcott
Age range: 2–13
No. of pupils: 600 B300 G300
Fees: KD1,750–KD3,060
Curriculum: National, UK
Language instr: English
(ECIS)

Universal American School
PO Box 17035, Khaldiya 72451, Kuwait
Tel: +965 1822827
Superintendent: James P Moras
Age range: 3–18
No. of pupils: 1600 B900 G700
Language instr: English
(CIS) (ECIS)

Kyrgyzstan

European School in Central Asia
67 Bronirovannaya, Bishkek, Kyrgyzstan
Tel: +996 3122 14406
Head of Education: Ian Martin
Language instr: English
(ECIS)

QSI International School of Bishkek
14A Tynstanova Street, Bishkek, 720055 Kyrgyzstan
Tel: +996 312 563139
Director: Arthur Hudson
Age range: 4–15
No. of pupils: 103
Curriculum: USA
Language instr: English

The Silk Road International School
Mikroregion 11, Aytieva 7a, Bishkek, 720049 Kyrgyzstan
Tel: +996 312 520290
Director: Emrullah Durmaz
Age range: 5–15
No. of pupils: 83 B54 G29
(ECIS)

Laos

VIENTIANE INTERNATIONAL SCHOOL
For further details see p. 98
PO Box 3180, Ban Saphanthong Tai, Vientiane, Laos
Tel: +856 21 486001
Email: contact@vislao.com admissions@vislao.com
Website: www.vislao.com
Director: Greg Smith
Age range: 3–18
No. of pupils: 447
Fees: US$6,650–US$17,720
Curriculum: IBDP, IBMYP, IBPYP
Language instr: English
(CIS) (EAR)

Lebanon

American Community School at Beirut
PO Box 8129, Riad Solh, Beirut 11072260, Lebanon
Tel: +961 1 374 370
Head of School: George Damon
Age range: 3–18
No. of pupils: 1023
Curriculum: IBDP, SAT, TOEFL
Language instr: English
(ECIS)

Antonine International School
PO Box 55035, Ajaltoun, Dekwaneh, Lebanon
Tel: +961 9 230969
Head of School: André Daher
No. of pupils: 1300
Curriculum: IBDP
Language instr: English

City International School
P.O.Box 11-472 Riad El Solh, Beirut, Lebanon
Tel: +961 137 5410
Principal: Nather Simhairi
Language instr: English
(ECIS)

Eastwood College
PO Box 100, Mansourieh el Metn / Kafarshima, Lebanon
Tel: +961 4 409307
Age range: 3–18
No. of pupils: B203 G123
Curriculum: AP, National, SAT, USA
Language instr: English

German School Beirut
Bliss Street, Ras Beirut, Beirut, PO Box 11-3888 Lebanon
Tel: +961 1 740523
Director: Omar Salloum
Age range: 3–18
No. of pupils: 1152
Fees: US$6,650
Curriculum: IBDP
Language instr: English

International College, Ain Aar
Bliss Street, PO Box 113-5373, Beirut, Lebanon
Tel: +96 149 28468
Head of School: John Johnson
Curriculum: IBPYP
Language instr: Arabic, English, French

International College, Ras Beirut
PO Box 113-5373, Beirut, Lebanon
Tel: +961 1 371 294
Head of School: John K Johnson
Age range: 3–18
No. of pupils: 3399 B1756 G1643
Fees: $6,300
Curriculum: IBDP, IBPYP
Language instr: Arabic, English, French
(CIS)

International School of Choueifat – Koura
Fih Village, Koura, Lebanon
Tel: +961 6 930740
Director: Saad Abou Chakna
Age range: 3–18
No. of pupils: 819 B462 G357
Curriculum: UK, IGCSE, ALevs

Makassed Houssam Eddine Hariri High School
PO Box 67, Saida, Lebanon
Tel: +961 7 739898
Head of School: Hanadi Jardaly Kotob
Age range: 3–18
No. of pupils: 1520 B835 G685
Curriculum: IBPYP, National, FrenchBacc, SAT, TOEFL
Language instr: Arabic, English, French

Sagesse High School
Aïn Saadeh, Metn, Lebanon
Tel: +961 1 872 145
School Rector: Gabriel Tabet
Age range: 2–18
No. of pupils: 1030
Curriculum: IBDP, National, USA
Language instr: English

Universal College-Aley
P.O. Box 284, Aley, Lebanon
Tel: +961 5 556665
Director: Walter Day
Language instr: English

Wellspring Learning Community
Al Mathaf, Main Street, Near National Museum, Beirut, PO Box 116-2134 Lebanon
Tel: +961 1 423 444
School Principal: Kathleen Battah
Age range: 3–16
No. of pupils: B227 G220
Curriculum: IBPYP, National
Language instr: English, Arabic

Malaysia

Alice Smith School
No 2, Jalan Bellamy, 50460 Kuala Lumpur, Malaysia
Tel: +603 2148 3674/9543 3688
Director: Valerie Thomas-Peter
Age range: 3–18
No. of pupils: 1449 B737 G712
Fees: RM22,380–RM51,030
Curriculum: ALevs
Language instr: English
(COB)

Australian International School Malaysia
22 Jalan Anggerik, The Mones Resort City, 43300 Sri Kembangan, Selangor Darul Ehsan Malaysia
Tel: +603 8943 0622
Principal: David Kilpatrick
Age range: 5–18
(CIS)

Cempaka International Ladies' College
Persiaran Timur Satu, Bandar Enstek, Negeri Sembilan, Seremban, 71760 Malaysia
Tel: +603 9076 8400
Head of School: Freida Pilus
Age range: G11–18
Curriculum: IBDP
Language instr: English

Cempaka International School
No 19, Jalan Setiabakti 1, Damansara Heights, Kuala Lumpur, Malaysia
Tel: +60 3209 40623
Head of School: Farah Salizah Ahmad Sarji
Curriculum: IBDP
(ISA)

Dalat International School
Tanjung Bunga, Penang 11200, Malaysia
Tel: +60 4 899 2105
Director: Karl L Steinkamp
Age range: 3–18
No. of pupils: 400 B200 G200
Fees: US$2,000–US$10,000
Curriculum: ACT, SAT, USA
Language instr: English
(EAR)

elc International School
3664, Jalan Sierramas Barat, Sierramas, Sungai Buloh, 47000 Selangor, Malaysia
Tel: +60 3 6156 5001/2
Principle: Margaret A Kaloo
Age range: 3–16
No. of pupils: 650
Fees: RM8,400–RM28,500
Curriculum: UK
Language instr: English

Fairview International School
Lot 4178, Jalan 1/27D, Section 6, Wangsa Maju, Kuala Lumpur, 53300 Malaysia
Tel: +603 4142 0888
Head of School: Thilagavathy Navaratnam
Age range: 4–18
No. of pupils: 2500
Fees: RM4,500–RM15,000
Curriculum: IBDP, IBMYP, IBPYP
Language instr: English

Fairview International School Johor
Kompleks Mutiara Johor Land, Jalan Bukit Mutiara, Bandar Dato' Onn, Johor Bahru, Johor 88100 Malaysia
Tel: +607 358 5385
Head of School: P Leelavathy
Curriculum: IBMYP, IBPYP

Fairview International School Penang
Lot PT 1935, Mukim 13, Daerah Timur Laut, Tingkat Bukit Jambul 1, Bayan Lepas, Penang 11900 Malaysia
Tel: +60 464 06633
Head of School: R Gopinathan
Curriculum: IBDP, IBMYP, IBPYP

Fairview International School Subang
2A, Jalan TP 2, Sime UEP Industrial Park, Subang Jaya, Selangor 47600 Malaysia
Tel: +603 80237777
Head of School: Michael Chian
Curriculum: IBMYP, IBPYP

Garden International School
16 Jalan Kiara 3, Off Jln Bukit Kiara, Kuala Lumpur, 50480 Malaysia
Tel: +6 03 6209 6888
Principal: Stuart Walker
Age range: 3–18
No. of pupils: 2220
Fees: RM34,260–RM82,515
Curriculum: IPC, UK, IGCSE, ALevs
Language instr: English
(CIS) (EAR)

IGB International School
Jalan Sierramas Utama, Sungai Buloh, Kuala Lumpur, Selangor 47000 Malaysia
Tel: +60 367 307 788
Head of School: Anne Fowles
Curriculum: IBDP

Kinabalu International School
PO Box 12080, Sabah 88822, Kota Kinabalu, Malaysia
Tel: +60 88 224526
Principal: Stuart McLay
Age range: 3–18
No. of pupils: 250 B125 G125
(CIS)

Kolej Tuanku Ja'Afar
71700 Mantin, Negeri Sembilan, Malaysia
Tel: +606 7582561
Principal: Simon Watson
Age range: 3–19
No. of pupils: 792 B447 G345
Fees: RM5,850–RM40,140
Curriculum: IPC, National, UK, IGCSE, ALevs
Language instr: English
(CIS) (COB)

Marlborough College Malaysia
Jalan Marlborough, Nusajaya, Johor, 79250 Malaysia
Tel: +60 75602200
Head of School: Bob Pick
Curriculum: IBDP
Language instr: English

Mont'Kiara International School
22 Jalan Kiara, Off Jalan Bukit Kiara, Kuala Lumpur, 50480 Malaysia
Tel: +60 3 2093 8604
Head of School: Brian D Brumsickle
Age range: 3–18
No. of pupils: 1006 B430 G576
Fees: RM46,761–RM98,839
Curriculum: IBDP, SAT, USA
Language instr: English
(EAR)

Mutiara International Grammar School
Lot 707, Jalan Kerja Ayer Lama, Ampang Jaya, 68000 Ampang, Selangor Darul Ehsan Malaysia
Tel: +60 3 4252 1452
Principal: Stephen C Fulton
Age range: 3–16
No. of pupils: 450
Fees: RM8,000–RM19,000
Curriculum: UK
(COB)

Nexus International School, Putrajaya
No 1 Jalan Diplomatik 3/6, Presint 15, 62050 Putrajaya, Malaysia
Tel: +603 8889 3868
Principal: Alison Hampshire
Age range: 3–18
No. of pupils: 700
Fees: US$9,500–US$18,000
Curriculum: IBDP, IPC, UK, GCSE, IGCSE
Language instr: English
(🏛)

Prince of Wales Island International School
1 Jalan Sungai Air Putih 6, Bandar Baru Air Putih, Balik Pulau, 11000 Malaysia
Tel: +604 868 9999
Head of School: Philip Couzens
Curriculum: UK
Language instr: English
(COB)

Sri KDU International School
No 5, Jalan Teknologi 2/1, Kota Damansara, 47810 Petaling Jaya, Selangor Darul Ehsan Malaysia
Tel: +60 03 6145 3888
Principal: Margaret Rafee
Age range: 11–18
No. of pupils: 1001 B535 G466
Fees: RM31,000–RM45,000
Curriculum: IBDP, IGCSE
Language instr: English

St Christopher's International Primary School
10 Nunn Road, Penang 10350, Malaysia
Tel: +60 4 226 3589
Principal: John Gwyn Jones
Age range: 3–11
No. of pupils: 590 B287 G303
Fees: RM8,400–RM18,600
Curriculum: IPC, UK
Language instr: English

Taylor's College Sri Hartamas
G1 Ground Floor, No 62 Jalan Sri Hartamas 1, Sri Hartamas, 50480 Malaysia
Tel: +60 3 6203 0168
Head of School: Hariandra Muthu
Curriculum: IBDP, ALevs
Language instr: English
(🏛)

Tenby International School Miri
Lot 10700, Block 5, Jalan Desa Senadin, Miri, Malaysia
Tel: +60 085 491 526
Language instr: English

Tenby International School Setia Eco Gardens
7, Jalan Laman Setia Utama, Taman Setia Utama, Johor Bahru, 81550 Malaysia
Tel: +60 7 5588812
Language instr: English

Tenby Schools Ipoh
16 Persiaran Meru Utama, Bandar Meru Raya, Ipoh, 30020 Perak Malaysia
Tel: +60 55 252 628
Language instr: English
(EAR)

Tenby Schools Penang
No. 2, Lintang Lembah Permai 1, Tanjung Bungah, Pulau Pinang, 11200 Malaysia
Tel: +604 892 7777
Language instr: English

Tenby Schools Setia Eco Park
No.1, Jalan Setia Tropika U13/18T, Seksyen U13, Shah Alam, 40170 Malaysia
Tel: +60 03 3342 1535
Language instr: English

The British International School of Kuala Lumpur
No 1 Changkat Bukit Utama Bandar Utama, Petaling Jaya, Kuala Lumpur, Selangor 47800 Malaysia
Tel: +6 03 7727 7775
Headteacher: Janet Brock
Age range: 2–16
Fees: RM26,037–RM59,600
Curriculum: UK
(COB)

The International School of Kuala Lumpur
Jalan Kolam Air, Ampang, Selangor, 68000 Malaysia
Tel: +6 03 4259 5628/27
Head of School: Norma J Hudson
Age range: 3–18
No. of pupils: 1630
Curriculum: AP, IBDP, SAT
Language instr: English
(CIS) (EAR)

THE INTERNATIONAL SCHOOL OF PENANG (UPLANDS)
For further details see p. 97
Jalan Sungai Satu, Batu Feringgi, 11100 Penang, Malaysia
Tel: +604 8819 777
Email: info@uplands.org
Website: www.uplands.org
Principal: Ian Williams
Age range: 4–19
No. of pupils: 633 B331 G302 Vlth104
Fees: Day RM9,667–RM14,500 FB RM12,100–RM12,677
Curriculum: IBDP, IBPYP, GCSE, IGCSE, ALevs
Language instr: English
(🏛)

UCSI International School
1 Persiaran UCSI International School, Port Dickson, Negeri Sembalan 71010 Malaysia
Tel: +60 6653 6888
Head of School: Kathryn Farrell
Curriculum: IBDP
Language instr: English
(🏛)

Mongolia

American School of Ulaanbaatar
Khan Uul District, Post Office Box 2365, Central Post Office, Ulananbaatar, 15160 Mongolia
Tel: +976 11 348888
Head of School: Diane Field

British School of Ulaanbaatar
Post Office Box 80, Post Office Branch – 30, Ulaanbaatar, 17110 Mongolia
Tel: +976 11 347788
Principal: Anna Williams
Language instr: English
(COB)

International School of Ulaanbaatar
PO Box 36/10, Ulaanbaatar-36, 17032 Mongolia
Tel: +976 70160010
Director: Robert Stearns
Age range: 4–18
No. of pupils: 354 B170 G184
Fees: Day US$11,995–US$21,984
Curriculum: IBDP, IBMYP, IBPYP
Language instr: English
(CIS) (EAR)

Ulaanbaatar Elite International School
Seoul Street, 2nd Khoroo, Sukhbaatar District, Ulaanbaatar, 14523 Mongolia
Tel: +976, 11 462606
Director: Mustafa Uguz
Age range: 6–17
Curriculum: IBDP, UK
Language instr: English
(COB) (EDS)

Myanmar

Horizon International Education Center
25 Po Sein Road, Bahan Township, Yangon, 11201 Myanmar
Tel: +95 (1) 543926
Head of School: Adem Engin
Curriculum: IBDP
Language instr: English

International School of Yangon
20 Shwe Taungyar, Bahan Township, Yangon, 11181 Myanmar
Tel: +95 1 512793/94/95
Head of School: Stephen Plisinski
Age range: 4–20
No. of pupils: B245 G275
Curriculum: IBDP, SAT, TOEFL, USA
Language instr: English
(EAR)

Yangon International Educare Centre
No W-22, Mya Kan Thar Main Road, 5th Quarter, Hlaing Township, Yangon, Myanmar
Tel: +95 1 682231
Director: Tim Travers
Age range: 2–17
No. of pupils: 850
Curriculum: USA

Nepal

Kathmandu International Study Centre
PO Box 2714, Jawalakhel, Kathmandu, Nepal
Tel: +977 1 5538720
CEO: Judith Ellis
Age range: 4–18
No. of pupils: 170 B101 G84
Fees: US$7,000
Curriculum: National, UK, IGCSE, ALevs
Language instr: English
(🏛)

Lincoln School
PO Box 2673, Rabi Bhawan, Kathmandu, Nepal
Tel: +977 14 270482
Director: Allan Bredy
Age range: 3–19
No. of pupils: 340 B175 G165
Fees: US$15,900
Curriculum: AP, SAT, USA
Language instr: English

The British School Kathmandu
PO Box 566, Kathmandu, Nepal
Tel: +977 1 5521794
Principal: Sandj Wilderspin
Age range: 3–18
No. of pupils: 349 B173 G176
Fees: Day £4,680–£6,580 £1,200
Curriculum: UK, IGCSE, ALevs
Language instr: English
(COB)

Ullens School
Khumaltar-5, Lalipur, Post
Box Number 8975, EPC 1477,
Kathmandu, Nepal
Tel: +977 1 5570724
Head of School: Medin
Lamichhane
Curriculum: IBDP
Language instr: English

Pakistan

Aitchison College
The Mall, Lahore, 54000 Pakistan
Tel: +92 42 6363063
Principal: Shamim Khan
Age range: B4–18
Fees: Rs8,700–Rs12,300
Curriculum: ALevs

British Overseas School
AL 7/8, 14th/15th Lane, Off
Khayaban-e-Hilal, DHA Phase
VII, Karachi, Pakistan
Tel: +92 21 5845606
Principal: Andrew Williams
Age range: 3–18
Fees: Day £1,240–£4,280

Ilmesters Academy
32-C, 32nd Street, Block 6, PECHS,
Karachi, Sindh 74800 Pakistan
Tel: +92 21 3455 8986
Head of School: Alia Sajjad
Curriculum: IBPYP
Language instr: English, Urdu

International School of Islamabad
H-9/1, P.O. Box 1124,
Islamabad, 44000 Pakistan
Tel: +92 51 443 4950
Superintendent: R C Puffer
Age range: 2–18
No. of pupils: 255 B146 G109
Fees: US$5,760–US$18,708
Curriculum: ACT, AP, IBDP, SAT, USA
Language instr: English

Karachi International School
Amir Khusro Road, Karachi,
75350 Pakistan
Tel: +92 21 3453 9096
Age range: 3–18
No. of pupils: 336 B189 G147
Fees: US$8,025–US$12,333
Curriculum: USA
Language instr: English

Lahore American School
15 Upper Mall Canal Bank,
Lahore, 54000 Pakistan
Tel: +92 42 576 2406
Superintendent: Thomas Tunny
Age range: 4–18
No. of pupils: 410 B310 G100

Links Pre and Primary Schools
D101/1, Block 4, Clifton,
Karachi, Pakistan
Tel: +92 215874322
Head: Nausheen Leghari
Age range: 3–11
(COB)

Roots International Schools Islamabad Pakistan
Building 12 – K, G-8 Markaz,
Islamabad, 44000 Pakistan
Tel: +92 300 5061935
Head of School: Chaudry
Walid Mushtaq
Curriculum: IBDP
Language instr: English

The International School (TIS)
Executive, 51-C Old Clifton,
Near Mohatta Palace,
Karachi, 75600 Pakistan
Tel: +92 21 35835805-6
Head of School: Taymur Mirza
Age range: 3–18
No. of pupils: 250 B130 G120 VIth50
Fees: Day PKR250,000–PKR400,000
Curriculum: IBDP, IBMYP, UK, IGCSE
Language instr: English

The Lyceum School
78 Clifton, Karachi, 75600 Pakistan
Tel: +92 213 582 1741
Curriculum: ALevs
Language instr: English
(RS)

TNS Beaconhouse
1 H, Jail Road, Gulberg II,
Lahore, 54000 Pakistan
Tel: +92 (111) 867867
Head of School: Roger Clive Barnes
Curriculum: IBDP, IBMYP
(ISA)

Palestine

Al Mustaqbal Schools
P.O. Box 2422, Al Tireh,
Ramallah, Palestine
Tel: 2980636 / 2961853
Principal: Shaher Shanti
Age range: 2–18
No. of pupils: 630 B384 G246
Curriculum: IGCSE

Friends Boys School
PO Box 66, West Bank, Palestine,
Via Israel Palestine
Tel: +972 229 56230
Head of School: Mahmoud Amra
Age range: 4–18
No. of pupils: 1040
Curriculum: IBDP, IBMYP
Language instr: English

Philippines

Benedictine International School
Capitol Hills Drive,
Matandang Balara, Quezon
City NCR, Philippines
Tel: +632 951 7454
Director: Miladel Lourdes R Bondoc
Age range: 4–16
Language instr: English

Brent International School – Baguio
Brent Road, Baguio City,
2600 Philippines
Tel: +63, 74 442 2260
Headmaster: Dick Robbins
Age range: 4–19
No. of pupils: 353 B182 G171
Curriculum: IBDP
Language instr: English
(CIS) (EAR)

Brent International School – Manila
Brentville Subdivision, Mamplasan,
Biñan, Laguna 4024 Philippines
Tel: +63 2 6001-0300/9
Head of School: Dick Robbins
Age range: 4–18
No. of pupils: 1158 B599 G559
Curriculum: IBDP, SAT
Language instr: English
(CIS) (EAR)

Brent International School Subic
Building 6601 Binictican Drive,
Subic Bay Freeport Zone,
Zambales, Subic, 2222 Philippines
Tel: +63 47 252 6871/72
Head of School: Dick Robbins
Curriculum: IBDP
Language instr: English
(CIS) (EAR)

Britesparks International School
IDC Building, E Rodriguez Jr Ave,
Libis, Quezon City, Philippines
Tel: +632 633 8081
Age range: 2–15

Cebu International School
PO Box 735, Pit-os, Talamban,
Cebu City, 6000 Philippines
Tel: +63 32 401 1900/1/2/3
Superintendent: Tony Harduar
Age range: 3–18
No. of pupils: 460 B269 G191
Fees: Php76,000–Php571,000
Curriculum: IBDP, IBPYP
Language instr: English
(CIS) (EAR)

Chinese International School Manila
Upper McKinley Road, McKinley
Hill, Fort Bonifacio, Taguig
City, 1634 Philippines
Tel: +63 (2) 815 2476
Head of School: Ma Louisa Sian
Curriculum: IBDP

Domuschola International School
Dormitory 1, Philsports Complex,
Molave Street, Ugong,
Pasig City, Philippines
Tel: +63 2 6359743
Head of School: Jennifer
Mapua Banal
Curriculum: IBPYP
Language instr: English, Hindi

Esteban School
PO Box 1991, Makati Central Post
Office, Makati City, Philippines
Tel: +632 8449915/13
Headmistress: Eleanor Esteban
Age range: 3–16
No. of pupils: 147 B75 G72
Language instr: English

Eton International School
1839 Dr. Vasquez Street,
Malate, Manila, Philippines
Tel: +632 526 2994
President: Jacqueline Tolentino
Language instr: English
(ISA)

Faith Academy
MCPO 2016, 0706 Makati
City, Philippines
Tel: +632 651 7100
Superintendent: Tom Hardeman
Age range: 5–18
No. of pupils: 560 B294 G266
Fees: $2,121
Curriculum: ACT, AP, SAT, USA
(EAR)

Fountain International School
14-15 Annapolis St, North East
Greenhills, San Juan, Philippines
Tel: +63 2 723 73 078
Language instr: English
(ECIS)

German European School Manila
75 Swaziland Street, Better Living Subd, Paranaque, Metro Manila Philippines
Tel: +63, 2 776 1000
Head of School: Wolfgang Kollecker
No. of pupils: 350
Curriculum: IBDP, IBPYP
Language instr: English

International School Manila
University Parkway, Fort Bonifacio, Global City, Taguig, PO Box 1526 MCPO, 1255, Makati City, 1634 Philippines
Tel: +63 2 8408440
Head of School: David Toze
Age range: 3–18
No. of pupils: 2001
Curriculum: IBDP
Language instr: English
(CIS) (EAR)

Kids International Learning Academy
27 Jetta St. Village East Cainta Rizal., Cainta, Philippines
Tel: +63 655 9841
Director: Ivy Joan T. Ong
Language instr: English

Mahatma Gandhi International School
3270a Armstrong Avenue, Merville Access Road, Merville Park, Pasay City, 1300 Philippines
Tel: +63 2 7761 165
Founding Head of School: Lawrence M Buck
Age range: 2.6–18
No. of pupils: 155 B75 G80 VIth10
Curriculum: AP, IBDP, IPC, SAT, IGCSE, ALevs
Language instr: English

MIT International School
Alabang-Zapote Road, Alabang, Muntinlupa, Philippines
Tel: +63 2 807 0720
Head of School: Hyockchu Kwon
Language instr: English
(ISA)

Noblesse International School
Circumferential Roas, Friendship Highway, Barangay CutCut, Angeles City, Pampanga, 2009 Philippines
Tel: +63 (45) 459 9000
Curriculum: IBDP
Language instr: English
(⚓)

Reedley International School
JOSOL Building, E Rodriguez Avenue, Libis, Quezon City, Philippines
Tel: +63 2 571 5291
Founding Directress: Nellie Aquino-Ong
Age range: 6–18
No. of pupils: 476 B281 G195
Curriculum: National, USA
Language instr: English

Singapore School Manila
Lots 4 and 5, Block 5, Paseo de Magallanes, Makati City, Philippines
Tel: +632 851 0022
Age range: 5–18
Curriculum: National, UK, IGCSE, ALevs

Southville International School & Colleges
1281 Tropical Avenue Corner, Luxembourg Street, BF Homes International, Las Pinas City, Philippines
Tel: +63 2 820 8702
Head of School: Marl Ferenal
Age range: 2–21
No. of pupils: B596 G580
Curriculum: IBDP
Language instr: English

The Beacon Academy
PCPD Bldg, 2332 Chino Roces Ext, Taguig City, 1630 Philippines
Tel: +632 425 1326
Head of School: Martha Wilkins
Curriculum: IBDP, IBMYP

The Beacon School
PCPD Building, 2332 Chino Roces Extn, Taguig, Metro Manila, Philippines
Tel: +632 840 5040 loc 102
Head of School: Mary Catherine Chua
Age range: B5–14 G5–13
No. of pupils: 269 B144 G125
Curriculum: IBMYP, IBPYP
Language instr: English

The British School, Manila
36th Street, University Park, Bonifacio Global City, Taguig City, Makati, Metro Manila 1634 Philippines
Tel: +63, 2 860 4800
Head of School: Stephen Murray
Age range: 3–18
No. of pupils: 784 B369 G415
Curriculum: IBDP, National, UK, IGCSE
Language instr: English
(CIS)

The King's School Manila
Bradco Avenue, Aseana Business Park, Paranaque City, Metro Manila, Philippines
Tel: +63 2519 5799
Headteacher: Peter Lindsay
Curriculum: UK
Language instr: English

Westfields International School
21-2 Friendship Highway, Cutcut, Angeles City, 2009 Philippines
Tel: +63 453222862
Principal: Volet de Jesus
Language instr: English
(ISA)

Xavier School
64 Xavier Street, Greenhills West, San Juan City, Metro Manila 1500 Philippines
Tel: +632 7230481
Head of School: Johnny Go
Curriculum: IBDP
Language instr: English
(⚓)

Qatar

ACS Doha International School
PO Box 200568, Al Oyoun Street, Gharaffa, Doha, Qatar
Tel: +974 30260801
Head of School: Diane Hren
Age range: 3–14
Curriculum: AP, IBDP, IBMYP, USA
(ECIS)

Al Hekma International School
PO Box 11157, Dafna Doha, Qatar
Tel: +974 4493 5522
President: Mona Rashid Abdul Rahman Al Zayani
Age range: 3–11

Al Jazeera Academy
PO Box 22250, Mesaimeer, Doha, Qatar
Tel: +974 4469 3777
Academy Director: Denise Walsh
Age range: 3–19
No. of pupils: 1340
Fees: QR17,500
Curriculum: UK
Language instr: English

Al Khor International School
Al Khor Community, PO Box 22166, Doha, Qatar
Tel: +974 4473 4666
Principal: Lyal French-Wright
Age range: 4–18
No. of pupils: 1650 B950 G700
Curriculum: SAT, UK
Language instr: English

Al Wakra Independent Secondary School
PO Box 80150, Al Wakrah, Qatar
Tel: +974 464 3739
Head of School: Mohammad Ali M Mandani Al Emadi
Age range: B16–19
Curriculum: IBDP
Language instr: English
(⚓)

Al-Bayan Educational Complex for Girls
PO Box 23533, Doha, Qatar
Tel: +974 44591789
Head of School: Wadha Al Nuaimi
Age range: G3–18
Curriculum: IBDP
Language instr: English
(⚓) (CIS) (ECIS)

American School of Doha
PO Box 22090, Doha, Qatar
Tel: +974 4442 1777
Director: Deb Welch
Age range: 4–18
Fees: QR24,772–QR53,732
Curriculum: IBDP, USA
Language instr: English

Awsaj Institute of Education
PO Box 6639, Doha, Qatar
Tel: +974 4454 2111
Director: Ralph Pruitt
Age range: 7–16
No. of pupils: 181
Curriculum: USA
(CIS)

Compass International School Doha
PO Box 23479, Doha, Qatar
Tel: +974 4487 7445
Head of School: Robin Campbell
Age range: 3–16
No. of pupils: 1200
Fees: QR59,125–QR60,050
Curriculum: IBDP, IPC, National, IGCSE
Language instr: English
(ECIS)

Doha British School
PO Box 6142, Doha, Qatar
Tel: +974 4450 2257
Principal: Terry McGuire
Age range: 3–18
No. of pupils: 1200
Curriculum: IBDP, National, SAT, UK, IGCSE
Language instr: English
(CIS)

Doha College
PO Box 7506, Doha, Qatar
Tel: +974 4468 7379
Principal: Mark Leppard
Age range: 3–18
No. of pupils: 1167 B634 G533
Curriculum: UK
Language instr: English
(CIS) (COB)

Doha English Speaking School
PO Box 7660, Doha, Qatar
Tel: +974 4459 2750
Headteacher: Andy Yeoman
Age range: 3–11
No. of pupils: 708 B364 G344
Fees: QR29,130–QR29,130
Curriculum: UK
Language instr: English
(COB)

Dukhan English Speaking School
PO Box 100,001, Dukhan, Qatar
Tel: +974 4471 6231/147
Headmaster: Janson Harrison
Age range: 4–16
No. of pupils: 602 B296 G306
Curriculum: SAT, UK

INTERNATIONAL SCHOOL OF LONDON (ISL) QATAR
For further details see p. 85
PO Box 18511, North Duhail, Doha, Qatar
Tel: +974 4433 8600
Email: mail@islqatar.org
Website: www.islqatar.org
Head of School: Chris Charleson
Age range: 3–18
No. of pupils: 900
Fees: QR31,250–QR66,950
Curriculum: IBDP, IBMYP, IBPYP
(ECIS)

Park House English School
PO Box 22215, Doha, Qatar
Tel: +974 4468 3800
Director: Niall Brennan
Age range: 3–18
No. of pupils: 973 B474 G499
Curriculum: SAT, UK

Qatar Academy
PO Box 1129, Al Luqta Street, Doha, Qatar
Tel: +974 4454 2000
Director: Eric W Sands
Age range: 3–18
No. of pupils: 1683
Fees: QR16,145–QR42,678
Curriculum: IBDP, IBMYP, IBPYP
Language instr: English
(CIS) (ECIS)

Qatar Academy Al Khor
P.O. Box: 60774 – Doha, Al Khor, Qatar
Tel: +974 454 6752
Head of School: Ghada Bou Zeineddine
Curriculum: IBMYP
Language instr: English

Qatar Academy Al Wakra
PO Box 2589, Doha, Qatar
Tel: +974 4454 7418
Principal: Bedriyah Itani
Language instr: English
(ECIS)

Qatar International School
PO Box 5697, Doha, Qatar
Tel: +974 4483 3456
Principal: Joyce M Griffin
Age range: 2–18
No. of pupils: 1350 B720 G630
Fees: US$2,900–US$8,100
Curriculum: UK
Language instr: English

Qatar Leadership Academy
PO Box 24421, Doha, Qatar
Tel: +974 4454 2222
Head of School: Robert Trent
Age range: B11–17
No. of pupils: 90
Fees: QR50,000
Curriculum: IBDP, SAT, TOEFL
Language instr: English
(✈) (🏛) (ECIS)

Sherborne Qatar
PO Box 1108, Doha, Qatar
Tel: +974 4459 6400
Head Master: Michael Weston
Age range: 3–18
No. of pupils: B400 G400 VIth40
Curriculum: UK, IGCSE, ALevs
Language instr: English
(✈) (OOB)

The English Modern School
PO Box 875, Doha, Qatar
Tel: +974 4488 3806
Director: Judith Drotar
Age range: 3–18
Curriculum: UK, IGCSE, ALevs

THE GULF ENGLISH SCHOOL
For further details see p. 96
PO Box 2440, Doha, Qatar
Tel: +974 4457 8777
Email: info@gulfenglishschool.com
Website: www.gulfenglishschool.com
Managing Director's Advisor & Business Manager: Mona El Helbawi
Age range: 3–18
No. of pupils: 1535
Curriculum: IBDP, UK
Language instr: English
(CIS)

Republic of Korea

Asia Pacific International School
820 wolgye 2-dong Nowon-gu, Seoul, 139-724 Republic of Korea
Tel: +82 (0)2 907 2747
Director: Euysung Kim
Age range: 4–18
Curriculum: AP, National, USA
Language instr: English
(EAR)

Branksome Hall Asia
613 Gueok-ri, Daejung-eup, Seogwipo City, Jeju, 699-931 Republic of Korea
Tel: +82 26 456 8405
Principal: Glen Radojkovich
Curriculum: IBDP, IBMYP, IBPYP
(✈) (🏛)

Busan Foreign School
#1366-3, Jwa-Dong, Haeundae-Gu, Busan, 612-030 Republic of Korea
Tel: +82 51 747 7199
Principal: Scott Jolly
Age range: 4–18
No. of pupils: 200
Curriculum: USA
(EAR)

Busan International Foreign School
50 Gijang-daero, Gijang-eup, Gijang-gun, Busan, 619-902 Republic of Korea
Tel: +82 51 742 3332
Head of School: Kevin Baker
Age range: 2–18
No. of pupils: 465 B234 G231 VIth30
Fees: US$10,500–US$23,800
Curriculum: AP, IBDP, IBPYP, SAT, IGCSE
Language instr: English
(CIS) (EAR)

Chadwick International
17-4 SongdoDong, YeonsuGu, Incheon, 406-840 Republic of Korea
Tel: +82 32 250 5101
Head of School: Jeff Mercer
Curriculum: IBPYP
Language instr: English

Dulwich College Seoul
5-1 Banpo-2-dong, Seocho-Gu, Seoul 137-800, Republic of Korea
Tel: +82 2 3015 8500
Headmaster: Daryl Orchard
Age range: 1–13
No. of pupils: 400
Curriculum: UK

DWIGHT SCHOOL SEOUL
For further details see p. 81
21 World Cup Buk-ro 62-gil, Mapo-gu, Seoul, 121-835 Republic of Korea
Tel: +82 2 6920 8600
Email: admissions@dwight.or.kr
Website: www.dwight.or.kr
Head: Kevin Skeoch
Age range: 3–18
No. of pupils: B186 G145
Curriculum: IBDP, IBMYP, IBPYP, SAT

Gyeongam International Foreign School
49-22, Jodong-gil, Sanam-myeon, Sacheon-si, Gyeongnam, 664-942 Republic of Korea
Tel: +82 558 535 125
Director: John Ha
Language instr: English
(EAR)

Gyeonggi Academy of Foreign Languages
San 21-2 Gocheon-dong, Uiwang City, Gyeonggi Province 139206 Republic of Korea
Tel: +82 31 361 0560
Head of School: Sung Eun Jeon
Curriculum: IBDP
(🏛)

Gyeonggi Suwon International School
29-3 Youngtong-dong, Youngtong-gu, Suwon, Gyeonggi-do 443-808 Republic of Korea
Tel: +82 31 695 2838
Head of School: John Nelson
Curriculum: IBDP, IBMYP, IBPYP
Language instr: English
(🏛) (EAR)

Hyundai Foreign School
260 Sebudong, Dong-Gu, Ulsan, Kyung Nam, Republic of Korea
Tel: +82 52 250 2851/2
Head: Livingstone
Age range: 3–11
No. of pupils: 50 B25 G25
Curriculum: SAT, UK
(CIS) (ECIS)

International Christian School Pyongtaek
367-3 Shindae dong, Pyongtaek, 450-820 Republic of Korea
Tel: +82 316 511 376
Director: Meredith O'Hara
Language instr: English
(EAR)

International Christian School Uijongbu
375-2 Nogyang-dong, Gyeonggi-do, Uijeongbu-si, Republic of Korea
Tel: +82 318 551 276
Director: Rex Freel
Language instr: English
(EAR)

Korea International School
373-6 Baekhyun-dong, Bundang-gu, Seonhnam-si, Gyeonggi-do, 463-420 Republic of Korea
Tel: +82 31 789 0505
Director: Stephen Cathers
Age range: 4–18

North London Collegiate School Jeju
San 1-6 Gueok-lee, Daejeong-eup, Seogwipo City, Jeju-do 699931 Republic of Korea
Tel: +82 647938300
Head of School: Peter Daly
Curriculum: IBDP
(🏛)

Okpo International School
302 Okpo 1 Dong, Geoje-
Si, Kyungnam 656131
Republic of Korea
Tel: +82 55 687 3283
Principal: Myles Jackson
Age range: 4–14
No. of pupils: 150 B80 G70
Curriculum: SAT, UK, USA
Language instr: English
(ECIS)

Seoul Foreign British School
39 Yeonhui-ro 22 gil,
Seodaemun-gu, Seoul 120-
823, Republic of Korea
Tel: +82 2 330 3100
Headteacher: Timothy Grey
Age range: 3–14
No. of pupils: 300
Curriculum: SAT, UK
Language instr: English

Seoul Foreign School
39 Yeonhui-ro 22 gil,
Seodaemun-gu, Seoul 120-
823, Republic of Korea
Tel: +82 2 330 3100
Head of School: Colm Flanagan
Age range: 3–18
No. of pupils: 1450
Curriculum: ACT, AP, IBDP,
SAT, UK, USA, IGCSE
Language instr: English
(EAR)

Seoul International School
388-14 Bokjeong-dong, Sujeong-
gu, Seongnam, Gyeonggi-do,
Seoul, 461-200 Republic of Korea
Tel: +82 31 750 1200
Headmaster: Kim Hyung-Shik
Age range: 4–19
No. of pupils: 999 B490 G509
(EAR)

**Taejon Christian
International School**
77 Yongsan 2 Ro, Yuseong
Gu, Daejeon, 305-500
Republic of Korea
Tel: +82 42 620 9000
Head of School: Thomas J Penland
No. of pupils: 600
Curriculum: IBDP, IBMYP, IBPYP
Language instr: English
(⚓)(EAR)

**Yongsan International
School of Seoul**
San 10-213 Hannam 2 dong,
Yongsan ku, Seoul, 140-
210 Republic of Korea
Tel: +82 2 797 5104
Headmaster: Jeff Pinnow
Age range: 5–17
Curriculum: USA
Language instr: English
(EAR)

Saudi Arabia

**Advanced Learning
Schools**
PO Box 221985, Riyadh,
11311 Saudi Arabia
Tel: +966 1 207 0926
Superintendent: Iain Stirling
Age range: 4–18
No. of pupils: 437
Fees: SR55,000
Curriculum: IBDP, IBMYP, IBPYP
Language instr: English
(CIS)

**Ajial Aseer
International School**
PO Box 43, Khamis
Mushayt, Saudi Arabia
Tel: +966 7 237 5079
Principal: Hala Al-Hagan
Age range: 4–15
No. of pupils: 180 B100 G80
Language instr: English

Al Hussan Academy
PO Box 297, Dammam
31411, Saudi Arabia
Tel: +966 3 882 5425
Head Teacher: Chris Spedding
Age range: 3–18
No. of pupils: 684 B351 G333
Fees: SR9,500–SR18,000
Curriculum: UK, USA

**Al Waha International
School**
PO Box 12491, Jeddah,
21473 Saudi Arabia
Tel: +966 2 672 9660
Director: Zia Nadwi
Age range: 3–16
No. of pupils: 668 B388 G280

**Al-Hussan International
School**
PO Box 297, Dammam,
31411 Saudi Arabia
Tel: +966 3 858 7566/67/71
Director: Raed Abu-Rumman
Age range: 3–18
No. of pupils: 1100
Curriculum: IBDP, IGCSE, ALevs
(CIS)

**American International
School – Riyadh**
PO Box 990, Riyadh,
11421 Saudi Arabia
Tel: +966 11 491 4270
Superintendent: Brian Matthews
Age range: 4–18
No. of pupils: 1355
Fees: SR30,123
Curriculum: IBDP, USA
Language instr: English
(CIS)(ECIS)

**American International
School of Jeddah**
P.O. Box 127328, Jeddah
21352, Saudi Arabia
Tel: +966 2 662 0051
Superintendent: Mark A English
Age range: 3–19
No. of pupils: 600 B300 G300
Curriculum: AP, SAT

Bayan Gardens School
PO Box 180, Al Khobar,
31952 Saudi Arabia
Tel: +966 3 882 2645
Age range: 3–13
No. of pupils: 350
Curriculum: USA
Language instr: Arabic, English

**British International
School of Al Khobar**
PO Box 4359, Al Khobar
31952, Saudi Arabia
Tel: +966 3 882 5425
Principal: David Greetham
Age range: 3–18
No. of pupils: 450
Fees: SR31,000
Curriculum: SAT, UK, IGCSE
Language instr: English
(CIS)

**British International
School Riyadh**
PO Box 85769, Al Hamra,
Riyadh, 11612 Saudi Arabia
Tel: +966 11 248 2387/0386
Principal: Chris Mantz
Age range: 3–16
No. of pupils: 900
Curriculum: UK
Language instr: English

**Dhahran Baccalaureate
Centre**
PO Box 31677, Al-Khobar,
31952 Saudi Arabia
Tel: +966 3 330 0555 x 2420
Head of School: David Dorn
Curriculum: IBDP
(⚓)

**Dhahran British
Grammar School**
PO Box 31677, Alkhobar
31952, Saudi Arabia
Tel: +966 3 330 0555 ext 2003
Principal: Ian Jones
Age range: 4–16
No. of pupils: 400 B200 G200
(CIS)

**Dhahran Elementary/
Middle School**
PO Box 31677, Al Khobar,
31952 Saudi Arabia
Tel: +966 3 330 0555

Dhahran High School
PO Box 31677, Al Khobar,
31952 Saudi Arabia
Tel: +966 3 330 0555

**International
Schools Group**
PO Box 31677, Al Khobar,
31952 Saudi Arabia
Tel: +966 3 330 0555
Superintendent: Fred Bowen
Age range: 4–18
No. of pupils: 2126 B1168 G958
Curriculum: AP, SAT
(ECIS)

**International Schools
Group Jubail (ISG Jubail)**
PO Box 10059, Jubail,
31961 Saudi Arabia
Tel: +966 13 341 7550
Principal: Daniel Mock
Age range: Pre-K–Grade 11
No. of pupils: 410 B210 G200
Fees: SR14,070–SR54,090
Curriculum: USA
Language instr: English

**Jeddah Knowledge
International School**
Al Salamah District,
Mohammed Mosaud St. (Behind
Iceland), PO Box 7180, 21462
Jeddah, Saudi Arabia
Tel: +966 2 691 7367
**Executive Director
(Founder):** Elham Al Fadli
Age range: 3–18
No. of pupils: 2014
Curriculum: IBDP, IBMYP,
IBPYP, National, USA
Language instr: English, Arabic
(CIS)(ECIS)

**Jeddah Prep and
Grammar School**
PO Box 6316, Jeddah
21442, Saudi Arabia
Tel: +966 2 654 2354
Headmaster: Arshad Ashraf
Age range: 3–18 B3–18 G3–18
No. of pupils: 593 B450 G450 VIth83
Fees: Day £21,300–£61,500
SR21,300–SR55,815
Curriculum: UK, IGCSE, ALevs
Language instr: English

Jubail International School
PO Box 10957, Jubail,
31961 Saudi Arabia
Tel: +966 3 341 8710
Director: James Lepkowski
Age range: 3–18
No. of pupils: 357 B181 G176
Fees: SR9,500–SR18,000
Curriculum: UK, USA
(CIS)

KAUST Schools
PO Box 55455, Jeddah,
21534 Saudi Arabia
Tel: +966 2 808 6810
Head of School: Madeline Hewitt
Curriculum: IBDP, IBMYP, IBPYP
Language instr: English

King Faisal Pre-School
PO Box 94558, Riyadh,
11614 Saudi Arabia
Tel: +966 1 482 0802
Head of School: Sadeem Alkadi
Curriculum: IBPYP
Language instr: English, Arabic

King Faisal School
PO Box 94558, Riyadh,
11614 Saudi Arabia
Tel: +966 1 482 0802
Head of School: Sulaiman AlFraih
No. of pupils: 727
Fees: SR30,000–SR50,000
Curriculum: IBDP, IBMYP,
IBPYP, National, SAT, TOEFL
Language instr: English, Arabic

Nada International School
PO Box 1065, Al-Ahsa,
31982 Saudi Arabia
Tel: +966 3532 3338
Principal: Tony Flynn
Language instr: English

**Pakistan International
School (English
Section) Jeddah**
PO Box 4690, Al-Rehab District,
Jeddah 21412, Saudi Arabia
Tel: +966 50 564 5438
Principal: Sehar Kamran
Age range: 3–18
Fees: SR7,000–SR14,000
Curriculum: UK, IGCSE, ALevs

Riyadh Schools
An Namudhajiyah, Prince Fahd bin
Salman Road, Riyadh, Saudi Arabia
Tel: +966 01 4028411
Director General: Ron Lake
Language instr: English, Arabic

Saudi Aramco Schools
Dhahran 31311, Saudi Arabia
Tel: +966 3 877 1675
Principal: D Owen Harrison
Age range: 5–15
No. of pupils: 2040
Curriculum: SAT, USA

Tabuk Primary School
TGV Compound, PO Box
2, Tabuk, Saudi Arabia
Tel: +966 (0)4 428 2976/77
Head: David Holgate
Age range: 4–11
Curriculum: UK

**The British International
School of Jeddah**
PO Box 6453, Jeddah,
21442 Saudi Arabia
Tel: +966 1 2 699 0019
Director: Bruce Gamwell
Age range: 3–18
No. of pupils: B843 G688 VIth140
Fees: SR28,000–SR68,400
Curriculum: IBDP, IGCSE
Language instr: English

Singapore

**ACS (International),
Singapore**
61 Jalan Hitam Manis,
Singapore, 278475 Singapore
Tel: +658 6472 1477
Principal: Rob Burrough
Age range: 11–19
No. of pupils: 960
Fees: S$24,000–S$27,000
Curriculum: IBDP, IGCSE
Language instr: English

**Anglo-Chinese School
(Independent)**
121 Dover Road, Singapore,
139650 Singapore
Tel: +65 6773 1633
Principal: Winston Hodge
Age range: B13–18 G17–18
No. of pupils: 2898 B2664 G234
Curriculum: IBDP, UK
Language instr: English

**AUSTRALIAN
INTERNATIONAL
SCHOOL, SINGAPORE**
For further details see p. 76
1 Lorong Chuan,
556818 Singapore
Tel: +65 6883 5155
Email: enquiries@ais.com.sg
Website: www.ais.com.sg
Principal: Nick Miller
Age range: 3–18
No. of pupils: 2600
Fees: S$16,276–S$40,034
Curriculum: IBDP, IBPYP, National
Language instr: English

**Canadian International
School**
7 Jurong West Street 41,
Singapore, 649414 Singapore
Tel: +65 6467 1732
Head of School: Glenn Odland
Age range: 3–18
No. of pupils: 2500
Curriculum: IBDP, IBMYP, IBPYP
Language instr: English

**Canadian International
School, Tanjong
Katong Campus**
371 Tanjong Katong Road,
Singapore, 437128 Singapore
Tel: +65 6345 1573
Head of School: Glenn Odland
Curriculum: IBMYP, IBPYP

**Chatsworth
International School**
37 Emerald Hill Road, Singapore,
229313 Singapore
Tel: +65 6737 5955
Head of School: Tyler Sherwood
Age range: 3–18
No. of pupils: 715 B350 G365
Curriculum: IBDP, IBPYP, USA
Language instr: English

**Chatsworth International
School – East Campus**
25 Jalan Tembusu, Singapore,
438234 Singapore
Tel: +65 6344 5955
Head of School: Tyler Sherwood
Curriculum: IBPYP
Language instr: English

**Chinese International
School**
60-62 Dunearn Road,
Singapore, 309434 Singapore
Tel: +65 6254 0200
Principal: Zhong Hua
Age range: 3–19
No. of pupils: B199 G176
Curriculum: IBDP, IBPYP
Language instr: English

**Dover Court
Preparatory School**
Dover Court, Dover Road,
Singapore 139644, Singapore
Tel: +65 775 7664
Principal: Maureen Roach
Age range: 3–16
No. of pupils: 650 B350 G300
Fees: S$20,100
Curriculum: UK
Language instr: English

**EtonHouse International
Pre-School**
2 Orchard Boulevard,
Singapore, 248643 Singapore
Tel: +65 62523322
Head of School: Leanne Sunarya
Curriculum: IBPYP

**EtonHouse International
School**
51 Broadrick Road, Singapore,
439501 Singapore
Tel: +65 6346 6922
Head of School: Rob Stewart
Age range: 3–11
No. of pupils: 507
Curriculum: IBPYP
Language instr: English

**EtonHouse Preschool
– Newton Road**
39 Newton Road, Singapore,
307966 Singapore
Tel: +65 63523322
Head of School: Gabrielle
Macdonald
Age range: 18 months–6
Curriculum: IBPYP
Language instr: English

**German European
School Singapore**
72 Bukit Tinggi Road, Singapore,
289760 Singapore
Tel: +65 6469 1131
Head of School: Torsten Steininger
Curriculum: Abitur, IBPYP
Language instr: German, English

**German European School,
Singapore**
72 Bukit Tinggi Road, Singapore,
289760 Singapore
Tel: +65 6469 1131
Head of School: Torsten Steininger
Age range: 1.5–18
No. of pupils: 1471
Fees: S$22,100–S$25,610
Curriculum: Abitur, IBDP,
IBMYP, IBPYP, National
Language instr: English, German

**Global Indian
International School**
1 Mei Chin Road, Singapore,
149253 Singapore
Tel: +65 6479 1511
Head of School: Meenakshi Mehta
Age range: 2–18
No. of pupils: 3900
Curriculum: IBDP
Language instr: English

**Hwa Chong
International School**
663 Bukit Timah Road,
Singapore, 269783 Singapore
Tel: +65 6464 7077
Head of School: Chin Nguang Koh
Curriculum: IBDP, GCSE
Language instr: English, Mandarin

ISS International School
21 Preston Road, Singapore,
109355 Singapore
Tel: +65 6475 4188
Head of School: Margaret Alvarez
Age range: 4–18
No. of pupils: 800 B392 G408
Fees: S$10,500–S$30,700
Curriculum: IBDP, IBMYP, IBPYP
Language instr: English

Nexus International School
201 Ulu Pandan Road,
Singapore, 596468 Singapore
Tel: +65 6536 6566
Head of School: Paul Beach
Age range: 2–18
No. of pupils: 350
Fees: S$14,910–S$25,920
Curriculum: IBDP, IBPYP,
UK, IGCSE, ALevs
Language instr: English

NPS International School
10 & 12 Chai Chee Lane,
Singapore, 468201 Singapore
Tel: +65 62942400
Head of School: Matthew Sullivan
No. of pupils: 1400
Fees: S$12,000–S$15,000
Curriculum: IBDP
Language instr: English

Odyssey, The Global Preschool Pte Ltd
101 Wilkinson Road,
436559 Singapore
Tel: +65 6346 1820
Head of School: Kelly Hor Siew Fun
Curriculum: IBPYP
Language instr: English

One World International School
696 Upper Changi Road East,
Singapore, 486826 Singapore
Tel: +65 65422285
Head of School: Elaine
Goddard-Tame
Curriculum: IBPYP

Overseas Family School
25F Paterson Road, Singapore,
238515 Singapore
Tel: +65 6 738 0211
Head of School: Pat Keenan
Age range: 3–18
No. of pupils: 3670 B1893 G1782
Fees: S$20,000–S$25,000
Curriculum: IBDP, IBMYP,
IBPYP, IGCSE
Language instr: English

Pasir Ridge International School
c/o UNOCAL, Locked Bag 3,
Tampines Central Post Office,
Singapore, 91586 Singapore
Tel: +65 542 543474
Principal: Seamus Marriott
Age range: 3–15
Language instr: English
(EAR)

School of the Arts, Singapore
1 Zubir Said Drive, Administration
Office #05-01, Singapore,
227968 Singapore
Tel: +65 63389663
Head of School: Geok Cheng Lim
Curriculum: IBDP, IBCC
Language instr: English

Singapore American School
40 Woodlands Street 41,
Singapore 738547, Singapore
Tel: +65 6363 3403
Principal: Don Bergman
Age range: 3–21
No. of pupils: 2196
Curriculum: ACT, AP,
SAT, TOEFL, USA
(EAR)

St Joseph's Institution International
490 Thomson Road, Singapore,
298191 Singapore
Tel: +65 6353 9383
**Principal of High
School:** Bradley Roberts
Age range: 6–18
No. of pupils: 675
Fees: S$19,998
Curriculum: IBDP, IGCSE
Language instr: English
(icon)

STAMFORD AMERICAN INTERNATIONAL SCHOOL
For further details see p. 92
1 Woodleigh Lane (off
Upper Serangoon Road),
357684 Singapore
Tel: +65 6602 7247
Email: admissions@sais.edu.sg
Website: www.sais.edu.sg
Superintendent: Malcolm Kay
Age range: 2–18
No. of pupils: 1650
Curriculum: IBDP,
IBMYP, IBPYP, USA
Language instr: English
(CIS)

TANGLIN TRUST SCHOOL, SINGAPORE
For further details see p. 94
92 Portsdown Road,
139299 Singapore
Tel: +65 67780771
Email: admissions@tts.edu.sg
Website: www.tts.edu.sg
Head of School: Peter
Derby-Crook
Age range: 3–18
No. of pupils: 2730
Fees: *Day* S$23,754–S$39,467
Curriculum: IBDP, ALevs
Language instr: English

UWC South East Asia
1207 Dover Road, Singapore,
139654 Singapore
Tel: +65 6 775 5344
Head of College: Julian Whiteley
Age range: 4–18
No. of pupils: 2998
Curriculum: IBDP
Language instr: English
(icon) (CIS) (EAR) (ECIS) (RS)

UWC South East Asia
East Campus, 1 Tampines Street
73, Singapore, 528704 Singapore
Tel: +65 63055344
Head of College: Julian Whiteley
Age range: 4–18
No. of pupils: 2400
Curriculum: IBDP
Language instr: English
(icon) (EAR) (ECIS) (RS)

Sri Lanka

Colombo International School
28 Gregory's Road,
Colombo 7, Sri Lanka
Tel: +94 11 2697 587
Principal: David Sanders
Age range: 2–18
No. of pupils: 1443 B781
G662 VIth280
Fees: *Day* US$2,500–US$4,000
Curriculum: SAT, UK, IGCSE, ALevs
Language instr: English

Elizabeth Moir School
4/20 Thalakotuwa Gardens,
Colombo 5, Sri Lanka
Tel: +941 1 2512275
Head of School: Elizabeth Moir
Age range: 2–18
No. of pupils: 400 B200 G200 VIth80
Fees: US$2,000–US$5,000
Curriculum: SAT, TOEFL,
UK, IGCSE, ALevs
Language instr: English

The British School in Colombo
63 Elvitigala Mawatha, Mawatha,
Colombo 08, Sri Lanka
Tel: +94 (11) 532 9329
Principal: John Scarth
Age range: 2–18
Curriculum: IBDP, UK, IGCSE, ALevs
Language instr: English

The Overseas School of Colombo
PO Box 9, Pelawatte,
Battaramulla, 10120 Sri Lanka
Tel: +94 11 2784 920-2
Head of School: Areta Williams
Age range: 3–18
No. of pupils: 420
Fees: US$8,270–US$18,840
Curriculum: IBDP, IBMYP, IBPYP
Language instr: English
(AISA) (CIS)

Sultanate of Oman

ABA – An IB World School
PO Box 372, Medinat Al Sultan
Qaboos, Post Code 115, Muscat,
115 Sultanate of Oman
Tel: +968 24603646
Superintendent: Mona
Nashman-Smith
Age range: 3–18
No. of pupils: 996 B521 G475 VIth66
Fees: *Day* £4,345–£10,540
Curriculum: IBDP, IBMYP,
IBPYP, SAT, IGCSE
Language instr: English
(ECIS)

Al Batinah International School
PO Box 193, Postal Code 321,
Sohar, Sultanate of Oman
Tel: +968 26850001
Head of School: Neil Tomalin
Curriculum: IBDP, IBPYP

Al Sahwa Schools
PO Box 644, PC 116, Mina-Al-Fahal,
Muscat, Sultanate of Oman
Tel: + 968 24607620
Director: Simon Head
Age range: 3–17
No. of pupils: 1191 B595 G620
Fees: RO1,500–RO3,100
Curriculum: IBPYP,
National, UK, IGCSE
Language instr: English/Arabic

Al Shomoukh International School
Sheikh Salim Al Hashimy Al Seeb
Al Khoud Street Building, Number
381, Muscat, Sultanate of Oman
Tel: +96 89 29 62 715
Language instr: English
(ECIS)

American International School of Muscat
PO Box 584, Azaiba Postal Code
130, Sultanate of Oman
Tel: +968 2459 5180
Director: Kevin Schafer
Age range: 3–19
No. of pupils: 635 B312 G323
Fees: $8,925
Curriculum: AP, USA
(CIS)

Muscat International School
PO Box 1031, Postal Code 112,
Ruwi, Sultanate of Oman
Tel: +968 24565550
Principal: Brian McCormack
Age range: 3–18
No. of pupils: 880 B502 G378
Curriculum: National, SAT,
TOEFL, UK, IGCSE, ALevs
Language instr: English
(CIS)

The British School – Muscat
PO Box 1907 Ruwi, Postal Code
112, Sultanate of Oman
Tel: +96 82 460 842
Principal: Steve Howland
Age range: 3–18
No. of pupils: 900 B450 G450
Fees: OMR2,400–OMR5,880
Curriculum: UK, ALevs
Language instr: English

The British School Salalah
PO Box 71, Salalah 214,
Sultanate of Oman
Tel: +968 23235242
Head Teacher: Norah O'Neill
Age range: 4–12
No. of pupils: 40
Curriculum: UK

The Indian School
PO Box 1887, CPO Seeb,
Postal Code 111, Muscat,
111 Sultanate of Oman
Tel: +968 24491587
Principal: Papri Ghosh
Age range: 3–18
No. of pupils: 3125 B1596 G1529
Fees: US$1,272
Curriculum: TOEFL
Language instr: English

The Sultan's School
PO Box 665, Seeb, 121
Sultanate of Oman
Tel: +968 24536 777
Principal: Graham Garrett
Age range: 3–18
No. of pupils: 1300
Fees: RO1,400–RO3,000
Curriculum: IBDP, IGCSE
Language instr: Arabic, English

Syrian Arab Republic

ICARDA International School of Aleppo
PO Box 5466, Aleppo,
Syrian Arab Republic
Tel: +963 21 574 3104
Head of School: Shirley Davis
Age range: 3–17
No. of pupils: 281 B179 G102
Fees: US$3,933–US$13,486
Curriculum: IBDP, IBPYP, SAT, TOEFL
Language instr: English

Taiwan

American School in Taichung
406 Beitun District,
Taichung City, Taiwan
Tel: +886 4 2239 7532
Director: Andrew W. Corcoran
Language instr: English

Dominican International School
76 Tah Chih Street,
Taipei 104, Taiwan
Tel: +886 2 2533 8451
Headmistress: Maria Begona Divinagracia OP
Age range: 4–17
No. of pupils: 465

Hsinchu International
Niu Pu East Road, #290,
Hsinchu 30091, Taiwan
Tel: +886 3 538 8113
Head of School: Rowena Lines
Age range: 4–18
No. of pupils: 260 B122 G128
Fees: NT$255,000–NT$480,000
Curriculum: AP, SAT, USA
Language instr: English

I-Shou International School
No 6, Sec 1, Xuecheng Rd., Dashu
Dist., Kaohsiung City, 840 Taiwan
Tel: +886 7 657 7115
Principal: Yu-Yi Huang
Age range: 5–18
No. of pupils: 600
Fees: NT$120,000–NT$150,000
Curriculum: IBDP, IBMYP, IBPYP, SAT, TOEFL
Language instr: English, Chinese

Ivy Collegiate Academy
320, Lane 165, Section 1,
Tan-Hsing Rd, Tan-Tzu Shiang/
Taichung, Taiwan
Tel: +886 4 25395011
Head: John Cheska
Age range: 12–17

Kaohsiung American School
35 Sheng Li Road, Zuo-Ying
District, Kaohsiung, Taiwan
Tel: +886 7 583 0112
Head of School: Thomas Farrell
Age range: 4–18
No. of pupils: 505
Curriculum: AP, IBDP, USA
Language instr: English

Morrison Academy
System Services, 136-1 Shui Nan
Road, Taichung 40679, Taiwan
Tel: +886 4 2297 3927
Superintendent: Tim McGill
Age range: 5–18
No. of pupils: 800 B400 G400
Fees: US$12,000–US$14,000
Curriculum: AP, SAT, USA
Language instr: English

Pacific American School
3F, No. 151, Section 2, Kuang-Fu
Road, Hsinchu, 30071 Taiwan
Tel: +886 3 571 7070
Head of School: Pamela Chu

Taipei Adventist American School
No. 64 Lane 80 Zhuang Ding
Rd., Shihlin 111, Taipei, Taiwan
Tel: 02-2861-6400
Principal: David Robinson
Curriculum: USA

Taipei American School
800 Chung Shan North Road,
Sec 6, Taipei, Taiwan
Tel: +886 22 873 9900
Superintendent: Sharon Hennessy
Age range: 4–17
No. of pupils: 2235 B1115 G1120
Fees: NT$508,415–NT$563,855
Curriculum: AP, IBDP, SAT, USA
Language instr: English

Taipei European School
Swire European Campus, 31
Jian Ye Road, Yang Ming Shan,
Shihlin, Taipei 11193 Taiwan
Tel: +886 2 8145 9007
CEO: Allan Weston
Age range: 3–18
No. of pupils: 1157
Fees: US$4,000–US$15,000
Curriculum: IBDP, SAT, UK
Language instr: English, French, German

Tajikistan

Dushanbe International School
Bofande Ulitsa 9,
Dushanbe, Tajikistan
Tel: +992 372 214947
Superintendent: Hamza Akturkoglu
Age range: 5–18
No. of pupils: 135 B84 G51
Fees: US$2,000–US$9,000

QSI International School of Dushanbe
Sovetskaya 85, Dushanbe,
734001 Tajikistan
Tel: +992 37 224 8559/8560
Director: Lois Bridenback
Age range: 3–13
No. of pupils: 30
Curriculum: USA
Language instr: English

Thailand

Adventist International Mission School
195 Moo 3, Muaklek,
Saraburi 18180, Thailand
Tel: +66 036 720 675

AIT International School
Km. 42, Phaholyothin
Highway, Klong Luang,
Patumthani 12120, Thailand
Tel: +66 (0)2 524 5984
Principal/Head: Kevin Mauritson
Age range: 3–12
No. of pupils: 285
Curriculum: National

American Pacific International School
158/1 Moo 3, Hangdong-Samoeng
Road, Banpong, Hangdong,
Chiang Mai 50230, Thailand
Tel: +66 53 365 303/5
Headmaster: Ross Hall
Age range: 3–18
No. of pupils: 121 B70 G51
Curriculum: IBPYP
Language instr: English

Anglo Singapore International School
341 Sukhumvit 31 (Soi Si Yak
Sawatdee), Klongtan, Wattana,
Bangkok, 10110 Thailand
Tel: +66 02 662 3105 6
Director: Julie Sutanto
Age range: 3–12
No. of pupils: 211 B107 G104
Curriculum: National, UK
Language instr: English, Thai, Chinese

Ascot International School
Soi Ramkamhaeng 118, Sapansung,
Bangkok, 10240 Thailand
Tel: +66 2 373 4400
Headmistress: Vanessa Armstrong
Age range: 2–18
No. of pupils: 169 B145 G124
Curriculum: UK

Bangkok Adventist International School
P.O. Box 234 Prakhanong,
Klongtan Nua, Wattana,
Bangkok, 10110 Thailand
Tel: +66 2 381 9406
Director: Panuwat Kattiya
Age range: 4–17
No. of pupils: B54 G46
Fees: Baht127,000
Curriculum: USA
Language instr: English

Bangkok Christian International School
53 Soi 44 Pattanakarn Road, Suan
Luang, Bangkok 10250, Thailand
Tel: +662 322 1979
Principal: Moonsu Song
Age range: 4–18
No. of pupils: 300
Curriculum: AP, USA

Bangkok Grace International School
79/3-12 Latphrao Soi 112,
Wangthonglang, Bangkok,
10310 Thailand
Tel: +66 2 539 4516/7/8
Principal: Sirima
Age range: 3–18
No. of pupils: 92 B48 G44
Curriculum: USA
Language instr: English

Bangkok International Preparatory & Secondary School
23 Sukhumvit 53 Wattana,
Bangkok, 10110 Thailand
Tel: +66 2 260 7890
Headmaster: Keith Wecker
Age range: 3–16
No. of pupils: 700 B380 G320
Curriculum: UK, ALevs
Language instr: English

Bangkok Patana School
643 La Salle Road, Sukhumvit
105, Bangkok, 10260 Thailand
Tel: +66 2 785 2200
Head of School: Matthew G Mills
Age range: 2–18
No. of pupils: 2185 B1100 G1085
Fees: THB411,615–THB738,600
Curriculum: IBDP, IGCSE
Language instr: English
(CIS) (EAR)

**Berkeley International
School**
123 Bangna-Trad Road, Bangna,
Bangkok, 10260 Thailand
Tel: +662(0)2 747-4788
Head of School: Michael Gohde
(EAR)

**British Columbia
International School**
608/1 Kalaprapruk Road,
Bangwar, Phasicharoen,
Bangkok, 10160 Thailand
Tel: +66 2 802 1188
Principal: Brenda Krause
Age range: 12–18
Curriculum: National

**BRITISH INTERNATIONAL
SCHOOL, PHUKET**
For further details see p. 80
59 Moo 2, Thepkrasattri
Road, Koh Kaew, Muang,
Phuket 83000 Thailand
Tel: +66 (076) 335555
Email: info@bisphuket.ac.th
Website: www.bisphuket.ac.th
Head of School: Neil M Richards
Age range: 18 months–18 years
No. of pupils: 840
Fees: *Day* THB245,000–
THB600,600 *WB* THB251,200–
THB294,800 *FB* THB300,300–
THB327,600
Curriculum: IBDP, UK, IGCSE
Language instr: English
(金) (CIS)

British School Bangkok Ltd
36 Sukhumvit Soi 4, Soi Nana,
Bangkok, 10110 Thailand
Tel: +66 2 656 7734
Principal: June Bond
Age range: 2–11
No. of pupils: 178 B102 G76
Curriculum: SAT, UK
Language instr: English
(CIS)

**Bromsgrove
International School**
Windsor Park & Golf Club, 55 Mu
9 Suwinthawong Road, Minburi,
Bangkok, 10510 Thailand
Tel: +66 2989 4873
Headmaster: Jon Wingfield
Age range: 2–18
No. of pupils: 400 B200 G200
Fees: Baht60,000–Baht480,249
Curriculum: UK, IGCSE, ALevs
Language instr: English
(金) (CIS)

**Charter International
School**
36 Chalermprakiat Ror 9 Road,
Pravate, Bangkok, 10250 Thailand
Tel: +66 2 7268283/4
Headteacher: Jon Lane
Age range: 3–16
No. of pupils: B103 G117
Curriculum: IGCSE, ALevs
Language instr: English
(CIS)

**Chiang Mai
International School**
PO Box 38, 13 Chetupon Road,
Chiang Mai 50000, Thailand
Tel: +66 (53) 306152-3
Principal: Lance Potter
Age range: 4–18
Curriculum: AP, USA
(EAR)

**Concordian
International School**
918 Moo 8, Bangna-Trad Highway
Km 7, Bangkaew, Bangplee
Samutprakarn, 10540 Thailand
Tel: +66 2 706 9000
School Director: Varnnee Ross
Age range: 2–18
No. of pupils: B361 G309
Fees: THB397,200–THB62,760
Curriculum: IBDP, IBMYP, IBPYP
Language instr: English, Chinese
(CIS) (EAR)

**Ekamai International
School**
57 Ekamai 12 (Soi Charoenjai),
Sukhumvit 63 Road, Klongtan Neua,
Wattana, Bangkok, 10110 Thailand
Tel: +66 023 913 593
**Principal of Academic
Administration:** Harold Dawat
Language instr: English
(EAR)

**Garden International
School (Bangkok campus)**
2/1 Yen Akart Soi 2, Yen Akart Road,
Sathorn, Bangkok 10120 Thailand
Tel: +66 2249 1880
Principal: Jeremy Stokes
Age range: 2–16
No. of pupils: 200 B99 G101
Fees: THB60,000–THB404,000
Curriculum: IGCSE
Language instr: English

**Garden International
School (Rayong Campus)**
188/24 Pala-Ban Chang Road,
Tambol Pala, Amphur Ban
Chang, Rayong 21130 Thailand
Tel: +66 38 880 360
Principal: Stuart Tasker
Age range: 2–18
No. of pupils: B210 G220 VIth36
Fees: THB70,000–THB404,000
Curriculum: IBDP, UK, IGCSE
Language instr: English
(金) (CIS)

**Harrow International
School**
45 Soi Kosonruamchai 14,
Kosonruamchai, Road,
Kwaeng Sikun, Don Muang,
Bangkok 10110, Thailand
Tel: +66 02 503 7222
Headmaster: Kevin Riley
Age range: 3–18
No. of pupils: 1081 B582 G499
Fees: Baht305,380–Baht556,880
Curriculum: UK
(金) (CIS)

**Heathfield International
School**
10/22 Moo 4, Sukhapiban
3 (Rakhambaeng Road),
Saphansung, Bangkok, Thailand
Tel: +662 372 2678
Head: Peter Hartnell
Age range: 2–15
No. of pupils: 154 B74 G80
Curriculum: UK
(CIS)

**International School
Bangkok**
39/7 Soi Nichada Thani,
Samakee Road, Pakkret,
Nonthaburi, 11120 Thailand
Tel: +66 2 963 5800
Head of School: Andrew Davies
Age range: 4–18
No. of pupils: 1800
Fees: Baht427,000–Baht773,000
Curriculum: AP, IBDP
Language instr: English
(EAR)

**International School
Eastern Seaboard**
PO Box 6, Banglamung,
Chonburi, 20150 Thailand
Tel: +66 (0) 38 372 591
Head of School: Robert Brewitt
Age range: 3–18
No. of pupils: 350
Curriculum: IBDP
Language instr: English
(EAR)

**Kevalee International
School**
Benjarong Villa, Ramkhamhaeng
178, Thailand
Tel: +66 2916 7594
Age range: 4–12

**Kiddykare International
Kindergarten**
59/34 Sukhumvit 26, Klongton,
Bangkok 10110, Thailand
Tel: +66 2665 6777
Age range: 18 months–6 years
No. of pupils: B11 G29
Fees: $4,100
Curriculum: UK
Language instr: English

**Kids Academy
International Pre-School**
52/1-2 Sukhumvit 63, Soi 2,
Bangkok 10110, Thailand
Tel: +66 2 714 3636
Curriculum: UK

**Kincaid International
School of Bangkok**
205/73-74, Pasooksanti3,
Pattanakarn 69, Pravej,
Bangkok 10250, Thailand
Tel: +66 2 321 7010
Age range: 4–17

**KIS INTERNATIONAL
SCHOOL**
For further details see p. 88
999/124 Pracha Utit Road,
Samsennok, Huay Kwang,
Bangkok, 10320 Thailand
Tel: +66 (0)2 2743444
Email: admissions@kis.ac.th
Website: www.kis.ac.th
Head of School: Sally Holloway
Age range: 2–18
No. of pupils: 550
Fees: Baht281,000–Baht591,000
Curriculum: IBDP, IBMYP, IBPYP
Language instr: English
(CIS)

**Ladybird International
Kindergarten**
21 Soi Promsri 2, Sukhumvit 39,
Bangkok 10110, Thailand
Tel: +66 2382 3338
Age range: 18 months–5
Curriculum: UK, USA
Language instr: English

**Lanna International
School Thailand**
300 Grandview Moo 1, Chiang
Mai to Hang Dong Road,
Chiang Mai, 50100 Thailand
Tel: +66 53 806230/1
Head of School: Roy Lewis
Age range: 3–18
No. of pupils: B166 G139 VIth35
Curriculum: SAT, UK, IGCSE, ALevs
Language instr: English
(EAR)

**Lycee Francais
International de Bangkok**
498, soi Rhamkhamhaeng 39
(Thep Leela 1), Wangthonglang,
Bangkok 10310, Thailand
Tel: +66 2 934 8008
Language instr: French

**Magic Years International
Kindergarten**
59/307-308 Muangthong Thani,
Chaengwattana Soi 29, Pakkred,
Nonthaburri, 11120 Thailand
Tel: +66 2 573 4597
Head of School: Khanum Thampi
No. of pupils: 100
Curriculum: IBPYP

Meta International School
66 Moo 1, Baan-Suantarn,
Pethkasaem Rd., Tapraya,
Nakhonchaisri Dist.,
Nakhonpathom Province,
73120 Thailand
Tel: +66 34 339310

Mulberry House International Pre-school
7 Soi Tonson, Ploenchit Road,
Lumpini Sub-district, Pathumwan
District, Bangkok 10330, Thailand
Tel: 0 2684 5900
Age range: 2–6
Curriculum: UK
Language instr: English

Nakorn Payap International School
240 M.6 San Phi Sua, Muang,
Chiangmai, 50300 Thailand
Tel: +66 (0) 53 110 680
Principal: John Allen
Age range: 3–17
Curriculum: USA
Language instr: English
(EAR)

New Sathorn International School
289/2, 289/5 Soi Naradhiwas
Rajanakharindra 24, Naradhiwas
Rajanakarindra Rd, Chongnonsri,
Yannawa, Bangkok, 10120 Thailand
Tel: +66 26 722 100-1
Executive Director: Chong Ik Rhee
Age range: 2–17
Curriculum: UK, USA

NIST INTERNATIONAL SCHOOL
For further details see p. 90
36 Soi 15 Sukhumvit Road,
Wattana, Bangkok,
10110 Thailand
Tel: +66 2 651 2065
Email: admissions@nist.ac.th
Website: www.nist.ac.th
Headmaster: James MacDonald
Age range: 3–18
No. of pupils: 1538
Fees: US$12,000–US$22,000
Curriculum: IBDP, IBMYP, IBPYP
Language instr: English
(CIS) (EAR)

Niva International School
2537 Ladprao 101 Road,
Klongchan, Bangkapi,
Bangkok, 10240 Thailand
Tel: +66 2 948 4605-9
Chief Administrator: Ronald Anderson
Age range: 3–18
No. of pupils: 327

Pan-Asia International School
100 Moo 3, Charaemprakiat, Rama
9 St, Soi 67, Kwang Dokmai Prawet
District, Bangkok, 10250 Thailand
Tel: +66 2 726 6273-4
Head of School: Mohammad Noman
Curriculum: IBDP
Language instr: English

Phuket International Academy Day School
115/15 Moo 7 Thepkasattri
Road, Thepkasattri, Thalang,
Phuket, 83110 Thailand
Tel: +66 76 336 076
Head of School: Dennison J MacKinnon
Curriculum: IBDP, IBPYP

Prem Tinsulanonda International School
234 Moo 3, Huay Sai, A.Mae Rim,
Chiang Mai, 50180 Thailand
Tel: +66 503 301 500
Head of School: Maxine Driscoll
Age range: 2–19
No. of pupils: B231 G172
Fees: THB274,060–THB537,660
Curriculum: IBDP, IBMYP, IBPYP, IBCC
Language instr: English
(♨) (CIS) (EAR)

QSI International School of Phuket
81/4 Moo1, Chalermprakiat
r.9 Road, T. Kathu, A. Kathu,
Phuket, 83120 Thailand
Tel: +66 76 304 312
Director: Patrick Buckley
Age range: 3–16
No. of pupils: 126
Curriculum: USA
Language instr: English

Redeemer International School Thailand
6/2 Ramkhamhaeng 184 Road,
Minburi, Bangkok, 10510 Thailand
Tel: +66 2916 6257
Head of School: Somphong Teowtrakul
Age range: 8–17
Curriculum: USA
Language instr: English
(EAR)

Ruamrudee International School
6, Ramkamhaeng 184,
Bangkok, 10510 Thailand
Tel: +662 791 8900
Head of School: Peter Toscano
Age range: 3–20
No. of pupils: 1611 B843 G768
Fees: Baht328,400–Baht477,960
Curriculum: AP, IBDP,
SAT, TOEFL, USA
Language instr: English
(♨) (EAR)

SHREWSBURY INTERNATIONAL SCHOOL
For further details see p. 91
1922 Charoen Krung Road, Wat
Phrayakrai, Bang Kholame,
Bangkok 10120, Thailand
Tel: +66 2 675 1888
Email:
admissions@shrewsbury.ac.th
Website: www.shrewsbury.ac.th
Principal: Stephen Holroyd
Age range: 3–18
No. of pupils: 1600
Curriculum: UK
(CIS)

Singapore International School of Bangkok
Pracha Utit Campus, 498/11 Soi
Ramkhamhaeng 39 (Tepleela 1),
Wangthonglang, Wangthonglang,
Bangkok 10310 Thailand
Tel: +66 2 158 9191
Age range: 2–18
Curriculum: IGCSE, ALevs
Language instr: English,
Chinese, Thai

St Andrews International School (Green Valley)
PO Box 54, Banchang,
Rayong, 21130 Thailand
Tel: +66 (0) 38 030 701-3
Head of School: Andrew Harrison
Age range: 2–18
Curriculum: IBDP, UK, IGCSE
Language instr: English

St Andrews International School Bangkok
9 Pridi Banomyong 20,
Sukhumvit 71, Prakanong,
Bangkok, 10110 Thailand
Tel: +662 381 2387, 4925-6
Head of School: Paul Schofield
Age range: 2–18
No. of pupils: 800
Fees: Baht168,000–Baht415,800
Curriculum: IBDP, IGCSE
Language instr: English
(CIS)

St Andrews International School, Bangna
7 Sukhumvit 107 Road, Bangna,
Bangkok, 10260 Thailand
Tel: +66 2 13933883
Head of School: Iain Colledge
Curriculum: IBDP

St John's International School
1124/1 Phaholyothin Road,
Ladprao, Bangkok, 10900 Thailand
Tel: +66 25138575
Head teacher: David Lowder
Age range: 2–18
No. of pupils: 240 B120 G120
Fees: Baht212,300–Baht366,200
Curriculum: UK, IGCSE, ALevs
Language instr: English

St Stephen's International School
107 Viphavadi-Rangsit
Road, Ladyao, Chatuchak,
Bangkok, 10900 Thailand
Tel: +66 2 513 0270
Superintendent: Richard A Ralphs
Age range: 2–11
No. of pupils: 342 B187 G155
(CIS)

St Stephen's International School, Khao Yai
49/1-3 Moo 4, Thanarat
Road, Nongnamdaeng, Pak
Chong, Nakhon Ratchasima,
30130 Thailand
Tel: +66 (0)864688040
School Principal: Jane Deotrakul
Age range: 5–18
No. of pupils: B60 G50 VIth9
Fees: Baht210,000–Baht392,500
Curriculum: IPC, IGCSE, ALevs
Language instr: English
(♨)

Thai Sikh International School
1799 Rim Thang Road, Fai Kao Moo
1, Samrong Nua, Samutprakarn,
Bangkok, 10270 Thailand
Tel: +66 2 748 5454
Headmaster: M George
Age range: 5–16
No. of pupils: 342
(CIS)

Thai-Chinese International School
101/177 Moo 7 Soi Mooban
Bangpleenives, Prasertsin
Road, Bangplee Yai,
Samutprakarn, 10540 Thailand
Tel: +66 2 751 1201
Curriculum: USA
Language instr: English
(EAR)

The American School of Bangkok
59-59/1 Sukhumvit Road Soi 49/3
Wattana, Bangkok 10110, Thailand
Tel: +66 (0) 2620 8600
Director: John McGrath
Age range: 4–18
Curriculum: USA
(EAR)

The Early Learning Centre International School
18 Soi 49/4 Sukhumvit Road,
Bangkok, 10110 Thailand
Tel: +662 381 2919
Principal: Jacqueline Alexander
No. of pupils: 200
(CIS)

The International School of Samui
141/21 Moo 6, Bophut, Koh Samui, Surat Thani 84320 Thailand
Tel: +66 (0)77 48 45 48
Headmistress: Lisa Taylor Hawkins
Age range: 2–18
No. of pupils: 235 B120 G115
Fees: Baht157,500–Baht310,407
Curriculum: UK, IGCSE, ALevs
Language instr: English
(COB)

The Regent's School
Pattaya, PO Box 33 Naklua, Banglamung, Chonburi, 20150 Thailand
Tel: +66 38 4 734 777
Head of School: Michael Walton
Age range: 2–18
No. of pupils: 1228 B568 G660
Fees: Baht225,000–Baht465,000
Curriculum: IBDP, UK, ALevs
Language instr: English
(symbol)

The Regent's School, Bangkok
592 Pracha-Uthit Road, Huai Kwang, Bangkok, 10310 Thailand
Tel: +66 2 690 3777
Head of School: Martin Kneath
Curriculum: IBDP
Language instr: English
(symbol) (CIS)

Traill International School
36 Soi 18, Ramkangheng Road, Huamark, Bangkok, Thailand
Tel: +66 2 314 5250
Principal: A M Traill
Age range: 5–16
No. of pupils: 160
Curriculum: UK
(ECIS)

Wells International School – On Nut Campus
2209 Sukhumvit Road, Bangchak, Prakanong, Bangkok, 10260 Thailand
Tel: +66 2 730 3366
Curriculum: IBDP
Language instr: English

Turkmenistan

QSI Ashgabat International School
Berzengi, Ataturk St, Ashgabat, Turkmenistan
Tel: +993 12 519027
Director: Francis Redmon
Age range: 3–18
No. of pupils: 190
Curriculum: USA
Language instr: English

United Arab Emirates

Abu Dhabi International Pvt School
Karamah Street, PO Box 25898, Abu Dhabi, United Arab Emirates
Tel: +971 2 4434433
Superintendent: Jihan Nasr
Age range: 3–18
No. of pupils: 3225
Curriculum: IBDP
Language instr: English

Ajman Academy
PO Box 639, Sheikh Ammar Street, Mowaihat, Ajman, United Arab Emirates
Tel: +971 6 731 4444
Director: Anthony Cashin

Al Ain English Speaking School
PO Box 17939, Al – Ain, United Arab Emirates
Tel: +971 3 7678636
Principal: James G Crawford
Age range: 3–18
No. of pupils: 440

Al Bateen Secondary School
PO Box 128484, Abu Dhabi, United Arab Emirates
Tel: +971 2 501 4777
Head of School: Tamra Bradbury
Curriculum: IBDP

Al Dhafra Private School
PO Box 25801, Abu Dhabi, United Arab Emirates
Tel: +971 2 610 8400/1
Principal: Nada Saab
Age range: 3–18
Fees: DHS7,500–DHS13,800
Curriculum: National, UK, USA

Al Ittihad Private School Jumeirah
PO Box 37090, Jumeirah-Dubai, United Arab Emirates
Tel: +971 43 945 111
Director General: Nehad Al Shamsi
Curriculum: USA
Language instr: English
(CIS)

Al Ittihad Private School Mamzar
Cairo Road, Mamzar-Dubai, United Arab Emirates
Tel: +971 42 966 314
Director General: Amna Rafi
Curriculum: USA
Language instr: English
(CIS)

Al Khaleej National School
PO Box 26780, Dubai, United Arab Emirates
Tel: +971 4 2822707
Principal: Nigel Cropley
Age range: 3–18
Fees: AED12,290–AED23,518
Curriculum: SAT, TOEFL, USA
Language instr: English

Al Mawakeb School
PO Box 10799, Dubai, United Arab Emirates
Tel: +971 4 285 1415
President: Nouhad Nasr
Age range: 3–18
Curriculum: National, SAT, TOEFL, USA

Al Nahda International Schools
PO Box 815, Abu Dhabi, United Arab Emirates
Tel: +971 2 445 4200/447
Directors: Jihad Abdul Ghani & Basema Saeed Abdulkh AlJuneibi
Age range: 4–18
No. of pupils: 3500 B1200 G3300
Curriculum: SAT, TOEFL, ALevs
(CIS) (ECIS)

Al Najah Private School
PO Box 284, Abu Dhabi, United Arab Emirates
Tel: +971 2 553 0935
Head of School: Baria Abou Zein
Curriculum: IBDP

Al Rabeeh School
PO Box 41807, Abu Dhabi, United Arab Emirates
Tel: +971 2 4482856
Principal: H J Kadri
Age range: 3–12
No. of pupils: 798 B425 G373
Fees: AED16,000–AED19,200
Curriculum: National, UK
Language instr: English, Arabic

Al Shohub School
PO Box 31515, Abu Dhabi, United Arab Emirates
Tel: +971 2 446 4800
Principal: Elizabeth Bromfield
Age range: B3–9 G3–18
No. of pupils: 435 B115 G320
Fees: AED15,000–AED38,000
Curriculum: UK, ALevs
Language instr: English
(symbol)

Al Yasmina School
PO Box 128484, Abu Dhabi, United Arab Emirates
Tel: +971 2 501 4888
Head of School: Gale
Age range: 3–18
Curriculum: UK

Al-Mizhar American Academy for Girls
PO Box 78484, Dubai, United Arab Emirates
Tel: +971 4 288 7250
Principal: Delice A Scotto
Age range: G4–19
No. of pupils: 650
Fees: AED28,580–AED44,170
Curriculum: USA
(symbol) (CIS)

Al-Worood School
PO Box 46673, Abu Dhabi, United Arab Emirates
Tel: +971 2 444 7655/8855/8990
Academic Controller: Ahmed Osman
Age range: 3–19
No. of pupils: 2092 B1204 G888
Curriculum: SAT, TOEFL, UK
(ECIS)

American Community School, Abu Dhabi
PO Box 42114, Abu Dhabi, United Arab Emirates
Tel: +971 2 681 5115
Head of School: George Robinson
Age range: 4–18
Curriculum: IBDP, USA
Language instr: English

American International School in Abu Dhabi
PO Box 5992, Abu Dhabi, United Arab Emirates
Tel: +971 2 4444 333
Director: Gareth Jones
Age range: 3–18
No. of pupils: 1330
Fees: DHS28,000–DHS50,000
Curriculum: IBDP, IBPYP, SAT, USA
Language instr: English
(CIS) (ECIS)

American School of Dubai
PO Box 7118, Dubai, United Arab Emirates
Tel: +971 4 395 0005
Superintendent: Roger G Hove
Age range: 4–18
No. of pupils: 910
Curriculum: AP, SAT, USA

Arab Unity School
PO Box 10563, Rashidiya, Dubai, United Arab Emirates
Tel: +971 4 2886226/7
Executive Director: Arwa A Taher
Age range: 3–18
No. of pupils: 3321 B1742 G1579
Curriculum: UK, IGCSE, ALevs
(ECIS)

Australian International School
PO Box 43364, Sharjah, United Arab Emirates
Tel: +971 6 558 9967
Head of School: Annette Wilson
No. of pupils: 1200
Curriculum: IBDP
Language instr: English

Australian School of Abu Dhabi
Khalifa City B, PO Box 36044, Abu Dhabi, United Arab Emirates
Tel: +971 2 5866980
Head of School: Salah Salman
Curriculum: IBDP, IBMYP, IBPYP
Language instr: English

Brighton College Abu Dhabi
PO Box 129444, Abu Dhabi, United Arab Emirates
Tel: +971 2 815 6500
Head Master: Ken Grocott
Curriculum: UK
Language instr: English
(COB)

Brighton College Al Ain
PO Box 14000, Al Ain, United Arab Emirates
Tel: +971 (0)3 7133 999
Head Master: Alun Yorath
Curriculum: UK
Language instr: English
(COB)

British International School Abu Dhabi
PO Box 60968, Abu Dhabi, United Arab Emirates
Tel: +971 2 5100 100
Curriculum: IBDP
Language instr: English
(RS)

Cambridge International School – Dubai
PO Box 60835, Dubai, United Arab Emirates
Tel: +971 4 282 4646
Headmaster: David McLaughin
Age range: 3–18
No. of pupils: 2009 B1200 G809
Fees: AED14,667–AED19,914
Curriculum: UK, ALevs
Language instr: English

Dar Al Marefa Private School
Mirdif, street 71, corner 58C, P.O.Box 112602, Dubai, 112602 United Arab Emirates
Tel: +971 42885782
Head of School: Shirine Al Khudari
Curriculum: IBPYP

Deira International School
PO Box 79043, Dubai, United Arab Emirates
Tel: +9714 2325552
Director: Jeff Smith
Age range: 3–18
No. of pupils: 1530 B750 G780 VIth140
Curriculum: IBDP, IBCC, UK, IGCSE
Language instr: English
(CIS)

Dubai American Academy
PO Box 32762, Dubai, United Arab Emirates
Tel: +971 4 347 9222
Superintendent: Robin Appleby
Age range: 3–18
No. of pupils: 2500 B1255 G1245
Fees: AED15,740–AED65,270
Curriculum: IBDP, USA
Language instr: English
(CIS) (ECIS)

Dubai British School
Springs 3, Emirates Hills, Dubai, PO Box 37828 United Arab Emirates
Tel: +971 4361 9361
Principal: Andrew Homden
Age range: 3–18
No. of pupils: 1039 B531 G508
Fees: AED35,400–AED53,100
Curriculum: GCSE, IGCSE, ALevs
Language instr: English
(CIS)

Dubai College
PO Box 837, Dubai, United Arab Emirates
Tel: +971 4 399 9111
Headmaster: Peter Hill
Age range: 11–18
No. of pupils: 830 VIth220
Fees: AED67,773–AED76,743
Curriculum: UK, IGCSE, ALevs
Language instr: English
(COB)

Dubai English Speaking School
PO Box 2002, Dubai, United Arab Emirates
Tel: +971 4 3371457
Head Teacher: David Hammond
Age range: 3–11
No. of pupils: 875 B450 G425
Curriculum: UK
Language instr: English

Dubai International Academy
PO Box 118111, Dubai, United Arab Emirates
Tel: +971 4 368 4111
Head of School: Poonam Bhojani
Age range: 3–18
No. of pupils: 1660 B830 G830
Fees: AED29,520–AED52,800
Curriculum: IBDP, IBMYP, IBPYP
Language instr: English, Arabic

Dubai Modern High School
PO Box 53663, Nad Al Sheba 3,4, Dubai, United Arab Emirates
Tel: +971 4 326 3339
Head of School: Darryl Bloud
Age range: 5–18
Curriculum: IBDP

Emirates International School – Jumeirah
PO Box 6446, Dubai, United Arab Emirates
Tel: +971 4 3489804
Principal: David Charles Hicks
Age range: 4–18
No. of pupils: 1850
Curriculum: IBDP, IBMYP, IBPYP, IGCSE
Language instr: English

Emirates International School – Meadows
PO Box 120118, Dubai, United Arab Emirates
Tel: +971 4 362 9009
Principal: David Hicks
Age range: 3–18
No. of pupils: 1500 B800 G700
Fees: AED2,050–AED65,400
Curriculum: IBDP, IGCSE
Language instr: English
(CIS)

Emirates National School – Abu Dhabi City Campus
P.O. Box 44759, Abu Dhabi, United Arab Emirates
Tel: +971 2 642 5993
Head of School: John DeFelice
Curriculum: IBPYP
Language instr: English

Emirates National School – Al Ain City Campus
PO Box 69392, Al Ain, United Arab Emirates
Tel: +971 3 761 6888
Curriculum: IBPYP
Language instr: English

Emirates National School – Mohammed Bin Zayed Campus
PO Box 44321, Mussafah, Abu Dhabi, United Arab Emirates
Tel: +971 2 559 00 00
Director: Alan Benson
Age range: 3–17
No. of pupils: 1151 B626 G525
Curriculum: IBPYP, National
Language instr: Arabic, English

Fujairah Academy
PO Box 797, Fujairah, United Arab Emirates
Tel: +971 9 2224001
Principal: Jan Brettingham
Age range: 3 –18
Fees: DH13,000–DH29,730

GEMS American Academy – Abu Dhabi
PO Box 110273, Abu Dhabi, United Arab Emirates
Tel: +971 2 557 4880
Superintendent and CEO: Dan Keller
Age range: 4–16
Fees: AED31,500–AED66,780
Curriculum: IBPYP, USA
Language instr: English
(CIS)

GEMS Cambridge International School – Abu Dhabi
Abu Dhabi, United Arab Emirates
Tel: +971 4 347 7770
Principal & CEO: Rebecca Plaskitt
Curriculum: UK

GEMS Jumeirah Primary School
PO Box 29093, Dubai, United Arab Emirates
Tel: +971 4 3943500
Principal: Chris McDermott
Age range: 3–18
No. of pupils: 1150 B560 G590
Fees: AED30,920–AED38,976
Curriculum: UK
Language instr: English

GEMS Millennium School – Sharjah
Sharjah School Zone Area, PO Box – 31910, Sharjah, United Arab Emirates
Tel: +971 6 5358176
Principal: Anthony Joseph
Age range: 5–18

GEMS Royal Dubai School
PO Box 121310, Dubai, United Arab Emirates
Tel: +971 4 288 6499
Principal: Kevin Loft
Age range: 3–11
No. of pupils: 965
Fees: AED31,438–AED39,639
Curriculum: UK
Language instr: English

GEMS Wellington Academy – Silicon Oasis
Silicon Oasis, Dubai, United Arab Emirates
Tel: +971 4 342 4040
Principal & CEO: Michael Gernon
Age range: 3–18
Curriculum: IBDP, IBCC, UK

GEMS Wellington International School
PO Box 37486, Dubai, United Arab Emirates
Tel: +971 4 348 4999
Principal & CEO: Keith Miller
Age range: 4–18
Fees: AED33,249–AED72,335
Curriculum: IBDP, UK
Language instr: English

GEMS Wellington Primary School
PO Box 114652, Dubai, United Arab Emirates
Tel: +971 4 343 3266
Principal: Leo Spaans
Age range: 5–11
Fees: AED36,063–AED45,458
Curriculum: UK
Language instr: English

GEMS Westminster School, Sharjah
Sharjah, United Arab Emirates
Tel: +971 6 542 6323

GEMS Winchester School
Oud Metha, Dubai,
United Arab Emirates
Tel: +971 4 337 4112
Principal: Lee Davies
Age range: 3–18
Curriculum: UK, ALevs
Language instr: English
(AISA)

GEMS World Academy – Abu Dhabi
PO Box 110273, Abu Dhabi,
United Arab Emirates
Tel: +971 2 641 6333
Principal & CEO: Jay Roy
Age range: 3–11
No. of pupils: 500 B225 G225
Fees: AED25,000–AED55,650
Curriculum: IBPYP, USA
Language instr: English
(CIS)

GEMS World Academy – Dubai
PO Box 126260, Al Barsha South,
Dubai, United Arab Emirates
Tel: +971 4 373 6373
Head of School: Jason McBride
Age range: 3–18
No. of pupils: B997 G866
Fees: AED53,000–AED92,000
Curriculum: IBDP, IBMYP, IBPYP
Language instr: English
(CIS)

Greenfield Community School
Dubai Investments Park, PO
Box 282627, Dubai, 282627
United Arab Emirates
Tel: +971 4 885 6600
Principal: Angela Hollington
Age range: 4–18
No. of pupils: 1036 B558 G478
Fees: AED36,000–AED66,000
Curriculum: IBDP, IBMYP, IBPYP, IBCC
Language instr: English,
Arabic, German

Horizon School
PO Box 6749, Dubai,
United Arab Emirates
Tel: +9714 3422891
Headteacher: Marion Sinclair
Age range: 3–11
No. of pupils: 415
Fees: UDh31,800
Curriculum: UK
Language instr: English

Indian High School
Oud Metha Rd, Dubai,
United Arab Emirates
Tel: +971 4 337 7475
Chief Executive Officer: Ashok Kumar
Language instr: English
(RR)

International Community School Abu Dhabi
PO Box 55022, Abu Dhabi,
United Arab Emirates
Tel: +971 2 633 0444
Principal: Hayat Hmoud
Age range: 3–18
No. of pupils: 1349 B762 G587
Fees: AED15,515
Curriculum: National, SAT,
TOEFL, UK, USA, IGCSE, ALevs
Language instr: English

International School of Choueifat
PO Box 21935, Dubai,
United Arab Emirates
Tel: +971 4, 3999 444
Director: A Shaw
Age range: 3–19
No. of pupils: 3210 B1745 G1465
Curriculum: AP, SAT, ALevs

International School of Choueifat
PO Box 2077, Sharjah,
United Arab Emirates
Tel: +971 6 558 2211
Acting Director: Janet Haley
Age range: 3–18
No. of pupils: 3338 B1935 G1403
Curriculum: AP, UK, ALevs
Language instr: English

International School of Choueifat
PO Box 7212, Abu Dhabi,
United Arab Emirates
Tel: +971 2 446 1444
Director: Marilyn Abu Esber
Age range: 3–18
No. of pupils: 2876 B1639 G1237

International School of Choueifat
PO Box 15997, Al Ain,
United Arab Emirates
Tel: +971 3 767 8444
Deputy Director: Fawaz Dabboussi
Age range: 3–18
No. of pupils: 618 B387 G231

Jebel Ali Primary School
PO Box 17111, Dubai,
United Arab Emirates
Tel: +971 4 884 6485
Acting Head Teacher: Ann Jones
Age range: 4–11
No. of pupils: 650
Curriculum: UK

Jumeira Baccalaureate School
PO Box 211829, Dubai, 211829
United Arab Emirates
Tel: +971 4 344 6931
Principal: Andy Homden
Age range: 3–18
No. of pupils: B515 G497 VIth68
Curriculum: IBDP
Language instr: English

Jumeirah College
PO Box 74856, Dubai,
United Arab Emirates
Tel: +971 4 395 5524
Principal & CEO: Fiona Cottam
Age range: 11–18
No. of pupils: 991 B519 G472
Curriculum: UK, ALevs
Language instr: English

Jumeirah English Speaking School
PO Box 24942, Dubai,
United Arab Emirates
Tel: +971 4 3619019
Director: Robert Stokoe
Age range: 3–18
No. of pupils: 1376 B672
G704 VIth184
Fees: AED32,043–AED78,741
Curriculum: IBDP, IBCC, UK, IGCSE
Language instr: English
(ECIS)

King's Dubai
PO Box 38199, Dubai,
United Arab Emirates
Tel: +971 4 348 3939
Headteacher: Alison Wilkinson
Age range: 5–11

Latifa School for Girls
PO Box 11533, Dubai,
United Arab Emirates
Tel: +971 4 3361065
Headmistress: Carol Green
Age range: G3–18
Curriculum: ALevs
(symbol)

Providence English Private School
PO Box 25532, Sharjah,
United Arab Emirates
Tel: +971 6 5340443
Principal: M Diaa
Age range: 3–18
Fees: DHS8,500–DHS17,000
Curriculum: National, UK, IGCSE

Raffles World Academy
PO Box 122900, Dubai,
United Arab Emirates
Tel: +971 4 4271351/2
Principal: Julian Williams
Age range: 3–18+
Fees: AED26,125–AED31,350
Curriculum: IBDP, IBPYP, SAT, IGCSE
Language instr: English

Raha International School
PO Box 34150, Abu Dhabi,
United Arab Emirates
Tel: +971 2 556 1567
Head of School: Wayne MacInnis
Curriculum: IBDP, IBMYP, IBPYP
Language instr: English
(ECIS)

Ras Al Khaimah English Speaking School
PO Box 975, Ras Al Khiamah,
United Arab Emirates
Tel: +971 7 236 2441
Executive Principal: Ross Hall
Age range: 2.5–18
No. of pupils: 1300 B700 G600
Fees: AED9,000–AED26,000
Curriculum: IBDP, IBPYP, SAT, UK
Language instr: English

Rashid School for Boys
PO Box 2861, Dubai,
United Arab Emirates
Tel: +971 4 3361300
Headmaster: Glyn Kilsby
Age range: B3–18
No. of pupils: 450
Curriculum: SAT, TOEFL, UK, ALevs
Language instr: English, Arabic
(symbol)

Regent International School
The Greens, Emirates Living
Community, PO Box 2487,
Dubai, United Arab Emirates
Tel: +971 4 360 8830
Director: Janet O'Keeffe
Age range: 3–18
Curriculum: UK, ALevs

Repton School, Dubai
PO Box 300331, Nad Al Sheba 3 &
4, Dubai, United Arab Emirates
Tel: +971 4 426 9300
Head of School: Jonathan
Hughes-D'Aeth
Age range: 3–18
No. of pupils: 2158 B1227 G931
Curriculum: IBDP, UK, IGCSE
Language instr: English
(symbol) (COB)

Safa School
PO Box 71091, Dubai,
United Arab Emirates
Tel: +971 4 3947879
Principal: Jane Knight
Age range: 3–11

School of Modern Skills
PO Box: 57475, Dubai,
United Arab Emirates
Tel: +971 42887765
Head of School: Mohd Fliti
Language instr: English
(ISA)

Sharjah American International School
PO Box 5201, Sharjah,
United Arab Emirates
Tel: +971 6 5380000
Principal: Saleh Jadayel
Age range: 4–18
No. of pupils: 1600 B900 G700
Fees: AED14,000–AED32,000
Curriculum: AP, SAT, USA
Language instr: English

Sharjah English School
PO Box 1600, Sharjah,
United Arab Emirates
Tel: +971 (6) 558 9304
Headmaster: G B C Savage
Age range: 3–11
No. of pupils: 320 B165 G155
Curriculum: UK

Star International School
PO Box 51008, Dubai,
United Arab Emirates
Tel: +971 4 348 3314
Principal: David Wilson
Age range: 3–13
Fees: AED16,500–AED29,700

Taaleem
PO Box 76691, Dubai,
United Arab Emirates
Tel: +971 4 349 8806
CEO: Ziad J Azzam
Age range: 3–19
No. of pupils: 4280 B1828 G2452
Fees: AED20,000–AED66,000
Curriculum: IBDP, IBMYP, IBPYP,
National, UK, USA, IGCSE, ALevs
Language instr: English

The British School – Al Khubairat
PO Box 4001, Abu Dhabi,
United Arab Emirates
Tel: +971 2 4462280
Principal: Paul Coakley
Age range: 3–18
No. of pupils: 1284 B673 G611
Curriculum: UK
(COB)

The Cambridge High School – Abu Dhabi
PO Box 27602, Abu Dhabi,
United Arab Emirates
Tel: +971 2 552 1621
Principal: Peter A Lugg
Age range: 3–19
No. of pupils: 1600 B866 G734
Fees: AED12,216–AED25,800
Curriculum: UK, ALevs
Language instr: English

The English College
PO Box 11812, Dubai,
United Arab Emirates
Tel: +971 4 3943465
Headmaster: Michael Biggs
Age range: 4–18
No. of pupils: 750 B400 G350
Curriculum: ALevs

The Millennium School
P.O. Box 32446, Dubai,
United Arab Emirates
Tel: +971 4 298 8567
Principal: Michael Gudzer
Language instr: English
(RS)

The Pearl Primary School
ALDAR Academies, PO Box 128484,
Abu Dhabi, United Arab Emirates
Tel: +971 2 641 8887
Principal: Maureen Chapman
Age range: 3–11
Curriculum: National, UK

The School of Research Science
44 Baghdad Street, Dubai,
United Arab Emirates
Tel: +971 4 6011011
Principal: Nan Billingham
Age range: 3–18
No. of pupils: B1086 G987
Fees: Day UDh27,588–UDh51,790
Curriculum: UK, ALevs
Language instr: English, Arabic

The Sheffield Private School
PO Box 92665, Dubai,
United Arab Emirates
Tel: +971 4 2678444
Principal: Robin Campbell
Age range: 4–18
No. of pupils: 740 B408 G332
Fees: AED18,560–AED35,000
Curriculum: UK
Language instr: English

The Sheikh Zayed Private Academy
PO Box 42989, Abu Dhabi,
United Arab Emirates
Tel: +971 2 446 9777
Principal: Heather Mann
Age range: G3–18
No. of pupils: 305
Curriculum: USA
(♿)(CIS)

The Westminster School
Al Ghusais School Zone, PO Box
27016, Dubai, United Arab Emirates
Tel: +971 4 2988333
Principal: Neville Sherman
Age range: 3–17
No. of pupils: 5100 B2800 G2300
Curriculum: UK
Language instr: English

The Winchester School
The Gardens, Jebel Ali, Dubai,
United Arab Emirates
Tel: +971 4 8820444
Principal: Ranju Anand
Age range: 3–18
Curriculum: UK

Universal American School, Dubai
PO Box 79133, Al Rashidiya,
Dubai, United Arab Emirates
Tel: +971 4 232 5222
Director: Andrew Torris
Age range: 3–18
No. of pupils: 1100 B616 G484
Fees: AED23,500–AED56,000
Curriculum: IBDP, IBPYP, SAT, USA
Language instr: English, Arabic
(CIS)

Uptown School
Corner Algeria Road and Road
15, Uptown Mirdif, PO Box 78181,
Dubai, United Arab Emirates
Tel: +971 4 288 6270
Principal: Tim Waley
Age range: 3–11
No. of pupils: 720
Curriculum: IBPYP
Language instr: English
(ECIS)

Victoria English School
PO Box 25549, Sharjah,
United Arab Emirates
Tel: +971 6 5227770
Headmaster: Roy Hart
Age range: 2–18
No. of pupils: 582 B309 G273
Curriculum: UK
Language instr: English

Victoria International School of Sharjah
PO Box 68600, Al Mamzar,
Sharjah, United Arab Emirates
Tel: +971 6 577 1999
Head of School: Roderick Crouch
Curriculum: IBDP

Wesgreen International School
PO Box 40658, Sharjah,
United Arab Emirates
Tel: +971 6 534 6333
Headmaster: J Calafato
Age range: 1–17
No. of pupils: 1388 B720 G668
Fees: DHS9,000–DHS25,000
Curriculum: UK
Language instr: English
(CIS)

Uzbekistan

Tashkent International School
38 Sarikulskaya Street, Tashkent,
100005 Uzbekistan
Tel: +998 71 291 9670
Director: David G. Henry
Age range: 3–19
No. of pupils: 457 B232 G225
Curriculum: ACT, IBDP, IBMYP,
IBPYP, SAT, TOEFL, USA
Language instr: English
(CEE)(CIS)(ECIS)

Tashkent Ulugbek International School
Jamshid Shoshoy street 5-A,
100100 Tashkent, Uzbekistan
Tel: +998 71 255 17 24
Director: Rustam Yahiyaev
Age range: 6–16
No. of pupils: 200 B118 G82
Curriculum: ALevs
(ECIS)

The British School of Tashkent
Yassi Street Bld 15-a Mirzo-Ulugbeck
District, Tashkent, Uzbekistan
Tel: +998 712 626 020
Headmaster: David Kirkham
Language instr: English

Vietnam

ABC International School
28 Troung Dinh Street, District
3, Ho Chi Minh City, Vietnam
Tel: +84 8 4311 833
Headteacher: Lynda Marsall
Age range: 2–18
No. of pupils: 280 B135 G145
Fees: US$5,000–US$11,500
Curriculum: UK, IGCSE, ALevs
Language instr: English
(COB)

American International School
781/C1-C2 Le Hong Phong
(extended) Street, Ho Chi
Minh City, Vietnam
Tel: +848 3868 1001
Head of School: Van Tran
Curriculum: IBDP, USA
Language instr: English

Australian International School (AIS)
264 Mai Chi Tho (East-West
Highway), An Phu Ward, District
2, Ho Chi Minh City, Vietnam
Tel: +84 8 3742 4040
Executive Principal: Clive Keevil
Curriculum: IBDP, IBPYP, IGCSE

BRITISH INTERNATIONAL SCHOOL, HO CHI MINH CITY
For further details see p. 79
An Phu Secondary Campus,
246 Nguyen Van Huong,
Thao Dien Ward, District 2,
Ho Chi Minh City, Vietnam
Tel: +84 83 744 2335 (Ext:230)
Email: info@bisvietnam.com
Website: www.bisvietnam.com
CEO & Principal: Shaun Williams
Age range: 2–18
No. of pupils: 1859
B909 G950 Vlth137
Fees: US$9,300–US$25,000
Curriculum: IBDP, IGCSE
Language instr: English

Hanoi Academy
D45 – D46, Ciputra International
City, Hanoi, Vietnam
Tel: +84 43 7430135
Director: Anne-Maree Rolley
Age range: 2–18
Curriculum: National

Hanoi International School
48 Lieu Giai Street, Ba Dinh
District, Hanoi, Vietnam
Tel: +84 4 3832 8140
Head of School: Terry Hamilton
Age range: 4–18
No. of pupils: 270 B130 G140
Fees: US$14,000–US$20,000
Curriculum: IBDP, IBPYP
Language instr: English
(CIS)

Horizon International Bilingual School
02 Luong Huu Khanh Street,
Pham Ngu Lao ward District
1 (Main), Hanoi, Vietnam
Tel: +84 8 925 7023
General Director: Ali Kutlu
Age range: 14–17
No. of pupils: 207 B135 G72
Fees: Day £3,200 WB £6,350
Curriculum: National
Language instr: English,
Vietnamese

International School Ho Chi Minh City (ISHCMC)
28 Vo Truong Toan St, An Phu,
District 2, Ho Chi Minh City, Vietnam
Tel: +84 8 3898 9100
Head: Simon Leslie
Age range: 2–18
No. of pupils: 779 B424 G355
Curriculum: IBDP, IBMYP,
IBPYP, UK, IGCSE, ALevs
Language instr: English
(CIS) (EAR) (ECIS)

International School Saigon Pearl
92 Nguyen Huu Canh Street,
Ward 22, Binh Thanh District,
Ho Chi Minh City, Vietnam
Tel: +84 8 2222 7788/99
Campus Principal: Lisa Johnson
Language instr: English

QSI International School of Haiphong
Unit G6A-B, Me Linh Quarter,
Km2 Pham Van Dong Road, Anh
Dung Commune, Duong Kinh
District, Haiphong City, Vietnam
Tel: +84 31 381 4258
Director: Susan Seaman
Age range: 3–18
No. of pupils: 5
Curriculum: USA
Language instr: English

Renaissance International School Saigon
74 Nguyen Thi Thap Street,
Binh Thuan Ward, District 7,
Ho Chi Minh City, Vietnam
Tel: +848 3 77 33 171
Head of School: Alun Rees Thomas
Age range: 2–18
No. of pupils: 528 B280 G248 VIth10
Fees: US$6,500–US$14,000
Curriculum: IBDP, UK, ALevs
Language instr: English
(⛪) (RS)

Saigon South International School
78 Nguyen Duc Canh, Tan
Phong Ward, District 7, Ho Chi
Minh City, 70000 Vietnam
Tel: +84 8 5413 0901
Head of School: Mark Iver Sylte
Age range: 3–18
No. of pupils: 760
Fees: $14,000–$18,000
Curriculum: AP, IBDP, USA
Language instr: English
(EAR)

United Nations International School of Hanoi
GPO Box 313, Hanoi, 1000 Vietnam
Tel: +84 4 3758 1551
Head of School: Charles P Barder
Age range: 3–18
No. of pupils: 883 B470 G413
Fees: US$7,360–US$19,070
Curriculum: IBDP, IBMYP, IBPYP
Language instr: English
(CIS) (EAR) (ECIS)

Yemen

Mohammed Ali Othman School
PO Box 5713, Taiz, Yemen
Tel: +967 4203 950
Principal: Abdulla Ahmad
Age range: 3–18
No. of pupils: 1000
Curriculum: UK, IGCSE, ALevs
(COB)

Sana'a British School
PO Box 15546, Sana'a, Yemen
Tel: +967 1 203950
Head: Gary Gibbons
Age range: 3–18
No. of pupils: 201 B91 G110
Fees: US$12,158
Curriculum: National,
UK, IGCSE, ALevs
Language instr: English

Sanaa International school
Box 2002, Sanaa, Yemen
Tel: +967 1 370 191/2
Director: Gordon B Blackie
Age range: 3–18
No. of pupils: 203 B123 G80
Curriculum: AP, SAT, USA
Language instr: English

International schools in Australasia

Schools ordered A–Z by Country

Key to directory

Country	———
Name of school or college	———
Indicates that this school has a profile	———
Address and contact number	—
Head's name	———
Age range	
Number of pupils. B = boys G = girls VIth = sixth form	———
Fees per annum. Day = fees for day pupils. WB = fees for weekly boarders. FB = fees for full boarders.	
Curriculum	
Language of instruction	
Memberships/Accreditation	

Whereford

College Academy

For further details see p.00

Which Street, Whosville, Wherefordshire AB12 3CD

Tel: 01000 000000

Head Master: Dr A Person

Age range: 11–18

No. of pupils:
660 B330 G330 VIth 200

Fees: Day £11,000
WB £16,000 FB £20,000

Curriculum:
National, IBDP, ALevs

Language instr:
English, French

(AISA) (COB) (EAR)

Key to icons

Key to symbols:
- Boys' school
- Girls' school
- Boarding accommodation

Member of:
- (AISA) Association of International Schools in Africa
- (CEE) Central and Eastern European Schools Association
- (EAR) East Asia Regional Council of Overseas Schools
- (ECIS) European Council of International Schools
- (RS) Round Square

Accreditation:
- (CIS) Council of International Schools
- (COB) Council of British International Schools

Please note: Schools are coeducational day schools unless otherwise indicated

Australia

Adelaide High School
West Terrace, Adelaide,
SA Australia
Tel: +61 8 8231 9373
Principal: Stephen Dowdy
Age range: 12–18
Language instr: English
(CIS)

Adelaide Secondary School of English
253 Torrens Road, West
Croydon, SA 5008 Australia
Tel: +61 8 8340 3733
Principal: Maria Adanza
Age range: 12–18
No. of pupils: 447 B220 G227
Language instr: English
(CIS)

Al Zahra College
3-5Wollongong Road, Arncliffe,
NSW 2205 Australia
Tel: +061(002)9599-0161
Head of School: Ahmad Mokachar
Curriculum: IBDP, IBPYP

All Saints College
PO Box 165, Ewing Avenue, Bull
Creek, Willetton, WA 6151 Australia
Tel: +61 8 9313 9333
Principal: Geoffrey Shaw
Age range: 3–18
Fees: $11,070–$20,630

Annesley Junior School
28 Rose Terrace, Wayville,
SA 5034 Australia
Tel: +61 8 8422 2288
Principal: Cherylyn Skewes
Age range: 2–12
No. of pupils: 147 B72 G75
Fees: AUS$7,950
Curriculum: IBPYP
Language instr: English

Ascham School
188 New South Head Road,
Edgecliff, NSW 2027 Australia
Tel: +61 2 8356 7000
Headmistress: Helen Wright
Age range: G3–18
No. of pupils: 1000
Curriculum: National
(♦)(♠)

Australian International Academy
56 Bakers Road, North
Coburg, VIC 3058 Australia
Tel: +61 3 9350 4533
Head of Academy: Salah
Salman AM
Age range: 5–18
No. of pupils: 2545
Curriculum: IBDP, IBMYP, IBPYP
Language instr: English

Australian International Academy – Kellyville Campus
57-69 Samantha Riley
Drive, Kellyville, Sydney,
NSW 2155 Australia
Tel: +612 8801 3100
Principal: Mona Abdel-Fattah
Age range: 5–16
Curriculum: National
Language instr: English

Australian International Academy – Sydney Campus
420 Liverpool Road, Strathfield,
Sydney, NSW 2135 Australia
Tel: +61 2 9642 0104
Principal: Mafaz Alsafi
Age range: 5–18
No. of pupils: 418 B243 G175
Curriculum: IBDP, IBMYP, National
Language instr: English

Ballarat Grammar School
201 Forest Street, Wendouree,
Victoria 3355 Australia
Tel: + 61 3 5338 0700
Head of School: Stephen Higgs
Language instr: English
(♠)(RS)

Barker College
91 Pacific Highway, Hornsby,
NSW 2077 Australia
Tel: +61 2 9847 8399
Head of School: P Heath
Age range: B3–18 G16–18
Fees: $22,796
(♦)

Bendigo Senior Secondary College
PO Box 545, Bendigo,
VIC 3550 Australia
Tel: +61 03 5443 1222
Principal: Dale Pearce
Age range: 15–21
No. of pupils: 1750
Language instr: English
(CIS)

Bendigo South East College
Ellis St, Flora Hill, VIC 3550 Australia
Tel: +61 354 434 522
Principal: Ernie Fleming
Language instr: English
(CIS)

Berwick Grammar School
80 Tivendale Rd Officer,
Victoria, 3809 Australia
Tel: +61 3 9703 8111
Principal: Doug Bailey
Age range: B3–18
Curriculum: National
Language instr: English
(♦)

Billanook College
197-199 Cardigan Road,
Mooroolbark, Vic 3138 Australia
Tel: +61 397 255 388
Principal: Roger Oates
Language instr: English
(RS)

Brighton Grammar School
90 Outer Crescent, Brighton,
VIC 3186 Australia
Tel: +61 3 8591 2200
Headmaster: Michael Urwin
Age range: B3–18
Fees: $13,830–$23,260
(♦)

Brighton Primary School
Wilson Street, Brighton,
VIC 3186 Australia
Tel: +61 39592 0177
Head of School: Anny Lawrence
Age range: 5–12
No. of pupils: 800
Curriculum: IBPYP
Language instr: English
(CIS)

Brisbane Grammar School
Gregory Terrace, Brisbane
QLD, AA 4000 Australia
Tel: +617 3834 5200
Headmaster: Anthony Micallef
Age range: B10–18
Language instr: English
(♦)(♠)

Camberwell Grammar School
PO Box 151, Balwyn, Victoria,
VIC 3186 Australia
Tel: +61 3 9835 1777
Headmaster: P Hicks
Age range: B4–18
No. of pupils: B1300
Fees: AU$12,860–AU$22,500
Language instr: English
(♦)

Cambridge Primary School
Carruthers Drive, Hoppers
Crossing, VIC 3029 Australia
Tel: +61 (03) 9748 9011
Principal: Meenah Marchbank
Age range: 5–12
Language instr: English

Canberra Girls' Grammar School
Melbourne Avenue, Deakin,
ACT 2600 Australia
Tel: +61 2 6202 6400
Principal: Anne Coutts
Age range: B3–8 G3–17
No. of pupils: 1600
Curriculum: IBDP, IBPYP
Language instr: English
(♦)(♠)

Canberra Grammar School
40 Monaro Crescent, Red Hill,
Canberra, ACT 2603 Australia
Tel: + 61 2 6260 9700
Head of School: Justin Garrick
Age range: B4–18 G4–7
No. of pupils: 1570
Curriculum: IBDP
Language instr: English
(♦)(♠)

Carey Baptist Grammar School
349 Barkers Road, Kew
3101 Vic, Australia
Tel: +61 3 9816 1222
Principal: Philip Grutzner
Age range: 3–18
No. of pupils: 2300 B1150 G1150
Curriculum: IBDP
Language instr: English

Caulfield Grammar School
PO Box 610, 217 Glen Eira Road
East, St Kilda, VIC 3185 Australia
Tel: +61 3 9524 6300
Principal: Stephen Newton
Age range: 3–18
Language instr: English
(♠)

Caulfield Junior College
186 Balaclava Rd, Caulfield
North, VIC 3161 Australia
Tel: +61 395 096 872
Principal: Tim Douglas
Language instr: English
(CIS)

Charles Campbell College
3 Campbell Rd, Paradise,
SA 5075 Australia
Tel: +61 881 654 700
Principal: Sue George-Duif
Language instr: English
(CIS)

Christ Church Grammar School
PO Box 399, Claremont,
WA 6010 Australia
Tel: +61 8 9442 1555
Headmaster: Garth Wynne
Age range: B5–18
No. of pupils: 1610
Fees: AUS$14,800–AUS$20,820
Curriculum: National
Language instr: English
(♦)(♠)

Cleveland District State High School
Russell Street, Cleveland,
QLD 4163 Australia
Tel: +61 738 249 222
Principal: Paul Bancroft
Language instr: English
(CIS)

Concordia College
45 Cheltenham Street,
Highgate, SA 5063 Australia
Tel: +61 8 8272 0444
Principal: Lester Saegenschnitter
No. of pupils: 860 B452 G408
Fees: AU$13,140–AU$14,360
Curriculum: IBDP, IBMYP
Language instr: English

Cornish College
63 Riverend Road, Bangholme,
VIC 3175 Australia
Tel: +61 03 9773 1011
Principal: Kerry Bolger
Age range: 3–16
No. of pupils: 313 B164 G149
Curriculum: IBPYP
Language instr: English

Cranbrook School
6 Kent Road, Rose Bay,
NSW 2029 Australia
Tel: +61 2 9327 9100
Head of School: Michael Dunn
Age range: B5–12
No. of pupils: 462
Fees: $19,000–$23,000
Curriculum: IBPYP, National
Language instr: English

Elonera Montessori School
21 Mount Ousley Road,
Wollongong, NSW 2519 Australia
Tel: +61 2 4225 1000
Head of School: Elizabeth Goor
Curriculum: IBDP

Fintona Junior School
79 Balwyn Road, Balwyn,
VIC 3103 Australia
Tel: +61 3 9830 1388
Principal: Suzy Chandler
Fees: Day £0
Curriculum: IBPYP

Firbank Grammar School, Junior School – Brighton Campus
51 Outer Crescent, Brighton,
VIC 3186 Australia
Tel: +61 3 9591 5141
Head of School: Michelle Phillips
No. of pupils: 290
Fees: AU$13,803–AU$18,900
Curriculum: IBPYP
Language instr: English

Geelong Grammar School
50 Biddlecombe Avenue,
Corio, VIC 3214 Australia
Tel: +61 3 5273 9200
Head of School: Stephen Donald Meek
Age range: 3–18
No. of pupils: 1522 B923 G599
Curriculum: IBDP, IBPYP, National, SAT
Language instr: English

Geraldton Grammar School
134 George Road, Geraldton,
WA 6530 Australia
Tel: +61 899 657 800
Principal: Susan Shaw
Language instr: English

German International School Sydney
33 Myoora Road, Terrey Hills, NSW 2084 Australia
Tel: +61 (0) 2 94851900
Principal: Erhard Seifert
Age range: 3–18
No. of pupils: 202
Fees: AU$4,300–AU$17,660
Curriculum: IBDP, National
Language instr: English, German

Glenunga International High School
L'Estrange Street, Glenunga,
SA 5064 Australia
Tel: +61 88 379 5629
Principal: Wendy Johnson
Age range: 11–18
No. of pupils: 1540
Curriculum: IBDP
Language instr: English

Good Shepherd Lutheran College – Noosa
115 Eumundi Road, Noosaville,
QLD 4566 Australia
Tel: +61 7 5455 8600
Head of School: Anthony Dyer
Curriculum: IBPYP

Good Shepherd Lutheran College – Palmerston
PO Box 1146, Howard Springs,
NT 0835 Australia
Tel: +61 8 89830300
Principal: Julian Denholm
Curriculum: IBMYP, IBPYP

Good Shepherd Lutheran School, Angaston
7 Neldner Avenue, Angaston,
SA 5353 Australia
Tel: +61 8 8564 2396
Head of School: Steven Seidel
Curriculum: IBPYP
Language instr: English

Grimwade House
67 Balaclava Road, Caulfield,
VIC 3161 Australia
Tel: +61 3 9865 7800
Headmaster: Andrew Boyd
Age range: 5–11
No. of pupils: 680

Haileybury
855-891 Springvale Road,
Keysborough, VIC 3173 Australia
Tel: +61 3 9213 2222
Principal: Derek Scott
Age range: 3–18
No. of pupils: B2104 G1401
Fees: AU$12,970–AU$23,055
Curriculum: National
Language instr: English

Helena College
PO Box 52, Glenn Forrest,
WA 6071 Australia
Tel: +61 89 298 9100
Head of School: Ian Lyons
Curriculum: IBMYP

Henley High School
Cudmore Terrace, Henley Beach, SA 5022 Australia
Tel: +61 883 557 000
Principal: Liz Schneyder
Language instr: English

Hills International College
Lot 4 Johanna Street, Jimboomba, Queensland 4280 Australia
Tel: +61 7 5546 0667
Principal: Joseph Marinov
Age range: 4–18
No. of pupils: 427 B255 G172
Curriculum: IBPYP, National, SAT
Language instr: English

Immanuel College
32 Morphett Road, Novar Gardens, SA 5040 Australia
Tel: +61 08 8294 3588
Principal: Kevin Richardson
Curriculum: IBMYP, National
Language instr: English

Immanuel Lutheran School, Gawler
11 Lyndoch Road, Gawler East, South Australia 5118 Australia
Tel: +61 8 8522 5740
Head of School: Sue De Biasi
Curriculum: IBPYP

Immanuel Primary School
Saratoga Drive, Novar Gardens, SA 5040 Australia
Tel: +61 (0)8 8294 8422
Principal: Robert Hoff
Fees: AU$6,200
Curriculum: IBPYP
Language instr: English

International School of Western Australia
22 Kalinda Drive, City Beach, Western Australia 6015 Australia
Tel: +61 8 9285 1144
Principal: Melissa Powell
Age range: 4–18
No. of pupils: 350 B175 G175
Fees: AU$14,768–AU$21,208
Curriculum: ACT, AP, IBDP, IBPYP, SAT
Language instr: English

Ivanhoe Grammar School
The Ridgeway, Ivanhoe 3079, 730 Bridge Inn Road, Mernda 3754, Melbourne, VIC 3079 Australia
Tel: +61 3 9490 1877
Principal: Roderick Fraser
Age range: 3–18
No. of pupils: 1846 B1220 G626 VIth210
Fees: AU$4,845–AU$19,455
Curriculum: IBDP
Language instr: English

John Paul College
John Paul Drive, Daisy Hill, Queensland, 4127 Australia
Tel: +61 7 3826 3333
Headmaster: Peter Foster
Age range: 4–18
No. of pupils: 2200
Fees: AU$6,800–AU$11,200
Curriculum: IBDP, IBPYP
Language instr: English

John Wollaston Anglican Community School
Centre Road, Kelmscott,
WA 6111 Australia
Tel: +61 (08) 9495 1133
Head of School: Anne Ford
Curriculum: IBPYP

Kambala
794 New South Head Road, Rose Bay, Sydney, NSW 2029 Australia
Tel: +612 93886777
Head of School: Debra Kelliher
No. of pupils: 1000
Curriculum: IBDP
Language instr: English

Kardinia International College
PO Box 17, Geelong,
VIC 3220 Australia
Tel: +61 3 52 789999
Principal: John Goodfellow
No. of pupils: 1800
Curriculum: IBDP, IBPYP
Language instr: English

Kormilda College
PO Box 241, Berrimah,
NT 0828 Australia
Tel: +61 8 8922 1611
Principal: Helen Spiers
Age range: 12–18
No. of pupils: 670 B335 G335
Fees: Day AU$6,989–AU$7,957 FB AU$26,405–AU$27,126
Curriculum: IBDP, IBMYP
Language instr: English

Lauriston Girls' School
38 Huntingtower Road, Armadale VIC 3143, Australia
Tel: +61 3 9864 7555
Principal: Susan Just
Age range: G3–18
No. of pupils: 920
Fees: AU$16,852–AU$25,556
Curriculum: IBDP
Language instr: English

Loreto College
316 Portrush Road, Marryatville,
SA 5068 Australia
Tel: +61 8 8334 4200
Principal: Rosalie Gleeson
Curriculum: IBMYP, IBPYP
Language instr: English
(symbols)

Lycée Condorcet – The International French School of Sydney
758 Anzac Parade, Maroubra,
NSW 2035 Australia
Tel: +61 2 9344 8692
Head of School: Loïc Bernard
Age range: 3–19
No. of pupils: 620 B310 G310 VIth57
Fees: AU$9,000–AU$14,200
Curriculum: IBDP
Language instr: French, IB in English

Macarthur Anglican School
PO Box 555, Camden,
NSW 2570 Australia
Tel: +61 2 4647 5333
Headmaster: David Nockles
Age range: 4–18
No. of pupils: 924 B467 G457 VIth87
Fees: AU$8,170–AU$11,480
Curriculum: National
Language instr: English

Macedon Grammar School
PO Box 176, Macedon,
VIC 3440 Australia
Tel: +61 3 5426 1751
Principal: Mark Smith
Age range: 4–18
No. of pupils: 160 B80 G80
Curriculum: IBDP
Language instr: English

Mater Christi College
28 Bayview Road, Belgrave,
VIC 3160 Australia
Tel: +61 3 9754 6611
Head of School: Mary Fitz-Gerald
Curriculum: IBMYP
(symbols)

MENTONE GIRLS' GRAMMAR SCHOOL
For further details see p. 104
11 Mentone Parade, Mentone,
VIC 3194 Australia
Tel: +61 3 9581 1200
Email:
info@mentonegirls.vic.edu.au
Website:
www.mentonegirls.vic.edu.au
Head of School: Fran Reddan
Age range: G3–18
No. of pupils: 730
Fees: AUS$10,903–AUS$24,565
Curriculum: IBPYP, National
Language instr: English
(symbols)

Mercedes College
540 Fullarton Road, Springfield
SA, 5062 Australia
Tel: +61 8 8372 3200
Principal: Peter Daw
Age range: 5–18
No. of pupils: 1226
Fees: AU$6,000–AU$11,000
Curriculum: IBDP, IBMYP, IBPYP
Language instr: English
(symbols)

Methodist Ladies' College
207 Barkers Road, Kew,
VIC 3101 Australia
Tel: +61 3 9274 6316
Principal: Diana Vernon
Age range: B0–4 G0–18
No. of pupils: 2204 B46 G2126
Fees: Day £14,434–£24,596
AU$14,049–AU$22,810
Curriculum: IBDP, National
Language instr: English
(symbols)

MLC School
Rowley Street, Burwood,
Sydney, NSW 2134 Australia
Tel: +61 2 9747 1266
Principal: Denice Scala
Age range: G4–18
No. of pupils: 1200
Fees: AU$24,768
Curriculum: IBDP
Language instr: English
(symbols)

Monte Sant' Angelo Mercy College
PO Box 1064, 128 Miller Street,
North Sydney, NSW 2059 Australia
Tel: +61 2 9409 6200
Principal: Catherine Alcock
Age range: G12–18
No. of pupils: 1100
Fees: AU$13,000
Curriculum: IBDP, IBMYP
Language instr: English

Moreton Bay Boys' College
302 Manly Road, Manly
West, QLD 4179 Australia
Tel: +61 07 3906 9444
Head of School: Tony Wood
Curriculum: IBMYP, IBPYP
(symbols)

Mosman Church of England Preparatory School
PO Box 950, Spit Junction,
NSW 2088 Australia
Tel: +61 2 9968 4044
Headmaster: Garry Brown
Age range: B4–11
No. of pupils: 290
Fees: $15,000
Curriculum: National
(symbols)

Mount Carmel Christian School
20 Kinchington Road, Leneva,
Mellboune, VIC 3691 Australia
Tel: +61 02 6056 2288
Head of School: Larry Gunn
Curriculum: IBDP
Language instr: English
(symbols)

Mount Scopus Memorial College
245 Burwood Highway,
Burwood, VIC 3125 Australia
Tel: +61 3 9808 5722
Head of School: James Kennard
No. of pupils: 1503
Curriculum: IBMYP, IBPYP
Language instr: English

Mt Zaagham International School
PO Box 616, Cairns,
Queensland Australia
Tel: +62 901 434803
Head of School: Stephen Wilkin
Age range: 3–12
Curriculum: IBPYP
Language instr: English
(symbols)

Navigator College
PO Box 3199, Port Lincoln,
SA 5606 Australia
Tel: +61 8 86825099
Head of School: Kaye Mathwin-Cox
Curriculum: IBPYP

New England Girls' School
Uralla Road, Armidale,
NSW 2350 Australia
Tel: +61 2 6772 5922
Principal: Rebecca Ling
Age range: G4–18
No. of pupils: 400 B40 G360
(symbols)

Newington College
200 Stanmore Road, Stanmore,
NSW 2048 Australia
Tel: +61 2 9568 9333
Headmaster: David Mulford
Age range: B5–18
No. of pupils: 1900
Fees: AU$14,463–AU$27,369
Curriculum: IBDP, IBPYP, TOEFL
Language instr: English, French
(symbols)

Newington College – Lindfield
26 Northcote Road, Lindfield,
New South Wales, 2070 Australia
Tel: +61 2 9416 4280
Head of School: Chris Wyatt
Curriculum: IBPYP
(symbols)

Pedare Christian College
2-30 Surrey Farm Drive, Golden
Grove, SA 5125 Australia
Tel: +61 8 8280 1700
College Principal: Mike Millard
No. of pupils: 335 B163 G172
Curriculum: IBMYP
Language instr: English

Pembroke School
342 The Parade, Kensington
Park, SA 5068 Australia
Tel: +61 8 8166 6225
Principal: Luke Thomson
Age range: 4–18
No. of pupils: 1550 B800 G750
Curriculum: IBDP, IBPYP, National
Language instr: English
(symbols)

Penrith Anglican College
PO Box 636, Kingswood,
NSW 2747 Australia
Tel: +61 247 36 8100
Headmaster: Barry Roots
Age range: 5–18
No. of pupils: 1300 B650 G650
Fees: AU$8,500
Curriculum: IBDP, National
Language instr: English

Plenty Valley Christian College
840 Yan Yean Road, Doreen,
VIC 3754 Australia
Tel: +61 3 9717 7400
Head of School: Douglas Peck
Age range: 5–12
No. of pupils: B194 G155
Curriculum: IBPYP
Language instr: English

Presbyterian Ladies' College – Perth
14 McNeil Street, Peppermint
Grove, Perth, WA 6011 Australia
Tel: +61 8 9424 6444
Principal: Beth Blackwood
Age range: G3–18
No. of pupils: 1200
Fees: AU$8,500–AU$23,000
Curriculum: IBDP, IBMYP, IBPYP
Language instr: English
(symbols)

Presbyterian Ladies' College Melbourne
141 Burwood Highway,
Burwood, VIC 3125 Australia
Tel: +61 3 9808 5811
Principal: Elaine Collin
Age range: G1–18
No. of pupils: 1400
Fees: AU$20,216
Curriculum: IBDP, National
Language instr: English
(symbols)

Prince Alfred College
PO Box 571, Kent Town,
SA 5071 Australia
Tel: +61 8 8334 1275
Headmaster: Kevin Tutt
Age range: B2–18
No. of pupils: 1050
Curriculum: IBDP, IBPYP
Language instr: English

Queenwood School for Girls
Locked bag 1, Mosman,
NSW 2088 Australia
Tel: +61 2 89687777
Principal: Elizabeth Stone
Age range: G5–18
No. of pupils: 850
Curriculum: IBDP, National
Language instr: English

Radford College
College Street, Bruce,
Canberra, 2617 Australia
Tel: +61 2 6162 5332
Head of School: Paul Southwell
Curriculum: IBPYP

Ravenswood
Henry Street, Gordon,
NSW 2072 Australia
Tel: +612 9498 9898
Principal: Vicki Steer
Age range: G5–18
No. of pupils: 1120
Fees: AU$14,000–AU$23,300
Curriculum: IBDP, National
Language instr: English

Redeemer Lutheran School, Nuriootpa
Box 397, Nuriootpa, SA
5355 Australia
Tel: +61 885 621655
Head of School: Steven Wilksch
Curriculum: IBPYP
Language instr: English

Redlands
272 Military Road, Cremorne,
NSW 2090 Australia
Tel: +61 2 9908 6479
Principal: Peter Lennox
Age range: 3–19
Curriculum: IBDP, National
Language instr: English

Sacred Heart College Geelong
Retreat Road, Newtown,
VIC 3220 Australia
Tel: +61 3 52214211
Head of School: Anna Negro
Age range: G11–16
No. of pupils: 1350
Fees: AU$3,350–AU$3,950
Curriculum: IBMYP
Language instr: English

Sandringham House Firbank Grammar
45 Royal Avenue, Sandringham,
VIC 3191 Australia
Tel: +61 3 9533 5711
Head of School: Anne Sarros
Curriculum: IBPYP
Language instr: English

Scotch College
76 Shenton Road, Swanbourne,
Perth, WA 6010 Australia
Tel: +61 8 9383 6800
Head of School: Alec O'Connell
Age range: B5–18
No. of pupils: 1270
Curriculum: IBDP, IBMYP, IBPYP
Language instr: English

Scotch Oakburn College
85 Penquite Road, Newstead,
TAS 7250 Australia
Tel: +61 363 363 300
Principal: Andy Müller
Language instr: English

Somerset College
Somerset Drive, Mudgeeraba,
QLD 4213 Australia
Tel: +61 0755 304100
Head of School: Craig Bassingthwaighte
Curriculum: IBDP, IBMYP, IBPYP
Language instr: English

Sophia Mundi Steiner School
St. Mary's Abbotsford
Convent, 1 St Heller's Street,
Abbotsford, 3067 Australia
Tel: +61 3 9419 9229
Head of School: Jennifer West
No. of pupils: 200
Curriculum: IBDP

Spring Head Lutheran School
PO Box 444, Mt Torrens,
SA 5244 Australia
Tel: +61 (08) 8389 4334
Head of School: Victoria Weiss
Curriculum: IBPYP

St Andrew's Cathedral School
Sydney Square, Sydney,
NSW 2000 Australia
Tel: +61 2 9286 9500
Head of School: John Collier
No. of pupils: 1200
Curriculum: IBDP
Language instr: English

St Andrew's School
22 Smith Street, Walkerville,
SA 5081 Australia
Tel: +61 8 81685537
Head of School: Deb Dalwood
Curriculum: IBMYP, IBPYP

St Andrews Lutheran College
PO Box 2142, Burleigh BC,
QLD 4220 Australia
Tel: +61 7 5568 5900
Head of College: Timothy Kotzur
Age range: 5–18
No. of pupils: 1105
Curriculum: IBPYP
Language instr: English

St Brigid's College
200 Lesmurdie Road, Lesmurdie,
Perth, WA 6076 Australia
Tel: +61 8 9290 4200
Principal: Amelia Toffoli
No. of pupils: 1300
Curriculum: IBMYP, IBPYP
Language instr: English

St John's Lutheran School, Eudunda, Inc.
8 Ward Street, Eudunda,
5374 Australia
Tel: +61 8 8581 1282
Head of School: Paula Skinner
Age range: 5–13
No. of pupils: 137
Curriculum: IBPYP
Language instr: English

St John's Lutheran School, Highgate
20 Highgate, Highgate,
SA 5063 Australia
Tel: +61 8 8271 4299
Head of School: Michael Paech
Age range: 4–12
Fees: $2,817–$5,359
Curriculum: IBPYP
Language instr: English

St Leonard's College
163 South Road, Brighton
East, VIC 3187 Australia
Tel: +61 3 9909 9300
Principal: Stuart Davis
Age range: 3–18
No. of pupils: 1424 B742 G682
Fees: AU$13,096–AU$23,480
Curriculum: IBDP, IBPYP, National
Language instr: English

St Margaret's School
27-47 Gloucester Avenue, Berwick,
Melbourne, 3806 Australia
Tel: +61 3 9703 8111
Principal: Doug Bailey
Age range: G3–18
Curriculum: IBPYP, National
Language instr: English

St Michael's Lutheran School
6 Balhannah Rd, Hahndorf,
SA 5250 Australia
Tel: +61 8 8388 7228
Head of School: Shane Paterson
No. of pupils: 290
Fees: AU$2,000
Curriculum: IBPYP
Language instr: English

St Paul's Grammar School
Locked Bag 8016, Penrith,
NSW 2751 Australia
Tel: +61 2 4777 4888
Principal: Paul Kidson
Age range: 4–18
No. of pupils: 1302 B660
G642 VIth120
Fees: AU$12,000
Curriculum: IBDP, IBMYP, IBPYP
Language instr: English

St Paul's School Brisbane
34 Strathpine Rd, Bald Hills,
QLD 4036 Australia
Tel: +61 732 611 388
Headmaster: Paul Browning
Language instr: English

St Peter's College
Hackney Road, St Peters,
SA 5069 Australia
Tel: +61 8 8404 0400
Head of School: Simon Murray
Age range: B3–18
Curriculum: IBDP
Language instr: English

St Peter's Collegiate Girls School
Stonyfell Road, Stonyfell,
SA 5066 Australia
Tel: +61 88 334 2200
Head of School: Fiona Godfrey
Curriculum: IBDP, IBPYP

St Peter's Lutheran School Blackwood
71 Cumming Street, Blackwood,
SA 5051 Australia
Tel: +61 8 8278 0800
Head of School: Margaret Linke
Age range: 4–12
No. of pupils: 244
Curriculum: IBPYP
Language instr: English

St Peter's Woodlands Grammar School
39 Partridge Street, Glenelg,
Adelaide, SA 5045 Australia
Tel: +61 (8) 8295 4317
Head of School: Christopher Prance
Curriculum: IBPYP

St Peters Lutheran College
66 Harts Road, Indooroopilly,
QLD 4068 Australia
Tel: +61 7 3377 6222
Head of College: Adrian Wiles
Age range: 5–18
No. of pupils: 2125
Fees: $16,600
Curriculum: IBDP
Language instr: English

St Philips College, Australia
Schwarz Crescent, Alice
Springs, NT 0870 Australia
Tel: +61 889 504 511
Language instr: English

The Armidale School
Locked Bag 3003, 87
Douglas Street, Armidale,
NSW 2350 Australia
Tel: +61 2 6776 5800
Headmaster: Murray Guest
Age range: B4–18 G4–11
Curriculum: National

The Essington School
PO Box 42321, Casuarina,
0811 NT Australia
Tel: +61 (08) 8948 1255
Principal: David Cannon
Age range: 3–16
No. of pupils: 3087 B2811 G276
Fees: AU$3,824–AU$4,500
Curriculum: National
Language instr: English

The Friends' School
PO Box 42, North Hobart,
TAS 7002 Australia
Tel: +61 3 6210 2200
Principal: Nelson File
Age range: 4–20
No. of pupils: 1330
Curriculum: IBDP, IBPYP
Language instr: English

The Hills Grammar School
43 Kenthurst Road, Kenthurst,
NSW 2156 Australia
Tel: +61 2 9654 2205
Head of School: Robert Phipps
Curriculum: IBPYP
Language instr: English

THE HUTCHINS SCHOOL
For further details see p. 100
71 Nelson Road, Sandy Bay,
Tasmania, 7005 Australia
Tel: +61 3 6221 4200
Email:
hutchins@hutchins.tas.edu.au
Website:
www.hutchins.tas.edu.au
Headmaster: Warwick Dean

**The Illawarra
Grammar School**
PO Box 225, Figtree,
NSW 2525 Australia
Tel: +61 2 4220 0253
Head of School: Stephen Kinsella
Curriculum: IBPYP

**The Kilmore
International School**
40 White Street, Kilmore,
VIC 3764 Australia
Tel: +61 3 5782 2211
Principal: Andrew Taylor
Age range: 11–20
No. of pupils: 400
Curriculum: IBDP
Language instr: English

**The King's School
Preparatory School**
PO Box 1, Parramatta,
NSW 2124 Australia
Tel: +61 2 9683 8444
**Head of the Preparatory
School:** Keith Dalleywater
No. of pupils: 365
Curriculum: IBPYP, National
Language instr: English

The Montessori School
PO Box 194, Landsdale,
WA 6065 Australia
Tel: +61 89 409 9151
Head of School: Bobbie Beasley
Curriculum: IBDP
Language instr: English

**The Norwood Morialta
High School**
Morialta Road, West,
Rostrevor, SA 5073 Australia
Tel: +61 8 83650455
Principal: Panayoula Parha
Age range: 12–19
No. of pupils: B853 G646
Fees: Day AU$750
Curriculum: IBMYP
Language instr: English

THE SCOTS COLLEGE
For further details see p. 102
Locked Bag 5001, Bellevue Hill,
Sydney, NSW 2023 Australia
Tel: +61 2 9391 7600
Email:
reception@tsc.nsw.edu.au
Website: www.tsc.nsw.edu.au
Principal: Ian PM Lambert
Language instr: English

The Southport School
2 Winchester Street, Southport,
QLD 4125 Australia
Tel: +61 755 319 911
Headmaster: Greg Wain
Language instr: English

Tintern Schools
90 Alexandra Road, Ringwood
East, VIC 3135 Australia
Tel: +61 3 9845 7777
Principal: Jenny Collins
Age range: 4–18
No. of pupils: 1000
Curriculum: IBDP
Language instr: English

Toorak College
PO Box 150, Mount Eliza,
VIC 3930 Australia
Tel: +61 3 9788 7200
Head of School: Helen Carmody
Age range: 3–18
Curriculum: IBPYP
Language instr: English

**Townsville Grammar
School**
45 Paxton Street, North
Ward, QLD 4810 Australia
Tel: +61 7 4722 4900
Principal: Richard Fairley
Age range: 4–18
No. of pupils: 1400 B700
G700 VIth160
Curriculum: IBDP
Language instr: English

Treetops Montessori School
PO Box 59, Darlington,
WA 6076 Australia
Tel: +61 8 9299 6725
Head of School: Jodi Kerslake
No. of pupils: 130
Curriculum: IBDP
Language instr: English

Trinity Anglican School
200-212 Progress Rd, White Rock,
Queensland, QLD 4868 Australia
Tel: +61 7 4036 8111
Principal: Christopher
Daunt Watney
Language instr: English

**Trinity Grammar School
Preparatory School**
115-125 The Boulevarde,
Strathfield, NSW 2135 Australia
Tel: +61 2 8732 4600
Head of School: Martin Lubrano
Curriculum: IBPYP

**Trinity Grammar
School, Sydney**
119 Prospect Road, Summer
Hill, NSW 2130 Australia
Tel: +61 2 9581 6000
Headmaster: Milton Cujes
No. of pupils: 2009
Curriculum: IBDP, IBPYP
Language instr: English

Trinity Lutheran College
PO Box 322, Ashmore City,
QLD 4214 Australia
Tel: +61 7 5556 8200
Head of College: Ann Mitchell
Age range: 4–18
No. of pupils: 1100
Curriculum: IBPYP, National
Language instr: English

Tudor House School
Illawarra Highway, Moss
Vale, NSW 2577 Australia
Tel: +61 2 4868 0000
Headmaster: John Stewart
Age range: B4–12
No. of pupils: 135
Fees: $8,000–$14,952

**Waikerie Lutheran
Primary School**
16 McCutcheon Street,
Waikerie, SA 5330 Australia
Tel: +61 8 8541 2344
Head of School: Adam Borgas
No. of pupils: 100
Curriculum: IBPYP
Language instr: English

**Walford Anglican
School for Girls**
316 Unley Road, Hyde
Park, SA 5061 Australia
Tel: +61 8 8272 6555
Principal: Rebecca Clarke
Age range: G1–18
No. of pupils: G720
Curriculum: IBDP, IBMYP, IBPYP
Language instr: English

**Wesley College –
Elsternwick Campus**
5 Gladstone Parade, Elsternwick,
VIC 3185 Australia
Tel: +61 3 8102 6800
Head of Campus: Gea Lovell
Curriculum: IBPYP
Language instr: English

**Wesley College – Glen
Waverley Campus**
620 High Street Road, Glen
Waverley, VIC 3150 Australia
Tel: +61 3 8102 6500
Head of Campus: Peter Dickinson
Curriculum: IBPYP
Language instr: English

**Wesley College,
Melbourne**
577 St Kilda Road, Melbourne,
VIC 3004 Australia
Tel: +61 3 8102 6100
Principal: Helen Drennen
Age range: 3–19
Curriculum: IBDP, IBPYP
Language instr: English

**Westminster School,
Adelaide**
1/23 Alison Avenue, Marion,
SA 5043 Australia
Tel: +61 882 760 276
Principal: Steve Bousfield
Language instr: English

Woodcroft College
PO Box 48, Bains Road, Morphett
Vale, SA 5162 Australia
Tel: +61 8 8322 2333
Head of the College: Mark Porter
Age range: 5–18
No. of pupils: 1468
Curriculum: IBDP, IBMYP, IBPYP
Language instr: English
(CIS)

Woodleigh School, Australia
485 Golf Links Road, Langwarrin,
SA 3911 Australia
Tel: +61 359 716 100
Principal: Jonathan Walter
Language instr: English
(RS)

Xavier College
Barkers Road, Kew, VIC
3101 Australia
Tel: +61 3 98 545411
Principal: Christopher Hayes
Age range: 3–18
No. of pupils: 2070 B1987 G83
Fees: AU$20,615
Curriculum: IBPYP, National
Language instr: English
(CIS)

Xavier College, Kostka Hall Campus
47 South Road, Brighton,
Melbourne, VIC 3186 Australia
Tel: +61 3 9592 2127
Head of School: Christopher Hayes
Curriculum: IBPYP

Fiji

International School Nadi
Box 9686 Nadi Airport, Nadi, Fiji
Tel: +679 6702 060
Head of School: Dianne Korare
Curriculum: IBDP, IBMYP, IBPYP
Language instr: English

International School Suva
PO Box 10828, Laucala
Beach Estate, Suva, Fiji
Tel: +679 339 3300
Principal: Anna Marsden
Age range: 3–18
No. of pupils: 502 B253 G249
Curriculum: ACT, IBDP,
IBPYP, SAT, TOEFL, IGCSE
Language instr: English
(EAR)

Pacific Harbour International School
PO Box 50, Pacific
Harbour, Deuba, Fiji
Tel: +679 3450005
Head Teacher: Janet Arone
Age range: 5–16
No. of pupils: 130 B70 G60
Fees: FJ$1,200
Curriculum: National
Language instr: English

Guam

St John's School
911 Marine Drive, Tumon
Bay, 96913 Guam
Tel: +1 (671) 646 8080
Head of School: Patricia A Bennett
Age range: 3–18
No. of pupils: 525 B253 G272 VIth42
Curriculum: ACT, IBDP, SAT
Language instr: English
(EAR)

New Zealand

ACG Senior College
66 Lorne Street, Auckland,
1141 New Zealand
Tel: +64 9 3074 474
Head of School: Kathleen Parker
Curriculum: IBDP
Language instr: English

Auckland International College
37 Heaphy Street, Blockhouse Bay,
Auckland, 0600 New Zealand
Tel: +64 9 309 4480
Principal: Carolyn Solomon
Age range: 15–18
No. of pupils: 371 B181 G190
Curriculum: IBDP
Language instr: English

Chilton Saint James School
PO Box 30090, Lower Hutt,
5040 New Zealand
Tel: +64 4 566 4089
Principal: Jude Fawcett
Age range: B3–4 G3–18
No. of pupils: 505 B15 G490
Curriculum: IBPYP
Language instr: English

Diocesan School for Girls
Clyde Street, Epsom, Auckland,
1051 New Zealand
Tel: +64 9 520 0221
Principal: Heather McRae
Age range: G4–18
Curriculum: IBDP, IBPYP
Language instr: English

John McGlashan College
2 Pilkington Street, Maori Hill,
Dunedin, 9010 New Zealand
Tel: +64 3 4676620
Principal: K M Corkery
Age range: B11–18
No. of pupils: 500 VIth80
Fees: NZ$1,600
Curriculum: IBDP
Language instr: English

King's College, Auckland
Golf Ave, Otahuhu, 1062
Auc New Zealand
Tel: +64 9276 0600
Language instr: English

Kristin School
PO Box 300-087, Albany,
Auckland New Zealand
Tel: +64 9 415 9566
Executive Principal: Peter Clague
Age range: k–13
No. of pupils: 1550
Curriculum: IBDP, IBMYP,
IBPYP, National
Language instr: English

Pinehurst School
PO Box 302-308, North Harbour,
North Shore City 0751, New Zealand
Tel: +64 9 414 0960
Executive Principal: Sherida
Penman Walters
Age range: 6–18
Curriculum: National, IGCSE

Queen Margaret College
53 Hobson Street, PO Box
12274, Thorndon, Wellington,
6144 New Zealand
Tel: +64 4 473 7160
Principal: Carol Craymer
Age range: G3–18
No. of pupils: 680
Curriculum: IBDP, IBPYP
Language instr: English

Saint Kentigern College
PO Box 51060, Pakuranga,
Manukau 2010 New Zealand
Tel: +64 9 576 9019
Head of School: Steve Cole
Curriculum: IBDP
Language instr: English

Scots College
PO Box 15064, Strathmore,
Wellington 6243 New Zealand
Tel: +64 4 388 0850
Headmaster: Graeme Yule
Age range: B5–18
No. of pupils: 845
Fees: NZ$16,000
Curriculum: IBDP, IBPYP
Language instr: English

Selwyn House School
122 Merivale Lane, 8104,
Christchurch, New Zealand
Tel: +64 3 3557299
Head of School: Jane Lapthorn
Curriculum: IBPYP
Language instr: English

St Cuthbert's College
122 Market Road, Epsom,
Auckland 1051, New Zealand
Tel: +64 9 520 4159
Principal: Lynda Reid
Age range: G5–18
No. of pupils: 1470
Fees: NZ$16,376
Curriculum: IBDP
Language instr: English

St Margaret's College
28 Winchester Street, Merivale,
Christchurch, 8144 New Zealand
Tel: +64 3 379 2000
Executive Principal: Gillian Simpson
Age range: G7–17
No. of pupils: 740
Curriculum: IBDP
Language instr: English

St Mark's Church School
13 Dufferin Street, Mt Victoria,
Wellington, 6021 New Zealand
Tel: +64 4 385 9489
Head of School: Tony Batchelor
Curriculum: IBPYP

St Peter's School, Cambridge
1716 Hamilton Road, Private
Bag 884, Cambridge
3450, New Zealand
Tel: +64 7 827 9899
Head of School: Steve Robb
Age range: 11–18
No. of pupils: 1108 B510 G550
Fees: NZ$17,250
Curriculum: IBDP, National, IGCSE
Language instr: English

Papua New Guinea

International School of Lae
PO Box 2130, Lae, MP 411
Papua New Guinea
Tel: +675 479 1425
Principal: Michael Johnson
Age range: 1–19
No. of pupils: 318
Curriculum: ACT

Kimbe International School
PO Box 307, Kimbe,
Papua New Guinea
Tel: +675 983 5078
Principal: Ifor John Jones
Age range: 5–18
No. of pupils: 300

Port Moresby International School
PO Box 276, Boroko,
Papua New Guinea
Tel: +675 325 3166
Principal: Christopher West
Age range: 3–18
No. of pupils: 990
Curriculum: ACT, IBDP
Language instr: English

Star Mountains Institute of Technology International School (SMITIS)
PO Box 408, Tabubil 332, Western Province Papua New Guinea
Tel: +675 649 9233
Principal: Ken Darvall
Age range: 3–13
No. of pupils: 300

The Ela Murray International School
PO Box 1137, Boroko, Papua New Guinea
Tel: +675 325 22729
Principal: Suzanne Savage
Age range: 2–14
No. of pupils: 585 B300 G285
Language instr: English

Solomon Islands

Woodford International School
PO Box R44, Honiaro, Solomon Islands
Tel: +677 30186
Principal: Greg Hollis
Age range: 3–12
No. of pupils: 220 B110 G110
Curriculum: IBPYP, SAT

International schools in Europe

Schools ordered A–Z by Country

Key to directory

Country

Name of school or college

Indicates that this school has a profile

Address and contact number

Head's name

Age range

Number of pupils.
B = boys G = girls VIth = sixth form

Fees per annum.
Day = fees for day pupils.
WB = fees for weekly boarders.
FB = fees for full boarders.

Curriculum

Language of instruction

Memberships/Accreditation

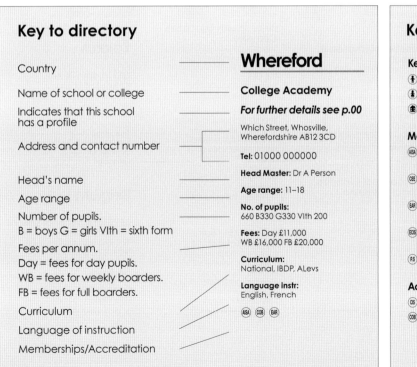

Whereford

College Academy

For further details see p.00

Which Street, Whosville,
Wherefordshire AB12 3CD

Tel: 01000 000000

Head Master: Dr A Person

Age range: 11–18

No. of pupils:
660 B330 G330 VIth 200

Fees: Day £11,000
WB £16,000 FB £20,000

Curriculum:
National, IBDP, ALevs

Language instr:
English, French

(AISA) (COB) (EAR)

Key to icons

Key to symbols:

(♂) Boys' school

(♀) Girls' school

(🛏) Boarding accommodation

Member of:

(AISA) Association of International Schools in Africa

(CEE) Central and Eastern European Schools Association

(EAR) East Asia Regional Council of Overseas Schools

(ECIS) European Council of International Schools

(RS) Round Square

Accreditation:

(CIS) Council of International Schools

(COB) Council of British International Schools

Please note: Schools are coeducational day schools unless otherwise indicated

Albania

Memorial International School of Tirana
PO Box 143, Tirana, Albania
Tel: +355 4 2237 379
Principal: Birol Inaltekin
Age range: 6–17
No. of pupils: 161 B71 G90
Fees: €5,500–€6,600
Curriculum: National, UK
Language instr: English

Tirana International School
Rruga Vilat Gjermane, Kutia
Postare 1527, Tirana, Albania
Tel: +355 4 236 5239
Director: Mark Hemphill
Age range: 3–17
No. of pupils: 130
Curriculum: AP, USA
Language instr: English

Armenia

Anania Shirakatsy Lyceum
Artem Mikoyan 35, Nor Nork
5, Yerevan, 0079 Armenia
Tel: +37410 640102
Principal: Ashot Alikhanyan
Curriculum: National
(AISA)

QSI International School of Yerevan
PO Box 82, Astarak Highway
49/15, Yerevan, 0088 Armenia
Tel: +374 10 349130
Director: Carol Hoffman
Age range: 3–13
No. of pupils: 61
Curriculum: USA
Language instr: English

Quantum College
Bagratuniats 23/2, Shengavit,
Yerevan, 0046 Armenia
Tel: +37410 422217
Head of School: Robert Vardanyan
Curriculum: Abitur, IBDP, National
Language instr: English

UWC Dilijan
6 Baghramyan Avenue,
Yerevan, 0019 Armenia
Tel: +374 10 52 40 40
Head of School: John Puddefoot
Curriculum: IBDP
Language instr: English
(⚑)

Yerevan Lycée after Anania Shirakatsy
35 Artem Mikoyan,
Yerevan, 0079 Armenia
Tel: +374 10 640 102
Curriculum: IBPYP
Language instr: Armenian

Austria

AMADEUS International School Vienna
Bastiengasse 36-38, Haus
3, 1180 Vienna, Austria
Tel: +43 1 470 30 37 -37
Principal: Günter Boos
Curriculum: IBDP
Language instr: English

American International School
Salmannsdorferstrasse 47,
Vienna, 1190 Austria
Tel: +43 1 40132-0
Director: Steve Razidlo
Age range: 4–18
No. of pupils: 780
Fees: €10,410–€19,039
Curriculum: AP, IBDP, SAT, USA
Language instr: English
(CEE) (CIS) (ECIS)

American International School – Salzburg
Moosstrasse 106, 5020
Salzburg, Austria
Tel: +43 662 824617
Headmaster: Paul McLean
Age range: 13–19
No. of pupils: 84
Curriculum: AP, SAT
(⚑) (ECIS)

Campus Wien West
Seuttergasse 29, Wien, 1130 Austria
Tel: +43 680 5577 573
Curriculum: IBDP
Language instr: English

Danube International School
Josef Gall-Gasse 2, 1020
Vienna, Austria
Tel: +43 1 7203110
Director: Ian Piper
Age range: 3–19
No. of pupils: 530 B260 G270
Fees: €10,925–€20,598
Curriculum: IBDP, IBMYP, IBPYP
Language instr: English
(CIS) (ECIS)

International Christian School of Vienna
Wagramer Strasse 175, Panethgasse
6A, Vienna, A-1220 Austria
Tel: +43 1 25122
Director: James Devenish
Age range: 5–19
No. of pupils: 253 B128 G125
Fees: €10,950
Curriculum: USA
(ECIS)

St. Gilgen International School GmbH
Ischlerstrasse 13, 5340
St. Gilgen, Austria
Tel: +43 62 272 0259
Head of School: Michael Chapman
Age range: 8–18
No. of pupils: 200
Curriculum: IBDP, IGCSE
Language instr: English
(⚑) (CIS) (ECIS)

Vienna International School
Strasse der Menschenrechte
1, 1220 Vienna, Austria
Tel: +43 1 203 5595
Director: Peter M J Murphy
Age range: 3–18
No. of pupils: B743 G657
Fees: Day €5,688–€17,556
Curriculum: IBDP, IBMYP, IBPYP
Language instr: English
(CIS) (ECIS)

Azerbaijan

Baku International School
Darnagul Qasabasi, Str Ajami
Nakchivani, Block 3097,
Baku, 1108 Azerbaijan
Tel: +994 12 440 66 16
Director: Gary Tuttle
Age range: 2–18
No. of pupils: 151
Curriculum: AP, SAT, USA
Language instr: English

Baku Talents Education Complex
Sabail District, Salyan Highway
(New Bibiheybet mosque),
Baku, 1023 Azerbaijan
Tel: +994 50 292 22 95
Principal: Hasan Hasanov
Language instr: English, Azeri

British School in Baku
13 Koroglu Ragimov Str,
Baku AZ1072, Azerbaijan
Tel: +99412 465 80 86
Head: David Draper
Age range: 4–18
No. of pupils: 500 B250 G250
Curriculum: UK
Language instr: English
(COB) (ECIS)

CET Gunar – Baku Oxford School
8 A Abbaszadeh Str., AZ
1073, Baku, Azerbaijan
Tel: +994 12 510 80 01
Vice President: Naila Rzayeva
Age range: 4–18
Curriculum: National,
UK, IGCSE, ALevs

Dunya School
2 Alatava street, Baku,
AZ1102 Azerbaijan
Tel: +994 12 430 3315
Head of School: Naila Isayeva
Curriculum: IBDP
Language instr: English

European Azerbaijan School
7 Basti Bagirova, Yasamal
District, Baku City, Azerbaijan
Tel: +994 1253 98936
Director: Shaundele Leatherberry
Language instr: English
(ECIS)

The International School of Azerbaijan, Baku
AIOC-TISA, c/o BP Azerbaijan,
Chertsey Road, Sunbury on
Thames, TW16 7LN, UK Azerbaijan
Tel: +994 12 4973 028
Director: John Gillespie
Age range: 2–17
No. of pupils: 592 B360 G336
Fees: $10,755–$34,830
Curriculum: IBDP, IBMYP, IBPYP
Language instr: English
(CIS)

XXI Century International Education and Innovation Center
30 Inshaatchilar Avenue,
Baku, 1065 Azerbaijan
Tel: +994 12 510 0205
Head of School: Vafa Mammadova
Curriculum: IBDP

Belarus

QSI International School of Minsk
Perioluk Bogdanovicha, 15,
Minsk, 220040 Belarus
Tel: +375 17 265 1216
Director: Robert Jackson
Age range: 3–18
No. of pupils: 45
Curriculum: USA
Language instr: English

Belgium

BEPS International School
Av Franklin Roosevelt 23,
1050 Brussels, Belgium
Tel: +32 2 648 43 11
Head of School: Mandy Porrett
Age range: 2–11
No. of pupils: 200
Curriculum: IPC
Language instr: English

British Junior Academy of Brussels
83 Boulevard St Michel,
B-1040 Brussels, Belgium
Tel: +32 2 732 5376
Headteacher: Diane Perry
Age range: 3–11
No. of pupils: 150
Fees: €8,098–€17,241
Curriculum: SAT, UK
(COB)

Da Vinci International School
Verbondstraat 67, Antwerp,
2000 Belgium
Tel: +32 (0)3 216 1232
Headmaster: Ian Stanley
Age range: 2–18
No. of pupils: B83 G85
Fees: €10,000–€17,500
Curriculum: UK, IGCSE, ALevs
Language instr: English

DYP International School, Belgium
Kontichsesteenweg 40, 2630
Aartselaar, Belgium
Tel: +32 3 271 0943
Head of School: Edmond Maher
Curriculum: IBDP
(ECIS)(CIS)

European School (Brussels I)
Avenue du Vert Chasseur 46,
B-1180 Bruxelles, Belgium
Tel: +32 2 373 8611
Director: Antonia Ruiz-Esturla
Age range: 4–18
No. of pupils: 3100

International Montessori School Tervuren
Rotselaerlaan 1, 3080
Tervuren, Belgium
Tel: +32 2 721 2111
Head of School: Rinze Hoekstra
Age range: 1–17
No. of pupils: 380
Fees: €9,240–€27,120
Curriculum: IBDP, IBMYP
Language instr: English, French

International School of Brussels
19 Kattenberg, Boitsfort,
Brussels, 1170 Belgium
Tel: +32 2 661 4211
Director: Kevin Bartlett
Age range: 3–18
No. of pupils: 1459 B749 G710
Fees: €12,400–€27,500
Curriculum: AP, IBDP, SAT, USA
Language instr: English
(CIS)

ISF Waterloo International School
280 Chaussee de Waterloo,
Rhode-St-Genese, 1640 Belgium
Tel: +32 2 358 56 06
Head: Belinda Yates
Age range: 2–18
No. of pupils: 109 B54 G55
Fees: €8,600–€19,800
Curriculum: IPC, IGCSE
Language instr: English
(ECIS)

Scandinavian School of Brussels
Square d'Argenteuil 5,
Waterloo, 1410 Belgium
Tel: +32 2 357 06 70
Head of School: Kristy Lundström
Age range: 3–20
No. of pupils: 400 B200 G200
Curriculum: IBDP, National
Language instr: English
(🏛)

St John's International School
146 Drève Richelle,
Waterloo, 1410 Belgium
Tel: +32 2 352 0610
Head of School: Tom Hawkins
Age range: 3–19
No. of pupils: 800 B400 G400
Fees: €8,500–€30,520
Curriculum: AP, IBDP, IBPYP
Language instr: English
(CIS)(ECIS)

St Paul's British Primary School
Stationsstraat 3, 3080 Vossem-
Tervuren, Belgium
Tel: +32 2 767 3098
Head Teacher: Brett Neilson
Age range: 3–11
No. of pupils: 90
Fees: €8,500–€23,300
Curriculum: UK
Language instr: English
(COB)

The Antwerp International School
Veltwijcklaan 180, B-2180
Ekeren, Antwerp, Belgium
Tel: +32 (0)3 543 93 00
Headmaster: Geoffrey Fisher
Age range: 2–18
No. of pupils: 450
Fees: €7,615–€24,930
Curriculum: IBDP, IPC, IGCSE
Language instr: English
(CIS)(ECIS)

The British International School of Brussels
163 Av Emile Max, B-1030
Brussels, Belgium
Tel: +32 2 736 8981
Headteacher: Stephen Prescott
Age range: 3–11
No. of pupils: 121 B63 G58
Fees: €7,000–€14,750
Curriculum: UK
Language instr: English
(COB)(ECIS)

Bosnia & Herzegovina

QSI International School of Sarajevo
Omladinska #16, 71320, Vogosca-
Sarajevo, Bosnia & Herzegovina
Tel: +387 33 424450
Director: Karin Noll
Age range: 3–17
No. of pupils: 136
Curriculum: USA
Language instr: English

UWC in Mostar
Spanjolski Trg 1, Mostar, 88000
Bosnia & Herzegovina
Tel: +387 36 320 601
Headmistress: Valentina Mindoljevic
Age range: 16–19
No. of pupils: 154 B57 G97
Fees: €25,000
Curriculum: IBDP
Language instr: English
(🏛)

Bulgaria

American College Arcus
16 Dragoman Street, 5000,
Veliko Turnovo, Bulgaria
Tel: +359 62 619959
Director: Peter Ivanov
Age range: 14–19
No. of pupils: 189 B82 G107
Fees: €2,000
Curriculum: IBDP, National
Language instr: English
(🏛)(ECIS)

American College of Sofia
PO Box 873, Sofia, 1000 Bulgaria
Tel: +359 2 434 10 08
President: Paul K Johnson
Age range: 13–19
No. of pupils: 640 B300 G340
Fees: €12,000
Curriculum: AP, IBDP, SAT
Language instr: English
(🏛)

British International School Classic
7 Lady Strangford Street,
Plovdiv, 4000 Bulgaria
Tel: +359 32 625 220
Principal: Milanova Reni
Age range: 6–19
Curriculum: National, UK, IGCSE
(COB)

British School of Sofia
Lozenets, quarter;, 1. Ekaterina
Nencheva str, Sofia, 1700 Bulgaria
Tel: +359 2 979 19 49
Director: Ralitsa Voynova
Curriculum: UK
Language instr: English, Bulgarian
(COB)

International School UWEKIND
136 Voivodina Mogila Street,
Knyajevo, Sofia, 1619 Bulgaria
Tel: +359 2 8572000
Head of School: Julia Radoslavova
Curriculum: IBMYP
Language instr: English

Private English Language High School 'Meridian 22'
Mladost 2 bl.227, Sofia
1799, Bulgaria
Tel: +359 2 8876 423; +359 2 8840 238
Head of School: Radka Stamenova
Curriculum: IBDP
Language instr: English

Professor Vassil Zlatarski Private School – Sofia
49 Kliment Ohridski Boulevard,
BG-Sofia, 1756 Bulgaria
Tel: +359 2 876 67 67
Head of School: Tsvetanka Kardasheva
Age range: 13–19
No. of pupils: 300 B150 G150
Curriculum: IBDP, National
Language instr: English

Croatia

American International School of Zagreb
Vorcarska 106, Zagreb,
10000 Croatia
Tel: +385 1 4680 133
Director: David Harris
Age range: 3–18
No. of pupils: 211 B108 G103
Fees: €13,500–€14,500
Curriculum: AP, IBDP, SAT, USA
Language instr: English
(CEE) (ECIS)

Bright Horizons – International School of Zagreb
Sveti Duh 122, Zagreb, Croatia
Tel: +385 915379711
Head of School: Milena Prodanić Ti ma
Curriculum: UK
Language instr: English
(COB)

Cyprus

American Academy Larnaca
PO Box 40112, Gregoris Afxentiou Avenue, Larnaca, 6301 Cyprus
Tel: +357 24 815400
Director: Tom Widdows
Age range: 4–19
No. of pupils: 937 B470 G467 VIth116
Fees: Day £2,500
Curriculum: GCSE, ALevs

American Academy Limassol
PO Box 1867, 3509 Limassol, Cyprus
Tel: +357 25 337054/7777 22 77
Principal: Robert Swan
Age range: 2–19
No. of pupils: 750 B450 G300 VIth60
Fees: €1,950–€6,630
Curriculum: UK, GCSE, IGCSE, ALevs
Language instr: English
(🏛)

American International School in Cyprus
PO Box 23847, 11 Kassos Str,
Nicosia, 1686 Cyprus
Tel: +357 22 316345
Head of School: Michelle Kleiss
Age range: 3–19
No. of pupils: 315
Fees: €10,370
Curriculum: IBDP, SAT, USA
Language instr: English
(ECIS)

Falcon School
P O Box 23640, Nicosia, 1685 Cyprus
Tel: +357 22 424 781
Head of School: G Hajivarnava
Age range: 4–18
No. of pupils: 235 B225 G210 VIth60
Curriculum: GCSE, IGCSE, ALevs

Foley's Grammar and Junior School
40 Homer Street, Limassol,
3095 Cyprus
Tel: +357 25 582191
Headmaster: C J Bailey
Age range: 4–18
No. of pupils: 480
Fees: €5,400–€9,780
Curriculum: UK, GCSE, IGCSE, ALevs
Language instr: English

International School of Paphos
100 Aristotelous Savva Ave,
Anavargos, PO Box 62018,
8060 Paphos, Cyprus
Tel: +357 26 821700
Head: Litsa Olympiou
Age range: 3–18
No. of pupils: 610 B293 G317 VIth24
Fees: €3,560–€6,680
Curriculum: UK, IGCSE, ALevs
Language instr: English

Logos Boarding School
33-35 Agialousa Street, PO Box 51075, Limassol 3501, Cyprus
Tel: +357 253 36061
Headmaster: Gary Love
Age range: 3–18
No. of pupils: 273 B142 G131
Curriculum: UK, GCSE, IGCSE, ALevs

PASCAL English School – Larnaka
PO Box 45077, Aradippou,
7110 Cyprus
Tel: +357 22 509 300
Head of School: Despina Lioliou
Age range: 12–18
No. of pupils: 620
Curriculum: IBDP, UK, IGCSE, ALevs
Language instr: English

PASCAL English School – Lefkosia
PO Box 24746, Kopenhagis 177, 2306 Lakatamia, Lefkosia 1303 Cyprus
Tel: +357 22 509 000
Headmistress: Ariana Milutinovic
Age range: 12–18
No. of pupils: 718
Fees: €6,000–€8,000
Curriculum: IBDP, National, IGCSE, ALevs
Language instr: English

The English School, Cyprus
P O Box 23575, 1684 Nicosia, Cyprus
Tel: +357 22 799 300
Headteacher: S J Haggett
Age range: 11–19
No. of pupils: 836 B501 G335 VIth238
Fees: Day £2,700
Curriculum: ALevs

The Junior School
P O Box 23903, Ayie Omoloyitae, Nicosia, 1687 Cyprus
Tel: +357 22 664 855
Age range: 3–18
No. of pupils: 850 B450 G400
Fees: CYP£2,800–CYP£3,800
Curriculum: SAT, UK
Language instr: English

Czech Republic

1st International School of Ostrava
Gregorova 2582/3, Ostrava,
702 00 Czech Republic
Tel: +420 599 442 085
Head of School: Brett Gray
Age range: 3–19
No. of pupils: 260 B130 G130
Curriculum: IBDP, IBMYP, IPC, National, UK
Language instr: English
(COB)

International Montessori School of Prague
Hrudickova 2107, Prague 4 – Roztyly, 148 00 Czech Republic
Tel: +420 272 937 758
Executive Director: Katerina Becková
Age range: 1.5–12

International School of Brno
Cejkovicka 10, Brno-Vinohrady 628 00, Czech Republic
Tel: +420 544 233 629
Head: Jan Svihálek
Age range: 3–16
No. of pupils: 68
Curriculum: National
Language instr: English

International School of Prague
Nebusicka 700, Prague 6,
Nebusice 16400 Czech Republic
Tel: +420 2 203 84111
Director: Arnold Bieber
Age range: 3–18
No. of pupils: 780 B410 G370
Fees: €10,000–€15,400
Curriculum: AP, IBDP, SAT
Language instr: English
(CEE) (CIS) (ECIS)

International School Olomouc
Roosveltova 101, Olomouc,
779 00 Czech Republic
Tel: +420 585 754 880
Director: Petr Pospisil
Language instr: English
(COB)

Meridian International School
Frydlantska 1350/1, Prague 8 – Kobylisy, Prague, 182 00 Czech Republic
Tel: +420 286 581 805
Principal: Ahmet H Gursoy
Curriculum: UK
Language instr: English
(COB)

Open Gate – Boarding School
Babice 5, Ricany, 251 01 Czech Republic
Tel: +420 323 616 405
Head of School: Peter Nitsche
Curriculum: IBDP
Language instr: English
(🏛)

Park Lane International School
Norbertov 3, Prague 6 – Stresovice, 162 00 Czech Republic
Tel: +420 220 512 653
Age range: 3–13
Curriculum: UK, IGCSE
(COB)

PORG – gymnazium a zakladni skola, o.p.s.
Pod Krcskym lesem 1300/25, Praha 4 – Krc, 142 00 Czech Republic
Tel: +420 773 963 650
Head of School: Vaclav Klaus
Curriculum: IBDP

Riverside School, Prague
Roztocka 9/43, Sedlec, 160 00 Praha 6, Czech Republic
Tel: +420 2 24315336
Director: Peter Daish
Age range: 3–18
No. of pupils: 290
Fees: Day £3,363–£7,437
Curriculum: AP, IBDP, National, IGCSE, ALevs
Language instr: English
(CIS) (COB) (ECIS)

The English College in Prague
Sokolovska 320, 190 00
Prague 9, Czech Republic
Tel: +420 2 8389 3113
Headmaster: Mark Waldron
Age range: 13–19
No. of pupils: 360 VIth140
Fees: Day £9,000
Curriculum: IBDP, IGCSE
Language instr: English
(COB)

The English International School, Prague
Brunelova 960/12, Libus, Prague 4, 142 00, Czech Republic
Tel: (+420) 272 181 911
Principal: David Rowsell
Age range: 2–18
No. of pupils: 179 B92 G87
Curriculum: IBDP, SAT, UK
Language instr: English
(COB) (ECIS)

The Prague British School
K Lesu 558/2, 142 00 Prague 4, Czech Republic
Tel: +420 226 096 200
**Head of Senior
School:** Timothy Roberts
Age range: 1–18
No. of pupils: 650 B320 G330
Fees: €13,000–€15,800
Curriculum: IBDP, SAT
Language instr: English
(COB) (ECIS)

Townshend International School
Hradcany 1070, 37341
Hluboka, Czech Republic
Tel: +420 387688113
Director: Vivek Williams
Age range: 3–18
Curriculum: UK, IGCSE, ALevs
Language instr: English
(𝄞) (COB)

Denmark

Bernadotte Skolen
Hellerupvej 11, 2900 Hellerup,
Copenhagen, Denmark
Tel: +45 396 21215/22837
School Leader: Lars
Stubbe Teglbjerg
Age range: 6–16
No. of pupils: 560 B270 G290

Bjorn's International School
Gartnerivej 5, Copenhagen,
2100 Denmark
Tel: +45 39 292937
Head/Principal: Pia Drabowicz
Age range: 6–16
No. of pupils: 165
Fees: Day £2,000
Curriculum: National, IGCSE
Language instr: English, Danish
(ECIS)

Copenhagen International School
Hellerupvej 22-26, Hellerup,
2900 Denmark
Tel: +45 39463300
Director: Walter Plotkin
Age range: 4–19
No. of pupils: 700
Fees: DKK92,000–DKK132,000
Curriculum: IBDP, IBMYP,
IBPYP, SAT, USA
Language instr: English
(CIS) (ECIS)

Herlufsholm Skole
Herlufsholm Allé 170,
Naestved, 4700 Denmark
Tel: +45 55 75 35 00
Head of School: Klaus
Eusebius Jakobsen
Age range: 15–20
No. of pupils: 500 B250 G250
Curriculum: IBDP, National
Language instr: English
(𝄞) (RS)

International School of Aarhus
Engtoften 22, 8260 Viby J, Denmark
Tel: +45 86 11 45 60
Head: Megan Oliver Winther
Age range: 5–16
Curriculum: UK
(COB)

NGG International School
Cirkelhuset, Christianshusvej 16,
DK 2970 Hørsholm, Denmark
Tel: +45 45 57 26 16
Director: Jan Thrane
Age range: 4–16
No. of pupils: 220
Curriculum: IGCSE
Language instr: English
(ECIS)

Rygaards School
Bernstorffsvej 54, Hellerup,
2900 Denmark
Tel: +45 39 62 10 53
**Head of International
School:** Charles Dalton
Age range: 4–16
No. of pupils: 460
Curriculum: UK, IGCSE
Language instr: English
(COB) (ECIS)

Estonia

Audentes School
Tondi str 84, Tallinn, 11316 Estonia
Tel: +372 6996 591
Head of School: Ahto Orav
Age range: 2–18
No. of pupils: 520
Fees: €2,000–€6,300
Curriculum: IBDP
(𝄞)

International School of Estonia
Juhkentali 18, Tallinn, 10132 Estonia
Tel: +372 666 4380
Head of School: Kathleen Naglee
Age range: 3–19
No. of pupils: 130 B62 G68
Fees: €15,015–€16,766
Curriculum: IBDP, IBPYP
Language instr: English
(CEE) (CIS)

Finland

Helsingin Suomalainen Yhteiskoulu
Isonnevantie 8, Helsinki,
00320 Finland
Tel: +358 94774 1814
Head of School: Jukka-Pekka Tanska
Age range: 9–19
No. of pupils: 1081 B465 G616
Curriculum: IBDP, National
Language instr: English

International School of Helsinki
Selkämerenkatu 11,
Helsinki, 00180 Finland
Tel: +358 9 686 6160
Head of School: Peter Welch
Age range: 4–18
No. of pupils: 320
Curriculum: IBDP, IBMYP, IBPYP, SAT
Language instr: English
(CEE) (CIS) (ECIS)

International School of Vantaa
Hagelstamintie 1, 01520,
Vantaa, Finland
Tel: +358 9 8392 4810
Principal: Heli-Hanna Filppula
Age range: 6–16
No. of pupils: 350
Language instr: English

Oulu International School
Kasarmintie 4, Oulu, 90130 Finland
Tel: +358 50 371 6977
Principal: Raija Johnson
No. of pupils: 280
Curriculum: IBMYP, IBPYP
Language instr: English

France

American School of Grenoble
Cité Scolaire Internationale,
4 Place de Sfax BP 1570,
Grenoble, 38000 France
Tel: +33 438 12 25 47
Head of School: Carol-Margaret Bitner
Age range: 10–18
No. of pupils: 38 B22 G16
Fees: €4,000
Curriculum: AP, SAT, USA
Language instr: English
(CIS) (ECIS)

American School of Paris
41 rue Pasteur, BP 82, Saint-Cloud Cedex, 92216 France
Tel: +33 1 41 12 82 82
Head of School: Mark Ulfers
Age range: 4–18
No. of pupils: 796 B411 G385
Fees: €15,320
Curriculum: ACT, AP, IBDP, SAT, USA
Language instr: English
(CIS) (ECIS)

BORDEAUX INTERNATIONAL SCHOOL
For further details see p. 109
252 Rue Judaïque, 33000
Bordeaux, France
Tel: +33 5 57870211
Email:
bis@bordeaux-school.com
Website:
www.bordeaux-school.com
Principal: Cussac
Age range: 3–19
No. of pupils: 130 B64 G66
Fees: Day €3,180–€13,980
FB €6,110–€9,100
Curriculum: National,
UK, IGCSE, ALevs
Language instr: English, French
(𝄞) (CIS) (ECIS)

Centre International de Valbonne, Anglophone Section
Buropolis 2, 1240 Route des
Dolines, 06560 Valbonne,
Sophia Antipolis, France
Tel: +33 4 97 23 92 30
Head: Phyllis Brante
Age range: 6–18
No. of pupils: 1500
(ECIS)

Cite Scolaire Internationale de Lyon
Section Anglophone, 2
Place de Montreal, 69361
Lyon Cedex 07, France
Tel: +33 4 7869 6006
**Head of Anglophone
Section:** John Cadden
Age range: 6–18
No. of pupils: 1600
Curriculum: SAT
(ECIS)

Colegio Internacional SEK-Los Alpes
Saint Nicolas La Chappelle,
73590 Flumet, France
Tel: +33 479 317491
Principal: Íñigo Yvorra
Age range: 13–16
No. of pupils: 50 B27 G23

College International de Fontainebleau

Anglophone Section, 48 Rue Geurin, Fontainbleau, 77300 France
Tel: +33 1 6422 1177
Head of Section: Shaun Corrigan
Age range: 6–18
No. of pupils: 450 VIth 44
Curriculum: FrenchBacc, UK
(ECIS)

EAB International

The Victor Hugo School, 23 rue de Cronstadt, Paris, 75015 France
Tel: +33 (0)1 5656 6070
Head of School: Marie-France Conchard
Age range: 4–18
Curriculum: IBDP
Language instr: English

Ecole Active Bilingue

Administration, 117 Boulevard Malesherbes, Paris 75008, France
Tel: +33 1 45 63 62 22
Head: Delesalle
Age range: 3–18
No. of pupils: 3000
Curriculum: AP, IBDP, SAT, ALevs
(ECIS)

ECOLE ACTIVE BILINGUE JEANNINE MANUEL
For further details see p. 115
70 rue du Théâtre,
Paris, 75015 France
Tel: +33 1 44 37 00 80
Email: admissions@eabjm.net
Website: www.eabjm.org
Principal: Elisabeth Zéboulon
Age range: 4–18
No. of pupils: 2390 B1148 G1242
Fees: Day €5,118–€5,414
Curriculum: IBDP, IGCSE
Language instr: English, French
(ECIS)

Ecole Active Bilingue Jeannine Manuel (Lille)

418 bis, rue Albert Bailly, Marcq-en-Baroeul, 59700 France
Tel: +33 3 2065 9050
Head of School: Francis Gianni
Age range: 6–19
No. of pupils: 700 B350 G350
Fees: €2,685–€9,750
Curriculum: IBDP, National, FrenchBacc
Language instr: French, English
(symbol)

Ecole Des Roches

Stages F.L.E., BP 710, 27130 Verneuil-sur-avre, France
Tel: +33 232 6040 16
Director: Chantal Collomb
Age range: 11–18
(symbol)

EPIM – Marseille International School

27 Boulevard de la Corderie, F13007, Marseille, France
Tel: +33 (0) 491 53 00 00
Headmaster: Bruno Corgnier
Age range: 2–11
No. of pupils: 65
Curriculum: National
(ECIS)

Ermitage International School of France

46 Avenue Eglé, 78600 Maisons-Laffitte, France
Tel: +33 1 39 62 81 75
Head of School: Chris Hunter
Age range: 3–18
No. of pupils: 1100
Curriculum: IBDP
Language instr: English, French
(symbol) (RS)

Eurecole

5 rue de Lubeck, 75116 Paris, France
Tel: +33 1 40 70 12 81
Headmistress: Claude Duval
Age range: 2–15
No. of pupils: 190
Curriculum: National
(ECIS)

Forest International School

28 Chemin du Tour d'Echelle du Mur, de Cloture de la Foret de Marly, Mareil Marly, 78750 France
Tel: +33 1391 68735
Principal: Mariane Wyler
Language instr: English
(ECIS)

International School of Béarn

Rue des Fougères, 64160 Morlaas, France
Tel: +33 6 12 56 68 67
Head of School: Maria Elias
Age range: 2–10
No. of pupils: 265
Curriculum: SAT
(ECIS)

International School of Lyon

80 Chemin du Grand Roule, 69110 Sainte Foy Lès Lyon, France
Tel: +33 (0) 478 866 190
Director: Donna Philip
Age range: 3–18
No. of pupils: 252
Fees: €4,082–€15,201
Curriculum: IBDP, IBPYP, IGCSE
Language instr: English
(ECIS)

International School of Nice

15 avenue Claude Debussy, Nice, 06200 France
Tel: +33 4 93 21 04 00
Director: David Johnson
Age range: 4–18
No. of pupils: 369 B181 G188
Fees: €10,350–€15,945
Curriculum: ACT, AP, IBDP, IBPYP, SAT, USA, IGCSE
Language instr: English
(CIS) (ECIS)

International School of Paris

6 rue Beethoven, Paris, 75016 France
Tel: +33 1 4224 0954
Head of School: Ray Holliday-Bersegeay
Age range: 3–18
No. of pupils: 700
Fees: €17,900–€27,100
Curriculum: IBDP, IBMYP, IBPYP
Language instr: English
(CIS) (ECIS)

International School of Toulouse

Route de Pibrac, Colomiers, 31770 France
Tel: +33 562 74 26 74
Principal: Carolyn Steinson
Age range: 3–18
No. of pupils: B237 G238
Fees: €10,200–€17,900
Curriculum: IBDP, IPC, UK, IGCSE
Language instr: English
(CIS) (ECIS)

Lycee de Sevres, International Sections

Rue Lecocq, 92310 Sevres, France
Tel: +33 1 46 23 9635
Director: Kevin Jones
Age range: 11–18
No. of pupils: 620

Lycee International of St Germain-en-Laye, American Section

BP 70107, 78101 St Germain-en-Laye Cedex, France
Tel: +33 1 34 51 74 85
Director: Kelly Herrity
Age range: 4–19
No. of pupils: 700 B350 G350
Fees: €3,410–€8,900
Curriculum: National, FrenchBacc, USA
Language instr: French, English
(ECIS)

Marymount School

72 boulevard de la Saussaye, 92200 Neuilly sur Seine, France
Tel: +33 1 46 24 10 51
Head of School: Ronald Roukema
Age range: 3–14
No. of pupils: 432 B218 G214
Fees: €12,000–€23,700
Curriculum: USA
Language instr: English
(ECIS)

MOUGINS SCHOOL
For further details see p. 131
615 Avenue Dr Maurice Donat, CS 12180, 06252 MOUGINS Cedex, France
Tel: +33 (0)4 93 90 15 47
Email: information@mougins-school.com
Website: www.mougins-school.com
Headmaster: Brian G Hickmore
Age range: 3–18
No. of pupils: 518 B275 G243 VIth 79
Fees: €5,600–€15,520
Curriculum: UK, GCSE, IGCSE, ALevs
(COB)

Ombrosa, Lycée Multilingue de Lyon

95 Quai Clemenceau, Caluire, 69300 France
Tel: +33 4 78 23 22 63
Head of School: Luc Vezin
Age range: 2–18
No. of pupils: 1007 B528 G479
Fees: €3,160
Curriculum: AP, IBDP, National
Language instr: English, Spanish

Sainte Victoire International School

Domaine Sainte Victoire, Fuveau, 13710 France
Tel: +33 688 168 768
Head of School: Frederic Fabre
Curriculum: IBDP
Language instr: English, French
(symbol)

The British School of Paris

38 Quai De L'Ecluse, 78290 Croissy-sur-Seine, 78290 France
Tel: +33 (0)1 34 80 45 96 (admissions)
Headmaster: Steffen Sommer
Age range: 3–18
No. of pupils: 800 B400 G400 VIth 100
Fees: €10,000–€22,583
Curriculum: GCSE, ALevs
Language instr: English
(COB)

The International Bilingual School of Provence

500 Route de Bouc-Bel-Air, Domaine des Pins, Luynes, Aix en Provence, 13080 France
Tel: +33 (0)4 4224 0340
General Director: Jean-Marc Gobbi
Age range: 11–18
No. of pupils: 500
Fees: €8,920–€10,290
Curriculum: AP, IBDP, National, FrenchBacc, SAT, TOEFL, UK, USA, GCSE, IGCSE, ALevs
Language instr: English, French
(symbol) (ECIS)

Georgia

Buckswood International School Tbilisi
52 Rustaveli Street, Tskneti, Tbilisi, 0189 Georgia
Tel: +995 877 992 993
General Director: Archil Sumbadze
Language instr: English, Russian
ECIS

European School
34g Kazbegi Avenue, Tbilisi 0177, Georgia
Tel: +995 32 2140041
Head of School: Nana Mosidze
Age range: 3–18
No. of pupils: 580
Curriculum: IBDP, IBMYP
Language instr: English

New School
35 Tskneti Highway, Bagebi, Tbilisi, 0162 Georgia
Tel: +995 32 225 7079
Head of School: Marina Zhgenti
Curriculum: IBDP, IBMYP, IBPYP
Language instr: English, Georgian

QSI International school of Tbilisi
Village Zurgovani, Tbilisi, Georgia
Tel: +995 32 253 7670
Director: Thomas Tunny
Age range: 4–18
No. of pupils: 146
Curriculum: SAT, USA
Language instr: English

St George's British Georgian School
3 Aleksidze Street, Tbilisi, Georgia
Tel: +995 32 2609989
Headmaster: Christopher Greenfield
Curriculum: UK
Language instr: English
COB

Germany

Bavarian International School e.V.
Schloss Haimhausen, Hauptstrasse 1, Haimhausen, D-85778 Germany
Tel: +49 8133 917111
Director: Martin van Rijswijk
Age range: 4–18
Curriculum: IBDP, IBMYP, IBPYP, IGCSE
Language instr: English
CIS ECIS

BBIS Berlin Brandenburg International School GmbH
Am Hochwald 30, 14532 Kleinmachnow, Germany
Tel: +49 (0)33203 8036 0
Head of School: Peter Kotrc
Age range: 3–19
No. of pupils: 680
Fees: €10,700–€17,100
Curriculum: IBDP, IBMYP, IBPYP, IBCC
Language instr: English
CIS ECIS

Berlin British School
Dickensweg 17-19, Berlin, 14055 Germany
Tel: +49 (0)30 35109 190
Head: Graham Lacey
Age range: 3–18
No. of pupils: 400
Fees: €3,685–€14,083
Curriculum: IBDP, UK, IGCSE
Language instr: English
COB ECIS

Berlin Cosmopolitan School
Rückerstr 9, Berlin, 10119 Germany
Tel: +49 30 688 33 23 0
Head of School: Yvonne Wende
Curriculum: IBDP, IBPYP

Berlin International School
Lentzeallee 8/14, Berlin, 14195 Germany
Tel: +49 (0) 30 8200 7790
Director: Hubert Keulers
Age range: 6–18
No. of pupils: 825 B410 G415
Fees: €10,000
Curriculum: IBDP, IBPYP, SAT, IGCSE
Language instr: English
CIS ECIS

Berlin Metropolitan School
Linienstraße 122, 10115 Berlin, Germany
Tel: +49 30 8872 7390
Executive Director: Silke Friedrich
Age range: 5–11
No. of pupils: 424 B192 G232
Fees: €3,600–€7,200
Curriculum: IBDP, IBPYP, National
Language instr: English, German
ECIS

Bertolt-Brecht-Gymnasium Dresden
Lortzingstraße 01, Dresden, 01307 Germany
Tel: +49 351 449040
Head of School: Marcello Meschke
Curriculum: IBDP
Language instr: English

Black Forest Academy
Postfach 1109, 79396 Kandern, Germany
Tel: +49 7626 91610
Director/Head of School: Scott Jones
Age range: 10–19
No. of pupils: B160 G164
Fees: €8,640–€14,400
Curriculum: ACT, AP, SAT, USA
Language instr: English
CIS

Bonn International School EV
Martin-Luther-King Str 14, Bonn, 53175 Germany
Tel: +49 228 30854 0
Director: Chris Müller
Age range: 3–19
No. of pupils: 750 B375 G375
Fees: Day €8,050–€16,883
Curriculum: IBDP, IBMYP, IBPYP, SAT
Language instr: English
CIS ECIS

Cologne International School
Neue Sandkaul 29, 50859 Köln, Germany
Tel: +49 221 31 06 34 0
Managing Director: Sonja Guentner
Age range: 2–18
Language instr: English

Dresden International School e.V
Annenstr 9, 01067 Dresden, Germany
Tel: +49 351 440070
Head of School: Chrissie Sorenson
Age range: 1–19
No. of pupils: 530
Fees: €5,200–€11,000
Curriculum: ACT, IBDP, IBMYP, IBPYP, USA
Language instr: English
CIS ECIS

Erasmus International School
Flotowstrasse 10, 14480, Potsdam, Germany
Tel: +49 331 237 2790
Director: Stephen Wilkerson
Age range: 4–18
No. of pupils: 80 B37 G43
Curriculum: UK, IGCSE
Language instr: English

Franconian International School
Marie Curie-Strasse 2, 91052, Erlangen, Germany
Tel: +49 9131 940390
Acting Director: Petra Niemczyk
Age range: 4–18
No. of pupils: 168 B86 G82
Curriculum: IBDP
Language instr: English
CIS ECIS

Frankfurt International School
An der Waldlust 15, Oberursel, 61440 Germany
Tel: +49 6171 2024 0
Head of School: Paul M Fochtman
Age range: 3–18
No. of pupils: 1730 B865 G865
Fees: Day €16,940–€20,100
Curriculum: IBDP, IBPYP, SAT
Language instr: English, German
CIS ECIS

Frankfurt International School Wiesbaden Campus
Rudolf-Dietz-Strasse 14, Wiesbaden-Naurod, 65207 Germany
Tel: +49 6127 99400
Principal: Andrea Rosinger
Age range: 3–11
No. of pupils: B100 G100
Fees: €16,500
Curriculum: IBPYP
Language instr: English, German

Hansa-Gymnasium, Hamburg-Bergedorf
Hermann-Distel-Straße 25, Hamburg, 21029 Germany
Tel: +49 (0)40 724 18 60
Head of School: Hildegund Remme
Age range: B10–19 G10–19
No. of pupils: Vlfh185
Curriculum: Abitur, IBDP, TOEFL
Language instr: German/English

Heidelberg International School
Villa Heinstein, Wieblinger Weg 7, 69123 Heidelberg, Germany
Tel: +49 6221 75 90 600
School Director: Kathleen Macdonald
Age range: 4–19
No. of pupils: 182 B85 G97
Fees: €11,475–€15,860
Curriculum: IBDP, IBMYP, IBPYP
Language instr: English
ECIS

Herder Schule
Luisenstrasse 136, Wuppertal, D 42103 Germany
Tel: +49 202 313170
Headmaster: Dirk Norpoth
Age range: 10–19
No. of pupils: 240
Fees: €10,400
Curriculum: Abitur, National, TOEFL
Language instr: German/English
ISA

Hessen International Day & Boarding School
Postfach 2523, Schwalbach im Taunus, 65818 Germany
Tel: +49 (0) 6196 9998964
Director: Pelina Achimu-Heinzel
Age range: 3–18
No. of pupils: 37 B20 G17
Fees: €9,800–€11,600

Independent Bonn International School
Tulpenbaumweg 42,
53177 Bonn, Germany
Tel: +49 228 323 166
Headteacher: Irene Bolik
Age range: 3–11
No. of pupils: 225 B110 G115
Fees: Day £10,500
Curriculum: UK
Language instr: English
(COB) (ECIS)

International Kids Campus
Lerchenaurstrße 197,
München, 80935 Germany
Tel: +49 170 198 8896
Head of School: James Hamilton
Curriculum: IBPYP
Language instr: English, German

International Kindergarten/Pre-School
Sandstrasse, 64342 Seeheim-Jugenheim, Germany
Tel: +49 6257 944220
Head Teacher: Wende McCabe-Teichert
Age range: 3–6
No. of pupils: 72 B37 G35
Fees: €650
Curriculum: IPC, National
Language instr: English, German
(ECIS)

International School Augsburg (ISA)
Wernher-von-Braun-Str 1a,
86368 Gersthofen, Germany
Tel: +49 821 45 55 60 0
Head of School: Cathie Mullen
Age range: 4–18
No. of pupils: 315
Curriculum: IBDP, IBPYP
Language instr: English
(CIS)

International School Braunschweig-Wolfsburg
Helmstedter Straße 37,
Braunschweig, 38126 Germany
Tel: +49 531 889210 0
Head of School: Ursula Hellert
Age range: 4–19
No. of pupils: 256
Fees: €9,360
Curriculum: IBDP, IGCSE
Language instr: English
(⚖)

International School Hannover Region
Bruchmeisterallee 6,
Hannover, 30169 Germany
Tel: +49 511 270 416 50
Director: Patricia Baier
Age range: 3–19
No. of pupils: 539 B281 G258
Fees: €6,990–€12,020
Curriculum: IBDP, IBMYP, IBPYP
Language instr: English
(CIS) (ECIS)

International School Mainfranken
Cuspinianstrasse 3, Unterspiesheim,
97509 Germany
Tel: +49 9723 934250
Curriculum: IBDP
Language instr: English

INTERNATIONAL SCHOOL OF BREMEN
For further details see p. 122
Badgasteiner Str 11, D-28359
Bremen, Germany
Tel: +49 421 5157790
Email: office@isbremen.de
Website: www.isbremen.de
Director: Malcolm Davis
Age range: 3–18
No. of pupils: 400
Fees: €9,950–€15,150
Curriculum: ACT, IBDP, IPC, SAT, TOEFL, IGCSE
Language instr: English
(ECIS)

INTERNATIONAL SCHOOL OF DUSSELDORF E.V.
For further details see p. 124
Niederrheinstrasse 336,
Düsseldorf, 40489 Germany
Tel: +49 211 (0) 9406 712
Email: info@isdedu.de
Website: www.isdedu.de
Head: Simon Head
Age range: 4–19
No. of pupils: B540 G542
Curriculum: ACT, IBDP, IBMYP, IBPYP, SAT
Language instr: English
(CIS) (ECIS)

International School of Hamburg
Hemmingstedter Weg 130,
Hamburg, 22609 Germany
Tel: +49 40 8000 50 0
Head of School: Andreas Swoboda
Age range: 3–18
No. of pupils: 712 B372 G340 VIth52
Fees: €9,870–€19,230
Curriculum: IBDP, IPC, SAT
Language instr: English
(CIS) (ECIS)

International School of Neustadt
Maximilianstr 43, Neustadt,
Weinstrasse 67433 Germany
Tel: +49 6321 890 0960
Head of School: Nicolas Puga
Curriculum: IBDP, IBPYP
Language instr: English

International School of Stuttgart
Sigmaringer Str 257, Stuttgart,
70597 Germany
Tel: +49 711 769 6000
Director: Timothy Kelley
Age range: 3–18
No. of pupils: 602 B289 G313
Fees: €8,400–€13,350
Curriculum: IBDP, IBMYP, IBPYP, SAT
Language Instr: English
(CIS) (ECIS)

International School of Ulm/Neu Ulm
Schwabenstraße 25, D-89231
Neu-Ulm, Germany
Tel: +49 731 379 353-0
Director: Rob DeWolf
Age range: 3–14
No. of pupils: 175 B87 G88
Curriculum: IBDP, IBPYP
Language instr: English
(ECIS)

International School Ruhr
Villa Koppers, Moltkeplatz
61, Essen, 45138 Germany
Tel: +49 (0)201 479 10409
Head of School: Frank van Poucke
Curriculum: IBPYP

International School Villa Amalienhof
Heerstrasse 465, 13593
Berlin, Germany
Tel: +49 30 36 43 98 20
Head of School: Susanne Ak
Age range: 3–18
Curriculum: UK, ALevs
Language instr: English

Internationale Friedensschule Koln
Neue Sandkaul 29, Köln,
50859 Germany
Tel: +49 221 310 6340
Head of School: Sonja Guentner
Curriculum: IBPYP
Language instr: English, German
(ECIS)

ISF Internationale Schule Frankfurt-Rhein-Main Verwaltungs-GmbH
Strasse zur Internationalen
Schule 33, 65931 Frankfurt
am Main, Germany
Tel: +49 69 954319-710
Director: Angus Slesser
Age range: Pre-school–Grade 12
No. of pupils: 915 B526 G389
Fees: €12,105–€18,375
Curriculum: Abitur, AP, IBDP, SAT, IGCSE
Language instr: English
(ECIS)

ISR International School on the Rhine
Konrad-Adenauer-Ring 2,
41464 Neuss, Germany
Tel: +49 2131 403880
Head of School: Eileen Lyons
Age range: 3–19
Fees: €10,965–€16,890
Curriculum: AP, IBDP, SAT, IGCSE
Language instr: English
(ECIS)

John F Kennedy School
Telltower Damm 87-93,
14167 Berlin, Germany
Tel: + 49 30 90299 5711
Managing Director: Reinhard Roth
Age range: 5–19
No. of pupils: 1712

Leipzig International School eV
Koenneritzstrasse 47, 04229
Leipzig, Germany
Tel: +49 341 337 5580
Headmaster: David Smith
Age range: 3–19
Fees: €6,000–€10,000
Curriculum: IBDP, IGCSE
Language instr: English
(CIS) (ECIS)

Leonardo Da Vinci Campus
Zu den Luchbergen 13,
Brandenburg, Nauen,
14641 Germany
Tel: +49 3321 74 878 20
Head of School: Irene Petrovic-Wettstaedt
Curriculum: IBDP
Language instr: English, Spanish
(⚖)

Metropolitan School Frankfurt
Eschborner Landstrasse 134-138,
60489 Frankfurt, Germany
Tel: +49 69 96 86 405-0
Headteacher: Peter Ferres
Age range: 3–11
No. of pupils: 351
Fees: €4,392–€9,528
Curriculum: IBPYP
Language instr: English

Munich International School E.V.
Schloss Buchhof, Percha,
Starnberg, 82319 Germany
Tel: +49 8151 366 0
Head of School: Simon Taylor
Age range: 4–18
No. of pupils: 1217
Fees: €12,900–€16,210
Curriculum: IBDP, IBMYP, IBPYP
Language instr: English
(CIS) (ECIS)

Nymphenburger Schulen
Sadelerstraße 10, München,
80638 Germany
Tel: +49 89 15912200
Head of School: Monika Florian
Age range: 10–18
Curriculum: IBDP, National
Language instr: German, English

Phorms Berlin Mitte Bilingual School
Ackerstrasse 76, 13355
Berlin, Germany
Tel: +49 30 4679 8630
Director: Herbert Klassen
Age range: 3–19
No. of pupils: 570 B280 G290
Curriculum: Abitur, National, UK
Language instr: English, German
(ECIS)

Schillerschule Hannover
Ebellstrasse 15, Hannover,
30625 Germany
Tel: +49 511 16848777
Head of School: Beate Günther
Curriculum: IBDP
Language instr: English

Schule Birklehof
Birklehof 1, Hinterzarten,
79856 Germany
Tel: +49 7652 1220
Principal: Henrik Fass
Language instr: German

Schule Schloss Salem
Schloss Salem (Castle District),
88682 Salem, Germany
Tel: +49 7553 919 352
Principal: Bernd Westermeyer
Age range: 10–19
No. of pupils: 620
Fees: €32,000–€35,000
Curriculum: Abitur, IBDP, National
Language instr: English, German

St George's School Duisburg
Am Neuen Angerbach
90, Duisburg-Ungelsheim,
47259 Germany
Tel: +49 203 456860
Director: Edward Connolly
Age range: 3–18
No. of pupils: 376 B196 G180
Fees: €8,120
Curriculum: IBDP, UK, ALevs

St George's The English International School Cologne
Husarenstrasse 20, Cologne,
50997 Germany
Tel: +49 2233 80887 0
School Director: S Jaggard
Age range: 2–18
No. of pupils: 830 B415 G415
Fees: €9,420–€15,450
Curriculum: IBDP, GCSE,
IGCSE, ALevs
Language instr: English

State International School Seeheim-Jugenheim
Schuldorf Bergstraße, c/o
Wetterich/Szartowicz, Seeheim-
Jugenheim, D-64342 Germany
Tel: +49 6257 9703 13
Director: Ronald Seffrin
Age range: 6–15
No. of pupils: 203 B150 G153
Fees: €220–€270
Curriculum: National, UK, IGCSE
Language instr: English

Stiftung Landheim Schondorf am Ammersee
Country Home 1-14, Schondorf
am Ammersee, 86938 Germany
Tel: +49 8192 8090
Headmistress: Friederike Lenssen
Language instr: German

Stiftung Louisenlund
Güby 24357, Germany
Tel: +49 4354 999685
Head of School: Werner Esser
No. of pupils: 370
Fees: €2,455
Curriculum: IBDP

Strothoff International School Rhein-Main Campus Dreieich
Frankfurter Strasse 160-166,
Dreieich, 63303 Germany
Tel: +49 6103 8022523
Head of School: Andreas Koini
Age range: 3–18
Curriculum: IBDP, IBPYP
Language instr: English

Taunus International Montessori School
Zimmersmuehtenweg 77,
61440 Oberursel, Germany
Tel: +49 6171 91330
Director: Kathleen McClean
Age range: 1 –6
No. of pupils: 60

Thuringia International School – Weimar
Belvederer Allee 40, Weimar,
99425 Germany
Tel: +49 (0)3643 776904
Director: Philip Armstrong
Age range: 4–18
No. of pupils: 270 B135 G135 VIth25
Fees: €6,300–€8,000
Curriculum: IBDP, IBPYP, IGCSE
Language instr: English

UWC Robert Bosch College
Gauchstraße 1, Freiburg,
79098 Germany
Tel: +4976142963526
Head of School: Laurence Nodder
Curriculum: IBDP
Language instr: English

Gibraltar

Loreto Convent School
13 Europa Road, Gibraltar
Tel: +350 200 75781
Headteacher: Louise Napoli
Age range: 2–12
No. of pupils: 450 B220 G230
Fees: Day £3,555
Curriculum: UK
Language instr: English

Greece

American Community Schools of Athens
129 Aghias Paraskevis, Ano
Xalandri, Athens, GR 152 34 Greece
Tel: +30 210 639 3200
Director: Stefanos Gialamas
Age range: JK–12
No. of pupils: 792
Fees: €6,000–€13,000
Curriculum: IBDP
Language instr: English

American Farm School
Marinou Antipa 54, PO Box 23,
Thessaloniki, 551 02 Greece
Tel: +30 23104 92700
Curriculum: USA

Anatolia College
PO Box 21021, Pylea,
Thessaloniki, 55510 Greece
Tel: +30 231 0 398222
Head of School: Theodoros Filaretos
Age range: 12–18
No. of pupils: 1273 B567 G706
Curriculum: IBDP
Language instr: English

Byron College
7 Filolaou Street, 15344
Gerakas, Greece
Tel: +30 210 60 47 722 – 5
Head of School: Matthew Burfield
Age range: 3–18
Fees: €6,350–€11,350
Curriculum: UK, IGCSE, ALevs

Campion School
PO Box 67484, Pallini, 15302 Greece
Tel: +30 210 6071700
Head: Stephen Atherton
Age range: 3–18
No. of pupils: 510
Curriculum: IBDP
Language instr: English

Costeas-Geitonas School
Pallini – Attikis, Athens,
15351 Greece
Tel: +30 210 6030 411
Head of School: Christos Geitonas
Curriculum: IBDP, IBMYP, IBPYP
Language instr: English

Doukas School SA
151 Mesogion Street,
15125 Paradissos, Marousi,
Athens, 15125 Greece
Tel: +30 210 618 6000
Head of School: Konstantinos
I Doukas
No. of pupils: 2152
Curriculum: IBDP
Language instr: English

Geitona School
International Baccalaureate
Diploma Programme, PO
Box 74128, Sternizes, Koropi,
Attiki 166 02 Greece
Tel: +30 210, 9656200-10
Head of School: Eleftherios
Geitonas
Age range: 4–19
No. of pupils: 2147 B1100 G1047
Curriculum: IBDP
Language instr: English

H.A.E.F (Psychico College)
Psychico College, PO Box 65005,
Psychiko, Athens, 15410 Greece
Tel: +30 210 6798208
Head of School: Apostolos
Athanasopoulos
Age range: 17–18
No. of pupils: 243 B122 G121
Curriculum: IBDP
Language instr: English

I.M. Panagiotopoulos School
14 Nikiforou Lytra St, 154 52 Psychico,
Athens, GR-154 52 Greece
Tel: +30 210 677 6010
Head of School: Alkis
Panagiotopoulos
Age range: 3–18
Curriculum: National
Language instr: English

International School of Athens
PO Box 51051, Kifissia,
Athens, 14510 Greece
Tel: +30 210 6233 888
Head of School: Spiridon Molfetas
Age range: 3–18
No. of pupils: 324 B189 G135 VIth25
Fees: €4,700–€11,300
Curriculum: AP, IBDP, SAT
Language instr: English

Ionios School
PO Box 13622, Filothei,
15202 Greece
Tel: +30 210 6857130
Head of School: Zanis Margetis
Curriculum: IBDP

Moraitis School
A Papanastasiou & Ag
Dimitriou, Paleo Psychico,
Athens, 15452 Greece
Tel: +30 210 679 5000
Head of School: Chryssanthi
Moraiti-Kartali
Age range: 4–18
No. of pupils: 1800
Fees: €8,000–€13,000
Curriculum: IBDP,
National, SAT, TOEFL
Language instr: English

Pinewood American International School of Thessaloniki, Greece
14th km Thessalonikis – N. Moudanion, P.O. Box 60606, Thermi – Thessaloniki, GR-57001 Greece
Tel: +30, 2310 301 221
Director: Roxanne Giampapa
Age range: 3–18
No. of pupils: 206 B98 G108
Curriculum: IBDP
Language instr: English
🏛

Platon School
Eleytheriou Venizelou Street, Glyka Nera, Attika, 15354 Greece
Tel: +30 210 6611 793
Head of School: Panagiotis Papadopoulos
Curriculum: IBDP, IBMYP, IBPYP

St Catherine's British School
Leoforos Venizelou 77, Lykovrissi, Athens, 141 23 Greece
Tel: +30 210 2829 750
Head of School: Stuart Smith
Age range: 3–18
No. of pupils: 1060
Fees: €8,050–€13,040
Curriculum: IBDP, UK
Language instr: English
(COB)

St Lawrence College
PO Box 70151, 16610 Glyfada, Athens, Greece
Tel: +30 21 0891 7000
Headmaster: Phil Holden
Age range: 3–19
No. of pupils: 755 B372 G383
Fees: €7,410–€12,030
Curriculum: UK, IGCSE, ALevs
Language instr: English

The American College of Greece
Deree College, 6 Gravias Street, Gr-153 42 Aghia Paraskevi, Greece
Tel: +30 210 600 9800
President: David G Horner
🏛

Hungary

American International School of Budapest
Nagykovácsi út 12, Nagykovácsi, 2094 Hungary
Tel: +36 26 556 000
Director: Jan Wood
Age range: 3–20
No. of pupils: B434 G429
Fees: US$12,550–US$23,950
Curriculum: IBDP, SAT, USA
Language instr: English
(CEE) (OIS) (ECIS)

Britannica International School
Kakukk Way 1-3, 1121 Budapest, Hungary
Tel: +36 1 466 9794
Headmaster: Ken Baines
Age range: 5–18
No. of pupils: B150 G140
Curriculum: National, UK, IGCSE, ALevs
Language instr: English

International Christian School of Budapest
H-2049 Diosd, Ifjusag 11, Hungary
Tel: +36 23 381 986
Director: David M Welsh
Age range: 6–18
No. of pupils: 210
Curriculum: USA
Language instr: English
(CEE)

International School of Budapest
Konkoly Thege M u 21, Budapest 1121, Hungary
Tel: +36 1 395 6534
Principal: Susan Ballantyne
Age range: 5–12
No. of pupils: 160 B80 G80
Fees: €9,000–€10,500
Curriculum: National
Language instr: English

SEK Budapest International School
Hüvösvölgyi út 131, Budapest, 1021 Hungary
Tel: +36 1 394 2968
Head of School: Gabriella Gidró
Curriculum: IBDP
Language instr: English
(ISA)

The British International School, Budapest
Kiscelli koz 17, Budapest, 1037 Hungary
Tel: +36 1 200 8488
Head of School: John Hart
Age range: 3–18
No. of pupils: 500
Fees: Day £4,896–£11,318
Curriculum: IBDP, UK, GCSE
Language instr: English
(COB) (ECIS)

Iceland

International School of Iceland
Löngulínu 8, 210 Gar abœr, Iceland
Tel: +354 590 3106
Headmistress: Berta Faber
Age range: 5–13
Curriculum: IPC, National
(ECIS)

Ireland

Aravon School
Old Conna House, Ferndale Road, Old Conna, Bray, County Wicklow Ireland
Tel: +353 1 2821355
Headmaster: K W J Allwright
Age range: 3–12
No. of pupils: 162 B103 G59 VIth19
Fees: Day £1,320–£2,736
WB £5,337 FB £6,036
🏛

Castle Park School
Castle Park Road, Dalkey, Co Dublin, Ireland
Tel: +353 1 280 3037
Headmaster: D McSweeney
Age range: 3–12
No. of pupils: 286 B162 G124
Fees: €7,950
Language instr: English

Colegio Internacional SEK-Dublin
Belbedere Hall, Windgate, Bray, Co Wicklow Ireland
Tel: +353 1 287 4175
Principal: Mary McKey
Age range: 11–14
No. of pupils: 99 B48 G51

Headfort School
Kells, Co Meath Ireland
Tel: +353 4692 40065
Headmaster: Dermot Dix
Age range: 7–13
No. of pupils: 105 B65 G40
Fees: €8,500
🏛

International School of Dublin
Barclay Court, Temple Road, Blackrock, Dublin, Ireland
Tel: +353 1 668 9255
Head of School: Sarah Pepper
Age range: 3–13
No. of pupils: 55 B23 G32
Fees: €8,200
Curriculum: IBPYP
Language instr: English, Spanish

ST ANDREW'S COLLEGE
For further details see p. 137
Booterstown Avenue, Blackrock, County Dublin Ireland
Tel: +353 1 288 2785
Email: information@st-andrews.ie
Website: www.st-andrews.ie
Headmaster: Peter Fraser
Age range: 4–18
No. of pupils: 1264 B634 G630 VIth176
Fees: €6,400–€8,450
Curriculum: IBDP, National, SAT
Language instr: English
(AISA) (OIS) (ECIS)

ST COLUMBA'S COLLEGE
For further details see p. 138
Kilmashogue Lane, Whitechurch, Dublin 16, Ireland
Tel: +353 1 4906791
Email: admin@stcolumbas.ie
Website: www.stcolumbas.ie
Warden: L J Haslett
Age range: 11–18
No. of pupils: 295 B159 G136 VIth137
Fees: Day €3,452–€4,944
FB €6,207–€7,450
Curriculum: National
Language instr: English
🏛

Sutton Park School
St Fintan's Road, Sutton, Dublin 13, Ireland
Tel: +353 1 8322940
Head of School: Michael Moretta
Age range: 4–18
No. of pupils: 278 B167 G111
Curriculum: SAT
🏛 (OIS)

The King's Hospital
Palmerstown, Dublin 20, Ireland
Tel: +353 1 643 6500
Headmaster: Michael D Hall
Age range: 12–18
No. of pupils: 698 B355 G343 VIth120
Fees: €5,680
Curriculum: National
🏛

Italy

Ambrit International School
Via F Tajani 50, 00149 Rome, Italy
Tel: +39 06 5595 305/301
Headmaster: Bernard C Mullane MS
Age range: 3–14
No. of pupils: 450 B225 G225
Fees: €8,700–€14,200
Curriculum: IBPYP, National
Language instr: English

American Overseas School of Rome
Via Cassia 811, Rome, 00189 Italy
Tel: +39 06 334 381
Head of School: Beth Pfannl
Age range: 3–20
No. of pupils: 626
Fees: €8,900–€18,700
Curriculum: AP, IBDP, SAT, USA
Language instr: English
(ECIS)

American School of Milan
Via Karl Marx 14, Noverasco di Opera, Milano, 20090 Italy
Tel: +39 02 5300 001
Director: Alan Austen
Age range: 3–18
No. of pupils: 657 B337 G320
Fees: €7,684–€16,065
Curriculum: IBDP, SAT
Language instr: English

Andersen International School
Via Don Carlo, San Martino 8, Milan, 20133 Italy
Tel: +39 02 70 00 65 80
Consultant Head: Sheila Stokes
Age range: 2–11
No. of pupils: 250 B110 G140
Curriculum: UK
Language instr: English
(COB)

Anglo-Italian School Montessori Division
Viale Della Liberazione Comando NATO, 90125 Bagnoli Naples, Italy
Tel: +39 081 721 2266
Director: Alba Fedele
Age range: 2–15
No. of pupils: 346 B180 G166
Fees: €2,755–€4,940
Curriculum: National, USA
(ECIS)

Bilingual European School
Via Val Cismon 9, Milan, 20162 Italy
Tel: +39 02 6611 7449
Head of School: Day Jones
Curriculum: IBPYP
Language instr: English, Italian

Castelli International School
Via Degli Scozzesi 13, 00046 Grottaferrata, Rome, Italy
Tel: +39, 06 94315779
Head: Marianne Palladino
Age range: 6–14
No. of pupils: 130 B70 G60
Fees: €10,500
Curriculum: IPC, National, SAT
Language instr: English

CEI International School Palermo
Centro Educativo Ignaziano, Via Piersanti Mattarella, 38/42, Palermo, 90141 Italy
Tel: +39 0917 216111 ext 3
Curriculum: IBPYP
Language instr: English

Deledda International School
IB Diploma Course, Via Bertani, 6, Castelletto, Genova, Liguria 16125 Italy
Tel: +39 010 811634
Head of School: Ignazio Venzano
No. of pupils: 770
Curriculum: IBDP
Language instr: English

English International School
Via Segafredo 50, 36027, Rosà (VI), Italy
Tel: +39 0424 582191
Principal: Francesca Eger
Age range: 4–14
No. of pupils: 276 B137 G139
Fees: €6,000
Curriculum: National, TOEFL
Language instr: English, Italian
(ECIS)

Greenwood Garden School
Via Vito Sinisi 5, Rome 00189, Italy
Tel: +39 06 3326 6703
Age range: 2–6
No. of pupils: 44 B22 G22
Curriculum: USA
Language instr: English

International School of Bologna
Via della Libertà 2, Bologna, 40123 Italy
Tel: +39 051 6449954
Head of School: Denise Walsh
Age range: 3–12
Fees: €7,000–€11,500
Curriculum: IBMYP, IBPYP
Language instr: English
(CIS)

International School of Brescia
Via Don Orione, 1, 25082 Botticino, Italy
Tel: +39 030 2191182
Director: Patrick Arcuri
Age range: 1–7
Fees: €7,500–€10,000
Curriculum: IBPYP
(ECIS)

International School of Como
Via Adda 25, 22073 Fino Mornasco (Como), Italy
Tel: +39 031 576186
Head of School: Emanuela Ferloni
Age range: 2–14
No. of pupils: 217
Curriculum: IBPYP
Language instr: English
(ECIS)

International School of Europe Srl
P.I. 11794570157, Villa Parigini-Loc., Basciano, Monteriggioni, Milan, 20146 Italy
Tel: +39 0577 328103
Head of School: Victoria Watson
Curriculum: IBPYP
Language instr: English

International School of Florence
Via del Carota 23/25, Bagno a Ripoli, Florence, 50012 Italy
Tel: +39 055 6461 007
Head of School: Christopher C Maggio
Age range: 3–18
No. of pupils: 439 B216 G223 VIth28
Curriculum: IBDP, IBPYP, National, SAT, USA
Language instr: English, Italian
(CIS) (ECIS)

International School of Milan
Sede in Via I Maggio, 20, 20021 Baranzate, Milano, Italy
Tel: +39 02 872581
Headmaster: Terence Haywood
Age range: 3–18
No. of pupils: 1300 B650 G650 VIth120
Fees: €8,000–€16,000
Curriculum: IBDP, IBMYP, IBPYP
Language instr: English
(ECIS)

International School of Milan – Monza Section
Via Santo Stefano, 4, Vedano al Lambro, Milan, 20057 Italy
Tel: +39 039 2497937
Head of School: Martina Geromin
Curriculum: IBMYP, IBPYP
Language instr: English

International School of Modena
Piazza Montessori 1/A, Montale Rangone, Modena, 41051 Italy
Tel: +39 059 530 649
Head of School: Sarah Rimini
Age range: 5–16
No. of pupils: 50 B24 G26
Curriculum: IBMYP, IBPYP
Language instr: English
(ECIS)

International School of Naples
Viale della Liberazione, 1, Bagnoli 80125, Naples, Italy
Tel: +39 081 762 8429
Principal: Josephine Sessa
Age range: 4–18
No. of pupils: 203 B113 G90
Curriculum: National, SAT, USA
(CIS) (ECIS)

International School of Treviso
Via Milano 1, Olmi di San Biagio di Callalta, TV 31048 Italy
Tel: +39 0422 794061
Headteacher: Katriona Hoskins
Age range: 3–14
No. of pupils: 163 B104 G57
Curriculum: IBPYP
Language instr: English, Italian
(ECIS)

International School of Trieste
Via Conconello 16, Opicina, 34016 Trieste, Italy
Tel: +39 040 211452
Principal: Jason Anklowitz
Age range: 2–14
No. of pupils: 335 B165 G170
Curriculum: AP, USA
Language instr: English
(ECIS)

International School of Turin
Strada Pecetto 34, 10023 Chieri, Turin, Italy
Tel: +39 011 645 967
Head of School: Tomm J Elliott
Age range: 3–18
No. of pupils: 470
Curriculum: IBDP, IBMYP, IBPYP
Language instr: English
(CIS) (ECIS)

International School of Venice
Via Terraglio, Mestre-Venice, 30 Italy
Tel: +39 041 983 711
Language instr: English, Italian
(ECIS)

International School of Verona Aleardo Aleardi
Aleardo Aleardi, Via Segantini 20, Verona, 37138 Italy
Tel: +39 04557 8200
Head of School: Maria Grazia Nalin
Age range: 3–18
No. of pupils: 730
Curriculum: IBDP, National, IGCSE
Language instr: English
(ECIS)

Istituto Marymount
Via Nomentana, 355, Bagno a Ripoli, Rome, 00162 Italy
Tel: +39 06 8622571
Head of School: Andrea Forzoni
Language instr: English, Italian

Kendale International Primary School
Via Gradoli 86, Tombe di Nerone, Rome 00189, Italy
Tel: +39 06 3326 7608
Directress: Gloria Hughes Fabriani
Age range: 3–11
No. of pupils: 100 B48 G52
Fees: €5,000–€9,300
Curriculum: UK
Language instr: English

Marymount International School
Via di Villa Lauchli, 180, (Via Cassia) km 7, Rome, 00191 Italy
Tel: +39 06 3629101
Head of School: Maire Castelluccio
Age range: 3–18
No. of pupils: 650 B325 G325
Fees: €9,900–€19,000
Curriculum: AP, IBDP
Language instr: English
(CIS) (ECIS)

New School Rome
Via Della Camilluecia 669, Rome 00135, Italy
Tel: +39 06 329 4269
Headteacher: Domini MacRory
Age range: 3–18
No. of pupils: 170
Curriculum: UK, ALevs
(COB)

O.M.C. – Collegio Vescovile Pio X
Borgo Cavour 40, Treviso, 31100 Italy
Tel: +39 0422 411725
Head of School: Mauro Bordignon
Curriculum: IBDP
Language instr: English

Play English & The Bilingual School of Monza
Via Confalonieri 18, Monza, Milan 20052, Italy
Tel: +39 039 231 2282
Headteacher: Eugenia Papadaki
Age range: 1–11
No. of pupils: 111 B51 G60
Curriculum: IBPYP
Language instr: English
(ECIS)

QSI International School of Brindisi
Via Benvenuto Cellini 25, 72100 Brindisi, Italy
Tel: +39 0831 518764
Director: Steve Christensen
Age range: 3–13
No. of pupils: 34
Curriculum: USA
Language instr: English

Rome International School
Via Gugliemo Pecori Giraldi n.137, Rome, 00135 Italy
Tel: +39 06 8448 2651
Principal – Primary: Patricia Martin-Smith
Age range: 2–18
No. of pupils: 475 B238 G237
Fees: €9,940–€18,000
Curriculum: IBDP, IBPYP, UK, GCSE, IGCSE
Language instr: English
(ECIS)

Sir James Henderson British School of Milan
Via Pisani Dossi 16, Milan, 20134 Italy
Tel: +39 02 210941
Principal & CEO: Carlo Ferrario
Age range: 3–18
Fees: €9,300–€14,650
Curriculum: IBDP, IBCC, UK, IGCSE
Language instr: English
(COB)

Southlands English School in Rome
Via Teleclide 20, Casal Palocco, Rome 00124, Italy
Tel: +39 06 505 3932
Principal: Deryck M Wilson
Age range: 3–14
No. of pupils: 400 B200 G200
Fees: €6,370–€11,590
Curriculum: UK, GCSE
Language instr: English
(COB)

St George's British International School
Via Cassia, La Storta, Roma, 00123 Italy
Tel: +39 06 30860021
Principal: Martyn J Hales
Age range: 3–18
No. of pupils: 660 B340 G320 VIth1300
Fees: €11,160–€17,680
Curriculum: IBDP, GCSE, IGCSE
Language instr: English
(CIS) (COB) (ECIS)

St Louis School
Via Caviglia 1, 20139, Milan, Italy
Tel: +39 02 552 31235
Head of School: Gerry Rafferty
Age range: 2–14
No. of pupils: 330 B183 G147
Curriculum: IBDP
(COB) (ECIS)

ST. STEPHEN'S SCHOOL
For further details see p. 141
Via Aventina 3, Rome, 00153 Italy
Tel: +39 06 575 0605
Email: ststephens@ststephens-rome.com
Website: www.sssrome.it
Head of School: Eric Mayer
Age range: 14–19
No. of pupils: 270
Fees: €21,900
Curriculum: ACT, AP, IBDP, SAT, USA
Language instr: English
(⚑) (CIS) (ECIS)

The English International School of Padua
Via Forcellini 168, Padova, Veneto, 35128 Italy
Tel: +39 049 80 22 503
School Director: Rossella Gilli
Age range: 2–18
No. of pupils: B383 G355
Fees: €5,970–€11,910
Curriculum: IBDP, National, SAT, UK, IGCSE, ALevs
Language instr: English
(ECIS)

The International School in Genoa
Via Romana Della Castagna 11A, Genoa 16148, Italy
Tel: +39 010 386528
Head of School: Samer Khoury
Age range: 3–18
No. of pupils: 244 B126 G118
Curriculum: IBDP, National, SAT
Language instr: English
(CIS) (ECIS)

The Udine International School
Via Martignacco 187, Udine, 33100 Italy
Tel: +39 0432 541119
Head of School: Matthew Conn
Age range: 2–13
Language instr: English
(CIS)

United World College of the Adriatic/ONLUS
Via Trieste 29, Duino, Trieste, 34011 Italy
Tel: +39 040 3739 111
Head of School: Mike Price
Age range: 16–19
No. of pupils: 200 B100 G100
Curriculum: IBDP
Language instr: English
(⚑)

Villa Grimani International School
Via Leonardo da Vinci 4, 35027 Noventa Padovana PD, Italy
Tel: +39 049 8933833
Director: Stefano Amarilli
Age range: 3–13
(ECIS)

Vittoria International School
Via delle Rosine 14, Turin 10123, Italy
Tel: +39 011 889870
Head of School: Marcella Margaria
Age range: 14–19
No. of pupils: 85
Fees: €7,800–€8,700
Curriculum: IBDP, ALevs
Language instr: English

Westminster International School
Piazza Toniolo 4, Pisa, 56125 Italy
Tel: +39 050 28466
Head of School: Wendy Fish
Curriculum: IBPYP

Kosovo

International School of Prishtina
Marigona Residence, Pristina, Kosovo
Tel: +386 49 770513 / +386 49 425216
Principal: Mustafa Guven
Age range: 6–18
No. of pupils: 425
Curriculum: National
(ECIS)

Mehmet Akif College
Banullë, Lipjan, Kosovo
Tel: +38138581999 / +38649770514
Principal: Yusuf Karabina
No. of pupils: 563
(⚑) (ECIS)

Latvia

International School of Latvia
Meistaru 2, Pinki, Babītes novads, Jurmala, LV-2107 Latvia
Tel: +371 6775 5146
Director: Mary Russman
Age range: 2–18
No. of pupils: 325
Fees: €6,500–€14,700
Curriculum: IBDP, IBMYP, IBPYP, SAT
Language instr: English
(CEE) (CIS)

International School of Riga
Zvejnieku iela 12, Riga, 1048 Latvia
Tel: +371 6762 4622
Head of School: Lee Chalkly
Age range: 2–14
No. of pupils: 1847 B80 G104 VIth16
Fees: LVL4,195–LVL8,375
Curriculum: IBPYP
Language instr: English
(CIS)

Lithuania

Kaunas Jesuit High School
RotuÅ¡Ä—s a. 9, 4428 Lithuania
Tel: +370 37423098
Head of School: Virgilijus Saulius
Curriculum: IBDP

The American International School of Vilnius
Subaciaus 41, Vilnius, 11350 Lithuania
Tel: +370 5 212 1031
Director: David W. Christenbury
Age range: 3–16
No. of pupils: 171 B25 G34
Fees: €1,050–€17,750
Curriculum: IBDP
(CEE) (CIS) (ECIS)

Vilnius International School
Turniskiu Str 21, Rusu Str 3, Vilnius, 01125 Lithuania
Tel: +370 5 276 1564
Head of School: Rebecca Toth Juras
Curriculum: IBMYP, IBPYP

Luxembourg

Fräi-Öffentlech Waldorfschoul Lëtzebuerg
45 rue de l'Avenir, Luxembourg, 1147 Luxembourg
Tel: +352 466932
Head of School: Dominique Schlechter
No. of pupils: 349
Curriculum: IBDP
Language instr: French

International School of Luxembourg
36 Boulevard Pierre Dupong,
1430 Luxembourg, Luxembourg
Tel: +352 26 04 40
Director: Christopher Bowman
Age range: 3–18
No. of pupils: 1198
Fees: €10,500–€17,500
Curriculum: IBDP, SAT, IGCSE
Language instr: English
(CIS) (ECIS)

ST GEORGE'S INTERNATIONAL SCHOOL LUXEMBOURG A.S.B.L.
For further details see p. 139
11 Rue des Peupliers, L-2328
Luxembourg, Luxembourg
Tel: +352 423224
Email: reception@st-georges.lu
Website: www.st-georges.lu
Principal: Christian Barkei
Age range: 3–18+
No. of pupils: 674 B332 G342
Fees: €5,625–€13,715
Curriculum: IPC, UK, IGCSE, ALevs
Language instr: English
(CIS) (COB) (ECIS)

Macedonia

Anglo-American School Skopje
Str. Frederik Shopen 10,
Skopje, Macedonia
Tel: +389 23 216 944
Principal: Natali Ilievska
Language instr: English, Macedonian

NOVA International Schools
Praska BB, Skopje, 1000 Macedonia
Tel: +389 2 3061 907
Head of School: Venera Novakovska
Age range: 16–18
No. of pupils: 530 B272 G258
Fees: €5,050
Curriculum: IBDP
Language instr: English
(IB) (CEE)

QSI International School of Skopje
Zenevska #51, 1000 Skopje, Macedonia
Tel: +389 2 305 1844
Director: Robert Tower
Age range: 5–13
No. of pupils: 103
Curriculum: USA
Language instr: English

Malta

QSI International School of Malta
Triq Durumblat, Mosta, 4815 Malta
Tel: +356 21 423067
Director: Howell Iles
Age range: 5–18
Curriculum: USA
Language instr: English

RBSM International Boarding School
Triq Il-Gifen, San Pawl Il-Bahar, Bugibba, SPB 2847 Malta
Tel: +356 21584448
Principal: Snezhana Bodishtianu
Language instr: English, Russian
(IB) (ECIS)

St Edwards College, Malta
St Edward's Street, Birgu (Città Vittoriosa), BRG 9039 Malta
Tel: +356 2182 5978
Headmaster: Michael Chittenden
Age range: 16–18 B3–16
No. of pupils: B524 G20
Fees: €1,600–€5,000
Curriculum: IBDP, National
Language instr: English
(IB)

Verdala International School
Fort Pembroke, Pembroke, PBK 1641 Malta
Tel: +356 21375133
Head of School: Roy Crawford
Age range: 3–18
No. of pupils: 320 B166 G154
Curriculum: IBDP, IPC, SAT, IGCSE
Language instr: English
(IB) (ECIS)

Moldova

QSI International School of Chisinau
48/2 Nicolae Costin Street, Chisinau, MD 2051 Moldova
Tel: +373 22 588 346
Director: Valerie Mullen
Age range: 3–13
No. of pupils: 47
Curriculum: USA
Language instr: English

Monaco

International School of Monaco
12 quai Antoine 1er, Monte Carlo, 98000 Monaco
Tel: +377 9325 6820
Head of School: John Price
Age range: 3–18
No. of pupils: 525 B247 G278
Fees: €8,340–€20,300
Curriculum: IBDP, UK, IGCSE
Language instr: English, French
(CIS) (ECIS)

International Section of Monaco
Avenue de L'Annociade, 98000 Monaco, Monaco
Tel: +377 93 15 89 60
Principal: Madame Lamblin
Age range: 4–18
No. of pupils: 365

Montenegro

Arcadia Academy
Donja Lastva, Jadranska magistrala, Tivat, 85332 Montenegro
Tel: +382 32 662 662
Headteacher: Milija Bozovic
Language instr: English

KSI MONTENEGRO
For further details see p. 128
Seljanovo bb, Porto Montenegro, Tivat, Montenegro
Tel: +382 32 672 655
Email: info@KSI-Montenegro.com
Website: www.KSI-Montenegro.com
Head of School: Linda Winch
Age range: 3–16
Fees: *Day* €11,850–€13,500 *FB* €11,500
Curriculum: IBPYP
(IB)

QSI International School of Montenegro
Ul. Romanovih 33, Zabjelo, 81000 Podgorica, Montenegro
Tel: +382 20 641 734
Director: Mitchell Elswick
Age range: 5–13
No. of pupils: 42 B20 G22
Fees: $16,100
Language instr: English

Netherlands

AFNORTH International School
Ferdinand Bolstraat 1, Brunssum 6445 EE, Netherlands
Tel: +31 455 278 221
International Director: Elsie Stresman
Age range: 4–19
No. of pupils: 1000
Fees: €15,405–€17,570
Curriculum: ACT, AP, SAT, UK, USA
Language instr: English, German, French
(ECIS)

American International School of Rotterdam
Verhulstlaan 21, Rotterdam 3055WJ, Netherlands
Tel: +31 10 422 5351
Director: Neal Dilk
Age range: 3–18
No. of pupils: 130
Curriculum: IBDP, SAT, USA, IGCSE
Language instr: English
(CIS) (ECIS)

American School of The Hague
Rijksstraatweg 200, 2241BX Wassenaar, Netherlands
Tel: +31 70 512 1080
Director: Richard Spradling
Age range: 3–18
No. of pupils: 1230
Fees: €15,750–€22,855
Curriculum: ACT, AP, IBDP, SAT, TOEFL, USA
Language instr: English
(CIS) (ECIS)

Amsterdam International Community School
Prinses Irenestraat 59, 1077 WV Amsterdam, Netherlands
Tel: +31 20 577 1240
Principal: Kees van Ruitenbeek
Age range: 4–19
No. of pupils: 920
Fees: €5,045–€7,735
Curriculum: IBDP, IBMYP, IPC
Language instr: English
(CIS) (ECIS)

Arnhem International School
Groningensingel 1245, Arnhem, 6835 HZ Netherlands
Tel: +31 26 3200111/4
Head of School: J Katzer
Age range: 12–18
No. of pupils: 155 B80 G75
Fees: €5,550
Curriculum: IBDP, IBMYP
Language instr: English
(ECIS)

British School in The Netherlands
Admissions Office, BSS Building, Vrouw Avenweg 640, Den Haag, 2493 WZ Netherlands
Tel: +31 (0) 70 315 4077
Head of School: Peter Simpson
Age range: 3–18
No. of pupils: 1962 B1006 G956 VIth221
Fees: €12,510–€17,430
Curriculum: IBDP, National, TOEFL, GCSE, ALevs
Language instr: English
(COB)

British School of Amsterdam
Anthonie van Dijckstraat 1, 1077
ME Amsterdam, Netherlands
Tel: +31 (0)20 679 7840
Principal: J Goyer
Age range: 3–18
No. of pupils: 800 *B*420 *G*380 *VIth*40
Curriculum: SAT, UK, IGCSE, ALevs
Language instr: English
(COB)

De Blijberg (International Department)
Graaf Florisstraat 56, 3021 CJ,
Rotterdam, Netherlands
Tel: +31 10 448 2266
Head of School: Lorraine Boyle
Age range: 4–12
No. of pupils: 170 *B*90 *G*80
Fees: €2,850
Language instr: English

European School Bergen
Molenweidtje 5, Bergen, North
Holland, 1862 BC Netherlands
Tel: +31 72 589 0109
Director: Steve Lewis
Age range: 4–18
No. of pupils: 600 *B*300 *G*300
Fees: €3,374–€6,326
Language instr: French,
Dutch, English, German

Haagsche School Vereeniging, International Department
Nassaulaan 26, The Hague
E 2514 JT, Netherlands
Tel: +31 70 3638531
Head of International Dept: L Dean
Age range: 4–11
No. of pupils: 250
Fees: €3,750
Language instr: English
(ECIS)

International School Almere
Heliumweg 61, Almere Poort,
1362 JA Netherlands
Tel: +31 36 7600750
Head of School: Rynette de Villiers
Age range: 11–18
No. of pupils: 150 *B*76 *G*74
Curriculum: IBDP, IBMYP
Language instr: English

International School Eerde
Kasteellaan 1, Ommen,
PJ 7731 Netherlands
Tel: +31 529 451452
Principal: D Peek
Age range: 4–18
No. of pupils: 130
Fees: €21,000
Curriculum: IBDP, IGCSE
Language instr: English
(英) (CIS) (ECIS)

International School Eindhoven
Oirschotsedijk 14b, 5651GC
Eindhoven, Netherlands
Tel: +31 (0)40 251 9437
Director of School: David Gatley
Age range: 3–18
Fees: €3,570
Curriculum: IBDP, IBMYP, IPC
Language instr: English, Dutch
(CIS) (ECIS)

International School Groningen
PO Box 6105, 9702 HC
Groningen, Netherlands
Tel: +31 50 5340084
Head of School: Mike Weston
Age range: 11–19
No. of pupils: 130 *B*65 *G*65 *VIth*45
Fees: €6,700
Curriculum: National
Language instr: English
(ECIS)

International School Hilversum 'Alberdingk Thijm'
Emmastraat 56, Hilversum,
1213 AL Netherlands
Tel: + 31, 35 6729931
Head of School: Jetty van Driel
Age range: 5–19
No. of pupils: 550 *B*281 *G*269 *VIth*170
Curriculum: IBDP, IBMYP, IBPYP
Language instr: English
(CIS) (ECIS)

International School of Amsterdam
PO Box 920, Sportlaan 45,
Amstelveen, 1180 AX Netherlands
Tel: +31 20 347 1111
Director: Edward E Greene
Age range: 3–18
No. of pupils: 1070 *B*558 *G*512
Fees: Day €6,400–€22,700
Curriculum: IBDP, IBMYP, IBPYP
Language instr: English
(CIS) (ECIS)

International School The Rijnlands Lyceum Oegstgeest
Apollolaan 1, Oegstgeest,
BA 2341 Netherlands
Tel: +31 71 5193 555
Head of School: John Swieringa
Age range: 11–18
No. of pupils: 1200
Fees: €4,600
Curriculum: IBDP, IBMYP
Language instr: English
(ECIS)

IPS Violenschool
Rembrandtlaan 30, Hilversum,
BH 1213 Netherlands
Tel: +31 35 6216 053
Head of School: Robert Westlake
Age range: 4–12
No. of pupils: 250 *B*140 *G*110
Curriculum: IBPYP

Laar & Berg
Langsakker 4, Laren (NH),
1251 GB Netherlands
Tel: +31 3553 95422
Head of School: Bart van den Haak
Age range: 11–18
No. of pupils: 800 *B*406 *G*394
Fees: €178–€1,441
Curriculum: IBMYP, National
Language instr: English and Dutch
(CIS)

Maartenscollege
PO Box 6105, Groningen,
HC 9702 Netherlands
Tel: +31 50 534 0084
Head of School: Michael Weston
No. of pupils: 130
Fees: €6,700
Curriculum: IBDP, IBMYP
Language instr: English

Marcanti College
Jan van Galenstraat 31, 1051
KM Amsterdam, Netherlands
Tel: +31 020 6069000
Director: PJA Henry

Rotterdam International Secondary School
Bentincklaan 294, Rotterdam,
3039 KK Netherlands
Tel: +31 10 890 7744
Head of School: Jane Forrest
Age range: 11–19
No. of pupils: *B*93 *G*92 *VIth*60
Fees: €6,000–€8,000
Curriculum: IBDP, IGCSE
Language instr: English
(CIS) (ECIS)

The International School of The Hague
Wijndaelerduin 1, The Hague,
2554 BX Netherlands
Tel: +31 70 328 1450
Secondary Principal: David Butcher
Age range: 11–18
No. of pupils: 900
Fees: €6,250–€7,200
Curriculum: IBDP, IBMYP
Language instr: English
(CIS) (ECIS)

United World College Maastricht
Nijverheidsweg 25, Maastricht,
6201 BD Netherlands
Tel: +31 43 24 10 410
Head of College: Peter Howe
Age range: 11–18
No. of pupils: 230 *B*12 *G*110
Fees: €5,300
Curriculum: IBDP, IBMYP, IGCSE
Language instr: English
(ECIS)

Norway

Arendal International School
Julius Smiths Vei, His 4817,
Aust Agder, 4806 Norway
Tel: +47 37 055 104
Head of School: Bente Pedersen
Curriculum: IBMYP, IBPYP
Language instr: English

Birralee International School
Bispegata 9c, Trondheim,
7012 Norway
Tel: +47 73 87 02 60
Principal: Trude Farstad
Age range: 4–16
No. of pupils: 175 *B*80 *G*95
Fees: NOK13,500–NOK24,750
Curriculum: UK, IGCSE
Language instr: English
(ECIS)

British International School of Stavanger
Gauselbakken 107, Gausel,
N-4032 Norway
Tel: +47 519 50 250
Principal: Anne Howells
Age range: 2–16
No. of pupils: 500 *B*250 *G*250
Fees: NOK135,000
Curriculum: IBMYP
Language instr: English
(COB)

International School of Bergen
Vilhelm Bjerknesvei 15,
Bergen, 5081 Norway
Tel: +47 55 30432
Director: June Murison
Age range: 3–16
No. of pupils: 220
Fees: NOK24,000–NOK180,000
Curriculum: IBDP, IBMYP,
IBPYP, National
Language instr: English
(CIS) (ECIS)

International School of Stavanger
Treskeveien 3, Hafrsfjord,
4043 Norway
Tel: +47 51554300
Head of School: Linda Duevel
Age range: 3–19
No. of pupils: 725
Curriculum: ACT, IBDP, SAT
Language instr: English
(CIS) (COB) (ECIS)

International School Telemark
Hovet Ring 7, Porsgrunn,
3931 Norway
Tel: 00 47 35291400
Principal: Richard Caffyn
Age range: 6–16
No. of pupils: 133 *B*73 *G*60
Fees: NOK24,300
Curriculum: IBMYP, IBPYP
Language instr: English

Kongsberg International School
Dyrmyrgata 39-41,
Kongsberg, 3611 Norway
Tel: +47 32 29 93 80
Principal: Robert Clarence
Age range: 3–16
No. of pupils: 194
Fees: NOK25,465–NOK26,020
Curriculum: IBMYP, IBPYP
Language instr: English

Kristiansand International School
Kongsgård alle 20,
Kristiansand, 4631 Norway
Tel: +47 38 10 2811
Head of School: Sonya Eriksson
Curriculum: IBMYP, IBPYP
Language instr: English, Norweigan

Oslo International School
PO Box 53, Bekkestua, 1318 Norway
Tel: +47 67 8182 90
Head of School: Janecke Aarnæs
Age range: 3–18
No. of pupils: 600 B320 G280
Curriculum: IBDP, SAT
Language instr: English
(CIS) (ECIS)

Red Cross Nordic United World College
N – 6968 Flekke, Fjaler Norway
Tel: +47 5773 7005
Head of School: Richard Lamont
Age range: 16–21
No. of pupils: 200
Curriculum: IBDP, SAT
Language instr: English
(♔)

Skagerak International School
Framnesveien 7, Sandefjord,
3222 Norway
Tel: +47 33456500
Head of School: Michael L Meszaros
Age range: 4–19
No. of pupils: 345 B158 G187
Curriculum: IBDP
Language instr: English
(ECIS)

Skagerak Primary and Middle School
Framnesveien 7, Sandefjord,
3222 Norway
Tel: +4733456500
Age range: 4–16
No. of pupils: 200 B100 G100
Fees: NOK25,500
Curriculum: IBMYP, IBPYP
Language instr: English

The Children's House
Kornbergveien 23, Sola,
4050 Norway
Tel: +47 51 651696
Age range: 2–7
No. of pupils: 158 B86 G72
(ECIS)

Tromsø International School
4 Breiviklia, Tromso, 9019 Norway
Tel: +47 99200780
Head of School: Tonje Hofsoy
Curriculum: IBPYP
Language instr: English

Trondheim International School
Festningsgata 2, Trondheim
7014, Norway
Tel: +47 7351 4800
Head of School: James Hamilton
No. of pupils: 197
Curriculum: IBMYP, IBPYP
Language instr: English

Poland

American School of Warsaw
Bielawa, ul Warszawska 202,
Konstancin-Jeziorna, 05-520 Poland
Tel: +48 22 702 8500
Director: Terry Gamble
Age range: 4–18
No. of pupils: 920 B460 G460
Curriculum: ACT, AP, IBDP, SAT
Language instr: English
(CEE) (CIS) (ECIS)

British International School of Cracow
Ul Smolensk 25, Kraków,
31-108 Poland
Tel: +48 12 292 64 78
Head of School: Stanislaw Kwiecinski
Age range: 3–19
No. of pupils: 161 B85 G76
Curriculum: IBDP
Language instr: English
(ECIS)

British International School Wroclaw
Al, Akacjowa 10/12, 53-134 Wroclaw, Poland
Tel: +48 71 7966861
Headteacher: Derek Smith
Age range: 3–18
No. of pupils: B55 G54
Curriculum: National,
UK, IGCSE, ALevs
Language instr: English
(ECIS)

British International School, Lodz
ul Sterlinga 26, 90-212
Lódz Polska, Poland
Tel: +48 42 631 59 23
Head Teacher: Marzena Podsiedlik
Age range: 5–16
Curriculum: UK
Language instr: English

British School Vocandus
ul. Woronicza 16, 91-030 Lodz, Poland
Tel: +48 696 050 078
Principal: Grazyna Miller
Age range: 5–18
Curriculum: UK, IGCSE
(ECIS)

Canadian School of Warsaw
Kanadyjska Szkola Podstawowa, Ul.
Belska 7, Warszawa, 02-638 Poland
Tel: +48 22 646 92 89
Head of School: Monika Chandler
Curriculum: IBPYP
Language instr: English

International American School
Ul Dembego 18, Warszawa,
02-796 Poland
Tel: +48 22 649 1442
Head of School: Steven Weeks-Johnson
Curriculum: IBDP
Language instr: English

International European School Warsaw
ul. Wiertnicza 140, Warsaw,
02-952 Poland
Tel: +48 22 842 44 48
Head of School: Mira Ciechowska
Curriculum: IBDP
Language instr: English

International High School of Wroclaw
Fundacja Edukacji
Miedzynarodowej, ul. Zielinskiego
38, 53-534 Wroclaw, 53-534 Poland
Tel: +48 71 782 26 26
Head of School: Jolanta Slawska
Curriculum: IBMYP
Language instr: English

International School of Krakow
ul Sw Floriana 57, Lusina,
30-698 Krakow, Poland
Tel: +48 12 270 1409
Director: Mamie Heard
Age range: 3–18
No. of pupils: 160 B76 G84
Fees: €4,815
Curriculum: AP, IBDP, SAT
Language instr: English
(CEE) (CIS)

International School of Poznan
Ul Taczanowskiego 18,
Poznan, 60-147 Poland
Tel: +48 61 646 37 60
Head of School: Iwona Richter
Curriculum: IBDP, IBPYP
Language instr: English

Kolegium Europejskie
Kazimierza Wielkiego 33,
Krakow, 30-074 Poland
Tel: +48 12 632 46 29
Head of School: Zbigniew Koloch
Age range: 12–18
No. of pupils: 130 B50 G80
Fees: Day £1,500
Curriculum: IBDP, National
Language instr: English

Meridian International School
Stoklosy 3, Ursynow,
Warsaw, 02-787 Poland
Tel: +48 22 457 24 24
Principal: Lokman Cakir
Curriculum: IBDP
Language instr: English

Monnet International School: Prywatne LO nr 32
Abramowskiego 4,
Warsaw, 00740 Poland
Tel: +48 22 852 31 10
Head of School: Hanna Bukiewicz-Piskorska
No. of pupils: 67
Curriculum: IBDP, IBMYP, IBPYP
Language instr: English

Paderewski Private Grammar School
ul Symfoniczna 1, Lublin,
20-853 Poland
Tel: +48 81 740-75-43
Head of School: Adam Kalbarczyk
Age range: 13–19
No. of pupils: 220
Fees: Day £1,100 FB £1,500
Curriculum: IBDP, IBMYP, ALevs
Language instr: English

Poznan British International School
ul Darzyborska 1a, 61-303 Poznan, Poland
Tel: +48 61 870 97 30
Principal: Danuta Koscinska
Age range: 2 –15
Curriculum: IPC, National
(COB)

Private Primary School 97
Abramowskiego Street 4,
Warsaw, 02-659 Poland
Tel: +48 22 646 85 71
Head of School: Alina Wozniak
Curriculum: IBPYP
Language instr: English

Prywatne Liceum Ogólnoksztalcace im. Melchiora Wankowicza
ul. Witosa 18, Katowice,
40832 Poland
Tel: +48 322549194
Head of School: Jolanta Kaluza
Curriculum: IBDP
Language instr: English

Szczecin International School
ul Starzynskiego 3-4,
Szczecin, 70506 Poland
Tel: +48 91 4240 300
Head of School: Maria Sawka
Curriculum: IBDP
Language instr: English

Szkola Europejska – Gimnazjum / Liceum
ul Tuszynska 31, Lódz,
93 – 020 Poland
Tel: +48 42 682 3696
Head of School: Urszula Moryc
Curriculum: IBDP
Language instr: English

The British School
Ul Limanowskiego 15,
Warsaw, 02 943 Poland
Tel: +48 22 842 32 81
Head of School: Terry Creissen
Age range: 2–18
No. of pupils: 800 B400 G400
Curriculum: IBDP,
National, UK, IGCSE
Language instr: English
(COB) (ECIS)

The Nazareth Middle and, High School in Warsaw
ul. Czerniakowska 137,
Warszawa, 00-720 Poland
Tel: +48 22 841 3854/+48 601 644 102
Head of School: Karolina Luczak
Age range: G13–19
No. of pupils: 250
Fees: €2,257–€4,860
Curriculum: IBDP
Language instr: English, Polish
(symbols)

VIII Prywatne Akademickie Liceum Ogólnoksztalcace
ul Karmelicka 45, Krakow,
31-128 Poland
Tel: +48 12 633 96 57
Head of School: Jerzy Waligóra
No. of pupils: B19 G25
Fees: 14,400
Curriculum: IBDP
Language instr: English

Wroclaw International School
Zielinskiego Street No 38, PL
53-534 Wroclaw, Poland
Tel: +48 71 782 26 26
Head of School: Hewa Thompson
Age range: 3–15
No. of pupils: 104 B47 G57
Curriculum: IBMYP, IBPYP
Language instr: English, Polish
(ECIS)

Zespól Szkól Ogólnoksztalcacych im. Pawla z Tarsu
ul Poezji 19, Warsaw, 04-994 Poland
Tel: +48 22 789 14 02
Head of School: Wieslawa Sanecka-Tombacher
No. of pupils: 75
Fees: €200
Curriculum: IBDP
Language instr: English

Portugal

Carlucci American International School of Lisbon
Rua Antonio dos Reis, 95, Linhó,
Sintra, 2710-301 Portugal
Tel: +351 21 923 9800
Director: Blannie Curtis
Age range: 3–18
No. of pupils: 550
Fees: €7,064–€16,480
Curriculum: IBDP, SAT, USA
Language instr: English

CLIB – The Braga International School
R da Igreja Velha – Gualtar,
4710-069 Braga, Portugal
Tel: +351 253 679 860
Principal: Helena Pina Vaz
Age range: 3–18
No. of pupils: 249 B124 G125
Fees: €3,950–€6,190
(ECIS)

CLIP – Colegio Luso-Internacional do Porto
Rua de Vila Nova 1071, 4100
– 506, Porto, Portugal
Tel: +351 22 619 9160
Principal: Paul Turner
Age range: 5–18
No. of pupils: 497 B282 G215
(CIS) (ECIS)

Colégio Luso-Internacional do Centro
Rua D João Pereira Venâncio,
2430-291 Marinha Grande, Portugal
Tel: +351 244 503710
Age range: 3–18
Curriculum: UK
Language instr: English, Portuguese

Colegio Planalto
Rua Armindo Rodrigues, 28,
Lisbon, 1600-414 Portugal
Tel: +351 21 754 15 30
Director: António José Sarmento
Age range: B3–18
No. of pupils: 500
Curriculum: IBDP, National
Language instr: English
(symbol)

Escola Internacional São Lourenço
Caixa Postal 445N, Sitio da Rabona
8135, Almancil, Algarve Portugal
Tel: +351 289 398 328
Head Teacher: Jean Chinn
Age range: 3–18
No. of pupils: 261 B143 G118
Curriculum: UK, ALevs
(ECIS)

International Christian School of Cascais
Avenida de Sintra, 1154,
2750-494 Cascais, Portugal
Tel: +351 214 842 279
Director: Pastor Carlos de Freitas
Age range: 4–18
No. of pupils: B23 G22
Curriculum: SAT, USA
Language instr: English

International Preparatory School
Rua do Boror 12, Carcavelos,
2775 Parede, Portugal
Tel: +351 21 457 0149
Head Teacher: Robert Taylor
Age range: 3–11
No. of pupils: 240 B110 G130
Fees: €7,075–€10,075
Curriculum: UK
Language instr: English

International School of Palmela
International School of Palmela
Amelia Avenue, Lot 171/172, Quinta
do Anjo, 2950-805 Portugal
Tel: +351 212 110530
Director: Rachid Ismael
Language instr: English, Portuguese
(ECIS)

OEIRAS INTERNATIONAL SCHOOL
For further details see p. 132
Quinta Nossa Senhora da
Conceicao, Rua Antero de
Quental no 7, Barcarena,
2730-013 Portugal
Tel: +351 211935330
Email: info@oeiras
internationalschool.com
Website: www.oeiras
internationalschool.com
Principal/IBCC
Coordinator: Chari Empis
Age range: 10–18
No. of pupils: B128 G94
Fees: €10,700–€17,900
Curriculum: IBDP, IBMYP, IBCC
Language instr: English

Oporto British School
Rua da Cerca 326, 4150-
201 Porto, Portugal
Tel: +351 22 616 6660
Head Master: Michael
William Clack
Age range: 3–18
No. of pupils: 404
Fees: Day £6,572–£9,657
Curriculum: IBDP, UK, IGCSE
Language instr: English
(CIS) (COB) (ECIS)

St Dominic's International School
Rua Maria Brown, Outeiro de
Polima, 2785-816 S Domingos
de Rana, Portugal
Tel: +351 21 444 0434
Principal: Dinah Hawtree
Age range: 3–18
No. of pupils: 397
Fees: €7,613–€15,300
Curriculum: IBDP, IBMYP, IBPYP
Language instr: English
(CIS) (ECIS)

St James' Primary School
Rua dos Depósitos de
Agua, No 339, Cobre, 2750-
561 Cascais, Portugal
Tel: +351 21 486 4754/5
Principal: Sofia Moniz
Age range: 6–10

St Julian's School
Secondary School, Quinta
Nova, Carcavelos Codex,
2776-601 Portugal
Tel: +351 21 4585300
Head of School: David Smith
Age range: 3–18
No. of pupils: 1070 B553
G517 VIth122
Fees: €10,950
Curriculum: IBDP, National, SAT, UK
Language instr: English
(CIS) (COB) (ECIS)

The British School Madeira
Caminho Dos Saltos 6, 9050-219
Funchal, Madeira, Portugal
Tel: +351 291 773218
Head: Jane Gordon
Age range: 3–15
No. of pupils: 80 B40 G40
Fees: €4,300–€7,000
Curriculum: National, UK
Language instr: English, Portuguese

THE INTERNATIONAL SCHOOL OF THE ALGARVE
For further details see p. 145
Apartado 80, 8401-901
Lagoa, Algarve, Portugal
Tel: +351 282 342547
Email: geral@eialgarve.com
Website: www.eialgarve.com
Head: Graciete de Sá e Cid
Age range: 3–18
No. of pupils: B373 G365 VIth110
Fees: €3,624–€13,400
Curriculum: AP, UK,
GCSE, IGCSE, ALevs
Language instr: English
(ECIS)

Vale Verde International School
Apartado 125, Luz-Lagos
8601-907, Portugal
Tel: +351 282 697205
Headmaster: Blaine Harris
Age range: 11–16
No. of pupils: 50 B20 G30
Curriculum: UK, IGCSE, ALevs
(ECIS)

Vilamoura International School
Apartado 856, 8125 – 911
Vilamoura, Portugal
Tel: +351 289 303 280
Director: Cidalia Ferreira Bicho
Age range: 2–18
No. of pupils: 500 B267 G233
Fees: €5,020–€9,265
Curriculum: National, UK, IGCSE
Language instr: English, Portuguese
(ECIS)

Romania

Acorns British Style Nursery
63 Popa Soare Street, Sector 2,
Bucharest, 031122 Romania
Tel: +40 788 418 186
Headteacher: Fiona Dutu
(COB)

American International School of Bucharest
Sos Pipera-Tunari 196, Voluntari, Jud
Ilfov, Bucharest, 077190 Romania
Tel: +40 (21) 204 4300
Director: David Ottaviano
Age range: 3–19
No. of pupils: 695 B326 G369
Fees: €13,300–€18,605
Curriculum: IBDP, IBMYP, IBPYP, SAT
Language instr: English
(CEE) (DIS) (ECIS)

British School of Bucharest
42 Erou Iancu Nicolae
Street, 077190, Ilfov County,
Bucharest Romania
Tel: +40 21 267 89 19
Principal: Joanne Puddy Wells
Age range: 1–18
No. of pupils: B250 G250 VIth23
Fees: €13,225–€20,190
Curriculum: UK, IGCSE, ALevs
Language instr: English
(COB) (ECIS)

International British School of Bucharest
Str Agricultori no 21-23, Sector 2,
Bucharest, 021481 Romania
Tel: +40 21 253 16 98/252 56 04
Principal: Kendall Peet
Age range: 3–19
No. of pupils: B140 G165 VIth45
Fees: €7,500–€13,860
Curriculum: SAT, UK, IGCSE, ALevs
Language instr: English
(CEE) (COB) (ECIS)

International School for Primary Education
72 Petre Aurelian, Greenlake
Residences, Bucharest
Sector 1, Romania
Tel: +40 21 380 3535
Head of School: Kirsty Davidson
Age range: 1–11
Fees: €10,890–€12,650
Curriculum: National, UK
Language instr: English
(ECIS)

International School of Cluj
400 434, Baisoara 2A, Cluj-
Napoca, Romania
Tel: +40 (0) 264 418 990
Director: Julian Hingley
Age range: 1–18
Curriculum: National,
UK, IGCSE, ALevs
(COB) (ECIS)

Mark Twain International School
25 Erou Iancu Nicolae
Street, Baneasa, Bucharest,
077190 Romania
Tel: +40 72 320 0702
Head of School: Anca
Macovei Vlasceanu
Age range: 2–19
No. of pupils: 440 B225 G215
Fees: €3,500–€8,200
Curriculum: IBDP, IBMYP,
IBPYP, National
Language instr: English, Romanian
(DIS) (ECIS)

Olga Gudynn International School
5 Erou Iancu Nicolae Street,
Voluntari, Ilfov, Bucharest, Romania
Tel: +40 212674025
Principal: Bogdan N Lazar
Age range: 3–15
Curriculum: National
(CEE) (COB) (ECIS)

Scoala Europeana Bucuresti
33 Baiculesti st., Bucharest,
013913 Romania
Tel: +40 21 3117 770
Curriculum: IBDP
Language instr: English

The International School of Bucharest
Sos Gara Catelu, Nr 1R, Sector 3,
032991, Bucharest, Romania
Tel: +40 21 306 9530
Director: Faruk Erduran
Age range: 3–18
No. of pupils: 573 B283 G290
Fees: €5,000–€8,900
Curriculum: SAT, UK, ALevs
Language instr: English
(DIS) (COB)

Transylvania College
Baisoara, 2A, Cluj-Napoca,
400445 Romania
Tel: +40 (0) 264 418 990
Director: Gillian Greenwood
Age range: 1–18
No. of pupils: B281 G276 VIth48
Fees: Day €3,090–€6,820
WB €60,500–€7,150 FB €7,150–€8,250
Curriculum: UK, IGCSE, ALevs
Language instr: English, Romanian
(COB) (RS)

Russian Federation

Atlantic International School
Moscovskaya oblast, Zarech'e,
Berezovaya Street, 6a, Moscow,
Russian Federation
Tel: +7 903 726 2811
**Development
Director:** Damian Butters
Curriculum: IGCSE, ALevs
Language instr: English, Russian
(ECIS)

British International School, Moscow
Novoyasenevsky prospekt 19/5,
Moscow, 117593 Russian Federation
Tel: +7 495 425 5100
Head of School: Andrew Short
Age range: 3–18
No. of pupils: 1200 B650 G550
Fees: €11,040–€18,230
Curriculum: IBDP,
National, UK, ALevs
Language instr: English
(ECIS)

'Education through Dialogue' School
Nekrasova Street, 19, St Petersburg,
191014 Russian Federation
Tel: +7 812 272 0360
Head of School: Vladimir Andreev
Curriculum: IBDP
Language instr: English

European Gymnasium
House 3, 3rd Sokolnicheskaya St,
Moscow, 107014 Russian Federation
Tel: +7 495 268 4404
Head of School: Irina Bogantseva
Age range: 4–18
No. of pupils: 170
Curriculum: IBDP, IBMYP, IBPYP
Language instr: Russian, English

Lyceum-Boarding School No 2 – Municipal Autonomous Educational Institution
11 Shamil Usmanov Street, Kazan,
420095 Russian Federation
Tel: +7 8435 543234
Director: Mukhametov
Ildar Rinatovich
Language instr: English, Russian
(ECIS)

Moscow Economic School, Campus Zaitsevo
29 Zamorenova Street, Moscow,
123022 Russian Federation
Tel: +7 495 780 5230
Head of School: Natalia Kadjaya
Curriculum: IBDP, IBMYP, IBPYP
Language instr: English
(ECIS)

Moscow Economic School, Presnya Campus
29 Zamorenova Street, Moscow,
123022 Russian Federation
Tel: +7 499 255 55 66
President: Yury Shamilov
Age range: 3–18
No. of pupils: B324 G293 VIth29
Curriculum: IBDP, IBMYP, IBPYP
Language instr: English, Russian
(CEE) (DIS) (ECIS)

Moscow International Gymnasia
111123 3rd Vladimirskaya Str, House
5, Moscow, Russian Federation
Tel: +7 495 304 3794
Director: Tatania Goumennik
Age range: 6–10
No. of pupils: 65 B30 G35

President School
OK Sosny, P/O Uspenskoye,
Odintsovski r-n, Moscow Region
143030 Russian Federation
Tel: +8 (495) 940 70 15
Head of School: Lyubov Mashina
Age range: 4–18
No. of pupils: 158 B81 G77
Curriculum: IBDP
Language instr: Russian, English

QSI International School of Novosibirsk
#4 Vyazemkaya 4, Novosibirsk,
630117 Russian Federation
Tel: 7-913-000-50-55
Director: Jay Loftin
Age range: 3–17
Language instr: English

Slavic Anglo-American School 'Marina'
6 Panferov St, Building 2, Moscow,
117261 Russian Federation
Tel: +7 499 134 1096
School Principal: Tatiana
A Yurovskaya
Age range: 6–17
No. of pupils: 280 B140 G140 VIth13
Fees: RUB280,000
Curriculum: AP, National,
SAT, TOEFL, USA
Language instr: Russian, English

The Anglo-American School of Moscow
1 Beregovaya Street, Moscow, 125367 Russian Federation
Tel: +7 (495) 231-44-88
Director: Jon P Zurfluh
Age range: 4–18
No. of pupils: 1250
Fees: US$15,000–US$28,000
Curriculum: ACT, AP, IBDP, IBPYP, SAT
Language instr: English
(CEE) (CIS) (ECIS)

The English International School Moscow
Zeleny prospect 66-a, Moscow, 111396, Russian Federation
Tel: +7 495 301 2104
Headmaster: R D Hunter
Age range: 3–18
Curriculum: UK, IGCSE, ALevs
(COB)

The International School of Moscow
Buildings 5 & 6, Krylatskaya Street 12, Krylatskoe, Moscow 121552, Russian Federation
Tel: +7 499 149 4434
Age range: 2–13
No. of pupils: 359 B185 G174
Fees: €11,685–€19,380
Language instr: English
(COB)

XXI Century Integration International Secondary School
16 Katukova Street, Building 3, Moscow, 123592 Russian Federation
Tel: +7 495 750 3102
Head of School: Svetlana Kulichenko
Age range: 5–18
No. of pupils: 242
Fees: €15,500–€22,800
Curriculum: IBDP, IBMYP
Language instr: English

Serbia

Anglo-American International School
Andre Nikolica 29, Senjak, Belgrade, 11000 Serbia
Tel: +381 11 369 2064
Principal-owner: Tijana Mandic
Age range: 6–18
Curriculum: AICE, AP, SAT, UK, USA, IGCSE, ALevs
Language instr: English
(ECIS)

British International School Belgrade
Radoja Dakica 44, 11000, Belgrade, Serbia
Tel: +381 11 637515
Director of Education: Martin Scott
Age range: 4–18
No. of pupils: 51 B29 G22
(OOO) (ECIS)

Chartwell International School
Teodora Drajzera 38, 11000 Belgrade, Serbia
Tel: +381 11 3675 340/299
Executive Director: Michael O'Grady
Age range: 2–14
Fees: €3,200–€9,800
(COB)

Crnjanski High School
Djordja Ognjanovica 2, Belgrade, 11030 Serbia
Tel: +381 11 23 98 388
Head of School: Svetlana Zivkovic
Age range: 16–19
Fees: €6,500–€12,500
Curriculum: IBDP
Language instr: English

Gimnazija Ruder Bo kovic
Kneza Vi eslava 17, Belgrade, 11000 Serbia
Tel: + 381 11 35 407 86
Head of School: Nada Vukovic
Curriculum: IBDP, IGCSE
Language instr: English
(書)

International School of Belgrade
Temisvarska 19, Belgrade, 11040 Serbia
Tel: +381 11 206 9999
Director: Robert Risch
Age range: 4–18
No. of pupils: 364
Curriculum: IBDP, IBMYP, IBPYP, SAT
Language instr: English
(CEE) (CIS) (ECIS)

Slovakia

British International School Bratislava
Peknikova 6, Bratislava, 84102 Slovakia
Tel: +421 2 69307081/2
Principal: Matthew Benjamin Farthing
Age range: 2–18
No. of pupils: 600
Fees: €6,734–€14,688
Curriculum: IBDP, UK, ALevs
Language instr: English
(COB)

QSI International School of Bratislava
Karloveská 64, 842-20 Bratislava, Slovakia
Tel: +421 2 6542 2844
Director: Britt Brantley
Age range: 2–18
No. of pupils: 242
Curriculum: AP, IBDP, SAT, USA
Language instr: English

QSI International School of Kosice
Drabova 3, 040 23, Kosice, Slovakia
Tel: +421 55 625 0040
Director: Lisa Haberman
Age range: 5–13
No. of pupils: 49
Curriculum: USA
Language instr: English

Slovenia

British International School of Ljubljana
Podmilscakova ulica 18, Ljubljana, 1000 Slovenia
Tel: +386 40 486 548
Headmaster: Jeremy Hibbins
Age range: 3–18
No. of pupils: 70 B36 G34
Fees: €7,950–€11,450
Curriculum: IPC, SAT, UK, IGCSE, ALevs
Language instr: English
(COB)

Gimnazija Bezigrad
Periceva 4, Ljubljana, 1000 Slovenia
Tel: +386 1 3000 400
Head of School: Janez Sustersic
Age range: 14–19
No. of pupils: 74
Curriculum: IBDP, IBMYP, National
Language instr: English
(ECIS)

QSI International School of Ljubljana
Dolgi most 6A, 1000 Ljubljana, Slovenia
Tel: +386 1 244 1750
Director: Jay Loftin
Age range: 4–17
No. of pupils: 56
Curriculum: USA
Language instr: English

Spain

Academy International School
Camí de Son Ametler Vell, Marratxi, Mallorca, Spain
Tel: +34 971 605008
Head of Education: Clare Mooney
Age range: 2–16
No. of pupils: 260 B125 G135
Curriculum: UK, IGCSE
Language instr: English

Agora International School Barcelona
Puig de Mira, 15-21 – Urb Masia Bach, Sant Esteve Sesrovires, Barcelona, 08635 Spain
Tel: +34 93 779 89 28
Director: Ignasi Bau
Language instr: English, French, German
(ISA)

Agora Portals International School
Carretera vella d'Andratx, s/n, Portals Nous, Mallorca, 078181 Spain
Tel: +34 971684042
Head of School: Rafael Barea Roig
Curriculum: IBDP
(ISA)

Agora Sant Cugat International School
C / Ferrer y Guardia s / n, 08174 – Sant Cugat del Valles, Barcelona, Spain
Tel: 93 590 26 00
Director: Vicenç Gandol Casado
Curriculum: IBDP, National
Language instr: English, Spanish
(ISA)

Aloha College
Urbanización el Angel, Nueva Andalucía, 29660 Marbella, (Málaga) Spain
Tel: +34 95 281 41 33
Senior School
Headmistress: Elizabeth Batchelor
Age range: 3–18
No. of pupils: 800
Curriculum: IBDP
Language instr: English, Spanish
(COB) (ECIS)

American School of Barcelona
Calle Balmes 7, 08950 Esplugues de Llobregat, Barcelona, Spain
Tel: +34 93 371 4016
Director: Mark Pingitore
Age range: 3–18
No. of pupils: 660
Curriculum: IBDP, National, SAT
Language instr: English
(ECIS)

American School of Bilbao
Soparda Bidea 10, Berango, Bizkaia, 48640 Spain
Tel: +34 94 668 0860/61
Director: John F Larner
Age range: 2–18
No. of pupils: 357 B172 G185 Vlth35
Fees: €4,394–€7,149
Curriculum: IBDP
Language instr: English
(CIS) (ECIS)

American School of Las Palmas
Carretera de los Hoyos, Km 1.7, Las Palmas de Gran Canaria, 35017 Spain
Tel: 928 430 023
Director: Alex Hernández-Stalder
Age range: 3–18
Curriculum: AP, USA

**American School
of Madrid**
Apartado 80, Madrid, 28080 Spain
Tel: +34 91 740 19 00
Head of School: William O'Hale
Age range: 3–18
No. of pupils: 900
Curriculum: IBDP, SAT, USA
Language instr: English
(ECIS)

**American School
of Valencia**
Urbanización Los Monasterios,
Apartado de Correos 9, Puzol,
Valencia 46530 Spain
Tel: +34 96 140 5412
Director: Michael L. Smith
Age range: 2–18
No. of pupils: 750 VIth98
Fees: €6,000
Curriculum: IBDP, National, SAT, USA
Language instr: English,
Spanish, Valencia
(ECIS)

Aquinas American School
Calle Transversal Cuatro, 4,
Pozuelo de Alarcon, 28223 Spain
Tel: +34 91 352 31 20
Director: Antonio Arcones
Language instr: English

Aula Escola Europea
Avinguda Mare de, Déu de Lorda,
34-36, Barcelona, 08034 Spain
Tel: +34 93 203 03 54
Head of School: Joaquim Guerola
Curriculum: IBDP
Language instr: Spanish

**Baleares International
College**
Crta. Cala Figuera, 3A, Sa
Porassa, 07182 Calvia, Spain
Tel: +34 971 133167
Principal: John Barrie Wiggins
Age range: 3–18
No. of pupils: 230
Curriculum: AP, SAT, TOEFL, ALevs

Bell-lloc Del Pla
Can Pau Birol, 2-6, 17005,
Girona, 17005 Spain
Tel: +34 972 232 111
Head of School: Miquel
Riera Casadevall
Curriculum: IBDP
Language instr: Spanish
(♦)

**Bellver International
College**
5 Jose Costa Ferrer, Palma,
Mallorca 07015 Spain
Tel: +34 971 401679
Principal: Albert Loddo
Age range: 3–18
No. of pupils: 300 B153 G147
Fees: €5,325–€8,625
Curriculum: UK, IGCSE, ALevs
Language instr: English

**Benjamin Franklin
International School**
Martorell i Pena 9, 08017
Barcelona, Spain
Tel: +34 93 434 2380
Head of School: William Knauer
Age range: 3–18
No. of pupils: 602
Curriculum: AP, IBDP,
National, SAT, TOEFL
Language instr: English
(ECIS)

**BRITISH COUNCIL
SCHOOL**
For further details see p. 110
Calle Solano, 5 – 7, Pozuelo de
Alarcon, Madrid, 28223 Spain
Tel: +34 91 337 3612
Email: school@britishcouncil.es
Website:
www.britishcouncilschool.es
Head of School: Gillian Flaxman
Age range: 3–18
No. of pupils: 1950
B987 G963 VIth233
Curriculum: National,
SAT, UK, IGCSE
Language instr: English, Spanish
(ECIS)

British School Alzira
La Barraca de Aguas Vivas,
Alzira -Valencia, Spain
Tel: +034 96 258 93 68
Head: Patricia Tarrant
Age range: 1–18
Curriculum: UK

British School of Alicante
Glorieta del Reino Unido no.
5, Alicante 03008, Spain
Tel: +34 965 106 351
Head: Derek Laidlaw
Age range: 3–18
No. of pupils: 860
Curriculum: UK, ALevs
(COB)

British School of Cordoba
Calle México 4, 14012
Córdoba, Spain
Tel: +34 957 767 048
Headteacher: Howard Thomas
Age range: 3–18
Curriculum: UK

**British School of
Gran Canaria**
Apartado 11, Tafira Alta,
35017 Las Palmas Spain
Tel: +34 9 28 351167
Headmaster: S Hardes
Age range: 3–18
No. of pupils: 569
Fees: €4,010–€5,375
Curriculum: UK, ALevs
Language instr: English
(COB)

British School of Lanzarote
Calle, 1 Juan Echevarria 10,
35509 Tahiche, Lanzarote,
Grand Canaria Spain
Tel: +34 928 810085
Headteacher: Gill Crew
Age range: 4–16
No. of pupils: 200 B100 G100

British School of Valencia
Avda Peris y Valero 53, 55,
57, 46006 Valencia, Spain
Tel: +34 96 374 29 30
Age range: 2–18
Curriculum: UK, ALevs

British Yeoward School
Parque Taoro, Puerto de
la Cruz, 38400, Tenerife,
Canary Islands Spain
Tel: +34 922 384685
Headmaster: Derek Smith
Age range: 2–18
No. of pupils: 249 B132 G117

Caxton College
C/ Mas de León, 5, 46530
Puzol, Valencia, Spain
Tel: +34 96 142 4500
Age range: 1–18
No. of pupils: 1469 B738
G731 VIth140
Fees: €4,750–€6,250
Curriculum: IGCSE, ALevs
Language instr: English
(♠)

**Centre Cultural I
Esportiu Xaloc**
Gran Vía 100, L'Hospitalet de
Llobregat, Barcelona, 08902 Spain
Tel: +34 93 335 1600
Head of School: Esteve Darnés Vilà
Curriculum: IBDP
Language instr: Spanish
(♦)

**Chester College
International School**
Travesá de Montouto 2, Santiago
de Compostella, 15894 Spain
Tel: +34 981 819 160
Director: Dolores Peleteiro
Language instr: English, Spanish
(♠)

Colegio Arenas Atlántico
Paseo San Patricio, No 20,
Gran Canaria, 35416 Spain
Tel: +34 928 629 140
Head of School: Pino Afonso Ponce
Age range: 3–18
No. of pupils: 306 B179 G127
Fees: €4,080
Curriculum: IBDP, National
Language instr: Spanish

**Colegio Arenas
Internacional**
Avenida del Mar 37, Costa
Teguise, Lanzarote, Canary
Islands 35509 Spain
Tel: +34 928 590 835
Head of School: Delfina
Rodriguez Cavero
Curriculum: IBDP
Language instr: Spanish

Colegio Arenas Sur
Las Margaritas s/n, San
Agustín, 35290 Spain
Tel: +34 928 765 934
Curriculum: IBDP
Language instr: Spanish

Colegio Brains
Calle Salvia, Nº 48, Alcobendas,
Madrid, 28109 Spain
Tel: +34 91 650 43 00
Curriculum: IBDP
Language instr: English

**Colegio de San
Francisco de Paula**
C/ Santa Angela de la Cruz,
11, Sevilla, 41003 Spain
Tel: +34 95 422 4382
Head of School: Luis Rey Goñi
Age range: 3–18
Curriculum: IBDP, IBMYP, National
Language instr: Spanish, English

Colegio El Planet
Partida Planet 71, Altea,
03590 Spain
Tel: +34 965 844 224
Curriculum: IBDP
Language instr: English

**Colegio El Valle
II – Sanchinarro**
Calle Ana De Austria, 60,
Madrid, 28050 Spain
Tel: +34 91 7188426
Head of School: Eva Hurtado
Curriculum: IBDP

Colegio Gaztelueta
PO Box 2, Las Arenas,
Vizcaya, 48930 Spain
Tel: +34 94 463 3000
Head of School: Imanol Goyarrola
Age range: B1–18
No. of pupils: 1220
Curriculum: IBDP
Language instr: Spanish
(♦)

Colegio Heidelberg
Apartado de Correos 248,
Barranco Seco 15, Las Palmas
de Gran Canaria, 35090 Spain
Tel: +34 928 350 615
Head of School: Miguel
Angel Montenegro
Age range: 3–18
No. of pupils: 1140 B570 G570
Curriculum: IBDP, IBMYP
Language instr: Spanish

Colegio Internacional de Levante
C/Río Jalón 23 Urb Calicanto,
Valencia, 46370 Spain
Tel: +34 961980650
Director: Consuelo Rodriguez
Language instr: Spanish
(ISA)

Colegio Internacional Eiris
Castanos de Eirís, La
Coruna, 15009 Spain
Tel: +34 981 284400
Director General: Angela
Ortiz Iglesias
Language instr: Spanish
(ISA)

Colegio Internacional Meres
Meres S/N, (Siero) 33.199,
Asturias, 33199 Spain
Tel: +34 985 792 427
Head of School: D Antonio-
Manuel González Garcia
Curriculum: IBDP
(†)

Colegio Internacional Peñacorada
Calle Bandonilla 32, CP
Armunia, León 24009 Spain
Tel: +34 987 202352
Head of School: Luis José
Cillero Pedrero
Curriculum: IBDP
Language instr: Spanish

Colegio Internacional SEK – Atlántico
Urb. A Caeira, Illa de
Arousa, 4 Boa Vista, Poio,
Pontevedra, 36005 Spain
Tel: +34 98 687 2277
Head of School: Jacobo
Olmedo Suárez-Vence
Curriculum: IBMYP, IBPYP
Language instr: Spanish, English

Colegio Internacional SEK-Alborán
C/Barlovento s/n Urb Almerimar,
El Ejido, Almeria, 04711 Spain
Tel: +34 950 497273
Head of School: Luis Carlos
Jiménez Gámez
Age range: 1–18
No. of pupils: 900 B450 G450
Curriculum: IBDP, IBMYP, IBPYP
Language instr: Spanish, English

Colegio Internacional SEK-Catalunya
Av Els Tremolencs, 24-26, La
Garriga, Barcelona, 08530 Spain
Tel: +34 938 71 84 48
Head of School: Philip Hudson
Age range: 3–18
No. of pupils: 1000 B475
G525 VIth100
Curriculum: IBDP, IBMYP, IBPYP
Language instr: Spanish,
Catalan, English
(CIS)

Colegio Internacional SEK-Ciudalcampo
Avd de las Perdices, No 2,
San Sebastián de los Reyes,
Madrid, 28707 Spain
Tel: +34 91 659 6303
Head: Mª Cruz Lagar
Age range: 1–18
No. of pupils: 1900 B960
G940 VIth180
Curriculum: IBDP, IBMYP, IBPYP
Language instr: Spanish
(CIS)

Colegio Internacional Torrequebrada
C/ Ronda del Golf Este, 7-11,
Urbanización Torrequebrada,
Benalmádena, 29639 Spain
Tel: +34 952 57 60 65
Head of School: Sonia Diez Abad
Age range: 3–18
No. of pupils: 550
Curriculum: IBDP
(†)(ISA)

Colegio Liceo Europeo
C/ Camino Sur 10,
Alcobendas, 28100 Spain
Tel: +34 91 650 00 00
Curriculum: IBDP
Language instr: Spanish

Colegio Marcote
Avda del Puente, 80 (Cabral),
Vigo, Pontevedra 36318 Spain
Tel: +34 986 251 511
Head of School: Maria
Elena Marcote
No. of pupils: 350
Curriculum: IBDP
Language instr: Spanish

Colegio Mirabal
Calle Monte Almenara, s/n,
Madrid, 28660 Spain
Tel: +34 916 331 711
Curriculum: IBDP
Language instr: Spanish

Colegio Montserrat
Av Vallvidrera, 68,
Barcelona, 08017 Spain
Tel: +34 932 038 800
Head of School: Montserrat
Del Pozo Rosello
Curriculum: IBDP
Language instr: English, Spanish

Colegio Nuestra Señora de Europa
C/ Estrada de Goñi, 3, 48993
Getxo, Vizcaya, Spain
Tel: +34 94 491 03 92
Head of School: Fernando Lecanda
Age range: 3–18
No. of pupils: 750
Curriculum: IBDP
Language instr: Spanish

Colegio Obradoiro
Rua Obradoiro 49, La
Coruña, 15190 Spain
Tel: +34 981 281 888
Head of School: Jose Varela Nuñez
Curriculum: IBDP
Language instr: Spanish

Colegio Retamar
Madrid España, c / Pajares
22, Madrid, 28223 Spain
Tel: +34 91 714 10 22
Head of School: Jose
Luis Alier Gándaras
Age range: B6–18
No. of pupils: 2100
Curriculum: IBDP
Language instr: Spanish
(†)

Colegio San Fernando
Avenida San Agustín, s/n,
Avilés, 33400 Spain
Tel: +34 985 565 745
Head of School: Javier
Martínez Gutiérrez
Curriculum: IBDP

Colegio San Patricio
Calle Jazmin 148, El Soto de
la Moraleja, Alcobendas,
Madrid, 28109 Spain
Tel: +349 16500602
Head of School: D Borja
Aguilar González-Babé
Curriculum: IBDP

Colegio Zuloaga
C/ Duero 35 Urb El Bosque,
Madrid, 28670 Spain
Tel: +34 91 616 72 68
Director: Isabel Palacios
Language instr: Spanish, English
(ISA)

El Centro Ingles
Apartado Correos 85, Carretera
Fuentebravia KM1.2, Puerto de
Santa Maria, 11500 Cadiz Spain
Tel: +34 956 850560
Headmistress: Linda Randell
Age range: 2–18
No. of pupils: 805 B404 G401 VIth77
Fees: €4,220–€5,820

El Limonar International School Murcia (El Palmar)
/c Colonia Buenavista s/n,
El Palmar, 30120 Spain
Tel: +34 902 999 070
Principal: Christopher Eversden
Language instr: English, Spanish

El Limonar International School Murcia (La Alberca)
c/ General Sanjurjo, 2, Santo
Ángel, 30151 Spain
Tel: +34 902 999 070
Principal: Christopher Eversden
Language instr: English, Spanish

El Limonar International School Murcia (Montepríncipe)
/c María zambrano s/n Urb.
Montepríncipe, Molina de
Segura, 30500 Spain
Tel: +34 902 999 070
Principal: Christopher Eversden
Curriculum: UK
Language instr: Spanish

El Limonar International School, Alicante (Villamartin)
c/ Filipinas, 15 – Urb. Blue Lagoon,
San Miguel de Salinas, 03193 Spain
Tel: +34 902 999 070
Principal: Justine Brown
Language instr: English, Spanish

El Plantío International School of Valencia
Calle 233 No36 Urb El Plantío,
La Cañada, Paterna,
Valencia 46182 Spain
Tel: +34 96 132 14 10
Head of School: Richard Stevens
Age range: 2–18
No. of pupils: 650
Curriculum: IBDP,
National, UK, IGCSE
Language instr: English, Spanish
(†)

ES International School
Apartado de Correos 176,
Barcelona, 08820 Spain
Tel: +34 93 479 1611
Director: Joanne Burns
Language instr: English

Eurocolegio Casvi
Avenida de Castilla, 27, Villaviciosa
de Odón, Madrid, 28670 Spain
Tel: +34 91 616 22 18
Head of School: Juan
Luis Yagüe Del Real
Curriculum: IBDP
Language instr: English

Europa International School
Av Pla del Vinyet 110, 08172 Sant
Cugat del Vallés, Barcelona Spain
Tel: +34 93 589 8420
General Director: Esther Herranz
Age range: 1–18
No. of pupils: 1315 B625 G690 VIth80
Fees: €7,000
(ECIS)

Fundacion Privada Oak House School
Sant Pere Claver 12-18,
Barcelona, 08017 Spain
Tel: +34 932 524 020
Headteacher: Julie Harris
Age range: 3–17
Curriculum: IBDP, UK
Language instr: English

Hamelin-Internacional Laie
C/ Núria, 30, Alella, 8328 Spain
Tel: +34 93 5556717
Head of School: Sonia Sas Sanjur
Curriculum: IBDP
Language instr: English, Spanish

Hastings School
c/ Azulinas 8, 28036 Madrid, Spain
Tel: +34 91 359 99 13/359 06 21
Headmaster: Michael B Mellor
Age range: 3–18
No. of pupils: 384 B198 G186 VIth50
Curriculum: ALevs

Institucion Educativa SEK (San Estenislao de Kostka)
Ciudalcampo Urb. San Sebastian de los Reyes, Madrid, 28707 Spain
Tel: +34 91 659 63 00
Director: Victoria Steffen
Language instr: Spanish
(ECIS) (ISA)

INTERNATIONAL COLLEGE SPAIN
For further details see p. 120
C/Vereda Norte, 3, La Moraleja, 28109 Alcobendas, (Madrid) Spain
Tel: +34 91 650 2398
Email: icsinfo@wclschools.org
Website: www.icsmadrid.org
Director: Jeremy Singer
Age range: 3–18
No. of pupils: 705
Fees: €8,700–€16,530
Curriculum: IBDP, IBMYP, IBPYP
Language instr: English
(CIS) (ECIS)

International School of Barcelona
Passeig Isaac Albeniz s/n, Vallpineda, Sitges, 08870 Spain
Tel: +34 93 894 20 40
Head of School: Carmen Gassol
Age range: 2–18
Curriculum: IBDP, National, SAT, UK
Language instr: English

International School of Catalunya
Passeig 9, La Garriga, 08530 Barcelona, Spain
Tel: +34 93 841 40 77
Age range: 3–18
Curriculum: UK
(COB)

International School of Madrid
Rosa Jardon 3, Madrid 28016, Spain
Tel: +34 91 359 2121/0722
Principal: Anne Mazon
Age range: 3–18
No. of pupils: 700 B350 G350 VIth87
Curriculum: UK, IGCSE, ALevs
Language instr: English

International School SEK-EL Castillo
Urbanizción Villafranca del Castillo, Calle Castillo de Manzanares s/n, Villanueva de la Cañada, 28692 Madrid Spain
Tel: +34 91 815 08 92
Director: Mercedes Pereda Tarrazona
Age range: 1–18
No. of pupils: 1436
Curriculum: IBDP, IBMYP, IBPYP, National
Language instr: Spanish, English
(image)

Kensington School
Avenida de Bularas n° 2, Pozuelo de Alarcón, 28224 Madrid, Spain
Tel: +34 91 7154 699
Age range: 3–14

King Richard III College
Calle Oratorio 4, Portals Nous, 07181, Mallorca, Spain
Tel: +34 971 675 850/1
Director: James Berry
Age range: 2–18
No. of pupils: 270 B150 G120
Fees: €6,000–€11,850
Curriculum: National, UK, IGCSE, ALevs
Language instr: English

King's College Murcia
Calle Pez Volador s/n, Urbanización La Torre Golf Resort, Roldán (Murcia), 30709 Spain
Tel: +34 968 032 500
Head of School: Stefan Rumistrzewicz
Age range: 1–18
No. of pupils: 471 B250 G221 VIth15
Curriculum: UK, GCSE, ALevs
Language instr: English
(COB)

King's College School, La Moraleja
Paseo de Alcobendas, 5, La Moraleja, 28109 Spain
Tel: +34 916 585 540
Headteacher: Dawn Akyurek
Curriculum: UK
Language instr: English
(COB)

KING'S COLLEGE, THE BRITISH SCHOOL OF MADRID
For further details see p. 126
Paseo de los Andes 35, 28761 Soto de Viñuelas, Madrid, Spain
Tel: +34 918 034 800
Email: info@kingscollege.es
Website: www.kingscollege.es
Head: Andrew Rattue
Age range: 2–18
No. of pupils: 1405
Curriculum: UK, GCSE, IGCSE, ALevs
Language instr: English
(image) (COB)

King's Infant School
Prieto Urena 9E, Madrid, 28016 Spain
Tel: +34 913 505 843
Headteacher: Kay Seward
Language instr: English
(COB)

Laude British School of Vila-real
Carretera de Vila-real a Burriana, 3er Sedeny, Villa-real 12540 (Castellón), Spain
Tel: +34 964 500 155
Head: Kevin Livesey
Age range: 2–18
Curriculum: UK

Laude The Lady Elizabeth School
Entrada Norte de La Cumbre del Sol, 03726 Benitachell, Alicante, Spain
Tel: + 34 671698764
Headmaster: Richard Wijeratne
Age range: 4–17
Curriculum: UK, GCSE, ALevs

Les Alzines
La Creu de Palau 2, Girona, 17003 Spain
Tel: +34 972 212162
Head of School: Ester Latre Mendez
Curriculum: IBDP
Language instr: Spanish
(image)

Lledó International School
Camino Caminàs, 175, Castellón, 12003 Spain
Tel: +34 964723170
Head of School: Luis Madrid Giménez
No. of pupils: 720
Curriculum: IBDP
(ISA)

Manuel Peleteiro
Monte Redondo – Castiñeiriño, Santiago de Compostela, 15702 Spain
Tel: +34 98 1591475
Head of School: Luis Peleteiro Ramos
Curriculum: IBDP
(image)

Morna International College
Apartado 333, Santa Gertrudis, Ibiza 07814, Spain
Tel: +34 971 19 76 72
Age range: 3–18
Curriculum: UK, IGCSE, ALevs
Language instr: English

New Castelar College
Las Palmas S/N 30740, San Pedro del Pinatar, Murcia, Spain
Tel: +34 968 178 276
Principal: Matías Martínez Garrido
Language instr: English, Spanish
(ECIS)

Newton College
Camino Viejo Elche Alicante km3, Partida de Maitino P-1, Elche (Alicante), 03295 Spain
Tel: +34 965 451 428
Head of School: Rosa Maria Tortosa
Age range: 3–18
No. of pupils: 800
Curriculum: IBDP, IBMYP
Language instr: Spanish, English

Novaschool Sunland International
Cartera Cartama-Pizarra, Nueva Aljaima, Cartama Estacion, Malaga, Spain
Tel: +34 952 42 4253
Principal: Glen Mundy
Age range: 3–18
No. of pupils: 180 B90 G90
Curriculum: National, UK

Numont School
C/ Parma, 16, 28043 Madrid, Spain
Tel: +34 91 300 24 31/388 20 85
Head: Joan Gemmell
Age range: 3–11
No. of pupils: 320

Oakley College
C/Z Zuloaga 17, Tafira Alta 35017, Las Palmas, Canary Islands Spain
Tel: +34 928 354247
Head: Donat Morgan
Age range: 2–18
No. of pupils: 500 B230 G240 VIth30
Curriculum: GCSE, IGCSE, ALevs

Orgaz Nursery School
Frascuelo n°2, 28043 Parque Conde Orgaz, Madrid, Spain
Tel: +34 91 300 2883
Head: María Hita
Curriculum: UK
Language instr: English

Queen's College, The English School
Juan de Saridakis 64, Palma de Mallorca, 07015 Spain
Tel: +34 971 401011
Headteacher: H R Muntaner
Age range: 3–18
No. of pupils: 399 B195 G204 VIth60
Fees: Day €5,549–€9,860
Curriculum: National, UK, GCSE, IGCSE, ALevs
Language instr: English

Runnymede College
c/Salvia 30, 28109 La Moraleja, Madrid, Spain
Tel: +34 916 508 302
Head: Frank M Powell
Age range: 3–18
No. of pupils: 702 B361 G341
Fees: €5,859–€11,454
Curriculum: UK, IGCSE, ALevs
Language instr: English

Scandinavian School of Madrid
Camino Ancho 14, La Moraleja,
Alcobendas, Madrid 28109, Spain
Tel: +34 91 650 01 27
Headmaster: Per Celander
Age range: 2–18
Curriculum: National
(CIS)

SEK Santa Isabel
Calle San Ildefonso, 18,
Madrid, 28012 Spain
Tel: +34 91 527 9094
Head of School: Javier
Presol Castillo
Curriculum: IBPYP
Language instr: English, Spanish

Sierra Bernia School
San Rafael S/N, Alfaz del Pi,
Alicante, 03580 Spain
Tel: +34 96 687 5149
Director: Duncan M Allan
Age range: 3–18
No. of pupils: 100 B50 G50
Curriculum: UK, GCSE, IGCSE, ALevs
Language instr: English
(COB)

Sotogrande International School
Apartado 15, Sotogrande,
Provincia de Cádiz, 11310 Spain
Tel: +34 956 795 902
Head: Chad Fairy
Age range: 3–18
No. of pupils: 660
Fees: €7,596–€16,773
Curriculum: IBDP, IBMYP,
IBPYP, National
Language instr: English, Spanish
(🏛) (CIS) (ECIS)

Sunny View School
c/ Tereul No 32, Cerro de Toril,
Torremolinos, 29620 Spain
Tel: +34 952 383164
Head: Jane Barbadillo
Age range: 4–18
No. of pupils: 300
Curriculum: ALevs

Swans International Sierra Blanca
c/lago de los Cisnes s/n,
Urb. Sierra Blanca, Marbella,
Malaga 29602 Spain
Tel: +34 952902755 / +34 952773248
Head of Secondary: Catherine
Davies
Age range: 3–18
No. of pupils: B340 G340 VIth55
Curriculum: IBDP, IGCSE
Language instr: English

The British College
Urbanización Torremuelle, C/ Paseo
del Genil s/n, 29630 Benalmádena
Costa, Málaga Spain
Tel: +34 952 44 22 15
Principal: Pilar Sainz
Age range: 1–18
Curriculum: National,
UK, IGCSE, ALevs

The British School of Barcelona
Calle Ginesta 26, Castelldefels,
Barcelona, 08860 Spain
Tel: +34 93 665 1584
Principal: Josep González
Age range: 3–18
No. of pupils: B489 G481
Curriculum: IGCSE, ALevs
Language instr: English

The British School of Marbella
Calle Jacinto Benavente S/N,
Marbella, 29601 Spain
Tel: +34 952 779 264
Headmistress: Sian Kirkham
Curriculum: UK
Language instr: English

The British School of Navarra
Avenida Juan Pablo II, Pamplona,
Navarra, 31004 Spain
Tel: +34 948 242 826
Headteacher: Nieves Sciulli
Curriculum: UK
Language instr: English

The English International College
Urb Ricmar, Crtr de Cádiz Km
189.5, 29600 Marbella, Spain
Tel: +34 952 83 1058/9
Principal: Y Stevenson
Age range: 3–18
No. of pupils: 500
Curriculum: UK
(COB)

Xabia International College
Apartado de Correos 311,
Javea Alicante, 03730 Spain
Tel: +34 96 647 1785
Directorr: Michael Bayes
Age range: 4–18
No. of pupils: 320 B150 G170 VIth40
Curriculum: ALevs

Sweden

Aranäsgymnasiet
Gymnasiegatan 44,
Kungsbacka, 43442 Sweden
Tel: +46 (0) 300 83 3200
Sector 4 Head: Christer Olofsson
No. of pupils: 1400
Curriculum: IBDP
Language instr: English

Bladins International School of Malmö
Box 20093, Själlandstorget 1,
S-200 74 Malmö, Sweden
Tel: +46 40 987970
Head of School: Darryll Lottering
Age range: 3–16
No. of pupils: 371
Curriculum: IBDP, IBMYP, IBPYP
Language instr: English
(ECIS)

British International Primary School of Stockholm
Östrka Valhallavagen 17,
Djursholm, 18268 Sweden
Tel: +46 8 755 2375
Principal: Carl Hutson
Age range: 3–11
No. of pupils: 140 B66 G74
Curriculum: SAT, UK
(COB) (ECIS)

Europaskolan in Södermalm
Gotlandsgatan 43,
Stockholm, 116 65 Sweden
Tel: +46 8 335054
Principal: Ulf Jonsson
Curriculum: IBMYP, IBPYP

Futuraskolan International School of Stockholm
Erik Dahlbergsgatan 58,
Stockholm, 115 57 Sweden
Tel: +46 736 001 314
Principal: Chris Mockrish
Language instr: English, Swedish
(ECIS)

Grennaskolan Riksinternat
Borgmästargården, Gränna,
SE-563 22 Sweden
Tel: +46 390 56150
Head of School: Mats Almlöw
Age range: 13–19
No. of pupils: 300 B149 G151
Curriculum: IBDP, National, UK
Language instr: English
(🏛) (ECIS)

Hvitfeldtska Gymnasiet
Rektorsgatan 2, Göteborg,
41133 Sweden
Tel: +46 31 36 70 608
Head of School: Peter Larsson
Age range: 16–19
No. of pupils: 1900
Curriculum: ACT, IBDP, National, SAT
Language instr: English

International School of Helsingborg
Östra Vallgatan 9, Helsingborg
SE-25437, Sweden
Tel: +46 42 105 705
Head of School: Michael Moore
Age range: 3–20
No. of pupils: 423 B220 G203
Curriculum: IBDP, IBMYP, IBPYP, SAT
Language instr: English
(ECIS)

International School of the Gothenburg Region
PO Box 2667, Gothenburg,
403 14 Sweden
Tel: +46 31 367 29 00
Head of School: Mark Mayer
Age range: 6–16
No. of pupils: 831
Curriculum: IBMYP, IBPYP
Language instr: English, Swedish
(CIS) (ECIS)

International School of the Stockholm Region
Bohusgatan 24-26, Stockholm,
116 67 Sweden
Tel: +46 8 508 426 50
Head of School: Karin
Henrekson Ahlberg
No. of pupils: 750
Curriculum: IBDP
Language instr: English
(ECIS)

Internationella Engelska Gymnasiet
Allhelgonagatan 4,
Stockholm, 11858 Sweden
Tel: +46 8 562 28 701
Head of School: Margret Benedikz
Curriculum: IBDP
Language instr: English

Kungsholmen's Gymnasium, International Section
Hantverkargatan 67-69, PO Box
12601, Stockholm, 11292 Sweden
Tel: +46 8 508 38 006
**Head of International
Section:** Lesley Brunnman
Age range: 16–20
No. of pupils: 450 B175 G275
Curriculum: IBDP, National
Language instr: English
(ECIS)

Lund International School
Warholmsväg 10, Lund,
22465 Sweden
Tel: +46 46140767, +46737087926
Head of School: Melani
Moniharapon
Curriculum: IBPYP
Language instr: English

Malmö Borgarskola
Box 17029, Malmö, 200 10 Sweden
Tel: +46 4034 1000
Head of School: Martin Roth
Age range: 16–19
No. of pupils: 240 B90 G150
Curriculum: IBDP
Language instr: English
(ECIS)

Malmö International School (formerly Söderkulla International School)
Klerkgatan 2, Malmö, Sweden
Tel: +46 708818195 / +46 723736074
Age range: 6–16
No. of pupils: 170
Curriculum: IBPYP
Language instr: English
(ECIS)

Sigtunaskolan Humanistiska Läroverket
Box 508, Sigtunase, 19328 Sweden
Tel: +46 8 592 571 20
Head of School: Lena Månsson
Age range: 13–19
No. of pupils: 590
Curriculum: IBDP, IBMYP
Language instr: English, Swedish

Stockholm International School
Johannesgatan 18, SE-111
38 Stockholm, Sweden
Tel: +46 (0)8 412 40 00
Head of School: Marta Medved Krajnovic
Age range: 3–18
No. of pupils: 550
Curriculum: IBDP, IBMYP, SAT
Language instr: English

Uppsala International School – Kvarngärdesskolan
Thunmansgatan 47, 75421, Uppsala, Sweden
Tel: +46 18 727 5900
Principal: Marianne Löwenstad
Age range: 6–16
No. of pupils: 104 B52 G52

Switzerland

AIGLON COLLEGE
For further details see p. 108
Avenue Centrale 61, 1885
Chesières-Villars, Switzerland
Tel: +41 (0)24 496 6161
Email: admissions@aiglon.ch
Website: www.aiglon.ch
Head Master: Richard McDonald
Age range: 9–18
No. of pupils: 341 B180 G161 VIth113
Fees: Day CHF31,150–CHF70,180 FB CHF63,000–CHF97,280
Curriculum: IBDP, SAT, UK, GCSE, IGCSE
Language instr: English

Bilingual Middleschool Zurich
Arbenzstrasse 19, Postfach, 8034 Zürich, Switzerland
Tel: +41 43 456 77 77
Principal: Remo Kaspar
Age range: 11–14
Language instr: English, German

Bilingual School Terra Nova
Florastr 19, 8700, Küsnacht, Switzerland
Tel: +41 44 910 4300
Age range: 4–14
No. of pupils: 200 B102 G98
Fees: SFR12,600
Curriculum: National
Language instr: German, English

Brillantmont International School
Avenue Secrétan 16, 1005 Lausanne, Switzerland
Tel: +41 21 310 04 00
Director: Philippe Pasche
Age range: 11–18
No. of pupils: 140
Fees: CHF25,000–CHF28,000
Curriculum: AP, SAT, UK, USA, IGCSE, ALevs
Language instr: English

Collège Alpin Beau Soleil
Route Du Village 1, Villars sur Ollon, 1884 Switzerland
Tel: +41 24 496 2626
Headmaster: Frances King
fking@beausoleil.ch
Age range: 12–19
No. of pupils: 210 B103 G107
Fees: SFR81,000
Curriculum: IBDP, National, FrenchBacc, SAT, TOEFL, UK, IGCSE
Language instr: English, French

COLLÈGE CHAMPITTET
For further details see p. 112
Ch. de Champittet, PO Box 622.
Pully-Lausanne, 1009 Switzerland
Tel: +41 21 721 0505
Email: info@champittet.ch
Website: www.champittet.ch
Director General: Steffen Sommer
Age range: 3–18
No. of pupils: 800
Fees: CHF18,100–CHF31,550 FB CHF70,500–CHF77,750
Curriculum: IBDP, National, FrenchBacc
Language instr: English, French

COLLÈGE DU LÉMAN INTERNATIONAL SCHOOL
For further details see p. 113
74, route de Sauverny, 1290 Versoix, Geneva, Switzerland
Tel: +41 22 775 55 55
Email: admissions@cdl.ch
Website: www.cdl.ch
Director General: Yves Thézé
Age range: 2–18
No. of pupils: 2002
Fees: CHF19,900–CHF32,900
Curriculum: AP, IBDP, IPC, National, FrenchBacc, SAT, IGCSE, ALevs
Language instr: English, French

Ecole D'Humanité
Hasilberg-Goldern, CH-6085 Switzerland
Tel: +41 33 972 9292
Director: Kathleen Hennessy
Age range: 7–20
No. of pupils: 145 B72 G73
Fees: SFR19,000
Curriculum: AP, National, SAT, USA
Language instr: German, English

Ecole des Arches
Chemin de Mornex 2-4, PO Box 566, Lausanne, Vaud 1001 Switzerland
Tel: +41 21 311 09 69
Head of School: Christian Hofer
Age range: 16–21
No. of pupils: B120 G80
Fees: CHF10,400–CHF21,000
Curriculum: IBDP
Language instr: French

Ecole Lémania
Chemin de Préville 3, CP 550, 1001 Lausanne, Switzerland
Tel: +41 21 320 15 01
Head of School: Jean-Pierre Du Pasquier
Curriculum: IBDP
Language instr: English, French

Ecole Mosaic
23, avenue Dumas, Geneva, CH – 1206 Switzerland
Tel: +41 22 346 21 69
Head of School: Sylvie Johannot
Language instr: English, French

Ecole Nouvelle de la Suisse Romande – Chailly
Chemin de Rovéréaz 20, CP 161, 1000 Lausanne 12, Switzerland
Tel: +41 21 654 65 00
General director: Nicolas Catsicas
Age range: 3–18
No. of pupils: 620
Fees: CHF10,400–CHF22,400
Curriculum: IBDP
Language instr: French, English

ELA Basel
Gartenstrasse 93, Basel, CH-4052 Switzerland
Tel: +41 61 313 05 80
Director: Bernadette Allison
Language instr: English

GEMS WORLD ACADEMY – ETOY INTERNATIONAL SCHOOL
For further details see p. 119
La Tuilière 18, Etoy, 1163 Switzerland
Tel: +41 (0)21 964 18 18
Email: registrar_gwe@gemsedu.com
Website: www.gemsworld academy-etoy.com
Founding Principal: Audrey Peverelli
Age range: 2–16

Geneva English School
36 Route de Malagny, 1294 Genthod, Geneva, Switzerland
Tel: +41 22 755 18 55
Headmaster: Stephan Baird
Age range: 4–11
No. of pupils: 180 B90 G90
Language instr: English

Haut-Lac International Bilingual School
14 route du Tirage, St-Légier-la Chiesaz, 1806 Switzerland
Tel: +41 21 943 06 60
Head of School: Denise Coates
Age range: 3–18
No. of pupils: 640
Curriculum: IBDP, IBMYP
Language instr: English

Institut auf dem Rosenberg
Hohenweg 60, Ch-9000 St Gallen, Switzerland
Tel: +41 71 277 77 77
Director General: O Gademann
Age range: 7–19
No. of pupils: 150 B90 G60

Institut Florimont
37 Avenue du Petit-Lancy, Petit-Lancy, 1213 Switzerland
Tel: +41 2287 90000
Head of School: Sean Power
Curriculum: IBDP
Language instr: English, French

Institut International de Lancy
Avenue Eugene-Lance 24, Grand-Lancy, Genève 1212 Switzerland
Tel: +41 22 794 2620
Head of School: Norbert Foerster
Age range: 3–19
No. of pupils: 1533 B779 G754
Fees: CHF10,650–CHF24,600
Curriculum: IBDP, FrenchBacc, IGCSE
Language instr: English, French

Institut Le Rosey
Château du Rosey, 1180
Rolle, Switzerland
Tel: +41 21 822 5500
Headmaster: Rob Gray
Age range: 8–18
No. of pupils: 400 B200 G200
Fees: SFR75,300
Curriculum: ACT, IBDP, IPC,
FrenchBacc, SAT, TOEFL
Language instr: English, French

Institut Montana Zugerberg
Zugerberg, Zug, 6300 Switzerland
Tel: +41 41 729 1177
Director: Gerhard Pfister
Age range: 6–18
No. of pupils: 300
Curriculum: IBDP, USA
Language instr: English, German

Institut Monte Rosa
Avenue de Chillon 57, 1820
Montreux-Territet, Switzerland
Tel: +41 21 965 4545
Director: Bernhard Gademann
Age range: 8–20
No. of pupils: 70 B45 G25
Fees: CHF61,000
Curriculum: AP, SAT, TOEFL, USA
Language instr: English

Institut Villa Pierrefeu
Route de Caux 28, Ch-1823 Glion
Sur Montreux, Switzerland
Tel: +41 21 963 73 11
Principal: Philippe Néri
Age range: G15–30+
No. of pupils: 30

Inter-Community School Zurich
Strubenacher 3, 8126
Zumikon, Switzerland
Tel: +41 44 919 8300
Head of School: Mary-
Lyn Campbell
Age range: 3–18
No. of pupils: 744 B447 G397
Fees: SFR14,500–SFR31,900
Curriculum: IBDP, IBMYP, IBPYP
Language instr: English

International School Basel
Fleischbachstrasse 2, Reinach,
BL 2 4153 Switzerland
Tel: +41 61 715 33 33
Head of School: Lesley Barron
Age range: 3–18
No. of pupils: 1150
Curriculum: IBDP, IBMYP, IBPYP, SAT
Language instr: English

International School of Berne
Mattenstrasse 3, 3073
Gümligen, Switzerland
Tel: +41 (0)31 951 23 58
Director: Wayne Haugen
Age range: 3–19
No. of pupils: 305
Fees: CHF8,500–CHF31,500
Curriculum: IBDP, IBMYP, IBPYP
Language instr: English

International School of Central Switzerland
Lorzenparkstrasse 8, Cham,
6330 Switzerland
Tel: +41 41 781 44 44
Head of School: Jacqueline
Webb-Archibald
Curriculum: IBPYP

International School of Geneva (Campus des Nations)
11 route des Morillons, CH-1218
Grand Saconnex, Switzerland
Tel: +41 22 770 4700
Head of School: Elyane Ruel
Age range: 3–11
No. of pupils: 963
Fees: SFR17,925–SFR30,755
Curriculum: IBDP, IBMYP, IBPYP, IBCC
Language instr: English, French

International School of Geneva (La Châtaigneraie Campus)
2, chemin de la Ferme, 1297
Founey, Switzerland
Tel: +41 22 960 9111
Campus Principal: David Woods
Age range: 3–19
No. of pupils: 1538
Fees: SFR17,925–SFR30,755
Curriculum: IBDP, IBPYP, IGCSE
Language instr: English, French

International School of Geneva (La Grande Boissière Campus)
62, route de Chêne, 1208
Geneva, Switzerland
Tel: +41 22 787 2400
Head of School: Michael
Featherstone
Age range: 3–19
No. of pupils: 1879
Fees: SFR17,925–SFR30,755
Curriculum: IBDP
Language instr: English, French

International School of Kreuzlingen Konstanz
Villa Doldenhof, Hauptstrasse
27, Kreuzlingen, Thurgau
8280 Switzerland
Tel: +41 71 672 2727
Head of School: Sanjay Teelluck
Curriculum: IBDP, IBPYP
Language instr: English

International School of Lausanne
Chemin de la Grangette 2, 1052 Le
Mont-sur-Lausanne, Switzerland
Tel: +41 21 560 02 02
Director: Lyn Cheetham
Age range: 3–18
No. of pupils: 623 B309 G314
Fees: CHF24,700–CHF33,400
Curriculum: IBDP, IBMYP, IBPYP, SAT
Language instr: English

International School of Monts-de-Corsier
Champ des Pesses, CH-1808, Les
Monts-de Corsier, Switzerland
Tel: +41 21 948 0808
Director: Andy Croft
Age range: 3–12
No. of pupils: 100 B50 G50
Curriculum: UK

International School of Schaffhausen
Mühlentalstrasse 280,
Schaffhausen, 8200 Switzerland
Tel: +41 52 624 1707
Head of School: Gundula Kohlhaas
Age range: 3–19
No. of pupils: B125 G98 VIth10
Fees: Day SFR23,000–
SFR28,000 FB SFR21,000
Curriculum: IBDP, IBMYP, IBPYP
Language instr: English

International School of St. Gallen
ISSG, Höhenweg 1, St.
Gallen, 9000 Switzerland
Tel: +41 71 220 84 11
Head of School: Hamid Chowdery
Curriculum: IBPYP
Language instr: English

International School of Zug & Luzern, Luzern Campus
Villa Kramerstein, St Niklausen
strasse 59, Kastanienbaum,
6047 Switzerland
Tel: +41 41 342 0090
Head of School: Dominic Currer
Curriculum: IBPYP
Language instr: English

International School of Zug & Luzern, Riverside Campus
Rothustrasse 4b, 6331
Hünnenberg, Switzerland
Tel: +41 41 768 2950
Director: Dominic Currer
Age range: 12–18
Fees: SFR26,000–SFR30,000
Curriculum: AP, IBDP,
IBMYP, SAT, TOEFL
Language instr: English

International School of Zug & Luzern, Zug Campus
Walterswil, Baar, 6340 Switzerland
Tel: +41 41 768 1188
Director: Dominic Currer
Age range: 3–18
No. of pupils: 1006 B490 G516
Fees: SFR21,500–SFR31,500
Curriculum: IBPYP, UK, USA
Language instr: English

International School Rheintal
Aeulistrasse 10, Buchs,
9470 Switzerland
Tel: +41 81 750 6300
Director: Meg Sutcliffe
Age range: 3–19 B3–19 G3–19
No. of pupils: 145 B72 G73
Fees: Day £22,000–£31,000
Curriculum: IBDP, IBMYP, IBPYP
Language instr: English

International School Winterthur
Zum Park 5, CH-8404
Winterthur, Switzerland
Tel: +41 52 203 50 00
Head of School: Rhonda L Mott-Hill
Age range: 3–17
Curriculum: IBDP, IBMYP, IBPYP
Language instr: English

John F Kennedy International School
CH-3792 Saanen,
Gstaad, Switzerland
Tel: +41 (0)33 744 1372
Age range: 5–14
No. of pupils: 60 B30 G30
Fees: CHF30,000
Curriculum: UK

Juventus Schule Zürich
Lagerstrasse 45, Postfach 3021,
Zürich, 8021 Switzerland
Tel: +41 43 268 25 11
Head of School: Ralph Schlaepfer
Age range: 16–21
No. of pupils: 1000 B500 G500
Curriculum: IBDP
Language instr: English,
German, French, Italian

Kumon Leysin Academy of Switzerland
CH – 1854 Leysin, Switzerland
Tel: +41 24 4935 335
Principal: Hiroshi Watanabe
Age range: 16–19
No. of pupils: 182 B85 G97
Curriculum: AP, SAT, TOEFL

La Côte International School
Route de l'Etraz 54-60, En-Clarens-
Vich, Gland, 1196 Switzerland
Tel: +41 22 823 2626
Head of School: Alison Piguet
Curriculum: IBDP, IBMYP

Lakeside Bilingual Dayschool Zurich
Seestrasse 5, Postfach, 8700 Kusnacht, Switzerland
Tel: +41 44 914 2050
Head of School: Stefan Urner
Age range: 3–12
No. of pupils: 154 B78 G76
Fees: CHF23,880
Curriculum: National
Language instr: English, German

Lemania College Sion – Switzerland
Rue de Saint Guérin 24, Sion, Valais, 1950 Switzerland
Tel: +41 27 322 55 60
Head of School: Lionetto Lucien
Curriculum: IBDP

Leysin American School
Bâtiment Savoy, Leysin, 1854 Switzerland
Tel: +41 24 493 4888
Head of School: Marc-Frédéric Ott
Age range: 13–19
No. of pupils: 360
Fees: CHF77,500
Curriculum: ACT, AP, IBDP, SAT, TOEFL
Language instr: English

Lyceum Alpinum Zuoz
Agüel 185, CH-7524 Zuoz, Switzerland
Tel: +41 81 851 30 00
Head of School: Beat Sommer
Age range: 12–19
No. of pupils: 300 B183 G117
Fees: FB CHF72,100–CHF80,000
Curriculum: Abitur, ACT, IBDP, National, SAT
Language instr: English, German

Mutuelle d'études secondaires
7bis boulevard Carl-Vogt, Genève, 1205 Switzerland
Tel: +41 22 741 0001/52
Head of School: Michel Dubret
Age range: 15–25
No. of pupils: 84 B35 G49
Curriculum: IBDP
Language instr: French

Neuchatel Junior College
Cret-Taconnet 4, 2002 Neuchatel, Switzerland
Tel: +41 32 722 1860
Head of School: William Boyer
Age range: 16–19
No. of pupils: 77 B26 G51
Curriculum: AP, SAT
Language instr: English

SIS Swiss International School
at Lernstudio Junior, Schaffhauserstr 18, CH-8400 Winterthur, Switzerland
Tel: +41 52 202 8211
Head of School: Lawrence Wood
Age range: 3–13
No. of pupils: 51 B28 G23

SIS Swiss International School
Scheuchzerstrasse 2, Zürich, 8006 Switzerland
Tel: +41 44 368 4020
Head of School: Marcel Stähli
No. of pupils: 700
Curriculum: IBDP
Language instr: English

SIS Swiss International School
Erlenstrasse 15, CH-4058 Basel, Switzerland
Tel: +41 61 683 71 40
Head of School: Andrew Wulfers
Age range: 3–16
No. of pupils: 235 B123 G112
Fees: SFR15,000–SFR25,000
Curriculum: IBDP, National, UK, IGCSE
Language instr: German, English

SIS Swiss International School Zurich
Seestrasse 271, CH-8038 Zurich, Switzerland
Tel: +41 43 399 88 44
Principal: Ivo Müller-Läuchli
Age range: 4–13
No. of pupils: 163 B80 G83
Curriculum: National, UK
Language instr: German, English

ST. GEORGE'S SCHOOL IN SWITZERLAND
For further details see p. 140
Chemin de St Georges 19, CH 1815 Clarens/ Montreux, Switzerland
Tel: +41 21 964 3411
Email: admissions@stgeorges.ch
Website: www.stgeorges.ch
Head of School: Ian Tysoe
Age range: 3–18
No. of pupils: 400
Curriculum: IBDP, SAT, TOEFL, USA, IGCSE
Language instr: English

Stiftsschule Engelberg
Wydenstrasse, Engelberg, 6390 Switzerland
Tel: +41 41 639 62 11
Head of School: Thomas Ruprecht
Curriculum: IBDP

Surval Montreux
Route de Glion 56, Montreux, 1820 Switzerland
Tel: +41 21 966 16 16
Headmistress: Penelope Penney
Language instr: English

Swiss International School – Zurich North
Industriestrasse 50, Wallisellen, CH-8304 Switzerland
Tel: +41 44 830 7000
Head of School: Rob Butler
Age range: 3–16
No. of pupils: 200 B100 G100
Curriculum: IBPYP, IGCSE
Language instr: English

The American School in Switzerland
Via Collina D'Oro, 6926 Montagnola-Lugano, Switzerland
Tel: +41 91 960 5151
Headmaster: Charles Skipper
Age range: 4–19
No. of pupils: 700
Curriculum: IBDP
Language instr: English

The British School of Geneva
Avenue de Châtelaine 95A, Châtelaine, Geneva, 1219 Switzerland
Tel: +41 22 795 7510
Principal: Raji Sundaram
Curriculum: ALevs
Language instr: English

The British School, Bern
Hintere Dorfgasse 20, 3073 Gumligen, Switzerland
Tel: +41 31 952 7555
Head: Enid Potts
Age range: 3–12
No. of pupils: 100 B50 G50
Fees: SFR19,000
Curriculum: UK
Language instr: English

Zurich International School
Steinacherstr 140, 8820 Wädenswil, Switzerland
Tel: +41 58 750 2500
Director: Peter Mott
Age range: 2–18
No. of pupils: 1420
Fees: SFR23,050–SFR32,750
Curriculum: AP, IBDP, IBPYP, SAT, USA
Language instr: English

Zurich International School – Baden
Burghaldenstrasse 6, Baden, 5400 Switzerland
Tel: +41 58 750 2280
Head of School: Ji Han
Curriculum: IBPYP
Language instr: English, German

Turkey

Açi Schools
Bahçeköy Valide Sultan Cad Su Kemeri Mevkii No:2, 34473 Sariyer / Istanbul, Turkey
Tel: +90 (212) 349 07 00
Age range: 3–17
Curriculum: National, IGCSE, ALevs

Adapazari Enka Private Primary School
Camyolu Mah, Adapazari Sakarya, 54100 Turkey
Tel: +90 264 323 37 74
Head of School: Ozlem Mecit
Curriculum: IBPYP
Language instr: English

Ahmet Ulusoy College
Menderes Cad, Anda Sok No 16, Incek, Ankara, 06000 Turkey
Tel: +90 312 460 20 20
Head of School: Hayri Avar
Age range: 14–18
Curriculum: IBDP, National, SAT, TOEFL, IGCSE
Language instr: English

Aka School
Radyum Sok No 21 Basin Sitesi, Bahcelievler, Istanbul, Turkey
Tel: +90 2125572772
Head of School: Zubeyde Karip
Age range: 5–18
No. of pupils: 503 B238 G265
Curriculum: IBDP, National
Language instr: Turkish, English

American Collegiate Institute
Inonu Caddesi, No 476, Goztepe, Izmir, 35290 Turkey
Tel: +90 232 285 3401
Head of School: Todd Cuddington
Age range: 15–18
No. of pupils: 520
Curriculum: IBDP, SAT, TOEFL
Language instr: English

AREL Primary School
Merkez Mah, Haci Arif Bey Sok, No:1 Yenibosna – Bahcelievler, Istanbul, 34197 Turkey
Tel: +90 212 550 4930
Head of School: Munevver Gozukara
Age range: 3–14
No. of pupils: B297 G214
Fees: US$7,600–US$11,255
Curriculum: IBMYP, IBPYP
Language instr: Turkish, (English as a Second Language)

Avrupa Koleji
Prof Muammer Ahsoy Cad No 10, Zeytinburnu, Istanbul, Turkey
Tel: +90 212 547 8010
Principal: Ebru Gunay Arpaci
Age range: 5–19
No. of pupils: 508

Beykoz Doga Koleji
Fener Cad. No: 6 Dereseki, Akbaba
Koyu Beykoz, Istanbul, Turkey
Tel: + 90 (216) 320 52 00
Head of School: Nurten Balkan
Curriculum: IBPYP
Language instr: English

Bilkent Laboratory &
International School
East Campus, Ankara, 06800 Turkey
Tel: +90 312 2905361
Director: Christopher Green
Age range: 4–18
No. of pupils: 575 B264 G311
Fees: US$10,350–US$21,825
Curriculum: IBDP, IBPYP,
National, SAT, UK
Language instr: English, Turkish
(CIS) (ECIS)

Bilkent Primary School
Bilkent Universitesi, Dogu Kampusu,
Bilkent, Ankara, 06800 Turkey
Tel: +90 312 266 4864
Head of School: Oya Kerman
No. of pupils: 1060
Fees: TL22,000
Curriculum: IBPYP

British Embassy
School Ankara
Sehit Ersan Caddesi 46/A,
Çankaya, Ankara, 06680 Turkey
Tel: +90 (312) 468 6563
Headteacher: Ken Page
Age range: 3–11
No. of pupils: 136 B65 G71
Fees: Day £4,250–£7,500
Curriculum: SAT, UK
Language instr: English
(COB)

British International
School – Istanbul
PDI-ER Uluslararasi Ozel
Egitim, Hizmetleri Ticaret AS,
Maslak Meydan SK. Spring
Giz Plaza, K-5 No: 29/B 34398
Istanbul, Maslak Turkey
Tel: +90 212 202 7027
Director: William Bradley
Age range: 2–18
No. of pupils: 690
Fees: €3,750–€22,470
Curriculum: IBDP, SAT, UK
Language instr: English
(CIS) (COB)

Cakir Ilkogretim Okulu
(Cakir Primary School)
Orhaneli Yolu, Egitimciler Cd
15, Nilufer, Bursa, Turkey
Tel: +90 224 451 9330
School Governor: Cem Cakir
Curriculum: IBPYP
Language instr: Turkish

Darussafaka Schools
B.dere cad. Derbent Mevkii,
Sariyer, Istanbul, 34457 Turkey
Tel: +90 212 286 2200
Head of School: Adnan Ersan
Curriculum: IBMYP
(⚖)

Dogus Schools
Zeamet sok No 17 Acibadem,
Kadiköy, Istanbul, 81010 Turkey
Tel: +90 216 339 52 16
Head of School: Dogu Gözaçan
Age range: 16–19
No. of pupils: 118
Curriculum: IBDP, National, TOEFL
Language instr: English
(CIS) (ECIS)

Edirne Beykent Schools
Ayse Kadin Tren Gari Yani,
Edirne, 22100 Turkey
Tel: +90 506 301 7073
Head of School: Bahattin Erel
Curriculum: IBMYP
(⚖)

Emine Ornek Schools
Bademli Mah, Egitim Cad 12
Sokak No 2, Bursa, 16940 Turkey
Tel: +90 2245 491600
**Chief Executive
Officer:** Emine Ornek
Language instr: English, Turkish
(CIS) (ECIS)

Enka Schools
Sadi Gülçelik Spor Sitesi, Istinye,
Istanbul, 34460 Turkey
Tel: +90 212 705 65 00
Director of Schools: Judith Guy
Age range: 3–18
No. of pupils: B638 G627 VIth165
Fees: TL32,000–TL35,000
Curriculum: IBDP, IBPYP,
National, IGCSE
Language instr: English, Turkish
(CIS) (ECIS) (RS)

Eyüboglu Atasehir
Primary School
2 Cadde 59 Ada Manolya 4,
Bloklari yani No 6, Atasehir,
Istanbul, 34758 Turkey
Tel: +90 216 522 1222
Head of School: Firuze Vanlioglu
Curriculum: IBPYP

Eyüboglu Schools
Esenevler Mah, Dr Rüstem
Eyüboglu sok 3, Ümraniye,
Istanbul, 34762 Turkey
Tel: +90 216 522 12 12
Head of School: Ayşegül Erbil
Age range: 3–18
No. of pupils: 2228
Fees: TL32,500
Curriculum: IBDP, IBMYP,
IBPYP, National
Language instr: Turkish, English
(CIS)

Feyziye Mektepleri
Vakfi Isik Okullari
Tesvikiye Cad 152, Nisantasi,
Istanbul, Turkey
Tel: +90 212 233 1203
General Manager: Hasan
Turgu Binzet
Age range: 3–18
No. of pupils: 3947
(CIS)

FMV Erenköy Isik
High School
Sinan Ercan Cad. No: 17, Kazasker
Erenköy, Istanbul, 34736 Turkey
Tel: +90 216 355 22 07
Head of School: Özden Soyer
Curriculum: IBDP
Language instr: English

FMV Özel Ayazaga
Isik High School
Buyukdere Cad. No:106,
Istanbul, 34460 Turkey
Tel: +90 0212 2861130
Head of School: Omer Orhan
Curriculum: IBDP
Language instr: English

Gazi University Foundation
Private High School
Ali Suavi Street, Eti Quarter No 15,
Maltepe, Ankara, 06570 Turkey
Tel: +90 312 232 28 12
Head of School: Serap Kosedag
Curriculum: IBDP

Hisar School
Göktürk Merkez Mahallesi Istanbul
Caddesi No:3 Eyüp/Istanbul 34077,
Kemerburgaz, Istanbul, Turkey
Tel: +90 212 364 00 00
Age range: 4–17
No. of pupils: 1248 B661 G587
Curriculum: AP, National, SAT
Language instr: Turkish
(CIS) (ECIS)

Horizon International
College, Ozel Tarabya
Ingiliz Okullari
Salcikir cd., No:44 Tarabya,
Sariyer, Istanbul, 34457 Turkey
Tel: +90 212 280 41 07
Director: Janet Williams-Ipek
Language instr: English, Turkish

International Pre-
School PLUS
Bagdat Cad. Kadiköy.,
Istanbul, Turkey
Tel: +90 216 350 0606
Director: Sema Sever
Language instr: English,
German, French
(ISA)

Irmak School
Cemil Topuzlu Cad No
112, Caddebostan,
Istanbul, 34728 Turkey
Tel: +90 216 411 3923/4/5
Director: Meral Bilgin
Age range: 5–18
No. of pupils: 620 B310 G310
Fees: $1,350
Curriculum: IBPYP, National, SAT
Language instr: Turkish, English
(ECIS)

Isikkent Egitim Kampusu
6240/5 Sokak No. 3, Karacaoglan
Mah, Yesilova, Izmir, 35070 Turkey
Tel: +90 232 462 7100
General Manager: F. Okan Sezer
Age range: 3–18
No. of pupils: 546 B278 G268
Fees: TL12,500–TL17,900
Curriculum: IBPYP, National
Language instr: Turkish, English
(CIS)

Istanbul Beykent Schools
Gurpinar E-5 Yol Ayrimi,
Beykent Büyükçekmece,
Istanbul, 34500 Turkey
Tel: +90 212 872 6432
Head of School: Fatma Gunal
Curriculum: IBMYP

Istanbul Coskun College
Sema Egitim Hiz. A.S, Zümrütevler
Mah. Emek Cad. Maltepe,
Istanbul, 34852 Turkey
Tel: +90 216 370 55 55
Curriculum: IBDP, IBMYP
Language instr: English

Istanbul International
Community School
Karaagac Koyu, Istanbul,
34866 Turkey
Tel: +90 212 857 8264
Director: Jane Thompson
Age range: 3–18 B3–18 G3–18
No. of pupils: 520 B285 G302
Fees: $13,450–$26,850
Curriculum: IBDP, IBMYP, IBPYP
Language instr: English
(CEE) (CIS) (ECIS)

Istanbul International
School (Ozel Camilica
Park Uluslar Arasi
Okulu) Diyalog
Turistik Camilica Cad. No:12
Büyük Camilica, Istanbul, Turkey
Tel: +90 216 335 0055
Head of School: John Lees
Language instr: English, Turkish
(ISA)

ISTEK Baris Schools
Bagdat Cad. No: 238/1,
Ciftehavuzlar – Kadiköy,
Istanbul, 34730 Turkey
Tel: +90 216 360 12 18
Head of School: Burcu Akyol
Age range: 3–11
No. of pupils: 350
Fees: TL18,500–TL23,500
Curriculum: IBPYP
Language instr: Turkish, English

ISTEK Kemal Atatürk Schools (Kindergarten & Primary School)
Tarabya Bayiri Cad., Tarabya,
Istanbul, 34457 Turkey
Tel: +90 212 262 7575
**Head of Primary
School:** Zeynep Belendir
Age range: 3–10
Curriculum: IBPYP
Language instr: Turkish, English

ITU Gelistirme Vakfi Özel Ekrem Elginkan Lisesi
ITU Ayazaga Kampusu, Maslak,
Istanbul, 34469 Turkey
Tel: +90 212 367 1300
Head of School: Kudret Ulukoy
Curriculum: IBDP
Language instr: English

Jale Tezer Private School
Vedat Dalokay Cad No 105
GOP, Ankara, 6100 Turkey
Tel: +90 312 446 4446
Head: Bahar Tezer Alanya
Age range: 3–18
No. of pupils: B387 G322
Fees: TL51,000
Curriculum: National
Language instr: English, Turkish

Kultur 2000 College
Alkent 2, Faz yani, Karaagaç
Koyu Yolu, Buyukçekmece,
Istanbul, 34500 Turkey
Tel: +90 212 857 8466
Head of School: Mufide
van der Hoeven
Curriculum: IBDP, IBMYP
Language instr: English, Turkish

Kultur High School
Ataköy 9-10. Kisim, Ataköy,
Istanbul, 34156 Turkey
Tel: +90 212 5705444
Head of School: Erdogan Yilmaz
No. of pupils: 332
Curriculum: IBDP
Language instr: English

Marmara Education Group
Marmara Egitim Köyü, Basibüyük,
Maltepe, Istanbul, 34857 Turkey
Tel: +90 216 626 10 00
Head of School: Mehmet Alkan
Curriculum: IBDP
Language instr: English

MEF INTERNATIONAL SCHOOL
For further details see p. 130
Ulus Mah. Öztopuz Cad.,
Leylak Sok. 34340, Ulus/
Besiktas, Istanbul, Turkey
Tel: +90 (212) 287 6900 ext 1340
Email: contact@mef.k12.tr
Website: www.mefinternational
schools.com
Head of School: Figen Sönmez
Age range: 3–18
No. of pupils: 425
Fees: US$10,066–US$25,817
Curriculum: IBDP, IBPYP, IGCSE
Language instr: English

MEF Schools of Turkey
Amberlidere Mevkii -Dereboyu,
Cad-Ortakoy, OrtaKöy,
Istanbul, 34340 Turkey
Tel: +90 212 2876900/237
Head of School: Dilara Sougstad
Curriculum: IBDP
Language instr: English

Ozel Acarkent Doga Anadolu Lisesi
Acarkent Mah, 3 Kisim 3
Cadde, T25 Villa 34820,
Kavacik, Istanbul, Turkey
Tel: +90 216 4853580
Head of School: Ugur Gazanker
Curriculum: IBDP
Language instr: English

Özel Antalya Lisesi
Il Jandarma Komutanligi
Arkasi, Antalya, Turkey
Tel: +90 242 238 2300
Principal: Munire Yildiz
Age range: 5–18
No. of pupils: 1886 B944 G942 VIth71

Özel Bilkent Lisesi
Bilkent University, East Campus,
Bilkent, Ankara 06533, Turkey
Tel: +90 312 266 5001/02
Director: John O'Dwyer
Age range: 0–14
No. of pupils: 278
Curriculum: IBDP
Language instr: English, Turkish

Özel Büyük Kolej
Baglar Caddesi No 184, Hulya
Sokak No 7, Gaziosmanpasa,
Ankara, 06700 Turkey
Tel: +90 312 446 6676
Director: C Rumi Dogay
Age range: 5–17
No. of pupils: 1859 B947 G912

Özel Çag Lisesi
Adana-Mersin Kayayolu Uzeri
33800, Yenice, Tarsus, Mersin, Turkey
Tel: +90 324 651 3386-9
General Director: Fatma Eroglu
Age range: 6–17
No. of pupils: 510 B270 G240
Curriculum: National

Ozel Caglayan Murat High Schools
imambakir mah., Veterinerlik Cad.
no:29, Sanliurfa, 63040 Turkey
Tel: +90 414 316 35 30
Head of School: Ahmet Arslan
Curriculum: IBDP
Language instr: English

Ozel Kilicaslan Liseleri
Sivas yolu 10.km, KumarlÄ±
Mevkii, Kayseri, 38110 Turkey
Tel: +90 3522410326
Head of School: Salih Ongul
Curriculum: IBDP

Özel Nesibe Aydin Okullari
Haymana Yolu 5. Km, Karsiyaka
Mahallesi 577, Sokak No:1,
Gölbasi, Ankara, 06830 Turkey
Tel: +90 312 498 2525
Head of School: Semsettin Beser
Curriculum: IBDP
Language instr: English

Privatschule Der Deutschen Botschaft Ankara
Tunus Cad 56, Cankaya,
Ankara, Turkey
Tel: +90 312 426 63 82
Head of School: Violetta
Schrammel
No. of pupils: 184
Curriculum: IBDP
Language instr: English, German

Robert College of Istanbul
Kuruçesme Cad No 87, Arnavutkoy,
Istanbul, 34345 Turkey
Tel: +90 212 359 2222
Head of School: John R Chandler
Age range: 14–19
No. of pupils: 997 B499 G498
Fees: $17,000
Curriculum: AP, National, SAT, USA
Language instr: English, Turkish

Tarsus American School
Cengiz Topel Caddesi,
Caminur Mahallesi No 66,
Tarsus, Mersin 33440 Turkey
Tel: +90 324 613 54 02/3/4
Head of School: Charles C Hanna
Age range: 5–18
No. of pupils: 551 B287 G264
Curriculum: IBDP, SAT, TOEFL
Language instr: English

Tas Private Elementary School
Cevizlik Mah. Hallaç Hüseyin, Sk.
No:11, Bakirköy, 34142 Turkey
Tel: +90 (212) 543 6000
Head of School: Ali Akdogan
Curriculum: IBPYP
Language instr: Turkish, English

TED Ankara College Foundation High School
Golbasi Taspinar Koyu Yumrubel,
Mevkii No:310, Ankara, 06830 Turkey
Tel: +90 (312) 5869000
Head of School: Sedef Eryurt
Age range: 5–18
No. of pupils: 1499
Fees: £4,159
Curriculum: IBDP, National
Language instr: English

TED Bursa College
21 Yüzyil Cad Mürsel, Köyü
Mevkii, Bademli, Bursa, Turkey
Tel: +90 224 549 2100
Head of School: Zeynep Karslioglu
Curriculum: IBDP
Language instr: English

TED Istanbul College Foundation
Cavusbasi Acarkent D Girisi,
81686, Istanbul, Turkey
Tel: +90 216 485 0333
Principal: Atilla Küçükkayikç
Age range: 4–18
No. of pupils: 1311 B671 G640

Terakki Foundation Schools Sisli Terakki Private High School
Ebulula Mardin Cad. 12/A
34335, Levent, 34335 Turkey
Tel: +90 212 351 0060
Curriculum: IBDP
Language instr: English

Tev Inanc Turkes High School For Gifted Students
Muallimkoy Mevkii, PK 125,
Gebze, Kocaeli, 41490 Turkey
Tel: +90 262 759 11 95
Head of School: Azmi Özkardes
No. of pupils: 202
Curriculum: IBDP
Language instr: English

The English School of Kyrenia
Bilim Sokak, Bellapais, North Cyprus
Via Mersin 10, Kyrenia, Turkey
Tel: +90 533 861 2277
Head of School: David Charman
Curriculum: IBDP

The Koç School
Koc Ozel Ilkogretim ve Lisesi, PO Box 60, Tuzla, Istanbul, 34941 Turkey
Tel: +90 216 585 6282
Head of School: Koray Özsaraç
Age range: 5–18
No. of pupils: 2019
Fees: US$20,580–US$20,580
Curriculum: IBDP, National
Language instr: Turkish, English

Uskudar American Academy
Vakif Sk., No: 1 Baglarbasi, Uskudar, Istanbul, 33664 Turkey
Tel: +90 (216) 553 1818
Head of School: Eric Trujillo
Curriculum: IBDP
Language instr: English

Uskudar American Academy & SEV Elementary School
Vakif Sokak No 1, 34664 Baglarbasi, Istanbul, Turkey
Tel: +90 216 333 1100
Director: Whitman Shepard
Age range: 4–19
No. of pupils: 1644 B822 G822 Vlth150
Fees: $18,000
Curriculum: AP, National, SAT, USA
Language instr: English, Turkinsh

YUCE Schools
Ozel YUCE Okullari, Zuhtu Tigrel Caddesi, Ismet Eker Sokak No 5, Oran-Ankara, 06450 Turkey
Tel: +90 312 490 02 02
Head of School: Saadet Roach
Curriculum: IBDP, IBPYP
Language instr: English

UK

Abbots Bromley School
High Street, Abbots Bromley, Rugeley, Staffordshire, WS15 3BW UK
Tel: 01283 840232
Executive Head: Victoria Musgrave
Age range: B3–11 G3–18
No. of pupils: 250
Fees: Day £4,518–£15,357
WB £17,040–£21,552
FB £20,904–£25,725
Curriculum: UK, GCSE, IGCSE, ALevs
Language instr: English

Abbotsholme School
Rocester, Uttoxeter, Staffordshire, ST14 5BS UK
Tel: 01889 590217
Headmaster: Steve Fairclough
Age range: 2–18
No. of pupils: 310 B165 G145 Vlth55
Fees: Day £8,040–19,620
WB £19,095–£24,135
FB £21,430–£28,800
Curriculum: GCSE, IGCSE, ALevs
Language instr: English

Abingdon School
Park Road, Abingdon, Oxfordshire, OX14 1DE UK
Tel: 01235 521563
Head: Felicity Lusk
Age range: B11–18
No. of pupils: B950
Fees: Day £16,650–£35,190
Curriculum: UK, GCSE, IGCSE, ALevs
Language instr: English

Ackworth School
Barnsley Road, Ackworth, Pontefract, West Yorkshire, WF7 7LT UK
Tel: 01977 611401
Head: Kathryn Bell
Age range: 2–18
No. of pupils: 451 B227 G224 Vlth96
Fees: Day £7,809–£12,573
FB £22,437 £29,130
Curriculum: GCSE, IGCSE, ALevs
Language instr: English

ACS Cobham International School
Heywood, Portsmouth Road, Cobham, Surrey, KT11 1BL UK
Tel: +44 (0) 1932 867251
Head of School: A Eysele
Age range: 2–18
No. of pupils: 1399
Fees: Day £9,990–£23,150
FB £33,460–£40,370
Curriculum: AP, IBDP, USA
Language instr: English

ACS Egham International School
Woodlee, London Road, Egham, Surrey, TW20 0HS UK
Tel: +44 (0) 1784 430 800
Head of School: Jeremy Lewis
Age range: 3–18
No. of pupils: 630
Fees: Day £9,920–£21,990
Curriculum: AP, IBDP, IBMYP, IBPYP, IBCC, USA
Language instr: English

ACS Hillingdon International School
Hillingdon Court, 108 Vine Lane, Hillingdon, Uxbridge, Middlesex, UB10 0BE UK
Tel: +44 (0) 1895 259 771
Head of School: Linda LaPine
Age range: 4–18
No. of pupils: 600
Fees: Day £9,820–£21,490
Curriculum: AP, IBDP, IBMYP, USA
Language instr: English

Adcote School for Girls
Little Ness, Shrewsbury, Shropshire, SY4 2JY UK
Tel: 01939 260202
Headmaster: Gary Wright
Age range: G4–18
No. of pupils: 280
Fees: Day £4,635–£13,320
WB £15,495–£18,645
FB £17,160–£24,325
Curriculum: GCSE, IGCSE, ALevs

Aldenham School
Elstree, Hertfordshire, WD6 3AJ UK
Tel: 01923 858122
Headmaster: James C Fowler
Age range: 3–18
No. of pupils: 700 B515 G185 Vlth158
Fees: Day £13,626–£19,500
FB £18,768–£28,410
Curriculum: GCSE, ALevs

Alexanders College
Bawdsey Manor, Bawdsey, Woodbridge, Suffolk, IP12 3AZ UK
Tel: 01394 411633
Principal: Alister Laidlaw
Age range: 11–18
No. of pupils: B60 G40
Curriculum: ALevs

Ampleforth College
York, North Yorkshire, YO62 4ER UK
Tel: 01439 766000
Headmaster: Gabriel Everitt
Age range: 13–18
No. of pupils: B468 G175 Vlth255
Fees: Day £17,265 FB £27,375
Curriculum: GCSE, ALevs

Ardingly College
College Road, Ardingly, Haywards Heath, West Sussex, RH17 6SQ UK
Tel: +44 (0)1444 893000
Headmaster: Peter Green
Age range: 13–18
No. of pupils: 555 B322 G233 Vlth241
Fees: Day £20,925–£22,065
FB £27,930–£29,535
Curriculum: IBDP, National, UK, GCSE, IGCSE, ALevs
Language instr: English

Ashford School
East Hill, Ashford, Kent, TN24 8PB UK
Tel: 01233 739030
Head: M R Buchanan
Age range: 3 months–18 years
No. of pupils: 835 B426 G409 Vlth170
Fees: Day £6,384–£14,763
WB £23,709 FB £27,225–£28,581
Curriculum: GCSE, ALevs
Language instr: English

Ashville College
Green Lane, Harrogate, North Yorkshire, HG2 9JP UK
Tel: 01423 566358
Headmaster: D M Lauder
Age range: 4–18
No. of pupils: 768
Fees: Day £6,894–£11,769
FB £17,970–£26,010
Curriculum: UK, GCSE, IGCSE, ALevs
Language instr: English

Badminton School
Westbury-on-Trym, Bristol, Bristol, BS9 3BA UK
Tel: 0117 905 5271
Headmistress: Rebecca Tear
Age range: G3–18
No. of pupils: G450
Fees: Day £8,040–£16,920
FB £20,190–£32,070
Curriculum: GCSE, IGCSE, ALevs

Bales College
742 Harrow Road, Kensal Town, London, W10 4AA UK
Tel: 020 8960 5899
Principal: William Moore
Age range: 11–19
No. of pupils: 90 B60 G30
Fees: Day £7,950–£8,550 FB £16,050
Curriculum: GCSE, IGCSE, ALevs

Barnard Castle Senior School
Barnard Castle, Durham, DL12 8UN UK
Tel: 01833 690222
Headmaster: Alan D Stevens
Age range: 11–18
No. of pupils: 570 B370 G200 Vlth160
Fees: Day £10,980 FB £19,716
Curriculum: GCSE, IGCSE, ALevs
Language instr: English

Bath Academy
27 Queen Square, Bath, Bath & North-East Somerset, BA1 2HX UK
Tel: 01225 334577
Principal: Tim Naylor
Age range: 16–20+
No. of pupils: 160 B80 G80 Vlth120
Fees: Day £8,450–£9,700 FB £15,000
Curriculum: IGCSE, ALevs

Battle Abbey School
Battle, East Sussex, TN33 0AD UK
Tel: 01424 772385
Headmaster: R C Clark
Age range: 2–18
No. of pupils: 286 B140 G146 Vlth48
Fees: Day £6,630–£13,390 FB £23,190
Curriculum: GCSE, ALevs

Bearwood College
Bearwood Road, Wokingham,
Berkshire, RG41 5BG UK
Tel: 0118 974 8300
Headmaster: S G G Aiano
Age range: 0–18
No. of pupils: 487 B338 G149 VIth80
Fees: Day £13,890–£16,365
FB £24,360–£28,080
Curriculum: UK, GCSE, ALevs
Language instr: English

Bedales School
Church Road, Steep, Petersfield,
Hampshire, GU32 2DG UK
Tel: 01730 711733
Head: Keith Budge
Age range: 13–18
No. of pupils: 444 B209 G235 VIth166
Fees: Day £25,035 FB £31,845
Curriculum: GCSE, ALevs

Bede's School
The Dicker, Upper Dicker, Hailsham,
East Sussex, BN27 3QH UK
Tel: +44 (0)1323843252
Head: Richard Maloney
Age range: 12–18+
No. of pupils: 800 B485 G315 VIth295
Fees: Day £15,450 FB £25,725
Curriculum: UK, GCSE, IGCSE, ALevs
Language instr: English

Bedford Girls' School
Cardington Road, Bedford,
Bedfordshire, MK42 0BX UK
Tel: 01234 361900
Headmistress: Jo MacKenzie
Age range: G7–18
No. of pupils: 1200
Fees: Day £7,602–£10,683
Curriculum: IBDP, GCSE, ALevs
Language instr: English

Bedford School
De Parys Avenue, Bedford,
Bedfordshire, MK40 2TU UK
Tel: +44 (0)1234 362216
Head Master: John Moule
Age range: B7–18
No. of pupils: 1090 VIth278
Fees: Day £10,806–£16,674
WB £18,330–£27,270
FB £19,230–£28,200
Curriculum: IBDP, GCSE,
IGCSE, ALevs
Language instr: English

Bedstone College
Bedstone, Bucknell,
Shropshire, SY7 0BG UK
Tel: 01547 530303
Headmaster: M S Symonds
Age range: 3–18
No. of pupils: B150 G120 VIth34
Fees: Day £3,960–£11,550
FB £13,800–£20,955
Curriculum: GCSE, ALevs

Beechwood Sacred Heart
12 Pembury Road, Tunbridge
Wells, Kent, TN2 3QD UK
Tel: 01892 532747
Headmaster: Aaron Lennon
Age range: G3–18
No. of pupils: 400 B190 G210 VIth70
Fees: Day £8,880–£15,525
WB £22,845 FB £25,770
Curriculum: GCSE, IGCSE, ALevs

Benenden School
Cranbrook, Kent, TN17 4AA UK
Tel: 01580 240592
Headmistress: C M Oulton
Age range: G11–18
No. of pupils: 543
Fees: FB £31,410
Curriculum: GCSE, ALevs
Language instr: English

Berkhamsted School
Overton House, 131 High
Street, Berkhamsted,
Hertfordshire, HP4 2DJ UK
Tel: 01442 358001
Principal: M S Steed
Age range: 3–18
No. of pupils: 1594 VIth344
Fees: Day £9,195–£18,000
WB £24,090 FB £28,660
Curriculum: GCSE, ALevs

Bethany School
Curtisden Green, Goudhurst,
Cranbrook, Kent, TN17 1LB UK
Tel: 01580 211273
Headmaster: Francie Healy
Age range: 11–18
No. of pupils: B293 G136 VIth128
Fees: Day £14,184
WB £21,504 FB £22,143
Curriculum: GCSE, ALevs

Bingham Academy
PO Box 4937, Addis Ababa, UK
Tel: +251 11 27 91 791
Director: Brad Adams
Language instr: English

Bishop's Stortford College
10 Maze Green Road, Bishop's
Stortford, Hertfordshire,
CM23 2PJ UK
Tel: 01279 838575
Headmaster: Jeremy Gladwin
Age range: 13–18
No. of pupils: B315 G263 VIth240
Fees: Day £16,338–£16,452
WB £23,550–£23,664
FB £23,787–£24,714
Curriculum: GCSE, IGCSE, ALevs

Bloxham School
Bloxham, Banbury,
Oxfordshire, OX15 4PE UK
Tel: 01295 720222 or 724301
Headmaster: Mark E Allbrook
Age range: 11–18
No. of pupils: 424 B270 G154 VIth140
Fees: Day £15,750–£22,320
WB £20,460 FB £28,845
Curriculum: ALevs

Blundell's School
Tiverton, Devon, EX16 4DN UK
Tel: 01884 252543
Head: N Huggett
Age range: 11–18
No. of pupils: 579 B340 G239
Fees: Day £11,955–£18,930
WB £18,135–£25,800
FB £20,040–£29,340
Curriculum: GCSE, ALevs
Language instr: English

Bootham School
York, North Yorkshire, YO30 7BU UK
Tel: 01904 623261
Headmaster: Jonathan Taylor
Age range: 11–18
No. of pupils: 468 B270 G198 VIth162
Fees: Day £14,985–£16,515
FB £16,935–£28,485
Curriculum: National, GCSE, ALevs

Box Hill School
Old London Road, Mickleham,
Dorking, Surrey, RH5 6EA UK
Tel: 01372 373382
Acting Headmaster: Corydon
Lowde
Age range: 11–18
No. of pupils: 425 B280 G145 VIth96
Fees: Day £14,520–£16,050
FB £27,690–£32,400
Curriculum: IBDP, GCSE, IGCSE
Language instr: English

Bradfield College
Bradfield, Reading,
Berkshire, RG7 6AU UK
Tel: 0118 964 4516
Headmaster: Simon Henderson
Age range: 13–18
No. of pupils: 770 B482 G288 VIth310
Fees: Day £25,752 FB £32,190
Curriculum: IBDP, UK,
GCSE, IGCSE, ALevs
Language instr: English

Bramdean School
Richmond Lodge, Homefield
Road, Heavitree, Exeter,
Devon, EX1 2QR UK
Tel: 01392 273387
Head: D Stoneman
Age range: 3–18
No. of pupils: 180 B97 G83 VIth12
Fees: Day £4,740–£7,875
Curriculum: GCSE, ALevs

Bredon School
Pull Court, Bushley, Tewkesbury,
Gloucestershire, GL20 6AH UK
Tel: 01684 293156
Headmaster: John Hewitt
Age range: 4–18
No. of pupils: 224 B153 G71 VIth40
Fees: Day £6,045–£16,410
WB £17,715–£25,260
FB £18,180–£25,740
Curriculum: GCSE, ALevs

Brentwood School
Middleton Hall Lane, Brentwood,
Essex, CM15 8EE UK
Tel: 01277 243243
Headmaster: I Davies
Age range: 11–18
No. of pupils: B612 G463 VIth321
Fees: Day £15,390 FB £29,385
Curriculum: IBDP, GCSE,
IGCSE, ALevs
Language instr: English

Brighton College
Eastern Road, Brighton,
East Sussex, BN2 0AL UK
Tel: 01273 704200
Head Master: Richard Cairns
Age range: 3–18
No. of pupils: 945 B497 G448 VIth340
Fees: Day £4,890–£18,675
WB £24,729–£25,884
FB £28,575–£30,141
Curriculum: National,
GCSE, IGCSE, ALevs

Brockwood Park & Inwoods School
Brockwood Park, Bramdean,
Hampshire, SO24 0LQ UK
Tel: +44 (0)1962 771744
Age range: 4–19
No. of pupils: 92 B46 G46
Fees: Day £3,150 FB £17,270
Curriculum: IGCSE, ALevs

Bromsgrove School
Worcester Road, Bromsgrove,
Worcestershire, B61 7DU UK
Tel: +44 (0)1527 579679
Headmaster: Chris Edwards
Age range: 7–18
No. of pupils: 1300 VIth374
Fees: Day £14,175
FB £19,755–£29,985
Curriculum: IBDP, ALevs
Language instr: English

Bruton School for Girls
Sunny Hill, Bruton,
Somerset, BA10 0NT UK
Tel: 01749 814400
Headmistress: Nicola Botterill
Age range: G2–18
No. of pupils: 250
Fees: Day £6,690–£14,031
FB £17,067–£25,554
Curriculum: GCSE, ALevs

Bryanston School
Blandford Forum, Dorset,
DT11 0PX UK
Tel: 01258 484633
Head: S J Thomas
Age range: 13–18
No. of pupils: 664 B379 G285 VIth275
Fees: Day £26,415 FB £32,214
Curriculum: IBDP, GCSE, ALevs
Language instr: English

Buckswood School
Broomham Hall, Rye Road,
Guestling, Hastings, East
Sussex, TN35 4LT UK
Tel: 01424 813813
Headteacher: Mark Redsell
Age range: 10–19
No. of pupils: 420
Curriculum: IBDP, GCSE, ALevs

Burgess Hill School for Girls
Keymer Road, Burgess Hill,
West Sussex, RH15 0EG UK
Tel: 01444 241050
Headmistress: Ann Aughwane
Age range: B2–4 G2–18
No. of pupils: 640 VIth65
Fees: Day £6,750–£14,250
FB £25,200
Curriculum: UK, GCSE, IGCSE, ALevs

Cambridge International School
Cherry Hinton Hall, Cherry
Hinton Road, Cambridge,
Cambridgeshire, CB1 8DW UK
Tel: 01223 416938
Principal: Harriet Sturdy
Age range: 3–16
No. of pupils: 260 B140 G120
Fees: Day £8,115–£9,645
Curriculum: IPC, UK, IGCSE
Language instr: English

Campbell College
Belfast, County Antrim, BT4 2ND UK
Tel: 028 9076 3076
Headmaster: Robert Robinson
Age range: B11–18
No. of pupils: 896 VIth200
Fees: Day £2,200 FB £10,951–£15,111
Curriculum: GCSE, ALevs

Canford School
Canford Magna, Wimborne,
Dorset, BH21 3AD UK
Tel: 01202 841254
Headmaster: B A M Vessey
Age range: 13–18
No. of pupils: B109 G110 VIth9
Fees: Day £7,954 FB £10,374
Curriculum: GCSE, IGCSE, ALevs

Casterton School
Kirkby Lonsdale, LA6 2SG UK
Tel: 01524 279200
Headmistress: M Lucas
Age range: B3–11 G3–18
No. of pupils: 283 B17 G266 VIth60
Fees: Day £6,570–£14,109
WB £17,478–£18,759
FB £17,949–£23,580
Curriculum: GCSE, ALevs

Caterham School
Harestone Valley, Caterham,
Surrey, CR3 6YA UK
Tel: 01883 343028
Head: J P Thomas
Age range: 11–18
No. of pupils: B474 G400 VIth313
Fees: £5,019–£12,915
Curriculum: UK, GCSE, IGCSE, ALevs
Language instr: English

CATS College Cambridge
13-15 Round Church Street,
Cambridge, Cambridgeshire,
CB5 8AD UK
Tel: 01223 314431
Principal: Glenn Hawkins
Age range: 14–19+
No. of pupils: 352
Fees: Day £14,480–£23,850
FB £20,270–£33,150
Curriculum: GCSE, ALevs

CATS College Canterbury
68 New Dover Road,
Canterbury, Kent, CT1 3LQ UK
Tel: +44 (0)1227866540
Principal: Jonathan Ullmer
Age range: 14–18
No. of pupils: 350
Fees: £20,695
Curriculum: IBDP, UK, ALevs
Language instr: English

CATS College London
43-45 Bloomsbury Square,
London, WC1A 2RA UK
Tel: 02078 411580
Principal: Mark Love
Age range: 14–20
No. of pupils: B135 G116 VIth235
Fees: Day £16,460–£35,740
FB £33,560–£52,840
Curriculum: National,
UK, IGCSE, ALevs
Language instr: English

CCSS Cambridge Centre for Sixth-form Studies
4-5 Bene't Place, Lensfield
Road, Cambridge,
Cambridgeshire, CB2 1EL UK
Tel: 01223 716890
Principal: Stuart Nicholson
Age range: 15–21
No. of pupils: B84 G80
Fees: Day £18,750–£23,655
FB £25,050–£37,200
Curriculum: National, UK,
GCSE, IGCSE, ALevs
Language instr: English

Centre Academy London
92 St John's Hill, Battersea,
London, SW11 1SH UK
Tel: 020 7738 2344
Principal: Duncan Rollo
Age range: 9–19
No. of pupils: 60 B45 G15
Fees: Day £28,000–£39,000
Curriculum: SAT, UK, USA, GCSE
Language instr: English

Charterhouse
Godalming, Surrey, GU7 2DX UK
Tel: 01483 291500
Headmaster: John Witheridge
Age range: B13–18 G16–18
No. of pupils: 803 B672 G131 VIth422
Fees: Day £22,809 FB £31,680
Curriculum: IBDP, National,
UK, GCSE, IGCSE, ALevs
Language instr: English

Chase Grammar School
Lyncroft House, St John's
Road, Cannock, Staffordshire,
WS11 0UR UK
Tel: 01543 501800
Principal: Mark Ellse
Age range: 11–18
No. of pupils: 219 B109 G100 VIth9
Fees: Day £2,940–£10,092 FB £13,320
Curriculum: GCSE, ALevs

Cheltenham College
Bath Road, Cheltenham,
Gloucestershire, GL53 7LD UK
Tel: 01242 265600
Headmaster: Alex Peterken
Age range: 13–18
No. of pupils: 640 B400 G240 VIth90
Fees: Day £22,275–£23,175
FB £29,727–£30,627
Curriculum: GCSE, IGCSE, ALevs

Cheltenham Ladies' College
Bayshill Road, Cheltenham,
Gloucestershire, GL50 3EP UK
Tel: +44 (0)1242 520691
Principal: Eve Jardine-Young
Age range: G11–18
No. of pupils: 855 VIth306
Fees: Day £20,442–£23,247
FB £30,450–£34,302
Curriculum: IBDP, GCSE,
IGCSE, ALevs
Language instr: English

Chetham's School of Music
Long Millgate, Manchester,
Greater Manchester, M3 1SB UK
Tel: 0161 834 9644
Head: C J Hickman
Age range: 8–18
No. of pupils: 296 B141 G155 VIth137
Fees: Day £23,988
WB £30,987 FB £30,987
Curriculum: GCSE, IGCSE, ALevs

Chigwell School
High Road, Chigwell,
Essex, IG7 6QF UK
Tel: 020 8501 5700
Headmaster: M E Punt
Age range: 7–18
No. of pupils: 740 VIth273
Fees: Day £8,391–£12,903
WB £17,493–£18,567 FB £19,611
Curriculum: GCSE, ALevs

Chilton Cantelo School
Chilton Cantelo, Yeovil,
Somerset, BA22 8BG UK
Tel: 01935 850555
Headmaster: John Price
Age range: 4–18
No. of pupils: B180 G127 VIth15
Fees: Day £5,787–£11,496
WB £16,125–£21,495
FB £16,125–£21,495
Curriculum: GCSE, ALevs

Christ College
Brecon, Powys, LD3 8AF UK
Tel: 01874 615440
Head: E Taylor
Age range: 7–18
No. of pupils: 347 B203 G144 VIth135
Fees: Day £13,275–£15,870
FB £18,270–£24,510
Curriculum: GCSE, ALevs
Language instr: English

Christ's Hospital
Horsham, West Sussex, RH13 0YP UK
Tel: 01403 211293
Head Master: John R Franklin
Age range: 11–18
No. of pupils: 870 B435 G435
Fees: Day £14,610–£18,300
FB £28,200
Curriculum: IBDP, National,
GCSE, IGCSE, ALevs

City of London Freemen's School
Ashtead Park, Ashtead,
Surrey, KT21 1ET UK
Tel: 01372 277933
Headmaster: Philip MacDonald
Age range: 7–18
No. of pupils: 877 VIth213
Fees: Day £10,872–
£14,598 FB £23,238
Curriculum: GCSE, ALevs

Clayesmore School
Iwerne Minster, Blandford
Forum, Dorset, DT11 8LL UK
Tel: 01747 812122
Headmaster: M G Cooke
Age range: 13–18
No. of pupils: B296 G174 VIth160
Fees: Day £22,560 FB £30,837
Curriculum: GCSE, ALevs

Clifton College
32 College Road, Clifton,
Bristol, Bristol, BS8 3JH UK
Tel: 0117 315 7000
Headmaster: Mark J Moore
Age range: 3–18
No. of pupils: 1330 B845
G485 VIth280
Fees: Day £5,460–£16,245
WB £16,305–£21,645
FB £17,070–£24,075
Curriculum: ALevs

Cobham Hall School
Cobham, Kent, DA12 3BL UK
Tel: 01474 823371
Headmaster: Paul Mitchell
Age range: G11–18
No. of pupils: 180
Curriculum: IBDP, UK, GCSE, IGCSE
Language instr: English

Colston's School
Stapleton, Bristol, Bristol, BS16 1BJ UK
Tel: 0117 965 5207
Headmaster: Peter Fraser
Age range: 3–18
No. of pupils: B408 G173 VIth138
Fees: Day £5,160–£7,110 FB £15,045
Curriculum: ALevs

Concord College
Acton Burnell Hall, Shrewsbury,
Shropshire, SY5 7PF UK
Tel: 01694 731631
Principal: N G Hawkins
Age range: 13–19
No. of pupils: B225 G230 VIth320
Fees: Day £11,940 FB £28,600
Curriculum: UK, GCSE, IGCSE, ALevs

Cranleigh School
Horseshoe Lane, Cranleigh,
Surrey, GU6 8QQ UK
Tel: 01483 273666
Head: G de W Waller
Age range: 13–18
No. of pupils: 606 B401 G205 VIth237
Fees: Day £21,225 FB £26,040
Curriculum: GCSE, IGCSE, ALevs

Culford School
Culford, Bury St Edmunds,
Suffolk, IP28 6TX UK
Tel: 01284 728615
Headmaster: J F Johnson-Munday
Age range: 13–18
No. of pupils: 650 B350 G300 VIth170
Fees: Day £16,995
FB £25,500–£27,255
Curriculum: GCSE, ALevs
Language instr: English

d'Overbroeck College
The Swan Building, 111
Banbury Road, Oxford,
Oxfordshire, OX2 6JX UK
Tel: 01865 310000
Age range: 11–18
No. of pupils: 351 B211 G140 VIth255
Fees: Day £19,260 FB £27,195–£29,115
Curriculum: GCSE, ALevs

Dauntsey's School
High Street, West Lavington,
Devizes, Wiltshire, SN10 4HE UK
Tel: 01380 814500
Head: Mark Lascelles
Age range: 11–18
No. of pupils: 790 B420 G370 VIth270
Fees: Day £16,800 FB £28,140
Curriculum: GCSE, ALevs

Dean Close School
Shelburne Road, Cheltenham,
Gloucestershire, GL51 6HE UK
Tel: 01242 258044
Headmaster: Jonathan Lancashire
Age range: 13–18
No. of pupils: B251 G231 VIth182
Fees: Day £21,645 FB £30,960
Curriculum: GCSE, IGCSE, ALevs

Denstone College
Uttoxeter, Staffordshire, ST14 5HN UK
Tel: 01889 590484
Headmaster: David Derbyshire
Age range: 11–18
No. of pupils: 591 B377 G214 VIth177
Fees: Day £10,083–£12,183
FB £14,601–£21,216
Curriculum: GCSE, ALevs

Deutsche Schule London
Douglas House, Petersham Road,
Richmond, Surrey, TW10 7AH UK
Tel: +44 20 8940 8776
Head of School: Marie-
Luise Balkenhol
Age range: 3–18
No. of pupils: 800 B398 G402
Fees: Day £5,420
Curriculum: Abitur, IBDP

Dollar Academy
Dollar, Clackmannanshire,
FK14 7DU UK
Tel: 01259 742511
Rector: David Knapman
Age range: 5–18
No. of pupils: 1200 B602
G598 VIth142
Fees: Day £7,974–£10,665
WB £20,637–£23,328
FB £21,978–£24,669
Curriculum: CSFS

Dover College
Effingham Crescent, Dover,
Kent, CT17 9RH UK
Tel: 01304 205969 Ext 201
Headmaster: Gerry Holden
Age range: 3–18
No. of pupils: 340 B170 G170 VIth100
Fees: Day £6,750–£14,250
WB £18,900–£22,200
FB £20,700–£27,900
Curriculum: SAT, UK,
GCSE, IGCSE, ALevs
Language instr: English

Downe House School
Hermitage Road, Cold
Ash, Thatcham, West
Berkshire, RG18 9JJ UK
Tel: 01635 200286
Headmistress: E McKendrick
Age range: G11–18
No. of pupils: VIth174
Fees: Day £23,040 FB £31,830
Curriculum: GCSE, ALevs

Downside School
Stratton-on-the-Fosse,
Radstock, Bath, Bath & North-
East Somerset, BA3 4RJ UK
Tel: 01761 235103
Head Master: Leo Maidlow Davis
Age range: 11–18
No. of pupils: 458 B286 G172 VIth140
Fees: Day £12,900–£14,352
FB £20,940–£26,361
Curriculum: GCSE, IGCSE, ALevs

Duke of Kent School
Peaslake Road, Ewhurst,
Surrey, GU6 7NS UK
Tel: 01483 277313
Head: Judith Fremont-Barnes
Age range: 3–16
No. of pupils: 234 B168 G66
Fees: Day £4,860–£14,130
WB £13,350–£16,770
FB £15,735–£18,855
Curriculum: GCSE

Dulwich College
London, SE21 7LD UK
Tel: 020 8693 3601
Master: J A F Spence
Age range: B7–18
No. of pupils: 1525 VIth429
Fees: Day £15,711
WB £30,747 FB £32,481
Curriculum: National,
GCSE, IGCSE, ALevs
Language instr: English

Durham School
, Durham, DH1 4SZ UK
Tel: 0191 386 4783
Headmaster: Martin George
Age range: 3–18
No. of pupils: 590 B416 G174 VIth143
Fees: Day £7,575–£15,450
WB £17,685–£21,615 FB £20,085–
£23,790 £21,015–£25,020
Curriculum: GCSE, ALevs

DWIGHT SCHOOL LONDON
For further details see p. 114
6 Friern Barnet Lane,
London, N11 3LX UK
Tel: +44 (0)20 8920 0600
Email:
admissions@dwightlondon.org
Website:
www.dwightlondon.org
Head: David Rose
Age range: 2–18+
Curriculum: IBDP,
IBMYP, IBPYP, GCSE
Language instr: English

Eastbourne College
Old Wish Road, Eastbourne,
East Sussex, BN21 4JX UK
Tel: 01323 452323 (Admissions)
Headmaster: S P Davies
Age range: 13–18
No. of pupils: 628 B360 G268 VIth282
Fees: £6,500
Curriculum: GCSE, ALevs

EF ACADEMY OXFORD
For further details see p. 116
Pullens Lane, Headington,
Oxfordshire, OX3 0DT UK
Tel: Admissions: +41 41 41 74 525
Email: admissionsia@ef.com
Website: www.ef.com/academy
Head of School: Ted McGrath
Age range: 16–19
No. of pupils: 180
Fees: *FB* £25,000
Curriculum: IBDP, ALevs
Language instr: English

EF ACADEMY TORBAY
For further details see p. 117
EF House, Castle Road,
Torquay, Devon, TQ1 3BG UK
Tel: Admissions: +41 41 41 74 525
Email: admissionsia@ef.com
Website: www.ef.com/academy
Head of School: Trevor Spence
Age range: 14–19
No. of pupils: 280
Fees: *FB* £22,650 £22,050
Curriculum: IBDP, IGCSE, ALevs
Language instr: English

Ellesmere College
Ellesmere, Shropshire, SY12 9AB UK
Tel: 01691 622321
Head: B J Wignall
Age range: 7–18
No. of pupils: *B*385 G188 VIth161
Fees: *Day* £9,756–£15,975
WB £20,079–£20,646
FB £21,564–£26,955
Curriculum: IBDP, UK, GCSE, ALevs
Language instr: English

Elmhurst School for Dance
249 Bristol Road, Edgbaston,
Birmingham, West
Midlands, B5 7UH UK
Tel: 0121 472 6655
Principal: Jessica Ward
Age range: 11–19
No. of pupils: *B*68 G118 VIth59
Fees: *Day* £18,015–£18,672
FB £23,091–£24,894
Curriculum: National,
UK, GCSE, ALevs
Language instr: English

Epsom College
Epsom, Surrey, KT17 4JQ UK
Tel: 01372 821234
Headmaster: Jay Piggot
Age range: 13–18
No. of pupils: 730
Fees: *Day* £21,255 *FB* £31,098
Curriculum: GCSE, IGCSE, ALevs

Eton College
Windsor, Berkshire, SL4 6DW UK
Tel: 01753 671249
Head Master: A R M Little
Age range: B13–18
No. of pupils: 1300 *B*1300 VIth520
Fees: *FB* £33,270
Curriculum: GCSE, IGCSE, ALevs
Language instr: English

Farlington School
Strood Park, Horsham, West
Sussex, RH12 3PN UK
Tel: 01403 254967
Headmistress: Louise Higson
Age range: G3–18
Fees: *Day* £7,050–£16,155
WB £20,970–£25,605
FB £22,035–£26,670
Curriculum: SAT, GCSE,
IGCSE, ALevs
Language instr: English

Farringtons School
Perry Street, Chislehurst,
Kent, BR7 6LR UK
Tel: 020 8467 0256
Headmistress: C E James
Age range: 3–18
No. of pupils: 650 *B*221 G429 VIth80
Fees: *Day* £9,060–£12,120
WB £21,900 *FB* £23,280
Curriculum: National,
GCSE, IGCSE, ALevs

Felsted School
Felsted, Great Dunmow,
Essex, CM6 3LL UK
Tel: +44 (0) 1371 822605
Headmaster: Michael Walker
Age range: 13–18
No. of pupils: 516 *B*294 G222 VIth236
Fees: *Day* £18,480
WB £22,377 *FB* £24,705
Curriculum: IBDP, GCSE,
IGCSE, ALevs
Language instr: English

Fettes College
Carrington Road, Edinburgh,
Edinburgh, EH4 1QX UK
Tel: 0131 332 2281
Headmaster: M C B Spens
Age range: 7–18
No. of pupils: 676 *B*365 G311 VIth232
Fees: *Day* £11,331–£17,838
FB £17,739–£24,348
Curriculum: IBDP, UK, GCSE,
IGCSE, ALevs, Scot Nat
Language instr: English

Finborough School
The Hall, Great Finborough,
Stowmarket, Suffolk, IP14 3EF UK
Tel: 01449 773600
Principal: J Sinclair
Age range: 2–18
No. of pupils: 226 *B*123 G103 VIth20
Fees: *Day* £5,220–£8,580
WB £10,860–£14,280
FB £13,200–£17,010
Curriculum: GCSE, ALevs

Framlingham College
Framlingham, Suffolk, IP13 9EY UK
Tel: 01728 723789
Headmaster: P B Taylor
Age range: 13–18
No. of pupils: 418 VIth195
Fees: *Day* £15,237
WB £23,706 *FB* £23,706
Curriculum: GCSE, IGCSE, ALevs

Frensham Heights
Rowledge, Farnham,
Surrey, GU10 4EA UK
Tel: 01252 792561
Headmaster: Andrew Fisher
Age range: 3–18
No. of pupils: 497 *B*267 G230 VIth105
Fees: *Day* £5,205–£15,300
FB £19,485–£22,680
Curriculum: GCSE, ALevs

Friends' School
Mount Pleasant Road, Saffron
Walden, Essex, CB11 3EB UK
Tel: 01799 525351
Head: Anna Chaudhri
Age range: 3–18
No. of pupils: 390 *B*200 G190 VIth50
Fees: *Day* £2,375–£5,305
WB £6,615–£7,690 *FB* £7,190–£8,590
Curriculum: GCSE, IGCSE, ALevs

Fulneck School
Fulneck, Pudsey, Leeds, West
Yorkshire, LS28 8DS UK
Tel: 0113 2570235
Principal: Deborah Newman
Age range: 3–19
No. of pupils: 440 VIth67
Fees: *Day* £6,210–£11,010
WB £15,390–£18,585
FB £16,725–£20,700
Curriculum: National,
UK, GCSE, ALevs

Fyling Hall School
Robin Hood's Bay, Whitby, North
Yorkshire, YO22 4QD UK
Tel: 01947 880353
Headmaster: Paul Griffin
Age range: 4–18
No. of pupils: *B*96 G69 VIth54
Fees: *Day* £6,552–£8,736
WB £15,288–£17,784
FB £15,912–£19,032
Curriculum: GCSE, IGCSE, ALevs

GEMS Bolitho School
Polwithen Road, Penzance,
Cornwall, TR18 4JR UK
Tel: +44 (0)1736 363271
Headmaster: Gordon McGinn
Age range: 1–19
No. of pupils: 175
Fees: *Day* £7,500–£14,760
FB £22,950–£26,000
Curriculum: IBDP, GCSE, IGCSE
Language instr: English

GEMS Sherfield School
Sherfield-on-Loddon, Hook,
Hampshire, RG27 0HU UK
Tel: +44 (0)1256 884 800
Headmaster: Dick Jaine
Age range: 3 months–18 years
No. of pupils: 445 *B*253 G192 VIth16
Fees: *Day* £7,350–£13,890 *FB* £20,946
Curriculum: GCSE, IGCSE
Language instr: English

George Watson's College
Colinton Road, Edinburgh,
Edinburgh, EH10 5EG UK
Tel: 0131 446 6000
Principal: Gareth H Edwards
Age range: 3–18
No. of pupils: 2336 *B*1260 G1076
Fees: *Day* £6,192–£9,606
Curriculum: IBDP, GCSE,
ALevs, Scot Nat, SVQ, CSFS

Giggleswick School
Giggleswick, Settle, North
Yorkshire, BD24 0DE UK
Tel: 01729 893000
Head: G P Boult
Age range: 13–18
No. of pupils: 320 *B*201 G119 VIth145
Fees: *Day* £14,730 *FB* £20,970
Curriculum: ALevs

Glenalmond College, Perth
Glenalmond, Perth, Perth
& Kinross, PH1 3RY UK
Tel: 01738 842000
Warden: G C Woods
Age range: 12–18
No. of pupils: 400 *B*230 G170 VIth176
Fees: *Day* £15,480–£20,640
FB £22,710–£30,300
Curriculum: GCSE, IGCSE, ALevs

Gordonstoun
Elgin, Moray, IV30 5RF UK
Tel: 01343 837829
Principal: Simon Reid
Age range: 8–18
No. of pupils: 603 *B*356 G247 VIth261
Fees: *Day* £12,420–£24,651
WB £20,199 *FB* £20,199–£29,985
Curriculum: GCSE, ALevs

Gosfield School
Cut Hedge Park, Halstead
Road, Gosfield, Halstead,
Essex, CO9 1PF UK
Tel: 01787 474040
Principal: Sarah Welch
Age range: 4–18
No. of pupils: B125 G83 VIth21
Fees: Day £4,740–£13,695
WB £15,465–£17,310
FB £17,985–£23,130
Curriculum: IGCSE, ALevs
🏛

Grantham Preparatory School
Gorse Lane, Grantham,
Lincolnshire, NG31 7UF UK
Tel: 01476 593293
Headmistress: K A Korcz
Age range: 3–11
No. of pupils: 119
Fees: Day £6,666–£8,139
(ISA)

Greenfields School
Priory Road, Forest Row,
East Sussex, RH18 5JD UK
Tel: 01342 822189
Headteacher: G Hudson
Age range: 2–19
No. of pupils: 125 B70 G55
Fees: Day £500–£10,800
FB £19,170–£20,850
Curriculum: National,
UK, GCSE, ALevs
🏛

Gresham's
Cromer Road, Holt,
Norfolk, NR25 6EA UK
Tel: +44 (0) 1263 714500
Headmaster: Nigel Flower
Age range: 13–18
No. of pupils: 485 B273 G212 VIth218
Fees: Day £22,425 FB £29,250
Curriculum: IBDP, GCSE,
IGCSE, ALevs
Language instr: English

Gresham's Pre-Prep School
Market Place, Holt,
Norfolk, NR25 6BB UK
Tel: 01263 714563
Headmistress: Janette Davidson
Age range: 3–8
No. of pupils: B52 G61
Fees: Day £8,100–£9,300

Gresham's Prep School
Cromer Road, Holt,
Norfolk, NR25 6EY UK
Tel: 01263 714600
Headmaster: J H W Quick
Age range: 8–13
No. of pupils: 219 B126 G93
Fees: Day £16,200 FB £21,300
🏛

Haberdashers' Monmouth School for Girls
Hereford Road, Monmouth,
Monmouthshire, NP25 5XT UK
Tel: 01600 711104
Head: H Davy
Age range: G7–18
No. of pupils: 582 VIth156
Fees: Day £9,537–£12,141
FB £18,171–£23,112
Curriculum: GCSE, IGCSE, ALevs
🏃 🏛

Haileybury
Haileybury, Hertford,
Hertfordshire, SG13 7NU UK
Tel: +44 (0)1992 706353
The Master: J S Davies
Age range: 11–18 (entry
at 11+, 13+ and 16+)
No. of pupils: 761 B432 G329 VIth309
Fees: Day £14,568–£21,924
FB £18,516–£29,190
Curriculum: IBDP, GCSE,
IGCSE, ALevs
Language instr: English
🏛

Halcyon London International School
33 Seymour Place,
London, W1H 5AU UK
Tel: 020 7258 1169
Director: Terry Hedger
Curriculum: UK
Language instr: English
(COB)

Hammond School
Hoole Bank, Mannings Lane,
Chester, Cheshire, CH2 2PB UK
Tel: 01244 305350
Principal: M Evans
Age range: 4–19
No. of pupils: 248 B103 G145
Fees: Day £10,359–£17,004
FB £17,499–£24,144
Curriculum: GCSE, ALevs
🏛

Hampshire Collegiate School
Embley Park, Romsey,
Hampshire, SO51 6ZE UK
Tel: 01794 512206
Principal: Emma-Kate Henry
Age range: 2–18
No. of pupils: 683 B388 G305
Fees: £2,453
Curriculum: GCSE, ALevs, CSFS
Language instr: English
🏛

Harrogate Ladies' College
Clarence Drive, Harrogate,
North Yorkshire, HG1 2QG UK
Tel: 01423 504543
Principal: S Brett
Age range: G11–18
No. of pupils: 350 G350
Fees: Day £14,370
FB £24,360–£30,855
Curriculum: GCSE, ALevs
🏃 🏛

Headington School
London Road, Oxford,
Oxfordshire, OX3 7TD UK
Tel: +44 (0)1865 759100
Headmistress: Caroline Jordan
Age range: G11–18
No. of pupils: 780
Fees: Day £7,002–£14,403
WB £19,287–£25,143
FB £20,937–£27,885
Curriculum: IBDP, GCSE, ALevs
🏃 🏛

Heathfield School
London Road, Ascot,
Berkshire, SL5 8BQ UK
Tel: 01344 898342
Head: Jo Heywood
Age range: G11–18
No. of pupils: 200 G200 VIth80
Fees: FB £29,991
Curriculum: GCSE, ALevs
Language instr: English
🏃 🏛

Hethersett Old Hall School
Hethersett, Norwich,
Norfolk, NR9 3DW UK
Tel: 01603 810390
Headmaster: S Crump
Age range: B3–11 G3–18
No. of pupils: 197 B24 G173 VIth29
Fees: Day £5,850–£12,450
WB £13,395–£17,850
FB £15,585–£23,175
Curriculum: GCSE, IGCSE, ALevs
Language instr: English
🏛

Holy Trinity International School
Birmingham Road, Kidderminster,
Worcestershire, DY10 2BY UK
Tel: 01562 822929
Headteacher: Pamela Leek-Wright
Age range: 0–18
No. of pupils: B76 G220 VIth22
Fees: Day £2,065–£3,510
Curriculum: IBDP, UK, GCSE, ALevs
Language instr: English

Hurst Lodge
Bagshot Road, Ascot,
Berkshire, SL5 9JU UK
Tel: 01344 622154
Principal: Victoria Smit
Age range: 3–18
No. of pupils: 195 B65 G124 VIth6
Fees: Day £6,600–£13,740
WB £19,620–£22,290
Curriculum: GCSE, IGCSE,
ALevs, Scot Nat
🏛

Hurstpierpoint College
Hurstpierpoint, West
Sussex, BN6 9JS UK
Tel: 01273 833636
Headmaster: T J Manly
Age range: 4–18
No. of pupils: 1030
Fees: Day £20,325 WB £25,635
FB £28,650–£30,240 £24,030
Curriculum: IBDP, GCSE, ALevs
🏛

International School of Aberdeen
Pitfodels House, North Deeside
Road, Pitfodels, Cults, Aberdeen,
Aberdeen, AB15 9PN UK
Tel: 01224 730300
Director: D A Hovde
Age range: 3–18
No. of pupils: B270 G268 VIth62
Fees: Day £17,875–£20,020
Curriculum: ACT, IBDP, SAT
Language instr: English
(CIS) (ECIS)

International School of London
139 Gunnersbury Avenue,
Acton, London, W3 8LG UK
Tel: +44 (0)20 8992 5823
Head of School: Huw Davies
Age range: 3–18
No. of pupils: B190 G170 VIth60
Fees: Day £16,750–£22,500
Curriculum: IBDP, IBMYP, IBPYP
Language instr: English
(CIS) (ECIS)

Ipswich School
Henley Road, Ipswich,
Suffolk, IP1 3SG UK
Tel: 01473 408300
Headmaster: Nicholas Weaver
Age range: 11–18
No. of pupils: 739 B471 G268 VIth218
Fees: Day £11,478–£12,582
WB £18,759–£21,099
FB £20,313–£23,289
Curriculum: GCSE, IGCSE, ALevs
Language instr: English
🏛

Kammer International Bilingual School
Lathusenstraße 11,
Hannover, 30539 UK
Tel: +49 5112 200890
Director: Andreas Schraknepper
Language instr: German, English
(ECIS)

Kelly College
Tavistock, Devon, PL19 0HZ UK
Tel: 01822 813127
Headmaster: G W R Hawley
Age range: 11–18
No. of pupils: B205 G148 VIth107
Fees: Day £3,950–£4,875
WB £6,450–£7,900 FB £7,175–£8,500
Curriculum: GCSE, ALevs
Language instr: English
(♠)

Kent College
Whitstable Road, Canterbury,
Kent, CT2 9DT UK
Tel: 01227 763231
Head Master: D J Lamper
Age range: 3–18
No. of pupils: 612
Fees: Day £14,988–£16,269
FB £29,367–£29,736
Curriculum: IBDP, UK,
GCSE, IGCSE, ALevs
Language instr: English
(♠)

Kent College Pembury
Old Church Road, Pembury,
Tunbridge Wells, Kent, TN2 4AX UK
Tel: +44 (0)1892 822006
Headmistress: Sally-Anne Huang
Age range: G3–18 Prep School 3–11
No. of pupils: 650 VIth102
Fees: Day £7,887–£17,322
FB £21,471–£27,924 £18,822
Curriculum: GCSE, ALevs
(♠)(♠)

Kilgraston School
Bridge of Earn, Perth, Perth
& Kinross, PH2 9BQ UK
Tel: 01738 812257
Principal: Carol Ann Lund
Age range: B2–5 G2–18
No. of pupils: 321 B8 G313 VIth88
Fees: Day £8,550–£14,925
FB £20,250–£25,455
Curriculum: GCSE, ALevs, Scot Nat
Language instr: English
(♠)(♠)

Kimbolton School
Kimbolton, Huntingdon,
Cambridgeshire, PE28 0EA UK
Tel: 01480 860505
Headmaster: Jonathan Belbin
Age range: 4–18
No. of pupils: B489 G467 VIth170
Fees: Day £8,625–£13,425 FB £22,215
Curriculum: GCSE, ALevs
Language instr: English
(♠)

King Edward's School
Edgbaston Park Road, Birmingham,
West Midlands, B15 2UA UK
Tel: 0121 472 1672
Chief Master: J A Claughton
Age range: B11–18
No. of pupils: VIth250
Fees: Day £112,506
Curriculum: IBDP, GCSE, IGCSE
Language instr: English
(♂)

King Edward's Witley
Petworth Road, Wormley,
Godalming, Surrey, GU8 5SG UK
Tel: +44 (0)1428 686700
Headmaster: John F Attwater
Age range: 11–18
No. of pupils: B240 G160 VIth145
Fees: Day £14,985–£19,950
FB £21,900–£28,500
Curriculum: IBDP, GCSE, IGCSE
Language instr: English
(♠)

King Fahad Academy
Bromyard Avenue, Acton,
London, W3 7HD UK
Tel: 020 8743 0131
**Acting Head of Primary
School:** Julie Benafif
Age range: 3–18
No. of pupils: 446
Fees: Day £3,000
Curriculum: IBDP, IBPYP, USA, ALevs
Language instr: English
(ECIS)

King William's College
Castletown, Isle of Man, IM9 1TP UK
Tel: +44 (0)1624 820400
Principal: Martin A C Humphreys
Age range: 11–18
No. of pupils: 377
Fees: Day £13,887–£19,746
FB £22,887–£28,746
Curriculum: IBDP, GCSE, IGCSE
Language instr: English
(♠)

King's Bruton
Bruton, Somerset, BA10 0ED UK
Tel: 01749 814200
Headmaster: I S Wilmshurst
Age range: 13–18
No. of pupils: 306 B221 G85 VIth145
Fees: Day £18,486 FB £25,455
Curriculum: GCSE, IGCSE, ALevs
(♠)

King's College
Taunton, Somerset, TA1 3DX UK
Tel: 01823 328204
Headmaster: R R Biggs
Age range: 13–18
No. of pupils: 440 B285 G155 VIth180
Fees: Day £13,650 FB £19,980
Curriculum: GCSE, ALevs
(♠)

King's College School
Southside, Wimbledon Common,
London, SW19 4TT UK
Tel: 020 8255 5300
Head Master: A D Halls
Age range: B7–18 G16+
No. of pupils: 762 VIth295
Fees: Day £18,900
Curriculum: IBDP, ALevs
Language instr: English
(♂)

King's Ely
Ely, Cambridgeshire, CB7 4DB UK
Tel: 01353 660700
Head: Susan Freestone
Age range: 3–18
No. of pupils: 971 B565 G406 VIth161
Fees: Day £11,946–£18,009
FB £19,047–£26,070
Curriculum: GCSE, IGCSE, ALevs
(♠)

KING'S SAINT MICHAEL'S COLLEGE
For further details see p. 127
Oldwood Road, Tenbury Wells,
Worcestershire, WR15 8PH UK
Tel: 01584 811300
Email: info@st-michaels.uk.com
Website:
www.st-michaels.uk.com
Principal: Stuart Higgins
Age range: 14–18
No. of pupils: 108
Fees: FB £24,995–£26,895
Curriculum: UK, GCSE,
IGCSE, ALevs
Language instr: English
(♠)(COB)

King's School, Rochester
Satis House, Boley Hill,
Rochester, Kent, ME1 1TE UK
Tel: 01634 888555
Headmaster: I R Walker
Age range: 13–18
No. of pupils: 688 B482 G206 VIth113
Fees: Day £7,655–£14,400
FB £17,145–£24,210
Curriculum: GCSE, IGCSE, ALevs
(♠)

Kingham Hill School
Kingham, Chipping Norton,
Oxfordshire, OX7 6TH UK
Tel: 01608 658999
Head of School: Nick Seward
Age range: 11–18
No. of pupils: 310 B194 G116
Fees: Day £4,965–£5,680
WB £7,075–£8,695 FB £7,340–£9,490
Curriculum: UK, USA,
GCSE, IGCSE, ALevs
Language instr: English
(♠)

Kingsley School
Northdown Road, Bideford,
Devon, EX39 3LY UK
Tel: 01237 426200
Headmaster: Simon Woolcott
Age range: 3 months–18 years
No. of pupils: 400 VIth80
Fees: Day £5,010–£11,640
FB £14,430–£22,200
Curriculum: GCSE, ALevs
(♠)

Kingsmead School
Bertram Drive, Hoylake, Wirral,
Merseyside, CH47 0LL UK
Tel: 0151 632 3156
Headmaster: M G Gibbons
Age range: 3–16
No. of pupils: B135 G81
Fees: Day £2,625–£9,105
WB £13,050–£15,345
FB £13,755–£16,050
Curriculum: GCSE
(♠)

Kingswood School
Lansdown, Bath, Bath & North-
East Somerset, BA1 5RG UK
Tel: 01225 734210
**Headmaster &
Principal:** Simon Morris
Age range: 11–18
No. of pupils: 642 B260 G193 VIth189
Fees: Day £9,789 WB £15,918–
£19,722 FB £18,222–£21,828
Curriculum: GCSE, ALevs
(♠)

Kirkham Grammar School
Ribby Road, Kirkham, Preston,
Lancashire, PR4 2BH UK
Tel: 01772 684264
Headmaster: RDW Laithwaite
Age range: 3–18
No. of pupils: 940 B467 G473 VIth157
Fees: Day £7,260–£9,675
WB £17,940 FB £18,375
Curriculum: GCSE, IGCSE, ALevs
Language instr: English
(♠)

Lancing College
Lancing, West Sussex, BN15 0RW UK
Tel: 01273 465805
Head Master: Dominic T Oliver
Age range: 13–18
No. of pupils: 546 B346 G200 VIth242
Fees: Day £7,260
WB £10,340 FB £10,340
Curriculum: GCSE, IGCSE, ALevs
Language instr: English
(♠)

Langley School
Langley Park, Loddon, Norwich,
Norfolk, NR14 6BJ UK
Tel: 01508 520210
Headmaster: Dominic Findlay
Age range: 10–18
No. of pupils: 461 B295 G166 VIth97
Fees: Day £12,555
WB £21,285 FB £25,515
Curriculum: GCSE, ALevs
(♠)

Lavant House
West Lavant, Chichester,
West Sussex, PO18 9AB UK
Tel: 01243 527211
Headteacher: C Horton
Age range: G7–18
No. of pupils: G130 VIth20
Fees: £10,938–£11,430
Curriculum: GCSE, ALevs

Leicester International School
16-20 Beal Street, Leicester,
Leicestershire, LE2 0AA UK
Tel: 0116 2515345
Principal: N Hussein
Age range: 5–11
No. of pupils: 146 B70 G76

Leighton Park School
Shinfield Road, Reading,
Berkshire, RG2 7ED UK
Tel: 0118 987 9600
Head: Nigel Williams
Age range: 11–18
No. of pupils: 489
Fees: Day £5,253–£6,363
FB £8,024–£9,910
Curriculum: IBDP, UK,
GCSE, IGCSE, ALevs
Language instr: English

Leweston School
Senior School, Sherborne,
Dorset, DT9 6EN UK
Head: A Aylward
Age range: G11–18
No. of pupils: 240 VIth70
Curriculum: GCSE, ALevs

Lichfield Cathedral School
The Close, Lichfield,
Staffordshire, WS13 7LH UK
Tel: 01543 306170
Headmaster: David Corran
Age range: 3–18
No. of pupils: 449 B242 G207
Fees: Day £6,258–£9,783
WB £12,111–£14,196
FB £13,875–£15,057

Lime House School
Holm Hill, Dalston, Carlisle,
Cumbria, CA5 7BX UK
Tel: 01228 710225
Headmaster: N A Rice
Age range: 3–18+
No. of pupils: 211 B128 G83 VIth40
Fees: Day £3,000–£7,050
WB £7,500–£15,000
FB £9,000–£16,500
Curriculum: GCSE, ALevs

Lincoln Minster Senior School
The Prior Building, Upper
Lindum Street, Lincoln,
Lincolnshire, LN2 5RW UK
Tel: 01522 551300
Principal: Clive Rickart
Age range: 2.5–18
No. of pupils: 840 B423 G417 VIth144
Fees: Day £6,510–£9,672
WB £14,289–£16,947
FB £15,417–£18,285
Curriculum: GCSE, ALevs

Liverpool College
Queen's Drive, Mossley Hill,
Liverpool, Merseyside, L18 8BG UK
Tel: 0151 724 4000
Principal: Hans van
Mourik Broekman
Age range: 3–18
No. of pupils: 806
Fees: Day £5,415–£8,595
Curriculum: UK, GCSE, ALevs
Language instr: English

Llandovery College
Queensway, Llandovery,
Carmarthenshire, SA20 0EE UK
Tel: +44 (0)1550 723005
Warden: Guy Ayling
Age range: Day 4–18 Boarding 7–18
No. of pupils: 320
Fees: Day £8,220–£16,002
FB £15,585–£23,970
Curriculum: GCSE, IGCSE, ALevs

Lomond School
10 Stafford Street, Helensburgh,
Argyll & Bute, G84 9JX UK
Tel: 01436 672476
Headmaster: Simon J Mills
Age range: 3–18
No. of pupils: B264 G256 VIth50
Fees: Day £4,470–£9,120 FB £20,030

Longridge Towers School
Longridge Towers, Berwick-
upon-Tweed, Northumberland,
TD15 2XH UK
Tel: 01289 307584
Headmaster: T M Manning
Age range: 3–18
No. of pupils: B140 G120 VIth45
Fees: Day £7,476–£11,682
WB £17,190–£18,477
FB £22,554–£23,799
Curriculum: GCSE, ALevs

Lord Wandsworth College
Long Sutton, Hook,
Hampshire, RG29 1TB UK
Tel: 01256 862201
Headmaster: Fergus Livingstone
Age range: 11–18
No. of pupils: 530 B360 G170 VIth160
Fees: Day £18,240–£19,200
WB £24,420–£25,770
FB £24,420–£27,090
Curriculum: GCSE, IGCSE, ALevs
Language instr: English

Loretto School
Linkfield Road, Musselburgh,
East Lothian, EH21 7RE UK
Tel: 0131 653 4455
Headmaster: Graham Hawley
Age range: 3–18
No. of pupils: 600 B310 G290 VIth160
Fees: Day £7,890–£20,011
FB £16,260–£29,460
Curriculum: GCSE, IGCSE,
ALevs, Scot Nat

Loughborough Grammar School
6 Burton Walks, Loughborough,
Leicestershire, LE11 2DU UK
Tel: 01509 233233
Headmaster: P B Fisher
Age range: B10–18
No. of pupils: 1010
Fees: Day £10,413 FB £19,356
Curriculum: GCSE, IGCSE, ALevs
Language instr: English

Luckley House School
Luckley Road, Wokingham,
Berkshire, RG40 3EU UK
Tel: 0118 978 4175
Headmistress: Jane Tudor
Age range: G11–18
No. of pupils: 300 VIth50
Fees: Day £13,476
WB £21,858 FB £23,586
Curriculum: GCSE, ALevs

Lucton School
Lucton, Leominster,
Herefordshire, HR6 9PN UK
Tel: 01568 782000
Headmistress: Gill Thorne
Age range: 7–19
No. of pupils: B179 G148 VIth53
Fees: Day £5,859–£11,430
WB £19,212–£22,530
FB £26,220–£26,220
Curriculum: National,
GCSE, IGCSE, ALevs
Language instr: English

LVS Ascot (Licensed Victuallers' School)
London Road, Ascot,
Berkshire, SL5 8DR UK
Tel: 01344 882770
Headmistress: Christine Cunniffe
Age range: 4–18
No. of pupils: 901 B542 G359 VIth150
Fees: Day £8,220–£15,435
FB £21,015–£24,900
Curriculum: GCSE, ALevs

Malvern College
College Road, Malvern,
Worcestershire, WR14 3DF UK
Tel: 01684 581500
Headmaster: Antony R Clark
Age range: 13–18
No. of pupils: 675 B371 G304 VIth49
Fees: Day £7,039 FB £11,027–£11,413
Curriculum: IBDP, GCSE,
IGCSE, ALevs
Language instr: English

Malvern St James
Avenue Road, Great Malvern,
Worcestershire, WR14 3BA UK
Tel: 01684 892288
Head Teacher: Patricia Woodhouse
Age range: G4–18
No. of pupils: 400
Fees: Day £8,310–£16,425
WB £16,005–£28,380
FB £17,775–£31,005
Curriculum: GCSE, IGCSE, ALevs

Manchester High School for Girls
Grangethorpe Road, Manchester,
Greater Manchester, M14 6HS UK
Tel: 0161 224 0447
Head Mistress: A C Hewitt
Age range: G4–18
No. of pupils: 923 VIth193
Fees: Day £7,053–£9,900
Curriculum: IBDP, GCSE, ALevs
Language instr: English

Marlborough College
Marlborough, Wiltshire, SN8 1PA UK
Tel: 01672 892300
the Master: Nicholas Sampson
Age range: 13–18
No. of pupils: 878 B548 G330 VIth388
Fees: Day £21,180 FB £28,245
Curriculum: IBDP, ALevs
Language instr: English

Merchiston Castle School

294 Colinton Road, Edinburgh,
Edinburgh, EH13 0PU UK
Tel: 0131 312 2201
Headmaster: A R Hunter
Age range: B7–18
No. of pupils: 470
Fees: Day £12,525–£20,190
FB £17,545–£27,465
Curriculum: GCSE, IGCSE,
ALevs, Scot Nat
Language instr: English

Methodist College

1 Malone Road, Belfast,
County Antrim, BT9 6BY UK
Tel: 028 9020 5205
Principal: J Scott W Naismith
Age range: 4–19
No. of pupils: 2307 B1258
G1049 VIth548
Fees: Day £130–£3,425
Curriculum: GCSE, ALevs

Michael Hall School

Kidbrooke Park, Forest Row,
East Sussex, RH18 5JB UK
Tel: 01342 822275
Age range: 3–19
No. of pupils: B267 G280
Fees: Day £7,900–£11,250
FB £5,400–£7,800
Curriculum: UK, GCSE, ALevs
Language instr: English

Mill Hill School

The Ridgeway, Mill Hill Village,
London, NW7 1QS UK
Tel: 020 8959 1176
Head: Dominic Luckett
Age range: 13–18
No. of pupils: 689 B492 G197 VIth259
Fees: Day £13,860 FB £21,900
Curriculum: TOEFL, UK, GCSE, ALevs

Millfield School

Street, Somerset, BA16 0YD UK
Tel: 01458 442 291/296
Headmaster: Craig A Considine
Age range: 13–18
No. of pupils: 1218 B756
G462 VIth566
Fees: Day £21,075 FB £31,260
Curriculum: GCSE, IGCSE, ALevs

Milton Abbey School

Blandford Forum,
Dorset, DT11 0BZ UK
Tel: 01258 880484
Headmaster: Magnus Bashaarat
Age range: 13–18
No. of pupils: 220 B188 G32
Fees: Day £16,485
Curriculum: GCSE, ALevs
Language instr: English

Moira House Girls School

Upper Carlisle Road, Eastbourne,
East Sussex, BN20 7TE UK
Tel: 01323 644144
Principal: L A Watson
Age range: G2–18
No. of pupils: 360 VIth105
Fees: Day £6,300–£14,655
WB £19,260–£24,060
FB £20,715–£26,550
Curriculum: TOEFL,
GCSE, IGCSE, ALevs
Language instr: English

Monkton Senior School

Monkton Combe, Bath, Bath &
North-East Somerset, BA2 7HG UK
Tel: +44 (0)1225 721102
Principal: Richard Backhouse
Age range: 11–19
No. of pupils: 375 B239 G136 VIth148
Fees: Day £12,753–£16,572
WB £14,998–£21,885
FB £17,997–£24,534
Curriculum: GCSE, IGCSE, ALevs

Monmouth School

Monmouth, Monmouthshire,
NP25 3XP UK
Tel: 01600 710433
Headmaster: Steven G Connors
Age range: B7–18
No. of pupils: 697 VIth188
Fees: Day £9,288–£13,116
FB £18,171–£23,112
Curriculum: GCSE, IGCSE, ALevs

Moreton Hall

Weston Rhyn, Oswestry,
Shropshire, SY11 3EW UK
Tel: 01691 773671
Head: Jonathan Forster
Age range: B3–11 G3–18
No. of pupils: B72 G413 VIth100
Fees: Day £8,250–£24,090
FB £18,270–£28,170
Curriculum: GCSE, ALevs

Mount St Mary's College

Spinkhill, Derbyshire, S21 3YL UK
Tel: 01246 433388
Headmaster: Laurence McKell
Age range: 11–18
No. of pupils: 344 B209 G135 VIth75
Fees: Day £10,470–£12,027
WB £16,332–£21,021
FB £19,602–£26,112
Curriculum: GCSE, IGCSE, ALevs
Language instr: English

Moyles Court School

Moyles Court, Ringwood,
Hampshire, BH24 3NF UK
Tel: 01425 472856
Headmaster: Dean
Age range: 3–16
No. of pupils: B83 G63
Fees: Day £3,285–£4,650
FB £6,690–£7,740

New Hall School

The Avenue, Boreham,
Chelmsford, Essex, CM3 3HS UK
Tel: 01245 467588
Principal: Katherine Jeffrey
Age range: 3–18
No. of pupils: 1132 B478
G654 VIth166
Fees: Day £7,392–£15,225
FB £16,110–£22,860
Curriculum: GCSE, ALevs

Newlands School

Eastbourne Road, Seaford,
East Sussex, BN25 4NP UK
Tel: 01323 490000
Headteacher: Tula Dyer
Age range: 0–18
No. of pupils: B94 G63 VIth4
Fees: Day £2,033–£3,960 WB £5,160–
£5,730 FB £5,735–£22,500
Curriculum: GCSE, ALevs
Language instr: English

North London Collegiate School

Canons, Canons Drive, Edgware,
Middlesex, HA8 7RJ UK
Tel: +44 (0)20 8952 0912
Headmistress: Bernice McCabe
Age range: G4–18
No. of pupils: 1080
Fees: Day £14,898–£17,625
Curriculum: IBDP, GCSE,
IGCSE, ALevs
Language instr: English

Oakham School

Chapel Close, Oakham,
Rutland, LE15 6DT UK
Tel: 01572 758758
Headmaster: Nigel M Lashbrook
Age range: 10–18
No. of pupils: B539 G526 VIth405
Fees: Day £15,930–£17,970
WB £20,655–£26,955
FB £24,435–£29,940
Curriculum: IBDP, GCSE,
IGCSE, ALevs
Language instr: English

Ockbrook School

The Settlement, Ockbrook,
Derby, Derbyshire, DE7 3RJ UK
Tel: 01332 673532
Head: Tom Brooksby
Age range: B2–14 G2–18
No. of pupils: 399 B76 G323 VIth50
Fees: Day £7,203–£10,613
WB £5,685 FB £6,174
Curriculum: GCSE, IGCSE, ALevs
Language instr: English

Oswestry School

Upper Brook Street, Oswestry,
Shropshire, SY11 2TL UK
Tel: 01691 655711
Headmaster: Douglas Robb
Age range: 4–19
No. of pupils: B240 G203 VIth92
Fees: Day £7,305–£13,140
WB £17,610–£21,390
FB £20,085–£23,385
Curriculum: GCSE, IGCSE, ALevs
Language instr: English

Oundle School

Oundle, Peterborough,
Northamptonshire, PE8 4GH UK
Tel: 01832 277 122
Headmaster: C M P Bush
Age range: 4–19
No. of pupils: 1104 B650
G454 VIth423
Fees: Day £19,035 FB £29,670
Curriculum: National,
GCSE, IGCSE, ALevs
Language instr: English

Padworth College

Padworth, Reading,
Berkshire, RG7 4NR UK
Tel: 0118 983 2644
Principal: John Aguilar
Age range: 13–19
No. of pupils: 116 B65 G51 VIth50
Fees: Day £14,250 FB £28,392
Curriculum: GCSE, IGCSE, ALevs

Pangbourne College

Pangbourne, Reading,
Berkshire, RG8 8LA UK
Tel: 0118 984 2101
Headmaster: Thomas J C Garnier
Age range: 11–18
No. of pupils: 387 B301 G86 VIth117
Fees: Day £7,500–£10,335
FB £10,710–£14,745
Curriculum: ALevs
Language instr: English

Plymouth College

Ford Park, Plymouth,
Devon, PL4 6RN UK
Tel: +44 (0)1752 505100
Headmaster: S J Wormleighton
Age range: 11–18
No. of pupils: 550 B325 G225 VIth180
Fees: Day £12,510–£14,700
FB £24,855–£28,200
Curriculum: IBDP, UK,
GCSE, IGCSE, ALevs
Language instr: English

Pocklington School
West Green, Pocklington, York,
North Yorkshire, YO42 2NJ UK
Tel: 01759 321200
Headmaster: Mark Ronan
Age range: 11–18
No. of pupils: 619 B290 G240 VIth206
Fees: Day £12,450
WB £21,699 FB £22,920
Curriculum: GCSE, IGCSE, ALevs
Language instr: English

Polam Hall School
Grange Road, Darlington,
Durham, DL1 5PA UK
Tel: 01325 463383
Headmaster: John Moreland
Age range: 11–18
No. of pupils: B55 G130 VIth50
Fees: Day £12,210
WB £22,545 FB £23,445
Curriculum: UK, GCSE, ALevs
Language instr: English

Princess Helena College
Preston, Hitchin,
Hertfordshire, SG4 7RT UK
Tel: 01462 432100
Headmistress: Jo-Anne Duncan
Age range: G11–18
No. of pupils: 194
Fees: Day £13,755–£17,220
FB £19,650–£28,350
Curriculum: GCSE, IGCSE, ALevs

Prior Park College
Ralph Allen Drive, Bath, Bath &
North-East Somerset, BA2 5AH UK
Tel: 01225 831000
Head: James Murphy-O'Connor
Age range: 11–18 Boarding 13–18
No. of pupils: 580 B310 G270 VIth180
Fees: Day £11,736–£13,077
WB £18,687 FB £23,583
Curriculum: National, ALevs

Prior's Field
Priorsfield Road, Godalming,
Surrey, GU7 2RH UK
Tel: 01483 810551
Head: J Roseblade
Age range: G11–18
No. of pupils: 450
Fees: Day £15,855 FB £25,575
Curriculum: GCSE, IGCSE, ALevs

Queen Anne's School
6 Henley Road, Caversham,
Reading, Berkshire, RG4 6DX UK
Tel: 0118 918 7300
Headmistress: Julia Harrington
Age range: G11–18
No. of pupils: 336 VIth100
Fees: Day £5,695 WB £7,545–
£7,975 FB £8,395
Curriculum: GCSE, IGCSE, ALevs

QUEEN ETHELBURGA'S COLLEGIATE FOUNDATION
For further details see p. 133
Thorpe Underwood Hall,
Ouseburn, York, North
Yorkshire, YO26 9SS UK
Tel: 01423 33 33 30
Email: info@qe.org
Website: www.qe.org
Principal: Steven Jandrell
Age range: 3–19
No. of pupils: 1278
B684 G594 VIth557
Fees: Day £7,185–£12,960
Curriculum: National, UK,
GCSE, IGCSE, ALevs
Language instr: English

Queen Margaret's School
Escrick Park, York, North
Yorkshire, YO19 6EU UK
Tel: 01904 728261
Headmaster: P R Silverwood
Age range: G11–18
No. of pupils: 332 VIth115
Fees: Day £17,100 FB £26,988
Curriculum: GCSE, IGCSE, ALevs

Queen Mary's School
Baldersby Park, Topcliffe, Thirsk,
North Yorkshire, YO7 3BZ UK
Tel: 01845 575000
Headmaster: R McKenzie Johnston
Age range: B3–8 G3–16
No. of pupils: 235 B8 G227
Fees: Day £5,445–£13,050
FB £14,400–£16,995
Curriculum: GCSE

Queen Victoria School
Dunblane, Stirling, FK15 0JY UK
Tel: 0131 310 2927
Head: W Bellars
Age range: 11–18
No. of pupils: 271 B137 G134 VIth26
Fees: FB £1,326
Curriculum: Scot Nat, SVQ, CSFS

Queen's College
Trull Road, Taunton,
Somerset, TA1 4QS UK
Tel: 01823 272559
Headmaster: Christopher J Alcock
Age range: 3–18
No. of pupils: 784 B404 G380 VIth150
Fees: Day £5,250–£14,700
FB £10,605–£23,400
Curriculum: GCSE, ALevs

Radley College
Radley, Abingdon,
Oxfordshire, OX14 2HR UK
Tel: 01235 543000
Warden: A W McPhail
Age range: B13–18
No. of pupils: 688
Fees: FB £30,900
Curriculum: GCSE, IGCSE, ALevs

Ratcliffe College
Fosse Way, Ratcliffe on the Wreake,
Leicester, Leicestershire, LE7 4SG UK
Tel: 01509 817000
Head: G Lloyd
Age range: 3–18
No. of pupils: 689 B392 G297 VIth154
Fees: Day £7,392–£13,644
FB £20,862 £7,392–£8,819
Curriculum: GCSE, ALevs
Language instr: English

Read School
Drax, Selby, North
Yorkshire, YO8 8NL UK
Tel: 01757 618248
Headmaster: J A Sweetman
Age range: 3–18
No. of pupils: B176 G112 VIth36
Fees: Day £6,480–£9,180
WB £15,447–£17,748
FB £17,295–£19,800
Curriculum: GCSE, ALevs
Language instr: English

Reed's School
Sandy Lane, Cobham,
Surrey, KT11 2ES UK
Tel: 01932 869001
Headmaster: D W Jarrett
Age range: B11–18 G16–18
No. of pupils: 650 B590 G60 VIth230
Fees: Day £16,938–£21,184
FB £22,582–£28,023
Curriculum: GCSE, IGCSE, ALevs
Language instr: English

Rendcomb College
Rendcomb, Cirencester,
Gloucestershire, GL7 7HA UK
Tel: 01285 831213
Headmaster: R Martin
Age range: 3–18
No. of pupils: 424 VIth90
Fees: Day £6,050–£19,350
FB £20,130–£26,625
Curriculum: National,
GCSE, IGCSE, ALevs

Repton School
The Hall, Repton, Derbyshire,
DE65 6FH UK
Tel: 01283 559222
Head: R A Holroyd
Age range: 13–18
No. of pupils: 658 B375 G283 VIth284
Fees: Day £21,726 FB £29,280
Curriculum: GCSE, IGCSE, ALevs

Rishworth School
Rishworth, Halifax, West
Yorkshire, HX6 4QA UK
Tel: 01422 822217
Headmaster: R A Baker
Age range: 3–18
No. of pupils: 600 B331 G269 VIth90
Fees: Day £4,905–£9,585
WB £15,285–£16,725
FB £16,830–£18,360
Curriculum: GCSE, ALevs

Rochester Independent College
Star Hill, Rochester, Medway,
Kent, ME1 1XF UK
Tel: 01634 828115
Age range: 11–19
No. of pupils: 240 B140 G100 VIth150
Fees: Day £9,990–£13,500
WB £21,000–£21,000
FB £23,718–£24,426
Curriculum: ALevs
Language instr: English

Rockport School
Craigavad, Holywood,
County Down, BT18 0DD UK
Tel: 028 9042 8372
Headmaster: George Vance
Age range: 3–16
No. of pupils: 200 B97 G103
Fees: Day £5,370–£11,790
WB £8,870–£13,040
FB £10,105–£14,275
Curriculum: GCSE

Roedean School
Roedean Way, Brighton,
East Sussex, BN2 5RQ UK
Tel: 01273 667500
Headmistress: Frances King
Age range: G11–18
No. of pupils: 375 VIth177
Fees: Day £15,750–£18,150
WB £24,450–£27,300
FB £28,200–£31,350
Curriculum: GCSE, IGCSE, ALevs
Language instr: English

Rookwood School
Weyhill Road, Andover,
Hampshire, SP10 3AL UK
Tel: 01264 325900
Headmistress: L Whetstone
Age range: 3–16
No. of pupils: B120 G189
Fees: Day £7,770–£12,780
FB £19,545–£22,875
Curriculum: GCSE

Rossall School
Broadway, Fleetwood,
Lancashire, FY7 8JW UK
Tel: +44 (0)1253 774260
Head: Elaine Purves
Age range: 2–18
No. of pupils: 655 B385 G270
Fees: Day £2,520–£4,060
WB £4,360–£6,980 FB £6,140–£11,500
Curriculum: IBDP, IBPYP,
National, GCSE, IGCSE, ALevs
Language instr: English

Royal Russell School
Coombe Lane, Croydon,
Surrey, CR9 5BX UK
Tel: 020 8657 3669
Headmaster: Christopher
Hutchinson
Age range: 11–18
No. of pupils: 590 B310 G280 VIth180
Fees: Day £15,285
FB £22,365–£30,240
Curriculum: GCSE, ALevs

RSA Academy
Bilston Road, Gospel Oak, Tipton,
West Midlands, DY4 0BZ UK
Tel: +44 (0)121 556 1351
Principal: Daulton Redmond
Curriculum: IBDP, IBCC
Language instr: English

Rugby School
Rugby, Warwickshire, CV22 5EH UK
Tel: +44 (0)1788 556274
Headmaster: P R A Green
Age range: 11–18
No. of pupils: 804 B444
G360 VIth366
Fees: Day £19,605 FB £31,245
Curriculum: National,
GCSE, IGCSE, ALevs

Ruthin School
Ruthin, Denbighshire, LL15 1EE UK
Tel: 01824 702543
Headmaster: T J Belfield
Age range: 3–18
No. of pupils: 240 B171 G69 VIth41
Fees: Day £5,550–£10,320
WB £13,965 FB £16,755
Curriculum: GCSE, ALevs

RYDAL PENRHOS SCHOOL
For further details see p. 134
Pwllycrochan Avenue, Colwyn
Bay, Clwyd, LL29 7BT UK
Tel: +44 (0)1492 530155
Email:
admissions@rydalpenrhos.com
Website:
www.rydalpenrhos.com
Headmaster: P A Lee-Browne
Age range: 2–18
No. of pupils: 547 B314 G233
Fees: Day £7,485–£15,210
WB £22,140–£27,300
FB £24,600–£30,315
Curriculum: IBDP, National,
IGCSE, ALevs
Language instr: English

Ryde School with Upper Chine
Queen's Road, Ryde, Isle
of Wight, PO33 3BE UK
Tel: 01983 617970
Headmaster: M. A. Waldron
Age range: 3–18
No. of pupils: 762 B401 G361 VIth144
Fees: Day £5,340–£11,376
WB £21,150–£22,170
FB £22,692–£23,712
Curriculum: IBDP, National,
GCSE, ALevs

Rye St Antony
Pullens Lane, Oxford,
Oxfordshire, OX3 0BY UK
Tel: 01865 762802
Headmistress: A M Jones
Age range: B3–8 G3–18
No. of pupils: 400 B20 G380 VIth60
Fees: Day £8,835–£13,425
WB £17,835–£20,985
FB £18,900–£22,065
Curriculum: National,
UK, GCSE, ALevs
Language instr: English

Sacred Heart School
17 Mangate Street, Swaffham,
Norfolk, PE37 7QW UK
Tel: 01760 721330/724577
Headmistress: Francis Ridler
Age range: 3–16
No. of pupils: 156 B33 G109
Fees: Day £7,005–£10,425
WB £14,850–£15,975 FB £19,350
Curriculum: UK, GCSE
Language instr: English

Saint Felix School
Halesworth Road, Southwold,
Suffolk, IP18 6SD UK
Tel: 01502 722175
Head: Fran D'Alcorn
Age range: 1–18
No. of pupils: 464 B220 G244 VIth74
Fees: Day £6,450–£13,980
WB £15,360–£19,590
FB £20,190–£24,420
Curriculum: GCSE, ALevs

Scarborough College
Filey Road, Scarborough,
North Yorkshire, YO11 3BA UK
Tel: +44 (0)1723 360620
Head of School: Isobel Nixon
Age range: 3–18
No. of pupils: 450
Fees: Day £5,580–£9,360
FB £16,140–£17,340
Curriculum: IBDP, ALevs
Language instr: English

SEAFORD COLLEGE
For further details see p. 135
Lavington Park, Petworth,
West Sussex, GU28 0NB UK
Tel: 01798 867392
Email: jmackay@seaford.org
Website: www.seaford.org
Headmaster: J P Green
Age range: 6–18
No. of pupils: 621 B436
G185 VIth143
Fees: Day £8,505–£17,850
WB £17,625–£23,850 FB £27,900
Curriculum: National,
GCSE, IGCSE, ALevs
Language instr: English

Sedbergh School
Sedbergh, Cumbria, LA10 5HG UK
Tel: 01539 620535
Headmaster: A Fleck
Age range: 3–18
No. of pupils: 490 B310 G180 VIth200
Fees: Day £21,519 FB £29,202
Curriculum: GCSE, IGCSE, ALevs

Sevenoaks School
High Street, Sevenoaks,
Kent, TN13 1HU UK
Tel: +44 (0)1732 455133
Head: Katy Ricks
Age range: 11–18
No. of pupils: 1025 B496
G524 VIth421
Fees: Day £19,287–£21,897
FB £30,798–£33,408
Curriculum: IBDP, National,
GCSE, IGCSE
Language instr: English

Shebbear College
Shebbear, Beaworthy,
Devon, EX21 5HJ UK
Tel: 01409 282000
Headmaster: S. D. Weale
Age range: 3–18
No. of pupils: 350 B210 G140 VIth54
Fees: Day £7,185–£11,400
WB £12,390–£17,190
FB £15,990–£22,245
Curriculum: GCSE, ALevs
Language instr: English

Sherborne Girls
Bradford Road, Sherborne,
Dorset, DT9 3QN UK
Tel: +44 (0)1935 818224
Headmistress: J Dwyer
Age range: G11–18
No. of pupils: 410 VIth144
Fees: Day £5,750–£6,865
FB £7,850–£9,450 £28,350
Curriculum: IBDP, GCSE,
IGCSE, ALevs
Language instr: English

SHERBORNE INTERNATIONAL
For further details see p. 136
Newell Grange, Newell,
Sherborne, Dorset, DT9 4EZ UK
Tel: 01935 814743
Email: reception@sherborne-
international.org
Website: www.sherborne-
international.org
Principal: Mary Arnal
Age range: 11–16
No. of pupils: 157 B100 G57
Fees: FB £37,500
Curriculum: National,
GCSE, IGCSE
Language instr: English

Sherborne School
Abbey Road, Sherborne,
Dorset, DT9 3AP UK
Tel: +44 (0)1935 812249
Headmaster: C Davis
Age range: B13–18
No. of pupils: 596 VIth210
Fees: Day £24,525 FB £30,300
Curriculum: IBDP, National,
GCSE, IGCSE, ALevs
Language instr: English

Shiplake College
Henley-on-Thames,
Oxfordshire, RG9 4BW UK
Tel: +44 (0)1189 402455
Headmaster: A G S Davies
Age range: B11–18 G16–18
No. of pupils: 405 B382 G23 VIth149
Fees: Day £14,925–£27,615
WB £27,615 FB £27,615
Curriculum: GCSE, IGCSE, ALevs
Language instr: English

Shrewsbury School
The Schools, Shrewsbury,
Shropshire, SY3 7BA UK
Tel: 01743 280552
Headmaster: Mark Turner
Age range: 13–18
No. of pupils: B600 G140 VIth359
Fees: Day £21,300 FB £30,420
Curriculum: GCSE, IGCSE, ALevs
Language instr: English

Sibford School
Sibford Ferris, Banbury,
Oxfordshire, OX15 5QL UK
Tel: 01295 781200
Head: Michael Goodwin
Age range: Day 3–18
Boarders 11–18
No. of pupils: B223 G178 VIth77
Fees: Day £7,758–£12,453
WB £15,555–£22,530
FB £23,718–£24,195
Curriculum: TOEFL, UK, GCSE, ALevs
Language instr: English

Sidcot School
Oakridge Lane, Winscombe,
North Somerset, BS25 1PD UK
Tel: 01934 843102
Head: Iain Kilpatrick
Age range: 3–18
No. of pupils: 515 B290 G225 VIth170
Fees: Day £6,150–£14,250
FB £22,050–£27,750
Curriculum: IBDP, GCSE, ALevs
Language instr: English

Slindon College
Slindon House, Slindon, Arundel,
West Sussex, BN18 0RH UK
Tel: 01243 814320
Headmaster: D Quick
Age range: B10–18
No. of pupils: 90 VIth6
Fees: Day £5,670
WB £9,080 FB £9,080
Curriculum: GCSE, ALevs
Language instr: English

Southbank International School – Hampstead
16 Netherhall Gardens,
London, NW3 5TH UK
Tel: 020 7243 3803
Principal: Shirley Harwood
Age range: 3–11
No. of pupils: 205 B104 G101
Fees: Day £13,200–£20,550
Curriculum: IBPYP
Language instr: English

Southbank International School – Kensington
36-38 Kensington Park Road,
London, W11 3BU UK
Tel: 020 7243 3803
Principal: Mark Case
Age range: 3–11
No. of pupils: B115 G105
Fees: Day £13,200–£20,550
Curriculum: IBPYP
Language instr: English

Southbank International School – Westminster
63-65 Portland Place,
London, W1B 1QR UK
Tel: 020 7243 3803
Principal: Terry Hedger
Age range: 11–18
No. of pupils: 348 B178 G170 VIth104
Fees: Day £22,140–£24,150
Curriculum: IBDP, IBMYP
Language instr: English

Southbank International School – Fitzrovia
17 Conway Street,
London, W1T 6BN UK
Tel: +44 2076 312600

St Catherine's School
Bramley, Guildford,
Surrey, GU5 0DF UK
Tel: 01483 893363
Headmistress: A M Phillips
Age range: G4–18
No. of pupils: 900
Fees: Day £7,695–£15,660 FB £25,770
Curriculum: UK, GCSE, IGCSE, ALevs

St Christopher School
Barrington Road, Letchworth,
Hertfordshire, SG6 3JZ UK
Tel: 01462 650 850
Head: Richard Palmer
Age range: 3–18
No. of pupils: 511 B294 G217 VIth78
Fees: Day £3,375–£14,505
FB £15,600–£25,470
Curriculum: GCSE, ALevs

St Clare's, Oxford
139 Banbury Road, Oxford,
Oxfordshire, OX2 7AL UK
Tel: +44 (0)1865 552031
Principal: Paula Holloway
Age range: 15–19
No. of pupils: 270
Fees: Day £15,843 FB £32,476
Curriculum: IBDP
Language instr: English

St David's College
Gloddaeth Hall, Llandudno,
Clwyd, LL30 1RD UK
Tel: 01492 875974
Headmaster: Stuart Hay
Age range: 9–19
No. of pupils: 254 B188 G66 VIth77
Fees: Day £10,425–£15,210
Curriculum: GCSE, ALevs

St Dominic's Priory School Stone
21 Station Road, Stone,
Staffordshire, ST15 8EN UK
Tel: +44 (0)1785 814181
Headteacher: Patricia Adamson
Age range: B3 months–11
G3 months–18
No. of pupils: 320 B20 G300 VIth40
Fees: Day £6,522–£10,242
Curriculum: GCSE, ALevs

St Dunstan's College
Stanstead Road,
London, SE6 4TY UK
Tel: 020 8516 7200
Headmistress: J D Davies
Age range: 3–18
No. of pupils: 870
Fees: £8,283
Curriculum: IBDP,
National, UK, ALevs
Language instr: English

St Edmund's College & Prep School
Old Hall Green, Nr Ware,
Hertfordshire, SG11 1DS UK
Tel: 01920 824247
Head: Paulo Durán BA
Age range: 3–18
No. of pupils: 799 B446 G353 VIth135
Fees: Day £9,465–£14,955
WB £19,830–£22,575
FB £21,855–£24,990
Curriculum: IBDP, GCSE, ALevs

St Edmund's School
St Thomas' Hill, Canterbury,
Kent, CT2 8HU UK
Tel: 01227 475601
Head: Louise Moelwyn-Hughes
Age range: 3–18
No. of pupils: 535
Fees: Day £18,651 FB £24,900
Curriculum: National, ALevs

St Edward's, Oxford
Woodstock Road, Oxford,
Oxfordshire, OX2 7NN UK
Tel: +44 (0)1865 319200
Warden: Stephen Jones
Age range: 13–18
No. of pupils: 680
Fees: Day £25,671 FB £32,082
Curriculum: IBDP, GCSE,
IGCSE, ALevs
Language instr: English

St Francis' College
Broadway, Letchworth Garden
City, Hertfordshire, SG6 3PJ UK
Tel: 01462 670511
Headmistress: D MacGinty
Age range: G3–18
No. of pupils: 460 VIth75
Fees: Day £8,370–£11,385
WB £15,555–£18,630
FB £19,140–£22,155
Curriculum: GCSE, ALevs
Language instr: English

St George's School
Wells Lane, Ascot,
Berkshire, SL5 7DZ UK
Tel: 01344 629900
Headmistress: Caroline Jordan
Age range: G11–18
No. of pupils: 280 VIth85
Fees: Day £16,440 FB £25,350
Curriculum: ALevs

St George's School for Girls
Garscube Terrace, Edinburgh,
Edinburgh, EH12 6BG UK
Tel: 0131 311 8000
Head: Anne Everest
Age range: B18 months–4
years G18 months–18 years
No. of pupils: 800 B10 G790
Fees: Day £7,050–£11,460 FB £23,265
Curriculum: UK, GCSE,
ALevs, Scot Nat, CSFS

St Helen's School
Eastbury Road, Northwood,
Middlesex, HA6 3AS UK
Tel: +44 (0)1923 843210
Headmistress: Mary Short
Age range: G3–18
No. of pupils: 1128 VIth153
Fees: £14,370
Curriculum: IBDP, UK, GCSE,
IGCSE, ALevs, CSFS
Language instr: English

St James Senior Boys School
Church Road, Ashford,
Surrey, TW15 3DZ UK
Tel: 01784 266930
Headmaster: David Brazier
Age range: B11–18
No. of pupils: VIth65
Fees: Day £14,400 WB £6,150
Curriculum: GCSE, IGCSE, ALevs

St James' School
22 Bargate, Grimsby, North-East
Lincolnshire, DN34 4SY UK
Tel: 01472 503260
Headteacher: S M Isaac
Age range: 2–18
No. of pupils: 238 B129 G109 VIth25
Fees: Day £4,605–£11,067
WB £11,775–£17,367
FB £13,125–£18,717
Curriculum: GCSE, ALevs
Language instr: English

St John's College
Grove Road South,
Southsea, Portsmouth,
Hampshire, PO5 3QW UK
Tel: 023 9281 5118
Headmaster: G J Best
Age range: 2–18
No. of pupils: 627 B401 G226 VIth105
Fees: Day £7,500–£9,765
FB £21,105–£22,500
Curriculum: GCSE, IGCSE, ALevs
Language instr: English

St John's International School
Broadway, Sidmouth,
Devon, EX10 8RG UK
Tel: 01395 513984
Headmaster: Simon Larter
Age range: 2–18
No. of pupils: 197 B102 G95 VIth5
Fees: Day £6,495–£10,215
WB £12,141 FB £15,570–£19,200
Curriculum: AICE, IBPYP, IGCSE

St John's School
Epsom Road, Leatherhead,
Surrey, KT22 8SP UK
Tel: 01372 373000
Headmaster: Martin A R Collier
Age range: 13–18
No. of pupils: 499 B429 G70 VIth236
Fees: Day £19,395
WB £24,252 FB £26,595
Curriculum: National, GCSE, ALevs
Language instr: English

St Joseph's College
Birkfield, Belstead Road,
Ipswich, Suffolk, IP2 9DR UK
Tel: 01473 690281
Principal: S Grant
Age range: 3–18
No. of pupils: 560 B403 G157 VIth109
Fees: Day £5,634–£9,510
WB £14,475–£15,825 FB £15,150–
£16,500 £15,150–£16,500
Curriculum: GCSE, IGCSE, ALevs

St Lawrence College
Ramsgate, Kent, CT11 7AE UK
Tel: 01843 572931
Principal: Antony Spencer
Age range: 3–18
No. of pupils: B298 G175 VIth127
Fees: Day £6,297–£15,882
FB £20,715–£27,564
Curriculum: GCSE, ALevs

St Leonards School
St Andrews, Fife, KY16 9QJ UK
Tel: 01334 472126
Headmaster: Michael Carslaw
Age range: 5–19
No. of pupils: B283 G263 VIth138
Fees: Day £8,259–£11,388
FB £27,114–£27,114
Curriculum: IBDP, UK, GCSE, IGCSE
Language instr: English

St Leonards-Mayfield School
The Old Palace, Mayfield,
East Sussex, TN20 6PH UK
Tel: 01435 874600
Head: Antonia Beary
Age range: G11–18
No. of pupils: 420 G420 VIth100
Fees: Day £15,285
WB £23,010 FB £23,010
Curriculum: GCSE, IGCSE, ALevs

St Margaret's School, Bushey
Merry Hill Road, Bushey,
Hertfordshire, WD23 1DT UK
Tel: 020 8416 4400
Head: Rose Hardy
Age range: G4–18
No. of pupils: 427 VIth90
Fees: Day £9,330–£14,730
WB £20,220–£23,670
FB £23,670–£27,600
Curriculum: GCSE, IGCSE, ALevs

St Mary's Calne
Curzon Street, Calne,
Wiltshire, SN11 0DF UK
Tel: 01249 857200
Headmistress: Felicia Kirk
Age range: G11–18
No. of pupils: 335 VIth110
Fees: Day £24,150–£23,001
FB £32,751–£31,500
Curriculum: GCSE, IGCSE, ALevs
Language instr: English

St Mary's Music School
Coates Hall, 25 Grosvenor Crescent,
Edinburgh, Edinburgh, EH12 5EL UK
Tel: 0131 538 7766
Headteacher: Jennifer Rimer
Age range: 9–19
No. of pupils: B27 G48 VIth17
Curriculum: ALevs, Scot Nat, CSFS

St Mary's School
Bateman Street, Cambridge,
Cambridgeshire, CB2 1LY UK
Tel: 01223 353253
Headmistress: Charlotte Avery
Age range: G4–18
No. of pupils: 650 G650 VIth105
Fees: Day £12,465
WB £23,100 FB £26,862
Curriculum: GCSE, ALevs

St Mary's School
Shaftesbury, Dorset, SP7 9LP UK
Tel: 01747 854005
Headmaster: Richard James
Age range: G11–18
No. of pupils: 325 G325 VIth86
Fees: Day £14,820–£15,570
FB £21,570–£22,650
Curriculum: GCSE, ALevs

St Mary's School Ascot
St Mary's Road, Ascot,
Berkshire, SL5 9JF UK
Tel: 01344 296614
Headmistress: Mary Breen
Age range: G11–18
No. of pupils: 380 G380 VIth120
Fees: Day £22,380 FB £31,440
Curriculum: GCSE, IGCSE, ALevs
Language instr: English

St Michael's School
Bryn, Llanelli, Carmarthenshire,
SA14 9TU UK
Tel: 01554 820325
Headmaster: Emma L Lewis
Age range: 3–18
No. of pupils: 420 B222 G198 VIth80
Fees: Day £4,179–£7,968 FB £18,250
Curriculum: ALevs

St Paul's School
Lonsdale Road, Barnes,
London, SW13 9JT UK
Tel: 020 8748 9162
High Master: Mark Bailey
Age range: B13–18
No. of pupils: 897
Fees: Day £19,674 FB £29,466
Curriculum: UK, IGCSE, ALevs

St Peter's School
Clifton, York, North
Yorkshire, YO30 6AB UK
Tel: 01904 527300
Head Master: L Winkley
Age range: 13–18
No. of pupils: 547 B329 G218 VIth238
Fees: Day £15,390 FB £25,185
Curriculum: National, UK,
GCSE, IGCSE, ALevs
Language instr: English

St Swithun's School
Alresford Road, Winchester,
Hampshire, SO21 1HA UK
Tel: 01962 835700
Headmistress: Jane Gandee
Age range: G11–18
No. of pupils: G446 VIth85
Fees: Day £17,640 FB £28,290
Curriculum: GCSE, ALevs

St Teresa's Effingham (Senior School)
Beech Avenue, Effingham,
Surrey, RH5 6ST UK
Tel: 01372 452037
Head: Michael Farmer
Age range: G2–18
No. of pupils: 450 VIth90
Fees: Day £14,190–£14,730
WB £22,800–£23,340
FB £22,800–£23,340
Curriculum: GCSE, ALevs

St. Bees School
St. Bees, Cumbria, CA27 0DS UK
Tel: 01946 828010
Head: James Davies
Age range: 4–18
No. of pupils: 271 B148 G123 VIth104
Fees: £4,105–£5,295
Curriculum: GCSE, IGCSE, ALevs

Stamford Endowed Schools
Brazenose House, St Paul's Street,
Stamford, Lincolnshire, PE9 2BS UK
Tel: 01780 750310
Principal: Stephen C Roberts
Age range: 2–18
No. of pupils: 1634 VIth400
Fees: Day £8,262–£13,446
£19,146–£24,909
Curriculum: GCSE, IGCSE, ALevs
Language instr: English

Stamford High School
St Martin's, Stamford,
Lincolnshire, PE9 2LL UK
Tel: 01780 428200
Principal: S C Roberts
Age range: G11–18
No. of pupils: 633 G633 VIth201
Fees: Day £12,252 WB £16,932–
£19,488 FB £22,356
Curriculum: GCSE, ALevs

Stanborough School
Stanborough Park, Garston,
Watford, Hertfordshire, WD25 9JT UK
Tel: 01923 673268
Head: Roger Murphy
Age range: 3–19
No. of pupils: 300 B128 G172 VIth20
Fees: Day £3,660–£5,500
WB £12,834–£15,846
Curriculum: GCSE, IGCSE
Language instr: English

Stewart's Melville College
Queensferry Road, Edinburgh,
Edinburgh, EH4 3EZ UK
Tel: 0131 311 1000
Principal: J N D Gray
Age range: B11–18 G16–18
No. of pupils: 864 B746 G118
Fees: Day £9,096 FB £18,249
Curriculum: National,
Scot Nat, CSFS

Steyning Grammar School
Shooting Field, Steyning,
West Sussex, BN44 3RX UK
Tel: +44 (0)1903 814555
Headteacher: C D Taylor
Age range: 11–18
No. of pupils: 1986
Fees: WB £8,250 FB £9,750
Curriculum: IBDP, GCSE, ALevs
Language instr: English

Stoke College
Stoke-by-Clare, Sudbury,
Suffolk, CO10 8JE UK
Tel: 01787 278141
Head: John Gibson
Age range: 3–16
No. of pupils: B143 G98
Fees: Day £6,732–£10,482
WB £14,586–£16,926
Curriculum: GCSE

Stonar School
Cottles Park, Atworth, Melksham,
Wiltshire, SN12 8NT UK
Tel: 01225 701740
Head: Toby Nutt
Age range: B2–11 G2–18
No. of pupils: 330 B29 G301 VIth46
Fees: Day £7,665–£14,895
WB £16,350–£19,050
FB £18,060–£26,880
Curriculum: GCSE,
IGCSE, ALevs, CSFS

Stonyhurst College
Stonyhurst, Clitheroe,
Lancashire, BB7 9PZ UK
Tel: 01254 827073
Headmaster: A Johnson
Age range: 3–18
No. of pupils: 470 VIth240
Fees: Day £16,884
WB £25,270 FB £30,332
Curriculum: IBDP, GCSE, ALevs

Stover School
Newton Abbot, Devon,
TQ12 6QG UK
Tel: 01626 354505
Principal: Sue Bradley
Age range: 3–18
No. of pupils: 423 B189 G234 VIth67
Fees: Day £6,879–£10,695
WB £15,183–£21,894
FB £16,575–£20,850
Curriculum: GCSE, ALevs

Stowe School
Buckingham, Buckinghamshire,
MK18 5EH UK
Tel: 01280 818000
Headmaster: Anthony Wallersteiner
Age range: 13–18
No. of pupils: 769 B504 G265 VIth318
Fees: Day £22,500 FB £30,975
Curriculum: GCSE, ALevs

Strathallan School
Forgandenny, Perth, Perth
& Kinross, PH2 9EG UK
Tel: 01738 812546
Headmaster: B K Thompson
Age range: 9–18
No. of pupils: 557 B318 G239 VIth195
Curriculum: GCSE, ALevs, Scot Nat

Sutton Valence School
North Street, Sutton Valence,
Kent, ME17 3HL UK
Tel: 01622 845200
Headmaster: B C W Grindlay
Age range: 11–18
No. of pupils: B318 G176 VIth165
Fees: Day £4,590–£6,005
WB £7,210–£9,450 FB £7,210–£9,450
Curriculum: UK, GCSE, IGCSE, ALevs
Language instr: English

Talbot Heath
Rothesay Road, Bournemouth,
Dorset, BH4 9NJ UK
Tel: 01202 761881
Head: A Holloway
Age range: G3–18
No. of pupils: 535 VIth80
Fees: Day £4,890–£10,665
WB £17,286 FB £17,763
Curriculum: GCSE, ALevs

TASIS THE AMERICAN SCHOOL IN ENGLAND
For further details see p. 142
Coldharbour Lane, Thorpe,
Surrey, TW20 8TE UK
Tel: +44 (0)1932 582316
Email: ukadmissions@tasisengland.org
Website: www.tasisengland.org
Head: Michael V McBrien
Age range: 3–18
No. of pupils: 750
Fees: Day £6,670–£21,630
FB £36,870
Curriculum: AP, IBDP, SAT, TOEFL, USA
Language instr: English

Taunton School
Staplegrove Road, Taunton,
Somerset, TA2 6AD UK
Tel: 01823 703703
Headmaster: John Newton
Age range: 0–18
No. of pupils: 604 B313 G291 VIth288
Fees: Day £16,485 FB £27,840
Curriculum: IBDP, GCSE, ALevs
Language instr: English

Tettenhall College
Wood Road, Tettenhall,
Wolverhampton, West
Midlands, WV6 8QX UK
Tel: 01902 751119
Head: D C Williams
Age range: 2–18
No. of pupils: B205 G122 VIth66
Fees: Day £7,002–£13,284
WB £15,156–£20,541
FB £19,044–£25,518
Curriculum: National, UK, GCSE, IGCSE, ALevs

The Abbey School
Kendrick Road, Reading,
Berkshire, RG1 5DZ UK
Tel: 0118 987 2256
Headmistress: Barbara Stanley
Age range: G3–18
No. of pupils: 1040 VIth163
Fees: Day £2,650–£4,200
Curriculum: IBDP, GCSE, IGCSE, ALevs
Language instr: English

THE AMERICAN SCHOOL IN LONDON
For further details see p. 143
One Waverley Place,
London, NW8 0NP UK
Tel: 020 7449 1221
Email: admissions@asl.org
Website: www.asl.org
Head: Coreen Hester
Age range: 4–18
No. of pupils: 1350 B696 G654
Fees: Day £21,950–£25,650
Language instr: English

The European School
Culham, Abingdon,
Oxfordshire, OX14 3DZ UK
Tel: 01235 522621
Head: S Sharron
Age range: 4–18
No. of pupils: 839 B396 G443
Fees: Day £1,918–£3,596
Language instr: English, French, German

The Godolphin and Latymer School
Iffley Road, Hammersmith,
London, W6 0PG UK
Tel: +44 (0)20 8741 1936
Head Mistress: R Mercer
Age range: G11–18
No. of pupils: 780 VIth113
Fees: Day £17,065
Curriculum: IBDP, GCSE, IGCSE, ALevs
Language instr: English

The Godolphin School
Milford Hill, Salisbury,
Wiltshire, SP1 2RA UK
Tel: 01722 430509
Headmistress: Emma Hattersley
Age range: G11–18
No. of pupils: 400 VIth100
Fees: Day £18,528
FB £27,024 £26,232
Curriculum: GCSE, IGCSE, ALevs

The Grammar School at Leeds
Alwoodley Gates, Harrogate Road,
Leeds, West Yorkshire, LS17 8GS UK
Tel: 0113 2291552
Principal and CEO: Michael Gibbons
Age range: 3–18
No. of pupils: 2120 B1168 G952 VIth418
Fees: Day £7,723–£11,282
Curriculum: GCSE, IGCSE, ALevs
Language instr: English

The King's School, Canterbury
The Precincts, Canterbury,
Kent, CT1 2ES UK
Tel: 01227 595579
Head: P Roberts
Age range: 13–18
No. of pupils: 826 B461 G365 VIth390
Fees: Day £25,290 FB £33,360
Curriculum: GCSE, IGCSE, ALevs
Language instr: English

The Leys School
Trumpington Road, Cambridge,
Cambridgeshire, CB2 7AD UK
Tel: 01223 508900
Headmaster: Martin Priestley
Age range: 11–18
No. of pupils: B327 G226 VIth199
Fees: Day £13,185–£18,480
WB £20,880–£20,880
FB £20,235–£27,780
Curriculum: GCSE, ALevs, CSFS

The Manchester Grammar School
Old Hall Lane, Fallowfield,
Manchester, Greater
Manchester, M13 0XT UK
Tel: 0161 224 7201
High Master: Christopher Ray
Age range: B7–18
No. of pupils: B1500
Fees: Day £9,996
Curriculum: IBDP, GCSE, IGCSE, ALevs
Language instr: English

The Mary Erskine School
Ravelston, Edinburgh,
Edinburgh, EH4 3NT UK
Tel: 0131 347 5700
Headmaster: J N D Gray
Age range: B16–18 G11–18
No. of pupils: B118 G751
Fees: Day £9,096 FB £18,249
Curriculum: Scot Nat, CSFS

The Mount School, York
Dalton Terrace, York, North
Yorkshire, YO24 4DD UK
Tel: 01904 667500
Headmistress: Diana Gant
Age range: G11–18
Curriculum: GCSE, ALevs

The New Eccles Hall School
Quidenham, Norwich,
Norfolk, NR16 2NZ UK
Tel: 01953 887217
Headmaster: Richard Allard
Age range: 5–18
No. of pupils: 150
Fees: Day £6,945–£11,370
FB £16,740–£19,785

The Oakland School, Abuja
No. 3 Volta Close, Off
Colorado Street, Ministers
Hills, Maitama, Abuja, UK
Tel: +234 8032 032294
Director: Baruka Saleh
Language instr: English

The Oratory School
Woodcote, Reading,
Berkshire, RG8 0PJ UK
Tel: 01491 683500
Head Master: C I Dytor
Age range: B11–18
No. of pupils: 420 VIth120
Fees: £5,350
Curriculum: GCSE, ALevs

The Park School
The Park, Yeovil, Somerset,
BA20 1DH UK
Tel: 01935 423514
Head: J Huntington
Age range: 3–18+
No. of pupils: B111 G108 VIth30
Fees: Day £4,350–£8,640
WB £14,385–£15,405
FB £15,750–£17,550
Curriculum: GCSE, ALevs

The Peterborough School
Thorpe Road, Peterborough,
Cambridgeshire, PE3 6AP UK
Tel: 01733 343357
Headmaster: A D Meadows
Age range: 6 weeks–18 years
No. of pupils: 410 VIth52
Fees: Day £9,188–£13,057
Curriculum: GCSE, ALevs

The Portsmouth Grammar School
High Street, Portsmouth,
Hampshire, PO1 2LN UK
Tel: +44 (0)23 9236 0036
Headmaster: J E Priory
Age range: 2–18
No. of pupils: 1645 VIth298
Fees: Day £8,379–£13,059
Curriculum: IBDP, GCSE,
IGCSE, ALevs
Language instr: English

The Primegate School
Primegate Avenue, off G.U.Ake
road, Eligbolo, Port Harcourt, UK
Tel: +234 80607 72006
Head of School: George Uloaku
Language instr: English

The Purcell School, London
Aldenham Road, Bushey,
Hertfordshire, WD2 3TS UK
Tel: 01923 331100
Headmaster: Peter Crook
Age range: 8–18
No. of pupils: 167 B57 G110 VIth70
Fees: WB £22,452 FB £28,716
Curriculum: GCSE, ALevs

The Red Maids' School
Westbury Road, Westbury-on-
Trym, Bristol, Bristol, BS9 3AW UK
Tel: +44 (0)117 962 2641
Headmistress: Isabel Tobias
Age range: G7–18
No. of pupils: 594 VIth100
Curriculum: IBDP, GCSE,
IGCSE, ALevs
Language instr: English

The Royal High School, Bath
Lansdown Road, Bath, Bath &
North-East Somerset, BA1 5SZ UK
Tel: +44 (0)1225 313877
Head: Rebecca Dougall
Age range: G3–18
No. of pupils: 680
Fees: Day £8,070–£11,685
FB £18,087–£21,747
Curriculum: IBDP, National,
GCSE, ALevs
Language instr: English

The Royal Hospital School
Holbrook, Ipswich,
Suffolk, IP9 2RX UK
Tel: +44 (0) 1473 326210
Headmaster: James Lockwood
Age range: 11–18
No. of pupils: 700 B410 G290 VIth220
Fees: Day £12,354–£16,770
WB £20,595–£25,437
FB £20,595–£25,437
Curriculum: GCSE, IGCSE, ALevs

The Royal Masonic School for Girls
Rickmansworth Park,
Rickmansworth, Hertfordshire,
WD3 4HF UK
Tel: 01923 773168
Headmistress: Diana Rose
Age range: G4–18 Pre-school 2–4
No. of pupils: 917 B26 G891 VIth188
Fees: Day £9,000–£14,700
WB £15,750–£23,760
FB £16,050–£25,050
Curriculum: ALevs
Language instr: English

The Royal School Dungannon
2 Ranfurly Road, Dungannon,
County Tyrone, BT71 6EG UK
Tel: 028 8772 2710
Headmaster: David Burnett
Age range: 11–18
No. of pupils: 660
Fees: Day £150 WB £13,200
FB £14,450 £7,000
Curriculum: GCSE, ALevs
Language instr: English

The Royal School, Haslemere
Farnham Lane, Haslemere,
Surrey, GU27 1BE UK
Tel: 01428 603052
Headmistress: Lynne Taylor-Gooby
Age range: B6 weeks–6
years G6 weeks–18 years
No. of pupils: 370 VIth50
Fees: FB £10,000
Curriculum: National, UK,
GCSE, IGCSE, ALevs
Language instr: English

The Royal Wolverhampton School
Penn Road, Wolverhampton,
West Midlands, WV3 0EG UK
Tel: 01902 341230
Head: Mark Heywood
Age range: 2–18
No. of pupils: 547 B340 G207 VIth116
Fees: Day £7,935–£12,255
WB £18,060–£21,120
FB £18,780–£26,265
Curriculum: ALevs

The Stephen Perse Sixth Form College
Shaftesbury Road, Cambridge,
Cambridgeshire, CB2 8AA UK
Tel: +44 (0)1223 488430
Head of School: Patricia Kelleher
Age range: 16–19
No. of pupils: 143
Fees: Day £13,470
Curriculum: IBDP, ALevs
Language instr: English

The Towers Convent School
Convent of the Blessed Sacrement,
Henfield Road, Upper Beeding,
Steyning, West Sussex, BN44 3TF UK
Tel: 01903 812185
Headmistress: Clare Trelfar
Age range: B2–8 G2–16
No. of pupils: 320
Fees: Day £6,960–£9,030
Curriculum: GCSE

Thornton College
Thornton, Milton Keynes,
Buckinghamshire, MK17 0HJ UK
Tel: 01280 812610
Headmistress: Agnes T Williams
Age range: B2–4+ G2–16
No. of pupils: 370 G370
Fees: Day £6,300–£10,095
WB £10,500–£13,305
FB £13,305–£16,545
Curriculum: GCSE

Tonbridge School
Tonbridge, Kent, TN9 1JP UK
Tel: 01732 365555
Headmaster: T H P Haynes
Age range: B13–18
No. of pupils: 781 VIth339
Fees: Day £25,602 FB £34,137
Curriculum: GCSE, IGCSE, ALevs

Trent College
Derby Road, Long Eaton,
Nottingham, Nottinghamshire,
NG10 4AD UK
Tel: 0115 8494949
Head: G Dixon
Age range: 11–18
No. of pupils: 1117 B650
G467 VIth200
Fees: Day £7,200–£13,500
WB £16,305–£17,685
FB £19,020–£20,625
Curriculum: GCSE, IGCSE, ALevs

Tring Park School for the Performing Arts
Tring Park, Tring, Hertfordshire,
HP23 5LX UK
Tel: 01442 824255
Principal: Stefan Anderson
Age range: 8–19
No. of pupils: 317 B88 G229 VIth217
Fees: Day £12,870–£20,100
FB £21,285–£30,090
Curriculum: National,
GCSE, IGCSE, ALevs

Trinity School
Buckeridge Road, Teignmouth,
Devon, TQ14 8LY UK
Tel: 01626 774138
Headmaster: Tim Waters
Age range: 3–19
No. of pupils: 495 B270 G225 VIth115
Fees: Day £7,650–£10,650
FB £17,700–£23,250
Curriculum: National, UK,
GCSE, IGCSE, ALevs, CSFS
Language instr: English

Truro School
Trennick Lane, Truro,
Cornwall, TR1 1TH UK
Tel: 01872 272763
Headmaster: A S Gordon-Brown
Age range: 3–18
No. of pupils: 751 B457 G294 VIth200
Curriculum: National,
GCSE, IGCSE, ALevs
Language instr: English

Tudor Hall School
Wykham Park, Banbury,
Oxfordshire, OX16 9UR UK
Tel: 01295 263434
Headmistress: W Griffiths
Age range: G11–18
No. of pupils: 336 VIth82
Fees: Day £17,862 FB £28,035
Curriculum: GCSE, IGCSE, ALevs
Language instr: English

Uppingham School
Uppingham, Rutland, LE15 9QE UK
Tel: 01572 822216 Admissions:
01572 820611
Headmaster: Richard Harman
Age range: 13–18
No. of pupils: 795 B450 G345 VIth350
Fees: Day £22,098 FB £31,569
Curriculum: GCSE, IGCSE, ALevs

UWC ATLANTIC COLLEGE
For further details see p. 146
St Donat's Castle, St Donat's, Llantwit Major, Vale of Glamorgan, CF61 1WF UK
Tel: +44 (0)1446 799000
Email: principal@atlanticcollege.org
Website: www.atlanticcollege.org
Principal: John Walmsley
Age range: 16–19
No. of pupils: 350
Fees: FB £27,025
Curriculum: IBDP
Language instr: English

Warminster School
Church Street, Warminster, Wiltshire, BA12 8PJ UK
Tel: +44 (0)1985 210160
Headmaster: Mark Mortimer
Age range: 3–18
No. of pupils: 550
Fees: Day £13,680 FB £28,350
Curriculum: IBDP, GCSE, ALevs
Language instr: English

Warwick School
Myton Road, Warwick, Warwickshire, CV34 6PP UK
Tel: 01926 776400
Head Master: A R Lock
Age range: B7–18
No. of pupils: 1214 VIth249
Fees: Day £8,505–£10,935
WB £21,870 FB £23,337
Curriculum: GCSE, IGCSE, ALevs

Wellington College
Duke's Ride, Crowthorne, Berkshire, RG45 7PU UK
Tel: +44 (0)1344 444000
Master: Anthony Seldon
Age range: 13–18
No. of pupils: 1050 B635 G415 VIth485
Fees: Day £24,330–£27,960 FB £32,940
Curriculum: IBDP, IBMYP, UK, GCSE, IGCSE, ALevs
Language instr: English

Wellington School
South Street, Wellington, Somerset, TA21 8NT UK
Tel: 01823 668800
Headmaster: M S Reader
Age range: 3–18
No. of pupils: B464 G369 VIth173
Fees: Day £10,974–£12,030
WB £14,976–£18,966
FB £18,720–£24,039
Curriculum: GCSE, IGCSE, ALevs
Language instr: English

Wells Cathedral School
Wells, Somerset, BA5 2ST UK
Tel: 01749 834200
Head: Elizabeth Cairncross
Age range: 3–18
No. of pupils: B369 G368 VIth197
Fees: Day £6,747–£16,002
Curriculum: GCSE, IGCSE, ALevs

West Buckland School
Barnstaple, Devon, EX32 0SX UK
Tel: 01598 760281
Headmaster: J Vick
Age range: 3–18
No. of pupils: B378 G351 VIth135
Fees: Day £2,280–£4,250
WB £6,760–£7,880 FB £6,760–£7,880
Curriculum: GCSE, ALevs

Westbourne School
Hickman Road, Penarth, Vale of Glamorgan, CF64 2AJ UK
Tel: 029 2070 5705
Head of School: K W Underhill
Age range: 3–18
No. of pupils: 162
Fees: Day £6,450–£11,700
FB £23,350–£25,850
Curriculum: IBDP, GCSE, IGCSE
Language instr: English

Westfield School
Oakfield Road, Gosforth, Newcastle upon Tyne, Tyne & Wear, NE3 4HS UK
Tel: 0191 255 3980
Headmistress: M Farndale
Age range: G3–18
No. of pupils: 315 VIth50
Fees: Day £1,372–£3,688
Curriculum: ALevs

Westminster School
17 Dean's Yard, Westminster, London, SW1P 3PF UK
Tel: 020 7963 1003
Headmaster: Stephen Spurr
Age range: B13–18 G16–18
No. of pupils: 754 B623 G131
Fees: Day £22,500–£24,390 FB £32,490
Curriculum: ALevs

Westonbirt School
Westonbirt, Tetbury, Gloucestershire, GL8 8QG UK
Tel: 01666 881301
Headmistress: Natasha Dangerfield
Age range: G11–18
Fees: Day £17,295–£21,300
FB £25,815–£31,500
Curriculum: GCSE, ALevs

Whitgift School
Haling Park, South Croydon, Surrey, CR2 6YT UK
Tel: +44 (0)20 8688 9222
Headmaster: Christopher Barnett
Age range: B10–18
No. of pupils: 1396
Fees: Day £17,340
WB £27,924 FB £33,396
Curriculum: IBDP, GCSE, IGCSE, ALevs
Language instr: English

Winchester College
College Street, Winchester, Hampshire, SO23 9NA UK
Tel: 01962 621247
Headmaster: R D Townsend
Age range: B13–18
No. of pupils: 690 VIth280
Fees: FB £34,740
Curriculum: GCSE, IGCSE
Language instr: English

Windermere School
Patterdale Road, Windermere, Cumbria, LA23 1NW UK
Tel: 015394 46164
Head of School: Ian Lavender
Age range: 2–18
No. of pupils: 403 B176 G227 VIth53
Fees: Day £8,205–£12,510
WB £18,630–£21,294
FB £19,680–£23,598
Curriculum: IBDP, GCSE, IGCSE
Language instr: English

Woldingham School
Marden Park, Woldingham, Surrey, CR3 7YA UK
Tel: 01883 349431
Headmistress: Jayne Triffitt
Age range: G11–18
No. of pupils: 530 VIth150
Fees: Day £23,700 FB £28,410
Curriculum: GCSE, ALevs

Woodbridge School
Marryott House, Burkitt Road, Woodbridge, Suffolk, IP12 4JH UK
Tel: 01394 615000
Headmaster: N P Tetley
Age range: 4–18
No. of pupils: B416 G431 VIth200
Fees: FB £26,700
Curriculum: GCSE, IGCSE, ALevs
Language instr: English

Woodhouse Grove School
Apperley Bridge, Bradford, West Yorkshire, BD10 0NR UK
Tel: 0113 250 2477
Headmaster: David Humphreys
Age range: 3–18
No. of pupils: 1055
Fees: Day £7,530–£11,385
FB £21,270–£21,420
Curriculum: GCSE, IGCSE, ALevs

Worksop College
Worksop, Nottinghamshire, S80 3AP UK
Tel: 01909 537100
Headmaster: G W Horgan
Age range: 3–18
No. of pupils: 586 B301 G285
Fees: Day £15,510
WB £24,120 FB £24,120
Curriculum: TOEFL, UK, GCSE, IGCSE, ALevs
Language instr: English

Worth School
Paddockhurst Road, Turners Hill, Crawley, West Sussex, RH10 4SD UK
Tel: +44 (0)1342 710200
Head Master: Gino Carminati
Age range: 11–18
No. of pupils: 580 VIth222
Fees: Day £20,235 FB £27,849
Curriculum: IBDP, National, GCSE, IGCSE, ALevs
Language instr: English

Wrekin College
Wellington, Telford, West Midlands, TF1 3BG UK
Tel: 01952 265600
Headmaster: R T F Fleming
Age range: 11–18
No. of pupils: 415 B240 G175 VIth140
Fees: Day £12,525–£15,132
FB £21,570–£24,975
Curriculum: National, UK, GCSE, ALevs
Language instr: English

Wychwood School
74 Banbury Road, Oxford, Oxfordshire, OX2 6JR UK
Tel: 01865 557976
Headmistress: A K Johnson
Age range: G11–18
No. of pupils: 130 VIth45
Fees: Day £13,650
WB £20,460 FB £21,450
Curriculum: ALevs

Wycliffe Preparatory & Senior School
Bath Road, Stonehouse, Gloucestershire, GL10 2JQ UK
Tel: 01453 822432
Senior School Head: M E Burnet Ward
Age range: 2–18
No. of pupils: B370 G240 VIth178
Fees: Day £5,295–£15,870
FB £13,620–£25,800
Curriculum: GCSE, IGCSE, ALevs

Wycombe Abbey School
High Wycombe,
Buckinghamshire, HP11 1PE UK
Tel: +44 (0)1494 897008
Headmistress: Rhiannon J Wilkinson
Age range: G11–18
No. of pupils: 559
Fees: Day £8,645 FB £11,525
Curriculum: GCSE, IGCSE, ALevs

Wynstones School
Whaddon Green, Gloucester,
Gloucestershire, GL4 0UF UK
Tel: 01452 429220
**Chair of the College of
Teachers:** Marianna Law-Lindberg
Age range: 3–18
No. of pupils: B127 G143 VIth9
Fees: Day £4,956–£7,236 FB £4,835
Curriculum: GCSE, ALevs

Yehudi Menuhin School
Stoke Road, Stoke d'Abernon,
Cobham, Surrey, KT11 3QQ UK
Tel: 01932 864739
Headmaster: Richard J Hillier
Age range: 7–19
No. of pupils: B37 G38 VIth29
Fees: Day £40,044 FB £41,106
Curriculum: GCSE, IGCSE, ALevs
Language instr: English

Ukraine

British International School, Kyiv
45 Tolbukhina Street,
Kyiv, 02190 Ukraine
Tel: +380 44 44 22110
Headteacher: Duveen Price
Age range: 3–18
No. of pupils: 352 B182 G170

Kyiv International School
3A Svyatoshinsky Provuluk,
Kyiv, 03115 Ukraine
Tel: +380 44 452 2793
Director: Scott D'Alterio
Age range: 4–18 B3–18 G3–18
No. of pupils: 567
Curriculum: AP, IBDP, USA
Language instr: English

Meridian International School
Provulok 5A, Kvitnevy,
Kiev, 04108 Ukraine
Tel: +380 44 433 9748
Director: Natalia Lymar
Age range: 3–18
No. of pupils: 315

Pechersk School International
7a Victora Zabily, Kiev, 3039 Ukraine
Tel: +380 44 455-95-85
Director: John Burns
Age range: 3–18
No. of pupils: 400 B210 G190
Fees: $9,000
Curriculum: IBDP, IBMYP, IBPYP
Language instr: English

Simferopol International School
Barrikadnaya 59A, Simferopol,
Crimea, 95000 Ukraine
Tel: +38 652 540606
Head: Olga Anatolyevna Kostruba
Age range: 2–17
No. of pupils: 185 B125 G60
Fees: $3,035
Curriculum: National, UK
Language instr: Russian,
Ukrainian, English

International schools in North America

Schools ordered A–Z by Country

Key to directory

Country

Name of school or college

Indicates that this school
has a profile

Address and contact number

Head's name

Age range

Number of pupils.
B = boys G = girls VIth = sixth form

Fees per annum.
Day = fees for day pupils.
WB = fees for weekly boarders.
FB = fees for full boarders.

Curriculum

Language of instruction

Memberships/Accreditation

Whereford

College Academy

For further details see p.00

Which Street, Whosville,
Wherefordshire AB12 3CD

Tel: 01000 000000

Head Master: Dr A Person

Age range: 11–18

No. of pupils:
660 B330 G330 VIth 200

Fees: Day £11,000
WB £16,000 FB £20,000

Curriculum:
National, IBDP, ALevs

Language instr:
English, French

(AISA) (COB) (EAR)

Key to icons

Key to symbols:
- (†) Boys' school
- (‡) Girls' school
- (♠) Boarding accommodation

Member of:
- (AISA) Association of International
  Schools in Africa
- (CEE) Central and Eastern European
  Schools Association
- (EAR) East Asia Regional Council of
  Overseas Schools
- (ECIS) European Council of
  International Schools
- (RS) Round Square

Accreditation:
- (CIS) Council of International Schools
- (COB) Council of British International
  Schools

Please note: Schools are coeducational day schools unless otherwise indicated

Antigua

Island Academy
PO Box W1884, St John's, Antigua
Tel: +1 268 460 1094
Head of School: Ronan Matthew
Age range: 3–18
Fees: $10,464–$21,000
Curriculum: IBDP, National
Language instr: English

Aruba

International School of Aruba
Wayaca 238A, Oranjestad, Aruba
Tel: +297 583 5040
Head: Sarah Putnam
Age range: 3–19
No. of pupils: 190
Fees: US$15,000–US$17,000
Curriculum: AP, SAT, TOEFL, USA
Language instr: English

Bahamas

Lucaya International School
Chesapeake Drive, PO Box, F-44066, Freeport, Grand Bahamas Island Bahamas
Tel: +1 242 373 4004
Head: Sharon E Wilson
Age range: 3–18
Fees: $5,400–$13,600
Curriculum: IBDP, IBPYP, IGCSE
Language instr: English
(CIS)

Lyford Cay International School
Lyford Cay Drive, PO Box N-7776, Nassau, NB Bahamas
Tel: +1 242 362 4774
Principal: Stacey Bobo
Age range: 3–18
No. of pupils: 273 B133 G140
Fees: US$14,040–US$20,490
Curriculum: IBDP, IBMYP, IBPYP, National, SAT, UK, USA
Language instr: English
(CIS) (ECIS)

St Andrew's School, The International School of the Bahamas
PO Box EE 17340, Nassau, NP, Bahamas
Tel: +1 242 677 7800
Head of School: Glenn Canterford
Age range: 4–18
No. of pupils: 802 B380 G422
Curriculum: AP, IBDP, IBPYP, SAT, UK, USA
Language instr: English
(CIS) (ECIS)

St Johns College
PO Box N 4858, Nassau
NP, Bahamas
Tel: +1 242 322 3249
Principal: Antoinette Storr
Age range: 4–17
No. of pupils: 1015
Curriculum: SAT

Barbados

The Codrington School
St John, BB 20008 Barbados
Tel: +1246 423 2570
Principal: Darryl Brown
Age range: 3–18
No. of pupils: 140 B80 G60
Fees: US$4,712–US$18,900
Curriculum: IBDP, IBMYP, IBPYP
Language instr: English
(ECIS)

Bermuda

Bermuda High School
19 Richmond Road, Pembroke, HM08 Bermuda
Tel: +441 295 6153
Head of School: Linda Parker
Age range: B16–18 G5–18
No. of pupils: 642
Fees: B$18,859
Curriculum: IBDP, SAT, IGCSE
Language instr: English

Saltus Grammar School
PO Box HM 2224, Hamilton
HM JX, Bermuda
Tel: +1 441 292 6177
Headmaster: E G Staunton
Age range: 5–18
No. of pupils: 1022 B613 G409
Curriculum: AP, SAT

Somersfield Academy
107 Middle Road, Devonshire, DV 06 Bermuda
Tel: +1 441 236 9797
Head of School: James Christopher
No. of pupils: 410
Curriculum: IBMYP
Language instr: English

The Chatmore Preparatory School
Windreach Recreation Facility, Windreach Lane, Warwick, WK04 Bermuda
Tel: +441 505 0464
Principal: Angela Fublar
Curriculum: IPC
Language instr: English
(COB)

Warwick Academy
117 Middle Road, Warwick, PG01 Bermuda
Tel: +1 441 236 1917/239 9452
Principal: Maggie McCorkell
Age range: 5–18
No. of pupils: 760
Fees: $17,208
Curriculum: IBDP, UK, IGCSE
Language instr: English

British Virgin Islands

Cedar International School
PO Box 3109, Road Town, Tortola VG1110 British Virgin Islands
Tel: +1 284 494 5262
Director: Scott Crawford
Age range: 3–18
No. of pupils: 240 B120 G120
Fees: US$10,306–US$15,371
Curriculum: IBDP, IBMYP, IBPYP
Language instr: English
(CIS)

Canada
*Ordered by State

Alberta

Lycee Louis Pasteur The International French School
4099 Garrison Boulevard SW, Calgary AB, T2T 6G2 Canada
Tel: +1 403 243 5420
Head of School: Benjamin Orillon
Age range: 3–17

Strathcona-Tweedsmuir School
RR 2, Okotoks AB, T1S 1A2 Canada
Tel: +1 403 938 4431
Head of School: William Jones
Age range: 6–18
No. of pupils: 661 B326 G335
Curriculum: IBDP, IBMYP, IBPYP
Language instr: English

British Columbia

Aspengrove School
7660 Clark Drive, RR2, Lantzville BC, V0R 2H0 Canada
Tel: +1 250 390 2201
Head of School: Zinda FitzGerald
No. of pupils: 193 B104 G89
Fees: $9,150–$12,400
Curriculum: IBDP, IBMYP, IBPYP
Language instr: English

Brentwood College School
2735 Mount Baker Road, Mill Bay BC, V0R 2P1 Canada
Tel: +1 250 743 5521
Head of School: Andrea Pennells
Age range: 14–18
No. of pupils: 435 B226 G109
Curriculum: AP, National
(符)

Brockton Preparatory School
3467 Duval Road, North Vancouver BC, V7J 3E8 Canada
Tel: +1 604 929 9201
Head of School: Alison Wall
Age range: 5–18
Fees: Day CAD$14,000–CAD$16,000
Curriculum: IBMYP, IBPYP, National
Language instr: English

DWIGHT SCHOOL CANADA
For further details see p. 154
2371 East Shawnigan Lake Road, Shawnigan Lake BC, V0R 2W5 Canada
Tel: +1 250 929 0506
Email: admissions@dwightcanada.org
Website: www.dwightcanada.org
Head: Jerry Salvador
Age range: 11–18
Curriculum: IBDP
Language instr: English
(符)

Glenlyon Norfolk School
801 Bank Street, Victoria BC, V8S 4A8 Canada
Tel: +1 250 370-6802
Head of School: Simon Bruce-Lockhart
Age range: 4–18
No. of pupils: 700
Fees: C$11,970–C$14,835
Curriculum: IBDP, IBMYP, IBPYP
Language instr: English

Island Pacific School
Box 128, Bowen Island BC, V0N 1G0 Canada
Tel: +1 604 947 9311
Head of School: Ted Spear
Age range: 11–14
No. of pupils: B34 G25
Fees: C$12,000
Curriculum: IBMYP
Language instr: English

MEADOWRIDGE SCHOOL
For further details see p. 157
12224 240th Street, Maple Ridge BC, V4R 1N1 Canada
Tel: +1 604 467 4444
Email: info@meadowridge.bc.ca
Website: www.meadowridge.bc.ca
Head of School: Hugh Burke
Age range: 4–18
No. of pupils: 530
Fees: C$17,800
Curriculum: IBDP, IBMYP, IBPYP
Language instr: English

MULGRAVE SCHOOL
For further details see p. 158
2330 Cypress Bowl Lane, West
Vancouver BC, V7S 3H9 Canada
Tel: +1 604 922 3223
Email:
admissions@mulgrave.com
Website: www.mulgrave.com
Head of School: John Wray
Age range: 3–18
No. of pupils: 800
Curriculum: IBDP, IBMYP, IBPYP
Language instr: English

Pacific Academy
10238 168th Street, Surrey
BC, V4N 1Z4 Canada
Tel: +1 604 581 5353
Head of School: Cliford Horban
Age range: 5–18
No. of pupils: 1400
Curriculum: IBDP
Language instr: English

Pearson College UWC of the Pacific
650 Pearson College Drive,
Victoria BC, V9C 4H7 Canada
Tel: +1 250 391 2411
Head of School: David Hawley
Age range: 16–19
No. of pupils: 200 B100 G100
Curriculum: IBDP, SAT
Language instr: English

Shawnigan Lake School
1975 Renfrew Road, Postal
Bag 2000, Shawnigan Lake
BC, V0R 2W1 Canada
Tel: +1 250 743 5516
Headmaster: David Robertson
Age range: 13–18
No. of pupils: 457 B254 G203
Fees: C$40,000–C$53,000
Language instr: English

Southridge School
2656 160th Street, Surrey
BC, V3S 0B7 Canada
Tel: +1 604 535 5056
Head of School: Drew Stephens
Age range: 4–17
No. of pupils: 667
Curriculum: AP, IBMYP, IBPYP
Language instr: English

St John's School
2215 West 10th Avenue,
Vancouver BC, V6K 2J1 Canada
Tel: +1 604 732 4434
Head of School: Steve Hutchison
Curriculum: IBDP, IBMYP
Language instr: English

Stratford Hall
3000 Commercial Drive,
Vancouver BC, V5N 4E2 Canada
Tel: +1 604 436 0608
Head of School: Jim McConnell
Age range: 5–18
No. of pupils: 465
Curriculum: IBDP, IBMYP, IBPYP
Language instr: English

New Brunswick

Rothesay Netherwood School
40 College Hill Road, Rothesay
NB, E2E 5H1 Canada
Tel: +1 506 847 8224
Head of School: Paul G Kitchen
Age range: 11–18
Curriculum: IBDP
Language instr: English

Nova Scotia

Halifax Grammar School
945 Tower Road, Halifax
NS, B3H 2Y2 Canada
Tel: +1 902 422 1287
Head of School: Paul Bennett
Age range: 4–18
No. of pupils: 525 B283 G242
Fees: C$10,466–C$14,541
Curriculum: IBDP
Language instr: English

King's-Edgehill School
11 King's-Edgehill Lane, Windsor
NS, B0N 2T0 Canada
Tel: +1 902 798 2278
Head of School: Joseph Seagram
Age range: 11–19
No. of pupils: 350
Fees: C$12,350
Language instr: English

Ontario

Académie de la Capitale
1010 Morrison Dr Suite 200,
Ottawa ON, K2H 8K7 Canada
Tel: +1 613 721 3872
Head of School: Lucie Lalonde
Fees: C$12,000
Curriculum: IBPYP
Language instr: French, English

Académie Ste Cécile International School
925 Cousineau Road, Windsor
ON, N9G 1V8 Canada
Tel: +1 519 969 1291
Head of School: Ann Marcotte
Age range: 5–19
No. of pupils: 260
Fees: C$12,750–C$13,750
Curriculum: IBDP, National
Language instr: English

Albert College
160 Dundas St West, Belleville
ON, K8OP 1A6 Canada
Tel: +1 (613) 968 5726
**Assistant Head of
School:** Keith Stansfield
Age range: 4–18

Appleby College
540 Lakeshore Road West,
Oakville ON, L6K 3P1 Canada
Tel: +1 905 845 4681 ext. 200
Age range: 12–18

Ashbury College
362 Mariposa Avenue, Ottawa
ON, K1M OT3 Canada
Tel: +1 613 749 5954
Head of School: Tam Matthews
Curriculum: IBDP

Bayview Glen
275 Duncan Mill Road, Toronto,
ON, M3B 3H9 Canada
Tel: +1 416 443 1030
Head of School: Eileen Daunt

Branksome Hall
10 Elm Avenue, Toronto
ON, M4W 1N4 Canada
Tel: +1 416 920 9741
Principal: Karen L. Jurjevich
Age range: Jr. Kindergarten–
Grade 12
No. of pupils: 880
Fees: C$27,620–C$29,620
Curriculum: IBDP, IBMYP, IBPYP
Language instr: English

CCI – THE RENAISSANCE SCHOOL
For further details see p. 152
59 Macamo Court, Maple,
Ontario L6A-1G1, Canada
Tel: +1 905 508 7108
Website: www.canadian
collegeitaly.com
Head of School: Marisa
DiCarlo D'Alessandro
Age range: 15–19
No. of pupils: 70 B30 G40

Elmwood School
261 Buena Vista Road, Ottawa
ON, K1M 0V9 Canada
Tel: +1 613 749 6761
Head of School: Cheryl Boughton
Age range: G4–18
Curriculum: IBDP, IBMYP, IBPYP
Language instr: English

Fern Hill School
801 North Service Road,
Burlington ON, L7P 5B6 Canada
Tel: +1 905 634 8652
Language instr: English

Kempenfelt Bay School
576 Bryne Drive, Barrie
ON, L4N 9P6 Canada
Tel: +1 705 739 4731
Head of School: Graham Hookey
Curriculum: IBMYP
Language instr: English

King Heights Acadamy
28 Roytec Road, Woodbridge
ON, L4L 8E4 Canada
Tel: +1 905 652 1234
Head of School: Elsa Norberto
Curriculum: IBPYP
Language instr: English

La Citadelle International Academy of Arts and Science
15 Mallow Road, North York
ON, M3B 1G2 Canada
Tel: +1 416 385 9685
Head of School: Alfred Abouchar
Curriculum: IBMYP
Language instr: English, French

Lakefield College School
4391 County Road 29, Lakefield
ON, K0L 2H0 Canada
Tel: +1 705 652 3324
Head of School: Struan Robertson
Language instr: English

Lynn-Rose Heights Private School
7215 Millcreek Drive, Mississauga
ON, L5N 3R3 Canada
Tel: +1 905 567 3553
Head of School: Marie Attard
Curriculum: IBMYP
Language instr: English

MacLachlan College
337 Trafalgar Road, Oakville
ON, L6J 3H3 Canada
Tel: +1 905 844 0372
Head of School: Michael Piening
Curriculum: AP, IBPYP
Language instr: English

Matthews Hall
1370 Oxford Street West, London
ON, N6H 1W2 Canada
Tel: +1 519 471 1506
Head: Ric Anderson
Age range: 4–14
No. of pupils: B126 G111
Fees: C$15,000
Language instr: English

Ridley College
PO Box 3013, 2 Ridley Road, St Catherines ON, L2R 7C3 Canada
Tel: +1 905 684 1889
Headmaster: J Edward Kidd
Age range: 4–18
No. of pupils: 620
Fees: $55,488
Curriculum: IBDP, IBPYP, National
Language instr: English

Springfield Preparatory and Nursery School
1444 Dundas Cres, Mississauga ON, L5C 1E9 Canada
Tel: +1 905 273 9717
Head of School: Janet Murphy
Curriculum: IBPYP
Language instr: English

St Andrew's College
15800 Yonge Street, Aurora ON, L4G 3H7 Canada
Tel: +1 905 727 3178
Headmaster: Ted Staunton
Age range: B11–18
No. of pupils: 546
Fees: $41,100

St Clement's School
21 St. Clements Avenue, Toronto ON, M4R 1G8 Canada
Tel: +1 416 483 4835
Principal: Martha Perry
Language instr: English

St John's – Kilmarnock School
2201 Shantz Station Road, Box 179, Breslau ON, N0B 1M0 Canada
Tel: +1 519 648 2183
Head of School: Norman Southward
Curriculum: IBDP, IBMYP, IBPYP
Language instr: English

St Jude's Academy
6670 Campobello Rd, Mississauga ON, L5N 2L8 Canada
Tel: +1 905 814 0202
Curriculum: IBPYP

St Mildred's Lightbourn School
1080 Linbrook Rd, Oakville ON, L6J 2L1 Canada
Tel: +1 905 845 2386
Language instr: English

Sunnybrook School
469 Merton Street, Toronto ON, M4S 1B4 Canada
Tel: +1 416 487 5308
Head of School: Irene Davy
Curriculum: IBPYP

TFS – Canada's International School
306 Lawrence Avenue East, Toronto ON, M4N 1T7 Canada
Tel: +1 416 484 6533
Headmaster: John Godfrey
Age range: 2–18
No. of pupils: 1375
Fees: CAD$15,480–CAD$28,900
Curriculum: IBDP, IBMYP, IBPYP
Language instr: French, English

The Leo Baeck Day School
36 Atkinson Avenue, Thornhill ON, L4J 8C9 Canada
Tel: +1 905 709 3636
Head of School: Eric Petersiel
Curriculum: IBMYP

The York School
1320 Yonge Street, Toronto ON, M4T 1X2 Canada
Tel: +1 416-646-5275 (Admissions) +1 416-926-1325 (Switchboard)
Head of School: Conor Jones
Age range: 4–18
No. of pupils: 568
Curriculum: IBDP, IBMYP, IBPYP
Language instr: English

Toronto Montessori Academy
8569 Bayview Avenue, Richmond Hill ON, L4B 3M7 Canada
Tel: +1 905 889 6882
Head of School: Glenn Zederayko
Curriculum: IBDP, IBMYP
Language instr: English

Upper Canada College
200 Lonsdale Road, Toronto ON, M4V 1W6 Canada
Tel: +1 416 484 8636
Head of School: James Power
No. of pupils: 680
Curriculum: IBDP, IBPYP
Language instr: English

Wheatley School
497 Scott Street, St Catharines ON, L2M 3X3 Canada
Tel: +1 905 641 3012
Head of School: Eda Varalli
No. of pupils: 180
Curriculum: IBMYP
Language instr: English

Quebec

Académie Antoine-Manseau
20 rue St Charles Borromée Sud, CP 410, Joliette QC, J6E 3Z9 Canada
Tel: +1 450 753 4271
Head of School: Robert Corriveau
No. of pupils: 612
Language instr: French

Académie François-Labelle
1227 rue Notre Dame, Repentigny QC, Quebec J5Y 3H2 Canada
Tel: +1 450 582 2020
Head of School: Michèle Beaudry
Curriculum: IBPYP

Académie Lafontaine
2171 boulevard Maurice, Saint-Jérôme, Québec, J7Z 4M7 Canada
Tel: +1 450 431 3733
Head of School: Claude Potvin
No. of pupils: 1293
Curriculum: IBMYP
Language instr: French

Académie Laurentienne
1200, 14th Avenue, Val-Morin QC, J0T 2R0 Canada
Tel: +1 819 322 2913
Head of School: Guy Richard
Age range: 12–16
No. of pupils: 10 B5 G5 VIth12
Fees: C$24,500
Curriculum: IBMYP, UK, IGCSE, ALevs
Language instr: English, French

Bishop's College School
80 Moulton Hill Road, PO Box 5001, Station Lennoxville, Sherbrooke QC, J1M 1Z8 Canada
Tel: +1 819 566 0227
Head of School: William Mitchell
Age range: 13–18
No. of pupils: 216

Centennial Academy
3641 Prud'homme Avenue, Montréal QC, H4A 3H6 Canada
Tel: +1 514 486 5533
Head of School: Angela Burgos
No. of pupils: 225
Fees: $16,195–$19,952
Curriculum: IBMYP
Language instr: English

Collège Charlemagne
5000 rue Pilon, Pierrefonds, Québec QC, H9K 1G4 Canada
Tel: +1 514 626 7060
Head of School: Julie Beaudet
No. of pupils: 1235
Curriculum: IBMYP
Language instr: French

College de l'Assomption
270 boulevard de l'Ange-Gardien, L'Assomption, QC, Quebec J5Y 3R7 Canada
Tel: +1 450 589 5621
Head of School: Yvon Tousignant
No. of pupils: 1336
Curriculum: IBMYP
Language instr: French

Collège de Lévis
9 rue Mgr Gosselin, Levis QC, G6V 5K1 Canada
Tel: +1 418 833 1249
Head of School: David Lehoux
Language instr: French

Collège Esther-Blondin
101 rue Sainte-Anne, Saint-Jacques, Québec QC, J0K 2R0 Canada
Tel: +1 450 839 3672
Head of School: Stéphane Mayer
Age range: 12–17
Curriculum: IBMYP
Language instr: French

Collège Jean-de-Brebeuf
3200, chemin de la Côte-Sainte-Catherine, Montréal QC, H3T 1C1 Canada
Tel: +1 514 342 9342
Director General: Michel April
Curriculum: IBDP, IBMYP
Language instr: French

Collège Jésus-Marie de Sillery
2047 chemin Saint-Louis, Québec QC, G1T 1P3 Canada
Tel: +1 418 687 9250
Head of School: Sylvie Gagné
Age range: B5,6,7 & 12+G5–17
No. of pupils: 1000
Fees: CN$3,070–CN$3,525
Curriculum: IBMYP
Language instr: French

Collège Laflèche
1687 boulevard du Carmel, Trois-Rivières QC, G8Z 3R8 Canada
Tel: +1 819 375 7346
Head of School: Luc Pellerin
Age range: 18–20
No. of pupils: 1300 B400 G900
Curriculum: IBDP
Language instr: French

Collège Marie-de-l'Incarnation
725 rue Hart, Trois-Rivières QC, G9A 4R9 Canada
Tel: +1 819 379 3223
Head of School: Réjean Lemay
Curriculum: IBPYP

Collège Mont Notre-Dame de Sherbrooke
114 rue Cathédrale, Sherbrooke, Québec QC, J1H 4MI Canada
Tel: +1 819 563 4104
Head of School: Eric Faucher
No. of pupils: 573
Curriculum: IBMYP
Language instr: French

Collège Northside
CP 5158, 750 Chemin Pierre-Péladeau, Sainte-Adèle, QC, J8B 1Z4 Canada
Tel: +1 450 229 9889
Head: Frédéric Fovet
Age range: 11–18
Curriculum: National, UK

Collège Notre-Dame-de-Lourdes
845 chemin Tiffin, Longueuil, QC, J4P 3G5 Canada
Tel: +1 450 670 4740
Head of School: Lucie D'Amour
No. of pupils: 791
Curriculum: IBMYP
Language instr: French

Collège Saint-Joseph de Hull
174 rue Notre-Dame-de-l'île, Gatineau QC, J8X 3T4 Canada
Tel: +1 819 776 3123
Head of School: Sandra Beauchamp
Curriculum: IBMYP
Language instr: French

Collège Saint-Maurice
630 rue Girouard Ouest, Saint-Hyacinthe QC, J2S 2Y3 Canada
Tel: +1 450 773-7478 #222
Head of School: Jean-Pierre Jeannotte
Age range: G12–17
No. of pupils: 700
Curriculum: IBMYP
Language instr: French

Collège Saint-Paul
235 rue Ste-Anne, Varenne, Québec QC, J3X 1P9 Canada
Tel: +1 450 652 2941
Head of School: Cathie Bouchard
No. of pupils: 786
Curriculum: IBMYP
Language instr: French

Collège Ville-Marie
2850 rue Sherbrooke Est, Montréal, QC, H2K 1H3 Canada
Tel: +1 514 525 2516
Head: Hélène Sirois
No. of pupils: 550
Curriculum: IBMYP
Language instr: French

École Marie-Clarac
3530 Boul Gouin Est, Montréal-Nord QC, H1H 1B7 Canada
Tel: +1 514 322 1160
Head of School: Ginette Dalpe
Curriculum: IBMYP
Language instr: French

École Plein Soleil (Association Coopérative)
300, rue de Montréal, Sherbrooke QC, J1H 1E5 Canada
Tel: +1 819 569 8359
Head of School: Marie-Josée Mayrand
Age range: 4–12
No. of pupils: B105 G97
Fees: C$4,735
Curriculum: IBPYP, National
Language instr: French

École secondaire Saint-Joseph de Saint-Hyacinthe
2875 Bourdages Nord, Saint-Hyacinthe QC, J2S 5S3 Canada
Tel: +1 450 774 3775
Head of School: Simone LeBlanc
Curriculum: IBMYP
Language instr: French

L'École des Ursulines de Québec
4 rue du Parloir, CP 820, Haute – Ville QC, G1R 4S7 Canada
Tel: +1 418 692 2612
Head of School: Serge Goyette
Curriculum: IBPYP

Le Collège Saint-Bernard
25 avenue des Frères, Drummondville QC, J2B 6A2 Canada
Tel: +1 819 478 3330
Head of School: Alexandre Cusson
Curriculum: IBMYP
Language instr: French

Le Petit Seminaire De Quebec
6 rue de la Vieille-Université, Québec QC, G1R 5X8 Canada
Tel: +1 418 694 1020
Head of School: Marc Dallaire
Age range: 12–18
No. of pupils: 810
Curriculum: IBMYP
Language instr: French

Lower Canada College
4090 Royal Avenue, Montreal QC, H4A 2M5 Canada
Tel: +1 514 482 9916
Headmaster: Christopher Shannon
Age range: 5–17
No. of pupils: 760
Curriculum: IBDP
Language instr: English

Miss Edgar's & Miss Cramp's School
525 Mount Pleasant Road, Westmount QC, H3Y 3H6 Canada
Tel: 514 935 6357
Head of School: Katherine Nikidis
Age range: G4–16
No. of pupils: G345
Fees: $14,500–$16,500
Language instr: English, French

Pensionnat du Saint-Nom-de-Marie
628 chemin de la Côte, St Catherine, Outremont QC, H2V 2C5 Canada
Tel: +1 514 735 5261
Head of School: Yves Petit
No. of pupils: 1030
Fees: C$2,550
Curriculum: IBMYP
Language instr: French

Stanstead College
450 Duferin Street, Stanstead QC, J0B 3E0 Canada
Tel: +1 819 876 2702
Headmaster: Michael Wolfe
Age range: 11–18
No. of pupils: 200
Fees: CN$17,700

Saskatchewan

Athol Murray College of Notre Dame
PO Box 100, Wilcox SK, S0G 5E0 Canada
Tel: +1 306 732 2080
Director: Rob Palmarin
Age range: 14–18
No. of pupils: 330 B240 G90
Curriculum: AP

Luther College High School
1500 Royal Street, Regina SK, S4T 5A5 Canada
Tel: +1 306 791 9150
Principal: Mark Anderson
Age range: 16–18+
No. of pupils: 420
Fees: C$21,120
Curriculum: IBDP
Language instr: English

Cayman Islands

Cayman International School
PO Box 31364, Grand Cayman, KY1-1206 Cayman Islands
Tel: +1 345 945 4664
Head of School: Jean Caskey
No. of pupils: 390
Curriculum: IBDP
Language instr: English

Costa Rica

American International School of Costa Rica
Apartado 4941-1000, San José, Costa Rica
Tel: +50 6 2293 2567
Director: Charles Prince
Age range: 4–18
No. of pupils: 170 B90 G80
Curriculum: AP, SAT

Colegio Internacional SEK Costa Rica
Cipreses de Curridabat del Servicentro 1.5km al norte, San José, 963 2050 Costa Rica
Tel: +506 2 272 5464
Language instr: Spanish, English

Country Day School
Apartado 1139-1250, Escazú, San José, Costa Rica
Tel: +506 2289 0919
Director: Greg L MacGilpin
Age range: 2–19
No. of pupils: 844 B424 G420
Curriculum: AP, SAT

Country Day School – Guanacaste
500 mts sur del Hotel Melia Conchal, Brasilito, Guanacaste, Costa Rica
Tel: +506 654 5042
Principal: Sarah Haun
Age range: 3–19
No. of pupils: 181 B82 G99
Fees: $7,460
Curriculum: AP, SAT, USA
Language instr: English

European School
Heredia, San Pablo, P.O. Box: 177, Heredia, Costa Rica
Tel: +506 2261 0717
Head of School: Anne C Aronson
Age range: 4–18
No. of pupils: 495
Curriculum: IBDP
Language instr: English

Iribó School
Del restaurante la casa de Doña, Lela 800 metros al sur, Curridabat, San José, 662-2050 S Costa Rica
Tel: +506 4000 8989
Head of School: Maureen Coto Alfaro
Curriculum: IBDP
Language instr: Spanish

La Paz Community School
500 metros sur de la ferreteria, Buenaventura, Flamingo, Guanacaste 50309 Costa Rica
Tel: +506 2654 4532
Curriculum: IBDP
Language instr: English

Lincoln School
PO Box 025216, Miami, FL 33102-5216, USA Costa Rica
Tel: +1 506 247 6623
Head of School: Jack J Bimrose
Age range: 4–19
No. of pupils: 632 Vlth632
Curriculum: ACT, IBDP, National, SAT, USA
Language instr: English

Pan-American School
632-4005 San Antonio de Belen, Heredia, Costa Rica
Tel: +506 2293 7393
General Director: Alegria Lores
Age range: 3–18
No. of pupils: 673 B355 G317
Fees: US$4,150–US$6,000

Saint Mary School
Apartado 1471, Escazu 1250, San
José, Escazú 1250 Costa Rica
Tel: +506 2215 2133
Head of School: Olman
Vargas Rojas
Curriculum: IBDP
Language instr: Spanish

The Blue Valley School
Apartado 1784-1250,
Escazú, Costa Rica
Tel: +50 6 2215 2204
Head of School: María Cristina
Gutiérrez de Urbina
Age range: 3–18
No. of pupils: 681 B313 G368
Fees: US$9,078
Curriculum: IBDP
Language instr: English

**The British School
of Costa Rica**
PO Box 8184, San José,
1000 Costa Rica
Tel: +506 2220 0131
Head of School: Trevor Davies
Age range: 4–18
No. of pupils: 910
Curriculum: IBDP, National, UK
Language instr: English, Spanish

**United World College
Costa Rica/Colegio
del Mundo Unido CR**
Santa Ana, 100M Este y100 Norte,
Supermercado Pali, Santa Ana,
San José, 678-6150 Costa Rica
Tel: +50 6 2282 1538
Head of School: Mauricio Viales
No. of pupils: 90
Curriculum: IBDP
Language instr: Spanish

Yorkín School
800 metros sur y 200 metros este
de la casa de Doña Lela, Lomas
de Ayarco Sur, Curridabat,
San José, 11801 Costa Rica
Tel: +506 2272 1547
Curriculum: IBDP
(symbol)

Cuba

**International School
of Havana**
Calle 18 #315 Miramar, esq
5ta Ave, Playa, Miramar, La
Habana, 11300 Cuba
Tel: +53 7 204 2540
Principal: Ian Morris
Age range: 2–18
No. of pupils: 330 B168 G162
Fees: US$3,700–US$11,500
Curriculum: IBDP, IPC, SAT,
USA, IGCSE, ALevs
Language instr: English
(CIS) (ECIS)

Dominican Republic

**American School of
Santo Domingo**
Calle C #7, Cuesta Hermosa III,
Arroyo Hondo, Santo Domingo,
Dominican Republic
Tel: +001 809 567 6824
Director: Abby Wynter
Age range: 5–18
Curriculum: AP, National, USA
Language instr: English, Spanish

Carol Morgan School
Avenida Sarasota, Apartado
1169, Santo Domingo,
Dominican Republic
Tel: +1 809 947 1005/6
Headmaster: Jack Delman
Age range: 4–18
No. of pupils: 1100 B506 G594
Fees: US$11,000–US$15,000
Language instr: English

**Colegio Internacional
SEK Las Americas**
C/ El Altar s/n y República de
Colombia, Santo Domingo,
Dominican Republic
Tel: +1809 2380737
Director: Mario Hinojosa Bozo
Language instr: Spanish
(ISA)

Notre Dame School
Manuel de Jesus Troncoso 52,
Ensanche Paraiso Z-7, Santo
Domingo, Dominican Republic
Tel: +1 8095652511
Head: Maria Lorraine de Ruiz-Alma
Age range: 4–18
No. of pupils: 441 B223 G218
Curriculum: National, USA
Language instr: English

**Puntacana
International School**
Punta Cana Village, Across from
Puntacana Int'l Airport, Punta
Cana, Dominican Republic
Tel: +1 809 959 3382
Age range: 2–18
(CIS)

Saint George School
1733 NW 79 Avenue, CPS
#404, Miami, FL 33126, USA
Dominican Republic
Tel: +809 562 5262
Head of School: Karina
Pablo de Redman
Age range: 2–18
Curriculum: IBDP
Language instr: English, Spanish
(CIS)

**The Americas
Bicultural School**
Calle Fernando Valerio No.
2, Ensanche La Julia, Santo
Domingo, Dominican Republic
Tel: +809 5353371
Director: Claudia Defillo Campeau
Language instr: English,
French, Spanish, Mandarin
(ISA)

El Salvador

**Academia Britanica
Cuscatleca**
Apartado Postal 121, Santa
Tecla, La Libertad, El Salvador
Tel: +503 2241 4400
Head of School: Graeme Keslake
Age range: 3–18
Fees: US$5,174–US$6,555
Curriculum: IBDP, IPC,
National, UK, IGCSE
Language instr: English
(PE, Art in Spanish)
(CIS)

**Colegio Internacional
de San Salvador**
Apartado 05-15, San
Salvador, El Salvador
Tel: +503 2224 1330
Head: Chester S Stemp
Age range: 4–19
No. of pupils: 330 B160 G170
Curriculum: ACT, AP,
National, SAT, USA

Colegio La Floresta
Km 13.5 Carretera al Puerto de
La Libertad, Call La Floresta,
Nueva San Salvador, El Salvador
Tel: +503 2229 5336/40
Head of School: Emilia de Guerrero
Age range: G6–17
No. of pupils: 642
Curriculum: IBDP, IBPYP
Language instr: Spanish
(symbol)

Colegio Lamatepec
Carretera al Puerto de La
Libertad Km 12.5, Calle Nueva
a Comasauga Santa Tecla, La
Libertad, San Salvador, El Salvador
Tel: +503 2534 8900
Head of School: Tulio Castillo Rivas
Age range: B6–18
No. of pupils: 615
Fees: $4,200–$4,900
Curriculum: IBDP, IBPYP
Language instr: Spanish, English
(symbol)

Colegio Maya
7a calle poniente Bis #4925,
Colonia Escalón, San
Salvador, El Salvador
Tel: +503 2263 2358
Director: Maris de los
Angeles de Parker
Age range: 4–19
Curriculum: National, USA
(CIS)

**Deutsche Schule – Escuela
Alemana San Salvador**
Apartado Postal 01-183, San
Salvador, CA El Salvador
Tel: +503 2243 2279
Head of School: Paul Hölzemann
No. of pupils: 588
Curriculum: IBDP
Language instr: Spanish

Escuela Americana
VIPSAL #1352, PO Box
025364, Miami, FL 33102-
5364, USA El Salvador
Tel: +503 2528 8300
General Director: Ken Templeton
Age range: 4–18
Curriculum: USA
Language instr: English

Escuela Panamericana
Final Pje Union, Calle El Carmen
#1348, Colonia Esculon, San
Salvador, El Salvador
Tel: +503 2209 6000
President: Jim Bosworth
Age range: 4–19
No. of pupils: 435 B220 G215
Fees: $3,761
Curriculum: National, SAT, USA
Language instr: English, Spanish

Guatemala

**American School
of Guatemala**
11 Calle 15-79 Zona 15 Vista
Hermosa III, Guatemala,
Guatemala
Tel: +502 236 907 91-95
General Director: Robert
E Gronniger
Age range: 4–18
Curriculum: USA
Language instr: Spanish, English

Centro Escolar 'El Roble'
11 Avenida Sur Final Las
Charcas, Zona 11, Guatemala
City, 01011 Guatemala
Tel: +502 2476 2973
Head of School: Julio Roberto
Asturias Arrivillaga
Curriculum: IBDP
Language instr: Spanish
(symbol)

**Centro Escolar
Campoalegre**
35 Calle and 12 Av Final, Zona
11, Código, 01011 Guatemala
Tel: +502 2380 3900
Head of School: Silvia
Valverde de Escobar
No. of pupils: 565
Curriculum: IBDP
Language instr: Spanish
(symbol)

Centro Escolar Entrevalles
Km 16.8 carretera a El Salvador,
Guatemala, Guatemala
Tel: +502 6685 4700 Ext 102
Head of School: Marìa del
Carmen de Camey
Curriculum: IBDP
Language instr: Spanish, English

Centro Escolar Solalto
Km 22.5, Carretera a
Fraijanes, Guatemala
Tel: +502 6634 9260
Head of School: José Guillermo
Mazariegos García
Curriculum: IBDP
Language instr: English, Spanish

**Colegio Internacional
SEK Guatemala**
Km 16.5 Carretera a El Salvador,
Guatemala, Guatemala
Tel: +502 66469999
Director: Javier Nuñez Diaz

**QSI International
School of Belize**
Mile 49.5, Western Highway,
Camalote Village, Cayo
District, Belize Guatemala
Tel: +501 668 8489
Director: Valerie Nathanson
Age range: 4–12
Curriculum: USA

Jamaica

**American International
School of Kingston**
2 College Green Avenue,
Kingston, Florida Jamaica
Tel: + 1 876 702 2070
Head of School: Shirley Davis
Age range: 3–18
No. of pupils: 290
Fees: $15,000
Curriculum: IBDP
Language instr: English

Hillel Academy
PO Box 2687, 51 Upper Mark
Way, Kingston 8, Jamaica
Tel: + 1 876 925 1980
Director: Bleyberg
Age range: 3–19
No. of pupils: 750 B420 G330
Fees: US$7,000–US$8,000
Curriculum: IBDP, IGCSE
Language instr: English

México

**American Institute
of Monterrey**
c/o 400 S 11th, McAllen,
TX 78501, USA México
Tel: +52 818303 3818
Director: Elizabeth Huergo
Age range: 3–16
No. of pupils: 1270 B653 G617

**American School
Foundation of
Guadalajara**
Colomos 2100, Col. Providencia,
Guadalajara, Jalisco 44630 México
Tel: +52 (33) 3648 0299
Superintendent: David McGrath
Age range: 3–18
No. of pupils: 1400 B700 G700
Fees: US$8,000
Curriculum: AP, National,
SAT, TOEFL, USA
Language instr: English, Spanish

**American School
Foundation of Monterrey**
Ave. Ignacio Morones Prieto
No. 1500, Col. San Isidro, Santa
Catarina, N.L., C.P. 66190 México
Tel: +52 81 5000 4400
Director: D Jeffrey Keller
Age range: 3–18
No. of pupils: 561

**American School
Foundation, AC**
Bondojito 215, Col Las Americas,
Mexico City, 01120 México
Tel: +52 55 5 227 4900
Executive Director: Paul Williams
Age range: 4–18
No. of pupils: 2481 B1325 G1156
Curriculum: ACT, SAT
Language instr: English

**American School
of Pachuca**
Blvd Valle de Anáhuac s/n,
Col San Javier, Pachuca,
Hgo. 42086, México
Tel: +771 7131058/7139608
General Director: Nicéforo
Ramírez Castillo
Age range: 4–14
No. of pupils: 830
Curriculum: USA

**American School of
Puerto Vallarta**
Albatros 129, Col. Marina Vallarta,
Puerto Vallarta, Jal. 48335 México
Tel: +52 322 226 7670/72
Superintendent: Gerald Selitzer
Age range: 3–18
No. of pupils: 337 B166 G171
Curriculum: AP, SAT

**Bachillerato
Alexander Bain, SC**
Las Flores 497, Tlacopac,
01049 México
Tel: +(5255) 5683 2911
Headmaster: Sergio
Riverio Benietez
Age range: 12–18
No. of pupils: 610
Curriculum: IBDP, IBMYP
Language instr: Spanish, English

**Bachillerato UPAEP
Angelópolis**
Avenida del Sol No 5, Concepción
La Cruz, Reserva Territorial
Atlixcáyotl, San Andrés Cholula,
72197 Puebla México
Tel: +52 (222) 225 2291
Head of School: Maria
Isabel Gómez Vallarta
Age range: 14–19
Curriculum: IBDP
Language instr: Spanish, English

**Bachillerato UPAEP
Santiago**
9 Poniente No 1508, Colonia
Santiago, Puebla, 72160 México
Tel: +52 (222) 246 58 50
Head of School: Érika
Cepeda Arvizu
Curriculum: IBDP, IBCC
Language instr: Spanish

**Bachillerato UPAEP,
Plantel Cholula**
Avenida Forjadores
#1804, Col Barrio de Jesús,
Puebla 72770 México
Tel: +52 (222) 4037373
Head of School: Carlos
Mauricio Aguila Cervera
Curriculum: IBDP
Language instr: Spanish

**Centro de Ensenanza
Tecnica y Superior**
PO Box 439042, San Diego, CA
92143-9042, USA México
Tel: +52 664 903 1800
Head of School: Arturo
Ponce Wilson
Curriculum: IBDP
Language instr: Spanish

**Centro de Enseñanza
Técnica y Superior –
Campus Mexicali**
Calzada del Cetys S/N,
Colonia Rivera, Mexicali, Baja
California 21259 México
Tel: +52 686 567 3704
Head of School: Patricia Pacho Ruiz
Curriculum: IBDP

**Centro Educativo
CRECER AC**
Calle del Vecino No 3,
Atlihuetzia, Yahuquehmecan,
Tlaxcala, 90459 México
Tel: +52 24 646 13 148
Head of School: Martha
Clara López-Jáuregui
Curriculum: IBPYP

**Centro Escolar
Instituto La Paz, SC**
Av Plan de San Luis 445, Col
Nueva Santa María, México
City, 02800 México
Tel: +52 55 55 56 66 46
Head of School: Francisco
Javier González García
Age range: 3–15
No. of pupils: 1200
Fees: US$4,000
Curriculum: IBMYP, IBPYP, National
Language instr: Spanish, English

Churchill College
Moctezuma 125, Colonia
San Pablo Tepetlapa,
México DF, 04620 México
Tel: +52 55 56 19 82 43
Head of School: Charlotte Crosland
Curriculum: IBDP,
National, UK, IGCSE
Language instr: Spanish, English

Colegio Álamos
Acceso al Aeropuerto 1000,
Colonia Arboledas, Santiago
de Querétaro, 76940 México
Tel: +52, 442 182 0222
Head of School: César Cruz Cortés
Curriculum: IBDP
Language instr: Spanish

**Colegio Alemán
de Guadalajara**
Av Bosques de los Cedros
N°32, Las Cañadas, Zapopan,
Jalisco 45132 México
Tel: +52 33 3685 00 60
Head of School: Rainer Quennet
Age range: 16–19
No. of pupils: 1037
Fees: Peso5,600
Curriculum: IBDP
Language instr: Spanish, German

**Colegio Alexander
Bain Irapuato**
Arquitecto Enrique del Moral
#335, Col Lo de Juárez, Irapuato,
Guanajuato 36540 México
Tel: +52 462 1442246
Head of School: José Prado Havaux
Curriculum: IBPYP
Language instr: English, Spanish

**Colegio Alexander
Bain S.C.**
Barranca de Pilares 29,
Tlacopac, 01760 México
Tel: +52 55 5595 0499
Head of School: Lourdes
Córdoba de Aburto
Age range: 3–12
Curriculum: IBPYP
Language instr: Spanish

**Colegio Alfonsino
de San Pedro AC**
Galeana 257 Pte, San Pedro, Garza
Garcia, NL CP, 68230 México
Tel: +52 81 8338 3818
Director: Ninfa Clariond
Reyes-Retana
Age range: 1–16

Colegio Americano de Durango
Francisco Sarabia 416
Pte, Apartado Postal 495,
Durango, 34000 México
Tel: +52 618 811 5098
Director General: Abel Valdez
Age range: 2–18
No. of pupils: 475 B240 G235
Curriculum: National, SAT, USA
Language instr: English, Spanish

Colegio Americano de Torreón
Paso del Algodón #500,
Fraccionamiento Los Viñedos,
Torreón, Coahuila 27019 México
Tel: +871 222 51 00
General Director: Makhlouf Ouyed
Age range: 4–12
Curriculum: ACT, AP, SAT,
TOEFL, USA, ALevs
Language instr: English

Colegio Anglo Mexicano de Chiapas
Avda. Querétaro # 238,
Fraccionamiento Residencial
La Hacienda, Tuxtla Gutiér+,
Chiapas, México
Tel: +52 961 60 232274
Head of School: Luz
María Ruiz González
Curriculum: IBPYP
Language instr: English

Colegio Arji
Avenida México # 2,
esquina Periférico, Colonia
del Bosque, Villahermosa,
Tabasco 86160 México
Tel: +52, 993, 3 510 250
Head of School: Graciela
Trujillo de Cobo
Age range: 3–18
No. of pupils: 1200
B600 G600 VIth80
Curriculum: IBDP, IBMYP, IBPYP
Language instr: English, Spanish

Colegio Atid AC
Carlos Echánove 224,
Colonia Lomas de Vista
Hermosa, Del Cuajimalpa,
Mexico DF, 05100 México
Tel: +52 55 5814 0800
Head of School: Jannette
Hamui Dichi
Age range: 4–18
Curriculum: IBDP, IBMYP, IBPYP
Language instr: English, Spanish

Colegio Bilingüe Carson de Ciudad Delicias
Ave 50 Aniversario 1709, Delicias,
Chihuahua, 33058 México
Tel: +52 (639) 472 9340
Head of School: Claudia Terrazas
Curriculum: IBPYP

Colegio Bilingüe Madison Chihuahua
Fuente Trevi #7001,
Fraccionamiento Puerta de Hierro,
z.c 31207 Chihuahua, México
Tel: +52 614 430 1464
Headmaster: Yolanda
Patricia Luna Márquez
Age range: 3–15
No. of pupils: 454
Fees: $3,100
Curriculum: IBPYP
Language instr: English, Spanish

Colegio Bosques
Prolongación Zaragoza No
218, Fracc Valle de las Trojes,
Aguascalientes, 20115 México
Tel: +52 449 162 0410
Head of School: Rita
Marcela Salinas Medina
Curriculum: IBMYP

Colegio Británico
Calle Pargo # 24, S.M. 3, Cancun,
Quintana Roo, 77500 México
Tel: +52 (998) 884 1295
Head of School: Clara
Silvia Barra Arias
Curriculum: IBPYP
Language instr: English, Spanish

Colegio Buena Tierra SC
Camino Viejo a San Mateo
273, San Salvador Tizatlalli,
Metepec, Toluca, 52172 México
Tel: +52 722 271 2500
Head of School: Dolores
Berumen y Riquelme
Curriculum: IBPYP
Language instr: English, Spanish

Colegio Celta Internacional
Libramiento Sur-Poniente
Km 4+200, Colonia Los
Olvera, Villa Corregidora,
Querétaro, 76902 México
Tel: +52 442 227 36 00
Head of School: Elizabeth
Melhado Cooke
No. of pupils: 840
Curriculum: IBMYP, IBPYP
Language instr: English, Spanish

Colegio Ciudad de México
Campos Elíseos, # 139, Col
Polanco, Mexico DF, 11560 México
Tel: +52 55 5203 7894
Head of School: Amparo
Lapiedra Barrón
Age range: 2–18
No. of pupils: 1400
Curriculum: IBDP, IBMYP, IBPYP
Language instr: Spanish

Colegio Ciudad de Mexico – Plantel Contadero
Calle de la Bolsa 456, El Contadero,
Cuajimalpa, CP 05500 México
Tel: +52 58 12 06 10
Head of School: Lorena Saenz
No. of pupils: 450
Fees: Day £0
Curriculum: IBPYP

Colegio Columbia
Poza Rica #507, Col Petrolera,
Tampico, CP 89110 México
Tel: +52 833 213 0054/1045
General Director: Eva Gil
Age range: 2–15
No. of pupils: 820 B429 G391
Curriculum: National
(CIS)

Colegio El Camino
Callejon del Jorongo 210, Col. El
Pedregal, Cabo San Lucas, Baja
California Sur 23458 México
Tel: +52 624 1432100
Head of School: Heath Sparrow
Curriculum: IBDP
Language instr: English

Colegio Euroamericano de Monterrey
Blvd Diaz Ordaz 250 Ote,
Colonia Santa Maria,
Monterrey, NL 64650 México
Tel: +52 81 8248 8400
Superintendent: Dorothee Cavazos
Age range: 2–15
No. of pupils: 1321 B691 G630
Curriculum: National, USA
Language instr: English,
Spanish, German
(CIS)

Colegio Fontanar
Camino al Fraccionamiento,
Vista Real 119, Corregidora,
Querétaro, 76900 México
Tel: +52 442 228 13 65
Head of School: Mónica
Cevallos Molina
No. of pupils: 630
Fees: US$2,900–US$5,000
Curriculum: IBDP
Language instr: Spanish

Colegio Hebreo Maguen David AC
Antiguo Camino a
Tecamachalco, #370 Col
Vista Hermosa, Cuajimalpa,
Mexico DF, 05100 México
Tel: +52 (55) 52 462600
Head of School: Liliana Pinto
No. of pupils: 1091 B536 G555
Curriculum: IBDP, IBMYP,
IBPYP, National, TOEFL
Language instr: Spanish,
English, Hebrew

Colegio Hebreo Monte Sinai AC
Av Loma de la Palma
133, Col Vista Hermosa,
Cuajimalpa, 05109 México
Tel: +52 55 5814 0500
Head of School: Daniel
Smeke Zwaiman
Curriculum: IBMYP
Language instr: Spanish, English

Colegio Hebreo Tarbut
Av. Loma del Parque 216, Colonia
Lomas de Vista Hermosa,
México DF, 05100 México
Tel: +52 55 5814 0500
Head of School: Eli Perez
Curriculum: IBMYP, IBPYP
Language instr: Spanish,
English, Hebrew

Colegio Inglés
Real San Agustin #100, Col San
Agustin Campestre, Garza
Garcia, NL 66270 México
Tel: +52 81 8133 1700
General Director: Alejandra
Garza Valero
Age range: 4–16
Curriculum: National
(CIS)

Colegio Internacional de México
Rio Magdalena 263, Tizapán,
México DF, 01090 México
Tel: +52 55 55 50 01 01
Head of School: Gabriela
Rojas Jimenez
Curriculum: IBPYP

Colegio Internacional Terranova
Av Palmira 705, Fracc.
Desarrollo del Pedregal, San
Luis Potosí, 78295 México
Tel: +52 444 8 41 64 22
Head of School: Margret Oettler
Curriculum: IBMYP, IBPYP

Colegio Internacional Tlalpan
Carretera Libre a Cuernavaca,
6867 Km 24, San Andrés Totoltepec,
Tlalpan 14400 México
Tel: +52, 55 58 491884
Head of School: Patricia
Galdames Jeria
No. of pupils: 220
Curriculum: IBDP
Language instr: Spanish

Colegio La Paz de Chiapas
Carretera Tuxtla, Villaflores
N° 1170, Tuxtla Gutiérrez,
Chiapas 29089 México
Tel: +52 6637000
Head of School: Raquel
Gutiérrez Zamora Vega
Curriculum: IBDP
Language instr: Spanish

Colegio Laureles IAP
Inzancanac s/n esq Jugueteros y
Canteros, Barrio Tlatel Xochitenco,
Chimalhuacan, 56330 México
Tel: +525 55852 9002
Head of School: Laura
Elena Franco Hernaiz
Curriculum: IBDP
Language instr: English, Spanish

Colegio Linares AC
Marina Silva de Rodriguez 1301
Pte, Colonia centro Linares,
Nuevo León, 67700 México
Tel: +52 821 212 0269
Head of School: Antonio
Benitez Coello
Curriculum: IBDP

**Colegio Lomas Hill –
Campus Contadero**
Av. Veracruz 158, Cuajimalpa,
México, D.F., 05100 México
Tel: +52 55 5812 0818
Head of School: Annette
Muench Garcés
Curriculum: IBPYP

**Colegio Maria Montessori
de Monclova**
Blvd Harold R Pape Nro 2002, Col
Jardines del Valle, Monclova,
Coah, 25730 México
Tel: +52 866 633 2993
Head of School: Aurora
Galaz Riojas
Curriculum: IBDP

Colegio Merici
Granjas 45, Col Palo Alto,
Cuajimalpa, Ciudad de
México 05110 México
Tel: +52 55 55703183
Director General: Adriana
Benavides Puente
Curriculum: IBMYP, IBPYP

Colegio Monteverde
Av Santa Lucia No 260, Col Prados
de la Montaña, Cualjimalpa,
México DF 05610 México
Tel: +52 55 50819700
Head of School: Amelia
García Casas
Age range: B2–6 G2–19
No. of pupils: 684 B80 G604
Curriculum: IBDP
Language instr: Spanish, English

Colegio Nuevo Continente
Nicolás San Juan 1141, Colonia Del
Valle, México, D.F., 03100 México
Tel: +52 55 5575 4066
Head of School: Iona
Luisa Astorga Hilbert
Curriculum: IBDP
Language instr: English, Spanish

Colegio Olinca Altavista
Av Altavista No 130, Colonia
San Angel, Delegación Álvaro
Obregón, México DF, 01060 México
Tel: +52 55 56160216
Head of School: María
Fernanda Carrera Compeán
Curriculum: IBPYP
Language instr: Spanish

Colegio Simón Bolivar
Av. Jacarandas No 176,
Colonia San Juan, Tepic,
Nayarit, 63130 México
Tel: +52 311 2144335
Head of School: José
Manuel Ramírez Gómez
Curriculum: IBPYP

Colegio Springfield, SC
Isidro Fabela Nte 1061, Col Tres
Caminos, Toluca, CP 50020 México
Tel: +52 722 272 0586
Head of School: Ing Luís
Enrique Durán Fernández
Curriculum: IBDP
Language instr: Spanish

**Colegio Suizo de México
– Campus Cuernavaca**
Calle Amates s/n, Col. Lomas
de Ahuatlán, Cuernavaca,
Morelos 62130 México
Tel: +52 777 323 5252
Head of School: Christian Zwingli
Curriculum: IBDP
Language instr: English

**Colegio Suizo de México
– Campus México DF**
Nicolás San Juan 917, Col del
Valle, México DF 03100, México
Tel: +52 55 43 78 62
Head of School: Walter Stooss
Age range: 3–19
No. of pupils: 726
Curriculum: IBDP
Language instr: English

Colegio Vista Hermosa
Bachillerato, Av Loma de Vista
Hermosa 221, Cuajimalpa,
Mexico City, DF 05100 México
Tel: +52, 55 50914630
Head of School: Maria Antonieta
Molina Garza Galindo
Age range: 13–18
No. of pupils: 900 B400 G500
Curriculum: IBDP, IBMYP, TOEFL
Language instr: Spanish

Colegio Williams
Mixcoac Campus, Empresa 8,
Col Mixcoac, Del. Benito Juárez,
México DF, CP 03910 México
Tel: +52 55 1087 9797
Head of School: Arturo
Camilo Williams Rivas
Curriculum: IBDP, IBMYP, IBPYP
Language instr: Spanish,
English, French

**Colegio Williams
de Cuernavaca**
Luna #32, Jardines de
Cuernavaca, Cuernavaca,
Morelos 62360 México
Tel: +52 (777) 3223640
Headmaster: Alfonso
Garcia Williams
Age range: 1–19
No. of pupils: 850 B460 G390
Curriculum: IBDP, IBMYP,
IBPYP, National, TOEFL
Language instr: English, Spanish

**Colegio Williams
Unidad San Jerónimo**
Presa Reventada No 53, Col
San Jerónimo Lídice, Del.
Magdalena Contreras, México
DF, CP 10400 México
Tel: +52 55 1087 9797
Head of School: Arturo
Camilo Williams Rivas
Curriculum: IBPYP
Language instr: Spanish, English

Colegio Xail
Calle Xail No 10, Col.
Lázaro Cárdenas, San
Francisco de Campeche,
Campeche, 24520 México
Tel: (52 981) 813 0322
Head of School: Ana
Florencia Heredia Ávila
Curriculum: IBMYP, IBPYP

**Columbus, Colegio
Bilingüe Madison**
Blvd del Mar #521, Fraccionamiento
Costa de Oro CP 94299, Boca
del Río, Veracruz México
Tel: +52 229 130 0714
Age range: 3–15
No. of pupils: 500
Fees: US$3,710–US$4,056
Curriculum: IBPYP
Language instr: English, Spanish

Discovery School
Chilpancingo No 102, Colonia
Vista Hermosa, Cuernavaca,
Morelos 62290 México
Tel: +52 777 318 5721
Head of School: Diana
Recio de Ramos
Curriculum: IBPYP
Language instr: English

**El Colegio Británico
(Edron Academy)**
Cal. al Desierto de los, Leones
5578, Col Olivar de los Padres,
Mexico DF, 01740 México
Tel: +52 (55) 5585 1920
Interim Head
Teacher: Eamonn Mullally
Age range: 2–18
No. of pupils: 1040 B540 G500
Fees: MEX$100,000–MEX$180,000
Curriculum: IBDP,
National, UK, IGCSE
Language instr: English, Spanish

Escuela Alexander Bain SC
Barranca de Pilares 4,
Tlacopac, 01049 México
Tel: +52 56 833 255
Head of School: María
Guadalupe Molina Ramos
Age range: 3–12
Curriculum: IBPYP
Language instr: Spanish

Escuela Ameyalli SC
Calzada de las Águilas 1972,
Col Axomiatla, Álvaro Obregón,
México DF 01820 México
Tel: +52, 55 12 85 70 20
Age range: 2–18
Curriculum: IBMYP, IBPYP
Language instr: Spanish, English

**Escuela Bancaria y
Comercial, SC**
Paseo de la Reforma No 202
Edif E 3er piso, Col Juárez,
Del Cuauhtemoc, México
DF, 06600 México
Tel: +52 (55) 91 49 20 79
Head of School: Ricardo
González Escobar
Curriculum: IBDP
Language instr: Spanish

Escuela John F. Kennedy
Av Sabinos 272, Jurica,
Querétaro, 76100 México
Tel: +52, 442 218 0075
Head of School: Mirtha
Stappung Ruff
Age range: 3–19
No. of pupils: 1444 B751 G693
Curriculum: IBDP
Language instr: English, Spanish

Escuela Lomas Atlas S.C.
Montañas Calizas #305,
Lomas de Chapultepec,
Mexico, DF 11000 México
Tel: +52 55 55 20 53 75/20 37 25
Principal of School: Isela Consuegra
Age range: 1 –13
No. of pupils: 260 B124 G136
Curriculum: IBPYP
Language instr: English, Spanish

Eton, SC
Santa Lucia 220, Prados de la
Montaña, Cujaimalpa de Morelos,
México DF, 05619 México
Tel: +52 5 261 5800
Head of School: Liz Panchuk
Age range: 2–18
Curriculum: IBDP, IBMYP
Language instr: Spanish, English

**Fundación Colegio
Americano de Puebla**
Apartado Postal 665,
Puebla, 72160 México
Tel: +52 222 3030400
Superintendent: Francisco
Galicia Ortega
Age range: 6 months–19 years
No. of pupils: 2325
Curriculum: IBDP, IBMYP,
IBPYP, National
Language instr: Spanish, English

Greengates School
Av. Circunvalación Pte. 102, Balcones de San Mateo, Naucalpan, Edo. de México, C.P. 53200 México
Tel: +52 55 5373-0088
Chief Executive Officer: Clarisa Desouches
Age range: 3–18
No. of pupils: 1200
Curriculum: IBDP, SAT
Language instr: English

Instituto Alexander Bain SC
Cascada 320, Jardines del Pedregal, México
Tel: +52 55 5595 6579
Head of School: Ofelia Arriaga de Nájera
Age range: 2–13
No. of pupils: B381 G382
Curriculum: IBPYP, National
Language instr: Spanish, English

Instituto Anglo Británico AC
Av. Isidoro Sepúlveda No. 555, Col. La Encarnación, Apodaca, NL México
Tel: +52 8183 21 5000
Headmistress: Imelda Jiménez Rocha
Age range: 2–15
No. of pupils: 1180
Fees: US$4,400
Curriculum: IBMYP, IBPYP
Language instr: English, Spanish

Instituto Bilingüe Rudyard Kipling
Cruz de Valle Verde No 25, Santa Cruz del Monte, Naucalpan, Edo. de México, 53110 México
Tel: +52 55 5572 6282
Head of School: Sebastián de Jesús Salcedo Aquino
Age range: 3–18
Curriculum: IBDP, IBMYP, IBPYP
Language instr: Spanish, English

Instituto Cervantes, A.C.
Prol. León García # 2355, Col. General I. Martínez, San Luis de Potosí, 78360 México
Tel: +52 444 815 91 50
Head Master: Joaquín Jasso Moreno
No. of pupils: 1200
Curriculum: IBMYP, IBPYP
Language instr: Spanish

Instituto D'Amicis, AC
Camino a Morillotla s/n, Colonia Bello Horizonte, Puebla, 72170 México
Tel: +52 222 303 2618
Head of School: Laura Montes de Oca Hernández
Curriculum: IBDP, IBMYP, IBPYP
Language instr: Spanish

Instituto Educativo Olinca
Periférico Sur 5170, Col Pedregal de Carrasco, Delegación Coyoacán, 04700 México DF, México
Tel: +52 55 5606 3113/5606 3371/5606 3510
Head: Maria Teresa Compeán de Carrera
Age range: 2–19
No. of pupils: 1600
Curriculum: IBDP, IBMYP, IBPYP
Language instr: Spanish, English, French

Instituto Educativo Olinca Plantel Cuernavaca
Paseo de Atzingo No 515, Colonia Lomas de Atzingo, Cuernavaca, Morelos, 62180 México
Tel: +52 777 313 1232
Head of School: Néstor Renedo Cámara
Curriculum: IBPYP

Instituto Internacional Octavio Paz
Calle Internacional 63 Fracc. Las Brisas el Jaguey, Col. Las RedesChapala, Jalisco, 45903 México
Tel: +52 376 766 0903
Head of School: Lily Ehlebracht
Curriculum: IBDP

Instituto Jefferson de Morelia
Av Fuentes de Morelia 666, Colonia Fuentes de Morelia, Morelia, Michoacán 58080 México
Tel: +52 443 324 3636
Head of School: Carlos Sandoval Cuellar
Age range: 2–15
No. of pupils: 730 B350 G380
Curriculum: IBDP, IBMYP, IBPYP
Language instr: Spanish

Instituto Kipling de Irapuato
Villa Mirador, 5724, Villas de Irapuato, Irapuato, Gto, 36670 México
Tel: +52 462 6230165
Principal: José González Ochoa
Age range: 2–18
No. of pupils: B611 G687
Curriculum: IBMYP, IBPYP
Language instr: Spanish, English

Instituto Kipling Esmeralda
Av Parque de los Ciervos No 1, Vallescondido, Atizapán de Zaragoza, 52937 México
Tel: 52 55 5308 1686
Head of School: Laura Labarthe Costas
Curriculum: IBMYP, IBPYP
Language instr: Spanish

Instituto Piaget
Nubes 413, Col Jardines del Pedregal, México DF, 01900 México
Tel: +52 55 55 68 71 28/32
Head of School: Gabriela Olavarría Cabrer
Age range: 2–16
No. of pupils: 660
Curriculum: IBPYP
Language instr: English, Spanish

Instituto San Roberto
Av Real San Agustín #4, Garza García, NL 66260 México
Tel: +52 81 8625 1500
CEO: Monica Lucia Garza Sada
Age range: 1–15
Language instr: English, Spanish

La Escuela de Lancaster A.C.
Av Insurgentes sur 3838, Col Tlalpan, CP 14000 México
Tel: +52 5556 6697 96
Head of School: Alan Downie
Curriculum: IBDP, IBPYP
Language instr: English, Spanish

Liceo de Apodaca Centro Educativo
Ave. Virrey de Velazco No. 500, Nuevo León, Apodaca, 66606 México
Tel: +52 81 83862089
Head of School: Luis Miguel Gónzalez Frías
Curriculum: IBMYP, IBPYP
Language instr: English

Liceo de Monterrey
Humberto Junco #400, Colonia Valle Ote, Garza Garcia, 66220 México
Tel: +52, 8187484112
Head of School: Bertha Alicia Larragoity
Fees: Day £0
Curriculum: IBDP
Language instr: Spanish

Liceo de Monterrey – Centro Educativo
Col Sendero San Jeronimo, Monterrey, Nuevo Leon 64659 México
Tel: +1 8122 8900
Head of School: José Portillo Ponce
Curriculum: IBDP
Language instr: Spanish

Liceo Federico Froebel de Oaxaca SC
Ajusco No 100, Colonia Volcanes, Oaxaca, 68020 México
Tel: +52 951 5200 675
Head of School: María Emma Rodríguez Gutiérrez
No. of pupils: 735
Curriculum: IBDP
Language instr: English, Spanish, French

Madison Campus Monterrey
Marsella #3055, Col Alta Vista CP 64840, Monterrey, Nuevo León, México
Tel: +52 81 8359 0627
Headmaster: José Angel Lozano Elizondo
Age range: 3–15
No. of pupils: 550
Fees: US$4,900
Curriculum: IBMYP, IBPYP
Language instr: English, Spanish

Madison International School
Camino Real #100, Col. El Uro 64986, Monterrey, Nuevo León, México
Tel: +52 81 82187909
Headmaster: Enrique David May Díaz
Age range: 3–15
No. of pupils: 750
Fees: US$7,100
Curriculum: IBPYP
Language instr: English, Spanish

Nuevo Colegio Israelita de Monterrey
Preescolar y Primaria, Canadá #207, Col Vista Hermosa – CP 64620, Monterrey, Nuevo Leon 64620 México
Tel: +52, 81 8346 9677
Head of School: Brenda Kirsch Kleiman
No. of pupils: 110

Peterson Lomas Preparatoria SC
Huizachito No 80 B, Colonia Lomas de Vista Hermosa, Delegación Cuajimalpa de Morelos, 05720 México
Tel: +55 58130114
Head of School: Kenneth Albert Peterson Marquart
Age range: 17–19
Curriculum: IBDP
Language instr: Spanish

Tecnológico de Monterrey
Ave Eugenio Garza Sada 2501, Sur Col Tecnológico C.P. 64840, Monterrey, Nuevo León México
Tel: +52 (81) 8358 1400
Head of School: Sel-Ha Bahena

Tecnológico de Monterrey – Campus Ciudad de México
Campus Ciudad de Mexico, Calle del Puente 222, Ejidos de Huipulco Tlalpan, Distrito Federal 14380 México
Tel: +52, 55 5483 2110
Head of School: Eugenio Aguilar Ibarra
Curriculum: IBDP
Language instr: Spanish

Tecnológico de Monterrey – Campus Cuernavaca
Autopista del Sol Km 104, Colonia Real del Puente, Xochitepec, Morelos, Cuernavaca, 62790 México
Tel: +52 777 362 0871
Head of School: Luis Raúl Domínguez Blanco
Curriculum: IBDP
Language instr: Spanish

Tecnológico de Monterrey – Campus Cumbres
Prol Alejandro de Rodas S/N, Col Cumbres Elite, Monterrey, NL 64349 México
Tel: +52 (81) 8158 4600
Head of School: Carlos Bejos
Curriculum: IBDP
Language instr: Spanish

Tecnológico de Monterrey – Campus Esmeralda
Fraccionamiento Conjunto Urbano, Manzana 7, Lote 1 y 2, Bosque Esmeralda S/N, Atizapán de Zaragoza, Estado de México 52900 México
Tel: +52 55 58 64 5370
Head of School: Carlos Lozano
Curriculum: IBDP
Language instr: Spanish

Tecnológico de Monterrey – Campus Estado de México – Sede Esmeralda
Carretera Lago de Guadalupe, km 3.5 col Margarita Maza de, Juárez, Atizapán deZaragoza 52916 México
Tel: +52 (55) 5864 5370/5864 5372
Head of School: Oscar Locayo
No. of pupils: 2358
Curriculum: IBDP
Language instr: Spanish

Tecnológico de Monterrey – Campus Eugenio Garza Lagüera
Topolobampo #4603, Valle de las Brisas, Monterrey, NL 64790 México
Tel: +52 (81) 8155 4445
Head of School: Alfredo Pena Marin
Age range: 15–18
No. of pupils: 5261 B2737 G2524
Curriculum: IBDP, SAT
Language instr: Spanish

Tecnológico de Monterrey – Campus Metepec
Avda Las Torres s/n casi esqu Avda Tecnológico, San Salvador Tizatlalli, Metepec, Estado de México 52172 México
Tel: +52 722 271 5977
Head of School: Guadalupe Gomez
Curriculum: IBDP
Language instr: Spanish

Tecnológico de Monterrey – Campus Puebla
Vía Atlixcáyotl # 2301, Col Reserva Territorial Atlixcayotl, 72453 Puebla, Puebla México
Tel: +52 222 303 2000
Head of School: Raúl Pérez Marcial
Age range: 15–18
No. of pupils: 1000
Curriculum: IBDP
Language instr: Spanish, English

Tecnológico de Monterrey – Campus Querétaro
Av Epigmenio González #500, Fracc San Pablo, Santiago de Querétaro, 76130 México
Tel: +52, 442 2383208
Head of School: Chrisantos Manuel Martinez Trujillo
Age range: 15–18
No. of pupils: 988
Curriculum: IBDP, SAT, TOEFL
Language instr: Spanish

Tecnológico de Monterrey – Campus San Luis Potosí
Av Eugenio Garza Sada No 300, Fraccionamiento Lomas del Tecnológico, San Luis Potosi, 78211 México
Tel: +52 4448 341000
Head of School: Paulino Miguel Napoleon Bernot Silis
Curriculum: IBDP
Language instr: English

Tecnológico de Monterrey – Campus Santa Catarina
Morones Prieto No 290 Pte, Col Jesús M Garza, Santa Catarina, Nuevo León 66180 México
Tel: +52 (81) 8153 4132
Head of School: Rafael Abrego Hinojosa
Curriculum: IBDP
Language instr: English, Spanish

Tecnológico de Monterrey – Campus Santa Fe
Av Carlos Lazo #100, Santa Fe, Delegación Alvaro Obregón, CP 01389 México
Tel: +52 55 9177 8000 x8131
Principal: Chandra Bhushan Choubey
Curriculum: IBDP
Language instr: Spanish, English

Tecnológico de Monterrey – Campus Valle Alto
Carretera Nacional Km 927, Monterrey, Nuevo León 64790 México
Tel: +52 (81) 8155 4445
Head of School: Blanca Dinorah Alanís Lozano
Curriculum: IBDP
Language instr: Spanish, English

Tecnológico de Monterrey – Prepa Tec
Dinamarca 451, Col del Carmen, Monterrey, Nuevo León 64710 México
Tel: +52 (81) 8151 4240
Head of School: Maria Jose Pineda
Curriculum: IBDP
Language instr: Spanish, English

The American School Foundation, A.C.
Calle Sur 136-135, Colonia Las Americas, Mexico DF, 01120 México
Tel: +52 55 5227 4900
Executive Director: Paul Williams
Age range: 3–18
No. of pupils: 2566 B1324 G1242
Fees: MPso145,200–MPso200,685
Curriculum: IBDP, IBMYP, IBPYP
Language instr: English

The Churchill School
Felipe Villanueva 36, Col Guadalupe Inn, Álvaro Obregón, 01020 México
Tel: +52 55 50288800
Head Teacher: Amanda Jacob
Age range: 2–16
No. of pupils: B547 G482
Fees: MEX$75,580–MEX$133,115
Curriculum: IBMYP, IBPYP
Language instr: English, Spanish

Universidad de Monterrey
Ave.Morones Prieto 4500 Pte, San Pedro Garza Garcia, NL 66238 México
Tel: +52 81 8215 1000
Head of School: Susana Cuilty Siller
Curriculum: IBDP
Language instr: Spanish

Universidad de Monterrey Unidad Valle Alto
Carretera Nacionala Salida Valle Alto Km1, Colonia Valle Alto, Monterrey, NL 64989 México
Head of School: Carlos Raymundo Cantú Cantú
Curriculum: IBDP
Language instr: English, Spanish

Westhill Institute SC
Domingo Garcia Ramos No 56, Prados de la Montaña, Santa Fe Cuajimalpa, México DF 05610 México
Tel: +52 (55) 8851 7000
Headmaster: Albert Wynder
Curriculum: IBDP

Winpenny School
José María Castorena 318, Colonia Cuajimalpa, México D. F., 05000 México
Tel: +52 55 8000 6100
Head of School: Marian Winpenny
Curriculum: IBMYP
Language instr: Spanish

Netherlands Antilles

International School of St Maarten
Oyster Pond, 4 Oyster Pond Road, St Maarten, Netherlands Antilles
Tel: +599 543 1205
Director: Catherine Kretzschmar
Age range: 3–18
Curriculum: ACT, AP, SAT, USA

Nicaragua

American Nicaraguan School
Frente al Club de Lomas de Montserrat, P.O. Box 2670, Managua, Nicaragua
Tel: +505 2278 0029
Secondary Principal: Timothy Gardina
Age range: 3–18
No. of pupils: 970
Curriculum: USA

Colegio Alemán Nicaragüense
Apartado 1636, Managua, Nicaragua
Tel: +505 2265 8449
Head of School: Marc-Thomas Bock
No. of pupils: 479
Curriculum: IBDP
Language instr: Spanish

Lincoln International Academy
Las Colinas Sur, Managua, Nicaragua
Tel: +505 2276 3000
General Director: Adolfo Gonzalez

Notre Dame School
Apartado 6092, Managua, Nicaragua
Tel: +505 22 760353
Head of School: Eduardo Soto
Age range: 2–19
Curriculum: IBDP
Language instr: English

Puerto Rico

Baldwin School
PO Box 1827, Bayamon, 00960-1827 Puerto Rico
Tel: +1 787 720 2421
Head of School: A R Cauz
Age range: 4–18
Curriculum: USA
Language instr: English

Caribbean School
Urb La Rambla, 1689 Calle Navarra, Ponce, 00730-4043 Puerto Rico
Tel: +1 787 843 2048
Age range: 4–18
No. of pupils: 600 B299 G301

Trinidad & Tobago

International School of Port of Spain
1 International Drive, Westmoorings, Port of Spain, Trinidad & Tobago
Tel: +1 868 633 4777
Head of School: Jeffrey Barney Latham
Age range: 4–19
No. of pupils: 452 B245 G207 VIth101
Fees: US$10,270–US$15,438
Curriculum: ACT, AP, IBPYP, SAT
Language instr: English

USA
*Ordered by State

Alabama

Cornerstone Schools of Alabama
118 55th Street North, Birmingham, Alabama AL 35232 USA
Tel: +1 205 591 7600
Head of School: Nita Thompson Carr
Curriculum: IBPYP
Language instr: English

Arizona

Rancho Solano Preparatory School
3540 West Union Hills Drive, Glendale, Arizona AZ 85308 USA
Tel: +1 623 825 2764
Head of School: Audrey C Menard
Curriculum: IBDP
Language instr: English

Verde Valley School
3511 Verde Valley School Road, Sedona, Arizona AZ 86351 USA
Tel: +1 928 284 2272
Head of School: Graham Frey
No. of pupils: 135
Fees: US$21,500
Curriculum: IBDP
Language instr: English

Westwind Prep Academy
2045 W Northern Avenue, Phoenix, Arizona AZ 85021 USA
Tel: +1 602 864 7731
Head of School: Debra Slagle
Curriculum: IBDP

Arkansas

Mount Saint Mary Academy
3224 Kavanaugh Blvd, Little Rock, Arkansas AR 72205 USA
Tel: +1 501 664 8006
Head of School: Deborah Troillett
Age range: G14–18
No. of pupils: 515
Curriculum: IBDP
Language instr: English

California

Al-Arqam Islamic School & College Preparatory
6990 65th Street, Sacramento, California CA 95823 USA
Tel: +1 916 391 3333
Head of School: A M Fain
Curriculum: IBDP
Language instr: English

Cate School
1960 Cate Mesa Road, Carpinteria, California CA 93013 USA
Tel: +1 805 684 4127
Headmaster: Benjamin D. Williams IV
Language instr: English

Escuela Bilingüe Internacional
410 Alcatraz Avenue, Oakland, California CA 94609 USA
Tel: +1 510 653 3324
Head of School: Jon Fulk
Curriculum: IBPYP

Fairmont Preparatory Academy
2200 West Sequoia Avenue, Anaheim, California CA 92801 USA
Tel: +1 714 999 5055
Head of School: Robert Mendoza
No. of pupils: 342
Curriculum: IBDP
Language instr: English

German American International School
275 Elliott Drive, Menlo Park, California CA 94025 USA
Tel: +1 650 324 8617
Head of School: Dominic Liechti
Age range: 3–14
No. of pupils: 280 B140 G140
Fees: $12,475
Curriculum: IBMYP, IBPYP
Language instr: German, English

International High School
Lycée International Franco-American, 150 Oak Street, San Francisco, California CA 94102-5812 USA
Tel: +1 415 558 2084
Head of School: Jane Camblin
Age range: 14–18
No. of pupils: 341
Fees: US$30,360
Curriculum: IBDP
Language instr: English

International School of Monterey
1720 Yosemite Street, Seaside, California CA 93955 USA
Tel: +1 831 583 2165
Director: Sean Madden
Age range: 4–14
No. of pupils: 416 B215 G201
Language instr: English

LYCÉE INTERNATIONAL DE LOS ANGELES (LILA)
For further details see p. 156
1105 W. Riverside Drive, Burbank, California CA 91506 USA
Tel: +1 626 695 5159
Email: admissions@lilaschool.com
Website: www.lilaschool.com
Interim CEO: John Fleck
Age range: 2–18
No. of pupils: 1003
Fees: $13,900–$16,700
Curriculum: ACT, AP, IBDP, FrenchBacc, SAT
Language instr: English

New Covenant Academy
3119 W 6th Street, Los Angeles, California CA 90020 USA
Tel: +1 213 487 5437
Head of School: Steven Chai
Age range: 6–19
No. of pupils: 137 B83 G55
Fees: $9,000–$11,000
Curriculum: ACT, IBDP, SAT, USA
Language instr: English

Pacific Rim International School
454 Peninsula Avenue, San Mateo, California CA 94401 USA
Tel: +1 650 685 1881
Head of School: Christinia Cheung
Curriculum: IBDP
Language instr: English

San Gabriel Mission High School
254 South Santa Anita Street, San Gabriel, California CA 91776 USA
Tel: +1 626 282 3181
Head of School: Jamie Collins
Curriculum: IBDP
Language instr: English

Santa Margarita Catholic High School
22062 Antonio Parkway, Rancho Santa Margarita, California CA 92688 USA
Tel: +1 949 766 6000
Head of School: Raymond R Dunne
Curriculum: IBDP
Language instr: English

Shu Ren International School
1333 University Avenue, Berkeley, California CA 94702 USA
Tel: +1 510 981 0320
Head of School: Nathan Pope
Curriculum: IBPYP
Language instr: English, Mandarin

St Mary & All Angels School
7 Pursuit, Aliso Viejo, California CA 92656 USA
Tel: +1 949 448 9027
Head of School: John O'Brien
No. of pupils: 621
Fees: $11,750
Curriculum: IBMYP, IBPYP
Language instr: French

THINK Global School
One Embarcadero Center, Suite 500, San Francisco, California CA 94111 USA
Tel: +1 347 281 6855
Head of School: Alun Cooper
Curriculum: IBDP

Vistamar School
737 Hawaii Street, El Segundo, California CA 90245 USA
Tel: +1 310 643 7377
Head: Jim Buckheit
Age range: 13–19
No. of pupils: 176 B90 G86
Fees: $25,850
Curriculum: USA
Language instr: English

Yew Chung International School of Silicon Valley
310 Easy Street, Mountain View, California CA 94043 USA
Tel: +1 650 903 0986
Principal: Kevin Reimer

Colorado

Boulder Country Day School
4820 Nautilus Court North, Boulder, Colorado CO 80301 USA
Tel: +1 303 527-4931
Head of School: Mike Shields
Curriculum: IBMYP
Language instr: English

Denver Montclair International School
206 Red Cross Way, Denver, Colorado CO 80230 USA
Tel: +1 303 340 3647
Head of School: Francois Penalver
Curriculum: IBMYP
Language instr: English

Fountain Valley School of Colorado
6155 Fountain Valley School Rd, Colorado Springs, Colorado CO 80911 USA
Tel: +1 719 390 7035
Head of School: William V. Webb
Language instr: English

Mackintosh Academy
7018 S Prince Street, Littleton, Colorado CO 80120 USA
Tel: +1 303 794 6222
Head of School: Renu Rose
Curriculum: IBMYP, IBPYP
Language instr: English

Connecticut

Cheshire Academy
10 Main Street, Cheshire,
Connecticut CT 06410 USA
Tel: +1 203 272 5396
Head of School: Doug Rogers
Curriculum: IBDP, National
🏛

The Hotchkiss School
11 Interlaken Road, Lakeville,
Connecticut CT 06039-2141 USA
Tel: +1 860 435 2591
Head of School: Kevin M. Hicks
Language instr: English
🏛 (RS)

Whitby School
969 Lake Avenue, Greenwich,
Connecticut CT 06831 USA
Tel: +1 203 869 8464 x141
Head of School: Doug Fainelli
Curriculum: IBMYP, IBPYP
Language instr: English

Delaware

Wilmington Friends School
101 School Road, Wilmington,
Delaware DE 19803 USA
Tel: +1 302 576 2900
Head of School: Bryan K Garman
Age range: 2–19
Curriculum: AP, IBDP, SAT
Language instr: English

District of Columbia

Archbishop Carroll High School
4300 Harewood Road NE,
Washington, District of
Columbia DC 20017 USA
Tel: +1 202 529 0900 x135
Head of School: Mary
Elizabeth Blaufuss
No. of pupils: 545
Curriculum: IBDP
Language instr: English

British School of Washington
2001 Wisconsin Ave NW,
Washington, District of
Columbia DC 20007 USA
Tel: +1 202 829 3700
Head of School: Ann McPhee
Age range: 3–18
Fees: $17,425–$22,475
Curriculum: IBDP, UK, IGCSE
Language instr: English
(COB) (ECIS)

Washington International School
3100 Macomb Street NW,
Washington, District of
Columbia DC 20008 USA
Tel: +1 202 243 1800
Head of School: Clayton Lewis
Age range: 4–18
No. of pupils: 900 B430 G470
Fees: US$28,930–US$32,250
Curriculum: IBDP, IBPYP
Language instr: English, French,
Spanish, Dutch, Chinese
(CIS) (ECIS)

Florida

Arthur I Meyer Jewish Academy
3261 N Military Trail, West Palm
Beach, Florida FL 33409 USA
Tel: +1 561 686 6520
Head of School: Nammie Ichilov
Curriculum: IBMYP

Boca Prep International School
10333 Diego Drive South, Boca
Raton, Florida FL 33428 USA
Tel: +1 561 852 1410
Head of School: Pelham
Lindfield Roberts
Curriculum: IBDP, IBMYP
Language instr: English
🏛 (ISA)

Cardinal Newman High School
512 Spencer Drive, West Palm
Beach, Florida FL 33409 USA
Tel: +1 561 683 6266
**Head of School &
President:** David Carr
No. of pupils: 870
Fees: US$6,950
Curriculum: IBDP
Language instr: English

Carrollton School of the Sacred Heart
3747 Main Highway, Miami,
Florida FL 33133 USA
Tel: +1 305 446 5673
Head of School: Suzanne Cooke
Curriculum: IBDP
Language instr: English
🏛

Carrollwood Day School
1515 W Bearss Avenue, Tampa,
Florida FL 33613 USA
Tel: +1 813 920 2288
Head of School: Mary L Kanter
Age range: 2–12
No. of pupils: 800
Fees: $3,500–$12,400
Curriculum: IBDP, IBMYP, IBPYP
Language instr: English

Clearwater Central Catholic High School
2750 Haines Bayshore Road,
Clearwater, Florida FL 33760 USA
Tel: +1 727 531 1449
Head of School: James Deputy
Curriculum: IBDP
Language instr: English

Gulliver Academy Middle School
12595 Red Road, Coral Gables,
Florida FL 33156 USA
Tel: +1 305 665 3593
Head of School: John Krutulis
Curriculum: IBMYP

Gulliver Preparatory School
6575 North Kendall Drive,
Miami, Florida FL 33156 USA
Tel: +1 305 666-7937
Head of School: Jerry Zank
Age range: 2–18
Fees: US$20,280
Curriculum: AP, IBDP
Language instr: English

Independent Day School
12015 Orange Grove Drive,
Tampa, Florida FL 33618 USA
Tel: +1 813, 961 3087
Head of School: Joyce
Burick Swarzman
Curriculum: IBMYP, IBPYP
Language instr: English

New Gate School
5237 Ashton Road, Sarasota,
Florida FL 34233 USA
Tel: +1 941 922 4949
Head of School: Tim Seldin
Curriculum: IBDP
Language instr: English

North Broward Preparatory School
7600 Lyons Road, Coconut
Creek, Florida FL 33073 USA
Tel: +1 954 247 0011
Head of School: Tom Marcy
Age range: 3–12
No. of pupils: 1400 B680 G720
Curriculum: ACT, AP, IBDP, SAT, USA
Language instr: English
🏛

Scheck Hillel Community School
19000 NE 25th Avenue, North Miami
Beach, Florida FL 33180 USA
Tel: +1 305 931 2831
Head of School: Pinchos Hecht
Curriculum: IBMYP

St Andrew's School
3900 Jog Road, Boca Raton,
Florida FL 33434 USA
Tel: +1 561 210 2000
Headmaster: Peter Benedict II
Curriculum: IBDP, IBMYP, IBPYP
Language instr: English
🏛

St Ann Catholic School
324 North Olive Avenue, West
Palm Beach, Florida FL 33401 USA
Tel: +1 561 832 3676
Head of School: Patrice Scheffler
Curriculum: IBMYP, IBPYP
Language instr: English

St John Vianney Catholic School
500 84th Avenue, St Pete
Beach, Florida FL 33706 USA
Tel: +1 727 360 1113
Principal: Jill Hudson
Age range: 3–12
Curriculum: IBMYP

St. Thomas the Apostle Catholic School
7303 S.W. 64th Street, Miami,
Florida FL 33143 USA
Tel: +1 305 661 8591
Head of School: Lisa M Figueredo
Curriculum: IBPYP
Language instr: English

The Biltmore School
1600 SW 57th Avenue, Miami,
Florida FL 33155 USA
Tel: (1) 305 266 4666
Head of School: Gina
Duarte-Romero
Curriculum: IBPYP

Windermere Preparatory School
6189 Winter Garden,
Vineland Road, Windermere,
Florida FL 34786 USA
Tel: +1 407 905 7737
Head of School: Tom Marcy
Curriculum: IBDP
Language instr: English
🏛

Georgia

Atlanta International School
2890 North Fulton Drive, Atlanta,
Georgia GA 30305 USA
Tel: +1 404 841 3840
Director: Kevin Glass
Age range: 4–19
No. of pupils: 935 B424 G511
Fees: $15,510–$17,830
Curriculum: IBDP, IBMYP, IBPYP, SAT
Language instr: English,
French, Spanish, German
(CIS) (ECIS)

High Meadows School
1055 Willeo Road, Roswell,
Georgia GA 30075 USA
Tel: +1 770 993 2940
Head of School: Jay Underwood
Age range: 3–12
No. of pupils: 400
Fees: $4,700–$14,500
Curriculum: IBPYP
Language instr: English

International Academy of Smyrna
2144 South Cobb Drive, Smyrna, Georgia GA 30080 USA
Tel: +1 678 370 0980
Principal: Kari Schrock
Curriculum: IBMYP, IBPYP
Language instr: English

Notre Dame Academy
4635 River Green Parkway, Duluth, Georgia GA 30096 USA
Tel: +1 678 387 9385
Head of School: Debra Orr
Curriculum: IBPYP
Language instr: English

St Andrew's School
601 Penn Waller Road, Savannah, Georgia GA 31410 USA
Tel: +1 912 897 4941
Head of School: Gil G Webb
Age range: 3–18
Fees: $6,095–$10,220
Curriculum: IBDP
Language instr: English

Hawaii

Island Pacific Academy
909 Haumea Street, Kapolei, Hawaii HI 96707 USA
Tel: +1 808 674 3523
Head of School: Benjamin Feinstein
Age range: 4–18
No. of pupils: B250 G250
Fees: US$13,700–US$15,700
Curriculum: IBDP, IBPYP
Language instr: English

Le Jardin Academy
917 Kalanianaole Highway, Kailua, Hawaii HI 96734 USA
Tel: +1 808 261 0707
Head of School: Louis Young
Age range: 3–17
No. of pupils: B411 G407
Fees: $17,130
Curriculum: IBDP, IBMYP, IBPYP, SAT
Language instr: English, French, Spanish, Japanese, Chinese

Mid-Pacific Institute
2445 Kaala Street, Honolulu, Hawaii HI 96822 USA
Tel: +1 808 973 5020
Head of School: Tom McManus
Age range: 4–18
No. of pupils: 1500
Curriculum: IBDP, SAT, TOEFL
Language instr: English

Idaho

Riverstone International School
5493 Warm Springs Avenue, Boise, Idaho ID 83716 USA
Tel: +1 208 424 5000
Head of School: Robert Carignan
Age range: 5–19
No. of pupils: 330
Fees: US$7,700–US$12,000
Curriculum: AP, IBDP, IBMYP, IBPYP, SAT
Language instr: English

Illinois

British School of Chicago
814 W Eastman Street, Chicago, Illinois IL 60622 USA
Tel: +1 773 506 2097
Headmaster: Michael Horton
Age range: 3–18
No. of pupils: 485 B243 G242
Fees: $21,380–$25,896
Curriculum: IBDP
Language instr: English

Hales Franciscan High School
4930 S Cottage Grove Avenue, Chicago, Illinois IL 60615 USA
Tel: 1 (773) 285-8400
Head of School: Erica Brownfield
Curriculum: IBDP

Lincoln Park High School
2001 North Orchard Street Mall, Chicago, Illinois IL 60614 USA
Tel: +1 773 534 8149
Principal: Michael Boraz
Age range: 13–19
No. of pupils: 2200
Curriculum: IBDP
Language instr: English

Lycée Français de Chicago
613 West Bittersweet Place, Chicago, Illinois IL 60613 USA
Tel: +1 773 665 0066
Curriculum: IBDP
Language instr: English

St. Matthias School
4910 N. Claremont Ave, Chicago, Illinois IL 60625 USA
Tel: +1 773 784 0999
Head of School: Adam Dufault
Curriculum: IBMYP
Language instr: English

Trinity College Preparatory High School
7574 West Division Street, River Forest, Illinois IL 60305 USA
Tel: +1 708 771 8383
Principal: Antonia Bouillette
Curriculum: IBDP
Language instr: English

Indiana

Cathedral High School
5225 East 56th Street, Indianapolis, Indiana IN 46226 USA
Tel: +1 317 542 1481
Principal: David L Worland
Curriculum: IBDP
Language instr: English

International School of Indiana
4330 North Michigan Road, Indianapolis, Indiana IN 46208 USA
Tel: +1 317 923 1951
Head of School: David Garner
Age range: 3–18
No. of pupils: 605 B274 G331
Fees: US$15,832
Curriculum: IBDP, IBMYP, IBPYP, USA
Language instr: English, French, Spanish, Mandarin

Saint Theodore Guerin High School
15300 Gray Road, Noblesville, Indiana IN 46062 USA
Tel: +1 317-582-0120
Principal: Rick Wagner
Curriculum: IBDP
Language instr: English

Kentucky

Sacred Heart Academy
3175 Lexington Road, Louisville, Kentucky KY 40206 USA
Tel: +1 502 897 6097
Head of School: Mary Lee McCoy
Age range: G14–18
No. of pupils: G828
Fees: $12,000
Curriculum: ACT, AP, IBDP, SAT, USA
Language instr: English

Sacred Heart Model School
3107 Lexington Road, Louisville, Kentucky KY 40206 USA
Tel: +1 502 896 3931
Head of School: Mary Beth Bowling
Curriculum: IBMYP
Language instr: English

Louisiana

BATON ROUGE INTERNATIONAL SCHOOL
For further details see p. 149
5015 Auto Plex Drive, Baton Rouge, Louisiana LA 70809 USA
Tel: +1 225 293 4338
Email: info@brisla.com
Website: www.brintl.com
Head of School: Nathalie Guyon
Age range: 6 weeks–18
Curriculum: ACT, AP, IBDP, IBMYP, SAT, USA
Language instr: English, French, Spanish, Chinese, Portuguese

Maryland

Archbishop Spalding High School
8080 New Cut Road, Severn, Maryland MD 21144 USA
Tel: +1 410 969 9105
Head of School: Kathleen Mahar
Curriculum: IBDP
Language instr: English

Our Lady of Good Counsel High School
17301 Old Vic Blvd, Olney, Maryland MD 20832 USA
Tel: +1 301 942 1155
Head of School: Patrick Bates
Age range: 13–17
No. of pupils: 1060 B509 G551
Curriculum: AP, IBDP, SAT
Language instr: English

Saint James Academy
3100 Monkton Road, Monkton, Maryland MD 21111 USA
Tel: +1 410 771 4816
Head of School: Karl Adler
Age range: 5–14
No. of pupils: 296 B151 G145
Curriculum: IBMYP
Language instr: English

Seneca Academy
15601 Germantown Road, Darnestown, Maryland MD 20874 USA
Tel: +1 301 869 3728
Head of School: E Brooke Carroll
Age range: 3–12
Curriculum: IBPYP

ST. TIMOTHY'S SCHOOL
For further details see p. 159
8400 Greenspring Ave, Stevenson, Maryland MD 21153 USA
Tel: +1 410 486 7400
Email: admis@stt.org
Website: www.stt.org
Head of School: Randy Stevens
No. of pupils: 180
Fees: $50,330
Curriculum: IBDP
Language instr: English

The Academy of the Holy Cross
4920 Strathmore Avenue, Kensington, Maryland MD 20895 USA
Tel: +1 301 929 6459
Head of School: Ann Nichols
Curriculum: IBDP
Language instr: English

The Boys' School of St Paul's Parish
PO Box 8100, Brooklandville, Maryland MD 21022-8100 USA
Tel: +1 410 825 4400
Head of School: Thomas Reid
Curriculum: IBDP
Language instr: English

The Calverton School
300 Calverton School Rd, Huntingtown, Maryland MD 20639 USA
Tel: +1 410 535 0216
Curriculum: IBDP

Massachusetts

British School of Boston
416 Pond Street, Boston, Massachusetts MA 02130 USA
Tel: +1 617 522 2261
Head of School: Paul Wiseman
Age range: 18 months–18 years
No. of pupils: 407 B193 G214
Fees: $13,900–$29,800
Curriculum: IBDP, UK
Language instr: English

Cathedral High School
260 Surrey Road, Springfield, Massachusetts MA 01095 USA
Tel: +1 413 782 5285
Head of School: John Miller
Curriculum: IBDP
Language instr: English

CHAMBERLAIN INTERNATIONAL SCHOOL
For further details see p. 150
1 Pleasant Street, PO Box 778, Middleboro, Massachusetts MA 02346 USA
Tel: +1 508 946 9348
Email: admissions@flcis.com
Website: www.chamberlainschool.org
Age range: 11–22
No. of pupils: 115
Language instr: English

Deerfield Academy
PO Box 87, Deerfield, Massachusetts MA 01342 USA
Tel: +413 772 0241
Head of School: Margarita O'Byrne Curtis
Language instr: English

International School of Boston
45 Matignon Road, Cambridge, Massachusetts MA 02140 USA
Tel: +1 617 499 1451
Head of School: Richard Bluementhal
Age range: 3–18
No. of pupils: 560 B260 G300
Fees: US$18,000
Curriculum: IBDP, FrenchBacc, USA
Language instr: French, English

STONELEIGH-BURNHAM SCHOOL
For further details see p. 160
574 Bernardston Road, Greenfield, Massachusetts MA 01301 USA
Tel: +1 413 774 2711
Website: www.sbschool.org
Head of School: Sally Mixsell
Age range: G11–20
No. of pupils: 155
Curriculum: IBDP, USA
Language instr: English

THE NEWMAN SCHOOL
For further details see p. 162
247 Marlborough Street, Boston, Massachusetts MA 02116 USA
Tel: +1 617 267 4530
Email: hlynch@newmanboston.org
Website: www.newmanboston.org
Head of School: J Harry Lynch
Age range: 13–18
No. of pupils: 240
Fees: US$32,000
Curriculum: IBDP
Language instr: English

Michigan

Detroit Country Day School
22305 West 13 Mile Road, Beverly Hills, Michigan MI 48025-4435 USA
Tel: +1 248 646 7717
Head of School: Glen Shilling
Age range: 3–18
No. of pupils: 1562 B847 G715
Curriculum: AP, IBDP, SAT
Language instr: English

Genesee Academy
9447 Corunna Road, Swartz Creek, Michigan MI 48473 USA
Tel: +1 810 250 7557
Curriculum: IBDP, IBMYP
Language instr: English

Huda School and Montessori
32220 Franklin Road, Franklin, Michigan MI 48025 USA
Tel: +1 248 626 0900
Head of School: Azra Ali
Curriculum: IBMYP

Kingsbury Country Day School
5000 Hosner Road, Oxford, Michigan MI 48370 USA
Tel: +1 248 628 2571
Head of School: Tom Mecsey
Curriculum: IBPYP
Language instr: English

Notre Dame Preparatory School & Marist Academy
1300 Giddings Road, Pontiac, Michigan MI 48340 USA
Tel: +1 248 373 5300
President: Leon M Olszamowski
Age range: 3–18
No. of pupils: 1126
Fees: US$13,212
Curriculum: ACT, AP, IBDP, IBMYP, IBPYP, SAT
Language instr: English

Minnesota

Rochester Arts and Sciences Academy
400 5th Avenue SW, Rochester, Minnesota MN 55902 USA
Tel: +1 507 206 4646
Principal: Vanessa Haluska
Age range: 3–12
No. of pupils: 55 B30 G25
Fees: $8,995
Curriculum: IBPYP, USA
Language instr: English

Rochester Montessori School
5099 7th Street NW, Rochester, Minnesota MN 55901 USA
Tel: +1 507 288 8725
Head of School: Paul Epstein
Curriculum: IBMYP

Saint John's Preparatory School
1857 Watertower Road, Collegeville, Minnesota MN 56321 USA
Tel: +1 320 363 3315
Head of School: Timothy Backous
Curriculum: IBDP
Language instr: English

St. Jude of the Lake School
600 Mahtomedi Ave, Mahtomedi, Minnesota MN 55115 USA
Tel: +1 651 426 2562
Curriculum: IBPYP
Language instr: English

Montana

Missoula International School
1100 Harrison Street, Missoula, Montana MT 59802 USA
Tel: +1 406 542 9924
Head of School: Julie Lennox
Age range: 3–14
No. of pupils: 186 B90 G96
Fees: $8,995
Curriculum: IBPYP
Language instr: Spanish, English

New Hampshire

New Hampton School
70 Main Street, New Hampton, New Hampshire NH 03256 USA
Tel: +1 603 677 3401
Headmaster: Andrew Menke
Age range: 14–19
No. of pupils: 320
Fees: US$51,700
Curriculum: IBDP
Language instr: English

New Jersey

Newark Academy
91 South Orange Avenue, Livingston, New Jersey NJ 07039 USA
Tel: +1 973 992 7000
Head of School: Donald M Austin
Age range: 11–18
No. of pupils: 582
Fees: $33,330
Curriculum: AP, IBDP
Language instr: English

St Dominic Academy
2572 Kennedy Boulevard, Jersey City, New Jersey NJ 07304 USA
Tel: +1 201 434 5938
Head of School: Barbara C Griffin
No. of pupils: 525
Curriculum: AP
Language instr: English

Waterfront Montessori
150 Warren St., Suite 108, Jersey City, New Jersey NJ 7302 USA
Tel: +1 201 333 5600
Curriculum: IBMYP
Language instr: English

New Mexico

Desert Academy at Santa Fe
7300 Old Santa Fe Trail, Santa Fe, New Mexico NM 87505 USA
Tel: +1 505 992 8284
Head of School: Terry Passalacqua
No. of pupils: 160 B80 G80
Fees: US$14,900
Curriculum: IBDP, IBMYP
Language instr: English

UNITED WORLD COLLEGE – USA
For further details see p. 163
PO Box 248, Route 65, Montezuma, New Mexico NM 87731 USA
Tel: +1 505 426 3394
Email: admission@uwc-usa.org
Website: www.uwc-usa.org
President: Mukul Kumar
Age range: 16–19
No. of pupils: 200 B100 G100
Curriculum: IBDP
Language instr: English

New York

Archbishop Walsh High School
208 North 24th Street, Olean, New York NY 14760 USA
Tel: +1 716 372 8122
Principal: Mykal Karl
Curriculum: IBDP

Brooklyn Friends School
375 Pearl Street, Brooklyn, New York, New York NY 11201 USA
Tel: +1 718 852 1029
Head of School: Larry Weiss
No. of pupils: 644
Curriculum: IBDP
Language instr: English

Convent of the Sacred Heart
1 East 91 Street, New York, New York NY 10128 USA
Tel: +1 212 722 4745
Headmistress: Mary Blake
Age range: G3–18
No. of pupils: 635

DWIGHT SCHOOL
For further details see p. 153
291 Central Park West, New York, New York NY 10024 USA
Tel: +1 212 724 7524
Email: admissions@dwight.edu
Website: www.dwight.edu
Chancellor: Stephen H. Spahn
Age range: 2–18
No. of pupils: 806
Fees: Day US$40,000
Curriculum: ACT, IBDP, IBMYP, IBPYP, IBCC, SAT, TOEFL
Language instr: English

EF ACADEMY NEW YORK
For further details see p. 155
100 Marymount Avenue, Tarrytown, New York NY 10591-3796 USA
Tel: Admissions: +1 914 597 7241
Email: admissionsia@ef.com
Website: www.ef.com/academy
Head of School: Brian Mahoney
Age range: 14–19
No. of pupils: 590
Fees: $44,700
Curriculum: IBDP
Language instr: English

French-American School of New York
525 Fenimore Road, Mamaroneck, New York NY 10543 USA
Tel: +1 914 250 0000
Head of School: Joël Peinado
Age range: 3–16
No. of pupils: 843 B431 G412
Curriculum: AP, National, FrenchBacc, SAT
Language instr: English, French

Hackley School
293 Benedict Ave, Tarrytown, New York NY 10591 USA
Tel: +1 914 631 0128
Headmaster: Walter C. Johnson
Language instr: English

International School of Brooklyn
477 Court Street, Brooklyn, New York, New York NY 11231 USA
Tel: +1 718 369 3023
Head of School: Rebecca Skinner
Curriculum: IBPYP
Language instr: English, French, Spanish

Léman Manhattan Preparatory School
41 Broad Street, New York, New York NY 10003 USA
Tel: +1 212 232 0266 (236)
Head of School: Drew Alexander
Curriculum: IBDP
Language instr: English

Lycée Français de New York
505 East 75th Street, New York, New York NY 10021 USA
Tel: +1 212 369 1400 ext 3103
Head of School: Sean Lynch
Age range: 3–18
No. of pupils: 1350
Curriculum: National, FrenchBacc
Language instr: French

Lyceum Kennedy – French American School
225 East 43rd Street, New York, New York NY 10017 USA
Tel: +1 212 681 1877
Head of School: Laurent Bonardi
Curriculum: IBDP
Language instr: English, French

Saint Edmund Preparatory High School
2474 Ocean Avenue, Brooklyn, New York, New York NY 11229 USA
Tel: +1 718 743 6100
Head of School: John P Lorenzetti
Curriculum: IBDP
Language instr: English

The British International School of New York
20 Waterside Plaza, New York, New York NY 10010 USA
Tel: +1 212 481 2700
Headmaster: William T Phelps
Age range: 3–14
No. of pupils: 225
Fees: $33,950
Curriculum: IBMYP, IBPYP, SAT, UK
Language instr: English

United Nations International School
24-50 Franklin D Roosevelt Drive, New York, New York NY 10010 USA
Tel: +1 212 684 7400
Head of School: Jane Camblin
Age range: 5–18
No. of pupils: 1573 B763 G778
Fees: $30,515–$33,975
Curriculum: IBDP
Language instr: English

North Carolina

British American School of Charlotte
7000 Endhaven Lane, Charlotte, North Carolina NC 28277 USA
Tel: +1 704 341 3236
Headmaster: Allan Strange
Age range: 3–14
No. of pupils: 118 B68 G50
Fees: US$8,745–US$16,635
Curriculum: UK

Charlotte Country Day School
1440 Carmel Road, Charlotte, North Carolina NC 28226 USA
Tel: +1 704 9434522
Head of School: Mark Reed
Age range: 4–18
No. of pupils: 1600
Curriculum: AP, IBDP
Language instr: English

Hickory Day School
2535 21st Ave NE, Hickory, North Carolina NC 28601 USA
Tel: +1 828 256 9492
Head of School: Janice Dollar
Curriculum: IBPYP
Language instr: English

Morganton Day School
305 West Concord Street, Morganton, North Carolina NC 28655 USA
Tel: +1 828 437 6782
Head of School: Melanie Mikusa
Age range: 4–13
No. of pupils: 100 B45 G55
Fees: $8,500
Curriculum: IBPYP
Language instr: English

Ohio

Central Catholic High School
2550 Cherry Street, Toldeo, Ohio OH 43608 USA
Tel: +1 419 255 2280
Head of School: Michael Kaucher
Age range: 13–18
Curriculum: IBDP
Language instr: English

Notre Dame Academy
3535 W Sylvania Avenue, Toledo, Ohio OH 43623 USA
Tel: +1 419 475 9359
Head of School: Mary Ann Culpert
Curriculum: IBDP

St Edward High School
13500 Detroit Avenue, Lakewood, Ohio OH 44107 USA
Tel: +1 216 221 3777
Head of School: Jim Kubacki
Curriculum: IBDP

The Montessori High School at University Circle
10923 Magnolia Drive, Apt C, Cleveland, Ohio OH 44106 USA
Tel: +1 216 421 3033
Head of School: David Kahn
Curriculum: IBDP
Language instr: English

Oregon

French American International School
8500 NW Johnson Street, Portland, Oregon OR 97229 USA
Tel: +1 503 292 9111
Head of School: Emmanuelle Burk
Curriculum: IBMYP, IBPYP
Language instr: English, French

Seven Peaks School
19660 SW Mountaineer Way, Bend, Oregon OR 97702 USA
Tel: +1 541 382 7755
Head of School: Megan Martin
Curriculum: IBMYP
Language instr: English

The International School
025 SW Sherman Street, Portland, Oregon OR 97210 USA
Tel: +1 503 226 2496
Head of School: Alfonso Orsini
Curriculum: IBPYP
Language instr: Chinese, Japanese, Spanish

Pennsylvania

George School
1690 Newtown Langhorne Rd, Newtown, Pennsylvania PA 18940 USA
Tel: +1 215 579 6703
Head of School: Nancy Starmer
Age range: 13–19
No. of pupils: 540 B270 G270
Fees: $32,860
Curriculum: ACT, AP, IBDP, SAT
Language instr: English

Mercyhurst Preparatory School
538 East Grandview Boulevard, Erie, Pennsylvania PA 16504 USA
Tel: +1 814 824 2323
Head of School: Deborah Laughlin
Age range: 13–19
No. of pupils: 600
Fees: $7,400
Curriculum: IBDP, SAT
Language instr: English

The Harrisburg Academy
10 Erford Road, Wormleysburg, Pennsylvania PA 17043 USA
Tel: +1 717 763 7811
Head of School: James Newman
Curriculum: IBDP
Language instr: English

Vincentian Academy
8100 McKnight Road, Pittsburgh, Pennsylvania PA 15237 USA
Tel: +1 412 364 1616
Head of School: John Fedko
No. of pupils: 230
Fees: $10,600
Curriculum: IBDP
Language instr: English

Westtown School
975 Westtown Rd, West Chester, Pennsylvania PA 19382 USA
Tel: +1 610 399 0123
Principal – Upper School: Eric Mayer
Language instr: English

Rhode Island

Prout School
4640 Tower Hill Road, Wakefield, Rhode Island RI 02879 USA
Tel: +1 401 789 9262
Head of School: Gary Delneo
Age range: 14–18
No. of pupils: 647
Curriculum: IBDP
Language instr: English

South Carolina

Christ Church Episcopal School
245 Cavalier Drive, Greenville, South Carolina SC 29607 USA
Tel: +1 864 299 1522
Headmaster: Leonard Kupersmith
No. of pupils: 990
Curriculum: IBDP, IBPYP
Language instr: English

Christ Our King-Stella Maris School
1183 Russell Drive, Mt Pleasant, South Carolina SC 29464 USA
Tel: +1 843 884 4721
Head of School: John Byrnes
Curriculum: IBMYP

Spartanburg Day School
1701 Skylyn Drive, Spartanburg, South Carolina SC 29307 USA
Tel: +1 864 582 8380
Head of School: Chris Dorrance
No. of pupils: 500
Curriculum: IBPYP
Language instr: English

Tennessee

Brown International Academy
718 East 8th Street, Chattanooga, Tennessee TN 37403 USA
Tel: +1 423 209 5760
Head of School: Jennifer Spates
Curriculum: IBPYP
Language instr: English, Spanish

Lausanne Collegiate School
1381 West Massey Road, Memphis, Tennessee TN 38120 USA
Tel: +1 901 474 1001
Head of School: Stuart McCathie
Curriculum: IBDP
Language instr: English

Texas

ALCUIN SCHOOL
For further details see p. 148
6144 Churchill Way, Dallas, Texas TX 75230 USA
Tel: +1 972 239 1745
Email: annie.villalobos@alcuinschool.org
Website: www.alcuinschool.org
Head of School: Walter Sorensen
Age range: 18 months–18 years
No. of pupils: 500
Fees: US$13,000–US$22,600
Curriculum: IBMYP, SAT
Language instr: English

British School of Houston
4211 Watonga Boulevard, Houston, Texas TX 77092 USA
Tel: +1 713 290 9025
Head Teacher: Stephen Foxwell
Age range: 3–19
No. of pupils: 850
Fees: $23,175
Curriculum: IBDP, IBCC, UK, GCSE, IGCSE
Language instr: English

CC Mason Elementary
1501 N. Lakeline Blvd, Cedar Park, Texas TX 78613 USA
Tel: +1 512 570 5500
Head of School: Jamie Klassen
Curriculum: IBPYP
Language instr: English

Cunae International School LLC
5655 Creekside Forest Drive, Spring, Texas TX 77389 USA
Tel: +1 281 516 3770
Head of School: Anji Price
Curriculum: IBDP

Dallas International School
6039 Churchill Way, Dallas, Texas TX 75230 USA
Tel: +1 972 991 6379
Head of School: Pierre Vittoz
No. of pupils: 550
Fees: $10,700–$17,000
Curriculum: IBDP, FrenchBacc, SAT
Language instr: English, French

International School of Texas
4105 Eck Lane, Austin, Texas, Texas TX 78734 USA
Tel: +1 512 351 3403
Headmistress: Grainne O'Rielly
Language instr: English

Jardín de Niños
8707 Mountain Crest Dr, Austin, Texas TX 78735 USA
Tel: +1 512 299 5731
Head of School: Adriana Rodriguez
Curriculum: IBPYP
Language instr: English

St Paul's Episcopal Day School
517 Columbus Avenue, Waco, Texas TX 76701 USA
Tel: +1 254 753-0246
Head of School: Matthew Blake
No. of pupils: 160
Curriculum: IBPYP
Language instr: English

St. Stephens Episcopal School Houston
1800 Sul Ross, Houston, Texas TX 77098 USA
Tel: +1 713 821 9101
Head of School: David Coe
Curriculum: IBDP
Language instr: English

The Awty International School
7455 Awty School Lane, Houston, Texas TX 77055-7222 USA
Tel: +1 (713) 686 4850
Head of School: Lisa A. H. Darling
Age range: 3–18
No. of pupils: 1557 VIth95
Curriculum: IBDP, FrenchBacc
Language instr: English, French

The Magellan International School
7938 Great Northern Boulevard, Austin, Texas TX 78757 USA
Tel: +1 512 782 2327
Head of School: María Isabel León
Age range: 3–11
No. of pupils: 275
Curriculum: IBPYP
Language instr: English, Spanish

The Post Oak School
4600 Bissonnet Street, Bellaire, Texas TX 77401 USA
Tel: +1 713 661 6688
Head of School: John Long
Curriculum: IBDP
Language instr: English

The Village School
13077 Westella Drive, Houston, Texas TX 77077 USA
Tel: +1 281 496 7900
Head of School: Bernard Mitchell
Curriculum: IBDP
Language instr: English

The Westwood School
14340 Proton Road, Dallas, Texas TX 75244 USA
Tel: +1 972 239 8598
Head of School: Pam Butler
Age range: 1–19
No. of pupils: 280
Fees: $7,000–$14,900
Curriculum: IBDP, IBMYP
Language instr: English

The Woodlands Academy Preparatory School
27440 Kuykendahl Road, Tomball, Texas TX 77375 USA
Tel: +1 281 516 0600
Head of School: Kenneth West
Curriculum: IBPYP
Language instr: English

Trent InternationalE School
2555 Cordes Dr, Sugarland, Texas TX 77479 USA
Tel: +1 281 980 5800
Age range: 3–19
Curriculum: ACT, AP, IPC, SAT, USA
Language instr: English

Westlake Academy
2600 Ottinger Road, Westlake, Texas TX 76262 USA
Tel: +1 817 4905757
Head of School: Clint Calzini
Age range: 5–18
No. of pupils: 418 B197 G221
Curriculum: ACT, AP, IBDP, IBMYP, IBPYP, SAT, USA
Language instr: English

Vermont

Long Trail School
1045 Kirby Hollow Road, Dorset, Vermont VT 05251 USA
Tel: +1 802 867 5717
Head of School: John Suitor
Age range: 10–19
Fees: $15,750
Curriculum: IBDP
Language instr: English

Virginia

Carlbrook School
PO Box 755, Halifax, Virginia VA 24558 USA
Tel: +1 434 476 2406
Headmaster: Tim Brace
No. of pupils: 100

Carlisle School

PO Box 5388, Martinsville,
Virginia VA 24115 USA
Tel: +1 276 632 7288
Head of School: Simon
Owen-Williams
Age range: 3–19
No. of pupils: 430
Curriculum: AP, IBDP,
IBMYP, IBPYP, SAT
Language instr: English

Islamic Saudi Academy

8333 Richmond Highway,
Alexandria, Virginia VA 22309 USA
Tel: +1 703 780 0606
Director General: Faridah Turkistani
Curriculum: IBDP, IBMYP
Language instr: English

Mary Passage Middle School

400 Atkinson Way, Newport
News, Virginia VA 23608 USA
Tel: +1 757 886 7600
Head of School: Janelle Spitz
Language instr: English

Saint Mary's Catholic School

9501 Gayton Road, Richmond,
Virginia VA 23229 USA
Tel: +1 804 740 1048
Head of School: Thomas Dertinger
Curriculum: IBMYP
Language instr: English

St Michael's Episcopal School

8706 Quaker Lane, Richmond,
Virginia VA 23235 USA
Tel: +1 804 272 3514
Head of School: Michael G Turner
Age range: 11–14
No. of pupils: 375
Curriculum: IBMYP
Language instr: English

Trinity Episcopal School

3850 Pittaway Road, Richmond,
Virginia VA 23235 USA
Tel: +1 804 272 5864
Head of School: Thomas Aycock
Age range: 13–18
No. of pupils: 350
Curriculum: AP, IBDP
Language instr: English

Trinity Lutheran School

6812 River Road, Newport
News, Virginia VA 23607 USA
Tel: +1 757 245 2576
Curriculum: IBPYP
Language instr: English

Washington

Annie Wright School

827 North Tacoma Avenue,
Tacoma, Washington
WA 98403 USA
Tel: +1 253 272 2216
Head of School: Christian Sullivan
Curriculum: IBDP
Language instr: English

Forest Ridge School of the Sacred Heart

4800 139th Avenue SE, Bellevue,
Washington WA 98006 USA
Tel: +1 425 641 0700
Head of School: Mark Pierotti
Curriculum: IBDP

Saint George's School

2929 W. Waikiki Road, Spokane,
Washington WA 99208 USA
Tel: +1 509 466 1636 (ext:331)
Head of School: Joseph Kennedy
Curriculum: IBDP
Language instr: English

Soundview School

6515 196th Street SW, Lynnwood,
Washington WA 98036 USA
Tel: +1 425 778 8572
Head of School: Inae Piercy
Curriculum: IBMYP
Language instr: English

West Sound Academy

16571 Creative Drive NE, Poulsbo,
Washington WA 98370 USA
Tel: +1 360 598 5954
Head of School: Barrie Hillman
Curriculum: IBDP

Wisconsin

Catholic Memorial High School

601 East College Avenue,
Waukesha, Wisconsin WI 53186 USA
Tel: +1 262 542 7101
Head of School: Paul Hartmann
No. of pupils: 750
Curriculum: IBDP
Language instr: English

Madison Country Day School

5606 River Road, Waunakee,
Wisconsin WI 53597 USA
Tel: +1 608 850 6000
Head of School: Luke Felker
Age range: 3–18
Curriculum: IBDP
Language instr: English

Notre Dame de la Baie Academy

610 Maryhill Drive, Green Bay,
Wisconsin WI 54303 USA
Tel: +1 920 429 6100
Principal: John Ravizza
Age range: 14–18
No. of pupils: 731 B377 G354
Fees: $6,700
Curriculum: ACT, IBDP, USA
Language instr: English

Wisconsin International School

405 Grant Street, De Pere,
Wisconsin WI 54115 USA
Tel: +1 920 632 7368
Head of School: Mary
Vanden Busch
Curriculum: IBPYP

Wyoming

Journeys School of Teton Science Schools

700 Coyote Canyon Road,
Jackson, Wyoming WY 83001 USA
Tel: +1 307 733 3729
Head of School: Nate McClennen
Curriculum: IBDP, IBMYP
Language instr: English

Virgin Islands (US)

Virgin Islands Montessori School

6936 Vessup Lane, St Thomas,
00802 Virgin Islands (US)
Tel: +1 340 775 6360
Head of School: Michael Bornn
Curriculum: IBDP, IBMYP
Language instr: English

International schools in South America

Schools ordered A–Z by Country

Key to directory

Country

Name of school or college

Indicates that this school
has a profile

Address and contact number

Head's name

Age range

Number of pupils.
B = boys G = girls VIth = sixth form

Fees per annum.
Day = fees for day pupils.
WB = fees for weekly boarders.
FB = fees for full boarders.

Curriculum

Language of instruction

Memberships/Accreditation

Whereford

College Academy

For further details see p.00

Which Street, Whosville,
Wherefordshire AB12 3CD

Tel: 01000 000000

Head Master: Dr A Person

Age range: 11–18

No. of pupils:
660 B330 G330 VIth 200

Fees: Day £11,000
WB £16,000 FB £20,000

Curriculum:
National, IBDP, ALevs

Language instr:
English, French

(AISA) (COB) (EAR)

Key to icons

Key to symbols:

(†) Boys' school

(♦) Girls' school

(⚑) Boarding accommodation

Member of:

(AISA) Association of International
Schools in Africa

(CEE) Central and Eastern European
Schools Association

(EAR) East Asia Regional Council of
Overseas Schools

(ECIS) European Council of
International Schools

(RS) Round Square

Accreditation:

(CIS) Council of International Schools

(COB) Council of British International
Schools

Please note: Schools are coeducational day schools unless otherwise indicated

Argentina

Asociación Cultural Pestalozzi
R Freire 1882, C1428CYB Ciudad de Buenos Aires, Argentina
Tel: +54 11 4555 3688
Rector: Luis A Mesyngier
Age range: 2–18
No. of pupils: 346
Curriculum: IBDP
Language instr: Spanish, German

Asociación Escuelas Lincoln
Andres Ferreyra 4073, B1637 AOS La Lucila, Buenos Aires, Argentina
Tel: +54 11 4851 1700
Superintendent: Philip Joslin
Age range: 4–18
No. of pupils: 830 B433 G397
Fees: $17,500
Curriculum: IBDP, USA
Language instr: English

Barker College
Mitre 131, Lomas de Zamora, Buenos Aires, 1832 Argentina
Tel: +54 11 4292 1107
Principal: Karen Thomas
Age range: 2–17
No. of pupils: 510 B222 G290
Curriculum: IGCSE
Language instr: Spanish, English

Belgrano Day School
Juramento 3035 (c1428doa), Ciudad de Buenos Aires, Argentina
Tel: +54 11 4781 6011
Director: Steven Page
Age range: 2–18
No. of pupils: 1160 B612 G548
Curriculum: National, UK, IGCSE, ALevs
Language instr: Spanish, English
(RS)

Colegio Carmen Arriola de Marin
Av del Libertador 17.115, San Isidro, Buenos Aires, 1642 Argentina
Tel: +54 11 4743 0028
Head of School: Carlos Espinosa
Curriculum: IBDP

Colegio De La Salle
Ayacucho 665, Buenos Aires, 1025 Argentina
Tel: +54 011 4374 0657/97
Head of School: Mata Ochoa
No. of pupils: 286
Curriculum: IBDP
Language instr: Spanish

Colegio de Todos Los Santos
Thames 798, Villa Adelina, 1607 Buenos Aires, Argentina
Tel: +54 114 766 3878
Head of School: María Teresa Mayochi de Arza
Age range: 2–18
No. of pupils: 700
Curriculum: IBDP
Language instr: Spanish, English

Colegio Franco Argentino
Lavalle 1067, Acassuso, San Isidro, Buenos Aires, B1641ALU Argentina
Tel: +54 11 4792 4628
Head of School: Patricia Elena Chama
Curriculum: IBDP
Language instr: Spanish

Colegio Lincoln
Olleros 2283, Buenos Aires, 1426 Argentina
Tel: +54 11 4778 1997
Head of School: Amalia C Lodi
Age range: 2–18
No. of pupils: 800 B400 G400 VIth35
Curriculum: IBDP, National, UK
Language instr: Spanish, English

Colegio Mark Twain
José Roque Funes 1525, Córdoba, 5009 Argentina
Tel: +543 514 830 664
Head of School: Pamela French
Age range: 3–17
No. of pupils: VIth25
Curriculum: IBDP
Language instr: Spanish

Colegio Padre Luis Maria Etcheverry Boneo
Juncal 2131, Buenos Aires, 1125 Argentina
Tel: +54 11 4822 3687
Head of School: Norah Armour
Curriculum: IBDP
Language instr: Spanish
(♣)

Colegio Palermo Chico A-871
Thames 2041/37, Buenos Aires, 1425 Argentina
Tel: +54 114 774 3975
Head of School: María Laura Pérez Maraviglia de Rebollo Paz
Curriculum: IBDP
Language instr: Spanish

Colegio San Ignacio
Guardias Nacionales 1400, Río Cuarto (Cba.), X5806DWJ Argentina
Tel: +54 (358) 464 8484/0802
Headmaster of School: Pablo Esteban Cedro
Age range: 12–18
No. of pupils: 125 B60 G65
Curriculum: IBDP, IGCSE
Language instr: Spanish, English

Colegio San Marcos
SECUNDARIA, Mariano Alegre 334, Monte Grande, Buenos Aires, 1842 Argentina
Tel: +54 114 296 4215
Head of School: Gabriela Alvarez de Martin
Curriculum: IBDP, National, UK, IGCSE
Language instr: Spanish

Colegio San Patricio
Moreno y Camino a las Higueritas, Yerba Buena, Tucumán, 4107 Argentina
Tel: +54 381 4250 708
Head of School: Diana Parrau de Pindar
Curriculum: IBDP
Language instr: Spanish

Colegio San Patricio de Luján
Provincia de Buenos Aires, Tucuman y Gaona sin / número, Luján, Buenos Aires, 6700 Argentina
Tel: +54 2323 437998
Head of School: Lucía Reneé Cornellá de Blanco
Curriculum: IBDP
Language instr: Spanish

Colegio San Pedro Apostol
Av Piamonte s/n, CP: X5016DQB, Córdoba, Argentina
Tel: +54 3 51 4846584
Head of School: Gabriela Cristina Peretti
Curriculum: IBDP

Colegio Santa María
Coronel Suárez 453, Salta, 4400 Argentina
Tel: +54 387 4213127
Head of School: María Andrea Domínguez de Abdo
Curriculum: IBDP
Language instr: Spanish
(OS)

Colegio Tarbut
Rosales 3019, Olivos, Buenos Aires, 1636 Argentina
Tel: +54 11 4794 3444
Executive Director: Roberto Dvoskin
Curriculum: IBDP, IGCSE
Language instr: Spanish

Deutsche Schule Temperley
Av Fernández 27, Temperley, Buenos Aires 1934 Argentina
Tel: + 54 11 4292-0959
Head of School: Mariana Vogt
Curriculum: IBDP
Language instr: English, Spanish

Dover High School
San Martín y Ruta 26, Ing Maschwitz, Buenos Aires, 1623 Argentina
Tel: +54 93488 441106
Head of School: Mirta Teruel
Curriculum: IBDP
Language instr: English, Spanish

Escuela Goethe Rosario – 8222
España 440, Rosario, España 430, Rosario, Santa Fe, 2000 Argentina
Tel: +54 3 414 263024
Head of School: María Luisa Dominato
Age range: 2–18
Curriculum: IBDP
Language instr: Spanish

Holy Trinity College
Gascón 544, Mar del Plata, 7600 Argentina
Tel: +54 223 486 3471
Age range: 2–18
No. of pupils: 637 B328 G309
Curriculum: IBDP
Language instr: English, Spanish

Instituto Ballester
San Martin 444, (1653) Villa Ballester, Buenos Aires, 1653 Argentina
Tel: +54 11 4768 0760
Head of School: Susanne Lutz
No. of pupils: 1583
Curriculum: IBDP
Language instr: Spanish

Instituto San Jorge
Godoy Cruz, Pedro J Godoy 1191, Mendoza, 5547 Argentina
Tel: +54 614 287 247
Head of School: Marcela Carrizo
Curriculum: IBDP
Language instr: Spanish

Instituto Santa Brigida
Av Gaona 2068, C 1416DRV, Buenos Aires, 1416DRV Argentina
Tel: +54 1 145 811 268
Head of School: Silvia Luppi
No. of pupils: B150 G141
Curriculum: IBDP
Language instr: Spanish

Islands International School
Amenábar 1840, Buenos Aires, 1428 Argentina
Tel: +54 11 4787 2294
General Director: Estela Irrera de Pallaro
Age range: 2–18
No. of pupils: 472 B201 G271
Curriculum: IBDP
Language instr: Spanish

New Model International School
El Salvador 3952/58, Buenos Aires, 1175 Argentina
Tel: +54 11 4825 2900
Head of School: Carlos Tonelli
Language instr: Spanish

Northern International School
Ruta 8km 61.5, Fátima, Pilar, Buenos Aires, 1633 Argentina
Tel: +54 2322 49 1208
Head of School: Estela Irrera de Pallaro
Age range: 2–18
Curriculum: IBDP
Language instr: Spanish, English, Italian

NORTHLANDS SCHOOL
For further details see p. 170
Olivos Site: Roma 1248,
Olivos, Provincia de
Buenos Aires, Argentina
Tel: +54 11 4711 8400
Email: admissionsolivos@
northlands.edu.ar
Website: www.northlands.edu.ar
Acting Principal: Marisa Perazzo
Age range: 2–18
Curriculum: IBDP, IBPYP,
National, IGCSE
Language instr: English, Spanish

Northlands School Nordelta
Nordelta site: Av de los Colegios
590, Nordelta, Privincia de Buenos
Aires, B1670NNN Argentina
Tel: +54 11 4871 2668/9
Head of School: Susana Magenta
Curriculum: IBDP, IBPYP,
National, IGCSE
Language instr: Spanish, English

Quilmes High School
Rivadavia 460, Quilmes,
Buenos Aires, 1878 Argentina
Tel: +54 11 4253 0123
Head of School: Juan Díaz
Age range: 5–18
No. of pupils: 650 B350 G300 VIth52
Curriculum: IBDP, ALevs
Language instr: Spanish

Saint Mary of the Hills School
Xul Solar 6650, San Fernando,
Buenos Aires, 1646 Argentina
Tel: +54 11 4714 0330
Head of School: Graciela
Borrás de Xanthopoulos
Curriculum: IBDP
Language instr: Spanish, English

Saint Mary of the Hills School Sede Pilar
Ruta 25 y Caamaño, Pilar,
Buenos Aires, 1644 Argentina
Tel: +54 2304 458181
Head of School: Graciela
Xanthopoulos
Curriculum: IBDP
Language instr: Spanish

Southern International School
Autopista BS As-La, Plata km 30.5,
Hudson, Berazategui, Prov de
Buenos Aires 1884 Argentina
Tel: +54 11 4215 3636
Head of School: Estela
María Irrera de Pallaro
Age range: 4–18
No. of pupils: 360
Curriculum: IBDP
Language instr: Spanish

St Andrew's Scots School
Roque Saenz Peña 601, Olivos,
Buenos Aires, 1636 Argentina
Tel: +54 114 790 5371
Headmaster: Gabriel Rshaid
Age range: 3–18
No. of pupils: 1866 B950 G916
Curriculum: IBDP, National, IGCSE
Language instr: English, Spanish

St Catherine's Moorlands – Tortuguitas
Ruta Panamericana Km 38
Ramal Pilar, Tortuguitas (1667),
Buenos Aires, Argentina
Tel: +54 (348) 463 9000
Head of School: Mabel
Mary Manzitti
Age range: 3–18
Curriculum: IBPYP,
National, UK, IGCSE
Language instr: English

St Catherine's School – Moorlands
Carbajal 3250, Buenos
Aires, 1426 Argentina
Tel: +54 11 4552 4353
Head of School: Mabel
Mary Manzitti
Age range: 3–18
No. of pupils: 1738 B792 G946
Curriculum: IBDP, IBMYP,
IBPYP, National, UK
Language instr: English, Spanish
(ISA)

St George's College
Guido 800, B1878WAA Quilmes,
Buenos Aires, B1878WAA Argentina
Tel: +54 11 4350 7900
Headmaster: Derek Pringle
Age range: 3–18
No. of pupils: B469 G351 VIth62
Curriculum: IBDP, IBPYP,
National, UK, IGCSE
Language instr: English, Spanish

St George's College North
Don Bosco y Mosconi S/N, Los
Polvorines, Buenos Aires, Prov.
Buenos Aires 1613 Argentina
Tel: +54 114 663 2494
Head of School: Ian Tate
Age range: 2–18
No. of pupils: 640 B340 G300 VIth82
Curriculum: IBDP, IBMYP,
IBPYP, National, IGCSE
Language instr: English, Spanish

St John's School
España 348/370, Beccar,
Buenos Aires, 1643 Argentina
Tel: +54 11 4513 4400
**Head of Secondary
School:** Florencia Noguera
Curriculum: IBDP
Language instr: Spanish, English

St John's School, Pilar
Panamericana, ramal Pilar
Km 48.8, Pilar, Buenos Aires,
B1629MYA Argentina
Tel: +54 2322 667 667
Head of School: María
Eugenia Duri de Oliden
Curriculum: IBDP
Language instr: English, Spanish

St Mary's International College
Martin Garcia 1435 / 1236
/ 1501, Ezeiza, Buenos
Aires, 1804 Argentina
Tel: +54 11 4295 2896
Head of School: Susana
Raquel Raffo
No. of pupils: 870
Curriculum: IBDP
Language instr: English

St Matthew's College
Moldes 1469, Buenos
Aires, 1426 Argentina
Tel: +54 11 4783 1110
Principal: Patricia Lische de Balboni
Age range: 2–18
Curriculum: IBDP, National, IGCSE
Language instr: Spanish, English

St Matthew's College North
Caamano 493, Pilar, Buenos
Aires, 1631 Argentina
Tel: +54 2322 693600
Head of School: Luz Balboni
Age range: 3–18
No. of pupils: 1100
Curriculum: IBDP
Language instr: English, Spanish

St Xavier's College
José Antonio Cabrera 5901,
Buenos Aires, 1414 Argentina
Tel: +54 114 777 5011/14
Head of School: Maria Luz
Paz de Bustamante
Curriculum: IBDP
Language instr: English

Sunrise School
Rio Negro, Casilla de
Correo 79 (8324) Cipolletti,
Río Negro, Argentina
Tel: +54 299, 4786590
Head of School: Anne
Lyons Buchanan
No. of pupils: 400
Curriculum: IBDP
Language instr: Spanish

Villa Devoto School
Pedro Morán 4441, Buenos
Aires, 1419 Argentina
Tel: +54 114 501 9419
Head of School: María
José Montenegro
Curriculum: IBDP
Language instr: English and Spanish

Washington School
Buenos Aires, Argentina,
Avenida Federico Lacroze 2012,
Buenos Aires, 1426 Argentina
Tel: +54 114 7728131
Head of School: Daniela Pérez
No. of pupils: 700
Fees: $528–$1,508
Curriculum: IBDP, IBPYP
Language instr: Spanish

Woodville School
Av de los Pioneros 2900, San Carlos
de Bariloche, 8400 Argentina
Tel: +54 2944 44 11 33
Head of School: Stephen Cohen
Age range: 16–18
No. of pupils: 169 B83 G86 VIth45
Curriculum: IBDP, IGCSE
Language instr: Spanish, English

Bolivia

American Cooperative School
c/o American Embassy,
La Paz, Bolivia
Tel: +591 2 279 2302
Superintendent: Sharon Schauss
Age range: 4–18

American International School of Bolivia
Casilla 5309, Cochabamba, Bolivia
Tel: +591 4 428 8577
Head of School: Selena Skelly
Age range: 3–18
No. of pupils: 240
Curriculum: IBDP
Language instr: English

Colegio Alemán Santa Cruz
Casilla 624, Av San Martin
s/n, Santa Cruz, Bolivia
Tel: +591 3 3326820
Head of School: Ulrich Lohrbach
Curriculum: IBDP
Language instr: Spanish

Colegio Saint Andrew's
Casilla 1679, Av Las Retomas
s/n, La Florida, La Paz, Bolivia
Tel: +591 2 2792484
Head of School: Alejandro
Zegarra Saldaña
Curriculum: IBDP
Language instr: English

Brazil

American School of Brasilia
SGAS 605, Conjunto E, Lotes
34/37, Brasilia 70200-650, Brazil
Tel: +55 61 3442 9700
Head of School: Barry Dequanne
Age range: 3–19
No. of pupils: 569 B262 G307
Curriculum: IBDP, USA
Language instr: English

American School of Campinas – Escola Americana de Campinas
Rua Cajamar, #35, Campinas, SP 13090-860 Brazil
Tel: +55 19 21021006
Head of School: Stephen Herrera
Age range: 3–18
No. of pupils: 444 B219 G225
Curriculum: ACT, IBDP, SAT

Associação Educacional Luterana Bom Jesus / IELUSC
Rua Princesa Isabel, 438, Joinville, Santa Catarina, 89201-270 Brazil
Tel: +55 47 3026 8000
Curriculum: IBDP

Associação Escola Graduada De São Paulo
Caixa Postal 1976, São Paulo, 01059-970 Brazil
Tel: +55 11 3747 4800
Superintendent: Lee Fertig
Age range: 2–18
No. of pupils: 1114 B566 G548
Curriculum: ACT, IBDP, SAT, USA
Language instr: English

Centro Internacional de Educaçào Integrada
Estrada do Pontal 2093, Recreio dos Bandeirantes, 22.785-560 Rio de Janeiro, 22785 Brazil
Tel: +55 21 2490 1673
Head of School: Claudia Stadelmann
Curriculum: IBDP, IBPYP
Language instr: English

Colégio Suíço-Brasileiro de Curitiba
Rua Wanda dos Santos Mallmann, 537, Jardim Pinhais, Pinhais, Paraná, 83323-400 Brazil
Tel: + 55 41 3225 9100
Head of School: Thomas Brulisauer
Curriculum: IBDP
Language instr: English

Escola Americana de Belo Horizonte
Av. Professor Mario Werneck, 3002, Bairro Buritis, Belo Horizonte, 30575-180 Brazil
Tel: +55 31 3378 6700
Head of School: Catarina Song Chen
Age range: 3–18
No. of pupils: 180 B95 G85
Curriculum: IBMYP, IBPYP
Language instr: English, Portuguese

Escola Americana do Rio de Janeiro
Estrada da Gávea 132, Gávea, Rio de Janeiro, 22451-263 Brazil
Tel: +55 21 2125 9002
Headmaster: Andrew Sherman
Age range: 3–19
No. of pupils: B600 G600
Fees: US$25,000
Curriculum: IBDP, National, USA
Language instr: English

Escola Beit Yaacov
Av Marques de Sao Vicente no 1748, Barra Funda, São Paulo, 1139 Brazil
Tel: +55 11 3611 0600
Head of School: Esther Dayan
Curriculum: IBDP, IBPYP
Language instr: English

Escola Cidade Jardim, São Paulo
Praça Professor Américo de Moura, 101, São Paulo, 05670-060 Brazil
Tel: +55 1138 129122
Principal: Guida Machado
Language instr: English, Portuguese

Escola Internacional SOCIESC
Rua Gothard Kaesemodel 833, 89203-400 Joinville, Santa Catarina Brazil
Tel: +55 47 34610500
Head of School: Elza Giostri
Age range: 6–18
No. of pupils: 220
Curriculum: IBDP

Escola Maria Imaculada (Chapel School)
Rua Vigário João de Pontes, 537, Chácara Flora, São Paulo, 04748-000 Brazil
Tel: +55 11 2101 7400
Superintendent: Gerald Clifford Gates
No. of pupils: 700
Curriculum: ACT, IBDP, SAT, TOEFL
Language instr: English

Escola Suiço Brasileira Rio de Janeiro
Rua Corrêa de Araújo, 81, Barra da Tijuca, Rio de Janeiro, 22611-060 Brazil
Tel: +55 (21) 3389-2089
Head of School: Luiza Maria Bokelmann
Curriculum: IBDP, IBPYP
Language instr: English, French

Escola Suiço-Brasileira de São Paulo
R Visconde de Porto Seguro 391, Alto da Boa Vista, São Paulo, 04642-000 Brazil
Tel: +55 11 5682 2140
Head of School: Marcel Brunner
No. of pupils: 650
Curriculum: IBDP, National
Language instr: German, Portuguese

ESFERA Escola Internacional
Av Anchieta, 908. Jardim Esplanada, Sao José dos Campos, Sao Paulo, 12242-280 Brazil
Tel: 55 12 3322 1255
Head of School: Andrea Andrade
Age range: 2–14
No. of pupils: 410
Curriculum: IBPYP

International School of Curitiba
Av Dr Eugenio Bertolli, 3900, Santa Felicidade, Curitiba, Paraná 82410-530 Brazil
Tel: +55 41 3525 7400
Superintendent: Bill Pearson
Age range: 2–19
No. of pupils: 560 B280 G280
Fees: FB 180–71,024
Curriculum: IBDP, SAT, USA
Language instr: English

Pan American School of Bahia
Av Ibirapitanga, Loteamento Patamares, s/n, Salvador, Bahia, 41680-060 Brazil
Tel: +55 71 3368 8400
Superintendent: Dennis Klumpp
Curriculum: IBDP

Pan American School of Porto Alegre
Av. João Obino 110, Porto Alegre, Rio Grande do Sul, 90470-150 Brazil
Tel: +55 513 334 5866
Director: Jeffrey M Jurkovac
Age range: 3–18
No. of pupils: 347 B163 G184
Curriculum: AP, IBPYP, National, SAT, USA
Language instr: English, Portuguese

Pueri Domus School
Rua Verbo Divino 993-A, Chacara Sto. Antonio, Sao Paulo, 04719 Brazil
Tel: +55 11 3512 2222
Head of School: Rose Mara Mernardi
Curriculum: IBDP

Saint Nicholas School
Av Eusébio Matoso 333, Pinheiros, São Paulo, CEP 05423-180 Brazil
Tel: + 55 11 3465 9666
Head of School: Nicholas Thody
Curriculum: IBDP, IBPYP
Language instr: English

Sidarta International School (Associacion Assistencial Educacional Sidarta)
Estrada Fernando Nobre, 1332 – km 28,5 da rodovia Raposo Tavares, sentido Coti+, Sao Paulo, Brazil
Tel: +55 11 4612 2711
(ISA)

St Francis College
Rua Bélgica 399, Jardim Europa, São Paulo, 01448-030 SP Brazil
Tel: +55 11 3905 6200
College Principal: Shirley Hazell
Age range: 2–18
No. of pupils: 820
Fees: US$18,000–US$23,000
Curriculum: IBDP, IBMYP, IBPYP
Language instr: English, Portuguese

St Francis School, Pinheiros Campus
Rua Joaquim Antunes, 678, Pinheiros, Sao Paulo, 05415 Brazil
Tel: +55 11 3728 8050
Head of School: Shirley Hazell

St Paul's School
Rua Juquiá 166, Jardim Paulistano, São Paulo, 01440-903 Brazil
Tel: +55 11 3087 3399
Headmaster: Crispin Rowe
Age range: 3–18
No. of pupils: 1094
Fees: US$30,000
Curriculum: IBDP, UK, IGCSE
Language instr: English
(COB)

The American School of Sao Paulo
Av. Presidente Giovanni Gronchi, 4710, Morumbi, Sao Paulo, 05724-002 Brazil
Tel: +55 11 3747 4800
Superintendent: Lee Fertig
Age range: 4–18
No. of pupils: 1170 B600 G570
Fees: US$25,000
Curriculum: IBDP, National, USA
Language instr: English

The British College of Brazil
Rua Engenheiro Oscar Americano, 630 Cidade Jardim, Sao Paulo, Brazil
Tel: +55 11 3031 4697
Headteacher: Stuart Young
Curriculum: UK

THE BRITISH SCHOOL, RIO DE JANEIRO
For further details see p. 174
Rua Real Grandeza 99, Botafogo, Rio de Janeiro, 22281-030 Brazil
Tel: +55 21 2539 2717
Email: edu@britishschool.g12.br
Website: www.britishschool.g12.br
Age range: 2–18
No. of pupils: 2166 B1052 G1108
Curriculum: IBDP, IPC, UK
Language instr: English
(GB)

The British School, Rio de Janeiro – Barra Site
Rua MÃ¡rio Autuori, 100, Barra da Tijuca, 22793 Brazil
Tel: +55 21 3329 2854
Head of School: Robert Franklin
Curriculum: IBDP

Chile

Bradford School
Avada Luis Pateur 6335, Vitacura, Chile
Tel: +56 218 6271/6753
Head of School: Patricia Artigues
Age range: 4–18
Curriculum: IBDP, UK

Colegio 'La Maisonette'
Avda Luis Pasteur 6076,
Vitacura, Santiago, Chile
Tel: +56 2 2185779
Head of School: Carmen
Echeverría Tortello
Curriculum: IBDP
Language instr: Spanish

**Colegio Alemán
de Concepción**
Camino El Venado 1075, Andalué,
San Pedro de la Paz, Concepción,
VIII Región del Bío Bío Chile
Tel: +56 41 2140000
Head of School: Dorothea
Schachtsiek
No. of pupils: 1080
Fees: US$4,200
Curriculum: IBDP
Language instr: Spanish

**Colegio Alemán
de Los Angeles**
Avenida Gabriela Mistral 1751,
Los Ángeles, 4440000 Chile
Tel: 56 43 533733
Head of School: Uwe
Schotte Schröder
Curriculum: IBDP

**Colegio Alemán de San
Felipe de Aconcagua**
60 CH N° 501 Panquehue,
San Felipe, Chile
Tel: +56 34 2 59 11 71
Head of School: Silvia Elgueta
Age range: 3–17
No. of pupils: 343 B173 G170
Curriculum: IBDP
Language instr: Spanish

**Colegio Alemán
de Temuco**
Avenida Holandesa
0855, Temuco, Chile
Tel: +56 45 963000
Head of School: Jürgen Mattmann
Curriculum: IBDP

**Colegio Alemán
de Valparaiso**
Alvarez 2950, El Salto,
Viña del Mar, Chile
Tel: +56 32 216 1531
Head of School: Franz Wägele
No. of pupils: 1252
Fees: US$4,500
Curriculum: IBDP, IBPYP
Language instr: Spanish

**Colegio Alemán St
Thomas Morus**
Casilla 16147, Correo 9, Providencia,
Santiago de Chile 16147 Chile
Tel: +56 02 7291600
Head of School: Sabine Trapp
Curriculum: IBDP

**Colegio de los
Sagrados Corazones,
Padres Franceses**
Independencia 2086,
Valparaiso, Chile
Tel: +56 32 381 196
Head of School: Patricia
Hola Chamy
No. of pupils: 1164
Curriculum: IBPYP
Language instr: Spanish

**Colegio Internacional
SEK Pacifico**
San Estanislao 50 Urbanización
Lomas de Montemar,
Concon, Chile
Tel: +56 32 2275700
Director: Nelson Becker
Language instr: Spanish
(ISA)

**Colegio Internacional
SEK-Chile**
Los Militares 6640, Las
Condes, Santiago, Chile
Tel: +56 2 212 7116
Head of School: Nelly Varella Lopez
Curriculum: IBDP, IBMYP
Language instr: Spanish
(ISA)

**Colegio Manquecura –
Ciudad de Los Valles**
Av. El Canal 19877, Ruta 68,
Santiago, 19877 Chile
Tel: +56 2601 6025
Language instr: Spanish

**Colegio Manquecura
– Ciudad del Este**
Avenida Diego Portales, Puente
Alto, Santiago, 07045 Chile
Tel: +56 2267 1421
Language instr: Spanish

**Colegio Manquecura
– Valle lo Campino**
Camino el Cerro, Quilicura,
Santiago, 2700 Chile
Tel: +56 2249 0005
Language instr: Spanish

**Colegio Pumahue
– Chicuero**
Camino Santa Elena
215, Santiago, Chile
Tel: +56 229 467 010
Language instr: Spanish

**Colegio Pumahue
– Curauma**
Nudo Curauma 495,
Valparaiso, Chile
Tel: +56 322 294 073
Language instr: Spanish

**Colegio Pumahue
– Huechuraba**
Santa Rosa de Huechuraba
7201, Santiago, Chile
Tel: +56 227 210 080
Language instr: Spanish

**Colegio Pumahue
– Peñalolen**
Av. Quilín 8200, Santiago, Chile
Tel: +56 222 988 412
Language instr: Spanish

**Colegio Pumahue
– Puerto Montt**
Volcán Puntiagudo 1700,
Puerto Montt, Chile
Tel: +56 652 435 766
Language instr: Spanish

**Colegio Pumahue
– Temuco**
Av. Martín Lutero 01200,
Temuco, Chile
Tel: +56 45 2 26 95 45
Language instr: Spanish

CRAIGHOUSE SCHOOL
For further details see p. 166
Casilla 20 007, Correo
20, Santiago, Chile
Tel: +56 2 756 0218
Email:
headmaster@craighouse.cl
Website: www.craighouse.cl
Headmaster: Peter Lacey
Age range: 3–18
No. of pupils: 1720
Curriculum: IBDP, IBMYP, IBPYP
Language instr: English, Spanish

Dunalastair
Av Las Condes 11931, Las Condes,
Santiago de Chile, Chile
Tel: +562 495 6600
Head of School: John Mackenzie
Age range: 3–18
No. of pupils: 1000
Fees: Day Peso3,200,000
Curriculum: IBDP, IBPYP
Language instr: Spanish

Dunalastair Valle Norte
Camino del Solar s/n, Valle Norte,
Chicureo, Colina, Santiago, Chile
Tel: +56 2 6736097
Headmistress: Mońica Le May
No. of pupils: 1070
Curriculum: IBPYP
Language instr: English, Spanish

**Instituto Alemán
Carlos Anwandter**
Los Laureles 050, Casilla
2-D, Valdivia, Chile
Tel: +56-63-2471100
Head of School: Cristoph
Rube-Vestweber
Curriculum: IBDP
Language instr: Spanish

**Instituto Alemán
de Osorno**
Los Carreras 818, Osorno, Chile
Tel: +56 2 64 331805
Head of School: Marianne Hohf
Curriculum: IBDP, IBPYP
Language instr: Spanish

**International
Preparatory School**
PO Box 20015, Las Condes,
Santiago, Chile
Tel: +56 2 321 5800
Headmistress: Lesley Easton Allen
Age range: 3–18
No. of pupils: 141 B83 G58
Curriculum: UK

**International School
Nido de Aguilas**
Casilla 162, Correo La
Dehesa, Santiago, Chile
Tel: +56 2 2339 8100
Headmaster: Donald Bergman
Curriculum: IBDP
Language instr: English

Mackay School
Casilla 558, Viña del Mar, Chile
Tel: +56 32 2386614
Headmaster: Mark Rosevear
Age range: B4–18
No. of pupils: 985
Curriculum: IBDP, National
Language instr: Spanish, English

Redland School
Camino El Alba 11357, Las Condes,
Santiago, 7600022 Chile
Tel: +56 2 9598500
Head of School: Mike Spooner
Age range: 4–18
No. of pupils: 800 B400 G400
Fees: US$5,700
Curriculum: IBDP, IBMYP
Language instr: Spanish

Saint Gabriel's School
Avda Fco Bilbao 3070,
Providencia, Santiago, Chile
Tel: +56 22 462 5400
Head of School: Odette
Boys Michell
Age range: 4–18
Curriculum: IBDP, National, IGCSE
Language instr: English,
Spanish (5th-12th grade)

SANTIAGO COLLEGE
For further details see p. 172
Av. Camino Los Trapenses 4007,
Lo Barnechea, Santiago, Chile
Tel: +56 2 27338800
Email: master@scollege.cl
Website: www.scollege.cl
Director: Lorna Prado Scott
Age range: 4–18
No. of pupils: 1846 VIth253
Curriculum: IBDP, IBMYP, IBPYP
Language instr: Spanish, English
(CIS) (ECIS)

St John's School
Fundo el Venado, San Pedro
de la Paz, Concepción, Chile
Tel: +56 41 2466440
Head of School: James Coulson
Age range: 4–18
No. of pupils: 1348
Fees: US$5,050
Curriculum: IBDP, National, IGCSE
Language instr: English, Spanish

St Margaret's British School For Girls
Casilla 392, Viña del Mar, Quinta Región Chile
Tel: +56 322 451701
Head of School: Carolyn Pettersen Cave
Curriculum: IBDP
Language instr: Spanish, English

St Paul's School
Merced Oriente 54, Viña del Mar, Casilla, 347 Chile
Tel: (56 32) 314 2200
Headmaster: Nicolás Gana
Curriculum: IBPYP
Language instr: English, Spanish

St Peter's School
Av. Libertad 575, Viña del Mar, Chile
Tel: (56 32) 238 1400
Headmaster: James Wilkins
Curriculum: UK

The Antofagasta British School
Pedro León Gallo 723, Antofagasta, Chile
Tel: 56 55 598930
Headmaster: Tim Deyes
Curriculum: IBPYP
Language instr: English, Spanish

The British School – Punta Arenas
Waldo Seguel 454, Punta Arenas, Chile
Tel: +56 61 22 33 81
Head of School: Alejandra Barrios Harmer
Age range: 4–18
No. of pupils: 600
Curriculum: IBDP, IBMYP, IBPYP
Language instr: Spanish, English

The Grange School
Príncipe de Gales 6154, La Reina, 687067, Santiago, 7850000 Chile
Tel: +56 2 2598 1500
Rector: Rachid Benammar
Age range: 4–17/18
No. of pupils: B1054 G961 VIth230
Curriculum: National, UK, IGCSE, ALevs
Language instr: English, Spanish

The Mayflower School
Avda Las Condes 12 167, Las Condes, Santiago, 668 2347 Chile
Tel: +56 2 3523100
Head of School: Gilda Tonini-Burgueño
Age range: 4–18
Curriculum: IBDP, ALevs
Language instr: Spanish

The Wessex School
Granada 314-A, Vilumanqu, Concepción, Chile
Tel: (56 41) 238 7280
Headmaster: Terrence Martin
Language instr: English

Trebulco School
Camino Carampangue 550, Talagante, Chile
Tel: +56 2 815 7550
Headmistress: Anemarie Hartwig
Age range: 3–17
Language instr: English

Wenlock School
Casilla 27169, Correo 27, Santiago, Chile
Tel: +56 2 363 1800
Headmaster: John Bell
Age range: 3–18
No. of pupils: 780 B390 G390
Curriculum: IBDP, National, UK, IGCSE
Language instr: Spanish

Colombia

Asociación Colegio Granadino
AA 2138, Manizales, Colombia
Tel: +57 (6) 874 57 74
Director: Michael Adams
Age range: 3–18
No. of pupils: 600 B295 G305
Language instr: English, Spanish

Aspaen Gimnasio Iragua
c/o Sra Ma Helena Jiménez, Coordinadora BI, Diagonal 170 # 66-51, Bogotá, Colombia
Tel: +57 1 667 9500
Head of School: María Eugenia Merizalde de Bermúdez
Curriculum: IBDP
Language instr: Spanish

Buckingham School
Cra 52 No 214 – 55, Bogotá, Colombia
Tel: +57 1 6760812
Head of School: Marta Teresa Rincon Reina
Age range: 3–17
Curriculum: IBDP, IBMYP, IBPYP, National
Language instr: English, Spanish

CIEDI – Colegio Internacional de Educación Integral
Km 3 vía Suba-Cota, Bogotá, Colombia
Tel: +57 1 683 0604
Head of School: Clara Gutiérrez de Palacios
Curriculum: IBDP, IBMYP, IBPYP
Language instr: Spanish, English

Colegio Albania
P.O. Box 02-5573, Miami, FL 33102, USA Colombia
Tel: +57 5 350 5648
Head of School: Ruth Allen
Curriculum: IBDP, IBMYP
Language instr: Spanish, English

Colegio Alemán
Autopista al Mar poste 89 Electricaribe, Baranquilla, Colombia
Tel: +57 5359 8520
Head of School: Wilhelm Binder
No. of pupils: 1000
Curriculum: IBDP
Language instr: Spanish

Colegio Alemán Medellin
Cra 61 No 34 – 62, Itagüi, Antioquía Colombia
Tel: +57 4 281 88 11
Head of School: Dominik Scheuten
Curriculum: IBDP
Language instr: Spanish

Colegio Anglo-Colombiano
Apartado Aéreo 253393, Avenida 19 Nº 152A-48, Santa Fé de Bogotá, Colombia
Tel: +57 1 259 5700
Head of School: Alan Shanks
Age range: 4–18
No. of pupils: 1826
Curriculum: IBDP, IBMYP, IBPYP, National, UK
Language instr: Spanish, English

Colegio Británico – The British School
Call 18 # 142-255 (Esquina), La Viga, Pance, Cali, Colombia
Tel: +572 555 7545
Head of School: Luis Alberto Sarria Tamayo
Curriculum: IBDP

Colegio Britanico Internacional
Apartado Aéreo 4368, Barranquilla, Colombia
Tel: +57 5 359 9243
Head of School: Guy Worthington
Curriculum: IBDP
Language instr: English

Colegio Colombo Britanico
Avenida La Maria 69 Pance, Pance, Cali, Colombia
Tel: +57 2 555 5385
Headmaster: John M. Wells
Age range: 2–18
No. of pupils: 1238 B622 G616
Curriculum: ACT, IBDP, IBMYP, IBPYP, National, SAT
Language instr: English, Spanish

Colegio Colombo Gales
Avenida Guaymaral, Costado sur Aeropuerto, Bogotá, 11001 Colombia
Tel: +57 1 6684910 ext 125
Head of School: Germán Gallo Grau
Curriculum: IBDP

Colegio de Inglaterra – The English School
Calle 170 #15-68, Bogotá, Colombia
Tel: +57 1 676 7700
Head of School: Sarah Osborne
Age range: 2–18
No. of pupils: 1700
Curriculum: IBDP, IBMYP, IBPYP
Language instr: English, Spanish

Colegio Gran Bretaña
Carrera 51 No 215-20, Bogotá, Colombia
Tel: +57 1 676 0391
Head of School: Maureen Fleming
Age range: 3–18
No. of pupils: 455 B235 G220
Fees: US$10,195
Curriculum: IBDP, National, UK
Language instr: Spanish

Colegio Hacienda Los Alcaparros
Carrera 12# 118-36, Verra El Salitre, Bogota, Colombia
Tel: +571 592 22 66
Age range: 3–18
Curriculum: USA

Colegio Internacional de Bogota
Carrera 49 no 202-85, Apartado Aereo 103314, Bogotá, Colombia
Tel: +57 1 676 2200
Head of School: Adriana Zárate
Curriculum: IBDP
Language instr: English

Colegio Internacional Los Cañaverales
Carrera 29 No 10-500, Arroyohonfo, Vía Dapa Km 1 Yumbo, Yumbo – Valle, Valle del Cauca 11297 Colombia
Tel: +57 2 6582818
Head of School: María Fernanda Girón
Curriculum: IBDP
Language instr: English

Colegio Karl C. Parrish
Km. 2 Antigua Via a Puerto Colombia, Barranquilla, Colombia
Tel: +57 5 359 8929

Colegio Los Nogales
Calle 202 # 56 – 50, Bogotá, 11 Colombia
Tel: +57 1 676 1128
Head of School: Ian Crossland
Age range: 4–18
No. of pupils: B451 G517
Fees: US$7,870
Curriculum: AP, National, SAT, USA
Language instr: English, Spanish

Colegio Los Tréboles
Vereda cerca de Piedra,
Finca Santa Elena, Chía,
Cundinamarca Colombia
Tel: +57 1 862 4830
Directora: Cristina Gaviria
de Valenzuela
Age range: 4–18
No. of pupils: 250
Curriculum: IBDP
Language instr: Spanish

**Colegio Marymount
Barranquilla**
Carrera 59B No 84-52,
Barranquilla, Colombia
Tel: +57 5 3554300
Head of School: Susan Kumnick
Age range: 3–19
No. of pupils: 1327
Curriculum: National, USA
(CIS)

**Colegio Mayor
de los Andes**
Kilómetro 3, Vía Chia Cajicá,
Verda Canelón, Cajicá
Cundinamarca, Colombia
Tel: +57 1 866 29 56
Head of School: Orlando Jiménez
Curriculum: IBDP

Colegio Nueva Granada
Cra 2 Este # 70-20,
Bogotá, Colombia
Tel: +57 1 212 3511
Director: Eric Habegger
Language instr: English

Colegio Panamericano
Calle 34 No. 8 -73 Cañaveral
Alto, Floridablanca,
Santander, Colombia
Tel: +57 7 638 6213
Director: John Hickey
Curriculum: National

Colegio Santa Maria
Carrera 11 #185B-17,
Bogota, Colombia
Tel: +57 1 671 4440
Principal: Ana María
Ternet de Samper
Age range: G4–18
No. of pupils: 1000
(*)

Colegio Tilatá
Kilómetro 9 vía La Calera,
Bogotá, Colombia
Tel: +571 5921414
Head of School: María
Isabel Casas Andrade
Curriculum: IBPYP

**Deutsche Schule –
Cali / Kolumbien**
Avenida Gualí N° 31, Barrio
Ciudad Jardín, Cali, Colombia
Tel: +57 2 6858900
Head of School: Andreas Irle
Curriculum: IBDP
Language instr: German, Spanish

**Fundación Nuevo
Marymount**
Calle 169B, No 74A-02,
Bogotá DC, Colombia
Tel: +57 1 669 9077
Head of School: María
Ángela Torres Soto
Age range: G3–18
Curriculum: IBDP
Language instr: Spanish
(*)

**George Washington
School**
Apartado Aereo 2899,
Cartagena, Colombia
Tel: +57 5665 3136
Director: Pete Nonnenkamp
Age range: 4–18
No. of pupils: 523 B257 G266
Curriculum: AP, SAT

GIMNASIO BRITÁNICO
For further details see p. 167
Calle 21 No 9A-58, Chia,
Cundinamarca, Colombia
Tel: +571 8615084
Email:
gb@gimnasio-britanico.edu.co
Website:
www.gimnasio-britanico.edu.co
Head of School: Jorge
Piraquive Arévalo
Age range: 2–16
No. of pupils: 1500
Curriculum: IBDP
Language instr: Spanish,
English, French

**Gimnasio Campestre
Los Cerezos**
Via Canelón, Finca Los Cerezos,
Cajicá, Bogota, 250247 Colombia
Tel: +57 (3) 168342410
Head of School: Orlando
Matiz Villamil
Curriculum: IBDP, IBPYP

**Gimnasio Campestre
San Rafael**
Km 6 Via Siberia – Tenjo,
Cundinamarca, Bogota, Colombia
Tel: +571 8646966
Head of School: Carolina
Parra García
Curriculum: IBDP
Language instr: Spanish

Gimnasio de Los Cerros
Calle 119 N° 0-68, Usaquén,
Santafé de Bogotá DC,
Cundinamarca, Colombia
Tel: + 57 1 657 6000
Head of School: Eduardo
Manrique Andrade
Curriculum: IBDP
Language instr: Spanish
(*)

Gimnasio del Norte
Calle 207 N° 70 – 50,
Bogotá, DC, Colombia
Tel: +57 1 6683939
Headmaster: José Contreras Tovar
Curriculum: IBDP, IBMYP, IBPYP
Language instr: Spanish, English

Gimnasio El Hontanar
Cra. 76 No. 150-26,
Bogotá, Colombia
Tel: +57 (1) 681 5287
Curriculum: IBDP
Language instr: English, Spanish

Gimnasio Femenino
Cr 7 # 128-40, Bella Suiza,
Bogotá, Colombia
Tel: +571 657 8420
Head of School: Sylvia Maldonado
Curriculum: IBDP
Language instr: Spanish
(*)

Gimnasio Fontana
Calle 221#108-20, Guaymaral,
Bogotá, 0000 Colombia
Tel: +57 1 742 0303 Ext 122-123
Director: Amparo Triana de Zuleta
Age range: 4–18
No. of pupils: 922 B465 G457
Curriculum: National, TOEFL
Language instr: Spanish,
English, French
(CIS)

Gimnasio Los Alcazares
Calle 63 sur 41-05 Sabaneta,
Antioquia, Colombia
Tel: +57 4 305 4000
Head of School: Omar
Giraldo Gómez
Curriculum: IBDP
Language instr: Spanish
(*)

Gimnasio Vermont
Cl 195 No 54-75, Bogotá, Colombia
Tel: +57 1 674 8070
Head of School: Raquel Lucía Rojas
Age range: 4–18
No. of pupils: 1577
Curriculum: IBDP
Language instr: Spanish

**International
Berckley School**
Km 5 – Vía al Mar, Poste 115,
Barranquilla, Colombia
Tel: + 575 3548131
Head of School: Tilsia Lara Baute
Curriculum: IBDP
Language instr: Spanish

**Jardín Infantil Tía Nora
y Liceo Los Alpes**
Av 8 Norte, No. 66-05 Urbanización
Menga, Cali, Colombia
Tel: 572 665 4120
Head of School: María Constanza
Velásquez de Fernández
Curriculum: IBMYP, IBPYP
Language instr: English, Spanish

La Colina School
Carrera 80 No. 147-50,
Bogota, Colombia
Tel: +57 1 6828417
Head of School: Maria
Claudia Mewndoza
Language instr: Spanish
(ISA)

Liceo Pino Verde
Vereda Los Planes kilometro, 5
Vía Cerritos Entrada 16, El Tigre,
Pereira, Risaralda, Colombia
Tel: +57 (6)3132668
Head of School: Diana
Inés Angel Arenas
Curriculum: IBDP

**Marymount School
– Medellín**
Calle 7 No 25-64,
Medellín, Colombia
Tel: +574 266 1555
Principal: Ana María Bernal
Age range: G3–18
No. of pupils: 835
Curriculum: National
(*) (CIS)

The Victoria School
Calle 215 N° 50-60,
Bogotá, Colombia
Tel: +57 1 676 1503
General Director: Mary
Hayes de Rojas
Age range: 3–18
No. of pupils: 510
Curriculum: IBDP, IBMYP, IBPYP
Language instr: English, Spanish

Curaçao

**INTERNATIONAL SCHOOL
OF CURAÇAO**
For further details see p. 168
PO Box 3090, Koninginnelaan
z/n, Emmastad, Curaçao
Tel: +599 9 737 3633
Email: info@isc.cw
Website: www.isc.cw
Director: Margie Elhage-Cancio
Age range: 2–19
No. of pupils: 454 B239 G216
Curriculum: ACT, AP,
IBDP, SAT, TOEFL, USA
Language instr: English
(CIS)

Ecuador

**Academia Cotopaxi
American International
School**
PO Box 17-11-6510, Quito, Ecuador
Tel: +593 2 246 7411
Head of School: William Johnston
Age range: 5–17
No. of pupils: B272 G266
Curriculum: IBDP, IBPYP
Language instr: English

Academia Naval Almirante Illingworth
Ave José Gómez Gault KM 8, Vía Daule, Guayaquil, 09013880 Ecuador
Tel: 593042250586
Head of School: Elías Sánchez Estrada
Curriculum: IBDP

Alliance Academy International
Casilla 17-11-06186, Quito, Ecuador
Tel: +593 2 226 7510
Director: David A Wells
Age range: 4–18
No. of pupils: 533 B287 G246

Centro Educativo Bilingue Internacional
Calle Alfredo Sevilla y Av Pedro Vásconez, Parroquia Izamba, Ambato, Ecuador
Tel: +593 3285 4400
Head of School: Verónica López Loayza
Curriculum: IBDP
Language instr: Spanish

Colegio Alemán Humboldt de Guayaquil
Dr Héctor Romero, #216, Los Ceibos, Guayaquil, Guayas 09-01-4760 Ecuador
Tel: +593 428 50260
Head of School: Werner Schiffer
No. of pupils: 1940
Fees: US$3,600
Curriculum: IBDP
Language instr: Spanish

Colegio Alemán Stiehle Cuenca Ecuador
Autopista Cuenca – Azogues, Km 11,5, Sector Challuabamba, Cuenca, Ecuador
Tel: +593 74 075 646
Head of School: Edda Mally
Curriculum: IBDP
Language instr: Spanish

Colegio Americano De Guayaquil
Direccion General, Casilla 3304, Guayaquil, Ecuador
Tel: +593 4 3082 020
Head of School: Jeffery A Berry
Curriculum: IBDP
Language instr: English, Spanish

Colegio Americano de Quito
Casilla 17-01-157, Pichincha Province, Quito, Ecuador
Tel: + 593 2 3976 300
Head of School: Susan Barba
Age range: 4–18
No. of pupils: 2806
Curriculum: AP, IBDP, IBMYP, SAT, TOEFL
Language instr: English

Colegio Balandra Cruz del Sur
Perimeter Road, The Prosperina, Guayaquil, Ecuador
Tel: +593 4 285 0020
Head of School: Margarita B Fioravanti
Curriculum: IBDP
Language instr: Spanish

Colegio Becquerel
Tulipanes E12-50 y Los Rosales, Quito, Pichincha Ecuador
Tel: +593 2 2257896
Head of School: Amada De Roldán
Curriculum: IBDP

Colegio Cap Edmundo Chiriboga
Av 9 de Octubre y Garcia Moreno, Chimborazo, Riobamba, Ecuador
Tel: +593 03 295 3406
Head of School: Ángel Silva Vallejo
Curriculum: IBDP
Language instr: Spanish

Colegio Católico José Engling
Calle Juan Montalvo s/n, Barrio La Dolorosa, Tumbaco, Quito, Pichincha 17-17-2010 Ecuador
Tel: +593 2 237 2871
Head of School: Mónica Cornish de Arteta
Curriculum: IBDP
Language instr: English, Spanish

Colegio Experimental Bilingüe SEK – Los Valles
León Febres Cordero s/n, y de los Rosales, San Juan de CumbayÄį, Quito, Pichincha 1717933 Ecuador
Tel: +593 2 2896848
Head of School: Eduardo Ahumada Jaña
Curriculum: IBDP

Colegio Experimental Británico Internacional
Amagasí del Inca, Calle de las Nueces E18-21, y Las Camelias, Quito, Ecuador
Tel: +593 2 3261 254
General Director: Scott Hibbard
Age range: 2–18
Curriculum: IBDP, IBMYP, IBPYP
Language instr: Spanish, English

Colegio Fiscomisional 'Madre Bernarda'
entre Pío Jaramillo, Alvarado y Francisco de Orellana, Zamora Chinchipe, EC190102 Ecuador
Tel: +593 7260 6568
Curriculum: IBDP

Colegio Internacional Rudolf Steiner
Calle Francisco Montalvo Nro 212, y Av Mariscal Sucre, (Av Occidental), Sector Cochabampa, Quito, Ecuador
Tel: +593 2244 3315
Head of School: Gustavo Ramos Vergara
Curriculum: IBDP, IBMYP, IBPYP
Language instr: Spanish

Colegio Internacional SEK-Ecuador, Guayaquil
PO Box 09-04-0878-Policentro, Guayaquil, Guayas 11373 Ecuador
Tel: +593 4 2738066
Head of School: Tomas Aznar
Age range: 2–18
Curriculum: IBDP
Language instr: Spanish and English

Colegio Internacional SEK-Ecuador, Quito
De los Guayacanes N51-69 y Carmen Olmo Mancebo, San Isidro de El Inca, Quito, Ecuador
Tel: +593 2 2401 896
Head of School: Jose Enrique Navas Zarzosa
Age range: 3–18
No. of pupils: 1630 B831 G799 VIth95
Curriculum: IBDP, IBMYP
Language instr: English, Spanish
(ISA)

Colegio Intisana
Avenida Occidental 5329, y Marcos Joffre, Quito, Pinchincha 8720 Ecuador
Tel: +593 2 2440 128
Head of School: Diego Javier Astudillo Cervantes
Curriculum: IBDP
Language instr: Spanish
(♦)(♨)

Colegio Los Pinos
Agustin Zambrano S/N y Vicente Pajuelo, Quito, POBox 8720 Ecuador
Tel: +593 2 246 3189
Head of School: Carmen Estupiñán de Félix
Age range: G4–18
No. of pupils: 595
Curriculum: IBDP
Language instr: Spanish
(♦)

Colegio Politécnico
Km 30.5 Vía Perimental, Campus Gustavo Galindo, Espol, 30,5 Via Perimetral, Guayaquil Ecuador
Tel: +593 4 2 269 653
Principal: MA Mario Luces Noboa
Age range: 3–18
No. of pupils: 1000
Fees: $2,800
Curriculum: IBDP, IBPYP
Language instr: Spanish

Colegio Stella Maris
Avenida 6 y Calle 14, Manta, Ecuador
Tel: +593 5 2611352
Head of School: Ana Rafaela Velasco Sarmiento
Curriculum: IBDP
Language instr: Spanish

Ecomundo Centro de Estudios
PO Box 09013807, Guayaquil, Ecuador
Tel: +593 4 2681 740
Head of School: Roberto Passailaigue Baquerizo
Curriculum: IBDP
Language instr: English

EMDI School
EMDI sector B, Parroquia Alangasi, Valle de los Chilos, Quito, Pichincha Ecuador
Tel: +593 2278 8652
Head of School: Karina Rueda
Curriculum: IBDP
Language instr: English, Spanish

Inter-American Academy Guayaquil
Puerto Azul, 10.5 via a la costa, Guayaquil, Ecuador
Tel: +593 4 3713360
Executive Director: Pete Nonnenkamp
Age range: 4–18
No. of pupils: 291
Curriculum: ACT, SAT

ISM International Academy
Calle Unión 886 y Ave Geovanny Calle, Sector Calderon, Quito, Ecuador
Tel: +593 2 282 0549
Head of School: Jenny Vinueza do López
Curriculum: IBDP
Language instr: English, Spanish

Logos Academy
Km 14.5 Via a la Costa, Guayaquil, Ecuador
Tel: +59 34 390 0125
Head of School: Susana Salcedo de Egas
Curriculum: IBDP, National
Language instr: Spanish, English

Ludoteca Elementary & High School, Padre Victor Grados
Av Simón Bolívar y Camino de los Incas # 5-6, Nueva Vía Oriental, Quito, Ecuador
Tel: +593 2 268 8142
Head of School: Nancy Albán
Curriculum: IBMYP
Language instr: English, Spanish

Plantel Educativo Particular Terranova
Calle De Los Rieles 507, y Ave Simón Bolívar, San Juan Alto de Cumbayá, Quito, Ecuador
Tel: +593 2 204 0252
Head of School: Inés Brioso
Curriculum: IBDP, IBMYP, IBPYP
Language instr: Spanish

The British School Quito
Casilla 17-21-52, Quito, Ecuador
Tel: +593 2 2 374 649
Head of School: Kerry Tyler-Pascoe
Age range: 3–19
No. of pupils: 218 B132 G86
Curriculum: IBDP, SAT, UK, USA
Language instr: English
(CIS)

Unidad Educativa 'Émile Jaques-Dalcroze'
Calle Río Pastaza No 777 y Av Ilaló de los Chillos, San Rafael, Quito, Ecuador
Tel: +593 (01) 2861500
Head of School: Antonio Díaz Sandoval
Curriculum: IBDP

Unidad Educativa Alberto Einstein
Av Diego Vásquez de Cepeda N77-157 y Alberto Einstein, Casilla Postal 17-11-5018, Quito, Pichincha Ecuador
Tel: +593 2 2477901
Head of School: Raquel Katzkowicz
Curriculum: IBDP, IBMYP, IBPYP
Language instr: Spanish, English

Unidad Educativa Atenas
Calle Gabriel Roman y Av. Pedro Vasconez, Yacupamba, Izamba, Ambato, 180156 Ecuador
Tel: +593 3 285 4297
Curriculum: IBDP
Language instr: English

Unidad Educativa Bilingüe Delta
Kilómetro 12.5 Vía Puntilla-Samborondón, Guayaquil, Ecuador
Tel: +593 4 251 1266
Head of School: Marilú Arosa de Ginattamena
Curriculum: IBDP
Language instr: English
(symbol)

Unidad Educativa Bilingüe Mixta Sagrados Corazones
El Oro 1219 y Avenida Quito, Guayaquil, Ecuador
Tel: +593 04 2440087
Head of School: Marina Guerrero Armas
Curriculum: IBDP

Unidad Educativa Bilingüe Nuevo Mundo
Km 2.5 Vía a Samborondón, Guayaquil, Ecuador
Tel: +593 4 2 830 095
Head of School: Sonya Rendón Blacio
Age range: 2–18
No. of pupils: 1300
Curriculum: IBDP
Language instr: English

Unidad Educativa Bilingüe Torremar
Km 14.5 via La Puntilla, La Aurotra (Perimetral), Al lado de Parques de la Paz, Guayaquil, Ecuador
Tel: +59 34 251 2512
Head of School: Jorge Coronel Jones
Curriculum: IBDP
Language instr: Spanish
(symbol)

Unidad Educativa Letort
Los Guayabos Nro E 13-05 y Farsalias, San Isidro del Inca, Quito, Ecuador
Tel: +593 2 326 0202
Head of School: Fernando Muñoz Vinueza
No. of pupils: 572
Fees: US$240
Curriculum: IBDP
Language instr: Spanish

Unidad Educativa Liceo de Valle
km 1 vía a Pintag, Valle de los Chillos, Quito, Ecuador
Tel: +593 2 2330703
Director: Patricio Cevallos Ponce
Age range: 3–18
No. of pupils: 500
Curriculum: IBDP
Language instr: Spanish

Unidad Educativa Monte Tabor Nazaret
Km 13.5 Via Samborondón, Guayaquil, Ecuador
Tel: 593 4 2145821
Head of School: María del Rocío Ycaza de Hall
Curriculum: IBDP

Unidad Educativa Santana
Av. De Los Cerezos y Via a, San Pedro del Cebollar s/n, Cuenca, Ecuador
Tel: +593 7 2857451
Head of School: Pablo Crespo Andrade
Curriculum: IBDP
Language instr: Spanish

Unidad Educativa Tomás Moro
Av De Las Orquideas E13-120, y De Los Guayacanes, Quito, Ecuador
Tel: +593 2 2405357
Head of School: Teodoro Álvarez Malo
Curriculum: IBDP, IBMYP, IBPYP
Language instr: Spanish

Guyana

Georgetown American International School
9-10 Delhi Street, Prashbad Nagar, Georgetown, Guyana
Tel: +592 226 1595
Director: Thurston Riehl
Age range: 4–18
No. of pupils: 64 B31 G33
Curriculum: AP, SAT

Honduras

Happy Days Bilingual School & Freedom High School
Carretera al Zapotal Km2, San Pedro Sula, Honduras
Tel: +504 2551 1501
Age range: 4–18
Curriculum: National, USA
Language instr: English, Spanish
(CIS)

Mazapan School
La Ceiba, Honduras
Tel: +1 504 443 2716
Director: Martha Counsil
Age range: 3–17
Curriculum: USA

The American School of Tegucigalpa
Col. Lomas del Guijarro, Avenida Republica Dominicana, Tegucigalpa, Honduras
Tel: +504 239 3333
Head of School: Liliana Jenkins
Curriculum: IBDP
Language instr: English

Panama

Balboa Academy
Apartado 0843-02777, Panama, Panama
Tel: +507 302 0035
Director: Jean Lamb
Age range: 3–18
Fees: US$4,776–US$8,752
Curriculum: USA
Language instr: English

Caribbean International School
Box 0301 03289, Cristobel, Colon, Panama
Tel: +507, 4450933/ 450961
Principal: Juana M Joly
Age range: 3–18
No. of pupils: 495 B245 G250
Curriculum: National, USA

Colegio Isaac Rabin
Edificio 130, Ciudad del Saber, Panama
Tel: +507 3170059
Head of School: Itzel Sayavedra
Curriculum: IBMYP, IBPYP
Language instr: Spanish

International School of Panama
Apartado 0819-02588, Panama, Panama
Tel: +507 293 3000
Director: Rajir Bhat
Age range: 3–18
No. of pupils: 1086 B532 G554
Fees: US$5,840–US$11,620
Curriculum: ACT, IBDP, National, SAT, USA
Language instr: English

KING'S COLLEGE, THE BRITISH SCHOOL OF PANAMA
For further details see p. 169
Edificio 518, Calle al Hospital, Clayton, Panama
Tel: +507 282 3300
Email: kcp.admissions@kingsgroup.org
Website: www.kingscollege.com.pa
Headteacher: Vanessa Whay
Age range: 3–18
No. of pupils: 176
Curriculum: UK
(COB)

Metropolitan School of Panama
Building #104, Avenida Vicento Bonilla, La Ciudad de Saber, Clayton, Panama City, Panama
Tel: +507 317 1130
Head of School: Nicholas Reeves
Curriculum: IBPYP
Language instr: English

Paraguay

American School of Asunción
Avenida España 1175, PO Box 10093, Asunción, Paraguay
Tel: +595(21)603 518/663 678
Director: Robert Beck
Age range: 4–18
No. of pupils: 640
Curriculum: National, USA

Colegio SEK – Paraguay
Casilla postal 1959, Asunción, Paraguay
Tel: +595 21 907649
Head of School: José Ignacio Fito Martínez
Curriculum: IBDP
Language instr: Spanish

Goethe Schule Asunción/ Colegio Goethe Asunción
Cnel Silva esq Tte Rocholl, Asunción, 232 Paraguay
Tel: +595 21 60 68 60
Head of School: Karl Ludwig Reinders
Curriculum: IBDP

Santa Teresa de Jesús
Avda. Mcal. López 237 c/ Brasil,
Asunción, 927 Paraguay
Tel: +595 21 224683
Curriculum: IBMYP
Language instr: English

St Anne's School
Tte. Manuel Pino Gonzalez y Eulalio
Facetti, Asunción, Paraguay
Tel: +595 21 295649
Head of School: Paula Monovasitis
Age range: 4–18
No. of pupils: 600 B300 G300
Curriculum: IBDP, IBMYP
Language instr: English, Spanish

Peru

Asociación Colegio Mater Admirabilis
Avenida Arica 898, San
Miguel, Lima, Peru
Tel: +51 1 460 8306
Head of School: Silvia
Rodríguez Escudero
Curriculum: IBMYP
Language instr: Spanish

Asociacion Educacional Williamson Newton College
Apartado 12-137, La
Molina, Lima, Peru
Tel: +51 1479 0460
Head of School: Andy Cino
No. of pupils: 1200
Curriculum: IBDP, IBPYP
Language instr: English

Ausangate Bilingual School
Urb. Santa María s/n, San
Sebastián, 0000 Cusco, Peru
Tel: +51 84 275135
Head of School: Patricia
Campana Zapata
Curriculum: IBPYP

Cambridge College – Peru
Alemeda se Los Molinos 728-
730, La Encantada de Villa,
Chorrillos, Lima 9, Peru
Tel: +51 1 254 0107
Age range: 4–15
Curriculum: National, UK
Language instr: English, Spanish

Casuarinas International College
Av Jacarandá 391, Valle
Hermoso Sur, Monterrico,
Surco, Lima, 00033 Peru
Tel: +51 1 344 4040
Director: Graham Gisby
Age range: 3–18
No. of pupils: 600 B300 G300
Curriculum: IBDP, IBMYP, IBPYP
Language instr: Spanish, English

CEP Altair
Avenida La Arboleda 385, Urb.
Sirius, La Molina, Lima 12, Peru
Tel: +511 365 0298
**School Founder and
Administrative Director:** Gina
Mantero Campodonico
Age range: 3–18
No. of pupils: 877 B448 G429
Fees: $215–$560
Curriculum: IBDP, IBMYP, IBPYP
Language instr: Spanish, English

Colegio Alpamayo
Calle Bucaramanga 145, Urb
Mayorazgo, Lima, Peru
Tel: +51 1 349 0111
Head of School: Renzo
Forlin Struque
Age range: B5–17
Curriculum: IBDP
Language instr: Spanish, English

Colegio Champagnat
Av Prolongación Paseo de la,
República 7930 – 7931, Lima,
Santiago de Surco 33 Peru
Tel: +511 247 1001/0300
Head of School: Arturo
Cajaleón Castilla
Curriculum: IBDP
Language instr: Spanish

Colegio Euroamericano
Parcela 183-187 Mz C, Fundo
Casablanca, Pachacámac, Peru
Tel: +51 1 231 1617
Head of School: Robert
Owen Jones
Age range: 3–18
No. of pupils: 490 B245 G245
Curriculum: IBDP, IBPYP
Language instr: Spanish, English

Colegio Franklin Delano Roosevelt
The American School of Lima,
Apartado 18-0977, Lima 18, Peru
Tel: +51 1 435 0890
Head of School: Russell Jones
Age range: 3–18
No. of pupils: 1218 B687 G531
Curriculum: AP, IBDP,
IBMYP, IBPYP, SAT
Language instr: English, Spanish

Colegio León Pinelo
Calle Maimonides 610, San
Isidro, Lima, 27 Peru
Tel: +51 1 2183040
Head of School: Daniel Trilnik
Age range: 3–17
Curriculum: IBDP
Language instr: Spanish

Colegio Los Álamos
Calle Estados Unidos 731,
Jesús María, Lima, 11 Peru
Tel: +51 1 4631044
Head of School: Jorge
Camacho Bueno
Curriculum: IBDP

Colegio Magister
Francisco de Cuéllar #686,
Surco, Lima, 33 Peru
Tel: +51 1 437 9029
Head of School: Yolanda de Belloni
Age range: 3–17
Curriculum: IBDP, National, TOEFL
Language instr: Spanish

Colegio Max Uhle
Av. Fernandini s/n, Sachaca,
Arequipa, Peru
Tel: +51 54 232921
Head of School: Gerhart Steinbach
No. of pupils: 1165
Curriculum: IBDP
Language instr: Spanish

Colegio Nuestra Señora del Pilar
Av Virgen del Pilar 1711,
Cercado, Arequipa, Peru
Tel: +5154226262
Head of School: Juan
Carlos Rivera Velazco
Curriculum: IBDP

Colegio Peruano – Alemán Reina del Mundo
Avenida Rinconada del Lago
675, La Molina, Lima, 12 Peru
Tel: +511 479 2191/+511 368
0495/+511 368 0496
Head of School: Schw
Viviana Orellano Labrin
Age range: 2–17
No. of pupils: 771
Fees: US$3,000–US$4,000
Curriculum: IBDP
Language instr: Spanish

Colegio Peruano Alemán Beata Imelda
Carretera Central Km. 29,
Chosica, Lima, 15 Peru
Tel: +51 1 360 3119
Head of School: Volker Allendorf
Curriculum: IBDP

Colegio Peruano Británico
Avda. Via Lactea 445, Monterrico,
Santiago de Surco, Lima 33 Peru
Tel: +51 1 436 0151
Headmaster: G J Crebbin
Curriculum: IBDP, IBPYP
Language instr: Spanish, English

Colegio Pestalozzi (Colegio Suizo del Peru)
Casilla 18-1027, Aurora-
Miraflores, Lima, 18 Peru
Tel: +51 1 241 4218
Head of School: Urs
Steiner Meerstetter
Age range: 4–18
No. of pupils: 574 B282 G292
Curriculum: IBDP
Language instr: Spanish

Colegio Sagrados Corazones 'Recoleta'
Av. Circunvalación del Golf
368, La Molina, Lima, Peru
Tel: +51 1 702 2500
Head of School: Francisco
Marcone Flores
Age range: 4–18
Curriculum: IBDP
Language instr: Spanish

Colegio San Agustín
Av. Javier Prado Este 980 San
Isidro, Lima, Lima 27 Peru
Tel: +51 1 616 4242 / +51 1 440 0320
Director General: Elías
Neira Arellano
Curriculum: IBDP

Colegio San Agustín de Chiclayo
Km 8 Carretera Pimentel,
Chiclayo, Lambayeque, Peru
Tel: +51 7 420 2948
Head of School: Homero
Cardozo Vargas
Age range: 3–17
No. of pupils: 1380
Fees: US$1,800–US$3,000
Curriculum: IBDP
Language instr: Spanish

Colegio San Ignacio de Recalde
Calle Géminis 251 San
Borja, Lima, Peru
Tel: +511 2119430
Head: María Inés Prado
Vargas-Machuca
Curriculum: IBDP
Language instr: English

Colegio Santa Úrsula
Calle Salamanca N° 125,
San Isidro, Lima, Peru
Tel: +51 202 7430
Head of School: Brigitte Nuyken
Curriculum: IBDP

Davy College
Avenida Hoyos Rubio 2684,
Cajamarca, Casilla 1 Peru
Tel: +51 76 36 7501
Superintendent: Peter Zeitoun
Age range: 2–18
No. of pupils: B359 G418 VIth8
Curriculum: IBDP
Language instr: Spanish, English

Hiram Bingham School
Paseo de la Castellana 919,
Surco, Lima, 33 Peru
Tel: +51 1 271 9880
Head of School: Thomas Lewis
No. of pupils: 485
Fees: US$2,640
Curriculum: IBDP, IBMYP, IBPYP
Language instr: English, Spanish

Lord Byron School
Jr Viña del Mar 375-379,
Urb. Sol de la Molina, 1era.
Etapa, Lima, 12 Peru
Tel: +511 4791717
Head of School: Janette
Urday Cáceres
Curriculum: IBDP
Language instr: English, Spanish

Markham College
Apartado 18-1048,
Miraflores, Lima, Peru
Tel: +51 1 315 6750
Director General: David Dowdles
Age range: 4–18
No. of pupils: 2100
Curriculum: IBDP
Language instr: English

Peruvian North American Abraham Lincoln School
Calle José Antonio 475, Urb
Parque de Monterrico, La
Molina Lima, 12 Peru
Tel: +51 1 617 4500
Headmaster: Luis Requena Pérez
Age range: 3–17
Fees: US$4,000
Curriculum: IBDP, IBMYP,
IBPYP, National
Language instr: Spanish, English

San Silvestre School Asociacion Civil
Apartado 18-0492,
Miraflores, Lima, 18 Peru
Tel: +51 1 2413334
Head of School: Rina Bayly
Age range: G3–18
No. of pupils: 1180
Curriculum: IBDP
Language instr: English

Sir Alexander Fleming College
Av América Sur 3701, Trujillo, Peru
Tel: +51 044 280395
Headteacher: Alan Nocker
Age range: 2–17
No. of pupils: B360 G360
Curriculum: National, IGCSE
Language instr: Spanish, English

St George's College
Av General Ernesto
Montagne 360, Urb La Aurora,
Miraflores, Lima, 18 Peru
Tel: +511 242 5747
Head of School: James Norbury
Curriculum: IBDP

Turks & Caicos Islands

The Ashcroft School
PO Box 278, Governor's Road,
Leeward, Providenciales,
Turks & Caicos Islands
Tel: +1 649 94 65523
Principal: Gabrielle Sullivan
Age range: 2–13
No. of pupils: 124

Uruguay

British Schools
Máximo Tajes 6400, esq Havre,
Montevideo, 11500 Uruguay
Tel: +598 2 600 3421
Principal: Alan Ripley
Age range: 4–18
No. of pupils: B720 G750
Curriculum: IBDP, National
Language instr: English, Spanish

Colegio Stella Maris
Máximo Tajes 7357/7359, CP 11500
Montevideo, 11500 Uruguay
Tel: +598 2 600 0702
Head of School: Juan
Pedro Toni Cavani
Age range: 4–17
No. of pupils: 1086 B576 G510
Curriculum: IBDP, IGCSE
Language instr: Spanish, English

Escuela Integral Hebreo Uruguaya
Jose Benito Lamas 2835,
Montevideo, 11300 Uruguay
Tel: +598 2 708 1712
Head of School: Cecilia Perazzo
Curriculum: IBDP
Language instr: Spanish

St Brendan's School
Av Rivera 2314, Montevideo,
CP 11200 Uruguay
Tel: +598 2409 4939
Head of School: Jimena Taboada
Age range: 3–17
Curriculum: IBDP, IBMYP, IBPYP
Language instr: English, Spanish

St Clare's College
California y los Médanos, Punta del
Este, San Rafael, 20000 Uruguay
Tel: +598 42 490200
Head of School: Daniel Reta
Curriculum: IBDP, ALevs
Language instr: Spanish, English

St Patrick's College
Camino Gigantes 2735,
Montevideo, 12100 Uruguay
Tel: +598 2 601 3474
Head of School: Manuel Varela
Age range: 3–18
Curriculum: IBMYP
Language instr: Spanish

Uruguayan American School
Saldún de Rodríguez
2375, Montevideo, Area
Code 11500 Uruguay
Tel: + (598) 2600 7681
Director: Michael Schramm
Curriculum: IBDP
Language instr: English

Woodlands School
San Carlos de Bolivar s/n
entre Havre y Cooper,
Montevideo, 11500 Uruguay
Tel: +59 82 604 27 14
Head of School: Sandra Senz
Curriculum: IBMYP, IGCSE
Language instr: Spanish

Woodside School
Punta del Este,
Maldonaldo, Uruguay
Tel: +598 42252552
Head of School: Claudia
Dominguez
Language instr: Spanish

Venezuela

Centro de Educación Valle Abierto
Calle Loma Azul, Urb San Luis, El
Cafetal, Caracas, Venezuela
Tel: +58 212 985 4552
Head of School: Blanca
Azpurua de Perelli
Age range: 1–18
No. of pupils: B189 G151
Curriculum: IBMYP, IBPYP, National
Language instr: Spanish

Colegio Bellas Artes
Zulia, Av 3F, con calle 71,
Maracaibo, Zulia, 4002 Venezuela
Tel: +58 0261 7911 175
Head of School: Milagros Viera
No. of pupils: 897
Curriculum: IBDP
Language instr: Spanish

Colegio Internacional de Caracas
Pakmail 6030, PO Box 025304,
Miami, FL 33102, USA Venezuela
Tel: +58 212 945 0444
Director: Carmen Sweeting
Curriculum: IBDP, IBMYP
Language instr: English, Spanish

Colegio Los Campitos
Ruta C, Urbanización Los
Campitos, Prados del Este,
Miranda, Venezuela
Tel: +58 212 977 1768
Head of School: Dominga
Antonuccio de Fernàndez
Fees: Day £0
Curriculum: IBDP
Language instr: Spanish

Colegio Moral y Luces
Final Ave. Los Chorros, SEDE CLUB
HEBRAICA (Frente al INAM), Los
Chorros, Caracas 1071 Venezuela
Tel: +58 212 273 6894/6807
Curriculum: IBDP

Escuela Bella Vista
Buzoom C-Mar-P-1815,
PO Box 02-8537, Miami, FL
33102, USA Venezuela
Tel: +58 261 794 0000
Head of School: Todd Zukewich
Curriculum: IBDP
Language instr: English

Escuela Campo Alegre
8424 NW 56th Street, Suite
CCS 00007, Miami, FL
33166, USA Venezuela
Tel: +1 58 212, 993 3922
Head of School: Jeff Paulson
Age range: 4–18
No. of pupils: 628 B311 G317
Fees: US$14,737–US$19,895
Curriculum: IBDP, USA
Language instr: English

Instituto Educacional Juan XXIII
Calle San Enrique No 85-70,
Trigal Centro, Valencia, Estado
Caraboo 2002 Venezuela
Tel: +58 241 8425732
Head of School: Virginia
Segovia de Bolivar
Curriculum: IBDP, IBMYP, IBPYP
Language instr: Spanish

Liceo Los Robles
Urbanización el Doral Norte,
Calle 34 esquina con Avenida,
Fuerzas Armadas, Mar, Estado
Zulia, 4002 Venezuela
Tel: +58 0261 7421833
Head of School: Adán
Jesús Rincón Rincón
Curriculum: IBDP
Language instr: Spanish

Morrocoy International School
c/o MUN-4385, PO Box
025352, Miami, FL 33102-
5352, USA Venezuela
Tel: +58 286 923 9742
Headmistress: Deborah de Azuaje
Age range: 3–15
No. of pupils: 38 B20 G18

QSI International School of El Tigre
Escuela las Americas,
El Tigre, Venezuela
Tel: +58 283 241 2005
Director: Michael Kempenich
Age range: 4–16
No. of pupils: 74
Curriculum: USA
Language instr: English

THE BRITISH SCHOOL CARACAS
For further details see p. 173
PO Box 668708, c/o Jet
International 489, Miami, Fl
33166, USA Venezuela
Tel: +58, 212 267 9443
Email:
headmaster@tbscaracas.com
Website: www.tbscaracas.com
Head of School: John Plommer
Age range: 3–18
No. of pupils: 350 B184 G166
Fees: US$8,050–US$19,923
Curriculum: IBDP, IPC, UK, IGCSE
(CIS) (ECIS)

Unidad Educativa Academia Washington
Coordinacion BI, Calle 'C', Colina
de Valle Arriba, Caracas, Estado
Miranda 1080 Venezuela
Tel: +58 0212 9757077
Head of School: Miranda Di Silvestri
No. of pupils: 482
Curriculum: IBDP
Language instr: Spanish

International school associations and groups

The Alliance for International Education (AIE)

The Alliance for International Education is committed to promoting international learning in any context. Its aim is always to balance theoretical discourse and research with practical action. Its conferences and activities bring together mainstream international schools with universities, researchers, providers of curriculum, resources and training, and representatives from state and private educational systems who are keen to internationalise learning in their own schools. Besides its 'world conferences' the AIE supports regional initiatives in several parts of the world – and in line with its vision that international education should be available to every child, it operates as an open access, open source organization where there are no membership fees for becoming a partners or for accessing resources.

For more information about the AIE, contact:

Beatrice Caston, Alliance for International Education, Niederrheinstrasse 336, 404089 Dusseldorf, Germany

Tel: +49 211 9406 712
Fax: +49 211 9406 804

Email: darlenef8@yahoo.co.uk
csalter.aie@btinternet.com

Website: www.intedalliance.org

Association of American Schools of Central America (AASCA)

The Association of American Schools of Central America (AASCA) was formed to support and encourage academic, artistic, athletic and cultural interaction between international schools that offer a US type education in Central America. It believes that through the organization and sponsorship of these types of activities that all young people involved will be exposed to and benefit from the multicultural interaction. It is the desire of AASCA to promote a better understanding of multiculturalism among all races of young people through these events.

AASCA also supports the continuing education of its member teachers and administrators through facilitating workshops and conferences that focus on the latest educational ideas and teaching methods from the United States. AASCA aims to improve the quality of all education in the countries in which they reside and create a greater awareness and appreciation for cultural diversity through the programs they sponsor.

AASAC has 23 schools in the following countries: Guatemala, El Salvador, Honduras, Nicaragua, Costa Rica and Panama. Any Central American school that provides a US curriculum is eligible to join this association.

President: Ron Vair (rvair@seishn.com)
Secretary: Adolfo González (adolfo@lincoln.edu.ni)

Website: www.aascaonline.net

Association of American Schools in South America (AASSA)

AASSA has 50 full member schools in 16 South American countries, namely: Argentina, Bolivia, Brazil, Chile, Colombia, Ecuador, Guyana, Jamaica, Netherlands Antilles, Nicaragua, Panama, Paraguay, Peru, Trinidad & Tobago, Uruguay and Venezuela. Its mission is to provide and promote programmes and services to their members, all of whom offer an American international education. In its mission statement, AASSA says that it values service leadership, quality and effectiveness.

Various services are provided for member schools including: a purchasing service; a recruiting fair in Central America and the Caribbean; four annual professional development conferences; a payroll processing service; awards to AASSA Heads; annual salary and benefits survey; and a quarterly newsletter.

AASSA member schools are all private, non-profit, institutions offering a mainly American curriculum; the language of instruction is English. Each of the schools combines US and host country courses of study, and many grant both host country and US diplomas. Some schools also offer the IB, Advanced Placement (AP) courses, and English as a Second Language (ESL).

AASSA schools who hold full membership are: elementary and/or secondary schools; have English as the primary language of instruction; are accredited by a recognised organization such as CIS or the IB; and agree to follow the principles, purposes and objectives of AASSA.

Contact: AASSA, 1911 NW 150 Avenue, Suite 101, Pembroke Pines, FL 33028, USA

Tel: +1 954 436 4034; Fax: +1 954 436 409

Website: www.aassa.com
Email: info@aassa.com

Association of British Schools Chile (ABSCH)

Founded in 1977 with just seven schools, this association now has 20 member schools, in Santiago, Viña del Mar, Casablanca, Concepción, Punta Arenas and Antofagasta. Its schools offer education for pupils aged four to 18 and all schools are bilingual with similar aims and practices. It believes in ongoing training for teaching staff and its mission is to 'encourage and support member schools in its endeavour to provide an education of quality that reflects the best of British practice, in co-operation with one another, and with Chilean and British educational authorities'.

For more information contact:

ABSCH, Juan Montalvo 80, Las Condes, Santiago, Chile CP 677 1083

Tel: +56 2 2121 953
Fax: +56 2 2121 944

Website: www.absch.cl
Email: absoffice@absch.cl

Association of China and Mongolia International Schools (ACAMIS)

Founded to promote and support the building of international schools in China and Mongolia, ACAMIS now has a membership that includes more than 50 of the 150+ international schools operating within China, Hong Kong, Macao, Taiwan and Mongolia.

The association hosts various student activities, professional development workshops for teachers and networking opportunities for Heads of schools, and other educational personnel within member schools. There is an annual meeting for ACAMIS Heads.

The association's aims are: to widen and evolve the curriculum of ACAMIS schools; to encourage the professional development of staff within their schools; to facilitate communication between member schools; to promote understanding and international friendship; to co-operate with others pursuing the same objectives; to encourage student exchanges; to collaborate on professional development; and to support national and regional networking.

For more information contact the Executive Officer:

Tel: +86 18706134540
Email: eo@acamis.org

Website: www.acamis.org

Association of Colombian-Caribbean American Schools (ACCAS)

ACCAS is one of the regional associations affiliated with the Tri-Association (www.tri-association.org).

It has 21 schools offering an American education in the Colombian and Caribbean region. Its core values include: school improvement and ongoing staff development.

All member schools must be US accredited candidates for accreditation. Currently it has schools in the Dominican Republic, Haiti, Ecuador, Venezuela and Colombia.

Website: www.tri-association.org

Association of German International Schools (AGIS)

The Association of German International Schools (AGIS) represents and supports the educational and public interest of member schools and their communities by promoting and improving international education. It currently has 25 members.

AGIS, Bruchmeisterallee 6, 30169 Hannover
Tel: +49 0511 10532406;
Fax: +49 0511 27041651;

Executive Secretary: Julia Brühöfner
Email: julia@agis-schools.org

Website: www.agis-schools.org

Association of International Schools in Africa (AISA)

AISA represents international schools on the continent of Africa. Its schools range in size from 20 to 3600 students. AISA schools tend to have an American or British-based curriculum; others have an eclectic mix but all have an international focus.

The association's goal is to serve the varying needs of its students, teachers and administrators. Its mission is to increase school effectiveness and inspire student learning by promoting communication, collaboration, and professional development.

AISA's objectives are: to enhance the quality of learning by promoting effective practice; foster intercultural and international understanding; promote an appreciation and understanding of Africa; support professional development within member schools; collate, analyse, and distribute information to help guide member schools; enable collaboration and networking between members; and to develop and maintain partnerships with organisations and institutions that complement the association's values and mission.

AISA, PO Box 14103-00800, Nairobi, Kenya

Tel: +254 (0) 20 269 7442;
Fax: +254 (0) 20 418 0596

Website: www.aisa.or.ke
Email: info@aisa.or.ke

Association of American Schools in Mexico (ASOMEX)

ASOMEX is a member of the Tri-Association (www.tri-association.org).

It was founded in 1957 and originally included eight American schools. Today, it is made up of 18 member schools throughout Mexico. These schools are private, non-profit establishments ranging in size from 42 to over 3000 students. It is committed to offering an American style curriculum, whilst meeting the criteria set down by the Mexican Secretariat of Education.

ASOMEX's main aims are: to develop a closer union of the American schools in Mexico; seek to resolve common problems of member schools; advance ideals and standards; assist member schools in establishing and maintaining high standards; encourage and enhance the multicultural/bilingual aspects of member schools; provide qualified consultants to teachers and administrators; select and procure quality educational materials and equipment; and develop communications and relations amongst member schools.

There are a wide variety of annual ASOMEX activities for members, including athletic tournaments, teacher and student workshops, model UN, and art and musical festivals.

Email: info@asomex.org
Website: www.asomex.org

British Association of Independent Schools with International Students (BAISIS)

The British Association of Independent Schools with International Students (BAISIS) is a group of educational centres which provide a full academic curriculum in the United Kingdom to students from other countries.

Members are drawn from independent schools, study centres and colleges. Originally founded in 1997 by Bedford, Rossall, Sherborne and Taunton Schools, membership has grown steadily and today the association is an influential organisation which occupies, and speaks for, an important niche sector in international education in the UK.

The Association exists to provide help in the form of training, development, and mutual support to its members and for quality assurance purposes. This is achieved through regular meetings, training from inside and outside the Association and through a bespoke annual conference. All member institutions provide a supportive pastoral framework and quality academic environment for international students.

The Association also represents the interests of schools and colleges with international students in the UK at the national level.

Website: www.baisis.org.uk

British Schools in the Middle East (BSME)

BSME has more than 70 schools in membership in 13 countries.

It provides a quality-assured network of schools helping Heads and Teachers share best practice and keep abreast of the latest educational developments. BSME runs its own Accreditation System, Annual Headteachers' Conferences, Continuing Professional Development (CPD) programme of over 100 courses per year and a range of inter-school sports, music, arts and other events.

All members schools are: an English Medium, essentially British Curriculum School in which the Principal/Head Teacher and the majority of teachers (apart from those teaching local languages) have qualifications recognised by the Division [sic] of Family and Children's Services (DFCS) in London.

Each year BSME holds a conference to discuss and learn about developments in UK education and school leadership and management issues.

BSME Head Office, PO Box 32052, Isa Town, Kingdom of Bahrain

Tel: +973 1759 8498
Fax: +973 1759 8493

Website: www.bsme.org.uk
Email: enquiries@bsme.org.uk

Central & Eastern European Schools Association (CEESA)

The Central & Eastern European Schools Association (CEESA) was founded as a result of the growth of American and International Schools in Central and Eastern Europe. In many cases, the schools were geographically isolated from each other and from the main stream of American and International Education.

CEESA was formed to broaden the horizons of schools and to promote professional growth. In addition to the CEESA Annual Conference in March, CEESA sponsors regional workshops, institutes and meetings to foster professionalism, scholarship, and a deeper understanding of improvements for leading, teaching and learning.

CEESA also sponsors student activities, focusing on a variety of academic and non-academic areas, and a full schedule of sports events.

CEESA, Vocarska 106, Zagreb 10000, Croatia

Tel: +385 91 181 7921;
Fax: +385 1 468 0171

Email: office@ceesa.org
Website: www.ceesa.org

Council of British International Schools (COBIS)

COBIS is a membership association of British schools of quality worldwide and is committed to a stringent process of quality assurance for all its member schools.

Founded more than 30 years ago, it is governed by an elected board of headteachers and governors from member schools worldwide. COBIS hosts a range of conferences and professional development events for teachers, middle leaders, support staff throughout the year plus an annual conference in London in May for school leaders and Governors

COBIS represents its members with the British Government, educational bodies, the corporate sector and Ministries of Education worldwide. It is a member of the Independent Schools Council (ISC) of the United Kingdom.

COBIS, St Mary's University, Strawberry Hill, Twickenham TW1 4SX

Tel: 0208 240 4142
Fax: 0208 240 4255

CEO: Colin Bell
Email: ceo@cobis.org.uk

Website: www.cobis.org.uk

Council of International Schools (CIS)

CIS is a not-for-profit organisation committed to supporting its member schools and colleges in achieving and delivering the highest standards of international education.

CIS provides accreditation to schools, teacher and leader recruitment and best practice development. CIS Higher Education assists member colleges and universities in recruiting a diverse profile of qualified international students.

CIS, Schipholweg 113, 2316 XC Leiden, The Netherlands.

Tel: +31 71 524 3300
Email: info@cois.org

Website: www.cois.org

European Association for International Education (EAIE)

The EAIE is a non-profit member-led organisation of more than 1800 international education professionals, whose aim is the promotion of the internationalisation of higher education in Europe and around the world.

The association aims to link international education professionals together. Professional development, an annual EAIE conference, and various groups work towards ensuring that attention is paid to the specific topics that concern EAIE members as well as the general topics challenging the international higher education arena.

EAIE, PO Box 11189, 1001 GD Amsterdam, The Netherlands

Tel: +31 20 3445 100
Fax: +31 20 3445 119

Email: info@eaie.nl
Website: www.eaie.org

East Asia Regional Council of Overseas Schools (EARCOS)

EARCOS is an organisation of 141 schools in East Asia, as well as 162 associate members and other individual members. Membership for schools is open to elementary and secondary establishments that offer English as the primary language of instruction.

The organisation has a vision that includes: developing collaborative educational partnerships worldwide; providing professional development opportunities for members; connecting schools, communities, and individuals through the use of technology; understanding, and access to broader educational opportunities; engaging all in learning activities that will promote friendship, understanding and global citizenship.

EARCOS, Brentville subdivision, Barangay Mamplasan, Biñan, Laguna, 4024, Philippines

Tel: +63 (02) 697 9170
Fax: +63 (49) 511 4694

Email: info@earcos.org
Website: www.earcos.org

European Council of International Schools (ECIS)

A network of schools and companies committed to promoting international education. Founded in 1965, ECIS is made up of regular member schools, affiliate members who provide services such as professional development for teachers, supporting members made up of commercial companies who supply/service the international schools market, and individual members.

ECIS, Fourth Floor, 146 Buckingham Palace Road, London

Tel: +44 (0)20 7824 7040

Email: ecis@ecis.org
Website: www.ecis.org

Federation of British International Schools in Asia (FOBISIA)

FOBISIA is a regional federation of the leading British international schools in Asia. Member schools have to meet a range of quality standards in order to be accepted into the federation and to retain membership.

Additionally, affiliate membership of FOBISIA is open to reputable educational organisations and suppliers whose services and products are of interest to member schools.

FOBISIA hosts a range of student events including the FOBISIA Games, a music festival, a primary performing arts carnival, mathematics competitions, a model United Nations conference and a short story writing competition.

It also organises conferences and workshops where teachers from across the region can meet to share good practice, swap ideas and receive professional training from invited university lecturers and consultants from around the world.

Contact: Shaun Williams, The British International School, Ho Chi Min City
246 Nguyen Van Huong Street, Thao Dien Ward District 2, Ho Chi Min City, Vietnam

Tel: +84 8744 23335
Fax: +84 8744 2334

Email: shaunwilliams@bisvietnam.com
Website: www.fobisia.org

International Schools Association (ISA)

The ISA is based in Geneva, with offices in India and the USA, and was established in Paris in 1951 as an international organisation for the development of co-operation among its member schools and with all those interested in promoting international understanding.

The ISA was instrumental in the development of the International Baccalaureate Organization and in creating a programme for middle schools, which later developed into the IBMYP. It publishes Internationalism in Schools – a Self-Study Guide, for schools and sponsor an annual 'Youth Encounter' for students from member and non-member schools. A biannual World Conference is organized around a theme dealing with international education and the association sponsors oral English examinations.

International Schools Association, 18, Avenue Louis Casaï – 1209 Geneva, Switzerland

Email: info@isaschools.org
Website: www.isaschools.org

International Schools Association of Thailand (ISAT)

This association was established in 1994 principally to act as a link between its member international schools, the Ministry of Education and the Office of the Private Education Commission. It is now involved in the joint marketing of international education both in Thailand and overseas.

ISAT has over 75 schools offering a range of curricula: American, British and international systems. They are committed to the promotion of the Thai language and culture in international schools along with support for culture and sporting links between international schools in Thailand and worldwide. ISAT member schools are accredited by WASC, NEASC and CIS.

ISAT, 39/7 Soi Nichada Thani, Samakee Road, Pakkret, Nonthaburi 11120

Tel: +66 (0)2 960 4101
Fax: +66 (0)2 960 4102

Email: isat@isat.or.th
Website: www.isat.or.th

Mediterranean Association of International Schools (MAIS)

The Mediterranean Association of International Schools strives to improve the quality of education in its member schools. It promotes the professional development of faculty, administrators, and school board members, effects communication and interchange, and creates international understanding.

MAIS serves as a liaison between its 39 member schools, 41 associate member organizations as well as other regional, professional, and in-service organizations.

Presently, MAIS is composed of schools from 15 different countries, including Austria, Cyprus, Egypt, France, Italy, Lebanon, Malta, Morocco, Oman, Portugal, Spain, Tunisia, Turkey, United Arab Emirates and the United Kingdom. In addition, several associate members, such as schools outside the Mediterranean region, colleges, businesses, and interested individuals, support MAIS endeavors and have joined the organization.

Tel: +34 91 352-0678
Fax: +34 91 352-7795

Email: rohale@mais-web.org
Website: www.mais-web.org

National Association of British Schools in Spain (NABSS)

The National Association of British Schools in Spain (NABSS) was founded in 1978 to promote, uphold and defend British education in Spain. The only schools permitted to be members of NABSS are those that are fully authorised British schools, recognised as such by the British Council and its official inspectorate.

NABSS insists on regular inspection of member schools, provides professional training for Heads and teachers and organises an annual conference with workshops.

The association aims to maintain contact with the British Council and the Spanish educational authorities as per the requirements of legislation referring to foreign schools in Spain.

NABSS's website lists all member schools. These schools follow the British National Curriculum and employ fully qualified staff. They range in age from early years to 16 and offer a broad selection of GCSE, AS and A level courses and generally administer UCAS entry to universities in the UK. Spanish authorities give full recognition to A levels and grant automatic access to spanish universities for NABSS A level students.

Email: info@nabss.org
Website: www.nabss.org

Near East South Asia Council of Overseas Schools (NESA)

NESA began informally in the early 1960s and has evolved into a world class organisation that serves more than 100 American international schools. The association promotes links between educators working in private, independent international schools in the Near East and South Asia region. Regular membership of the association is open to any American overseas or international overseas school located in the Near East South Asia geographical area, as long as they share the objectives and purposes of NESA and are accredited by a recognized agency.

NESA, Gravias 6, Aghia Paraskevia 153 42, Athens, Greece

Email: nesa@nesacenter.org
Website: www.nesacenter.org

Nordic Network of English Speaking Schools (NNESS)

Organisation that serves English speaking schools in the Nordic and Baltic regions. Originally founded by five international schools from Denmark, Norway and Sweden, it now offers membership to other schools in the region who provide an international education in English.

NNESS, Postbox 53, 1318 Bekkestua, Norway

Tel: +47 6781 8290
Email: admin@nordicnetworkonline.net
Website: www.nordicnetwork.net

Quality Schools International (QSI)

QSI is a group of 37 schools, in 27 countries, who are non-profit international schools serving diplomatic, development and business families. The association was first founded in 1971.

QSI schools have financial support from the US government and are accredited by the MSACS or the SACS. For further details: QSI, Langusova 16, 1000 Ljubljana, Slovenia

Tel: +386 1 200 7870; Fax: +386 1 200 7871
Email: qsi@qsi.org
Website: www.qsi.org

Round Square International Schools (RSIS)

Round Square is a world-wide association of schools on five continents. Students attending Round Square schools make a strong commitment, beyond academic excellence, to personal development and responsibility.

The Round Square approach promotes six IDEALS of learning: Internationalism, Democracy, Environment, Adventure, Leadership and Service. These are incorporated into the curriculum throughout all member schools.

Access to the Round Square network affords member schools the opportunity to arrange local and international student and teacher exchanges on a regular basis between their schools. Pupils also have the opportunity to participate in local and international community service projects and conferences

Tasks tackled through the community projects include building schools, classrooms and community centres; building clean water systems for remote hill-tribes or creating and maintaining trails in National Parks. Local materials are used, and teams always work with local people ensuring that they take ownership of the work once it has been completed

Round Square teams currently work in Thailand, Cambodia, Peru, Honduras, India, Kenya, South Africa, Romania, and Canada.

In 2014 The Sanskaar Valley School, Bhopal, India and King's Academy, Madaba, Jordan will jointly be hosting the Round Square International Conference.

Round Square, PO Box 105, Longfield DA3 9DA
United Kingdom

Tel: +44 (0) 1474 709843
Fax: +27 0865 5392 79
Email: enquire@roundsquare.org
Website: ww.roundsquare.org

Swiss Group of International Schools (SGIS)

The Swiss Group of International Schools (SGIS) is a non-profit organization. It exists to: promote closer links between the teachers, administrators, and students of its member schools and professional development; provide opportunities for arranging educational, cultural and sporting activities; represent the concerns of Swiss international schools; and co-operate and maintain professional contacts with other regional and international educational bodies and associations.

Each year it holds conferences and workshops, promote inter-school sports competitions at all levels, and hold an AGM that all members are encouraged to attend.

Email: info@sgischools.com
Website: www.sgischools.com

The Tri-Association – The Association of American Schools of Central America, Colombia-Caribbean and Mexico

Name of the joint association for AASCA, ACCAS and ASOMEX – see those entries for more information.

Contact: 1209 San Dario Ave, Suite 92-66, Laredo, TX, 78040, USA

Tel: (011) 52-81- 83384454

Email: skeller@tri-association.org
Website: www.tri-association.org

United World Colleges (UWC)

The concept for the first UWC (United World College) was conceived by Kurt Hahn at the end of the 1950s. As an educationalist himself, he believed that it was possible to create a curriculum that allowed students to study and learn about their own cultures but learn about the varied cultures of the world, without bias to any religious, cultural or racial misunderstanding, given them a more balanced education and allowing them to become truly global citizens of the world.

UWC of the Atlantic was opened in 1962, and there are now UWC schools and colleges in 13 countries, and national committees and selection contacts in over 140. UWC schools and colleges teach the IB Diploma and the organisation was instrumental in development of the IB.

Contact: UWC International, Second Floor, 17-21 Emerald Street, London WC1N 3QN

Tel: +44 (0) 20 7269 7800
Fax: +44 (0) 20 7405 4374

Email: uwcio@uwc.org
Website: www.uwc.org

Ministries of Education worldwide

Ministries of Education

Please note: every effort has been made to obtain information about all the Ministries of Education worldwide. However, some countries do not publish this information, others either do not have a specific education department or provide this information freely.

Most schools now refer to Years or Grades when talking about a specific age group. As a general guide the charts below outlines which Year/Grade denotes which age group.

UK SYSTEM

Year	Age
1	5-6
2	6-7
3	7-8
4	8-9
5	9-10
6	10-11
7	11-12
8	12-13
9	13-14
10	14-15
11	15-16
12	16-17
13	17-18

USA SYSTEM

Grade	Age
Preschool	
Pre-kindergarten	4-6
Elementary School	
Kindergarten	5-6
1st Grade	6-7
2nd Grade	7-8
3rd Grade	8-9
4th Grade	9-10
5th Grade	10-11
Middle School	
6th Grade	11-12
7th Grade	12-13
8th Grade	13-14
High School	
9th Grade – Freshman	14-15
10th Grade – Sophomore	15-16
11th Grade – Junior	16-17
12th Grade – Senior	17-18

ANGOLA
Angola Ministry of Education, Avenue Comandante Gika, Luanda
Tel: +244 222 320 502
Website: www.med.gov.ao
Primary school, ages 7-11
Secondary school, ages 11-19

ANTIGUA AND BARBUDA
Ministry of Education, Sports, Youth and Gender Affairs, Government Office Complex, St John's, Antigua
Tel: +1 268 462 4959
Website: www.education.gov.ag
Primary school, ages 5-12
Secondary school, ages 12-17
Post-16 education available at three colleges

ARGENTINA
Ministry of Education, Pizzurno 935, Segundo Piso, Oficina 143 (ala Marcelo T. de Alverar), CPA C1020ACA, Ciudad de Buenos Aires
Tel: +54 011 4129 1000
Website: www.me.gov.ar
Primary - Educación General Básica (EGB I), ages 6-8
Primary - Educación General Básica (EGB II), ages 9-11
Secondary - Educación General Básica (EGB III), ages 12-14
Secondary - Polimodal, ages 15-17
Other: some areas of Argentina have different names and criteria for secondary education.

ARMENIA
Ministry of Education and Science, Government Building 3, Republic Square, Yerevan
Tel: +374 (10) 52 7000
Website: www.gov.am/en
Elementary, ages 7-9
Basic secondary, ages 10-14
High school, ages 15-16
Post-16 education available in technical secondary colleges, universities

AUSTRALIA
Department of Education, Employment and Workplace Relations, GPO Box 9880, Canberra, ACT 2601
Tel: +61 1300 363 079
Website: www.deewr.gov.au
Compulsory education:
- Lower primary level education, ages 5-9
- Upper primary level education, ages 9-13
- Lower secondary phase education, ages 11-16
- Upper secondary level education, ages 16-18
Other: each state and territory in Australia has the responsibility for their own schools, including enrolment policies, curriculum content, course accreditation and certification, as well as the methods of assessment used. Australia also has part-time, pre-schools, which are available for up to two years before the age of six. However, during the second pre-school year there is the option to go full-time; this year is known as the preparatory year. Post-16 education in Australia is available in the form of secondary schools, technical or vocational colleges, senior colleges or rural training schools.

AUSTRIA
Federal Ministry for Education, Arts and Culture, Minoritenplatz 5, A-1014 Vienna
Tel: +43 (0)1 53120 0
Website: www.bmukk.gv.at/en
Pre-school, age 5
Elementary, ages 6-9
Lower secondary, ages 10-13
Upper secondary, ages 14-17
Vocational, ages 14-18

AZERBAIJAN REPUBLIC
Ministry of Education, 49 Khatai Avenue, Baku, AZ-1008
Tel: +994 12 496 0647
Website: www.edu.gov.az
Primary, ages 6-10
Basic, ages 10-15
Secondary, ages 15-17
Other: secondary schooling is free but parents of primary students are asked to pay a proportion of school fees etc.

THE BAHAMAS
Ministry of Education, Thompson Boulevard, PO Box N-3913, Nassau
Tel: Tel: +1 242 502 2700
Website: www.bahamaseducation.com
Nursery/kindergarten, ages 3-5
Primary, ages 5-11
Secondary, ages 12-15
Senior high school, ages 16-18

KINGDOM OF BAHRAIN
Ministry of Education, Pp B 43, Manama
Tel: +973 1727 8999
Website: www.moe.gov.bh
Pre-school, up to age 6
Basic, ages 6-14
Secondary, ages 15-17
Other: state run schools tend to be single sex, whereas private education offers coeducational schools.

BANGLADESH
Ministry of Education, Building 6, Floor 17th & 18th, Bangladesh Secretariat, Dhaka-1000
Tel: +880 716 8711
Website: www.moedu.gov.bd
Pre-primary, ages 3-6
Primary, ages 6-11
Secondary, ages 11-18
Other: the government partially subsidises private education.

BARBADOS
Ministry of Education and Human Resource Development, Elsie Payne Complex, St Michael, West Indies
Tel: +1 246 430 2700
Website: www.mes.gov.bb
Primary, ages 5-11
Secondary, ages 11-16
Other: some private secondary schools are government assisted.

REPUBLIC OF BELARUS
Ministry of Education, 9 Sovetskaya Street, 220010, Minsk
Tel: +375 17 227 4736
Website: www.minedu.unibel.by
Primary, ages 6-10
Basic, ages 10-15
General secondary, ages 15-17
Specialised secondary, ages 15-19
Vocational secondary, ages 15-18
Other: secondary education lasts between two and four years, depending on which type the student enrols for.

BELGIUM
Flemish Ministry of Education and Training, Hendrik Consciencegebouw, Koning Albert II-laan 15, 1210 Brussels
Tel: +32 2 553 5070
Website: www.ond.vlaanderen.be/English
Nursery: ages 2-6
Primary, ages 6-11
Secondary, ages 12-18
Other: VGO schools, which are privately owned and either religious (Catholic, Jewish etc) or method (Steiner, Freinet, Montessori); these schools are funded by the government.

BELIZE
Ministry of Education and Youth, West Block, Belmopan, Cayo
Tel: +11 501 822 2380/3315
Website: www.moes.gov.bz
Primary, ages 5-13
Secondary, ages 13-17
Other: Church-run schools. Secondary education in Belize is not free and students from many low-income families leave school before the age of 15.

BERMUDA
Ministry of Education, Dundonald Place, 14 Dundonald Street, PO Box HM 1185, HM Ex
Tel: +1 441 278 3300
Website: www.gov.bm
Pre-school, ages 4-5
Primary, ages 5-11
Middle, ages 11-14
Secondary, ages 14-18

BHUTAN
Ministry of Education, PO Box 112, Thimphu
Website: www.education.gov.bt
Primary, ages 5-12
Secondary, ages 12-16
Other: Monastic schools.

BOLIVIA
Ministry of Education, Avenida Arce No 2147, PO Box 3116, La Paz
Tel: +591 2244 2144
Website: www.minedu.gob.bo
Primary, ages 7-14
Intermediate, ages 14-17
Secondary, ages 17-21

BOSNIA AND HERZEGOVINA
Federal Ministry of Education and Science, Obala Maka Dizdara 2, Sarajevo
Tel: +387 33 276 370
Website: www.fmon.gov.ba
Pre-school, ages 3-5
Elementary, ages 6-15
Secondary, ages 15-19

BOTSWANA
Ministry of Education and Skills Development, Block 6 Building, Government Enclave, Gaborone
Tel: +0800 6006 78
Website: www.moe.gov.bw
Primary, ages 5-12
Junior secondary, ages 12-15
Senior secondary, ages 16-18

BRAZIL
Ministry of Education, Esplanada dos Ministeries, Bloeo L. Brasilia DF, 70047-900
Tel: +55 (61) 410 0444
Website: www.brasil.gov.br
Pre-school, ages 2-7
Fundamental, ages 7-14
Intermediate, ages 15-18

BRITISH VIRGIN ISLANDS
Ministry of Education and Culture, Road Town, Tortola
Tel: +1 s84 494 7739 40
Website: www.bvi.org.uk
Pre-primary, ages 3-5
Primary, ages 5-12
Secondary, ages 13-17

BRUNEI DARUSSALAM
Ministry of Education, Old Airport Road, Berakas BB3510
Tel: +673 238 1133
Website: www.moe.edu.bn
Pre-school, age 4
Primary, ages 6-13
Secondary, ages 13-17
Other: primary school is free to citizens but secondary school is not and students pay subsidised fees.

BULGARIA
Ministry of Education, Youth and Science, Str Prince Dondukov 2A, 1000 Sofia
Tel: +359 921 7799
Website: www.minedu.government.bg
Primary, ages 7-10
Lower secondary, ages 10-14
Upper secondary, ages 14-19
Vocational secondary, ages 15-19
Professional secondary, ages 15-19
Other: time spent in secondary education depends on which secondary school is attended.

BURMA
Ministry of Education, Theinbyu Street, Botahtaung Township, Yangon
Tel: (1) 28 55 88
Website: www.myanmar-education.edu.mm
Pre-school, ages 2-5
Kindergarten, ages 5-6
Primary, ages 6-11
Middle, ages 11-14
Secondary, ages 14-15

CAMBODIA
Ministry of Education, Youth and Sport, 30 Sangkat Psar Kandal 2, Khan Daun Pen, Phnom Penh
Tel: +855 2372 2234
Website: www.moeys.gov.kh
Pre-school, ages 3-5
Primary, ages 6-11
Secondary, ages 12-16

CAMEROON
Ministry of Education, rue Boulevard de la reunification, BP 1739, Yaounde
Tel: +237 2222 5176
Website: www.spm.gov.cm
Primary, ages 5-11
Secondary, ages 11-18
Other: primary schools are free but parents must pay for books and uniforms.

Ministries of Education

CANADA

New Brunswick Education, Place 2000, PO
Box 6000, Fredericton NB, E3B 5H1
Tel: +1 506 453 3678
Website: www.gnb.ca

Newfoundland and Labrador Department of
Education, PO Box 8700, St John's NL, A1B 4J6
Tel: +1 709 729 5097
Website: www.ed.gov.nl.ca/edu

Northwest Territories Ministry of Education, Culture and
Employment, PO Box 1320, Yellowknife NT, X1A 2L9
Tel: +1 867 873 7222
Website: www.gov.nt.ca

Nova Scotia Department of Education, PO Box
578, 2021 Brunswick Street, Halifax NS, B3J 2S9
Tel: +1 902 424 5168
Website: www.ednet.ns.ca

Government of Nunavut, Ministry of Education,
PO Box 1000, Statin 200, Iqaluit NU, X0A 0H0
Tel: +1 867 975 5600
Website: www.gov.nu.ca

Ministry of Education for Ontario, Mowat Block,
14th Floor, 900 Bay Street, Toronto ON, M7A 1L2
Tel: + 416 325 2929
Website: www.edu.gov.on.ca

Prince Edward Island Department of Education and Early
Childhood Development, Second Floor, Sullivan Building,
16 Fitzroy Street, PO Box 2000, Charlottetown PEI, C1A 7N8
Tel: +1 902 368 4600
Website: www.gov.pe.ca

Quebec - Ministry of Education, Recreation
and Sport, 1035 rue de la Chevrotière,
28th Floor, Quebec QC, G1R 5A5
Tel: +1 418 643 7095
Website: www.mels.gouv.qc.ca

Ministry of Education Manitoba, Education Administration
Services Branch, Portage Avenue, Winnipeg MB, R3G 0T3
Tel: +1 204 945 6897
Website: www.edu.gov.mb.ca

Alberta Education, Government of Alberta,
PO Box 1333, Edmonton AB, T5J 2N2
Tel: +1 780 427 7219
Website: http://education.alberta.ca

Government of Saskatchewan, Ministry of Education,

2220 College Avenue, Regina SK, S4P 4V9
Tel: +1 306 787 6030
Website: www.education.gov.sk.ca

Yukon Department of Education, Box
2703, Whitehorse, Yukon, Y1A 2C6
Tel: +1 867 667 5141
Website: www.education.gov.yk.ca
Primary education, or ages 6-13, or Years 1-8.
Secondary education, or ages 11-16, or Years 8-10.
Each territory or province in Canada has control over
their own School system. Most Local Authorities offer
publicly-funded kindergarten classes from age five.
Post-16 usually includes Years 10-12 or ages 16-19.

British Columbian Ministry of Education,
Parliament Buildings, Room 347, PO Box 9045,
Stn Prov Govt, Victoria BC, V8W 9E2
Tel: +1 604 660 2421
Website: www.gov.bc.ca

CAYMAN ISLANDS

Ministry of Education, Training and
Employment, 3rd Floor, Royal Plaza, Cardinall
Ave, George Town, Grand Cayman
Tel: +1 345 244 2417
Website: www.education.gov.ky
Primary, ages 4-11
Secondary, ages 11-16

CHILE

Ministry of Education, Alameda, 1371 Santiago
Tel: +56 2390 4000
Website: www.mineduc.cl
Pre-school, ages up to 6
Primary, ages 6-13
Secondary, ages 13-17
Other: some private schools are
subsidised by the government.

PR CHINA

Ministry of Education for PR of China, 37
Damucang Hutong, Xidan, Beijing 100816
Tel: +86 10 660 961 14
Website: www.moe.edu.cn
Pre-school or Kindergarten, ages 3-6
Elementary/primary school, ages 6-12
Junior middle school (secondary), ages 12-15
Senior middle school (secondary), ages 15-18

COLOMBIA
Ministry of Education, Calle 43 No 57-14, Bogota
Tel: +57 1222 2800
Website: www.mineducacion.gov.co
Nursery, ages 1-5
Primary, ages 6-11
Secondary (basic), ages 12-16
Secondary (vocational), ages 15-18
Other: there are non-profit schools that are
not state run and do not charge fees they
are largely funded by resources from outside
Colombia from countries such as the US.

COOK ISLANDS
Ministry of Education, Rarotonga
Website: www.education.gov.ck
Preschool, ages 3-5
Primary, ages 5-11
Secondary, ages 11-16

COSTA RICA
Ministry of Education, PO Box 10087-1000, San Jose
Tel: +506 2258 3745
Website: www.mep.go.cr
Elementary, ages 6-11
High School, ages 12-18
Other: Catholic schools

CROATIA
Ministry of Science, Education and Sports,
Donje Svetice 38, 10000 Zagreb
Tel: +385 1 4569 000
Website: http://public.mzos.hr
Pre-school, ages 6m-6
Elementary, ages 6-15
Secondary, ages 15+

CUBA
Ministry of Education, Calle 17 esquina a O, Vedado.
Plaza de la Revolución, Vedado Ciudad de la Habana
Tel: +53 7206 7765
Website: www.rimed.cu
Primary, ages 6-12
Secondary, ages 12-15

CYPRUS
Ministry of Education and Culture, Corner of Kimonos
and Thucydides, Acropolis, 1434 Nicosia
Tel: +357 2280 0913
Website: www.moec.gov.cy
Pre-school, ages 4-5
Primary, ages 5-11
Middle, ages 12-15
Secondary, ages 15-18

CZECH REPUBLIC
Ministry of Education, Youth and Sport,
Karmelitská 7, 118 12, Praha 1
Tel: +42 0234 811 111
Website: www.czech.cz/en/education
Pre-school, ages 4-6
Primary, ages 6-11
Secondary, ages 12-16

DENMARK
Danish Ministry of Education, Frederiksholms
Kanal 21, 1220 København K
Tel: +45 3392 5000
Website: www.eng.uvm.dk
Pre-primary/kindergarten
Primary school, grades 1-6, ages 7-12
Lower secondary, grades 7-10, ages 13-16
Upper secondary, which consists of either
general education towards higher education
or vocational/technical training.
Other: production schools, which are independent
schools approved and partially funded by the
Local Authority; they have representatives on
their school board from the local employers.

DOMINICAN REPUBLIC
Ministry of Education, Santiago,
No 2 Gazcue, Distrito Nacional
Tel: +1 809 731 1100
Website: www.seescyt.gov.do
Pre-school, age 4
Primary, ages 5-11
Secondary, ages 12-16
Other: Faith schools

Ministries of Education

EGYPT
Ministry of Education, 12 El-Falaky Street, Cairo
Tel: +20 4257 87643
Website: portal.moe.gov.eg/Pages/default.aspx
Kindergarten, ages 2-4
Primary, ages 4-10
Preparatory, ages 11-14
Secondary, ages 15-17

EL SALVADOR
Ministry of Education, Buildings A, Master Plan, Government Centre, Alameda Juan Pablo II & Calle Guadalupe, 503
Tel: +503 2281 0274
Website: www.mined.gob.sv
Pre-school, ages up to 5
Basic, ages 6-15
Middle, ages 15-18
Other: state education is not entirely free and charges are made on the basis of how much a family can afford, but only for the first child (second and subsequent children go free).

EQUATORIAL GUINEA
Ministry of Education and Sciences
Preschool, ages 0-6
Primary, ages 6-12
Secondary, ages 12-19
Other: education in Equatorial Guinea is very basic and not enforced, particularly for females.

ESTONIA
Ministry of Education, Munga Street 18, 50088 Tartu
Tel: +372 735 0222
Website: www.hm.ee
Preschool, ages 1-7
Basic, ages 7-16
General secondary, ages 16-19

ETHIOPIA
Ministry of Education, PO Box 1367, Addis Ababa
Tel: 00251 11 555 3133
Website: www.ethiopia.gov.et
Elementary, ages 5-11
Junior elementary, ages 11-13
Senior secondary, ages 13-16

FIJI
Ministry of Education, Marela House, Suva
Tel: +679 331 4477
Website: www.education.gov.fj
Pre-school/kindergarten, ages 3-5
Primary, ages 6-14
Secondary, ages 14-19
Other: church run schools.

FINLAND
Ministry of Education and Culture, PO Box 29, FI - 00023 Government
Tel: +358 2953 30004
Website: www.minedu.fi
Pre-primary, age 6
Primary or basic, ages 7-16
General upper secondary, ages 16-19
Other: most private schools follow the Finnish National Curriculum. However, Steiner schools and those offering education in languages other than Finnish, tend to follow their own curriculums.

FRANCE
Ministry of Education, 110 rue de Grenelle, 75357 Paris SP07
Tel: +33 01 5555 1010
Website: www.education.gouv.fr
Elementary school (école élémentaire), ages 6-11
Lower secondary school (college), ages 11-15
Lycée (general/technical or vocational) (lycée d'enseignement général et technologique, LEGT, or lycée professionnel, LP), ages 15-16
Other: the majority of the private fee-paying schools are Catholic schools. Some of these independent schools receive funding from the state to pay salaries and training costs and, in return, the schools must follow the same timetables and curriculum as the state schools. There are state-funded kindergartens available, for ages 2-6, called école maternelle or classe enfantine. There are also private pre-schools, which are fee paying. All pre-schools follow a National Curriculum. Post-16 education is covered by a lycée général et technologique, LEGT or a lycée d'enseignement professionnel, LP. Although the final year of compulsory state education (15-16 years old) usually takes place in a lycée.

GEORGIA
Ministry of Education and Science,
0102 Tbilisi, Dimitri Uznadze N52
Tel: +995 3231 8940
Website: www.mes.gov.ge
Elementary, ages 6-12
Basic, ages 13-15
Secondary, ages 16-18

GERMANY
Each state controls its own school system

Compulsory education:
Primary education, aged 6-10 (12 in
Berlin and Brandenburg)
Lower secondary education, ages 10-16 (12-16)
Upper secondary education, ages 15-19

Other: private schools receive some government funding
and are therefore subject to some state supervision.
Kindergärten is available for children between the
ages of 3-6. All such schools, whether state maintained
or private, are supervised by the state. There is also
a National Curriculum now for all pre-schools.
Post-16 education is compulsory in Germany up to the
age of 18; 19 in some areas.

Bundesministerium für Bildung und Forschung,
Dienstsitz Bonn, Heinemannstrasse 2, 53175 Bonn
Tel: +49 (0)228/9957-0

Bundesministerium für Bildung und Forschung - BMBF,
Dienstsitz Berlin, Hannoversche Strasse 28-30, 10115 Berlin
Tel: +49 (0) 30 1857-0

Bundesministerium für Bildung und Forschung,
Dienstsitz Berlin, Friedrichstrasse 130 B, 10117 Berlin
Tel: +49 (0) 30 1857-0

Website: www.bmbf.de/en

GHANA
Ministry of Education, PO Box M45, Accra, Greater Accra
Tel: +233 302 683627
Website: www.moe.gov.gh
Kindergarten, ages 3-4
Primary, ages 5-11
Secondary, ages 12-15

GIBRALTAR
Department of Education, 23 Queensway
Tel: +350 200 71048
Website: www.gibraltar.gov.gi
Pre-school, ages up to 4
Primary, ages 4-7
Middle school, ages 8-12
Secondary, ages 12-15

GREECE
Greek Ministry of Education and Religious Affairs,
Andrea Papandreou 37, Marousi 15180
Website: www.ypepth.gr
Pre-school, ages 2 1/2-5
Primary (Dimotiko), ages 6-12
Lower secondary (Gymnasio), ages 12-15
Secondary (Lykeio), ages 15-17
Other: private schools are supervised
by the Ministry of Education.

GRENADA
Ministry of Education and Human Resource
Development, Botanical Gardens,
Tanteen St George's, West Indies
Tel: +1 473 440 2737
Website: www.gov.gd/ministries/education.html
Pre-primary, ages 3-5
Primary, ages 5-11
Secondary, ages 11-16

GUATEMALA
Ministry of Education, 6a calle 1-87 zona 10, 01010
Tel: +502 2411 9595
Website: www.mineduc.gob.gt
Primary, ages 7-13
Middle, ages 13-16
Secondary, ages 16-18
Other: faith schools.

GUYANA
Ministry of Education, 21 Brickdam,
Georgetown, 413722 Demerara – Mahaica
Tel: +592 223 7900
Website: www.mineduc.gob.gt
Primary, ages 5-11
Secondary, ages 12-16

HONDURAS
Ministry of Education, 1a Avenida Entre 2a y 3a calle, Comayagüela, MDC
Tel: +504 238 4325
Website: www.se.gob.hn
Pre-primary, ages 5-6
Primary, ages 6-12
Middle, ages 12-15
Secondary, ages 15-18

HONG KONG
Education Bureau, 15/F, Wu Chung House, 213 Queen's Road East, Wan Chai, Hong Kong (SAR)
Tel: +852 2891 0088
Website: www.gov.hk/en
Kindergarten, ages 4-5
Primary, ages 6-12
Junior secondary, ages 12-15
Senior secondary, ages 15-17
Other: state schools are divided into three groups: government schools, subsidised schools (usually charities), and private schools run by organisations. Private, international schools tend to offer the IB. It is rare for an international student to take Hong Kong qualifications, particularly since they switched from the British to Chinese system.

HUNGARY
Ministry of National Resources, 1055 Budapest, Szalay u. 10-14
Tel: +36 1 795 1200
Website: www.okm.gov.hu/english
Pre-primary (Óvoda), ages 5-6
General school (Általános iskola), aged 6-14
General lower and upper secondary grammar school (Gimnázium), aged 10-19
Secondary or training school, ages 14-18
Other: for children aged 3-6 kindergarten is available and the final year is compulsory (for children aged 6). Post-16 education is compulsory in Hungary up to the age of 18.

ICELAND
The Ministry of Education, Science and Culture, Solvholsgata 4, Reykjavik
Tel: +354 545 9500
Website: eng.menntamalaraduneyti.is
Pre-primary, ages 1-6
Compulsory schools, ages 6-16
Upper secondary, ages 16-20

INDIA
Ministry of Human Resource Development, Shastri Bhawan, New Delhi-110001
Tel: +91 11 2338 3936
Website: www.education.nic.in
Primary, ages 6-14
Secondary, ages 14-18

INDONESIA
Ministry of Education, Jalan Jenderal Sudirman Senayan, Jakarta 10270
Tel: +62 021 5795 0226
Website: www.kemdiknas.go.id
Kindergarten, ages 3-5
Elementary, ages 6-11
Middle school, ages 12-14
High school, ages 14-16

IRAN
Ministry of Education
Tel: +98 8889 4024-021
Website: http://medu.ir
Pre-school, age 5
Primary, ages 6-11
Middle, ages 11-14
Secondary, ages 14-17

IRAQ
Ministry of Higher Education and Scientific Research
Website: www.mohesr.gov.iq
Pre-school, ages 4-5
Elementary, ages 6-11
Secondary, ages 12-17
Other: the educational system in Iraq was all but destroyed under the Hussein regime. The country is currently in the process of rebuilding its educational system.

IRELAND

Department of Education and Skills, Marlborough Street, Dublin 1

Tel: +353 1 8896 400

Website: www.education.ie

Primary level, ages 6-12

Second level (junior cycle), ages 12-16

Other: there are privately owned schools, usually by religious communities, which are state funded for the purposes of salaries and running costs. From the age of four, children can be enrolled in infant classes in primary schools. There is also a pre-school year for children aged from 39 months. Post-16 education for children aged 15-19 is called the second-level senior cycle and usually lasts two years. If they wish, students can opt for a further year of education, called a transition year, or undertake a two-year leaving certificate programme.

ISRAEL

Ministry of Education, Culture and Sports, 34 Shivtei Israel St, PO Box 292, Jerusalem 91911

Tel: +972 2 560 2222

Website: cms.education.gov.il/educationcms/units/owl/English

Kindergarten, ages 3-5

Primary, ages 6-12

Middle school, ages 12-15

High school, ages 15-18

Other: faith schools (Orthodox Jewish), and Arab schools.

ITALY

Ministry of Education, University and Research, Palazzo Gerini, Via M. Buonarroti, 50122 Firenze

Tel: +39 055 238 0325

Website: www.istruzione.it

Primary education, ages 6-11

Lower secondary education, ages 11-15

Other: there are private schools in Italy who are not bound by the same rules and who issue qualifications that are not legally recognised. Pre-schools/nurseries are available from the age of three. Post-16 education is covered by the liceo classico, (general academic), liceo scientifico (sciencies), liceo artistico or istituti d'arte (art), and istituti professionali (technical/vocational).

JAMAICA

Ministry of Education, 2a National Heroes Circle, Kingston 4

Tel: +876 922 1400 1

Website: www.moec.gov.jm

Early childhood, ages 1-5

Primary, ages 5-12

Secondary, ages 12-17

Other: independent education is strictly monitored and has its own department at the ministry: The Independent Schools Section. The schools are also required to be registered and regularly inspected.

JAPAN

Ministry of Education, Culture, Sports, Science and Technology (MEXT), 3-2-2 Kasumigaseki, Chiyoda-ku, Tokyo 100-8959

Tel: +81 03 5253 4111

Website: www.mext.go.jp/english

Kindergarten, ages 3-6

Elementary school, ages 6-12

Lower secondary school, ages 12-15

Upper secondary school, ages 15-18

Other: private schools receive public funding and they tend to follow the National Curriculum. The major difference between the state and private sectors are that the private schools tend to include religious education.

JORDAN

Ministry of Education, PO Box 1646, Amman

Tel: +962 568 4137

Website: www.moe.gov.jo

Basic, ages 6-16

Secondary/vocational, ages 16-18

KAZAKHSTAN

Ministry of Education and Science, 01000 Astana, Orenburgskaya St

Tel: +8 7172 74 24 28

Website: www.edu.gov.kz/en

Kindergarten, ages 5-6

Primary, ages 6-10

Basic, ages 10-15

General secondary, ages 15-17

Ministries of Education

KENYA
Ministry of Education, Jogoo House B,
Harambee Avenue, PO Box 30040, Nairobi
Tel: +254 318 581
Website: www.education.go.ke
Preschool, age 5
Primary, ages 6-14
Secondary, ages 14-18

DEMOCRATIC PEOPLE'S REPUBLIC OF KOREA
Department of Education
Kindergarten, ages 4-6
Primary, ages 6-9
Senior middle school, ages 10-15

SOUTH KOREA
The Ministry of Education, Science and
Technology, Central Government Complex,
77-6 Sejong-No, Jongno-Gu, Seoul, 110-760
Tel: +82 2 6222 6060
Website: http://English.mest.go.kr
Primary school, ages 6-12
Junior high school, ages 12-15
Senior high school, ages 15-18
Other: parents are expected to pay fees if their
child goes to senior high school. Private fee-
paying schools follow the National Curriculum.
Kindergartens are available for children aged
3-5. They too follow a National Curriculum.

KOSOVO
Ministry of Education, Science and Technology,
Rruga, Agim Ramadani, 10000 Prishtine
Tel: +381 038 213 327
Website: www.masht-gov.net

KUWAIT
Ministry of Education, PO Box 7, Shuwaikh,
Building No. 1, Al-Safat 13001
Website: www.moe.edu.kw
Tel: +965 483 5721
Kindergarten, ages 4-6
Primary, ages 6-11
Intermediate, ages 11-16
Secondary, ages 16-19

KYRGYZSTAN
Ministry of Education, Science and Culture,
720040 Biskek, Tynystanou St, 257, Bishkek
Website: edu.gov.kg/
Pre-school, ages 18m-3
Kindergarten, ages 3-7
Primary, ages 6-11
Secondary, ages 11-15
High school, ages 15-17

LAO
Ministry of Education,
Tel: +856 2121 6004
Website: www.moe.gov.la
Primary, ages 5-11
Secondary, ages 12-18

LATVIA
Ministry of Education and Science,
Valnu Street 2, Riga, LV-1050
Tel: +371 6722 6209
Website: http://izm.izm.gov.lv
Pre-school, ages up to 5
Primary, ages 5-7
Basic, ages 7-16
Secondary, ages 16-19

LEBANON
Ministry of Education and Higher Education,
B.P. 55264, Sin El-fil, Beyrouth
Tel: +961 1 683 089
Website: www.crdp.org
Primary, ages 5-6
Elementary, ages 6-11
Intermediate, ages 12-14
Secondary, ages 15-17

LESOTHO
Ministry of Education and Training, PO Box 47, Maseru 100
Tel: +266 2231 7900
Website: www.higher-edu.gov.lb/english
Pre-primary, up to age 6
Primary, ages 6-13
Secondary, ages 13-18

LIBYA
National Commission for Education, Science
and Culture, PO Box 1091, Tripoli
Website: www.higheredu.gov.ly
Primary, ages 6-12
Secondary, ages 12-15

LITHUANIA

Ministry of Education and Science, A Volano str 2/1, LT-01516, Vilnius
Tel: +370 5219 1190
Website: www.smm.lt/en
Primary, ages 6-11
Lower secondary, ages 10-17
Senior secondary, ages 16-19

LUXEMBOURG

Ministry of National Education and Training, 29 rue Aldringen, L-1118
Tel: +352 2478 5100
Website: www.men.public.lu
Pre-elementary, ages 4-5
Primary, ages 6-12
Secondary, ages 12-19

MACAU

Ministry of Education, Rua do Campo, no 162, Edificio Administração Pública, 26 andar
Tel: +853 8866 8866
Website: www.gov.mo
Primary, ages 6-12
Secondary, ages 12-18
Other: Macau does not have its own educational system at present. Different schools follow the Chinese, British and Portuguese systems and most schools are private or heavily subsidised schools. Therefore the years spent in each type of school will depend on which system the school follows. The Chinese and British schools have similar periods of attendance, the Portuguese schools tend to allow less time in primary, and more time in secondary and high school.

MACEDONIA

Ministry of Education and Science, st Mito Hadzivasilev - Jasmin bb, 1000 Skopje
Tel: +389 2 3117 896
Website: www.mon.gov.mk
Elementary, ages 7-15
General secondary, ages 15-19

MALAYSIA

Ministry of Education, Block E8, Complex E, Federal Government Administrative Centre, 62604, Putrajaya
Tel: +60 388 846 000
Website: www.moe.gov.my
Pre-school, ages 4-6
Primary, ages 6-13
Secondary, ages 13-16

REPUBLIC OF THE MALDIVES

Ministry of Education, Boduthakurufaanu Magu, Malé
Tel: +960 333 3234
Website: www.moe.gov.mv
Primary, ages 6-10
Middle school, ages 11-15
Secondary, ages 15-17
Other: some private schools, called Makthab, are traditional Islamic schools.

MALI

Ministry of Education, Place de la Liberté, Bamako
Tel: +223 223 1036
Website: www.education.gov.ml
Primary, ages 7-13
Secondary, ages 8-16

MALTA

Ministry of Education, Employment and the Family, Great Siege Road, Floriana, VLT2000
Tel: +356 21 221401
Website: www.education.gov.mt
Primary, ages 5-11
Secondary, ages 11-16
Post-secondary
Other: Malta also has Church schools.

MAURITIUS

Ministry of Education, IVTB House, Phoenix
Tel: +230 698 5349
Website: www.gov.mu/portal/site/education
Pre-primary, ages 4-5
Primary, ages 5-11
Secondary, ages 11-18

MOLDOVA

Ministry of Education, Piapa Maril Adunari Napioale nr 1, MD-2033, Chisinau
Tel: +373 2223 3348
Website: www.edu.md
Kindergarten, ages 3-4
Pre-school, ages 4-5
Primary, ages 6-10
Gymnasium, ages 10-15
Lyceum, ages 15-17

Ministries of Education

MONACO
Education, Youth and Sports Direction, Lycée Technique, Avenue de l'Annonciade, MC – 98000
Tel: +377 9898 8005
Website: www.education.gouv.mc
Elementary school (école élémentaire), ages 6-11
Lower secondary school (college), ages 11-15
Lycée (general/technical or vocational) (lycée d'enseignement général et technologique, LEGT, or lycée professionnel, LP), ages 15-18
Other: the majority of the private fee-paying schools are Catholic schools. Some of these independent schools receive funding from the state to pay salaries and training costs and in return the schools must follow the same timetables and curriculum as the state schools. There are state-funded kindergartens available, for ages 2-6, called école maternelle or classe enfantine. There are also private pre-schools, which are fee paying. Post-16 education is covered by a lycée général et technologique, LEGT or a lycée d'enseignement professionnel, LP. Although the final year of compulsory state education (15-16 years old) usually takes place in a lycée.

MONTENEGRO
Ministry of Education and Sports, Vaka Durovica, 81000 Podgorica
Tel: +382 20 410 100
Website: www.mpin.gov.me/en/ministry
Pre-school, up to age 6
Elementary, ages 6-14
Secondary, ages 14-18

MOROCCO
Ministry of National Education, 29 Avenue d'Alger, 10000, Rabat
Tel: +212 37 70 60 18
Website: www.men.gov.ma
Pre-school, ages 4-6
Primary, ages 6-12
Secondary, ages 12-18
Other: Morocco has three systems of education: a continuation of the French system; Islamic; and technical, skills and vocational training.

MOZAMBIQUE
Ministry of Education, Avenida 24 de Julho, No 167, PO Box 34, Maputo
Tel: +258 21 493 677
Website: www.mined.gov.mz
Pre-primary, ages 3-5
Primary, ages 5-13
Secondary, ages 13-18
Other: missionary schools.

NAMIBIA
Ministry of Education, Government Office Park (Luther Street), Private Bag 13186, Windhoek
Tel: +264 061 293 3358
Website: www.mec.gov.na
Primary, ages 6-13
Secondary, ages 13-19

NEPAL
Ministry of Education, Kaiser Mahal, Kathmandu
Tel: +977 1 4411704
Website: www.doe.gov.np
Pre-primary, ages 4-6
Primary, ages 6-10
Secondary, ages 11-15
Other: schools run by the local people that receive no grants or financial support.

NETHERLANDS
Ministry of Education, Culture and Science PO Box 16375, 2500 BJ Den Haag
Tel: +31 70 4123 456
Website: www.government.nl/ministries/ocw
Primary school, ages 4-12
Secondary school, ages 12-18
Other: private schools receive funding from the state and have to meet and maintain certain conditions to retain their funding, although they are allowed to set their own curriculum. There is no education on offer for children under the age of four.

NETHERLANDS ANTILLES
Ministry of Education and Culture, Fort Amsterdam 17, Curacao
Tel: +599 9 463 0484
Website: www.gov.an
Primary, ages 4-12
Secondary, ages 12-18

NEW ZEALAND
The Ministry of Education, National Office,
45-47 Pipitea Street, PO Box 1666,
Thorndon, Wellington 6011
Tel: +64 (04) 463 8000
Website: www.minedu.govt.nz
Primary school, ages 5-11, Standard 4.
Middle school, ages 11-13, Forms 1-2.
Secondary school, ages 13-18, Forms 3-7.
Other: integrated schools: private schools that
have been integrated into the state system and
are therefore state funded. These are usually
religious schools. Kindergarten/pre-school
education is available for children ages 3-4.

NIGERIA
Federal Ministry of Education, Federal
Secretariat Complex, Shehu Shagari Way,
Central Area, PMB 146, Garki, Abuja
Tel: +234 9 5232800
Basic, ages 6-12
Secondary, ages 12-18

NORWAY
Ministry of Education and Research,
Postboks 8119 Dep, 0032 Oslo
Tel: +47 2224 9090
Website: www.regjeringen.no/en/dep/kd.html?id=586
Kindergarten, ages 1-5
Primary and lower secondary, ages 6-16
Upper secondary, ages 16-19

OMAN
Ministry of Education, PO Box 3, Muscat 113
Website: www.moe.gov.om
Primary, ages 6-12
Preparatory, ages 12-15
Secondary, ages 15-18

PAKISTAN
Ministry of Education, Block D, Pakistan Secretariat,
Islamabad, 44000, Islamabad Capital Territory
Tel: +92 51 221 2020
Website: www.moptt.gov.pk
Primary, ages 5-10
Middle, ages 10-13
High, ages 13-15
Intermediate, ages 15-17

PALAU
Ministry of Education, PO Box 189, Koror
Tel: +680 767 1464
Website: www.palaumoe.net
Elementary, from age 6
High school, up to age 16

PALESTINE
Ministry of Education and Higher
Education, PO Box 719, Ramallah
Tel: +972 2296 9350
Website: www.moe.gov.ps
Pre-primary, ages 4-6
Primary, ages 5-15
Secondary, ages 15-17

PANAMA
Ministry of Education, PO Box 2440, Panama 3
Tel: +507 511 4400
Website: www.meduca.gob.pa
Primary, ages 6-12
Middle school, ages 12-15
Secondary, ages 15-18

PARAGUAY
Ministry of Education, Chile 849, Asunción
Tel: +595 21 450 014/5
Website: www.mec.gov.py
Pre-school, ages 3-6
Elementary, ages 6-15
High school, ages 15-18

PERU
Ministry of Education, National Library of Perus
- BNP, Av de la Poesia No160, San Borja
Tel: +51 1 215 5800
Website: www.minedu.gob.pe
Early years, ages 3-6
Primary, ages 6-12
Secondary, ages 12-17

PHILIPPINES
Department of Education, DepEd Complex,
Meralco Avenue, Pasig City
Tel: +63 032 632 1361
Website: www.deped.gov.ph
Nursery/kindergarten, ages 4-7
Elementary, ages 6-13
Secondary, ages 13-17

POLAND
Ministry of Education, al. J Ch Szucha 25, 00-918 Warsaw
Tel: +48 022 34 74 100
Website: www.men.gov.pl
Kindergarten, ages 5-6
Primary, ages 6-13
Lower secondary, ages 13-16
Upper secondary, ages 16-20

PORTUGAL
Ministry of Education, Avenida 5 de Outubro, 107 1069-018, Lisboa
Tel: +351 217 811 800
Website: www.min-edu.pt
Pre-primary, ages 3-5
Primary, ages 6-12
Secondary, ages 13-16

PUERTO RICO
Ministry of Education
Website: http://de.gobierno.pr
Primary, ages 5-11
Secondary, ages 11-18

QATAR
Supreme Education Council, PO Box 35111, Doha
Tel: +974 455 9362
Website: www.sec.gov.qa
Elementary, ages 6-12
Preparatory, ages 12-15
Secondary, ages 15-18

ROMANIA
Ministry of Education, Str Gen Berthelot 28-30, Sector 1, 010168, Bucharest
Tel: +40 562 00
Website: www.edu.ro
Kindergarten, ages 3-6
Primary, ages 6-10
Secondary, ages 11-14
High school, ages 15-19

RUSSIA
The Ministry of Education and Science of the Russian Federation, Tverskaya Street 11, Moscow GSP-3 125993
Tel: +7 495 629 7062
Website: http://eng.mon.gov.ru
Pre-school, ages up to 6 years
Primary school, ages 6-10
Middle school, ages 10-15
Secondary school, ages 15-17

RWANDA
Ministry of Education, PO Box 622, Kigali
Tel: +250 583 051
Website: www.mineduc.gov.rw
Primary, ages 6-12
Secondary, ages 12-18

SAUDI ARABIA
Ministry of Education, Riyadh 11148
Tel: +966 404 2888
Website: www.moe.gov.sa
Kindergarten, ages 3-5
Primary, ages 6-12
Intermediate, ages 12-15
High school, ages 15-18

SENEGAL
Ministry of Education, Rue Alpha Hachamiyou TALL, BP 4025
Tel: +221 33 849 54 54
Website: www.education.gouv.sn
Primary, ages 6-12
Secondary, ages 12-16
Other: Islamic schools.

SERBIA
Ministry of Education, Science and Technological Development, 24 Nemanjina Street, Belgrade
Tel: +381 011 3616 489
Website: www.mpn.gov.rs
Pre-primary, age 6
Primary, ages 6/7-15
High school, ages 15-18

SEYCHELLES
Ministry of Education, Mont Fleuri, PO Box 48
Tel: +248 283 283
Website: www.education.gov.sc
Early childhood, ages 3-8
Primary, ages 7-12
Secondary, ages 11-17
Other: private education and church-run schools were abolished in 1977. All education in the Seychelles is state-controlled.

SIERRA LEONE
Ministry of Education, Youth and Sports, New England, Freetown, Sierra Leone
Website: www.diasporaaffairs.gov.sl
Tel: +232 22 240881
Primary, ages 6-12
Junior secondary, 12-15
Senior secondary, 15-18

SINGAPORE
The Ministry of Education, Singapore, 1 North Buona Vista Drive, Singapore 138675
Tel: +65 6872 2220
Website: www.moe.gov.sg
Primary school, ages 6-13
Secondary school, ages 14-18
Other: there are also government-aided schools (formerly privately owned by churches or other organisations), who receive most of their funding from the state. Kindergartens (ages 3-6) and childcare centres (infant to age 7) are also available. These are privately run establishments, which have to be registered with the Ministry of Education.

SLOVAKIA
Ministry of Education, Science, Research and Sport, Stromová 1, 813 30, Bratislava
Tel: +421 2593 74111
Website: www.minedu.sk
Nursery, ages 3-6
First stage, ages 6-10
Second stage (primary), ages 10-15
Secondary, ages 15-19

SLOVENIA
Ministry of Education and Sport, Masarykova 16, SI-1000 Ljubljana
Tel: +386 1400 5200
Website: www.mss.gov.si
Pre-school, ages 1-6
Basic, ages 6-15
Secondary, ages 15-18

SOMALIA
Ministry of Education
Early childhood, ages up to 6
Elementary, ages 6-14
Secondary, ages 15-18
Other: there are three ministries handling education in Somalia, the national one and one each for Puntland and Somaliland.

SOUTH AFRICA
Department of Basic Education, Sol Plaatje House, 222 Struben Street, Pretoria
Tel: +27 012 357 300
Website: www.education.gov.za
Pre-primary, ages birth to 5
Reception, Grade R, ages 5-6
Primary, Grades 1-6, ages 6-12
Secondary, Grades 7-9, ages 12-15
Post secondary, Grades 9-12, ages 15-18
Other: South Africa runs a state school system that is unique. Schools are divided into five categories determined by the level of wealth in a particular area; the poorer schools are allocated larger funding than wealthier schools. Only the poorest state schools are completely free and entirely government funded, most charge some form of fee to top up their funding.

SPAIN
The Ministry of Education, Culture and Sport, C/Alcalá, 34, 28014, Madrid
Tel: +34 91 701 830
Website: www.educacion.es
Primary school, ages 6-12
Lower secondary school, ages 12-16
Other: there are also private schools that receive state funding and are therefore under the control of the state. Spain also offers pre-school education for children from birth to age six, which is free from the age of three. Post-16 education consists of either general upper secondary school or intermediate vocational training; both take place up to the age of 18. State colleges are free to students but parents are expected to pay for additional items such as meals, transport and various materials needed for their child's coursework.

SRI LANKA
Ministry of Education, Battaramulla
Tel: +94 11 2785141
Website: www.moe.gov.lk
Primary, ages 5-10
Junior, ages 11-15
Secondary, ages 16-18
Other: pirivenas (schools for Buddhist priests).

ST LUCIA

Ministry of Education and Culture,
Greaham Louisy Administrative Building
Waterfront, Castries
Tel: +1 758 468 2116
Website: www.education.gov.lc
Preschools, ages 3-5
Primary, ages 5-13
Secondary, ages 13-16

SUDAN

Ministry of Education, PO Box 284,
Sudan Khartoum, Alneer Avenue
Tel: +24 9122 838 009
Website: www.moe.gov.sd/english/index.html
Kindergarten, ages 3-5
Primary, ages 6-14
Secondary, ages 14-17

SWAZILAND

Ministry of Education and Training, PO Box 39, Mbabane
Tel: +268 404 2491
Website: www.gov.sz
Early childhood care and development,
ages up to 8
Primary, ages 6-13
Secondary, ages 13-18

SWEDEN

National Ministry of Education and
Research, SE-103 33, Stockholm
Tel: +46 8 405 1000
Website: www.Sweden.gov.se
Other: independent schools receive grants from
the NAE for each registered student, but they are
essentially fee-paying. Compulsory education runs
from age 6-16 and takes place in all-through schools,
which are coeducational and non-selective. There
are several varieties of pre-schools available for
children from birth to ages seven. These are: Daghem
(day nursery/pre-school), Familjedaghem (registered
childminders), Deltidsgrupp (part-time group), Oppen
förskola (pre-school/parent and toddler groups),
and Förskoleklass (pre-school for ages 6-7). Post-16 is
not compulsory but such education available is for
students, should they want it, up to the age of 20.

SWITZERLAND

State Secretariat for Education and Research
(SER), Hallwylstrasse 4, CH-3003, Bern
Tel: +41 031 322 9691
Website: www.sbf.admin.ch
Pre-school/kindergarten, ages 4-6
Primary, ages 6-12
Secondary I, ages 12-16
Secondary II, ages 16-20
Other: tertiary education is either general or
professional education. Professional education
applies to universities or occupational qualifications;
the latter tend to be supported/sponsored by the
relevant association (medical, law etc) who are
also responsible for setting the examinations.

TAIWAN

Ministry of Education, No 5 Zhongshan S Road,
Zhongzheng District, Taipei City 10051
Tel: +886 2773 66666
Website: http://english.moe.gov.tw
Preschool, ages 3-5
Primary, ages 5-11
Junior high, ages 12-15
Senior secondary, ages 15-18

TAJIKISTAN

Ministry of Education, 734024, Dushanbe,
Nisor Muhammad St, 13a
Tel: +992 37 227 35 76
Pre-school, ages 3-6
Primary, ages 7-11
Secondary, ages 11-18

TANZANIA

Ministry of Education and Vocational Training,
PO Box 9121, Dar es Salaam
Tel: +255 2120 403
Website: www.moe.go.tz
Pre-primary, ages 3-4
Primary, ages 5-11
Secondary, ages 12-16

THAILAND

Ministry of Education, Bangkok 10300
Tel: +66 2628 5620
Website: www.moe.go.th/english
Pre-school, ages 3-6
Elementary, ages 6-12
Secondary, ages 12-18

TIMOR-LESTE
Ministry of Education, Rua de Vila Verde, Dili
Tel: +670 333 9654
Website: http://timor-leste.gov.tl

TRINIDAD AND TOBAGO
Ministry of Education, 18 Alexandra Street, St Clair, Port of Spain
Tel: +1 868 628 7818
Website: www.moe.gov.tt
Pre-school, ages 3-5
Primary, ages 5-11
Secondary, ages 12-16
Other: religious schools.

TUNISIA
Ministry of Education, 3 Rue Asdrubal, 1002 Lafayette
Tel: +216 71 833 800
Website: www.edunet.tn/index.php?id=360&lan=3
Pre-school, ages 3-6
Primary, ages 6-12
Preparatory, ages 13-16
Secondary, ages 16-20

TURKEY
Ministry of National Education
Tel: +90 312 413 17
Website: www.meb.gov.tr/english/indexeng.htm
Primary, ages 6-14
Secondary, ages 14-17

TURKS AND CAICOS ISLANDS
Ministry of Education, Youth, Sports and Culture, Cockburn Town, Grand Turk
Primary, ages 5-11
Secondary, ages 12-16

UGANDA
Ministry of Education and Sports, PO Box 7063, Kampala
Tel: +256 4123 4451
Website: www.education.go.ug
Primary, ages 7-13
Secondary, ages 14-17

UK – ENGLAND
Department for Education, Castle View House, East Lane, Runcorn, WA7 2GL
Tel: 0370 000 2288
Website: www.education.gov.uk
Pre-school, 3-5
Infants, ages 4-6
Junior/preparatory, 7-10 (or 13 in private preparatory schools)
Secondary/senior, ages 11-16
Sixth form, ages 16-18
Other: faith schools, free schools, academies (nb: the latter two types are new, introduced in 2010).

UK – NORTHERN IRELAND
Department of Education, Rathgael House, Balloo Road, Rathgill, Bangor, BT19 7PR
Website: www.deni.gov.uk
Primary, ages 4-11
Secondary, ages 11-16
Sixth form, ages 16-18
Other: faith schools.

UK – SCOTLAND
Education and Lifelong Learning Directorate, St Andrew's House, Regent Road, Edinburgh, EH1 3DG
Website: www.scotland.gov.uk
Primary, ages 4-11
Secondary, ages 11-18
Other: faith schools.

UK – WALES
Department for Education and Skills, Cathays Park, Cardiff, CF10 3NQ
Website: http://new.wales.gov.uk
Pre-school, 3-5
Infants, ages 4-6
Junior/preparatory, 7-10 (or 13 in private preparatory schools)
Secondary/senior, ages 11-16
Sixth form, ages 16-18
Other: Welsh-speaking only schools.

UKRAINE
Ministry of Education, Science, Youth and Sports
Tel: +38 044 86 24 42
Website: www.mon.gov.ua
Primary, ages 6-10
Middle, ages 10-15
Secondary, ages 15-18

UNITED ARAB EMIRATES
Ministry of Education, PO Box 3962, Abu Dhabi
Tel: +971 4089 999-02
Website: www.moe.gov.ae/English
Primary, ages 6-12
Middle, ages 12-15
Secondary, ages 15-18

UNITED STATES OF AMERICA
Department of Education, 400 Maryland Avenue, SW, Washington, DC 20202
Website: www.ed.gov
Pre-school, ages 4-5
Kindergarten, ages 5-6
Elementary, ages 6-11, 1st-5th grade
Middle/junior high, ages 11-14, 6th-8th grade
High school, ages 14-18, 9th-12th grade
Other: in high school, ninth graders are called 'freshmen', tenth graders 'sophomores', eleventh graders 'juniors' and twelfth graders 'seniors'.

VIRGIN ISLANDS
Ministry of Education and Culture, Road Town, Tortola
Tel: +284 494 7739 40
Website: www.doe.vi
Junior high, ages 5-11
Senior high, ages 12-16

UZBEKISTAN
Ministry of Public Education, 5 Mustakillik Square, Taskent
Tel: +998 (71) 239-1735
Website: www.edu.uz/eng
Primary, ages 6-10
Secondary, ages 10-15
Upper secondary, ages 15-17

VENEZUELA
Ministry of Education, Salas Esq Caja de Agua, the MPPE Edif. Sede Parish Altagracia, Caracas, Dtto. Capital
Website: www.me.gob.ve
Preschool, ages up to 5
Primary, ages 6-11
Secondary, ages 11-15

VIETNAM
Ministry of Education and Training, 49 Dai Co Viet Street, Hanoi
Tel: +84 4869 2393
Website: en.moet.gov.vn
Pre-school, ages 3-6
Primary, ages 6-11
Lower secondary, ages 11-15
Upper secondary, ages 15-18

ZAMBIA
Ministry of Education, PO Box 50093, Lusaka, 10101
Tel: +260 1253 502
Website: www.moe.gov.zm
Primary, ages 5-12
Junior secondary. 12-14
Upper secondary, ages 14-17

ZIMBABWE
Ministry of Education, Sport, Arts and Culture, Head Office, Union Avenue, PO Box CY121, Causeway, Harare
Tel: +263 4 734071
Website: www.moesac.gov.zw
Primary, ages 5-12
Secondary, ages 12-16
High schools, ages 16-18

Curricula, examinations and tests

American College Testing (ACT)

The ACT is a test used to assess students' achievements before admission to college. It is widely accepted in the US, particularly in the midwestern and southern states. Students are tested in English, maths, reading and science reasoning with an optional writing test.

Like the US SAT, the American Mensa and other high IQ societies use scores from the ACT as a criteria for admission.

Scores range from one to 36; the English, maths and reading tests also have subscores ranging from 1 to 18. The composite score given to each student is the average of the four tests added together. Students taking the optional writing test can score from two to 12. The ACT is offered in the US four to six times a year (depending on the state in question) in September, October, December, February, April and June.

ACT scores compare to SATs as follows:

Contact ACT for further information or to register for a test, via their website: www.act.org

SAT	ACT	SAT	ACT
2400	36	1620	23
2340	35	1560	22
2280	34	1500	21
2220	33	1440	20
2160	32	1380	19
2100	31	1320	18
2040	30	1260	17
1980	29	1200	16
1920	28	1140	15
1860	27	1080	14
1800	26	1020	13
1740	25	960	12
1680	24	900	11

The Advanced Placement Program (AP)

The College Board's Advanced Placement Program (AP) provides an opportunity for willing and academically prepared to take rigorous, university-level courses that help them develop the skills necessary for success in college and their future careers. Students who succeed on AP Exams have the opportunity to earn college credit and/or advanced placement, helping them to reduce tuition costs and offering more time and flexibility to double major, study abroad or complete an internship. Research indicates that students who succeed on an AP Exam typically experience greater academic success in college, experience lower college costs and are more likely to earn a college degree than their peers.

AP courses are taught in secondary schools in more than 100 countries. AP courses include: art history, biology, calculus AB, calculus BC, chemistry, Chinese language and culture, comparative government and politics, computer science A, English language and composition, English literature and composition, environmental science, European history, French language and culture, German language and culture, human geography, Italian language and culture, Japanese language and culture, Latin, macroeconomics, microeconomics, music theory, physics C: electricity and magnetism, physics C: mechanics physics 1, physics 2, psychology, Spanish language and culture, Spanish literature and culture, statistics, studio art: 2D design, studio art: 3D design, studio art: drawing, US government and politics, US history, and world history.

AP Exams are available in secondary schools and in

authorized testing centers in China and India. AP Exams measure a student's mastery of university-level course content. The program allows students to develop a global perspective, as well as skills such as critical thinking and problem solving. Exams are administered each year in May, and scores can be sent directly to the universities of your choice. Outside the US, more than 600 universities in more than 65 countries recognize successful AP Exam scores in the admission process.

To find schools that offer AP around the world, visit:

https://apcourseaudit.epiconline.org/ledger/ and begin the search by entering a country in the 'Ledger Search' area. The AP Course Ledger is the official record of schools with authorized courses that can use the AP designation on secondary school transcripts. Courses that have not completed the AP Course Audit are not listed in the AP Course Ledger, cannot use the "AP" designation on students' transcripts, and are not recognized by universities as an AP course.

AP Capstone

AP Capstone™ is an innovative diploma program that provides students with an opportunity to engage in rigorous scholarly practice of the core academic skills necessary for successful college completion.

AP Capstone is built on the foundation of two courses — AP Seminar and AP Research. These two AP Capstone courses, with their associated performance tasks, assessments, and application of research methodology, complement the rigor of AP courses and exams by equipping students with the power to analyze and evaluate information with accuracy and precision in order to craft and communicate evidence-based arguments.

AP Capstone has collaborated with colleges and universities to define its content and standards. It utilizes frameworks and learning objectives uniquely aligned with core AP skills and practices and other skills-based learning objectives. For more information, visit collegeboard.org/apcapstone or email apcapstone@collegeboard.org.

Advanced Placement International Diploma (APID)

The Advanced Placement International Diploma (APID) is a globally recognized credential for students who embrace an international outlook. The APID also challenges a student to display exceptional achievement across several disciplines. Universities worldwide utilize the APID in admissions.

The APID is available to students attending secondary schools outside the United States and to US resident students applying to universities outside the country. The APID is not a substitute for a high school diploma, but provides additional recognition of outstanding academic excellence.

In addition, for students attending schools within the United States to be eligible for the APID scholar award, they must send their official AP score report to a university outside the United States. For a list of universities outside the US that recognize AP, visit: international.collegeboard.org/programs/ap-recognition

In order to earn the APID, students must earn scores of 3 or higher on five or more total AP Exams, based on the exam criteria requirements listed within each of the following content areas:

a) Two AP Exams from two different languages, either one selected from English and one from another world language OR two different world languages other than English: English language and composition, English literature and composition, French language and culture, German language and culture, Spanish language and culture, Spanish literature and culture, Italian language and culture, Chinese language and culture and Japanese language and culture

b) One AP Exam offering a global perspective: comparative government and politics, human geography and world history, and a new requirement in 2014 now includes art history, environmental science and macroeconomics in this content area.

c) One AP Exam from the sciences or mathematics and computer science content areas: biology, calculus AB, calculus BC, chemistry, computer science A, environmental science, physics B, physics C: mechanics, physics C: electricity and magnetism and statistics, physics 1 and physics 2

d) One additional exam from among any content areas except English and world languages. These include the content areas already described as well as history and social science and arts: art history, European history, Latin, macroeconomics, microeconomics, music theory, psychology, studio art: drawing, studio art: 2-D design, studio art: 3-D design, US government and politics, US history and world history.

Cambridge Advanced International Certificate of Education (AICE) Diploma

The Cambridge Advanced International Certificate of Education (AICE) Diploma prepares students for honours degree programmes. It requires the study of subjects drawn from three curriculum areas within an international curriculum framework: mathematics and sciences; languages; and arts and humanities. Subjects are available at Cambridge International Advanced Subsidiary (AS) level and Advanced (A) level. Cambridge International A levels count as double-credit qualifications, Cambridge International AS levels as a full (single) credit courses. In order to receive a Cambridge AICE Diploma, a candidate must earn six credits, with at least one course coming from each of the three curriculum areas.

Grading and points system

Cambridge International AS level – candidates are graded A to E.
Cambridge International A level – candidates are graded A* to E.
The Cambridge AICE Diploma is awarded on the basis of a points system:

Double credit study

Grade	Points
A*	140
A	120
B	100
C	80
D	60
E	40

Full credit study

Grade	Points
A*	n/a
A	60
B	50
C	40
D	30
E	20

Candidates who meet the requirements will receive a Cambridge AICE Diploma at one of three levels – pass, merit or distinction – on the basis of their overall AICE diploma score:
Distinction – 320-360 points
Merit – 220-319 points
Pass – 120-219 points
The maximum number of Cambridge AICE Diploma points is capped at 360.

Subjects

Group 1: Mathematics and sciences. Subjects available include biology, chemistry, computing, design and technology, environmental management, mathematics, physics, psychology, thinking skills.

Group 2: Languages. Subjects available include English language, first language Spanish, Afrikaans, Chinese, Portuguese, Spanish, French, German, Urdu.

Group 3: Arts and humanities. Subjects available include accounting, art and design, business studies, economics, geography, history, Chinese literature, English literature, French literature, Portuguese literature, Spanish literature, music, psychology, sociology, thinking skills.

Group 4: Global Perspectives. This new subject is available at Cambridge International AS and A level and develops independent research and thinking skills in preparation for university study. Schools with access to Cambridge Pre-U Global Perspectives and Research can also use entries for this subject to contribute to the diploma.

Note: The Cambridge AICE Diploma requirements are changing with effect from June 2017 to place more emphasis on the skills essential for success in university study and employment.
Website: www.cie.org.uk/aice

Cambridge International AS and A level

Cambridge International AS and A Level is an internationally benchmarked qualification, taught in over 125 countries worldwide. It is typically for learners aged 16 to 19 years who need advanced study to prepare for university. It was created specifically for an international audience and the content has been devised to suit the wide variety of schools worldwide and avoid any cultural bias.

Cambridge International A Level is typically a two-year course, and Cambridge International AS Level is typically one year. Some subjects can be started as a Cambridge International AS Level and extended to a Cambridge International A Level. Students can either follow a broad course of study, or specialise in one particular subject area.

Learners use Cambridge International AS and A Levels to gain places at leading universities worldwide, including the UK, Ireland, USA, Canada, Australia, New Zealand, India, Singapore, Egypt, Jordan, South Africa, the Netherlands, Germany and Spain. In places such as the US and Canada, good grades in carefully chosen Cambridge International A Level subjects can result in up to one year of university course credit.

Assessment options:

Option 1: take Cambridge International AS levels only – the Cambridge International syllabus content is half a Cambridge International A level.

Option 2: staged assessment, which means taking the Cambridge International AS Level in one exam session and the Cambridge International A Level at a later session. However, this route is not possible in all subjects.

Option 3: take all Cambridge International A Level papers in the same examination session, usually at the end of the course.

Grades and subjects

Cambridge International A Levels are graded from A* to E. Cambridge International AS Levels are graded from A to E.

Subjects: available in 55 subjects including accounting, Afrikaans, Afrikaans – first language (AS only), Afrikaans language (AS only), applied information and communication technology, Arabic, Arabic language (AS only), art and design, biology, business studies, chemistry, Chinese, Chinese language (AS only), classical studies, computing, design and technology, design and textiles, divinity, economics, English language, English literature, environmental management, food studies, French, French language (AS only), French literature (AS only), general paper 8001, general paper 8004, geography, German, German language (AS only), Global Perspectives & Research, Hindi, Hindi language (AS only), Hindi literature (AS only), Hinduism, history, Islamic studies, Japanese language (AS only), English language and literature (AS only), law, Marathi, Marathi language (AS only), marine science, mathematics, further mathematics, media studies, music, physical education, physical science, physics, Portuguese, Portuguese language (AS only), Portuguese literature (AS only), psychology, sociology, Spanish, Spanish first language (AS only), Spanish language (AS only), Spanish literature (AS only), Tamil, Tamil language (AS only), Telugu, Telugu language (AS only), thinking skills, travel and tourism, Urdu, Urdu language (AS only), Urdu Pakistan.
Website: www.cie.org.uk/alevel

Cambridge International Certificate of Education (ICE)

Cambridge ICE is the group award of Cambridge IGCSE (see below). In order to be awarded a Cambridge ICE certificate, a student must obtain at least grade G in seven subjects: two language subjects, one each from humanities and social sciences, sciences, mathematics and creative, technical and vocational and one other, taken from any subject group.

The certificates are awarded in the following levels:

Distinction – student must obtain grade A or above in five subjects and grade C or above in two further subjects.

Merit – student must obtain grade C or above in five subjects and grade F or above in two further subjects.

Pass – student must obtain grade G or above in seven subjects.

Cambridge International General Certificate of Education (IGCSE)

Cambridge IGCSE is the world's most popular international qualification for 14 to16 year olds. It develops skills in creative thinking, enquiry and problem solving, in preparation for the next stage in a student's education. Cambridge IGCSE is taken in over 160 countries, and is widely recognised by employers and higher education institutions worldwide.

Cambridge IGCSE is graded from A*-G. In the UK, Cambridge IGCSE is accepted as equivalent to the GCSE. It can be used as preparation for Cambridge International A and AS Levels, UK A and AS levels, IB or AP and in some instances entry into university. Cambridge IGCSE English as a Second Language (at grade C or above) is recognised by a number of UK universities as evidence of competence in the language for university entrance.

Subjects: available in over 70 subjects including accounting, Afrikaans – first language, Afrikaans – second language, agriculture, Arabic – first language, Arabic – foreign language, art and design, Baha Indonesia, Bangladesh studies, biology, business studies, chemistry, child development, Chinese – first language, Chinese – second language, Chinese (Mandarin) – foreign language, computer studies, Czech – first language, design and technology, development studies, drama, Dutch – first language, Dutch – foreign language, economics, English – first language, English – literature, English – second language, enterprise, environmental management, food and nutrition, French – first language, French – foreign language, geography, German – first language, German – foreign language, global perspectives, Greek – foreign language, Hindi as a second language, Italian – foreign language, history, India studies, Indonesian – foreign language, information and communication technology, IsiZulu as a second language, Japanese – first language, Japanese – foreign language, Kazakh as a second language, Korean (first language), Latin, Malay – foreign language, mathematics, mathematics – additional, international mathematics, music, Pakistan studies, physical education, physical science, physics, Portuguese – first language, Portuguese – foreign language, religious studies, Russian – first language, science – combined, sciences – co-ordinated (double), sociology, Spanish – first language, Spanish – foreign language, Spanish – literature, Thai – first language, travel and tourism, Turkish – first language, Urdu – second language, world literature.

Website: www.cie.org.uk/igcse

Cambridge Pre-U

Cambridge Pre-U is a post-16 qualification that equips students with the skills they need to succeed at university. Developed with universities, it was first introduced in UK schools in September 2008. It is now taught in 180 schools, including some schools outside the UK.

Cambridge Pre-U is a linear course, with exams taken at the end of two years. It encourages the development of well-informed, open and independent-minded individuals; promotes deep understanding through subject specialisation, with a depth and rigour appropriate to progression to higher education; and develops skills in independent research valued by universities.

Assessment

Cambridge Pre-U Principal Subjects are examined at the end of two years. Cambridge Pre-U Short Courses are typically examined at the end of one year. Students can study a combination of A Levels and Principal Subjects.

In order to gain the Cambridge Pre-U Diploma, students must study at least three Cambridge Pre-U Principal Subjects (up to two A Levels can be substituted for Principal Subjects) and Cambridge Pre-U Global Perspectives and Research (GPR). Cambridge Pre-U GPR includes an extended project in the second year, developing skills in research and critical thinking.

Subjects: available in 25 subjects including art and design, biology, business and management, chemistry, drama and theatre, economics, literature in English, French, further mathematics, geography, German, global perspectives and research, classical Greek, history, Italian, art history, Latin, Mandarin Chinese, mathematics, music, philosophy and theology, physics, psychology, Russian, Spanish.

Website: www.cie.org.uk/cambridgepreu

Cambridge Primary

Cambridge Primary is typically for learners aged 5 to 11 years. It develops learner skills and understanding through the primary years in English, mathematics and science. The flexible curriculum frameworks include optional assessment tools to help schools monitor learners' progress and give detailed feedback to parents. At the end of Cambridge Primary, schools can enter students for Cambridge Primary Checkpoint tests which are marked in Cambridge.

Website: www.cie.org.uk/primary

Cambridge Secondary 1

Cambridge Secondary 1 is typically for learners aged 11 to 14 years. It develops learner skills and understanding in English, mathematics and science for the first three years of secondary education, and includes assessment tools. At the end of Cambridge Secondary 1, schools can enter students for Cambridge Checkpoint tests which are marked in Cambridge and provide an external international benchmark for student performance.

Website: www.cie.org.uk/cambridgesecondary1

College Level Examination Program (CLEP)

CLEP gives students of any age the opportunity to demonstrate college level achievement through a programme of exams in undergraduate college courses. It enables students to earn college credit for learning gained through independent study, advanced high school courses, non-credit courses, or professional development. Students can use the CLEP examinations to demonstrate learning and earn placement, credit or exemption from entry-level courses.

Exams are offered in 33 subjects within the following areas: composition and literature, foreign languages, history and social science, science and mathematics, business. There are more than 2900 colleges that grant credit and/or advanced standing for CLEP exams. The exams themselves are 90 minutes long and are mostly multiple choice, covering material taught in courses that most students take during their first two years of college. Most examinations are designed to correspond to one-semester courses; some, however, correspond to full year or two year courses.

The exams are administered at over 1700 US test centres and at several international sites. There are no national test dates; students can work with their individual test centre to schedule the CLEP exam when they are ready.

The American Council on Education (ACE) has developed a recommended credit granting score and number of semester hours of credit for each CLEP exam. Bear in mind that the amount of credit you receive for each CLEP exam you take and the score you have to achieve to get that credit or exemption is determined by the credit granting policy of your college or university.

Common Entrance

The Common Entrance examinations are used in UK independent schools for transfer from junior to senior schools at the ages of 11+ and 13+. The papers are set centrally but the answers are marked by the senior school for which a candidate is entered. Candidates normally take the examination in their own junior or preparatory schools, either in the UK or overseas.

Common Entrance is not a public examination as, for example, GCSE, and candidates may normally be entered only in one of the following circumstances:
   a) they have been offered a place at a senior school subject to their passing the examination, or
   b) they are required to take the examination as a preliminary to sitting the scholarship examination, or
   c) they are entered as a 'trial run', in which case the papers are marked by the junior school concerned.
At 11+ the examination consists of English, mathematics

and science. The 11+ examination is designed so that it can be taken by candidates either from independent preparatory schools or by candidates from schools in the maintained sector who have had no special preparation. At 13+ most candidates come from independent preparatory schools, and the compulsory subjects are English, mathematics and science. Papers in French, geography, German, Greek, history, Latin, Mandarin, religious studies and Spanish are also available and candidates offer as many subjects as they can.

The 13+ examination came into being in the early part of the 20th century, and has for many years been used by the majority of boys' and coeducational senior schools admitting pupils at that age. The 11+ examination dates from 1947, when the Common Entrance Examination for Girls' Schools Ltd was founded by a group of headmistresses with the object of 'improving the standard of secondary education by the establishment of an accepted standard of attainment for the admission of pupils to girls' senior schools'. In recent years the distinction between the girls and the boys examinations has blurred, with a large number of girls taking the 13+ examination and some boys taking 11+. This blurring of distinctions has been accelerated by the increase in the number of coeducational preparatory and senior schools. In 1989 the Common Entrance Examination

Committee (Boys) and the Board of Common Entrance Examination for Girls' Schools Ltd joined forces to form the Common Entrance Board and subsequently the Independent Schools Examinations Board. The Board consists of members of HMC, GSA and IAPS. All the examinations are now available both to girls and boys.

Rapid changes in education nationally have resulted in regular reviews of the syllabuses for all the examinations. The introduction of GCSE and then the National Curriculum brought about a number of changes. Since preparation for GCSE starts at 11, and work for the National Curriculum Key Stage 3 starts at the same age, it is a guiding principle that Common Entrance should be part of the natural progression from 11-16, and not a diversion from it.

Details of the Common Entrance examinations are obtainable from the Chief Administrator at the address below. Copies of past papers and other publications are obtainable from Galore Park Publishing Ltd at www.galorepark.co.uk

Independent Schools Examinations Board, The Pump House,
16 Queen's Avenue, Christchurch, BH23 1BZ
Tel: +44 (0)1202 487538; Fax: +44 (0)1202 473728
Email: enquiries@iseb.co.uk Website: www.iseb.co.uk

European Baccalaureate (EB)

Not to be confused with the International Baccalaureate (IB) or the French Baccalaureate, this certificate is available in European schools and recognised in all EU countries.

To obtain the baccalaureate, a student must obtain a minimum score of 60%, which is made up from: coursework, oral participation in class and tests (40%); five written examinations (36%) – mother-tongue, first foreign language and maths are compulsory for all candidates; four oral examinations (24%) – mother tongue and first foreign language are compulsory (history or geography may also be compulsory here, dependant on whether the candidate has taken a written examination in these subjects).

Throughout the EU the syllabus and examinations necessary to achieve the EB are identical. The only exception to this rule is the syllabus for the mother tongue language. The EB has been specifically designed to meet, at the very least, the minimum qualification requirements of each member state.

Study for the EB begins at nursery stage (age 4)

and progresses through primary (age six) and on into secondary school (age 12).

Syllabus
Languages: Bulgarian, Czech, Danish, Dutch, English, Estonian, Finnish, Finnish as a second national language, French, German, Greek, Hungarian, Irish, Italian, Latvian, Lithuanian, Maltese, Polish, Portuguese, Romanian, Slovak, Slovenian, Spanish, Swedish, Swedish for Finnish pupils.

Literary: art education, non-confessional ethics, geography, ancient Greek, history, human sciences, Latin, music, philosophy, physical education.

Sciences: biology, chemistry, economics, ICT, integrated science, mathematics, physics.

For more information, contact:

Office of the Secretary-General of the European Schools, c/o European Commission, Rue Joseph II, 30-2ème étage, B-1049 Brussels, Belgium
Tel: +32 2295 3745; Fax: +32 2298 6298
Website: www.eursc.eu

French Baccalaureate

The French Baccalauréat or 'le bac', is an academic qualification taken at the end of the lycée (secondary education), usually when the student is 18. It is the required qualification in France for those students wishing to carry on their studies at university. Students not wishing to go on to higher education can, in theory, opt out of taking the baccalaureate and those who do not have one can instead take the higher education entrance exam, which leads to its own diploma.

There are three main types of baccalaureate in France:

- the baccalauréat général (general);
- the baccalauréat professionnel (professional);
- the baccalauréat technologique (technological).

General Baccalaureate

Students who sit for the baccalauréat général have to choose one of three specialised streams as follows:

S – scientifique (sciences)

Mathematics, physics and chemistry, also biology or engineering sciences

ES - sciences économiques et socials (economics and social sciences)

Equally split between literary and economic/social studies.

L – littéraire (literature)

French literature, philosophy, history and geography, as well as foreign languages.

The French baccalaureate exam is available in over 40 languages including French regional dialects such as Alsation and Catalan.

Exams take place in June each year, in the final year of the lycée, they are usually in the form of an essay and take between two and four hours to complete. Some options are more popular than others due to a weighting system that can have a significant effect on the student's final grade. There are exams in September each year as well, but these are for those students who missed the June exams for reasons such as illness. Students who fail their June exams cannot retake the baccalaureate in September that same year.

Option Internationale du Baccalauréat

This is an additional option to the general baccalaureate and offers further subjects. Extra exams are offered in literature, history and geography allowing a higher grade to be achieved towards the final baccalaureate mark. In general, this option is taken by students wishing to study at overseas universities.

Grades

In order to obtain a baccalaureate, the student must achieve at least ten out of a possible mark of 20. Above this, honours are awarded as follows:

- marks between 12 and 13.99 – assez bien (honours);
- marks between 14 and 15.99 – bien (high honours);
- marks between 16 and 20 – très bien (highest honours).

In addition, those students obtaining marks above 18 may also receive the félicitations du jury (jury's congratulations), which is an unofficial award given entirely at the panel's discretion.

For those students who score less than ten, but eight or more, they can opt for the épreuve de rattrapage, which is an oral exam given in two subjects of the student's choice. In this way, providing the student does well enough to raise his/her overall grade to ten, those students just missing the required pass mark are able to obtain their baccalaureate without having to repeat their final year at school.

Grade Point Averages (GPA)

Students at high schools in the US are given grades for each course they follow. The grading system is not standardised across school districts. However, in general they are:

Grade	level	points
A	excellent	4
B	above average	3
C	average	2
D	below average	1
F*	failure	0

* a student that fails a required course must take it again.

A student's high school GPA represents their accumulated grades throughout high school. It is calculated by adding the total of all points earned for each course, then dividing the total points by the total number of courses taken. Additional points may be awarded for extra work done in honors, AP or IB courses.

Graduate Record Examination (GRE)

GRE scores are used to evaluate a student's suitability for access into graduate programmes and business schools. The test consists of verbal reasoning, quantitative reasoning, critical thinking and analytical writing.

This test is used and accepted worldwide and is open to any student in any country.

The International Baccalaureate (IB)

The International Baccalaureate (IB) offers four challenging and high quality educational programmes for a worldwide community of schools, aiming to develop internationally minded people who, recognizing their common humanity and shared guardianship of the planet, help to create a better, more peaceful world.

The IB works with schools around the world (both state and privately funded) that share the commitment to international education to deliver these programmes.

Schools that have achieved the high standards required for authorization to offer one or more of the IB programmes are known as IB World Schools. There are over half a million students attending more than 3000 IB World Schools in 139 countries and this number is growing annually.

The Primary Years, Middle Years and Diploma Programmes share a common philosophy and common characteristics. They develop the whole student, helping students to grow intellectually, socially, aesthetically and culturally. They provide a broad and balanced education that includes science and the humanities, languages and mathematics, technology and the arts. The programmes teach students to think critically, and encourage them to draw connections between areas of knowledge and to use problem-solving techniques and concepts from many disciplines. They instil in students a sense of responsibility towards others and towards the environment. Lastly, and perhaps most importantly, the programmes give students an awareness and understanding of their own culture and of other cultures, values and ways of life.

A fourth programme called the IB Career Related Certificate (IBCC) became available to IB World Schools from September 2012.

All IB programmes include:

- a written curriculum or curriculum framework;
- student assessment appropriate to the age range;
- professional development and networking opportunities for teachers;
- support, authorization and programme evaluation for the school.

The IB Primary Years Programme

The IB Primary Years Programme (PYP), for students aged three to 12, focuses on the development of the whole child as an inquirer, both in the classroom and in the world outside. It is a framework consisting of five essential elements (concepts, knowledge, skills, attitude, action) and guided by six trans-disciplinary themes of global significance, explored using knowledge and skills derived from six subject areas (language, social studies, mathematics, science and technology, arts, personal, social and physical education) with a powerful emphasis on inquiry-based learning.

The most significant and distinctive feature of the PYP is the six trans-disciplinary themes. These themes are about issues that have meaning for, and are important to, all of us. The programme offers a balance between learning about or through the subject areas, and learning beyond them. The six themes of global significance create a trans-disciplinary framework that allows students to 'step up' beyond the confines of learning within subject areas:

- Who we are.
- Where we are in place and time.
- How we express ourselves.
- How the world works.
- How we organize ourselves.
- Sharing the planet.

The PYP exhibition is the culminating activity of the programme. It requires students to analyse and propose solutions to real-world issues, drawing on what they have learned through the programme. Evidence of student development and records of PYP exhibitions are reviewed by the IB as part of the programme evaluation process.

Assessment is an important part of each unit of inquiry as it both enhances learning and provides opportunities for students to reflect on what they know, understand and can do. The teacher's feedback to the students provides the guidance, the tools and the incentive for them to

Curricula, examinations and tests

become more competent, more skilful and better at understanding how to learn.

The IB Middle Years Programme (MYP)

The MYP, for students aged 11 to 16, provides a framework of academic challenge that encourages students to embrace and understand the connections between traditional subjects and the real world, and to become critical and reflective thinkers. Students are required to study their mother tongue, a second language, humanities, sciences, mathematics, arts, physical education and technology. In the final year of the programme, students also engage in a personal project, which they will use to demonstrate the understandings and skills they have developed throughout the programme.

Students study subjects from each of the eight subject groups through the five areas of interaction:

- Approaches to learning is concerned with developing the intellectual discipline, attitudes, strategies and skills that will result in critical, coherent and independent thought and the capacity for problem solving and decision-making.

- Community and service starts in the classroom and extends beyond it, requiring students to participate in the communities in which they live. The emphasis is on developing community awareness and concern, a sense of responsibility, and the skills and attitudes needed to make an effective contribution to society.

- Human ingenuity (formerly homo faber) allows students to focus on the evolution, processes and products of human creativity. It considers their impact on society and on the mind. Students learn to appreciate the human capacity to influence, transform, enjoy and improve the quality of life. This area of interaction encourages students to explore the relationships between science, aesthetics, technology and ethics.

- Environments aims to make students aware of their interdependence with the environment so that they become aware of their responsibility, and may take positive, responsible action for maintaining an environment fit for the future.

- Health and social education prepares students for a physically and mentally healthy life, aware of potential hazards and able to make informed choices. It develops in students a sense of responsibility for their own wellbeing and for the physical and social environment.

Assessment is criterion referenced, so students around the world are measured against pre-specified criteria for each subject group. Teachers may modify these criteria to be age-appropriate in the earlier years of the programme.

Teachers set assessment tasks that are assessed internally in the school. External checks (either moderation or monitoring of assessment by IB examiners) are carried out on this internal assessment to ensure worldwide consistency of standards. For schools that require official IB certification for their students, moderation is carried out every year.

The IB Diploma Programme (IBDP)

The IB Diploma Programme, for students aged 16 to 19, is an academically challenging and balanced programme of education with final examinations, which prepares students for success at university and life beyond.

IBDP students study six courses at higher level or standard level. Students must choose one subject from each of groups 1 to 5, thus ensuring breadth of experience in languages, social studies, the experimental sciences and mathematics. The sixth subject may be an arts subject chosen from group 6, or the student may choose another subject from groups 1 to 5. At least three and not more than four subjects are taken at higher level (recommended 240 teaching hours), the others at standard level (150 teaching hours). Students can study these subjects, and be examined, in English, French or Spanish.

In addition, three core elements – the extended essay, theory of knowledge and creativity, action, service – are compulsory and central to the philosophy of the programme.

Students take written examinations at the end of the programme, which are marked by external IB examiners. Students also complete assessment tasks in the school, which are either initially marked by teachers and then moderated by external moderators or sent directly to external examiners.

The marks awarded for each course range from one (lowest) to seven (highest). Students can also be awarded up to three additional points for their combined results on theory of knowledge and the extended essay. The diploma is awarded to students who gain at least 24 points, subject to certain minimum levels of performance across the whole programme and to satisfactory participation in the creativity, action, and service requirement. The highest total that a Diploma Programme student can be awarded is 45 points.

The IB Career Related Certificate (IBCC)

The IB Career Related Certificate, for students aged 16 to 19, accentuates and enhances skill development and the attainment of the competencies relevant to today's challenging work place. Students are able to develop a specific pathway into higher education in consultation with their school. A specially-designed IBCC core recognizes and emphasizes IB values, missions and the needs of career-related students.

IBCC students study a specialized IBCC core and a minimum of two Diploma Programme courses. The IBCC core consists of the following:

Community and Service: This element of the IBCC core is based on the principle of service learning, which uses community service as a vehicle for new learning that has academic value. The service learning model in the IBCC emphasises knowledge development, civic development, social development and personal development.

Approaches to learning (ATL): This course is designed to introduce students to life skills. At the heart of the ATL model is the learner who uses a range of skills to make sense of the world around them and develops skills with an emphasis on critical and ethical thinking and effective communication.

Language development: Language development ensures that all students have access to, and are exposed to, a second language that will assist and further their understanding of the wider world. Students are encouraged to extend or begin a second language that suits their needs, background and context.

Reflective project: Through a reflective project students identify, analyse, critically discuss and evaluate an ethical issue arising from their career-related studies. The project can be submitted in a variety of formats including an essay, web page or short film. This work allows the student to engage in personal inquiry, action and reflection and to develop strong research and communications skills.

The Diploma Programme courses are assessed in accordance with the standard Diploma Programme assessment process. However, the career-related courses are assessed by the career-related course provider, not the IB. Approaches to learning, community and service and language development are internally assessed by the school, while the reflective project is moderated by the IB.

For more information on IB programmes, visit: www.ibo.org

Africa, Europe, Middle East Global Centre, Churchillplein 6, The Hague, 2517JW, The Netherlands
Tel: +31 (0)70 352 6233

The International Middle Years Curriculum (IMYC)

The International Middle Years Curriculum (IMYC) provides an enriching, engaging and rigorous learning experience for 11-14 year olds. It is practical for the school to deliver, and inspiring and relevant for students, preparing them well for the next stage in their learning.

The IMYC is a curriculum that makes meaning, connects learning and develops minds. It delivers rigorous and transformational knowledge, skills and understanding of all subjects, linking all learning to a conceptual theme. The IMYC creates a challenging, student-led learning environment preparing students well for iGCSE, A levels and IB Diploma.

Each IMYC unit guides students to make meaning of the conceptual theme through a personal and global perspective which they represent at the end of their unit learning through a media project. Within each IMYC unit there is a learning process designed to engage and inspire teenagers, helping them to become confident, independent learners.

IMYC member schools and students are part of a worldwide IMYC community through which they share learning experiences, ideas and resources.

The IMYC is part of Fieldwork Education which, since 1984, has been helping schools around the world to develop children's learning. For more information about the IMYC or to talk with a school already using the IMYC contact Fieldwork Education at +44(0)20 7531 9696 or visit www.greatlearning.com/imyc

The International Primary Curriculum (IPC)

The International Primary Curriculum (IPC) is one of the only comprehensive curricula in the world equally committed to improving learning and developing international mindedness. It focuses on developing knowledge, skills and understanding of subjects set within child-friendly, relevant, cross-curricular thematic units of work that are creative and challenging for children of all abilities. The IPC, used in more than 1,500 schools worldwide, has over 80 different thematic units of learning; all modern-day topics appealing to all ages of primary children. This enables young children to remain motivated through the learning of science, geography, history and so on.

Within each theme, the IPC suggests many ideas for collaborative learning, for active learning, for learning outside the classroom, for role play, and for children learning from each other. The IPC's engaging approach also encourages parental involvement through a range of initiatives.

Each IPC unit incorporates most of the core subjects including science, history, geography, ICT, art and PE and provides opportunities to incorporate language arts and mathematics. Each subject then has a number of learning tasks to help teachers to help their children meet a range of learning goals set out in the curriculum. These learning goals are deliberately explicit, designed to make sure that teachers distinguish clearly between children's learning of knowledge, skills and understanding.

Each IPC unit has embedded within it learning-focused activities that help young children to start developing a global awareness and gain an increasing sense of the 'other'. Every unit creates opportunities to look at learning of the theme through a local perspective, a national perspective and an international perspective.

With schools in over 75 countries learning with the IPC, there are opportunities for children to share their local experiences related to an IPC unit with children in dramatically different environments.

Each IPC unit has a very structured yet flexible teaching framework providing teachers with a series of learning tasks. These are designed to achieve the learning goals through creative, meaningful and memorable learning activities that appeal to all learning styles and are relevant for all children of all abilities. However, the learning tasks are purely a guide and provide plenty of scope for creative teaching, personalisation to the class and locality, and development on the theme as well as linking with other schools learning with the IPC. With IPC member schools in countries as diverse as Swaziland, Malaysia, Qatar, Japan and Russia, this sharing of learning opportunities ensures that no school, however remote, feels isolated.

The IPC is part of Fieldwork Education. For more information about the IPC or to talk with a school already using the IPC contact Fieldwork Education at +44(0)20 7531 9696 or visit www.greatlearning.com/ipc

SATs (UK)

In UK schools, SATs (Standard Assessment Tests) occur at the end of Year 2 (age 7), Year 6 (age 11) and Year 9 (age 14). Used to show a child's progress compared with his/her classmates, the average score for each assessed age group is set at 100 and the standard deviation at 15.
The tests at each stage:

Key Stage 1 (Year 2). These take place throughout May each year. Each child is assessed in reading, writing, maths and science.

Key Stage 2 (Year 6). These also take place in May and cover the three core subjects: English, maths and science.

Key Stage 3 (Year 9). These tests cover: English, maths, science, history, geography, modern foreign languages, design and technology, ICT, art and design, music, physical education, citizenship, and religious education.

By Year 9, most students are expected to achieve level 5 in their SATs and it is at this stage that the results are often used to determine which GSCE set the student should be placed in. The key to the levels are:

Level W – working towards level 1, very weak
Level 1 – average for a typical 5-year-old
Level 2 – average for a typical 7-year-old
Level 3 – average for a typical 9-year-old
Level 4 – average for a typical 11-year-old
Level 5 – average for a typical 13-year-old
Level 6 – average for a typical 14-year-old
Level 7 – above average for typical 14-yr-old
Level 8 – only available in maths

Addition qualification, by using the letters 'a', 'b' and 'c', can be given within the levels; these indicate a range within the level with 'a' being the highest and 'c' being the lowest.

Website: www.direct.gov.uk

SATs (USA)

Developed with input from teachers and educators, the SAT® is a highly reliable and valid standardized measure of college readiness used in the admission process at nearly all four-year undergraduate colleges and universities in the United States.

The SAT is not only utilized by US universities, but also by universities in Canada, Singapore, Hong Kong, South Korea, Japan, Australia, the United Kingdom, and elsewhere. Hundreds of universities in more than 65 countries outside the US received SAT scores from students last academic year. Some require the test of all students. Examples of universities requiring the SAT of all applicants include Singapore Management University, located in Singapore; McGill University in Montreal, Canada; and Jacobs University Bremen in Germany.

The SAT is designed to predict a student's likely academic performance at a particular college or university in their first year and beyond. Studies regularly demonstrate that the best predictor of college success is the combination of SAT scores and high school grades. The SAT covers content areas deemed critical for success in college – critical reading, mathematics and writing – and SAT performance data illustrate that success on the SAT is linked to the type and rigor of course work completed during high school.

Nearly three million students take the SAT each academic year via nearly 7,000 test centers in more than 175 countries. SAT questions are prescreened on students from around the world to ensure fairness. Before any test question appears on a scored section of the SAT, it is included on one of the unscored test forms that are included in every SAT administration. By pretesting questions in this way, College Board researchers can be sure that each question is fair and valid for all students regardless of gender, race, ethnicity, country of origin or socio-economic status. The SAT is the only college entrance exam that prescreens test questions on a global population of test-takers. The SAT is offered six times a year outside the United States in October, November, December, January, May and June.

Dates for international test administrations, registrations requirements and deadlines can be found here: sat.collegeboard.org/register/sat-international-dates.

The Redesigned SAT

In March 2014, College Board President David Coleman announced changes to the SAT. The first administration of the redesigned exam will take place in spring 2016. Major changes to the exam include:

- focusing on words that students will use consistently in college and beyond
- students being asked to support answers with evidence, including questions that require them to cite a specific part of a passage to support their answer choice
- having the essay measure students' ability to analyze evidence and explain how an author builds an argument to persuade an audience
- having the math section focus on problem solving and data analysis; the heart of algebra; and passport to advanced math.
- having the reading section enable students to analyze a wide range of sources, including literature and literary non-fiction, science, history and social studies.
- analyzing data and texts in real world context including a passage drawn from the Founding Documents of America or the Great Global Conversation they inspire
- removing the penalty for wrong answers

Moving forward, the College Board will also work with teachers and college faculty to design course frameworks and modules for use in grades 6–12. In addition, the College Board has partnered with Khan Academy to provide free test-preparation programs and resources for all students. In this partnership, the organizations will continually work together to ensure that the practice materials are of the highest quality and truly focus on the work that matters most.

The College Board also shared for the first time the complete specifications of the exam, as well as sample items, two years before any student will take the exam. The College Board will continue to present updated information over the course of the two years leading up to the first administration of the redesigned exam. Updates will also be available on the organization's new microsite, deliveringopportunity.org.

Preliminary SAT/National Merit Scholarship Qualifying Test (PSAT/NMSQT)

The Preliminary SAT/National Merit Scholarship Test (PSAT/NMSQT®) is a standardized test that measures the critical reading, mathematics, and writing skills that students will need for higher education and careers after high school. Last year, over 23,000 schools opened the door to college for more than 3.5 million students by administering the PSAT/NMSQT.

Test results and their accompanying analysis are valuable tools that can help prepare students for the SAT® and education opportunities beyond high school. Each year, students around the world take the PSAT/NMSQT to prepare for the SAT, receive information from colleges, begin college and career planning and help assess academic skills necessary for college-level work.

In 2014, the PSAT/NMSQT will be administered on October 15 or on October 18 by schools around the globe. For more information about the PSAT/NMSQT, email international@collegeboard.org.

Index

Index

Index

H

I

Index

378

Index

M

N

Index

Index

Index

T

Index

Z